Between Crime and War

THE OXFORD SERIES IN ETHICS, NATIONAL SECURITY, AND THE RULE OF LAW

Series Editors
Claire Finkelstein and Jens David Ohlin
Oxford University Press

About the Series

The *Oxford series in Ethics, National Security, and the Rule of Law* is an interdisciplinary book series designed to address abiding questions at the intersection of national security, moral and political philosophy, and practical ethics. It seeks to illuminate both ethical and legal dilemmas that arise in democratic nations as they grapple with national security imperatives. The synergy the series creates between academic researchers and policy practitioners seeks to protect and augment the rule of law in the context of contemporary armed conflict and national security.

The book series grew out of the work of the Center for Ethics and the Rule of Law (CERL) at the University of Pennsylvania. CERL is a nonpartisan interdisciplinary institute dedicated to the preservation and promotion of the rule of law in twenty-first century warfare and national security. The only Center of its kind housed within a research university, CERL draws from the study of law, philosophy, and ethics to answer the difficult questions that arise in times of war and contemporary transnational conflicts.

Between Crime and War

Hybrid Legal Frameworks for Asymmetric Conflict

Edited by

CLAIRE FINKELSTEIN, CHRISTOPHER FULLER,
JENS DAVID OHLIN, MITT REGAN

OXFORD
UNIVERSITY PRESS

OXFORD
UNIVERSITY PRESS

Oxford University Press is a department of the University of Oxford. It furthers the University's objective of excellence in research, scholarship, and education by publishing worldwide. Oxford is a registered trade mark of Oxford University Press in the UK and certain other countries.

Published in the United States of America by Oxford University Press
198 Madison Avenue, New York, NY 10016, United States of America.

Library of Congress Cataloging-in-Publication Data

Names: Finkelstein, Claire Oakes, editor. | Fuller, Christopher J., editor. |
Ohlin, Jens David, editor. | Regan, Milton C., Jr., 1952– editor.
Title: Between Crime and War : hybrid legal frameworks for asymmetric conflict /
Claire Finkelstein, Christopher Fuller, Jens David Ohlin, Mitt Regan.
Description: New York, NY : Oxford University Press, [2022?] |
Series: Ethics national security rule law series |
Includes index. Identifiers: LCCN 2021056077 (print) | LCCN 2021056078 (ebook) |
ISBN 9780197638798 (hardback) | ISBN 9780197638811 (epub) |
ISBN 9780197638804 | ISBN 9780197638828
Subjects: LCSH: Terrorism (International law) | Non-state actors (International relations) |
Asymmetric warfare. | International and municipal law.
Classification: LCC KZ7220 .F54 2022 (print) |
LCC KZ7220 (ebook) | DDC 341.6/3—dc23/eng/20220202

DOI: 10.1093/oso/9780197638798.001.0001

1 3 5 7 9 8 6 4 2

Printed by Integrated Books International, United States of America

Note to Readers

This publication is designed to provide accurate and authoritative information in regard to the subject matter covered. It is based upon sources believed to be accurate and reliable and is intended to be current as of the time it was written. It is sold with the understanding that the publisher is not engaged in rendering legal, accounting, or other professional services. If legal advice or other expert assistance is required, the services of a competent professional person should be sought. Also, to confirm that the information has not been affected or changed by recent developments, traditional legal research techniques should be used, including checking primary sources where appropriate.

(Based on the Declaration of Principles jointly adopted by a Committee of the American Bar Association and a Committee of Publishers and Associations.)

Foreword

Lieutenant General Charles N. Pede[1]

The struggle against terrorism is the scourge of humanity and certainly our generation. But it is not a new phenomenon. In the twentieth century alone, the British government fought the Irish Republican Army, the Spanish government fought the Euskadi Ta Askatasuna (ETA), and Germany and Italy fought the Red Army Faction and the Red Brigades, respectively. Members of these terrorist organizations were predominately citizens of the nations they fought against. The nations treated the members of the terrorist organizations as criminals and, for the most part, utilized their domestic law enforcement system to investigate the terrorist acts and the judicial system to prosecute those apprehended.

However, the 1990s saw terrorism rise to an entirely new level. The Taliban gained control of most of Afghanistan. Al Qaeda and affiliated organizations conducted terrorist attacks around the world, including the attacks on U.S. embassies in Kenya and Tanzania in 1998, and the coordinated attacks on multiple targets in the United States in 2001, such as the World Trade Center and the Pentagon. In 2014, the Islamic State of Iraq and Syria (ISIS) broke with Al Qaeda and seized control of large portions of Iraq and Syria. Numerous attacks have been carried out in the name of ISIS by so-called "lone wolves."

Nations that have been the targets of these terrorist attacks have struggled to find the right approach against terrorism: either law enforcement or military force, or both. Terrorists often plan their operations in countries where there is little or no governance, making a law enforcement approach challenging, if not futile. These organizations have also grown in size and capacity to the point that most civilian law enforcement agencies are no match for them.

Just as the threat posed by terrorist groups rises and falls, the approach chosen by various nations to confront the threat has been fluid over the years. If the threat consists of a few dozen poorly equipped and loosely organized individuals, the nation's law enforcement and judicial systems may be an adequate response. However, as a terrorist group gains in strength and capability, those systems may prove to be unable to address the threat. This could result in a combined effort between law enforcement and the military to identify and detain

[1] The opinions expressed herein are solely those of the author and are not intended in any way to reflect an official position of the US Army, the US Department of Defense, or any branch of the US government.

terrorists. The existing penal code and court system could be used to prosecute terrorists for their criminal acts, or new criminal statutes and courts, such as the Anti-Terrorism Law issued by the Iraqi Council of Ministers in 2005, could be created.

But there is a tipping point where the size, capability, and the transnational nature of these terrorist organizations require a predominantly military response. State law enforcement agencies may be overmatched and national laws may restrict the ability to gather intelligence on terrorist activities domestically. Military forces may be the only option for staying a "step ahead" of a pending terrorist attack.

It is this Gordian knot intersection that seems to bedevil us.

Are normal law enforcement mechanisms sufficient to deal with the threat of modern terrorism, or is resort to armed force and the legal framework of the law of armed conflict the best medicine?

This book attempts to untangle the mythic knot by putting our current struggles in context and charting novel legal paths forward. If the enemies of civilization show an ever increasing agility in using our lawful and civilized approach to threats against us—now known as "lawfare"—must we not be more legally agile? If Somalis dropping their weapons and raising hands to a Cobra gunship in Mogadishu in 1993 was a manipulation of our rules of engagement, is it any surprise that ISIS matures the manipulation to create human shield "moments" of nation-state culpability?

That our enemies have become more sophisticated in fighting us asymmetrically—using our honorable adherence to law—is an expected outcome.

And so it should also be expected that a book such as this, and the embedded intellectual effort of this book, should drive evolution and understanding in how to defeat terrorists using the law. The law evolves. It does so through practice and through lawmaking. The wellspring for such evolution in practice and lawmaking is such a book as this.

The legal challenges we face are not insurmountable. Solutions and success start with ideas. And ideas matter. Ideas matter in the law as much as they matter in commercial product development. Ideas breed more ideas and more creative and faster innovation. Ideas challenge us to reflect, they challenge the status quo, and ideally, ideas envision a novel approach to a problem.

This book is fuel for innovation in the law. While conventional approaches to fighting the hideous and unfathomable cruelty of terrorists have, in my view, produced significant and salutary results both on the battlefield and in courtrooms, the law may, in its capacious quiver, have other arrows we have not tested. This book challenges each of us in the profession of arms and in the profession of law to understand the landscape better, to place it all in context, and to consider new and different legal approaches. This book should force uncomfortable conversations and produce as a result a more legally agile response to those who see our adherence to law as a vulnerability, not a strength.

While I view the law of armed conflict as immensely versatile and effective in the many environments in which we find ourselves in the modern world, I also believe we can all benefit from aggressive and relentless study and reflection.

This book is an incandescent starting point for that reflection.

Charles N. Pede
Lieutenant General, US Army

Contents

List of Contributors xi

Toward Principled Contextualism in Responding to Organized Non-State Violence 1
Jens David Ohlin & Mitt Regan

PART I: THE FRAMEWORK PROBLEM IN MODERN CONFLICT: CAN WE STILL DISTINGUISH WAR FROM CRIME?

1. Non-State Actors, Terrorism, and the War Paradigm Revisited 21
Seth Cantey
2. The Limits of Law and the Value of Rights in Addressing Terrorism: A Study of the UN Counterterrorism Architecture 45
Fionnuala Ní Aoláin
3. The Paradox of Discrimination 63
Jens David Ohlin
4. Fighting Terrorism under All Applicable Law 91
Joshua Andresen
5. When Conflict Recurs: Classification of Conflict when Hostilities Break Out Anew 125
Laurie R. Blank

PART II: WAR AS CRIMINAL ENFORCEMENT

6. Fighting State Actors with the Tools of Hybridized Warfare: Can the Law of Armed Conflict be Saved? 153
Claire Finkelstein
7. Urban Warfare: Policing Conflict 183
Kenneth Watkin
8. Ratchet Down or Ramp Up? Contemporary Threats, Armed Conflict, and Tailored Authority 223
Geoffrey S. Corn

9. Using Law as a Weapon against Nuclear Proliferation and Terrorism: The US Government's Financial Lawfare against Iran 265
Orde F. Kittrie

10. Human Rights Law as an Alternative to *Jus in Bello* 315
Christopher J. Fuller

PART III: FIGHTING CRIME AS WAR

11. National Security Policymaking in the Shadow of International Law 347
Laura A. Dickinson

12. Emerging Transnational Self-Defense Norms and Unrealized Liberal Values 369
John C. Dehn

13. Finding Peace in the Law of War 407
Bailey Brown

14. From Armed Conflict to Countering Threat Networks: Counterterrorism and Social Network Analysis 437
Todd Huntley & Mitt Regan

PART IV: CRIME AND WAR: PROSECUTING TERRORISM AND WAR CRIMES

15. Counting the Ripples: The Challenge of Extraterritorial Jurisdiction to Prosecute Non-State Actors 473
Evan R. Seamone

16. Diversifying the Sources of Evidence in Terrorism Cases before Criminal Courts in (Post-)Conflict and High-Risk Situations: The Role of the Military 491
Bibi van Ginkel, Christophe Paulussen, & Tanya Mehra

17. US Military Prosecutions during Non-International Armed Conflict 519
Chris Jenks

18. Conclusion 549
Jens David Ohlin & Mitt Regan

Index 559

List of Contributors

Joshua Andresen is Reader (Associate Professor) in National Security and Foreign Relations Law at the University of Surrey School of Law. His research focuses on the legal regulation of armed conflict in light of advanced weapons technology and the predominance of non-international armed conflicts.

Fionnuala Ní Aoláin is concurrently Regents Professor and Robina Professor of Law, Public Policy and Society at the University of Minnesota Law School, and Professor of Law at the Queens University, Belfast, Northern Ireland. Professor Ní Aoláin is currently the UN Special Rapporteur on the Protection and Promotion of Human Rights while Countering Terrorism (2017–Present).

Laurie R. Blank is Clinical Professor of Law, Director of the Center for International and Comparative Law, and Director of the International Humanitarian Law Clinic at Emory University School of Law.

Bailey Brown is an attorney who served twenty-one years with the US Army. Assignments included tours in Afghanistan, Italy, Germany, Korea, and the Pentagon. Lieutenant Colonel (Ret.) Brown holds a bachelor's degree in Political Science, a Law Degree, and a Master of Laws in Military Law.

Seth Cantey is an Associate Professor of Politics and core faculty member of the Middle East and South Asian Studies program at Washington and Lee University. He holds graduate degrees in Political Science and Latin American Studies from Duke and Georgetown, respectively, and a BA in Psychology and Spanish from Bucknell.

Geoffrey S. Corn is the George R. Killam Jr. Chair of Criminal Law Texas Tech University School of Law, and a retired US Army Lieutenant Colonel, who served as the Army's law of war expert. He is co-author of *The Law of Armed Conflict: An Operational Perspective*; *The Laws of War and the War on Terror*; and *Law in War: A Concise Overview* (with K. Watkin and J. Williamson).

John C. Dehn is an associate professor at Loyola University Chicago School of Law and Faculty Director of its National Security & Civil Rights Program. A West Point graduate, he served for over twenty-three years as an airborne artillery and logistics officer, Army judge advocate, and West Point faculty member.

Laura A. Dickinson is the Oswald Symister Colclough Research Professor and Professor of Law at George Washington University. Her work focuses on national security, human rights, the law of armed conflict, and foreign affairs privatization. She has authored numerous articles and book chapters, including scholarship that has appeared in the *American Journal of International Law*, the *Yale Journal of International Law*, the *NYU Journal of International Law and Politics*, the *William & Mary Law Review*, the *Emory Law Journal*, and the *Southern California Law Review*.

Claire Finkelstein is the Algernon Biddle Professor of Law and Professor of Philosophy at the University of Pennsylvania, where she is the Faculty Director of the Center for Ethics and the Rule of Law and a Distinguished Fellow at the Annenberg Public Policy Center. Her recent work focuses on the law of armed conflict, democratic governance, and national security law. She is a frequent media and print commentator.

Christopher J. Fuller is Associate Professor in Modern US History at the University of Southampton in the United Kingdom. He is the author of *See It/Shoot It: The Secret History of the CIA's Lethal Drone Program* (2017), and numerous chapters and articles on US and UK drone warfare.

Bibi van Ginkel, LLM is an international lawyer with expertise in counterterrorism and countering and preventing violent extremism. She is the owner and founder of the Glocal Connection—Platform for Shared Security and associate fellow of the International Centre for Counter Terrorism. She is also a member of the Advisory Committee on Public International Law of the government of the Netherlands.

Todd Huntley is the Director of the National Security Law Program and Lecturer in Law at Georgetown University Law Center. He previously served for twenty-three years on active duty as a US Navy Judge Advocate General.

Chris Jenks is a Professor of Law and Criminal Director at the SMU Dedman School of Law in Dallas, Texas, where he teaches criminal law, evidence, and international humanitarian law. His work considers accountability norms across the spectrum of conflict.

Orde Kittrie is a law professor at Arizona State University and a senior fellow at the Foundation for Defense of Democracies. He previously served for a decade as a US State Department attorney. He is the author of *Lawfare: Law as a Weapon of War* (2016).

Tanya Mehra LLM is a Senior Research Fellow and Programme Lead (Rule of Law Responses to Terrorism) at the International Centre for Counter-Terrorism – The Hague. Her main areas of interest are international (criminal) law and Rule of Law approaches in countering terrorism, with a special focus on accountability of terrorism-related crimes and human rights implications of countering terrorism. Other topics of interests include the repatriation of foreign fighters and their families, military evidence, and the use of administrative measures in a counterterrorism context.

Jens David Ohlin became the Allan R. Tessler Dean of Cornell Law School on July 1, 2021. His scholarly work stands at the intersection of four related fields: criminal law, criminal procedure, public international law, and the laws of war. Trained as both a lawyer and a philosopher, his research has tackled questions as diverse as criminal conspiracy and the punishment of collective criminal action, the philosophical foundations of international law, and the role of new technologies in warfare, including cyberwar, remotely piloted drones, and autonomous weapons.

Christophe Paulussen LLM MPhil is a senior researcher at the T.M.C. Asser Instituut, coordinator of its research strand "Human Dignity and Human Security in International and European Law," and research fellow at the International Centre for Counter-Terrorism – The Hague.

Charles N. Pede served as the 40th Judge Advocate General of the US Army from 2017 to 2021. As the Judge Advocate General, Lieutenant General (Ret.) Pede recruited, educated, assigned, and supervised the Army's law firm of about ten thousand lawyers and paralegals in over seventy legal offices around the world. He also provided daily advice to the senior leaders of the Army as it provided trained and ready forces for missions around the world.

Mitt Regan is McDevitt Professor of Jurisprudence, Director of the Center on Ethics and the Legal Profession, and Co-Director of the Center on National Security at Georgetown Law Center. He also serves as a Senior Fellow at the Stockdale Center for Ethical Leadership at the US Naval Academy. He is the author of *Drone Strike: Analyzing the Impacts of Targeted Killing (2022)* and numerous articles on international law, national security, and human rights.

Evan R. Seamone is the General Counsel of Trajector, Inc., a family of companies committed to assisting veterans and disabled persons in obtaining the benefits for which they are legally, morally, and ethically entitled. He is a retired officer with service in the US Army Judge Advocate General's Corps. As a Special Prosecutor at the Office of the Chief Prosecutor of Military Commissions, he represented the United States in capital litigation related to the laws of war.

Kenneth Watkin, QC, a former Canadian Judge Advocate General, and Brigadier-General (Ret.), has written extensively about contemporary conflict. His book *Fighting at the Legal Boundaries: Controlling the Use of Force in Contemporary Conflict* (2016) was awarded the 2017 Francis Lieber Prize by the American Society of International Law.

Toward Principled Contextualism in Responding to Organized Non-State Violence

Jens David Ohlin & Mitt Regan

Overview

The threat posed by the recent rise of transnational non-state armed groups does not fit easily within either of the two basic paradigms for state responses to violence. The crime paradigm focuses on the interception of demonstrable immediate threats to the safety of others. Its aim is to protect specific persons and members of the general public from violence by identifiable individuals, who may be acting alone or in concert. In pursuit of this aim, the state uses police operations and the criminal justice system. Both of these tools are governed by human rights principles that significantly constrain state power. A state may not restrict liberty unless it has clear evidence that an individual may pose a danger to others. It may not use force if other means will be effective to stop a threat. If using force is unavoidable, it must be the minimum amount necessary. Furthermore, a state generally may not take life unless no other measure will intercept an immediate threat to life.

The war paradigm focuses on threats posed by collective actors who pose a danger to the state's ability to maintain basic social order, its territorial integrity, or even its very existence. The threat to which it responds traditionally has been conceptualized as other states, whose aggression has the potential to inflict violence and achieve disruption on a scale beyond the capacity of ordinary police measures to respond effectively. Unlike the crime paradigm, the war paradigm does not adopt a presumption against taking life. Instead, it acknowledges that the state will kill others when acting in self-defense; its principle of necessity seeks to limit this by requiring that doing so will obtain a military advantage. The war paradigm generally authorizes the use of lethal force and detention without individualized determinations of culpability, but rather based on a "status," such as membership in a military organization. It also permits foreseeably but

Jens David Ohlin & Mitt Regan, *Toward Principled Contextualism in Responding to Organized Non-State Violence*
In: *Between Crime and War*. Edited by: Claire Finkelstein, Christopher Fuller, Jens David Ohlin, Mitt Regan,
Oxford University Press.
DOI: 10.1093/oso/9780197638798.003.0001

unintentionally taking innocent lives as long as their number is not excessive compared to the anticipated military benefit.

Transnational non-state armed groups can present a challenge to the binary framework of the crime and war paradigms. Such groups may inflict violence of scope and intensity that exceed ordinary crimes, and may use force to achieve political and psychological effects that differentiate them from individuals or criminal gangs with more limited capabilities and objectives. This can strain the crime paradigm's emphasis on the minimal use of force in response to immediate threats to individuals. At the same time, the disruption and fear caused by their attacks, while significant, often do not pose the kind of threat to the state itself that is presumed under the war paradigm. Furthermore, non-state groups' loose organizational structure and absence of readily observable indicia of group membership, along with their tendency to embed themselves within an innocent population, pose substantial challenges to the ability of a state to operate under the ground rules of the war paradigm.

While the United States has responded to the threat posed by non-state armed groups by using tools from both paradigms, it has placed substantially more emphasis than other states on the war paradigm. While there may be several reasons for this approach, one may be the assumption that a state must use each set of tools strictly according in accordance with the principles that underlie each paradigm. Implicit in this assumption is that the only alternative to the crime paradigm is the unqualified war paradigm.

This assumption is based on the belief that this is a more principled approach than borrowing from each paradigm based on pragmatic contextual factors. It is true that a pragmatic approach poses the risk of ad hoc determinations that are designed to justify whatever a state wants to do. It is also true, however, that decisions based on presumed consistency with principles can be formalistic and insensitive to the complex moral demands of particular settings. The chapters in this volume discuss the tensions between these paradigms, and examine whether there is a principled basis for determining when it is warranted to draw on both the crime and war paradigms and how a state might decide what features of each are appropriate to combine in which settings and why.

Rejecting a rigid binary framework in favor of a contextual approach may sometimes lead to a state acting more expansively than the conventional crime paradigm allows, but less expansively than the conventional war paradigm would permit. The legal categories of *jus ad bellum*, *jus in bello*, human rights law, and international humanitarian law (IHL) provide a useful orientation for this process. The chapters consider, however, whether they should serve as thresholds for triggering categorical authority, as opposed to expressing a mix of normative principles that can guide conduct in settings that feature complex forms of violence that do not fit neatly into these categories. Is it possible, in other words, to operate on the basis of a principled contextualism?

This notion of a principled contextualism is evident in the recent book authored by Kenneth Watkin, *Fighting at the Legal Boundaries: Controlling the Use of Force in Contemporary Conflict*, which was inspired by years of research and experience while Watkin was working as a legal officer with the Canadian Armed Forces.[1] Watkin's book takes as its point of departure the fact that most military engagements fought by modern states today involve a features of both war-fighting and law enforcement. This includes not just the identification and targeting of terrorists through targeted killing but also the law enforcement issues that arise when a military is engaged in operations in a particular locality with civilians who may be hostile, for whatever reason, to the presence of the outside military force.

Watkin's book argued for a more "holistic" approach to the application of international law, taking various elements of multiple bodies of law—human rights law, law of armed conflict, or international criminal law—as the context required. Instead of mechanically applying only one legal paradigm at a time, Watkin suggested a much more pragmatic approach designed to deal with operational realities of responding to security threats. However, unlike some other pragmatic approaches designed simply to achieve the maximum latitude for state powers, Watkin's pragmatism was aimed at promoting the underlying purpose of international law: to restrain, limit, and regulate how states exercise military force. Watkin's arguments inspired many of the authors in this volume to think critically about the relationship between the armed conflict and law enforcement paradigms, generating both support and disagreement for his methodology. And Watkin himself contributed a new essay for this volume reflecting on these themes.

This volume focuses in particular on the United States and the United Kingdom because they have conducted especially prominent counterterrorism campaigns in which this issue has come to the fore. It is therefore especially important to assess their experience because of its potential precedential effect. Related to this point, this volume does not engage with scholars who see vestiges of colonialism in Western counterterrorism campaigns, as well as assertion of the hegemony of the Global North. Nor does it address Third World theorists who question whether a liberal rules-based international order serves the purposes that proponents claim, and whether it is even normatively desirable. We believe that it is important to consider these perspectives. A volume that includes them, however, would significantly stray from the central focus of this book: the extent

[1] *See* Kenneth Watkin, Fighting at the Legal Boundaries: Controlling the Use of Force in Contemporary Conflict (2016).

to which states can work within the legal paradigms of the existing international order to effectively address non-state violence.

The volume's focus on the US and UK experience does not entail any deference to the approach taken by these governments. Indeed, contributors to our volume challenge the tendency of major Western powers to reach for what we describe as the war paradigm, and examine whether hybrid approaches that draw from both paradigms in some cases might be more faithful to liberal democratic values. In this respect, this book operates within the liberal international tradition and explores the resources that it can provide for effectively responding to non-state violence.

Part I: The Framework Problem in Modern Conflict: Can We Still Distinguish War from Crime?

The chapters in this part illuminate the ways in which violence by non-state groups can confound characterization as crime or war. One implication of this is that reliance primarily on the war paradigm may not do justice to the need for calibrated responses that reflect a proper balance between respect for life and effectively subduing violent collective threats. Modern conflicts with non-state groups often do not occur on segregated battlefields but in urban settings that contain hostile forces embedded in a large population. The need for a state to engage in individualized assessments of who may be attacked, for instance, and the ostensible precision of weapons to do so, raises the question whether something akin to liability under the crime paradigm should govern the use of force in some cases.

In addition, unqualified embrace of the war paradigm may be counterproductive in defeating non-state groups and reducing terrorism. The perception that a state has minimal regard for the deaths of innocent persons can seriously jeopardize a state's ability to prevail in the conflict, and to establish conditions for longer-term peace and security. Furthermore, while the intensity and organizational level of non-state groups may warrant characterizing hostilities with them as an armed conflict subject to the law of war, such conflicts may not end with formal surrender or cessation of hostilities. This can create uncertainty about when state operations should shift from the war to the crime paradigm. At some point organized violence will presumably dip below the threshold required for triggering the legal machinery of "armed conflict," but identifying this moment in time can be controversial.

These tensions and complexities underscore that how we conceptualize non-state violence in general, and terrorism in particular, can have profound consequences for states' ability to respond to violence while remaining faithful to the basic commitments of the rule of law. The chapters in this part thus lay the foundation for the discussion in the remainder of the book of how states might address these complications.

Seth Cantey's chapter, "Non-State Actors, Terrorism, and the War Paradigm Revisited," examines various definitions of both war and terrorism, and describes the differences between traditional wars and campaigns against terrorist organizations. He draws on scholarship on metaphors, analogies, and cognitive frames to suggest that conceptualizing and describing operations against non-state armed groups as warfare neglects important complexities of these struggles. Reliance on the war paradigm, he argues, has been counterproductive in several ways. It has conferred legitimacy on terrorists as official enemies, consistent with their own characterization of their activities as a military campaign. In addition, it has polarized political debate, creating a tendency to impugn the patriotism of those who object to characterizing the counterterrorism as war.

Further, the war paradigm exaggerates the threat of terrorism by framing it as an existential threat to the nation. This in turn can lead to a response that is disproportionate to the danger that it presents. Finally, it risks expanding the understanding of what constitutes war well beyond conventional parameters to encompass a potentially wider range of situations that warrant using military force. Cantey argues that the war paradigm has been unsuccessful in its goal of significantly weakening organized terrorist groups, and that it is time to rethink the extent to which greater reliance on the crime paradigm may be more effective.

In her chapter, "The Limits of Law and the Value of Rights in Addressing Terrorism: A Study of the UN Counterterrorism Architecture," Fionnuala Ní Aoláin describes the work of the UN Security Council after 9/11 in characterizing terrorism as a threat to international peace and security that requires regulation on the global level. She notes that the Security Council has granted considerable discretion to states to determine what constitutes terrorism and which domestic responses are appropriate to deal with it. The Council has taken these steps without sufficiently emphasizing, or in some cases even mentioning, the importance that counterterrorism measures abide by state human rights obligations.

The result is that many states have used the pretense of counterterrorism to stifle domestic dissent and political opposition, and to significantly infringe on human rights. Ní Aoláin maintains that such violations not only inflict harm on individuals but foster conditions conducive to the emergence of radical violent extremism by generating resentment of the state and alienation from it. Her chapter thus provides a valuable study of the interaction of counterterrorism initiatives on the international and domestic levels, and how human rights concerns can be marginalized in this process.

Jens David Ohlin's chapter, "The Paradox of Discrimination," presents the reader with a riddle regarding how targeted killings against terrorists are conceptualized. Ohlin takes as his departure the two paradigms of law enforcement and armed conflict and argues that a military power selecting between the two categories has a difficult decision to make. Under the armed conflict paradigm, IHL, as well as the moral principles underlying it, requires that states use as little military force as possible so as to reduce collateral damage while at the same time achieving a state's legitimate military objective. Drone strikes accomplish this task by replacing large-scale military campaigns with killing individuals with ostensible surgical accuracy. Once a state reduces force this far, however, the drone strike looks less "war-like" and more like law enforcement. The problem is that the law enforcement paradigm views lethal force as presumptively inappropriate as a form of extrajudicial execution. Taken as a whole, the state is caught in a difficult "paradox": reduce lethal force to be more "humane" as IHL demands, at which point the frame of reference switches suddenly to law enforcement where lethal force, especially against a single individual, suddenly looks "brutal" because it is extrajudicial. The irony is that the more force the state uses, the less restrictive the law becomes, because IHL is more permissive in its targeting rules than the law enforcement framework. Ohlin's chapter seeks to present rather than resolve this tension, ultimately concluding with his worry that the overall phenomenon might give states an incentive to use more—rather than less—military force, which is the exact opposite of what some human rights activists are hoping for.

Joshua Andresen's chapter, "Fighting Terrorism under All Applicable Law," argues that the level of force used in counterterrorism should not be based simply on the determination whether operations are occurring in an armed conflict governed by IHL. Even if they are, Andresen argues, permissions and constraints should depend on the circumstances in which force will be used. On one end of the spectrum is active combat in which combatants and civilians are clearly distinguishable, when full application of IHL is appropriate. On the other end is a situation far from an active battlefield, when combatants and civilians are intermingled, in which following international human rights law (IHRL) is preferable.

Andresen suggests seven factors to consider in determining where conditions fit on this spectrum. These are (1) the gravity of the threat that forces face; (2) whether operations are taking place in active combat areas; (3) whether civilians are absent or are readily distinguishable from combatants; (4) whether decisions must be made in the heat of battle; (5) whether the state exercises effective control over the area where the use of force is contemplated; (6) whether the state exercises authority and control over the people subject to the use of force; and (7) the reliability of the information that will be the basis for the use of force.

Based on these considerations, Andresen suggests, some combination of IHL and IHRL may be the most appropriate source of guidance on the use of force.

Laurie R. Blank's chapter, "When Conflict Recurs: Classification of Conflict when Hostilities Break Out Anew," discusses the challenge of determining when use of force under IHL is no longer an option because an armed conflict has ended. Hostilities with non-state groups may be especially likely to ebb and flow rather than follow the clear stages that tend to characterize conflicts between states. Should recurrence of violence be regarded as a continuation of an armed conflict, or should it be evaluated on its own to assess whether it meets the criteria of intensity and organization? Blank notes that states may have an incentive to take the former approach in order to enhance their authority, but this risks blurring the line between war and peace and creating an endless conflict. On the other hand, a history of violence may be relevant and ignoring it can be unrealistic.

Blank suggests that with internal hostilities it is reasonable for a state to rely first on domestic law enforcement measures to address violence, with resort to military force only when it becomes so intense and organized that it is necessary to declare the existence of an armed conflict. When violence is emanating from outside a state's borders, however, a conventional law enforcement response may be less feasible. Blank discusses other considerations that can be relevant in determining how the criteria for an armed conflict are interpreted in the face of a resurgence of violence. Since fighting between state and non-state groups continues to constitute the majority of hostilities, developing a framework for addressing this question is likely to grow in importance.

Part II: War as Criminal Enforcement

The chapters in this part consider whether the fluidity of armed conflicts with non-state groups calls into question the need to use the war paradigm in all circumstances. Might tools drawn from the crime paradigm complement or substitute for military measures? Should members of non-state groups with which a state is engaged in hostilities necessarily be characterized as combatants, for instance, or might treating them as criminals accomplish security goals while preventing harm to innocent persons? Even if a state is engaged in an armed conflict, are there instances in which using force under human rights principles rather than international humanitarian law is a wiser and more effective course of action?

In responding to violence by non-state groups, modern military forces are called upon to engage in many operations that do not conform to full-scale warfare. In this respect, the military may be used as a tool within the crime paradigm.

This can involve effectively serving as a police force that treats violent actors as criminals who must be brought to justice. Performing this function is guided by human rights principles with respect to detention and the use of force.

At the same time, military forces playing this role may quickly be required to deal with levels of violence that far exceed the normal law enforcement setting. How should the law address this increasingly common situation? When should the use of force be governed by human rights law and when by international humanitarian law? How should we conceptualize the role of the military in operations against non-state groups outside of active battlefields? Is it better to rely on the traditional rules of armed conflict with which the military is familiar and make restrictive adjustments as a matter of policy? Or should we incorporate these adjustments into legally binding rules? The chapters in this part examine how the fluid nature and location of hostilities with violent non-state groups give rise to these questions and how we might answer them.

Finally, the creative and aggressive use of law may provide a supplement or an alternative to the use of force in responding to non-state violence. This use of law as "lawfare" is an underexplored option that deserves more consideration. This part surveys the ways in which the goal of thwarting violence by non-state groups may rely on adjustments to the war paradigm in the course of hostilities or may be furthered by nonforcible means.

In "Fighting State and Non-State Actors in a Postwar World: Restoring the Rule of Law to the War on Terror," Claire Finkelstein examines how the United States has approached the challenge of characterizing individuals who are engaged on behalf of terrorist organizations in conflict with the United States. International law does not use the categories of combatants and civilians with respect to non-international armed conflicts between states and non-state groups. The United States has designated members of Al Qaeda and associated forces as unlawful combatants who may be targeted on the basis of their combatant status but who are not entitled to combatant immunity or treatment as prisoners of war. Finkelstein suggests that this application of the war paradigm poses the risk both of avoiding legal constraints on the use of force by one state against another, and of extending this paradigm into domestic law enforcement operations.

Finkelstein suggests that the former risk is reflected in the US targeted killing of Iran's Quds Forces commander Qasem Soleimani, in that the administration appeared to treat him as a dangerous individual rather than as a state official. She argues that the latter risk materializes in the militarized police responses to demonstrators on behalf of causes such as Black Lives Matter. Finkelstein proposes that non-state actors be regarded as members of criminal organizations rather than combatants. When they are engaged in hostilities in theaters of combat they may be targeted as civilians directly participating in hostilities on a continuous basis. Outside of such locations, however, states should use the criminal law to address the threat that they pose.

Kenneth Watkin's chapter, "Urban Warfare: Policing Conflict," notes that states are likely to confront major challenges from criminal, terrorist, and insurgent groups in major urban areas that are projected to grow at substantial rates over the next few decades. In some cases they will need to deal with major outbreaks of organized violence in the midst of densely populated areas with a significant number of innocent persons. Watkin argues that states should place priority on responding to these threats through law enforcement operations guided as much as possible by human rights law. This places a premium on policing as an essentially defensive activity rather than one that involves offensive operations. As violence intensifies, this may need to be supplemented by constabulary units experienced in operating in more volatile environments, as well as by military units engaged in policing.

The overall approach, however, should draw on counterinsurgency doctrine and its sensitivity to local population perception of forces' commitment to avoiding the loss of innocent human life and fair treatment of individuals. Watkin observes that some judicial decisions suggest flexible and potentially expansive authority under human rights law to take life and use intense levels of violence in some circumstances. He suggests, however, that at some point this may create the risk of the "militarization" of human rights law. It is preferable, he argues, to maintain a clear distinction between human rights law and the law of war—that is, the crime and the war paradigm—so that police do not begin to mirror military forces in their operations.

In "Ratchet Down or Ramp Up? Contemporary Threats, Armed Conflict, and Tailored Authority," Geoffrey S. Corn challenges the view that the existence of an armed conflict with non-state groups should automatically allow use of force as intensively and expansively as IHL permits.. He notes that such hostilities have become the most common form of modern conflict, but that they involve varying levels of violence that should not necessarily be met with full-bore military force. Instead, he argues, drawing on Watkin's work, that states should adopt a presumption of responding at least initially with operations governed by law enforcement standards, even in the course of a non-international armed conflict. Exceeding this level of force would require justification based on conditions on the ground that make proceeding under law enforcement authority likely to be ineffective under the circumstances. This would acknowledge that there may be what he calls "springing" armed conflicts of relatively brief duration that require operating under IHL.

This approach, says Corn, is most feasible on the operational level, which involves keener sensitivity to contextual factors than is available on the strategic level. This approach is already followed to some extent in formulating rules of engagement with respect to specific missions. It reflects the idea that using force as expansively as IHL permits is appropriate only in exceptional situations, and that many contemporary security challenges straddle the line between crime and armed conflict. It also allows commanders flexibility in tailoring the use of force to actual needs, rather than insisting that recognition of an armed conflict provides authority to use the maximum amount of force IHL would allow.

In "Using Law as a Weapon against Nuclear Proliferation and Terrorism: The US Government's Financial Lawfare against Iran," Orde Kittrie describes the use of what he calls "financial warfare" by the United States against states such as Iran, Russia, and North Korea as an instrument to serve national security goals. The US Treasury Department has been the lead agency in this effort, blocking access to the US economy and financial system for various states and individuals. This reflects greater willingness to use US financial regulatory authorities for national security objectives, and utilization of more widely available intelligence about global private sector business transactions. It has also involved directly contacting individual foreign private companies to induce them to stop doing business with designated parties, which can provide a more expeditious means of producing an impact.

Kittrie notes that, while companies in the finance, energy, and insurance sectors traditionally have been the targets of such efforts, major foreign companies in other sectors may be targets in the future. He cautions that the United States should carefully consider both the benefits of such measures and the risk of setting precedents that could be used against it in the future. Nonetheless, in appropriate cases, financial warfare may be an effective alternative to military options, allowing achievement of objectives with less loss of life and at lower cost.

Finally, Christopher J. Fuller's "Human Rights Law as an Alternative to *Jus in Bello*" examines the contrasting US and UK approaches to counterterrorism for much of the period following the 9/11 attacks. While the United States quickly adopted the war paradigm, the United Kingdom for the most part relied on the crime paradigm to address the threat of terrorism. Fuller suggests that the US approach has created an unduly elevated fear of terrorism among the American public, as well as an unrealistic expectation of virtually absolute protection against it. In addition, it has fostered involvement in an open-ended war based on the belief that terrorists pose an existential threat to the United States. This makes difficult the development of a sense of psychological resilience among the population that accepts the occurrence of at least some small-scale terrorist attacks for the foreseeable future.

By contrast, the United Kingdom generally has treated terrorists as criminals and has acknowledged the need to adhere to human rights obligations in its counterterrorism operations. Its strategy has been to reduce the risk of terrorism, not completely eliminate it, so that people generally can go about their daily lives with some confidence and sense of normality. This eschews the idea that the United Kingdom is involved in an existential conflict with terrorists who must be totally defeated. Fuller expresses concern, however, that the rise of ISIS and the prospect of returning foreign fighters has led the United Kingdom to embrace the kind of targeted killing program that the United States has conducted for several years. While relying solely on the crime paradigm may make this more aggressive approach appear necessary, Fuller argues that the United Kingdom should resist following the US example of treating current counterterrorism operations as activities conducted under the war paradigm. Instead, the United Kingdom should subject them to human rights law standards. He acknowledges that this will require clarifying the scope of extraterritorial jurisdiction under human rights law, as well as how those standards apply to such operations. Nonetheless, he maintains, doing so will be an important way in which the United Kingdom can continue to adopt a more realistic counterterrorism approach than US reliance on the war paradigm.

Part III: Fighting Crime as War

Chapters in this part are based on recognition that states following the crime paradigm must consider how to respond to non-state violence when it moves beyond threats to individuals and public order to challenge to the basic authority of the state and its ability to perform its core functions. In other words, when is a state engaged in policing and when is it engaged in self-defense? One dimension of this issue is when a state may adopt the latter posture in anticipation of an armed attack, rather than in response to an actual one. If some non-state groups are continuously engaged in planning violent attacks, at what point does their activity pose a sufficiently grave threat that a state may use military force against their members?

A related issue is the extent to which it is plausible to analogize non-state armed groups to state military forces. Is the loose affiliation of cells and members of a non-state group sufficiently similar to the hierarchical command and control structure of state forces to say that a state is at "war" with an identifiable collective enemy? If so, how do we know who are non-state "combatants" in the absence of the formal roles that characterize state militaries?

Finally, the law governing inter-state armed conflicts prescribes when a state may use force in the territory of a nonbelligerent state. Should we draw on this doctrine to analyze the ability of one state to use force in another state with which it is not at war, but in which violent non-state groups pose a threat to the first state? Can the threatened state bring war into another state without the latter's consent? As these questions indicate, the rules for initiating conflict under the war paradigm do not provide clear guidance for responding to violence by non-state groups that exceeds the level of intensity that characterizes ordinary crime.

In her chapter, "National Security Policymaking in the Shadow of International Law," Laura A. Dickinson suggests, drawing on the example of the Obama administration, that policy can be used to conduct activities in a more constrained fashion than legal authority would permit. She discusses the creation of the Presidential Policy Guidance on the use of direct action and of the Periodic Review Boards (PRB) to determine if continued confinement of prisoners at Guantánamo Bay is warranted. The former incorporated standards closely resembling requirements under human rights law to govern capture of or the use of lethal force against targets outside "areas of active hostilities." At the same time, the United States reserved the right as a legal matter to engage in direct action in these areas under the more permissive rules of IHL applicable in an armed conflict. Similarly, the PRB provided a review process for persons detained as non-state enemy combatants in an armed conflict that normally is required only for detention of civilians. Dickinson surmises that one important reason that these steps were taken is the need to respond to coalition allies' concern about compliance with their own human rights obligations when collaborating with the United States. These policies were continued with some revision during the Trump administration.

Policy, Dickinson argues, can be a pragmatic way of conforming operations more closely with human rights principles while avoiding the potential delay and controversy that may result from attempts to institute formal legal change. She asserts that policy may become embedded through organizational processes and institutional culture in a way that makes likely its continuation by subsequent administrations. She also notes that they may be framed in legalistic terms, containing rules and standards that must be interpreted by lawyers in advising operators on what is permissible. At the same time, she acknowledges that they elide differences of opinion on international law and can retard the development of customary norms. In any event, she concludes, the use of policy deserves greater attention as one way in which a state may achieve greater compliance with international norms.

John C. Dehn's chapter, "Emerging Transnational Self-Defense Norms and Unrealized Liberal Values," argues that recent trends in invocation of state self-defense pose a risk to liberal principles of respect for sovereignty, human rights, and strict limits on resort to and use of military force. The US declaration of an armed conflict against Al Qaeda and associated forces, he maintains, purports to enable the United States to use lethal force against non-state actors deemed enemy combatants in any location on the globe without demonstrating that they pose an imminent threat to the United States. Any such operation is deemed to be one in self-defense under the UN Charter and automatically governed by the law of armed conflict.

Coupled with this formulation is US insistence that it may undertake an operation in another state without its consent if that state is unable or unwilling to meet the threat emanating from its territory. The result, Dehn contends, is akin to the earlier view associated with Grotius that civilized states are bound to respect the sovereignty of their peers, but not of states regarded as "uncivilized," and therefore beyond the bounds of law. He expresses concern that recent interpretations of state self-defense perpetuate a hierarchy of states and of sovereignty that is inconsistent with principles of a liberal international order. This creates the risk that more powerful states will be able to use force against actors they deem threatening in any location in the world.

In his chapter, "Finding Peace in the Law of War," written before the Taliban reassumed power in Afghanstan, Bailey Brown draws on the experiences of Afghanistan and Colombia to emphasize that non-international armed conflicts may not involve a clear cessation of hostilities that triggers the displacement of IHL by civil law enforcement. Rather, such conflicts may involve a gradual transition from warfare to stability in which it is necessary to draw on both of these legal regimes. In Afghanistan, for instance, combat operations officially ended, but the official new government was not an established central regime that could exercise authority based on the rule of law and human rights principles throughout the country. Instead, it faced persistent violence by insurgents who found safe haven in various areas. This required continued use of force under IHL to provide security and seek greater control over the country. In this respect, de facto continuation of armed conflict was necessary in attempting tostabilize the nascent effort to establish and extend governmental authority. Brown suggests that the coexistence of armed conflict and civil law may continue for an extended period of time in some cases, until government is strong enough to exercise effective control.

In Colombia, guerillas, drug cartels, and criminal gangs control areas within the country and pose a challenge to establishing a stable government based on the rule of law. Columbia has relied on both IHL and human rights principles to govern the use of force in different circumstances. A striking reflection of this is the fact that the Colombian military has two different cards setting forth different rules of engagement: a blue card explaining law enforcement standards based on human rights principles, and a red card based on IHL. As in Afghanistan, Brown suggests, the existence of civil law based on human rights principles can be an emergent phenomenon, rather than a state of affairs that automatically comes into being formal end of an armed conflict. In these cases, IHL can help protect the civil law regime as it matures, fostering the kind of confidence and allegiance necessary for it to take root.

Todd Huntley and Mitt Regan discuss the use of social network analysis in counterterrorism operations in their chapter, "From Armed Conflict to Countering Threat Networks: Counterterrorism and Social Network Analysis." They describe how groups engaged in illegal activities such as terrorism or drug smuggling eschew traditional hierarchical organizational forms in favor of "dark networks" that can evade detection. This creates challenges for states in attempting to combat these groups because information that is readily available may simply consist of data on a large number of individuals without indication of any connection among them. Social network analysis can help connect the dots among these individuals. It relies on the accumulation of large amounts of information about individuals' affiliations and activities to identify and depict significant types of relationships among individuals who otherwise may seem unconnected with one another. This enables analysts to discern networks that serve as conduits for the flow of resources such as information, influence, services, and goods. It also allows identification of individuals who are "hubs" who play a crucial role in connecting parts of the network to one another.

Huntley and Regan argue that social network analysis is enabling the shift of US counterterrorism efforts from an "industrial age" model of armed conflict to an "information age" model of countering threat networks. This approach is described in US Department of Defense Joint Publication 3-25, "Countering Threat Networks." That publication sets forth an approach that focuses on using social network analysis to monitor activities across the globe that may eventually pose a threat to the United States. The emphasis is on identifying these threats and intervening to interrupt the flow of various types of resources that networks may use in strengthening their capabilities. Joint Publication 3-25 emphasizes the importance of nonkinetic measures in this process and cautions that it will rarely be the case that any network can be definitively defeated. On the one hand, this approach reflects a movement away from the emphasis on kinetic action that has characterized US reliance on the war paradigm for counterterrorism. On the other hand, Huntley and Regan note, it also contains the risk that in some cases lethal force may be used for preventive purposes rather than to address an imminent threat, or that it may serve to expand even further the US conception of when a threat is imminent.

Part IV: Crime and War: Prosecuting Terrorism and War Crimes

While the first three parts focus on forward-looking counterterrorism operations, the "paradigm question" also implicates the legal tools used to hold individuals responsible for acts of terrorism. Indeed, each paradigm has its own distinctive set of criminal law categories to hold people to account for wrongdoing; those categories are often related to the foundational assumptions implicit in each paradigm. So, for example, domestic criminal law provides the opportunity to prosecute individuals for offenses related to terrorism, while the law of war enables prosecution for war crimes that constitute grave breaches of the Geneva Conventions. With respect to prosecution under domestic law, is it possible to apprehend and prosecute violent non-state actors while respecting basic principles of sovereignty? To what extent should states be able to bring proceedings against persons who are not their citizens for conduct that did not occur within their territory? How feasible is it to gather evidence on terrorists that satisfies basic due process requirements in locations torn by conflict with only minimally functioning justice systems?

With respect to prosecution for war crimes, international law does not use the categories of combatant and civilian to characterize parties involved in non-international armed conflict. The standard "textbook" position regarding non-international armed conflict is that non-state actors do not enjoy the "privilege" of belligerency and therefore international law places no restriction on their domestic prosecution. At the same, thowever, international law has placed no restrictions on the ability of the government to exercise military force against rebels or terrorists, as long as that military action is consistent with *jus in bello* and does not violate the sovereignty of other nations. This creates the potential for disparate procedural protections in such conflicts for prosecution of one's own forces and of those regarded as the enemy. Finally, the military commission proceedings at Guantánamo Bay have prompted substantial criticism for their failure to abide by fundamental rule of law principles. Remedying its deficiencies would seem an especially important task in restoring the primacy of those principles and enhancing the perceived legality of the US counterterrorism campaign. How can this be done? The chapters in this part discuss issues that loom large for the rule of law in counterterrorism campaigns and implicate questions of how the two governing paradigms should interact with each other, particularly in the context of criminal prosecutions.

Evan R. Seamone's chapter, "Counting the Ripples: The Challenge of Extraterritorial Jurisdiction to Prosecute Non-State Actors," examines the potential of international law to permit a state to bring criminal prosecutions against terrorists who are neither citizens of that state nor commit terrorism within it. The protective principle of extraterritorial jurisdiction allows prosecution of aliens who commit offenses in foreign lands when the aliens have engaged in conduct that threatens the "security or other vital interests" of the prosecuting state. On the one hand, this may enable a state to rely on the crime paradigm in pursuing a counterterrorism strategy. On the other hand, as Seamone observes, the principle is susceptible to potential abuse by states that make expansive claims about the impact of foreign activities on their national interests.

Seamone analyzes how courts have interpreted the protective principle, focusing on the level of interference with important government interests sufficient to establish jurisdiction and the connection between the alien and those interests. He notes that, for instance, the mere fact that vessels containing contraband could find their way to a state is not in itself an adequate basis for jurisdiction, but that evidence of likely intent eventually to bring contraband to a state has been enough to do. He also observes that acts of terrorism by aliens abroad can be a basis for invocation of the protective principle if those acts have been done in preparation for an ultimate attack on the state. He poses a hypothetical set of events that raises a number of issues that need to be clarified in determining the scope of the principle as a basis for extraterritorial criminal prosecution.

The chapter by Bibi van Ginkel, Christophe Paulussen, and Tanya Mehra, "Diversifying the Sources of Evidence in Terrorism Cases before Criminal Courts in (Post-)Conflict and High-Risk Situations: The Role of the Military," discusses how conditions of conflict can create substantial challenges in investigating and prosecuting individuals for terrorist crimes in domestic courts. It may be difficult for civil investigators and prosecutors to travel to a conflict area, there may not be a cooperation agreement between the prosecuting state and the state where the possible crime has been committed, or there may not be an effective government in place where investigation needs to recur. As a practical matter, military forces are often first to arrive at a potential crime scene and may be in the best position to gather evidence in a timely fashion. Such forces, however, typically are not trained or equipped to perform this function, which creates the risk that what they gather may later be deemed inadmissible in a prosecution.

The authors suggest how to address this concern when it is necessary to rely on members of the military to gather information about terrorist crimes in high-risk situations. Military units engaged in counterterrorism operations should gain understanding of the legal frameworks that govern the collection of information in accordance with principles of evidence. They also should work as closely as possible with civilian investigators and prosecutors to learn about the criminal justice process to know how they can best contribute to it. The authors maintain in addition that judges confronted with some irregularity in military collection of evidence should take into account what is reasonable to demand of the military under the conditions that existed at the time, how close to the prosecuting entity the person involved in the irregularity is, and the significance of the norm from which there has been a departure.

The chapter by Chris Jenks, "US Military Prosecutions during Non-International Armed Conflict," discusses an activity during wartime that is based on the criminal justice model. This is the prosecution of war crimes, which are grave breaches of the Geneva Conventions regulating the conduct of armed conflict. The conventions require that a state's prosecution of both its own forces and those of the enemy for such crimes be conducted under identical proceedings when a state is involved in an armed conflict with another state. Such equivalence is not automatically required, however, in a non-international armed conflict with a non-state group. Common Article 3 of the conventions says simply that proceedings must involve judicial guarantees "recognized as indispensable by civilized peoples." Jenks notes that since 2001, the United States has tried what it regards as non-state combatants in military commissions that do not involve the same procedural protections as prosecutions of US service members.

The maximum penalties for the same offense diverge substantially under these two systems. For instance, a non-state enemy defendant can be subject to lifetime imprisonment without the possibility of parole for intentionally causing serious bodily injury, whereas, depending upon the instrument used to cause injury, a US service member could receive only a three-year sentence. Jenks finds that actual penalties that have been imposed by military commissions are much less severe than those available. This indicates that sentencing officials' temperament and judgment mitigate the risk posed by significantly different available maximum punishments. He argues, however, that we should not rely on such individual characteristics to reduce the risk of arbitrary imposition of punishment. Rule of law values of predictability and the desirability of equivalent treatment of comparably placed individuals should lead to equivalent procedural protections in prosecution of enemy and US service defendants for war crimes in non-international armed conflicts.

Conclusion

Overall, the chapters in this volume focus on the interplay between competing paradigms—law enforcement and armed conflict—and in so doing, they collectively raise a fundamental question about the nature of legal paradigms and how they structure legal and moral analysis. How should the selection of paradigm be accomplished? Lawyers are usually inclined to look for triggering conditions, that is, legal facts that establish which body of law should apply to the situation. Then, once the body of law is selected, it is applied to the legal question at issue to yield a particular answer. This structured type of analysis also finds expression in some, though not all, philosophical approaches to these questions, at least under "classical" just war theory, which recognizes a different set of rules governing the conduct of warfare.

But this is not the only way of proceeding. As some of the chapters in this volume explore, one can mix and match elements from multiple paradigms based on what is most appropriate for the particular context. While some lawyers might bristle at such a contextual approach and consider it unprincipled, or even worse, incoherent, there are competing values at stake. On the one hand, a rigid approach might serve a strict "gate-keeping" function, ensuring that the relatively permissive rules governing the conduct of armed conflict are only triggered in the rarest of circumstances. On the other hand, though, a contextual approach might give states, and the international community, the flexibility to come up with workable modus operandi that promote real change on the ground. While these proposed solutions might not go as far as some would hope, it is also the case that strict approaches that are never adopted by definition do not have a positive impact on the real world. The essays in this volume bring both conceptual and practical insights together to help foster an ongoing conversation about real solutions to modern non-state armed violence.

PART I

THE FRAMEWORK PROBLEM IN MODERN CONFLICT: CAN WE STILL DISTINGUISH WAR FROM CRIME?

1

Non-State Actors, Terrorism, and the War Paradigm Revisited

Seth Cantey

I. Introduction

President George W. Bush's address to Congress on September 20, 2001, shortly after the 9/11 attacks, marked the beginning of an ongoing conflict against an increasing variety of actors.[1] The past twenty years have seen invasions and occupations of Afghanistan and Iraq; regime change in Libya; airstrikes against Syria; and special operations in Pakistan, Somalia, Yemen, and elsewhere. Legal authorities to counter terrorism have evolved significantly: high-ranking state officials like Qasem Soleimani can now be designated terrorists and killed on that basis. By mid 2020, leading US officials had plenty to say about how to quell nationwide domestic protests. Secretary of Defense Mark Esper urged US states to "dominate the battlespace."[2] Attorney General Bill Bar explained that Washington would use its "joint terrorist task force" to address the problem.[3] President Donald J. Trump told governors: "You have to dominate. If you don't dominate, you're wasting your time. . . . These [protestors] are terrorists."[4] How does conceptual slippage like this happen? What are its implications?

International law does not provide a legally binding definition of war, so whether the United States is technically at war is a semantic matter.[5] But semantics matter. The nature of conflict influences the language we use to describe it, but the reverse is also true. Words affect how we think about and respond to threats, and they can be employed to move policy and public support for leaders'

[1] George Bush, "Address to a Joint Session of Congress and the American People," Washington, DC (Sept. 20, 2001).

[2] Missy Ryan & Dan Lamothe, *Trump Administration to Significantly Expand Military Response in Washington Amid Unrest*, WASH. POST, June 1, 2020.

[3] Donald Trump, "Transcript of President Trump's Call with US Governors over Protests" (June 1, 2020).

[4] *Id.*

[5] The US Constitution endows Congress with the authority to declare war, but the power to *initiate* hostilities rests with the president. Since the War Powers Resolution of 1973, the president has authorized military force absent Congressional authorization at least 132 times. *See* National Constitution Center Staff, "When Congress Last Used Its Powers to Declare War" (Dec. 8, 2016).

Seth Cantey, *Non-State Actors, Terrorism, and the War Paradigm Revisited* In: *Between Crime and War*. Edited by: Claire Finkelstein, Christopher Fuller, Jens David Ohlin, Mitt Regan, Oxford University Press. © Claire Finkelstein, Christopher Fuller, Jens David Ohlin, Mitt Regan 2023. DOI: 10.1093/oso/9780197638798.003.0002

decisions in nonintuitive directions. The experience of recent years proves that the *language* of fighting non-state actors has far-reaching legal, moral, and national security implications.

This chapter revisits a debate that emerged in the aftermath of 9/11 about how best to conceptualize the ongoing politico-military struggle against violent non-state actors—what so often has been called the "war on terror." It draws on literature from legal, academic, and policy circles to explain the allure of analogies and, in doing so, argues that the use of rhetorical devices related to war in recent years has been detrimental to our effort to counter violent extremism. The central claim is that the past two decades show that thinking about counterterrorism as war has been counterproductive for the United States.

The argument proceeds as follows. The next section defines terrorism and war for the purposes of this discussion. The third section reviews literature on metaphors, analogies, and the use of cognitive frames, illustrating both the allure and potential pitfalls of applying these devices to unfamiliar problems. The fourth section engages existing arguments *for* conceptualizing the struggle against terrorism as war, and the fifth makes a case *against* that conceptualization. The final section reflects on the evolution and implications of past and current policies for the future and questions whether existing legal architecture is sufficient to confront the challenges posed by non-state violent and terrorism today.

II. Terrorism and War

Terrorism. Long before 9/11, lawyers, judges, social scientists, policymakers, and others struggled to find consensus regarding the definition of terrorism. So far none of these efforts has proven successful. Experts continue to disagree about who can commit acts of terrorism, about who can be victimized by such acts, and about the validity of an oft-cited maxim: "One man's terrorist is another man's freedom fighter."[6] One of the world's preeminent experts on the subject, Bruce Hoffman, defines terrorism as "the deliberate creation and exploitation of fear through violence or the threat of violence in the pursuit of political change."[7] Though a useful starting point, this definition is incomplete because it encompasses what traditional armies do in conventional war. This conflation must be avoided; for a definition of terrorism to be useful, it must distinguish terrorist violence from other forms.

[6] Boaz Ganor, *Defining Terrorism: Is One Man's Terrorist Another Man's Freedom Fighter?*, 3 Police Practice & Research no. 4 (2002).

[7] Bruce Hoffman, Inside Terrorism 40 (2006).

For a political perspective, one might turn to the definition of terrorism proffered by the US State Department: "premeditated, politically motivated violence perpetrated against noncombatant targets by subnational groups or clandestine agents, usually intended to influence an audience."[8] This is a better description of the phenomenon but suffers from at least two problems. First, the State Department includes within the "non-combatant" element of its definition any "military personnel who at the time of the incident are unarmed or not on duty." This is a flawed and transparently self-interested distinction. As Claire Finkelstein notes in this volume, "In the traditional law of war, combatants have the rights, privileges and protections they do by way of their status. Their status, however, is also what puts them at risk. . . . Thus a combatant can be targeted when he is sleeping, watching a movie, taking a shower, etc., as long as he remains a combatant." Second, states have employed premeditated, politically motivated violence against noncombatant targets with the intention of influencing audiences throughout history.[9] One could reasonably argue that this definition thus limits terrorism to non-state actors to "define away" the possibility that a state could commit terrorist acts.

Among the most important legal definitions of terrorism are those in 18 USC 2331 and the USA PATRIOT Act.[10] Referring specifically to *international* terrorism, the US Code defines such activities as those that

A) involve violent acts or acts dangerous to human life that are a violation of the criminal laws of the United States or of any State, or that would be a criminal violation if committed within the jurisdiction of the United States or any State;
B) appear to be intended—
    i) to intimidate or coerce a civilian population,
    ii) to influence the policy of a government by intimidation or coercion; or
    iii) to affect the conduct of a government by mass destruction, assassination, or kidnapping; and
C) occur primarily outside the territorial jurisdiction of the United States, or transcend national boundaries in terms of the means by which they are accomplished, the persons they appear intended to intimidate or coerce, or the locale in which their perpetrators operate or seek asylum.[11]

[8] Office of the Coordinator for Counterterrorism, US Department of State, "Patterns of Global Terrorism," 2001.

[9] Alexander Downes, Targeting Civilians in War (2008).

[10] Uniting and Strengthening America by Providing Appropriate Tools Required to Intercept and Obstruct Terrorism (PATRIOT) Act of 2001.

[11] 18 U.S.C. 2331.

According to the USA PATRIOT Act, in Section 411, Part F, Subsection IV, the term 'engage in terrorist activity' means, in an individual capacity or as a member of an organization,

- (I) to commit or to incite to commit, under circumstances indicating an intention to cause death or serious bodily injury, a terrorist activity;
- (II) to prepare or plan a terrorist activity;
- (III) to gather information on potential targets for terrorist activity;
- (IV) to solicit funds or other things of value for—
  - (aa) a terrorist activity
  - (bb) a terrorist organization described in clause (vi)(I) or (vi)((II); or
  - (cc) a terrorist organization described in clause (vi)(III), unless the solicitor can demonstrate that he did not know, and should not reasonably have known, that the solicitation would further the organization's terrorist activity.[12]

These definitions suffer from problems similar to those outlined above. The US Code, for example, is expansive enough to make the definition of terrorism contingent on the laws of "any state." Separately, as in Hoffman's definition, Subparagraph B of the US Code describes violence that is common in conventional war. Indeed, the only clause that separates international terrorism from violence in conventional war claims that international terrorism necessarily violates criminal law in the United States or another state.

A more egregious problem exists in the text of the USA PATRIOT Act, which provides a tautological definition: terrorist activity occurs when one commits or incites terrorist activity. This reflects one of many problems associated with how we use language when we think about unfamiliar phenomena. Words do more than describe what we think; they influence what we think. This point is addressed in detail in the next section.

Enduring lack of consensus about the definition of terrorism is frustrating for two main reasons. First, without a common definition the term is imprecise and subjective, dependent on the perspective of the definer. An Israeli may argue that a suicide bombing committed by a Palestinian is a clear case of terrorism; a Palestinian may retort that indiscriminate bombing in retaliation for such attacks constitutes the same. Conor Gearty, who adheres to the idea that one man's terrorist *can* be another man's freedom fighter, has argued that the term has become "the rhetorical servant of the established order, whatever and however heinous its own activities are."[13]

[12] USA PATRIOT Act (HR 3162).

[13] Conor Gearty, *Terrorism and Morality*, RUSI J. 36–37 (2002).

A second problem is that definitional agreement is probably necessary for effective international coordination to combat terrorism. Some have gone so far as to argue that only on the basis of international understanding would it be possible to demand that all nations withhold support from terrorist organizations.[14] Yet the United Nations has failed to reach agreement about the definition, precluding that institution from adopting a proposed UN Comprehensive Anti-Terrorism Treaty.[15]

It would be too optimistic to proffer a definition of terrorism here in hopes that it may gain universal acceptance. Because conceptual clarity is both the motivation and the goal of this chapter, however, saying exactly what we mean by the term is necessary. An improved definition would entail three requisite elements: the use of violence, noncombatant targeting, and political motivation. It would also be as broad as possible, preventing selective use by interested parties while distinguishing terrorism from other forms of violence.

Consistent with these criteria, this discussion builds on Carsten Bockstette, who describes terrorism as "[p]olitical violence that is designed to induce terror and psychic fear (sometimes indiscriminate) through the violent victimization and destruction of noncombatant targets."[16] I define terrorism as "the intentional targeting of noncombatants for political purposes." Perhaps the principal attributes of this definition are that it distinguishes terrorism from insurgency[17] and applies a universal standard of responsibility to state and non-state actors that employ the tactic.

War. As with terrorism, consensus about the definition of war has eluded legal, academic, and policy circles. Traditionally, war has been a contest between states. According to Lassa Oppenheim's famous treatise on international law, "War is the contention between two or more states through their armed forces, for the purpose of overpowering each other and imposing such conditions of peace as the victor pleases."[18] Yoram Dinstein argues that, of the various elements of Oppenheim's definition, only one can be readily accepted today: "that war is a contest between states."[19]

[14] Ganor, *supra* note 6, at 287.

[15] Negotiations seeking to reach a "Comprehensive Convention on International Terrorism" began in 1996. They remain deadlocked.

[16] Carsten Bockstette, "Jihadist Terrorist Use of Strategic Communication Management Techniques," George C. Marshall European Center for Security Studies Occasional Paper Series, 20 (2008), 8.

[17] Consistent with this definition, Ganor, *supra* note 6, at 287, argues that the aims of terrorism and guerrilla warfare (i.e., insurgency) may be identical, but that they are distinguished by the targets of their operations. Guerrilla targets are military; terrorist targets are civilian. Lost here is the reality that most insurgencies target civilians as one among many tactics in their campaigns. What constitutes a "terrorist group," as opposed to an insurgency, thus remains a thorny definitional problem.

[18] Lassa Oppenheim, International Law, II, 56 (1906).

[19] Yoram Dinstein, War, Aggression and Self-Defence 14 (3d ed. 2001).

While Philip Bobbitt believes that the character of war is evolving such that states and non-state actors will increasingly go to war against each other, he observes that "[f]rom the time when the first modern states began to emerge, only states have made war . . . War is a matter between states—constitutional entities created by and wielding law—and war carries with it the constitutional evolution of five centuries of interstate conflict."[20]

Benjamin Wittes further highlights the role of the state when he contrasts policing with "warmaking," which he refers to as "radically different deployments of violence *by the state* [emphasis added], the former being the exercise of a legitimate near-monopoly of violence and the latter being the exercise of the level of violence dictated by military necessity in order to create a monopoly on the use of violence."[21]

Not all definitions require that states be on both sides of the phenomenon. J. David Singer and Melvin Small began the Correlates of War (COW) project[22] at the University of Michigan in the early 1960s seeking to define the scale of violence that constituted war—eventually settling on one thousand battle-related deaths per year—and to build a typology of war. They distinguished three kinds: inter-state wars (those between states), extra-systemic wars (those between states and non-state entities), and civil wars (those between a state and one or more non-state groups within a given state's borders). Despite some definitional overlap between the second and third types, in all cases they recognized war as combat between states and identifiable groups.

Some argue that efforts to reach consensus on a definition of war are both futile and moot, especially since formal declarations of war seem to be relics of the past.[23] The United States has not declared war since 1942, and there is little in the US Constitution that suggests what kinds of hostilities amount to war. The War Powers Resolution of 1973, which sought to claw back congressional war powers from the executive, did little to shed light on the matter. Indeed, the term "international armed conflict" has become more common than "war" in the realm of international law.

Though large-scale military action between the armed forces of internationally recognized states has come to be the most common understanding of war, this is clearly *not* the only way the term is used. Throughout history, "war" has

[20] Philip Bobbitt, Terror and Consent: The Wars for the Twenty-First Century 125 (2008).

[21] Legislating the War on Terror 350 (Benjamin Wittes ed., 2009).

[22] https://correlatesofwar.org.

[23] Nikolas Gvosdev and Andrew Stigler note, "[S]ince 'war' is forbidden by the charter of the United Nations except in self-defense or if authorized by the Security Council, states hardly ever declare military actions to be 'war' anymore—they are always self-defense, police actions, interventions or the like." Nikolas Gvosdev & Andrew Stigler, *Defining War in an Ill-Defined World*, N.Y. Times, June 28, 2011.

been used metaphorically to "heighten the effect of oral argument."[24] People sometimes refer to disagreements, controversies, and strife as war. For decades, the term has been used in the United States to reference campaigns against poverty, drugs, and crime. In recent years, this use has extended to discussion of terrorism, cyber operations, protest movements, and potential conflict in space.

Though metaphorical use of the term can in many cases be inappropriate, it is rarely dangerous. Whether the war metaphor is apt for treating the problem of poverty, for example, is not particularly consequential: use of the metaphor in that context does not have far-reaching implications. There is no danger that the government will "go to war" against employers who fire employees or against the poor. Whether the war metaphor is appropriate when dealing with the problems of crime and drugs is a more pressing question, because violence is associated with these phenomena. Still, there has historically been a natural barrier to "war on crime" morphing into war in the more traditional sense, given that armed state actors—the police and federal law enforcement—exist to combat these phenomena. The same cannot be said of the war metaphor as it relates to the struggle against non-state actors who engage in terrorism.

III. Metaphors as Shortcuts in Thinking about Problems

Given the dissimilarities between traditional wars and campaigns against terrorism since 9/11, it is fair to ask why so many have considered the latter "war." The answer to this question has at least two related parts. The first lies in how people organize and make sense of information. The second relates to incentives that policymakers have to structure information in specific ways for public consumption.

On the first point, research in the field of psychology has shown that people are "cognitive misers." Individuals have limited cognitive bandwidth, and so when confronted with new or unfamiliar information they tend to map that information onto more familiar, better-understood conceptual terrain.[25] This process simplifies complexity, allowing for the management of more information than would otherwise be possible.

This human characteristic is the reason that people use cognitive shortcuts, like political party affiliation, when determining positions on various issues. It is the reason that beliefs often come "bundled," sometimes in counterintuitive ways. It is why onc's opinion about the death penalty, for example, is predictive

[24] Dinstein, *supra* note 19, at 3.

[25] Dedre Gentner & Michael Jeziorski, *The Shift from Metaphor to Analogy in Western Science*," *in* METAPHOR AND THOUGHT 448–449 (A. Ortony ed., 2d ed. 1993).

of one's opinion about abortion, or why those who oppose strict gun control laws are more likely to be skeptical of accommodating transgender bathroom policy.

Charles Fillmore's work on "frames," defined as ideas and word groups "motivated by, founded on, and co-structured with specific, unified frameworks of knowledge or coherent schematizations of experiences" looms large here.[26] By providing packaged associations between words, situations, and events, frames facilitate both the interpretation and the structuring of information. In other words, they can serve as crutch or cudgel, promoting a certain understanding of phenomena and enabling the user to promote that understanding to others. This dynamic can lead to the adoption of narratives that organize and even mobilize reactions to events or experiences.

Metaphors and analogies are often drawn upon to frame information for these purposes. Both constructs are used to compare phenomena that have similarities. The principal difference between the two is that metaphors are abstract notions applied to concrete ones, whereas analogies generally compare historical events to other historical events or to current ones. To conceptualize the struggle against terrorism as war is to employ a metaphor.[27] When President John F. Kennedy considered the outbreak of World War I during the Cuban Missile Crisis, he drew an analogy. Lessons drawn from the use of metaphors can offer insights about the use of analogies and vice versa.[28]

Policymakers draw on metaphors and analogies for various reasons. Yuen Foong Khong suggests that analogies "help" policymakers perform six diagnostic tasks central to political decision-making. Analogies (1) help define the nature of the situation confronting the policymaker, (2) help assess the stakes, and (3) provide prescriptions. They help evaluate alternative options by (4) predicting their chances of success, (5) evaluating their moral rightness, and (6) warning about dangers associated with the options.[29]

This list points to the potential that metaphors and analogies have to enhance conceptual clarity, but the opposite may also occur. George Lakoff argues that metaphors may have the pernicious effect of hiding aspects of reality by

[26] Charles Fillmore, *Frames and the Semantics of Understanding*, 6 QUADERNI DI SEMANTICA no. 2, 223 (1985).

[27] Some argue that this conception is real, not metaphorical, as discussed later.

[28] For discussion of the use of these devices in discourse, *see* MARK JOHNSON & GEORGE LAKOFF, Metahpores We Live By (1980); METAPHOR AND Thought (Andrew Ortony ed., 1993); Veronika Koller, *Metaphor Clusters, Metapohor Chains: Analyzing the Multifunctionality of Metaphors in Text*, METAPHORIK.DE no. 5 (2003); ANDREAS MUSOLFF, METAPHOR AND POLITICAL DISCOURSE: ANALOGICAL REASONING IN DEBATES ABOUT EUROPE (2004); ELENA SEMINO, METAPHOR IN DISCOURSE (2008).

[29] YUEN KHONG, ANALOGIES AT WAR: KOREA, MUNICH, DIEN BIEN PHU AND THE VIETNAM DECISION OF 1965, at 10 (1992).

encouraging the selective perception of facts.[30] A strong commitment to a war metaphor in the struggle against terrorism, for example, could select against information that suggests the absence of war.

The late Earnest May would agree. In his 1973 book *"Lessons" from the Past*, May points out that policymakers, "when resorting to analogy, tend to seize upon the first that comes to mind. . . . Once persuaded that the War of 1812 or World War I or 'totalitarian aggression' is repeating itself, they may see only facts conforming to such an image."[31] This is particularly dangerous given May's observation that policymakers' knowledge of history is often "shallow or faulty, and [that] deficiencies in information breed greater deficiencies in reasoning."[32]

Khong, too, has written about the misuse of analogy in American foreign policy, noting that President Kennedy's effective use of the device during the Cuban Missile Crisis was an exception to a sobering rule. Though there is "striking proof [that] the power of ideas—mistaken or otherwise—[influences] policy decisions,"[33] he writes, analogies have historically not injected caution into executive committee decisions.[34]

Regardless of policymakers' motivations for using these devices, reality can be misconstrued to reinforce the validity of a metaphor. Years without a large-scale terrorist attack on the United States may call into question whether the United States is at war with terrorism, but the death of a US soldier may reinforce the notion that the United States is *at war*. This problem may be especially acute if the threat of terrorism is conflated with threats posed by more traditional enemies (e.g., Saddam Hussein in Iraq), or if terrorism is portrayed as a broader phenomenon than it actually is (e.g., when attacks on soldiers are described as terrorism).

To summarize, the virtue and danger of applying frames to foreign policy problems are one and the same. The simplification of complex realities makes them more mentally manageable, but it does so at the cost of inadequately representing the complexities of the problems at hand. Because these devices have the capacity, even the tendency, to create conceptual fog—exactly the opposite of their purported intent—they must be used with extraordinary caution. When this does not happen, the result is likely to be counterproductive policy.

[30] George Lakoff, *Metaphor in War: The Metaphor Used to Justify War in the Gulf*," 23 PEACE RESEARCH (1991).

[31] ERNEST MAY, "LESSONS" OF THE PAST: THE USE AND MISUSE OF HISTORY IN AMERICAN FOREIGN POLICY, at xi (1973).

[32] *Id.* 190. In fact, May went further, arguing that policymakers' analogies almost invariably misguide them (*id.* xi).

[33] Khong, *supra* note 29, at 7.

[34] *Id.* 5.

IV. The Case for War

Though the United States had endured terrorist violence in the past,[35] 9/11 was different. [36] These attacks claimed the lives of 2,996 people, roughly eighteen times the number lost in the Oklahoma City bombing in 1995. These were also the first large-scale terrorist attacks carried out by foreign actors on American soil. The magnitude of the event led policymakers in the United States to rethink how they would treat terrorism, both in their initial response and the longer term.[37] President Bush's message to "every nation in every region" on September 20, 2001—"Either you are with us, or you are with the terrorists"—forced policymakers around the world to do the same.[38]

Historically, terrorism had been understood as a criminal problem. With few exceptions, responses to threats and attacks had been a matter for state and federal police. President Bill Clinton's response to the August 1998 bombings of US embassies in Kenya and Tanzania, which killed more than 200 people and injured more than 4,000, is illustrative. "No matter how long it takes or where it takes us," Clinton pledged, "we will pursue terrorists until the cases are solved and justice is done."[39] This vocabulary reflects a conceptual paradigm of terrorism as criminal activity rather than war.

Almost immediately, it was clear that the Bush administration would shift to a war footing. Early evidence of the new theme came on 9/11 itself: "America and our friends and allies join with all those who want peace and security in the world, and we stand together to win the war against terrorism."[40] The next day, the president reinforced his message: "The deliberate and deadly attacks which were carried out yesterday against our country were more than acts of terror. They were acts of war."[41]

Versions of the metaphor abounded. From 2001 through 2008, the Bush administration claimed that it was waging a "war on terror," a "global war on terror,"

[35] The clearest examples include the World Trade Center bombing (1993) and the Oklahoma City bombing (1995). Other commonly cited examples include the targeting of a military barracks in Beirut (1983), in Khobar Towers in Saudi Arabia (1996), and aboard the *USS Cole* in Aden, Yemen (2000), though the latter attacks targeted military personnel. This demonstrates how ingrained the erroneous conflation of military and civilian targeting has become in discussion about terrorism.

[36] Several quotations in this section draw on the work of Adam Hodges, whose book, *The "War on Terror" Narrative: Discourse and Intertextuality in the Construction and Contestation of Sociopolitical Reality* (2011), is among the best resources on this topic.

[37] For an account of initial, critical deliberations, *see* Douglas Feith, War and Decision: Inside the Pentagon at the Dawn of the War on Terror 5–11 (2008).

[38] George Bush, "Address to a Joint Session of Congress and the American People," Washington, DC (Sept. 20, 2001).

[39] Bill Clinton, "The President's Radio Address," Washington, DC (Aug. 8, 1998).

[40] George Bush, "Remarks to the Nation on the Terrorist Attacks," Washington, DC (Sept. 11, 2001).

[41] George Bush, "Remarks to Cabinet and Advisers," Washington, DC (Sept. 12, 2001).

a "war on global terror," and a "war on terrorism." Repetition of this theme both normalized discussion of terrorism and counterterrorism as war and reinforced a guiding conception of how to deal with the problem.[42] When pushback from scholars and policymakers emerged, including from within the administration, adherence to the paradigm endured.[43] Ultimately, the president continued to believe that America was at war, as reflected in statements he made in 2004 and 2007:

> I know that some people question if America is really in a war at all. They view terrorism more as a crime, a problem to be solved mainly with law enforcement and indictments. After the World Trade Center was first attacked in 1993, some of the guilty were indicted, and tried, and convicted, and sent to prison. But the matter was not settled. The terrorists were still training and plotting in other nations, drawing up more ambitious plans. After the chaos and carnage of 9/11, it is not enough to serve our enemies with legal papers. The terrorists and their supporters declared war on the US, and war is what they got.[44]
>
> I stand before you as a wartime President. I wish I didn't have to say that, but an enemy that attacked us on 9/11/2001 declared war on the United States of America. And war is what we're engaged in.[45]

Washington's principal adversaries in this contest—Al Qaeda—has agreed with characterizing the conflict as war. In August 1996, Al Qaeda issued its *Declaration of War Against the Americans Occupying the Land of the Two Holy Places* in the Arabic-language London newspaper *Al-Quds Al-Arabi*.[46] Less than two years later, the group declared in the same newspaper that "to kill the Americans and their allies—civilians and military—is an individual duty for every Muslim who can do it in any country in which it is possible to do it."[47] The "Islamic State," a

42 As Norman Fairclough notes, "Different metaphors imply different ways of dealing with things: one does not arrive at a negotiated settlement with cancer, though one might with an opponent in an argument. Cancer has to be eliminated or cut out." NORMAN FAIRCLOUGH, LANGUAGE AND POWER 100 (2d ed. 1989). Hodges builds on this observation: "Although one launches a criminal investigation in response to a criminal act, one wages a military campaign in response to an act of war." ADAM HODGES, THE "WAR ON TERROR" NARRATIVE: DISCOURSE AND INTERTEXTUALITY IN THE CONSTRUCTION OF SOCIOPOLITICAL REALITY 27–28 (2011).

43 Early in Bush's second term, Secretary of Defense Donald Rumsfeld and Chairman of the Joint Chiefs of Staff General Richard Myers pushed for a revised slogan: "Global Struggle Against Violent Extremism (GSAVE)."

44 George Bush, "Transcript of State of the Union," Washington, DC (Jan. 21, 2004).

45 George Bush, "Speech at the Veterans of Foreign Wars Convention" Kansas City, MO (Aug. 27, 2007).

46 Osama bin Laden, *Declaration of War Against the Americans Occupying the Land of the Two Holy Places*," AL QUDS AL ARABI (London, United Kingdom), Apr. 23, 1996.

47 Osama bin Laden, *Jihad Against Jews and Crusaders*, AL QUDS AL ARABI (London, United Kingdom), Feb. 23, 1998.

derivative group that broke from Al Qaeda in 2013, has also declared war on the United States.[48]

For as much as parties to the conflict have agreed that they are at war, the strongest theoretical defenses of the claim have come from academic and legal scholarship. Writing from a political science perspective, and with extensive experience in the policy world, Peter Feaver and Eliot Cohen have separately argued that the United States is correct to treat its struggle against terrorism as war. From a legal perspective, Philip Bobbitt has offered a novel interpretation of the threat posed by Al Qaeda and believes that the United States *is* at war with that group. Bobbitt's logic applies even more forcefully to the Islamic State.

Writing shortly after 9/11, Feaver argues that the struggle against terrorism is properly conceived as a second Cold War. As during that historic conflict, he argues, (1) Americans will have to pay a heavy price in terms of life and fear to win; (2) domestic political support will be critical and cannot be assumed; and (3) the balance between national security and personal freedoms will be tested.[49] President Bush and others have also likened the struggle against terrorism to the Cold War.[50]

Though each of these analogies is arguably correct,[51] it does not follow that the United States is at war. One key distinction is the gravity of the threat posed by the enemy, a metric that Feaver signals *is* relevant. The Cold War was won, he writes, "because the American public quickly understood the gravity of the situation and successive administrations kept up the fight." But the difference in the scale of the threat across these different contexts is enormous. At the height of the Cold War, the Soviet Union had thousands of nuclear warheads pointed at the United States.[52] There was little disagreement among legal analysts, scholars, or policymakers that the superpowers posed existential threats to one another.

In contrast, the principal non-state opponents of the United States most associated with terrorism today are Al Qaeda and the Islamic State. Osama bin Laden once said that it was a religious duty for Muslims to seek nuclear and chemical weapons,[53] but there is no evidence that the group has attained anything of the kind. Presumably, if Al Qaeda or the Islamic State had acquired weapons that could pose an existential threat to the United States, they would have at least

[48] The clearest English-language explanation of the Islamic State's motivation for war appears in volume 15, pp. 30–33, of *Dabiq*, the group's now-defunct online magazine.

[49] Peter Feaver, *Cold War II*, THE WEEKLY STANDARD, Oct. 1, 2001.

[50] George Bush, "Remarks at a Reception for Congressional Candidate Dean Heller in Reno, Nevada" (Oct. 2, 2006), quoted in Hodges, *supra* note 43, at 36.

[51] Predictions that this struggle would test the balance between security and personal liberties have proven correct beyond any doubt, as detailed later in this volume.

[52] At one point in 1986, the Soviet Union had stockpiled more than 10,000 strategic nuclear warheads and some 30,000 nonstrategic nuclear weapons.

[53] PETER BERGEN, THE OSAMA BIN LADEN I KNOW 337 (2006).

made public that capability. None of this means that "war" requires existential threat; it only means that this particular analogy is flawed.

Cohen, also writing in 2001, has embraced the war paradigm in a different way, arguing that the United States is engaged in another "World War." Like Feaver, he believes that the current struggle is analogous to the Cold War, citing five parallels: (1) the current war is global; (2) it involves a mixture of violent and nonviolent efforts; (3) it requires the mobilization of skill, expertise, and resources; (4) it may go on for a long time; and (5) it has ideological roots.[54]

Again, though each parallel is arguably correct, none supports the case for "war" against terrorism unless war is considered purely metaphorically. Consider that the first four pillars of Cohen's analogy could be applied to the war on drugs. The war on drugs is global; it involves violent and nonviolent efforts; it requires the mobilization of skill, expertise, and resources; and it will go on for a long time. But by characterizing the struggle against terrorism as "world war," Cohen goes further to conjure images of the most destructive conflicts in history—wars that, together, claimed the lives of more than seventy million people.

The fifth pillar of Cohen's analogy, the idea that the struggle against terrorism has ideological roots, is correct. This was true during the Cold War and is true again today. But any dispute, not just war, can take shape for myriad reasons. Aside from ideology, politics, religion, and nationalism, conflicts have been fought for economic reasons, because of instinctual desires for power, for basic security, and more. In short, neither the claim that the United States is at war nor the evidence cited to support it demonstrate that countering ideological non-state actors who use terrorism may be appropriately construed as war.

Perhaps the most detailed case that the United States is at war against terrorism comes from legal scholar Philip Bobbitt. In *Terror and Consent: The Wars for the Twenty-First Century* (2008), Bobbitt argues that the nature of the state and the nature of war are evolving and that these evolutions intersect in a way that renders the war paradigm appropriate. Though he continues to believe that war remains the exclusive province of states, Bobbitt argues that "[t]he terror network that bin Laden has assembled might be described as a new and mutated form of the State."[55] It has a standing army, has a treasury and consistent source of finance, raises a significant amount of revenue, has an intelligence collection and analysis cadre, makes alliances with other states, and declares wars.[56]

These claims are dubious. First, Al Qaeda does not have a standing army. Though individuals across the world may claim to support the group, and while it does have affiliates in the Middle East, South Asia, North Africa, and elsewhere,

[54] Eliot Cohen, *World War IV*, WALL ST. J., Nov. 20, 2001.
[55] Bobbitt, *supra* note 20, at 126.
[56] *Id.* 127.

any "army" the group might claim is not hierarchical and cannot be effectively directed. As for a consistent source of finance and the ability to raise "significant" revenue (a vague term, though presumably this means revenue on par with what might be raised by a state), Al Qaeda has neither. The group does have an intelligence collection and analysis cadre, though not one analogous to those of states. Nor does Al Qaeda have formal alliances with state governments. If such alliances were to exist, presumably the United States and others would take steps against the allied governments, as happened to the Taliban after 9/11. The ability to declare war is something that anyone with a voice has, something that many militant groups have done. Statehood requires more.

Bobbitt's argument might have gotten more traction regarding the Islamic State, but only from 2014 to 2017 when that group had a defensible claim to statehood. At no point would such a claim have been grounded in the constitutive legal theory of statehood, where the *conditio sine qua non* is recognition from other states.[57] Legal grounding in declaratory theory, on the other hand, favored by most international legal theorists, would have been feasible. Based on criteria outlined in the 1933 Montevideo Convention on the Rights and Duties of States, declaratory theory holds that states are states when they have (1) a defined territory, (2) a government, (3) a population, and (4) the capacity to enter relations with other states. These criteria align with Bobbitt's thinking about statehood and do not depend on recognition.

At its height in late 2014, the Islamic State held territory the size of Great Britain.[58] Its government, which employed tens of thousands of salaried fighters,[59] had a clearly defined organizational structure. The Caliph had deputies for provinces in Syria and Iraq, and these men had deputies of their own. State councils included the Sharia Council, the Financial Council, the Military Council, the Fighter's Assistance Council, the Security and Intelligence Council, the Media Council, and others. This bureaucracy ruled over a population of some eight million people, roughly the population of Israel, and included Iraq's second-largest city, Mosul. Though no states entertained formal relations with the Islamic State, there can be little doubt that the group had this capacity.

With this in mind, was the Islamic State appropriately considered a state and, if so, was it is appropriate to conceptualize the fight against that group as war? Yes and no. Before 2014, the Islamic State did not have a defensible claim to statehood. Almost as soon as it did, the international community stepped in to deny

[57] Amy Eckert, *Constructing States: The Role of the International Community in the Creation of New States*, 13 J. Pub. & Int'l Aff. 21 (2002).

[58] Rick Noack, *Here's How the Islamic State Compares with Real States*, Wash. Post, Sept. 12, 2014.

[59] Estimates of the number of fighters in the ranks of the Islamic State have been wide-ranging. In late 2014, the CIA estimated that the group boasted 20,000 to 31,500 fighters. Around that time, the chief of staff to Kurdish President Massoud Barzani told Patrick Cockburn of *The Independent* that the group had at least 200,000 fighters.

the group that claim. What ensued is appropriately understood as war, but not war against terrorism. It more resembled conventional battle, with tanks and front lines, airstrikes and conventional artillery. Territorial control ebbed and flowed until the Islamic State could no longer defend itself as a state. The group continues to pose a terrorist threat, but since the end of 2017 the international community has no longer been "at war" against it. That is because the group lost the capacity to make war.

V. The Case against War

Adherence to the war paradigm has been counterproductive in four principal ways: (1) it has conferred legitimacy upon the enemy, (2) it has fostered division among people of good will, (3) it has magnified the threat beyond proportion, and (4) it has set a dangerous precedent by expanding accepted definitions of war. Taken together, these arguments constitute a case for renewed effort to abandon the war paradigm in both rhetoric and policy.

A. The War Paradigm Confers Legitimacy upon the Enemy

This observation is as old as the war on terror. British military historian Sir Michael Howard has argued that "to declare war on terrorists . . . is to accord terrorists a status and dignity that they seek and that they do not deserve."[60] John Nagl, coauthor of a US military counterinsurgency manual, has argued that the term "war on terror" was "enormously unfortunate because . . . it pulled together disparate organizations and insurgencies." "Viewing them all through one lens," he argues, "distorts the picture and magnifies the enemy."[61]

These are compelling reasons to reject the war paradigm. Howard's objection is theoretical: a declaration of war elevates terrorists' status from criminals to combatants.[62] "Combatant" carries with it the implication of more legitimacy—and indeed more capability—than "criminal" or "terrorist." Nagl's objection is practical: treating different groups as a unified enemy precludes a divide and conquer strategy and creates the illusion of a more capable and implacable adversary than actually exists.

[60] Michael Howard, *What's in a Name?*, 81 Foreign Aff. 8 (2002).

[61] John Nagl, quoted in Scott Wilson & Al Kamen, *"Global War on Terror" Is Given New Name*, Wash. Post, Mar. 25, 2009.

[62] For discussion of the principle of distinction in war, traditional requirements for combatancy, the term "unlawful combatant," and how international law applies to all of this, *see* Claire Finkelstein's chapter in this volume.

Both arguments suggest that militant responses to terrorism—through rhetoric, the curtailment of rights, or mobilization of the military—may reinforce public fear of the threat. Every successful attack, especially in the context of heightened alert, affirms the government's message that the threat is dire, that the steps being taken are necessary. Some will view attacks as evidence that measures in place are insufficient, that more needs to be done to ensure security at any cost. The absence of attacks, in contrast, serves as evidence that any steps taken to counter the threat are justified. News of drone strikes, images of military deployments, and the latest capture of high-level terrorist figures paradoxically reinforce the threat—perpetuating the continuation of the war footing and its attendant consequences.

B. The War Paradigm Fosters Division

"War" brings with it divisive rhetoric that is less common in times of peace. Words like warmonger, coward, fascist, traitor, peacenik, and appeaser are bandied about in national discourse.[63] Patriotism is impugned. Those who disagree with or who question government policies are accused of not having the country's best interests in mind. This kind of discourse exists not only among ordinary people but at the highest levels of government.

Just three months after 9/11, on December 6, 2001, Attorney General John Ashcroft sat before the Senate Judiciary Committee to discuss the detention of enemy combatants in the nascent war on terror. Having asserted, "we need honest, reasoned debate, not fear-mongering," the attorney general continued. "To those who scare peace-loving people with phantoms of lost liberty, my message is this: Your tactics aid terrorists, for they erode our national unity and diminish our resolve. [You] give ammunition to America's enemies, and pause to America's friends."[64]

Winston Nagan and Craig Hammer summarize the appeal to patriotism in the context of perceived insecurity. The war paradigm, they argue, can "rhetorically disguise the fear factor and promote the pride factor: if we have pride in our country, then we shall be proud of the war against terrorism; if we are proud of the war against terrorism, we will of course give unqualified support to the administration's agenda, and we shall then qualify as real national patriots."[65]

[63] *See* Philip Bobbitt at the Carnegie Council in New York (Sept. 17, 2008).

[64] John Ashcroft, "Testimony to the Senate Committee on the Judiciary," Washington, DC (Dec. 6, 2001).

[65] Winston Nagan & Craig Hammer, *Patriotism, Nationalism, and the War on Terror: A Mild Plea in Avoidance*, 56 FLA. L. REV. 947 (2004).

If we do not do these things, then logically the opposite must be true: we do not have pride in our country. We do not qualify as real patriots.

Supporters of the war paradigm are not alone in questioning patriotism. After John Ashcroft's statement, Democratic presidential nominee Howard Dean offered his thoughts about the attorney general: "John Ashcroft is not a patriot; John Ashcroft is a descendent of Joseph McCarthy."[66] Dean's rhetoric is as much the product of the adoption of the war paradigm as Ashcroft's. People take sides not only in but *about* wars, which can promote disunity as easily as unity.

C. The War Paradigm Magnifies the Threat beyond Proportion

By the time President Barack Obama arrived in the oval office, he understood what Brian Jenkins and others would observe in the years after 9/11: "the risk of death at the hands of terrorists in the United States approaches lottery-winning odds."[67] The principal threats of terrorism, he correctly believed, were the fear it would generate and the incentives it would create for overreaction on the part of the government. The president's advisers urged caution in how he spoke about the threat for political reasons, but he recognized that it was manageable, that resilience was a better strategy than war.

And yet the Obama administration maintained a war footing. Regardless of what explains that continuity—inertia, the allure of executive authority, or other politics—discussion of terrorism in quasi-apocalyptic terms endured. In 2016, for example, Secretary of State John Kerry characterized the Islamic State as "a threat to everybody in the world."[68] The group could cause a mass exodus from the Middle East to Europe, he explained, perhaps leading to the collapse of the European Union. "[E]veryone runs for cover and you've got the 1930s all over again, with nationalism and fascism and other things breaking out."

To some Kerry's words may seem prescient: there has been mass migration from the Middle East to Europe, and right-wing populism (even fascism) has taken root in several European countries. As the Trump administration

[66] Jonah Goldberg, *The Patriot Gap*, L.A. TIMES, Mar. 11, 2008.

[67] Brian Jenkins, *Fifteen Years On, Where Are We in the "War on Terror"?*, 9 CTC SENTINEL 8 (2016). Jeffrey Goldberg's 2016 interview with the president on this topic is illuminating. It conveys that the president frequently reminded his staff that "terrorism takes fewer lives in America than handguns, car accidents, and falls in bathtubs do." There is, of course, an important caveat to this line of argument. It is impossible to know what the number of dead Americans at the hands of terrorists would be in the absence of measures taken since 9/11 to keep that number as low as possible. This area is ripe for analysis, though commentary would necessarily be speculative. One could argue that the United States' offensive posture has allowed the country to fight those who would do it harm "over there." A sensible retort would be that fighting "over there," especially in unprovoked wars, has inspired further animosity against the United States both abroad and at home.

[68] Jonah Goldberg, *The Obama Doctrine*, THE ATLANTIC, Apr. 2016.

left office, fault lines in the United States were as deep as ever, the far right as emboldened as at any time in living memory. To attribute these developments to terrorism, however, rather than to the constellation of factors that have contributed to them, would be a mistake. Most displaced Syrians have not fled any individual actor but rather a multifaceted war to which dozens of major actors have contributed.[69] The same is true of displaced Afghans, Libyans, and Yemenis. In any case, no argument can be made that the Islamic State, or any terrorist organization, threatens everyone in the world. That kind of claim contributes to self-reinforcing hysteria.

Magnification of the threat has now catalyzed a disproportionate response to terrorism for two decades. Consider the record. On 9/11, terrorists killed nearly three thousand people and caused an estimated $178 billion in physical damage and other economic losses[70]—a horrific toll. Since that time, the wars in Afghanistan and Iraq have cost the lives of nearly seven thousand US service members; some fifty thousand more have been wounded. In dollar terms, the United States has spent $4–6 trillion on these wars alone. Then there are the costs that too often go unmentioned: hundreds of thousands of Iraqis dead, Iran dramatically better positioned in the Middle East than before 9/11, and the emergence of the Islamic State and its affiliates. None of this touches on policies that have contributed to animosity toward the United States, to disorder on the ground in places like Libya, Somalia, Pakistan, and Yemen, or to the costs of operations in those places. Nor do these observations touch on opportunity costs, which are incalculable.

D. The War Paradigm Expands Accepted Definitions of War

A direct consequence of adopting the war paradigm after 9/11 has been the gradual expansion of accepted understandings of war. War was once understood to be a contest between the armed forces of defined entities (usually states), as outlined above, but it is now understood as more. Counterterrorism, kinetic intelligence activity, and even disinformation campaigns are now commonly considered war. It is easy to see how the concept could expand further. Do regime-threatening economic sanctions constitute war? In an area with

[69] It is no secret that Bashar al-Assad is responsible for more internal displacement and refugee flows than any other party. He has received extensive help throughout the war from the Russian and Iranian governments. Gulf states have contributed money and arms to the conflict. Turkey allowed jihadists to filter through its border with Syria to fight Assad. The United States also bears responsibility. *See* Seth Cantey, *Obama Did Too Much in Syria, Not Too Little*, USA TODAY, July 21, 2016.

[70] Shan Carter & Amanda Cox, *One 9/11 Tally: $3.3 Trillion*, N.Y. TIMES, Sept. 8, 2011.

increasingly scarce natural resources, could diverting water by building a dam be considered war?

What constitutes war matters, because the expectations of governments, adversaries, and the public differ in times of war and peace. The law of armed conflict is based on this understanding, especially vis-à-vis the distinction between civilians and combatants, and the rights, privileges, and protections afforded these groups. The more we expand the definition of war, the more the law of armed conflict applies. That law is more forgiving of secrecy, surveillance, detention without trial, lack of transparency, and abuses of executive authority than is peacetime law.[71] By expanding notions of war, wartime authorities become anytime authorities, and the baseline from which the legal pendulum swings in the aftermath of the next attack is redefined.

Moreover, adoption of the war paradigm has bred the proliferation of government targets, objectives, and responsibilities. Brian Jenkins summarizes the point this way: "U.S. officials today speak variously of destroying the most dangerous terrorist adversaries, protecting those in peril, preventing terrorist atrocities, denying terrorists safe havens, fixing failing states, filling ungoverned spaces, countering violent extremism, altering the conditions that contribute to radicalization and recruitment to violence, and attacking the root causes of terrorism."[72] These goals are as complex as they are abstract, and in recent years responsibility for their achievement has fallen largely to the military, even when that institution has not been trained to carry out the relevant tasks. Consider the doctrine of counterinsurgency (COIN), which gained traction after the 2007 Iraq Surge. In addition to fighting enemies on the ground, the military has found itself forward deployed, distributing water, building schools, and serving as an informal diplomatic corp. With enough time, troops, and treasure, COIN has reduced violence in targeted areas, but it has done little to resolve political problems in places like Afghanistan and Iraq. And yet the massive investment that COIN demands creates incentives to stay, even as rationale for war fades. As of late 2020, the United States continues to fight a group in Afghanistan that has no aspirations beyond its borders. It does so with a troop presence that no one believes is capable of meeting its defined goals.

A final point about expanding conceptions of war merits emphasis. What happens when other countries take the same tack? The United States has more precedent-setting power than any other country. When it claims the right to fight terrorism anywhere, because terrorism is everywhere, other countries will eventually follow suit. What will be the response of the United States and the broader

[71] On this point, and for an excellent resource on the peril of expanding conceptualizations of war more generally, *see* Rosa Brooks, How Everything Became War and the Military Became Everything (2016).

[72] Jenkins, *supra* note 67, at 8.

international community when China, Russia, Iran, Israel, North Korea, or any other country crosses borders—with drones, special forces, or more—in the name of defending its people? In some cases, actions like these are already happening within these countries' borders.

VI. Sticky Paradigms and Unresolved Questions

Barack Obama's inaugural address on January 20, 2009, reiterated the message that fueled his rise to the presidency. *The New York Times* fairly characterized it as "a stark repudiation of the era of George W Bush and a vow to drive the United States into a 'new age' by reclaiming the values of an older one."[73] Obama spoke of a collective failure to make hard choices, a mistaken willingness to suspend national ideals, and a false choice between safety and values. During the campaign, he had argued that the "war on terror" had birthed counterproductive, illegal, and even immoral policies. It was time to take the nation off of a war footing, to make good on the promise of change.

Almost immediately, the new president banned torture and repudiated the legal opinions that served as its foundation. He closed CIA black sites and ordered the closure of the prison at Guantánamo Bay. In his first few months, Obama rescinded the vocabulary of the struggle against terrorism, directing the Pentagon and others "to avoid using the term 'long war' or 'global war on terror' [GWOT]"[74] in favor of the more anodyne "overseas contingency operations." By the end of his first term, he had ended US participation in the Iraq War and had begun drawing down troops in Afghanistan. By comparison with the Bush administration, the Obama administration appeared to be "deeply concerned with trying to justify to itself and to the world that its actions were rooted in the rule of law."[75]

What surprised many supporters was the extent to which President Obama maintained, sometimes expanded, and in any case entrenched a range of controversial national security policies. Extraordinary rendition, mass surveillance, and military commissions continued. Drone strikes and targeted killings surged, including in countries away from conventional battlefields. Military operations in Libya, Pakistan, Somalia, Syria, and Yemen proliferated. Over eight years, the administration prosecuted three times as many cases involving whistle-blowers and leakers as all previous administrations combined.[76] If the rhetoric of a nation at war had subsided, many of the policies of a nation at war remained.

[73] David Sanger, *Speech Spanned History and Confronted Bush*, N.Y. TIMES, Jan. 20, 2009.

[74] Wilson & Kamen, *supra* note 61.

[75] CHARLIE SAVAGE, POWER WARS: THE RELENTLESS RISE OF PRESIDENTIAL AUTHORITY AND SECRECY, at xxiv (2017).

[76] James Risen, *If Donald Trump Targets Journalists, Thank Obama*, N.Y. TIMES, Dec. 30, 2016.

Debate over whether the sum of these changes amounted to an abandonment of the "war on terror" is legitimate. Some have argued that the Obama administration "sharply changed direction," that it "rejected the Bush administration's disregard for the rule of law and disavowed extreme notions of commander-in-chief powers."[77] Perhaps more common is the assessment that national security policy during the Obama years reflected an adjustment. Especially when measured against the second term of the Bush administration, there seems to have been as much continuity as change. Quotations from 2007 and 2013 seem to reflect the evolution of the president's thinking on this matter as a consequence of his time in office:

> [The Bush-Cheney administration] puts forward a false choice between the liberties we cherish and the security we demand. I will provide our intelligence and law enforcement agencies with the tools they need to track and take out the terrorists without undermining our Constitution and our freedom (August 1, 2007).
>
> I think the American people understand that there are some trade-offs involved. . . . I think it's important to recognize that you can't have a hundred percent security and also then have a hundred percent privacy and zero inconvenience. You know, we're going to have to make some choices as a society (June 7, 2013).[78]

Regardless of disagreements over continuity and change, President Obama's embrace, and even expansion, of some national security policies from the Bush administration normalized conceptualizations of counterterrorism as war. De facto acceptance of the war paradigm, regardless of the vocabulary used to shorthand that posture, solidified a way of thinking about terrorism that the administration sought to undermine. This experience suggests that once a paradigm has been thoroughly adopted, it becomes sticky. President Obama sought to walk away from the language of war in counterterrorism; walking away from treating counterterrorism as war proved harder.

Excesses in national security policy after 9/11 were predictable. The United States had suffered an unprecedented terrorist attack, policymakers lacked information, and intelligence assessments suggested that far worse could be on the horizon.[79] Men and women trying to protect the country from the top down

[77] Dawn Johnsen, *The Lawyer's War: Counterterrorism from Bush to Obama to Trump*, Foreign Aff. 152 (2017).

[78] Both quotations borrowed from Savage, *supra* note 75, at viii.

[79] As Graham Allison explains, in October of 2001, the CIA reported to President Bush that Al Qaeda may have smuggled a nuclear weapon into Manhattan. Graham Allison, Nuclear Terrorism (2004).

made difficult decisions under pressure, and sometimes they got things wrong. In hindsight, the decision to adopt the war paradigm, perhaps understandable in context, facilitated and justified a series of legally and ethically dubious policies with legacies that endure today. UN Special Rapporteur Ben Emmerson characterized the problem this way in 2012, midway through the Obama administration: "The global war paradigm has done immense damage to a previously shared international consensus on the legal framework underlying both international human rights law and international humanitarian law. It has also given a spurious justification to a range of serious human rights and humanitarian law violations."[80]

Aside from legal and ethical damage, entrenchment of the war paradigm across Republican and Democratic administrations paved the way for a commander-in-chief openly hostile to legal oversight and traditional conventions of war.[81] Donald Trump campaigned on banning Muslims from the United States, killing the families of terrorists, and "a hell of a lot worse" than waterboarding. As president, he has cited the apocryphal story of General Pershing, who was said to execute Muslim prisoners with bullets dipped in pigs' blood, as an example of how the war against terrorism should be fought.

Indeed, the question of whether President Trump would explicitly resurrect the war paradigm has been resolved. Midway through his first year in office, he signed the "Global War on Terrorism War Memorial Act" (awkwardly incorporating the word "war" into the same legislation twice). As for the administration's approach to national security, policy advisor Stephen Miller's take is illuminating: "Our opponents, the media, and the whole world will soon see, as we begin to take further actions, that the powers of the president to protect our country are very substantial and we will not be questioned."[82] By the final year of his first term, the administration had killed a top Iranian general in a drone strike on Iraqi soil on the basis that he was a terrorist, and it had labeled domestic protestors in the United States the same.

For as long and rocky as the struggle against terrorism has already been, the key question about how to confront this phenomenon remains what it was on 9/11. Are terrorists "criminals who should be incapacitated through the civilian law enforcement process," "enemy belligerents engaged in war crimes who should be incapacitated through military detention," or "something in between for which

[80] Owen Bowcott, *UN to Investigate Civilian Deaths from US Drone Strikes*, THE GUARDIAN, Oct. 25, 2012.

[81] Consider a claim from then-candidate Trump in March 2016: "The problem is we have the Geneva Conventions, all sorts of rules and regulations, so the soldiers are afraid to fight. We can't waterboard, but they can chop off heads. I think we've got to make some changes, some adjustments." *See* Ben Schreckinger, *Trump Calls Geneva Conventions "The Problem,"* POLITICO, Mar. 30, 2016.

[82] Aaron Blake, *Stephen Miller's Authoritarian Declaration: Trump's National Security Actions 'Will Not Be Questioned*,' WASH. POST, Feb. 13, 2017.

we lack both a legal framework and an adequate vocabulary"?[83] In other words, how should the struggle against terrorism be conceptualized, and what is the relevant body of law? At a moment in history when individuals have proven capable of the kind of destruction once the reserve of states, is existing legal architecture sufficient? Can the evolution of law keep pace with the evolving challenges we face? If so, can that be done without stacking the deck in our favor?

This chapter has argued that treating terrorism and counterterrorism as war has proven to be a mistake. It has not tackled the difficult questions addressed immediately here, but other chapters in this volume do. Claire Finkelstein makes perhaps the strongest case to date that violent non-state actors are more properly thought of as international criminals than as combatants. Christopher Fuller convincingly argues that human rights law provides an adequate if imperfect model for the use of lethal force against terrorists plotting attacks from abroad. These and other scholars represented in these pages provide rare insight into the history and future of the intersection of law and terror. Scholars and policymakers alike would do well to consider their insights carefully.

[83] Robert Chesney, *The Sleeper Scenario: Terrorism-Support Laws and the Demands of Prevention*, 42 Harv. J. Legis. 2 (2005).

2

The Limits of Law and the Value of Rights in Addressing Terrorism

A Study of the UN Counterterrorism Architecture

Fionnuala Ní Aoláin[*]

Terrorism is paradoxically both an epiphenomenal and constant phenomenon. In its micro practice terrorism's predictability, durability and pathways are inconsistent, capricious, and defy easy capture. Terrorism is not a new practice. In fact, terrorism has long been experienced in national and international systems, a potent example being the murder of the Austrian crown prince by a Serbian nationalist triggering the outbreak of the First World War, and more recently the sustained transnational cooperation and exchange between terrorist organizations throughout the 1970s and 1980s.[1] Terrorism has also consistently woven across national borders, and terrorism has long been associated with various forms of armed conflict from high to low intensity, making disaggregation and conflation of applicable legal regimes challenging in practice.[2] States, scholars, and commentators have consistently struggled to define precisely what constitute the conditions that produce violence that, inter alia, primarily targets civilians and civilian objects to achieve its objectives.[3] Despite decades of labeling

* Regents Professor University of Minnesota Law School & Professor of Law, School of Law, The Queens University of Belfast, Northern Ireland. United Nations Special Rapporteur on the Promotion and Protection of Human Rights while Countering Terrorism. My thanks to Jesse Goldfarb for assistance with this research; any remaining faults or errors lie with the author.

[1] *See* Charles A. Russell, Leon J. Barket Jr., & Bowman H. Miller, *Out-Inventing the Terrorist*, *in* TERRORISM: THEORY AND PRACTICE (Yonah Alexander, David Carolton, & Paul Wilkinson eds., 1979); Sharon Harzenski, *Terrorism, A History: Stage 1*, 12 J. TRANSNAT'L L. & POL'Y (2003). I do not suggest that every act of political assassination constitutes a terrorist act, as there may be multiple causalities for such (illegal) actions.

[2] Examples of terrorism and armed conflict being interwoven (e.g., El Salvador, conflict is not recognised until the end as Protocol II, state insists it is terrorism throughout). *See* Andrea Bianchi, *Terrorism and Armed Conflict: Insights from a Law & Literature Perspective*, 24 LEIDEN J. INT'L L., no. 1, 8–12 (2011).

[3] Upendra D. Acharya, *War on Terror Wars: The Problem in Defining Terrorism*, 37 DENVER J. INT'L L. & POL'Y, no. 37, 653, 655 (2009); Reuven Young, *Defining Terrorism: The Evolution of Terrorism as a Legal Concept in International Law and Its Influence on Definitions in Domestic Legislation*, 29 B.C. INT'L & COMP. L. REV., no. 29, 23, 30 (2006); Danja Blöcher, *Terrorism as an International Crime: The Definitional Problem*, 8 EYES ON THE ICC, 109 (2011).

Fionnuala Ní Aoláin, *The Limits of Law and the Value of Rights in Addressing Terrorism* In: *Between Crime and War*. Edited by: Claire Finkelstein, Christopher Fuller, Jens David Ohlin, Mitt Regan, Oxford University Press. © Claire Finkelstein, Christopher Fuller, Jens David Ohlin, Mitt Regan 2023. DOI: 10.1093/oso/9780197638798.003.0003

the acts of various groups and organizations as "terrorist" in multiple parts of the globe, a comprehensive and agreed definition of terrorism by states is still elusive. That noted, states have moved closer to an agreed consensus on acts of terrorism,[4] and a significant list of treaties and security council resolutions attest to agreed language and frameworks in that regard.[5] In the aftermath of 9/11, I distinguish a number of distinct trends applicable to the global regulation of terrorism. First, it was agreed that a *global* framework was necessary and mandated and would be rooted in Chapter VII of the UN Charter. This was a new regulatory departure.[6] Second, the UN Security Council took the lead role in orchestrating and shaping that framework with broad support from the Permanent 5 (P5) members of the Council.[7] Third, where the Security Council's limits proved cumbersome to establishing global regulation, alternative fora were established to advance the work involved.[8] Fourth, the post 9/11 framework leaves considerable latitude and discretion to states in defining what constitutes "terrorism" domestically, placing few effective constraints on state's self-chosen definitions or national regulatory responses.[9] In establishing a global counterterrorism architecture post 9/11, human rights considerations were markedly sidelined, and remain profoundly marginal to state considerations particularly in the international, regional, and cooperative spaces where global security regimes dominate.

This chapter proceeds in the following way. Section I explores the global legal architecture that has emerged post 9/11. It addresses both the institutional elements of that architecture including the role of the Counter-Terrorism Committee (CTC), the Counter-Terrorism Executive Directorate (CTED), and the new UN Office of Counter-Terrorism (and attendant Counter-Terrorism Implementation Task ForceCTIFT committee structure). The global lawmaking process that has emerged from these structures is discussed with a particular emphasis on the exclusion of human rights and law of armed conflict into the emergent legal norms.

[4] For example, from the 1970s states articulated the need to cooperate to address the challenges of terrorism, *see* United Nations, "Declaration on Measures to Eliminate Terrorism" (General Assembly Resolution 34/145, Dec. 17, 1979), paras. 11, 17, http://www.un.org/en/ga/search/view_doc.asp?symbol=A/RES/34/145.

[5] United Nations Security Council, Resolution 1373 (Doc. S/RES/1373 Sept. 28, 2001); United Nations Security Council, Resolution 2178 (Doc. S/RES/2178 Sept. 24, 2014); United Nations Security Council, Resolution 2349 (Doc. S/RES/2178 Mar. 31, 2017); United Nations Security Council, Resolution 2368 (Doc. S/RES/2368 July 20, 2017); *Organization of American States: Inter-American Convention Against Terrorism*, 42 Int'l Legal Materials, 19 (2003); Council of Europe, Protocol Amending the European Convention on the Suppression of Terrorism (ETS 190, May 15, 2003).

[6] United Nations Security Council, Resolution 1373 (Doc. S/RES/1373 Sept. 28, 2001), para. 8.

[7] United Nations Security Council, Resolution 1373 (Doc. S/RES/1373 Sept. 28, 2001), para. 6.

[8] An example of an alternative is the Financial Action Task Force and Global Terrorism Task Force as it regulated Countering Terrorism Financing. *See* https://www.fatf-gafi.org.

[9] Reuven Young, *Defining Terrorism: The Evolution of Terrorism as a Legal Concept in International Law and Its Influence on Definitions in Domestic Legislation*, 29 B.C. Int'l & Comp. L. Rev., no. 29, 23, 71 (2006).

I define a new form of global-local interface in the counterterrorism sphere premised on the establishment of meta-norms but facilitated by extensive deference to national prerogatives in defining and regulating terrorism. The effect of that deference has been to enable systematic human rights violations in many countries premised on the risk of terrorism but, in reality for many states, legal regulation is directed at domestic dissent, political opponents, and disagreement with dominant elites. Section II, explores in a more comprehensive way what the effects of the normative outputs from the global counterterrorism architecture have been on the legal regimes of human rights and international humanitarian law. I claim that we have seen some distinct patterns since 2001. In the first instance, human rights and humanitarian law were largely excluded from the framework and the normative content of global counterterrorism law post 9/11. Much advocacy and some decisive action by human rights' standard bearing states have led to an increased reference to human rights standards in the normative content emerging from the Security Council. However, the content is devoid of any connection to implementation, benchmarking, or assessment in practice. Thus, it has a rhetorical and symbolic value but little practical effect. I make a broad claim that the effect of the legal norms produced since 9/11 has been to substantive weaken the international human rights treaty infrastructure by making its application irrelevant to much of the work states do in practice to enforce security (and increasingly simply to regulate by the resort to exceptional national security law over ordinary law). Section III addresses the costs of human rights exclusion. I claim that serious and sustained human rights violations can contribute in part to the creation of the conditions conducive to terrorism. By systematically disavowing human rights in practice, states in fact create the very conditions they state they wish to avoid, thereby enabling the kind of social and psycho-social conditions in which violence is more likely to emerge and undermining their own stated commitment to preventing and countering radical extremism and the conditions that give rise to violence in the first place.

I. The Global Counterterrorism Architecture and the Rule of Law

On September 12, 2001, the UN Security Council adopted Resolution 1368, which called upon the international community to "redouble its efforts" to prevent and suppress terrorist acts.[10] Close on its heels came Resolution 1373, which was adopted by the Security Council on September 28, 2001, under Chapter 7 of the UN Charter.[11] It requires states, among other things, to criminalize terrorist

10 United Nations Security Council, Resolution 1368 (Doc. S/RES/1368 Sept. 12, 2001), para. 4.

11 United Nations Security Council, Resolution 1373 (Doc. S/RES/1368 Sept. 28, 2001).

activities, to freeze the funds and financial assets of terrorists and their supporters, to ban others from making funds available to terrorists, and to deny safe heaven to terrorists. It can be described as one of the most wide-ranging Security Council resolutions ever passed, placing mandatory obligations upon states, and with an enormous weight of international political consensus behind it.[12] As Paul Szasz has noted, Resolution 1373 also manifests unusual legislative character in that it mandates compulsory action of a general nature for states with binding intent, and is unrelated to a specific situation of conflict affecting international peace and security.[13] He identifies this legislative mode as both unusual and momentous for the Security Council, effectively creating a new form of binding international legal obligations.

The resolution is framed by its affirmation that terrorist acts and acts of international terrorism constitute a threat to international peace and security, while no definition of these key terms is offered. This early lacuna was essential to the development of the deference doctrine to state counterterrorism practices that I identify in this chapter. This definitional lacuna reflects an ongoing tension at the United Nations, which until the events of September 11 were confined to the General Assembly and its Sixth (Legal) Committee, which had been working on several conventions related to terrorism.[14] The tension locates around the inability to agree a core treaty-based definition of terrorism.[15] The emphasis on Resolution 1373 on suppressing the sources of finance and support for terrorism points to greater clarity around these acts but evidence little consensus about the core definition itself. Evidently the measures contemplated by 1373 had far-reaching implications for the protection of human rights, but the resolution made no comprehensive or even specific reference to the need for states to comply with human rights standards in the suppression of terrorism.[16] Instead, the preamble to the resolution affirms the need to combat terrorist acts "by

[12] Wondwossen Kassa, *Rethinking the No Definition Consensus and the Would Have Been Binding Assumption Pertaining to the Security Council Resolution 1373*, 17 FLINDERS L.J., no. 17, 127, 128 (2015), "The Resolution has been a primary factor in setting the roadmap of the post 9/11 global counter-terrorism push."

[13] *See* Paul C. Szasz, *The Security Council Starts Legislating*, 96 AM. J. INT'L L. 901 (2002). This article identifies the unusual legislative character of 1373, and, also, specifically notes that many conventions languishing for a want of state ratification suddenly have the force of international law.

[14] *See* Eric Rosand, *Security Council Resolution 1373, The Counter-Terrorism Committee, and the Fight Against Terrorism*, 97 AM. J. INT'L L. 333, 333–34 (2003). Conventions drafted by the Sixth Committee include United Nations, *International Convention for the Suppression of Terrorist Bombings [Adopted New York, January 9, 1998]*, 37 INT'L LEGAL MATERIALS 249 (1998), and United Nations General Assembly, *International Convention for the Suppression of the Financing of Terrorism [Adopted December 9 1999; Opened for signature January 10, 2000]*, 39 INT'L LEGAL MATERIALS 270 (2000).

[15] *See* Danja Blöcher, *Terrorism as an International Crime: The Definitional Problem*, 8 EYES ON THE ICC107, 113 (2011)

[16] *See* International Helsinki Federation for Human Rights, "Anti-Terrorism Measures, Security and Human Rights" (Apr. 2003), 41–42, https://www.refworld.org/docid/46963adf0.html.

all means, in accordance with the Charter of the United Nations." As the UN Charter makes substantial references to human rights protection, such a reference could constitute an implicit reference to the need to promote and respect human rights norms. However, the obliqueness of this positive interpretation only serves to highlight the lack of an explicit statement in the resolution, and "leaves the impression that human rights protection is a secondary consideration in the campaign against terrorism, instead of an essential component of any counter-terrorism strategy."[17] Further, the only explicit reference to human rights norms in the operative paragraphs of the resolution arises in the context of refugee and asylum seekers where states are required to take appropriate measures, to ensure that such persons have not been involved in the commission of terrorist acts.[18]

Under Paragraph 6 of the resolution a Committee of the Security Council (Counter-Terrorism Committee) was established to monitor its implementation. States were initially required to report the Counter Terrorism Committee within ninety days, outlining what measures they had taken to conform with the resolution's requirements. The Counter-Terrorism Committee is made up of representatives of the fifteen countries currently sitting on the Security Council: the five permanent members of China, France, Great Britain, Russia, and the United States plus the ten non-permanent members. Its working arrangements are as follows. The Committee has been divided into three subcommittees of five members each. UN member states' reports have been assigned to one of the subcommittees alphabetically. No country sits on the subcommittee reviewing its own report. Each subcommittee is assisted by a group of experts employed by the UN Secretariat, and they are charged with the task of reviewing the reports submitted by states.[19]

The UN Security Council passed a number of additional resolutions between 2002 and 2006 to reauthorize and restructure the Counter-Terrorism Committee. Resolution 1456 (2003) reiterated the demands of Resolution 1373, and added a provision on legal concerns:

> States must ensure that any measure taken to combat terrorism comply with all their obligations under international law, and should adopt such measures in accordance with international law, in particular international human rights, refugee, and humanitarian law.[20]

[17] *Id.* note 42.

[18] United Nations General Assembly, Measures to Eliminate International Terrorism (A/Res/51/210 Jan. 16, 1997), para. 3(f), "Take appropriate measures in conformity with the relevant provisions of national and international law, including international standards of human rights, . . . of ensuring that the asylum-seeker has not planned, facilitated or participated in the commission of terrorist acts."

[19] *See generally* Security Council—Counter-Terrorism Committee, "Assessments" (United Nations), https://www.un.org/securitycouncil/ctc/content/assessments.

[20] United Nations Security Council, Resolution 1465 (Doc. S/Res/1465 13 February 2003), para. 6.

Resolution 1535 (2004) created the Counter-Terrorism Committee Executive Directorate (CTED) in order to "enhance the Committee's ability to monitor the implementation of resolution 1373 (2001) and effectively continue the capacity-building work in which it is engaged."[21] Resolution 1566 (2004) called upon states to cooperate with CTED and to continue to comply with the Al-Qaida/Taliban Sanctions Committee and the 1540 Committee. Resolution 1566 also directed the CTC to take specific initiatives to facilitate state cooperation with the Committee, including direction to "develop a set of best practices to assist States in implementing the provisions of resolution 1373 (2001) related to the financing of terrorism," and to "start visits to States, with the consent of the States concerned, in order to enhance the monitoring of the implementation of resolution 1373 (2001) and facilitate the provision of technical and other assistance for such implementation."[22] States continue to report to the CTC on their counterterrorism implementation but the new time frame is not public. The Reports submitted are also not public, and not shared within the UN system. Thus, neither the UN Special Rapporteur on Counter-Terrorism nor the Office of the High Commissioner for Human Rights OHCHR have had access to such reports to assess what if any implication for human rights protections follow from state counter-terrorism CT practice. Subsequent resolutions call upon states "to report to the Counter-Terrorism Committee, as part of their ongoing dialogue, on the steps they have taken to implement this resolution."[23] Resolution 1624 directed the CTC to take the following actions:

> (a) Include in its dialogue with Member States their efforts to implement this resolution; (b) Work with Member States to help build capacity, including through spreading best legal practice and promoting exchange of information in this regard; (c) Report back to the Council in twelve months on the implementation of this resolution. In total, 717 reports were submitted by member states to the CTC between 2001 and 2006. Each UN member state submitted at least one report in that time period.[24]

The CTC and CTED are but one cojoined element of the United Nation's counterterrorism architecture. In 2005, the Secretary-General established the

[21] United Nations Security Council, Resolution 1535 (Doc. S/Res/1535 Mar. 26, 2004); United Nations Security Council, Resolution 2395 (Doc. S/Res/2395 Dec. 21, 2017), and note the additional powers and requirements for CTED in that resolution.

[22] United Nations Security Council, Resolution 1566 (Doc. S/Res/1566 Oct. 8, 2004).

[23] United Nations Security Council, Resolution 1624 (Doc. S/Res/1624 Sept. 14, 2005).

[24] Reports by member states are not generally publicly available after 2006. Finland did release its briefing and details of its response to the CTC's visit recommendations in 2020. However, this document is no longer accessible. *See* Security Council—Counter-Terrorism Committee (CTC), "2020 Year in Review" (United Nations), https://www.un.org/securitycouncil/ctc/news/2020-year-review.

Counter-Terrorism Implementation Task Force (CTITF), which was endorsed by the General Assembly in the UN global counterterrorism strategy.[25] Its formal role is to strengthen coordination and coherence of counterterrorism within the United Nations.[26] It is made up of thirty-eight entities.[27] In 2017, mindful of the ongoing criticism that there was a lack of coherence and joined-up policy on counterterrorism in the UN system, the Secretary-General established the Office of Counter-Terrorism (OCT) headed by a new Under-Secretary General.[28] The CTIFT entities and committees are now supported by the OCT.[29]

This architecture has grown exponentially since 2001, and despite much criticism of the United Nations' effectiveness as a whole, close review of the CT architecture reveals a significant degree of compliance with its requirements by states.[30] This compulsion to compliance can be explained by intersecting factors including the institutionalism benefits conferred by engagement in these bodies to states,[31] the high value placed on compliance by P5 states (particularly the United States) creating a social solidarity network among states in the context of countering terrorism,[32] and access to certain goods for states including technical, military, policing, and data expertise when compliance is limited by technological or material factors. It is also increasingly clear that compliance is in the interests of states. The deference to state practice in the counterterrorism sphere has been a boon for states seeking to strengthen their national security apparatus.[33] It has enabled states to legitimately (and without external interference)

25 This task force no longer exists and has been replaced by a Global Counter-Terrorism Coordination Compact. *See* United Nations, "Office of Counter-Terrorism, The Compact," https://www.un.org/counterterrorism/global-ct-compact. Note that in 2006, the United Nations took further steps to emphasize the protection of human rights by establishing the Counter-Terrorism Implementation Task Force Working Group on "Protecting Human Rights While Countering Terrorism," which was specifically tasked with which was specifically tasked with investigating two specific issues: self-determination rights and targeted sanctions.

26 United Nations General Assembly, "60.288. The United Nations Global Counter-Terrorism Strategy" (Doc. A/Res/60/288, Sept. 20, 2006), https://undocs.org/A/RES/60/288, "[t]hrough its adoption that all Member States have agreed the first time to a common strategic and operational approach to fight terrorism, not only sending a clear message that terrorism is unacceptable in all its forms and manifestation but also resolving to take practical steps individually and collectively to prevent and combat it."

27 United Nations, "UN Global Counter-Terrorism Coordination Compact Entities," https://www.un.org/counterterrorism/global-ct-compact/entities.

28 United Nations, "Office of Counter-Terrorism: About Us," http://www.un.org/en/counterterrorism/.

29 *See* United Nations, *supra* note 25, for a description of the Compact and its work.

30 *See* Fionnuala Ní Aoláin, *The No-Gaps Approach to Parallel Application in the Context of the War on Terror*, 40 ISRAEL L. REV. 563, 567 (2007).

31 John W. Meyer, *The World Polity and the Authority of the Nation-State*, *in* STUDIES OF THE MODERN WORLD-SYSTEM (A. Bergesen ed., 1980).

32 RYAN GOODMAN & DEREK JINKS, SOCIALIZING STATES: PROMOTING HUMAN RIGHTS THROUGH INTERNATIONAL LAW (2013).

33 Tom Parker, *Fighting an Antaean Enemy: How Democratic States Unintentionally Sustain the Terrorist Movements They Oppose*, 19 TERRORISM & POL. VIOLENCE155, 173 (2006).

crackdown on domestic dissenters, troublesome insurgents (even if those internal conflicts reach the threshold of self-determination claims under international law or the thresholds of Protocols I and II of the Additional Protocols to the Geneva Conventions), and to modify domestic law on the basis of terrorism even if the proportionality and necessity for fundamental recalibration of legal norms at the domestic level remains empirically unproven.[34]

Clearly, then, effectiveness does not necessarily engage human rights protection or a high premium on adherence the rule of law dimensions of counterterrorism practice. The counterterrorism architecture has been consistently critiqued for its lack of attention to the human rights implications of counterterrorism.[35] Despite increasing references to human rights treaties in the most recent slew of Security Council Resolutions,[36] human rights are in practice "minimized to a generic line in a resolution, reduced to a few questions on a country visit survey, comprised of a small staff sprinkled throughout the Secretariat and Security Council bodies, securitized in the PVE agenda, and under-funded in its programming."[37] One can track the early assault on human rights in the immediate aftermath of 9/11, including: the lack of any formal institutional counterbalance to ensure the mainstreaming of human rights oversight of country action, reporting, and assessment through the CTC and CTED;[38] the lack of access in any meaningful and systematic way for civil society actors and human rights defenders to the counterterrorism architecture; the minimal capacity of

[34] "Protocol Additional to the Geneva Conventions of 12 August 1949, and relating to the Protection of Victims of International Armed Conflicts (Protocol I), adopted 8 June 1977" (1986) 1125 United Nations Treaty Series 3; "Protocol Additional to the Geneva Conventions of 12 August 1949, and relating to the Protection of Victims of Non-International Armed Conflicts (Protocol II), adopted 8 June 1977" (1986) 1125 United Nations Treaty Series 609.

[35] *See* United Nations General Assembly, Human Rights Impact of Counter-Terrorism and Countering (Violent) Extremism Policies and Practices on the Rights of Women, Girls, and the Family (Human Rights Council, A/HRC/46/36 Jan. 22, 2021); United Nations General Assembly, Human Rights Impact of Policies and Practices Aimed at Preventing and Countering Violent Extremism (Human Rights Council, A/HRC/43/46, Feb. 21, 2020); United Nations General Assembly, Impact of Measures to Address Terrorism and Violent Extremism on Civic Space and the Rights of Civil Society Actors and Human Rights Defenders (Human Rights Council, A/HRC/40/52, Mar. 1, 2019).

[36] United Nations Security Council, "Resolution 2396" (Doc. S/Res/2396 Dec. 21, 2017), https://undocs.org/S/RES/2396(2017); United Nations Security Council, "Resolution 2170" (Doc. S/Res/2170 Aug. 15, 2014).

[37] International Federation of Human Rights, "The United Nations Counter-Terrorism Complex: Bureaucracy, Political Influence, and Civil Liberties," 78 (Sept. 2017), https://www.fidh.org/IMG/pdf/9.25_fidh_final_compressed-2.pdf.

[38] Human Rights Advisors have been appointed to UNCTED, but overall this special political mission does not adopt a human-rights mainstreaming approach, has limited access to NGOs in consultation generally, and specifically when it conducts in-country assessments and human rights compliance, is not a benchmarked element of assessment in state practice. Working Group Established in 2008 in accordance with Security Council Resolution 1805. *See* Security Council Counter-Terrorism Committee, "Human Rights," https://www.un.org/sc/ctc/focus-areas/human-rights/.

existing human rights entities within the counterterrorism architecture including the cogent reality that the UN Special Rapporteur on Counter-Terrorism and Human Rights is a part-time, expert office holder who functions with minimal administrative support.[39]

Some important developments seek to stymie the exclusion of human rights in the global counterterrorism sphere. Positive developments include the establishment of human rights as one of four pillars within the global counterterrorism strategy,[40] the increased recognition that conditions conducive to terrorism include state abuses of individual and collective human rights,[41] and the willingness of national and regional courts to name state abuses of fundamental human rights in the course of counterterrorism practices.[42] As yet the influence of these developments on a largely securocratic architecture are unclear.

II. Human Rights Effects of the Global Counterterrorism Architecture

A pervasive theme of this chapter is the manner by which a lack of agreed treaty definition combined with deference to state articulations of what constitutes terrorism has laid the foundations for weakening human rights protections globally. What can be observed of state practice is an increasing tendency to lump various disaggregated experiences of violence under the banner of terrorism and the practice of numerous states in defining many forms of legitimate dissent as terrorism.

A focus on the practices of states in setting unacceptably broad definitions of terrorism helps elucidate the fundamental challenges at hand. For example, one of the broadest definitions of terrorism in Europe can be found in the Bulgarian criminal code.[43] In July 2016, the UN Human Rights Committee expressed concern as to the "vague terms criminalizing and defining actions constituting acts

[39] United Nations Human Rights Council, Report of the Special Rapporteur on the Promotion and Protection of Human Rights and Fundamental Freedoms while Countering Terrorism (Doc. A/HRC/31/6522 Feb. 2016); United Nations, Protection of Human Rights and Fundamental Freedoms While Countering Terrorism Human Rights Resolution 2005/80 (Commission on Human Rights, Doc. E/CN.4/RES/2005/80, Apr. 21, 2005).

[40] United Nations General Assembly, 70/291. The United Nations Global Counter-Terrorism Strategy Review (Doc. A/RES/70/291, July 19, 2016).

[41] *Pathways to Radicalization in Africa: Drivers, Incentives, and the Tipping Point for Recruitment* (United Nations Development Program, 2017); Fionnuala Ní Aoláin, *The Complexity and Challenges of Addressing the Conditions Conducive to Terrorism in Human Rights and Counter-Terrorism*, in Using Human Rights to Counter Terrorism (Manfred Nowak & Anne Charbord eds., 2018).

[42] El-Masri v. The Former Yugoslav Republic of Macedonia No. 39630/09 (ECtHR, November 13, 2012) 2067; Al Nashiri v. Poland No. 28761/11 (ECtHR, July 14, 2014) 875; Nasr and Ghali v. Italy No. 44883/09 (ECtHR, January 23, 2016) 210; Abu Zubaydah v. Lithuania No. 46454/11 (ECtHR, October 8, 2018); Al Nashiri v. Romania No. 33234/12 (ECtHR, May 31, 2018).

[43] *See* Article 108a: "[Anyone] who, in the view of causing disturbance or fear among the population or of threatening or forcing a competent authority, a representative of a public institution or

of terrorism" in Article 114 of Denmark's Criminal Code (2005).[44] New laws around the globe are also criminalizing freedom of expression or views that appear to praise, glorify, support, defend, apologize for, or seek to justify acts defined as "terrorism" under domestic law in ways that implicate both concerns of legality and limitations on freedom of thought and expression. The application of such provisions has inter alia been targeted at civil society, artists, and musicians.[45] While freedom of expression can legitimately be subject to derogation, restrictions increasingly shade from expression to presumed viewpoint and thought, enabled by criminal legislation that fails to define recognizable and distinct criminal acts, and lacking clear and direct causation between the statement/view/expression and an actual criminal act. Terminology such as "glorification" and "apology" remains notoriously vague and open to abuse.[46] The use of counterterrorism law to stifle domestic dissent in another persistent facet of the post-9/11 landscape. Another example is the Kingdom of Saudi Arabia's counterterrorism law, which has been so broadly and vaguely drafted as to raise substantial international concerns about the scope and content of the law.[47] Saudi Arabia's 2014 Law (the Law of Terrorism Crimes and its Financing) has a very broad definition of terrorist crimes, which encompassed any act "directly or indirectly intended to disturb the public order of the state, or to destabilise the security of society, or the stability of the state, or to expose its national unity to danger, or to suspend the basic law of governance or some of its articles, or to insult the reputation of the state or its standing, or to inflict damage upon one of its public utilities or its natural resources."[48] Anyone, whether Saudi Arabian or a

of a foreign state or international organization to perform or omit part of his/her duties commits a crime . . . [and] shall be punished by terrorism by deprivation of liberty from five to fifteen years."

[44] United Nations Human Rights Committee, Concluding Observations on the Sixth Periodic Report of Denmark (CCPR/C/DNK/CO/6, 7 Aug. 15, 2016), paras. 27–28.

[45] In Spain, the use of counterterrorism laws against artistic expression has been of particular concern. Raphael Minder, *Crackdowns on Free Speech Rise Across a Europe Wary of Terror*, N.Y. Times, Feb. 24, 2016, https://www.nytimes.com/2016/02/25/world/europe/spain-europe-protest-free-speech.html?_r=0.

[46] The French law on apology of terrorism is a relevant point of reference here as well as the statistics that indicate the large number of minors caught by the law, indicating that the targets may well be as guilty of immaturity and poor judgment as juveniles as they are of the crime of glorifying terrorism. *See* Human Rights Watch, *Preempting Justice: Counterterrorism Laws and Procedures in France* (July 2008), and Human Rights Watch, *"The Root of Humiliation": Abusive Identity Checks in France"* (2012).

[47] Office of the High Commissioner, "Special Rapporteur on the Promotion and Protection of Human Rights and Fundamental Freedoms while Countering Terrorism Concludes Visit to Saudi Arabia" (United Nations Human Rights, May 4, 2017), https://www.ohchr.org/EN/NewsEvents/Pages/DisplayNews.aspx?NewsID=21584&LangID=E; Human Rights Watch, "Saudi Arabia: New Counterterrorism Law Enables Abuse: Criminalizes Criticisms of King and Crown Prince as Terrorism Offense" (Nov. 23, 2017), https://www.hrw.org/news/2017/11/23/saudi-arabia-new-counterterrorism-law-enables-abuse.

[48] *See* Article 1.

foreign national, whether inside the country or abroad, who was accused of such conduct could be prosecuted as a "terrorist" inside Saudi Arabia.[49] This included those who attempted to "change the ruling system in the Kingdom" or "harmed the interests, economy, and national and social security of the Kingdom."[50] Under such a broad definition, anyone challenging the authority or policies of the state could qualify as a terrorist.[51] The Special Rapporteur on the Protection and Promotion of Human Rights While Countering Terrorism considers that the definition of terrorism in the 2014 Law on Counter Terrorism and its Financing is objectionably broad and fails to comply with international human rights standards.[52] Another data point is the comprehensive report by the Washington, DC–based Center for Strategic and International Studies, which has forcefully demonstrated that the pattern of targeting civil society, imprisoning human rights defenders, limiting the speech, movement, and assembly of those who critique repressive states has been enabled by national counterterrorism regimes, which are in turn enabled and facilitated by the regulatory dictates of the global counterterrorism architecture.[53]

There is an odd confluence at play in the symbiotic relationship between global demands to regulate terrorism and national responses, which use such laws to limit human rights protections. First, since 9/11, the scope and content of Security Council resolutions on terrorism have expanded and the operative aspects of such resolutions have become more pronounced.[54] States are mandated to regulate on particular issues (e.g., terrorist financing, foreign fighters) and the scope of formal state opt-out is limited given the high pressures to

[49] Human Rights Watch, "Saudi Arabia: New Counterterrorism Law Enables Abuse" (Nov. 23, 2017), https://www.hrw.org/news/2017/11/23/saudi-arabia-new-counterterrorism-law-enables-abuse.

[50] *See* Article 3.

[51] The introduction of new provisions by KSA in 2017 further expanded the scope of terrorist offenses, criminalizing describing, directly or indirectly, the king or the crown prince in "any way offensive to religion or justice" (Article 30) as well as conduct that may be deemed as supporting, advocating for, justifying, or praising terrorism (Article 34) and "anyone who broadcasts or publishes by any means news, statements, false or malicious propaganda, or the like, for the purpose of carrying out a terrorist offense" (Article 44). Unfortunately, even with the changes, the definition was not brought any closer to complying with human rights standards.

[52] Office of the High Commissioner, "UN Special Rapporteur on the Promotion and Protection of Human Rights and Fundamental Freedoms while Countering Terrorism Concludes Visit to Saudi Arabia" (United Nations Human Rights, May 4, 2017), https://www.ohchr.org/EN/NewsEvents/Pages/DisplayNews.aspx?NewsID=21584&LangID=E.

[53] Lauren Mooney, *Introduction*, *in* COUNTER-TERRORISM MEASURES AND CIVIL SOCIETY 1 (Lana Baydas & Shannon Green eds., Mar. 2018). "However, the world has witnessed an alarming rise in restrictions placed on civil society actors to curtail their space and operations, impending upon the realization of their rights to freedom of expression, association, and peaceful assembly—frequently in the name of countering terrorism and protecting national security, among other drivers."

[54] United Nations Security Council, Resolution 2395 (Doc. S/RES/2395, Dec. 21, 2017), para. 21, "[r]eminds Member States that effective measures to counter terrorism and violent extremism as and when conducive to terrorism and respect for human rights are complementary and mutually enforcing."

conform and be seen a "good" player in this arena.[55] Second, the opportunity to regulate, dictated in part by global political pressure and the institutional standing of the Security Council, allows states to act legislatively in ways that might not be possible without the prompt of the Security Council. Thus, states have an easy justification for expansive counterterrorism regulation, which then stymies national political debate on the need, form, and mechanisms involved. It may also expressly ouster national processes of review that have an explicit human rights component. This is not to say that the Security Council has in fact pronounced on the legality, proportionality, and necessity of all aspects of domestic legislative enactments. Rather, it gives convenient cover to states to do legislative work that might not otherwise be possible politically at home. Third, the perceived or articulated dictates of the Security Council have given some states the leeway to claim that legislative action needs to be "fast-tracked,"[56] and that certain kinds of domestic procedures can be sidestepped (even as those domestic procedures provide human rights benchmarking or review). Here the state can invoke its good standing and reputational need to conform to international law, even as that rhetoric is being used to nefarious domestic ends.[57] Fourth, the Security Council does not benchmark domestic legislative enactments by reference to the human rights obligations of states.[58] Countries increasingly understand is that the translation of Security Council exhortations into domestic law will be subject to limited scrutiny on the counterterrorism side.[59] So translation itself becomes a permissive site, in which states go far beyond the bounds of what has been deemed appropriate within the resolutions, but there is limited if no cost to the state for this approach. Even if there are embarrassment or litigation

[55] *See, e.g.*, Stephen A. Kocs, *Explaining the Strategic Behaviour of States: International Law as System Structure*, 38 INT'L STUD. Q., no. 4, 535–56 (1994). *See also* BETH SIMMONS, MOBILIZING FOR HUMAN RIGHTS: INTERNATIONAL LAW IN DOMESTIC POLITICS (2009), noting the rewards states seek as "good" actors.

[56] This bears an eerie similarity to the increased practice of "fast-tracking" that can be observed at the Security Council, a practice that has also been adopted at the regional level *see, e.g.*, "After a Fast-Track Process the European Parliament Takes a Troubling Position on Counterterrorism" (Open Society Foundations, July 13, 2016, https://www.opensocietyfoundations.org/press-releases/after-fast-track-process-european-parliament-takes-troubling-position; United Nations Security Council, Resolution 2395 (Doc. S/RES/2395, Dec. 21, 2017), "[r]eaffirming also the obligation of Member States to freeze without delay funds and other financial assets or economic resources of persons or entities who commit, or attempt to commit terrorist acts or participate in or facilitate the commission of terrorist acts."

[57] In a rather paradoxical twist, states then report the "efficiency" of their counterterrorism laws by reference to national statistics that sweep up all of those (including legitimate protesters, human rights defenders, indigenous leaders, women's rights activists) who have been processed under counterterrorism laws. United Nations, Report of the Special Rapporteur on the Promotion and Protection of Human Rights and Fundamental Freedoms while Countering Terrorism on the Human Rights Challenge of State of Emergency in the Context of Countering Terrorism (Doc. A/HRC/37/52, Feb. 27, 2018), para. 20.

[58] *Id.* para. 26.

[59] *Id.* para. 27.

costs with human rights bodies and regional human rights courts, these are bearable burdens, not least because one set of international legal obligations are being played off against the others. In this trade-off, human rights protections will inevitably lose out.

The insidious costs of an ever-expanding global security regime to human rights are in need of monitoring and evaluation. Some costs are easier to define than others. For example, it is relatively easy to undertake an institutional assessment of the global counterterrorism architecture and point out its human rights lacunae.[60] This is illustrated by a lack of sustained human rights hardwiring in the New York–based institutional structures.[61] It is demonstrated by the closed spaces in which counterterrorism policy and law is developed with virtually no access for civil society actors.[62] It is affirmed by the lack of transparency on country reports to CTED, whereby what any particular country is saying about its human rights adherence is not subject to external human rights input. The author is unaware of what kind of cross-referencing to human rights reporting (including for example Universal Periodic Review and the country reports of the UN Special Rapporteur for the Protection and Promotion of Human Rights while Countering Terrorism) is made in the evaluation of state reports to the CTC, but there is little external evidence to suggest robust cross-fertilization.[63] At the very least it is not required and states internalize the reality that the two systems of compliance are divorced from one another. The messaging that counterterrorism regulation has a higher and more sustained value for states is both obvious and nonobvious. As the next section will explore, a lack of concern about state adherence to the protection and promotion of human rights while countering terrorism as short-, medium-, and long-term consequences. In a fairly obvious contradiction, as states grapple with the reality that military and hard legal responses to terrorism hit a ceiling in addressing the causes conducive to terrorism and may in fact contribute to them, there is an obvious disjunction between two core strands of the global strategy to effectively prevent and manage terrorism.

[60] *See* United Nations, *Promotion and Protection of Human Rights and Fundamental Freedoms while Countering Terrorism* (Note by the Secretary-General, A/73/361, Sept. 3, 2018).

[61] International Federation for Human Rights, *supra* note 37, at 78; United Nations General Assembly, *Report of the Special Rapporteur on the Promotion and Protection of Human Rights and Fundamental Freedoms while Countering Terrorism* (Human Rights Council, Doc. A/HRC/31/65, Feb. 22, 2016).

[62] Alistair Millar, "Blue Sky IV: Clouds Dispersing" (Global Center on Cooperative Security, May 2018) 5, "[a] wider array of governmental agencies, intergovernmental actors, including civil society and the private sector, need to be engaged and involved to prevent and counter the threat of terrorism more effectively."

[63] The same might equally be said of the Mutual Evaluation Process for FATF membership.

III. The Costs of Ignoring Human Rights

The UN Global Counter-Terrorism Strategy adopted in 2006 established that all UN member states agree on a coordinated and comprehensive response to terrorism. Notably that strategy identified the following elements as conducive to the spread of terrorism: "prolonged unresolved conflicts, dehumanization of victims of terrorism in all its forms and manifestations, lack of the rule of law and violations of human rights, ethnic, national and religious discrimination, political exclusion, socio-economic marginalization and lack of good governance."[64] The strategy also identified the need to "strength[en] and make best possible use of the capacities of the United Nations in areas such as conflict prevention, negotiation, mediation, conciliation, judicial settlement, rule of law, peacekeeping and peacebuilding."[65] The General Assembly reaffirmed this strategy on September 8, 2010, and urged states to make greater and consistent efforts to implement it.[66]

Multiple and scalar macro-causes of terrorism have been identified by scholars and policy makers. They include: structural violence; socioeconomic exclusions;[67] poverty; sustained discrimination;[68] the systematic denial of civil and political rights; counterterrorism strategies;[69] the lack of meaningful participation in governance systems for groups and minorities; and persistent armed conflict. It would be naive to provide a linear explanation of terrorism in any

[64] United Nations, *supra* note 26).

[65] *Id.* sec. I, para. 1.

[66] United Nations General Assembly, "The United Nations Global Counterterrorism Strategy, Report of the Secretary General (A/64/818), Draft Resolution (A/64/L.69)" (117th Plenary Meeting, Doc. A/64/PV.117, Sept. 8, 2010), http://www.un.org/en/ga/search/view_doc.asp?symbol=A/64/PV.117.

[67] Raul Caruso & Friedrich Schneider, *The Socio-Economic Determinants of Terrorism and Political Violence in Western Europe (1994–2007)*, 27 Eur. J. Pol. Econ., S37 (2011). The article's objective is to empirically investigate the socioeconomic causes of terrorism and political violence in a sample of twelve countries in Western Europe. The findings conclude that in Western European countries the classical economic argument of opportunity cost can be confirmed—the larger is the set of economic opportunities for an individual the lower is the likelihood or the willingness for him to be involved in a terrorist activity.

[68] *See* James A. Piazza, *Poverty, Minority Economic Discrimination and Domestic Terrorism*, 48 J. Peace Research 339 (2011). Using data from the Minorities at Risk project, the author determines that countries featuring minority group economic discrimination are significantly more likely to experience domestic terrorist attacks, whereas countries lacking minority groups or whose minorities do not face discrimination are significantly less likely to experience terrorism. He also finds minority economic discrimination to be a strong and substantive predictor of domestic terrorism vis-á-vis the general level of economic development.

[69] *See* United Nations General Assembly, "Promotion and Protection of all Human Rights, Civil, Political, Economic, Social and Cultural Rights, Including the Rights to Development" (Human Rights Council Doc. A/HRC/6/17, Nov. 21, 2007), https://documents-dds-ny.un.org/doc/UNDOC/GEN/G07/149/48/PDF/G0714948.pdf?OpenElement. In this Report, the Special Rapporteur notes that terrorism and measures adopted to combat terrorist acts are both influenced by and have an impact upon economic, social, and cultural rights.

country setting. It is precisely the pernicious variable geometry of causes factoring in the precise relationship between poverty and political representation that might explain why in one setting the intersection of rights deprivations functions as a condition conducive to terrorist acts, whereas a slightly different vector of the same causes in another country setting does not have the same effect. There is also a danger that a focus on identifying simple causes translates into a cookie cutter approach that flattens out the real differences in mobilization to political violence.

I conclude by reflecting on one aspect of conditions conducive to terrorism, namely, the denial of the rule of law in general and in counterterrorism strategies as well as the systematic violations of human rights that can be experienced by individuals and populations at the national level. There is increased international recognition that combatting terrorism must be done in a way that affirms the enjoyment of human rights and secures rather than undermines both derogable and nonderogable rights.[70] Some international and regional institutions recognize (implicitly if not explicitly) that sustained deprivations of fundamental human rights may have significant implications for sustained and nurturing terrorist violence. For example, the Council of European Union's Revised EU Strategy for Combatting Radicalization and Recruitment to Terrorism affirms that preventative measures are critical and more effective than deradicalization.[71] A major new study by the United Nations Development Programme UNDP entitled *Journey to Extremism in Africa* cogently demonstrates how poor rule of law, trust in government, and a lack of confidence in the security sector provide tipping points to extremism.[72] The report is worth quoting at length:

> The research makes clear that a sense of grievance towards, and limited confidence in, government is widespread in the regions of Africa associated with the highest incidence of violent extremism. This may be an inevitable corollary of the life experience of growing up in the context of acute and relative multidimensional poverty, neglect and political marginalization affecting these areas. However, dissatisfaction with government is highest by significant margins among the *Journey to Extremism* respondents who were recruited by

[70] António Guterres, "Speech at SOAS, University of London, on "Counter-Terrorism and Human Rights: Winning the Fight While Upholding our Values," (United Nations Secretary General, Nov. 16, 2017), https://www.un.org/sg/en/content/sg/speeches/2017-11-16/speech-soas-university-london-counter-terrorism.

[71] Council of the European Union, "Revised EU Strategy for Combating Radicalisation and Recruitment to Terrorism" (Memo to COREPER/Council, Doc. 9956/14, May 19, 2004), http://register.consilium.europa.eu/doc/srv?l=EN&f=ST%209956%202014%20INIT.

[72] United Nations Development Programme, "Journey to Extremism in Africa: Drivers, Incentives, and the Tipping Point for Recruitment" (Regional Bureau for Africa, 2017), http://journey-to-extremism.undp.org/content/downloads/UNDP-JourneyToExtremism-report-2017-english.pdf.

> violent extremist groups across several key indicators. These include: belief that government only looks after the interests of a few; low level of trust in government authorities; and experience, or willingness to report experience, of bribe-paying. Grievances against security actors, as well as politicians, are particularly marked, with an average of 78 percent rating low levels of trust in the police, politicians and military.[73]

Human rights violations have been demonstrated in multiple studies to provide a measurable incentive to mobilization toward political violence.[74] The nexus of the abuse of state power, the abuse of legal process or ill-treatment at the hands of state agents shapes the individual and community's responses in ways that can mobilize protest, anomie, and violence.[75] In an obvious sense, this is entirely counterproductive to the goal of preventing and eradicating the conditions that produce and sustain violence. Human rights protection while countering terrorism has both an ethical and efficiency component. The ethical arguments have been well canvassed in debates concerning the use of torture, rendition, exceptional trial, and the deployment of the death penalty.[76] The efficiency arguments are equally compelling. Short-term gains from the abuses of human rights create long-term distrust between the state and individuals. The festering of grievance and the deep hurts that follow when groups (particularly ethnic, religious, and cultural minorities) are targeted under the guise of national security provoke deeper hostility and long-term animus for states. Moreover, when we view the conflation of legitimate governance grievances (whether involving internal or external self-determination) with state security crackdown, we enter the complex realm of fragile states, state insecurity, and cyclical driven by fundamental challenges to the legitimacy of the state. Increasingly, as states avoid

[73] *Id.* 5.

[74] Colm Campbell & Ita Connolly, *A Model for the "War Against Terrorism?" Military Intervention in Northern Ireland and the 1970 Fall Curfew*, 30 J.L. & Soc'y 341, 348 (2003), noting that unclear restrictions on governmental power lead to further lawlessness.

[75] Ted Robert Gurr, Why Men Rebel (1970); Violence Prevention: Changing Cultural and Social Norms that Support Violence (World Health Organization 2009), http://www.who.int/violence_injury_prevention/violence/norms.pdf; United Nations Development Program, "Journey of Young Africans into Violent Extremism Marked by Poverty and Deprivation: UNDP" (Sept. 7, 2017), http://www.undp.org/content/undp/en/home/presscenter/pressreleases/2017/09/07/vers-l-extremisme-violent-en-afrique.html; Sarah Mosoetsa, *Compromised Communities and Re-Emerging Civic Engagement in Mpumalanga Township, Durban, KwaZulu-Natal*, 31 J. Southern Africa Stud. 857, 858 (2005).

[76] Anaïs Reding et al., "Handling Ethical Problems in Counterterrorism: An Inventory of Methods to Support Ethical Decision Making" (Rand Europe 2014), https://www.rand.org/content/dam/rand/pubs/research_reports/RR200/RR251/RAND_RR251.pdf; Alex Bellmay, *No Pain, No Gain? Torture and Ethics in the War on Terror*, 82 Int'l Aff. 121, 123 (2006); Henry Frank Carey, *The Domestic Politics of Protecting Human Rights in Counter-Terrorism*, 27 East Eur. Pol. & Societies: and Cultures 429, 443 (2013); Jean Maria Arrigo, *A Utilitarian Argument Against Torture Interrogation of Terrorists*, 10 Sci. & Engineering Ethics 543, 557 (2010).

the application of international humanitarian law to low-intensity conflict and use the counterterrorism regulatory space to address such challenges, there are broader and deeper question of legal regime capacity and applicability to be addressed which are beyond the scope of this chapter. Nonetheless, the conflation of legal regimes, the overreach of national security or counterterrorism measures as a holdall for state responses to complex issues of legitimacy and representation should give pause to the global enthusiasm for counterterrorism as the preferred "holdall" capacity for state responses to violence of multiple forms.

IV. Conclusion

This chapter has explored the interface of global counterterrorism regimes with the protection and promotion of human rights post 9/11. The picture that emerges is not comforting from a right-based analysis. It affirms the institutional marginality of human rights norms and mechanisms within the global counterterrorism architecture and notes that the absence of rights based capacities is not an accidental oversight, but rather an institutional arrangement by design and deliberation. The chapter also affirms the complex interplay between a global cooperative model of addressing and regulating terrorism (from terrorist financing to airline passenger security) allied with a highly deferential model to state definitions of terrorism and assessments of threat. The operative mantra appears to be that states can generally label terrorists with latitude and that other states will defer under sovereignty and noninterference doctrines to domestic choices (even when the obvious targets are civil society and human rights defenders broadly defined). There are obviously necessary and well-defined global targets of counterterrorism regulation (including, for example, Al Qaeda, ISIS),[77] but beyond that specific consensus there is a broader universe of national practice where much of the powers given by Security Council mandate are exercised and where the range of individuals and groups targeted is far more diverse and multifaceted.

Given this rather sober assessment is there any likely recalibration of the global trend to security regime ascendency? The glimmers are few but worth noting. First, is the push-pull tension in global policymaking between hardline counterterrorism measures and more softly identified prevention and countering measures. As some states realize the necessity for the latter, the pull to human rights is stronger when there is considered engagement with "conditions conducive"

[77] United Nations Security Council, "Security Council Committee Pursuant to Resolution 1267 (1999) 1989 (2011) and 2253 (2015) Concerning Islamic State in Iraq and the Levant (Da'esh), Al-Qaida and Associated Individuals, Groups, Undertakings, and Entities," https://www.un.org/securitycouncil/sanctions/1267.

to terrorism.[78] Second, the increased lip service being paid to human rights language in Security Council resolutions affirms the sustained legitimacy pull of human rights norms, as well as a recognition that to entirely ouster human rights values from the counterterrorism space may be counterproductive as a matter of legitimacy and inconsistent with the national priorities of some vocal states.[79] Third, civil society activists continue to prod states and the counterterrorism architecture itself to be more transparent and accountable. These voices have not been muted by their isolation and many have found innovative ways to engage and put pressure on the CT architecture.[80] It remains astonishing that since 2001, the UN collective security apparatus could have been recalibrated in such profound ways. It is also noticeable that little scholarly or policy attention has been paid to the institutional changes.[81] This signals that scholars and policymakers need to pay more attention to where and how global security norms are being produced, which states have outsized influence on their content, and what kinds of constraining or limiting mechanisms are in place to prevent sovereignty overrides. To conclude, this chapter encourages much more attention to the UN counterterrorism architecture given its pivotal position in the creation of both local and national norms.

[78] Andrew Glazzard & Eric Rosand, *Is It All over for CVE?*, LAWFARE, June 11, 2017, https://www.lawfareblog.com/it-all-over-cve. "[T]hat CVE fails to deliver on its promise to 'tame' militarized and other hard-security approaches to counterterrorism; that it prioritizes Western security concerns over the needs of its supposed beneficiaries . . . that it provides a blank check to repressive governments to harass political opponents in the name of countering violent extremism."

[79] *Annual Report and Accounts 2016–2017* (Foreign and Commonwealth Office, Finance Directorate 2017); "Protection of Human Rights" (Permanent Mission of France to the United Nations and New York, June 9, 2020), https://onu.delegfrance.org/Protection-of-Human-Rights; "Human Rights—A Cornerstone of German Foreign Policy" (Federal Foreign Office, Dec. 3, 2020), https://www.auswaertiges-amt.de/en/aussenpolitik/themen/menschenrechte/01-menschenrechte-fundament.

[80] Noting the work of civil society to penetrate its processes and influence outcomes in the FATF context. *See* Financial Action Task Force, "Combating the Abuse of Non-Profit Organizations (Recommendation 8)" (June 2015) 6–7.

[81] A search on CT architecture reveals few scholarly interventions in the almost two decades since the CTC was established as indicated by the literature cited in this chapter and here. *See, e.g.*, Vincent-Joël Proulx, *An Incomplete Revolution: Enhancing the Security Council's Role in Enforcing Counterterrorism Obligations*, 8 J. INT'L DISP. SETTLEMENT 303 (2017); Marshall B. Lloyd, *Attacks, Conflicts, and Consensus: Institutional Developments to Combat Terrorism within the United Nations in Response to September 11, 2001*, 51 CRIM. L. BULL. 454 (2015); Isaac Kfir, *A Regime in Need of Balance: The UN Counter-Terrorism Regimes of Security and Human Rights*, 4 U. MIAMI NAT'L SECURITY & ARMED CONFLICT L. REV. 7 (2014); Howard Stoffer, *The Need for a United Nations Global Counter-Terrorism Coordinator* (International Centre for Counter Terrorism, The Hague, Policy Brief, Aug. 2013); "The Global Regime for Terrorism: Issue Brief" (Council on Foreign Relations, International Institutions and Global Government Program, 31 Aug. 31, 2011), https://www.cfr.org/report/global-regime-terrorism; Andrew Hudson, *Not a Great Asset: The UN Security Council's Counter-Terrorism Regime: Violating Human Rights*, 25 BERKELEY J. INT'L L. 203 (2007).

3
The Paradox of Discrimination

Jens David Ohlin

I. Introduction

In 1817, Abraham Thornton was placed on trial in England for murdering Mary Ashford. She was drowned, and the local authorities in Warwickshire determined that Thornton was the culprit. The indictment accused Thornton of drowning her "by the instigation of the Devil."[1] At trial, the case fell apart, and Thornton was acquitted. However, Ashford's surviving brother—still convinced of Thornton's guilt—managed to get the case reinstated. A second trial was ordered.

Thornton maintained his innocence and demanded to exercise an ancient right that endured in Britain but had fallen into disuse for many years: trial by combat. According to historian George Neilson, Thornton's invocation of this ancient right "was the last time that such a challenge was to be given in a British court of justice."[2] In making his challenge, Thornton *literally* threw down a gauntlet—this was how the right was triggered—and challenged the authorities to fight him to the death. The gauntlet was made from white leather with a red leather band and silk fringes, according to Neilson's description, calling it "as strange as the occasion."[3]

The authorities were perplexed and angered by this surprising turn of events in the murder case. Although trial by combat was once a recognized part of British criminal justice, it had long since fallen out of favor as an acceptable manner of resolving criminal allegations. When Thornton demanded trial by combat, he knew full well that no one would have the stomach to fight him. The practice was already regarded, in 1817, as cruel and barbaric and certainly not in keeping with the rule of law or evolving standards of civility. Thornton surely could not have been surprised by this reaction; indeed, he was counting on it. He was demanding a trial by combat that would never happen, so he would have to be released once his challenge went unmet.

[1] George Neilson, Trial by Combat 329 (1890).
[2] *Id.*
[3] *Id.*

Jens David Ohlin, *The Paradox of Discrimination* In: *Between Crime and War.* Edited by: Claire Finkelstein, Christopher Fuller, Jens David Ohlin, Mitt Regan, Oxford University Press. DOI: 10.1093/oso/9780197638798.003.0004

The authorities quickly realized that they had a problem on their hands. If other accused murderers realized that they could repeat Thornton's gambit, then soon they would all go free and a viable system of criminal justice might collapse. The right to trial by combat, once a mainstay of British justice, had quickly become an embarrassment. Parliament finally abolished it by statute in 1819.[4] Thornton was the last person in Britain to demand trial by combat.[5] His invocation of the right provided the impetus to finally dissolve the right and confine it to the dustbin of history. (Incidentally, the statute was enacted *after* American independence, past the point when Britain could legislate for its colony. So the repeal had no effect in the United States, leading some American defendants to suggest, a bit too cleverly, that the right still applies today in the United States.[6])

It is worth dwelling for a moment on why trial by combat should be regarded as anathema to a developed system of justice. Although the intuition seems obvious, of course, it is helpful to articulate it explicitly. In trial by combat, the outcome of the verdict is decided by brute force, by a physical contest. A weak individual is condemned to die, and a strong individual might survive. The contest is also circumscribed by luck and circumstance, neither of which gives anyone confidence in the legitimacy of the outcome. Trial by combat is an exercise in might makes right—a moral theory with little to recommend it.

In contrast, a criminal trial is supposed to be about evidence, reasons, and thoughtful deliberation. The outcome—the verdict—should be based on an objective presentation of facts and an unbiased application of the law. The result is an outcome determined by the rule of law. The result is a civilized process. Trial by combat is barbaric, precisely because law and brute force should not mix.

We have come a long way from trial by combat. But we still administer "justice" in some vague sense by brute force when we launch a drone attack against a suspected terrorist or send in the Navy Seals to Pakistan to kill Osama bin Laden. Perhaps it was a poorly chosen phrase, but President Barack Obama captioned the latter news event by declaring, during a nationally televised speech from the White House, that "justice" had been done.[7] And in places as diverse as Afghanistan, Yemen, Somalia, Libya, Iraq, and Syria, the United States and

[4] Act of 22 June 1819.

[5] Neilson, *supra* note 1.

[6] United States v. Luthmann, No. 17-CR-664, 2019 WL 5423570, at *4 (E.D.N.Y. Oct. 23, 2019) ("In 2010, Defendant returned to New York, and was employed as an associate at a trusts and estates law firm before starting his own firm. He gained notoriety as a lawyer for, among other things, his request for trial by combat to resolve a civil suit brought against him for allegedly assisting a client to fraudulently transfer assets.").

[7] President Obama, Address to the Nation, May 2, 2011 ("So Americans understand the costs of war. Yet as a country, we will never tolerate our security being threatened, nor stand idly by when our people have been killed. We will be relentless in defense of our citizens and our friends and allies. We will be true to the values that make us who we are. And on nights like this one, we can say to those families who have lost loved ones to al Qaeda's terror: Justice has been done.").

its allies have used targeted killings to kill specific individuals who have harmed American citizens and have threatened to harm more of them in the future.

Targeted killings enjoy broad support from the American public, as the poll numbers demonstrate.[8] However, a vocal minority takes strong umbrage to the attacks, which they describe with a variety of increasingly negative labels: targeted killings, unlawful executions, extrajudicial killings, assassinations, or simply murder. Indeed, the UN official who regularly issues unfavorable reports about the US policy of targeted killings is called the Special Rapporteur on extrajudicial, summary, or arbitrary executions.[9] To some, these are executions, handed down from 10,000 feet, without due process of law.

It is clear that targeted killings are transforming modern warfare. Gone is the war of yesteryear: a forced contest in a desert or forest with tanks and artillery fighting to wipe out the enemy with few or no civilians in close proximity. Now, battles are fought with terrorists and insurgents fighting in urban locations, hiding in and among civilians who are protected by the laws of war. Consequently, the United States uses drone technology to pick out specific individuals who are responsible for planning and conspiring to commit imminent terrorist attacks—and the military or the CIA kills them. These operations are often pursued covertly through the deployment of "unacknowledged force"—military operations that are an open secret in the world community but that remain officially unacknowledged by the US government.[10] In the past, unacknowledged force was the sole purview of the CIA and its Directorate of Clandestine Operations, but now the Defense Department, too, conducts drone operations, through its Joint Special Operations Command (JSOC), that remain unacknowledged by the government in particularly sensitive theaters of operation.[11]

The most unique aspect of these drone operations is the nature of the targeting process. Instead of launching indiscriminate force against a large collection of soldiers—essentially the paradigm of military operations in previous generations—the US government invests huge resources in collecting and analyzing intelligence regarding specific individuals who constitute a threat against

[8] Micah Zenko, *U.S. Public Opinion on Drone Strikes*, COUNCIL ON FOREIGN RELATIONS BLOG, Mar. 18, 2013.

[9] Philip Alston, Report of the Special Rapporteur on extrajudicial, summary or arbitrary executions, U.N. Doc. A/HRC/14/24/Add.6, May 28, 2010 (criticizing "a highly problematic blurring and expansion of the boundaries of the applicable legal frameworks").

[10] Philip Alston, *The CIA and Targeted Killings Beyond Borders*, 2 HARV. NAT'L SEC. J., 283, 284 (2011) ("Since 9/11, both the Central Intelligence Agency ("CIA") and the United States Department of Defense ("DOD") have rapidly expanded their covert operations around the world. Both are significantly engaged in extraterritorial targeted killings, neither operates with the degree of accountability officially envisaged under domestic law, and neither is in any meaningful way accountable for its actions in terms of the international legal obligations undertaken by the United States.").

[11] *Id.* 285 (referring to the Defense Department's JSOC as "an almost autonomous and at best minimally accountable force within its own ranks").

the United States.[12] In some instances, the intelligence is gathered through so-called HUMINT, or human intelligence—essentially assets on the ground that have agreed to provide information to the United States because of financial incentives (cash) or for ideological reasons. In other instances, intelligence is gathered through SIGINT, or signal intelligence—eavesdropping on telephone phone calls, emails, and other internet traffic collected in bulk by the National Security Agency or other agencies. Finally, the relevant intelligence might be collected by the drones themselves, as they hover over a location for extended periods of time, tracking the movements and behavior of specific targets as they associate with other individuals who might be members of a foreign terrorist organization.

II. The Obligation to Reduce Casualties

The key aspect of this targeting process is the individualized nature of the threat assessment. For example, the policy of the Obama administration was to kill specific terrorists who were plotting attacks or who were members of an organized armed group planning future attacks.[13] In doing so, the US military and the CIA are able to do more with less. They are allegedly able to promote security by killing the smallest number of persons—surgical, precise, military force against single individuals rather than the mass bombing or shelling that one might see during a conventional military campaign.[14]

For the US government, especially during the Obama administration, this surgical deployment of force against particular individuals was not only effective from a policy and strategic perspective but also morally and legally preferable to the conventional paradigm of deploying overwhelming force against an entire class of people—the entire military force of the enemy. Why would drone strikes be preferable to a conventional military attack? The answer lies in the ethical and philosophical constraints on killing embodied in the Just War Tradition, and

[12] Gregory S. McNeal, *Targeted Killing and Accountability*, 102 Geo. L.J., 681, 707 (2014) ("Although law delimits the categories of persons who can be killed, in practice, developing kill lists looks far beyond law to questions about the identity of a particular target and the accuracy and currency of the supporting intelligence. After intelligence is reviewed, a validation step revisits the initial legal determination to ensure that attacking an individual is lawful under the law of armed conflict or a particular covert action finding or executive directive.").

[13] US Government, "Procedures for Approving Direct Action Against Terrorist Targets Located Outside the United States and Areas of Active Hostilities," May 22, 2013, at 11 (stating that operations will be approved only when "the individual's activities pose a continuing, imminent threat to U.S. persons").

[14] Oren Gross, *The New Way of War: Is There a Duty to Use Drones?*, 67 Fla. L. Rev., 1, 13 (2015) ("And if, in fact, drones offer the twin promises of greater precision and reduced lethality, ought not the commander to deploy them rather than call for alternative methods of air support or bombardment or introduce 'boots on the ground'?").

the legal constraints on warfare imposed by international law. Specifically, both law and philosophy prohibit attacking forces from causing collateral damage to civilians that is disproportionate to the value of the military target.[15] Also, there is an emerging legal norm, one that is already well entrenched in philosophical thinking, that requires attacking forces to go even further, that is, to take all reasonable precautions to reduce collateral damage as far as possible.[16] For these reasons, the Obama administration articulated that its drone policy, in most situations, was to only act with lethal force if civilian casualties could be minimized to near zero.[17] True, the US government labeled this constraint as a policy directive (the PPG), rather than an acknowledged requirement of international law, though even as a pure policy directive, its impetus surely comes from a common-sense intuition that civilian casualties are unfortunate and should be reduced as much as possible.[18]

Furthermore, there are even ethical reasons to reduce the number of enemy soldiers killed during military action.[19] Drones help achieve that goal as well. For a moment, take the issue of killing civilians off the table and just imagine a situation where the only victims will be enemy soldiers. If the US military or CIA could keep the country safe by killing just one or two soldiers—say in a so-called decapitation strike—then that might be morally better than killing five thousand enemy soldiers by carpet-bombing an entire military installation. Some scholars and international lawyers argue that the law of war actually requires killing the fewest number of enemy soldiers possible while still accomplishing the mission, but the mainstream view is that international law is indifferent to how many enemy soldiers are killed in battle.[20]

Either way, though, it is good that drones allow the United States to accomplish its counterterrorism mission with surgical precision. For one thing, it may be more effective to kill fewer individuals. This may sound surprising, but it is undeniably true in some circumstances. For example, launching a military campaign

15 Protocol Additional to the Geneva Conventions of 12 August 1949, and Relating to the Protection of Victims of International Conflicts (Protocol I), art. 51(5)(b).

16 Additional Protocol I, art. 57(2)(a)(ii) (obligation to "take all feasible precautions in the choice of means and methods of attack, with a view to avoiding, and in any event to minimizing, incidental loss of civilian life, injury to civilians and damage to civilian objects").

17 "Procedures for Approving Direct Action Against Terrorist Targets Located Outside the United States and Areas of Active Hostilities" (*supra* note 13), 1 (directing that "absent extraordinary circumstances, direct action will be taken only if there is near certainty that the action can be taken without injuring or killing non-combatants").

18 *Id.*

19 Some of these moral considerations are canvassed in Larry May & Jens David Ohlin, Necessity in International Law (2016).

20 For a discussion of this issue, *see* Ryan Goodman, *The Power to Kill or Capture Enemy Combatants*, 24 Eur. J. Int'l L., 819, 819–20 (2013) (arguing that "[t]he modern law of armed conflict (LOAC) supports the following maxim: if enemy combatants can be put out of action by capturing them, they should not be injured; if they can be put out of action by injury, they should not be killed; and if they can be put out of action by light injury, grave injury should be avoided").

with overwhelming force might alienate the local population, even if civilian casualties are reduced or even eliminated.[21] If the local population witnesses widespread destruction and killing, even of individuals who are rightly described as soldiers or combatants, the population might resent the United States and end up supporting, rather than rejecting, extremist ideology.[22]

Of course, the most salient reason to use targeted force is that it usually reduces the risk of death to American military personnel. When the United States launches a drone strike against an Al Qaeda terrorist, an air force pilot who is safely out of harm's way operates the drone. Drones are the harbinger of a risk-free projection of power—action at a distance that allows for risk-free military engagements. It is true that the history of airpower is replete with examples of military force that allow soldiers to remain farther away from the enemy: strategic bombers, cruise missiles, and even artillery ordnance allow soldiers to kill the enemy without seeing them with the naked eye. Indeed, even the gun, which replaced the sword, created death at a distance.[23] The key difference between drones and missiles is that the risk is completely eliminated, not simply reduced, and the force is tightly targeted around specific individuals.

All of this adds up to an overlapping set of legal, ethical, policy, and strategic rationales for using targeted force. Instead of killing thousands of people with bombs and "dumb" air power, American military forces kill a small number with "smart" bombs fired from drones. Strategists refer to this type of force as smart power because it allows the United States to achieve its objectives with the smallest footprint possible. It sounds like a rosy picture. So why have drones and targeted killing gotten people so upset?

Upset they are. Although the use of drones is, in the main, popular among the majority of regular Americans, the practice has sparked intense criticism among some quarters of the population. Many of the critics are self-described leftist anti-military types who are skeptical of US military power. Some might even be pacifists. But the majority are just concerned citizens who think, in their gut, that the government is doing something wrong. Moreover, these criticisms are not limited to the Left. Those on the Far Right who describe themselves as libertarians object to the government's power to decide, from 10,000 feet, who lives and who dies. It smacks of royal authority. Rand Paul orchestrated a sustained filibuster in the US Senate, drawing attention to drone killings that he referred to as "executions"—a protest that eventually forced the Obama

[21] *See* Mara R. Revkin, *When Terrorists Govern: Protecting Civilians in Conflicts with State-Building Armed Groups*, 9 Harv. Nat'l Sec. J., 100, 135 (2018) ("The Islamic State has capitalized on the targeting of zakāt offices in densely populated areas—and accompanying civilian casualties and collateral damage—to fuel local anger toward the U.S.-led Coalition.").

[22] *Id.*

[23] For a longer discussion of this point, *see* Jens David Ohlin, *Remoteness and Reciprocal Risk*, *in* Research Handbook on Remote Warfare 15 (2016).

administration to be a bit more transparent about its legal process for selecting targets and carrying out the missions.[24]

Also, foreign allies are deeply suspicious of the American drone program. Although few European diplomats will speak openly about the issue, so as not to offend a critical strategic ally, many of them privately express doubts about the program and view it as an example of American exceptionalism. International lawyers who work for NGOs (as opposed to the government) are much more open about targeted killings, which they consider illegal.[25]

Taken together, the reactions to the drone program are deeply schizophrenic. On the one hand, targeted killings are justly heralded for their surgical precision and their reduction in the amount of killing—a requirement imposed by both international law and morality. On the other hand, targeted killings are deplored because they look too much like executions, which are barbaric. How can we square these divergent and simultaneous reactions?

This is the paradox of targeted killing. The United States is caught inside of it. The more the United States works to comply with international law and reduce the number of people killed in military strikes, the more the killings start to look like criminal law enforcement. That is because war usually involves killing a large number of people, often on the basis of their status as members of an enemy army.[26] In contrast, the criminal law involves imprisoning (or executing) a specific individual who has been prosecuted in a court of law for their conduct.[27] The problem is that as the United States tries to make the practice of war more humane, the practice of war starts to look more and more like criminal law enforcement, and not very humane at all. As American military force becomes more humane, it looks less warlike, and therefore triggers the operation of a nonwar paradigm, the framework of criminal law. And when viewed through that alternate lens, the force suddenly becomes the opposite. It becomes inhumane. There seems to be no way out of this paradox.

[24] *See* Ed O'Keefe & Aaron Blake, *Rand Paul Conducts Filibuster in Opposition to John Brennan, Obama's Drone Policy*, WASH. POST, Mar. 7, 2013 (filibuster was "aimed at drawing attention to deep concern on both sides of the aisle about the administration's use of unmanned aerial drones in its fight against terrorists and whether the government would ever use them in the United States").

[25] *See, e.g.*, Human Rights Watch, "'Between a Drone and Al-Qaeda': The Civilian Cost of US Targeted Killings in Yemen," Oct. 22, 2013 (stating that the "applicability of a war model to US operations against Al-Qaeda has increasingly been called into question"); Amnesty International, "'Will I Be Next?' US Drone Strikes in Pakistan," Oct. 2013, at 56 ("The USA's assertion that it is engaged in an ongoing, global armed conflict against al-Qa'ida and associated forces has deeply troubling implications for human rights and the rule of law. It appears to be an attempt to license the use of intentional lethal force when it is not strictly unavoidable to protect life.").

[26] Indeed, the definition of a non-international armed conflict between a state and a non-state actor requires that the level of violence reach a certain threshold.

[27] *See* Michael Scharf, *In the Cross Hairs of a Scary Idea*, WASH. POST, Apr. 25, 2004, B1.

This is the paradox of modern war. The paradigms of criminal law and war are collapsing in on each other.[28] More importantly, the impetus for this collision is entirely benign; it is born from the best of intentions. Diligent militaries will strive to reduce the amount of killing that they perform; when they do kill someone, they will strive to do so in a nonarbitrary manner. But this will involve selecting individual targets, based on the individual's level of threat to the nation. Once they do this, they will be accused of usurping the authority of the criminal justice system—acting like judge, jury, and executioner in a battlefield execution that violates every norm of civilized behavior that we hold dear.

Think again of old Abraham Thornton and his request for trial by combat in 1817. The idea of him fighting his way to an acquittal—or dying in the process—was viewed as barbaric because the contest would have replaced rule by law with rule by brute force. The idea that one man's fate should be decided by something so arbitrary as his capacity to swing a sword is utterly foreign to a civilized conception of justice. His fate should be determined by a judge and jury that listens to the facts of the case and makes a determination based on the law. Trial by combat is the opposite of a real trial; it is no trial at all.

Similarly, a terrorist who is at the wrong end of a Hellfire missile, fired from a Predator drone, should not have his or her fate decided by brute force. They should be arrested, detained, placed on trial, and punished if convicted. Or so some argue. Of course, there are crucial differences between Abraham Thornton's trial by combat and the execution of an Al Qaeda terrorist such as Anwar al-Awlaki, the US-born propagandist who was killed in Yemen in a CIA drone strike.[29] First, Thornton requested his own trial by combat, rather than having it forced upon him. (The request was not particularly sincere; he only requested it because he knew that no one would grant it, and so they would have to release him.) Second, a true trial by combat requires equality of arms. Both sides are on an equal playing field, armed with similar weapons, if not necessarily similar experience and strength. The outcome is not preordained but rather depends on how well the condemned prisoner succeeds in fighting off his attacker. Indeed, it is precisely this uncertainty—and drama—that transformed trials by combat into a ghoulish spectacle—a sport, if you will.

In contrast, the modern-day terrorist has little opportunity to outrun a Hellfire missile. And there is no equality of arms between a terrorist hiding in some remote region of Yemen or Afghanistan and a CIA-piloted drone. But the deeper point is that a drone strike looks like a trial by combat because it is so targeted. It

[28] ROSA BROOKS, HOW EVERYTHING BECAME WAR AND THE MILITARY BECAME EVERYTHING: TALES FROM THE PENTAGON (2016).

[29] Robert Chesney, *Who May Be Killed? Anwar al-Awlaki as a Case Study in the International Legal Regulation of Lethal Force*, Y.B. INT'L HUM. L. 13 (2010); Afsheen John Radsan & Richard Murphy, *The Evolution of Law and Policy for CIA Targeted Killing*, 5 J. NAT'L SEC. L. & POL'Y 439, 463 (2012).

decides someone's fate by military force, rather than adjudication by judge and jury. And most people have a gut feeling that when *one* person's life is at stake, the outcome should be determined by a judicial decision. If more people are being killed—well, that's war and we do not have the same expectation that outcomes will be determined by anything other than brute force, as long as that brute force complies with the law of war. So it is the targeted and individual nature of the killing—locating and killing a single individual for being a threat to the nation—that makes us feel that some due process is required.[30]

III. The Emergence of a Paradox

Herein lays the paradox for the United States of America. It is unclear how the nation can escape it. The more it reduces the amount of unnecessary killing in war, the more it ends up in the situation we have now: killing individual terrorists. But once it does that, the killing looks like it should be evaluated against the background requirements of criminal law enforcement. And so, the killing goes from being seen as extra humane to being extra barbaric. The killing looks more and more like a trial by combat, rather than a humane exercise of lawful military force.

I am not suggesting here that it is immoral or illegal under international law to kill a terrorist with a drone strike. Indeed, a close examination of international humanitarian law shows that, in fact, the United States was engaged in an armed conflict with Al Qaeda and other terrorist organizations at a certain point in time, and that the laws of war permit the killing of enemy combatants during an armed conflict.[31] Rather, the "paradox" here resides in our gut intuitions about these killings. The fact is a substantial percentage of the American population—embodied most eloquently in Senator Rand's complaints—consider the drone strikes problematic. If you look across the globe, drones are controversial and prompt objections that border on moral hysteria. The question is why. This chapter is a study of where these intuitions come from and what explains them. Indeed, I take these intuitions seriously as a barometer of something far deeper: a serious moral complaint about targeted killings. The more we make

[30] This issue is discussed in Jeremy Waldron & Tamar Meisels, Debating Targeted Killing: Counter-Terrorism or Extrajudicial Execution? 227 (2020) ("Targeted killing involves tight reference. One identifies an individual, usually by name, to be killed and we expect that individual to be hunted down and shot. . . . In my view this puts considerable pressure on Harold Koh's position that targeted killing is just an instance of ordinary combatant killing, where names just happen to be involved. The logic of targeting is quite different in the two cases.").

[31] Ryan J. Vogel, *Drone Warfare and the Law of Armed Conflict*, 39 Denv. J. Int'l L. & Pol'y 101, 102 (2010) (noting that "the United States has increasingly relied upon unmanned aerial vehicles (UAVs), or 'drones,' to target and kill enemies in its current armed conflicts").

warfare humane, the more we end up creating something that looks like inhumane criminal law. Unless the United States solves this paradox, it cannot win in the court of world opinion.

The paradox is not just about people's gut intuitions. The paradox is imbedded in the law as well, and recent debates about the legality of targeted killings demonstrate that the paradox is hard to resolve, even among the legal community. Here's why: there are two ways to examine the legality of a drone strike.

Under one view, the strikes are governed by international humanitarian law, or IHL, which is the body of law that governs how military operations are conducted during an armed conflict. This body of law has an ancient pedigree, embodied in professional notions of chivalry and honor, that were eventually codified in treaties such as the Hague Regulations of 1899 and 1907[32] and the four Geneva Conventions drafted immediately after World War II.[33] The basic pillars of this legal regime are relatively simple: military forces can target enemy combatants as much as they like, but they cannot target civilians. It is OK if civilians are killed as a side effect—collateral damage—but only if the anticipated collateral damage is proportionate to the value of the military target. In other words, disproportionate collateral damage to civilians is illegal. So as long as a drone strike takes place during an armed conflict, and the terrorist is considered an enemy combatant (both controversial assumptions), then the targeted killing might be lawful under IHL.[34]

However, there is another way to analyze drone strikes, using an alternative paradigm: international human rights law, or IHRL.[35] Human rights law is embodied in a serious of declarations, conventions, and treaties, most of which were signed in the aftermath of World War II. These rights are universal and protect the right to life, political and civil rights such as rights of free expression, due process, and freedom from torture and other forms of mistreatment. Summary executions violate these rights, for multiple reasons. They violate the right to

[32] Convention (II) with Respect to the Laws and Customs of War on Land and its Annex: Regulation Concerning the Laws and Customs of War on Land 1899, 32 Stat 1803; Convention (IV) Respecting the Laws and Customs of War on Land and Its Annex: Regulations Concerning the Laws and Customs of War on Land (Hague Convention IV) 1907, 36 Stat 2277.

[33] *See* Convention for the Amelioration of the Condition of the Wounded and Sick in Armed Forces in the Field, Aug. 12, 1949, art. 2, 6 U.S.T. 3114, 75 U.N.T.S. 31, 32 [Geneva I]; Convention for the Amelioration of the Condition of the Wounded, Sick, and Shipwrecked Members of Armed Forces at Sea, Aug. 12, 1949, art. 2, 6 U.S.T. 3217, 75 U.N.T.S. 85, 86 [Geneva II]; Convention Relative to the Treatment of Prisoners of War, Aug. 12, 1949, art. 2, 6 U.S.T. 3316, 75 U.N.T.S. 135, 136 [Geneva III]; Convention Relative to the Protection of Civilian Persons in Time of War, Aug. 12, 1949, art. 2, 6 U.S.T. 3516, 75 U.N.T.S. 287, 288 [Geneva IV].

[34] Michael N. Schmitt, *Drone Law: A Reply to UN Special Rapporteur Emmerson*, 55 Va. J. Int'l L. Dig., 13, 23 (2014) (stating that "[s]o long as the armed group in question is sufficiently 'organized' and the attendant hostilities cross the requisite intensity threshold, a NIAC exists, and status-based targeting is permissible").

[35] Michael Ramsden, *Assessing U.S. Targeted Killings Under an International Human Rights Law Framework*, 1 Groningen J. Int'l L. 19, 19 (2013).

have a fair trial. They violate the right to life. That is why the police are required to haul you to court and only a judge or jury can decide your punishment (if any) when the government alleges that you have committed a crime. Human rights law protects an individual's right to be subject to a civilized form of domestic criminal law. So, under the human rights paradigm, targeted killings are problematic because they are too summary and there is not enough due process.[36] Politicians, the military, or the CIA decide who lives and dies. There is no judge and no jury. No evidence and no reasons—only an execution. For many international human rights lawyers, drone strikes are an extrajudicial nightmare.[37]

For the moment, I do not want to resolve the question of which paradigm applies to drone strikes, and why. Is it IHL or human rights law? This is indeed the heart of the legal dispute over drones, but for the moment let us focus on the underlying conceptual tension: there are sound reasons for adopting each of the competing frameworks. When a drone strike is evaluated under the war paradigm, it looks humane and lawful because fewer people are killed than in most wars. But when a drone strike is evaluated under a human rights paradigm, it looks barbaric because the targets are not given a trial or a chance to exonerate themselves before they are executed. Ironically, the more that the practice of warfare becomes individualized, the less likely that we are to apply the war paradigm, and it becomes more likely that we will apply a human rights paradigm. But when we do that, the strikes look like they violate international human rights law, which enshrines a basic right to due process. So the paradox is not just a paradox about our gut intuitions, it is a paradox written into the very DNA of international law. Can war be made more humane without collapsing into criminal law enforcement? Or are we locked in a loop of perverse incentives, where we encourage the government to kill *more* people in order for them to demonstrate undeniably that they are operating under the war paradigm? That is hardly a good outcome.

This chapter will explore the paradox by considering the case of Anwar al-Awlaki. In drone strikes, the people who did the killing thought they were using discriminating force. They thought they were being humane. But paradoxically, they ended up being accused of carrying out an extrajudicial killing, an

[36] Ryan T. Williams, *The Road Most Travel: Is the Executive's Growing Preeminence Making America More Like the Authoritarian Regimes It Fights So Hard Against?*, 6 ALA. CR & CLL REV. 139, 143 (2015) (arguing that "[o]nce President Obama took office, the Executive accelerated the targeted killing of people, often destroying them remotely with predator drones" and stating that "[t]o effectuate this plan, the president formulated a 'kill list' comprising people, including Americans, targeted for death by the Executive Branch without trial or judicial due process").

[37] *See* Asma Jahangir, Special Rapporteur on Extrajudicial, Summary or Arbitrary Executions, "Civil and Political Rights, Including the Questions of Disappearances and Summary Executions, Extrajudicial, Summary or Arbitrary Executions" U.N. Doc. E/CN.4/2003/3, paras 37, 39; Saby Ghoshray, *Targeted Killing in International Law: Searching for Rights in the Shadow of 9/11*, 24 IND. INT'L & COMP. L. REV. 355, 418 (2014).

assassination—a trial by combat, as barbaric and unthinkable now as it was when Abraham Thornton demanded it in 1817.

IV. The Case of Anwar al-Awlaki

In the first months and years following 9/11, the George W. Bush administration's security apparatus was concerned about Islamic radicalization on multiple fronts. First, the administration wanted to prevent violence and discrimination against law-abiding American Muslims—to reassure them that their presence in the American body politic was secure. To do this, they had to show the country that Islam is a tolerant, peaceful religion. Second, the government needed leaders in the Muslim community to articulate that tolerant and peaceful vision—to prevent radicalization among impressionable and angry young men and to act as a counterbalance to extremist ideology flowing through the Internet from overseas. Both goals required buy-in from prominent religious leaders and required building bridges to Muslim community groups.

One of those leaders was Anwar al-Awlaki, a young preacher who grew up in New Mexico, born in 1971 to his Yemeni mother and his father who was attending graduate school at New Mexico State University.[38] When his parents returned to the home country in the late 1970s, Awlaki went with them and spent the rest of his childhood in Yemen.[39] But just as his parents had sought an American education, so too did Awlaki, who came back for college at Colorado State in 1991. Over the course of the next decade, Awlaki would hone his skills as an imam and preacher. He was charismatic and dynamic.

Then 9/11 happened. In the year following the attacks, Awlaki reportedly showed up at the Pentagon, invited to a lunch hosted by the General Counsel to the Secretary of Defense. This was a typical move for the US government. Enlisting moderate Muslim religious leaders in its effort—a counteroffensive in an ideological battle, if you will. There is no transcript of the meeting, but by all accounts, Awlaki was there to give Defense Department officials advice about understanding the Muslim community.

Roughly a decade after his lunch at the Pentagon, Awlaki and three other men were in a vehicle traveling through a remote region of Yemen.[40] They stopped for a meal—breakfast—but this time there would be no breaking bread with the Pentagon.[41] A US-piloted drone, probably launched from Saudi Arabia, fired a

[38] Scott Shane, Objective Troy: A Terrorist, a President, and the Rise of the Drone 51 (2016). The family moved to Nebraska shortly after Anwar was born.

[39] *Id.* at 52.

[40] Sudarsan Raghavan, *Anwar al-Aulaqi, U.S.-born Cleric Linked to al-Qaeda, Killed in Yemen*, Wash. Post, Oct. 1, 2011.

[41] *Id.*

Hellfire missile at the car.[42] Awlaki was killed instantly. The military he once advised had now killed him. What had Awlaki done to be marked for death by the US government?

Awlaki's journey from American kid to global terrorist was several decades in the making. But the key years in this transformation occurred in the early years after 9/11. Awlaki left the United States and moved to Britain, where he preached at several prominent British mosques.[43] In 2004, he returned to Yemen, where he would live for the rest of his brief life. Over time, his activities gained the attention of both the Yemeni and American authorities. His sermons became increasingly radical, exhorting young Muslims to wage jihad against the United States and the West. His sermons were distributed via the internet to a global audience of would-be jihadists. Government officials in both the United States and Yemen considered him a chief promoter, recruiter, ideologue, and propagandist for Al Qaeda.[44] In 2010, the Yemeni government prosecuted him in absentia because he was outside the reach of government forces.[45] At the time, Yemen was locked in an increasingly dire civil war against Islamic extremists who controlled broad swaths of Yemeni territory. The central government could charge Awlaki but could do little to arrest or imprison him.[46]

Meanwhile, there were extensive discussions among US security personnel over how to handle Awlaki.[47] He was an American, which made his betrayal particularly glaring. But his citizenship suggested—at least intuitively—that he was owed special procedural protections.[48] In any event, his "crimes" flowed from his advocacy—preaching—an activity that is usually protected by the Free Speech Clause of the US Constitution.[49] For most Americans, the First Amendment represents a bedrock principle that defines, in some sense, what it means to live under the rule of law. But, of course, the First Amendment does not protect all speech—verbal acts that constitute criminal offenses can be prosecuted. In this case, federal charges against Awlaki might have included incitement, conspiracy,

[42] Mark Mazzetti, Charlie Savage, & Scott Shane, *How a U.S. Citizen Came to Be in America's Cross Hairs*, N.Y. Times, Mar. 9, 2013.

[43] "Obituary: Anwar al-Awlaki," BBC News, Sept. 30, 2011.

[44] Mazzetti, Savage, & Shane, *supra* note 42 (quoting FBI official Philip Mudd as saying that Awlaki "was cropping up as a radicalizer—not in just a few investigations, but in what seemed to be every investigation").

[45] Chesney, *supra* note 29.

[46] *Id.* 27–28.

[47] Mark Mazzetti, *Killing of Americans Deepens Debate Over Use of Drone Strikes*, N.Y. Times, Apr. 23, 2015.

[48] Alessandra Grace, *Targeting U.S. Citizens in the Fight Against the Islamic State*, 53 Hous. L. Rev. 1435, 1461 (2016) (noting that "[b]ecause al-Awlaki was a U.S. citizen, the operation against him also had to be evaluated under the U.S. Constitution").

[49] Mohamed H. Aziz, *Counter Terrorism Measures Via Internet Intermediaries: A First Amendment & National Security Dilemma*, 4 J.L. & Cyber Warfare 1, 19 (2015) (remarking that "Al-Awlaki's case raises obvious Fifth Amendment due process questions, as well as First Amendment free speech questions").

or providing material support to terrorism.[50] He could have protested that his speech was constitutionally protected, but he would have lost that argument because he was engaged in more than mere advocacy.[51]

Awlaki was never charged by the federal government, and he was never arrested.[52] If a federal grand jury had indicted him, the FBI would have had great difficulty locating and arresting him, given the lack of control that the Yemeni government had in the areas where Awlaki was hiding. Capture was not feasible, according to US officials.[53] The only option to silence him, according to the federal government, was military engagement.[54] He would have to be killed.

At that point, US military and security officials made a factual and legal determination about Awlaki that was a game changer. They concluded that he had crossed the line from mere propagandist to operational leader in the hierarchy of Al Qaeda's regional affiliate, Al Qaeda in the Arabian Peninsula (AQAP).[55] He was not just inspiring terrorists, he was leading them.[56] Specifically, intelligence analysts tied him to a series of foiled terrorist plots, including the Christmas Day "underwear-bomber" who tried to detonate an explosive device, sewn into his underwear, while he was onboard a Detroit-bound airliner that had departed from Amsterdam's Schiphol Airport.[57] In 2010, a cargo plane departed from Yemen to Chicago with explosives hidden in toner cartridges.[58] Both plots were unsuccessful. It was later revealed that Awlaki corresponded over the internet with Major Nidal Hasan, the army psychologist who went on a shooting rampage

[50] 18 U.S.C., para. 2339A (West).

[51] Alexander Tsesis, *Foreword*, 86 FORDHAM L. REV. 367, 369 (2017) (noting that "[o]ne of the most respected principles of U.S. constitutional law is that the First Amendment does not prevent the government from enforcing criminal laws against speech aimed at inciting or likely to lead to an imminent harm"); United States v. Al Bahlul, 820 F. Supp. 2d 1141, 1249 (USCMCR 2011) (discussing the role of First Amendment in terrorism prosecutions).

[52] Jeffrey F. Addicott, *Rightly Dividing the Domestic Jihadist from the Enemy Combatant in the "War Against al-Qaeda"—Why It Matters in Rendition and Targeted Killing*, 45 CASE W. RES. J. INT'L L. 259, 296 (2012) (discussing the view that the targeted killing was "wrong for not operating under domestic criminal law to arrest al-Awlaki").

[53] K. Benson, *The Chaplaincy Exception in International Humanitarian Law: "American-Born Cleric" Anwar al-Awlaki and the Global War on Terror*, 20 BUFF. HUM. RTS. L. REV. 1, 8 (2014) (discussing the Obama Administration's view that "al-Awlaki could be legally killed if it was not feasible to capture him").

[54] Charlie Savage, *Secret U.S. Memo Made Legal Case to Kill a Citizen*, N.Y. TIMES, Oct. 8, 2011.

[55] Chesney, *supra* note 29 (noting US government view that Awlaki took an "operational leadership role in connection with specific attacks").

[56] *Id.*

[57] United States v. Abdulmutallab, 739 F.3d 891, 895 (6th Cir. 2014) ("During his time in Yemen, Abdulmutallab received training at an Al Qaeda camp under the direction of the radical Imam Anwar Awlaki and agreed to carry out a suicide attack by bombing a United States air carrier over the United States. The bomb given to Abdulmutallab was built into a pair of underwear and Abdulmutallab was assured that the bomb would defy airport security because it contained no metal parts.").

[58] DANIEL KLAIDMAN, KILL OR CAPTURE: THE WAR ON TERROR AND THE SOUL OF THE OBAMA PRESIDENCY 262 (2012).

at Fort Hood, murdering thirteen people in 2009.[59] Awlaki had officiated the funeral of Hasan's mother and provided religious advice in the ensuing years.[60]

Much of Awlaki's specific role in these plots is unknown to the general public and remains classified. What is publicly known is that Awlaki corresponded with individuals involved in these plots—something that Awlaki conceded during interviews—and that intelligence analysts viewed some of these interactions as "operational" in nature.[61] In other words, officials concluded that Awlaki had crossed a line from advocacy to implementation. That change was legally significant and ultimately paved the way for Awlaki's killing.[62]

In international law, the conduct of war is governed by the law of armed conflict (LOAC) as expressed in treaties and customary international law. Absent a specific rule to the contrary, enemy combatants—soldiers—can be targeted during war as long as they are not hors de combat.[63] However, civilians are immune from direct targeting under the LOAC.[64] Although civilians might die accidentally as collateral damage—which is lawful as long as there is not too much collateral damage—there is an absolute prohibition on intentionally targeting civilians.[65] It is a war crime.[66]

So, the cardinal separation in the LOAC is between combatants and civilians. Combatants can be intentionally targeted, but civilians cannot. The question is how Awlaki should be classified. Was he a combatant or a civilian? In common-sense terms, he seemed to fall in the middle. He certainly was not a professional soldier in the sense of wearing a uniform in a "conventional" army like the US Marines or the Russian Army. On the other hand, calling him a mere "civilian" would seem to understate his role in military affairs, if indeed US officials were correct that he had graduated to an operational role in attacks carried out by AQAP.

International law has long recognized that civilians should lose their immunity from attack when they start acting like a soldier. If a civilian were to pick up a

[59] David Johnston & Scott Shane, *U.S. Knew of Suspect's Tie to Radical Cleric*, N.Y. Times, Nov. 9, 2009.

[60] Evan Perez & Keith Johnson, *Hasan, Radical Cleric Had Contact*, Wall St. J., Nov. 10, 2009.

[61] Chesney, *supra* note 29.

[62] Nasser Al-Aulaqi v. Barack H Obama, Opposition to Plaintiff's Motion, 2010 WL 3863135 (D. D.C.) ("In addition, since late 2009, Anwar al-Aulaqi has taken on an increasingly operational role in AQAP, including preparing Umar Farouk Abdulmutallab in his attempt to detonate an explosive device aboard a Northwest Airlines flight from Amsterdam to Detroit on Christmas Day 2009.").

[63] Robert M. Chesney, *Who May Be Held? Military Detention Through the Habeas Lens*, 52 B.C. L. Rev. 769, 824 (2011).

[64] Nils Melzer, Int'l Comm. of the Red Cross, Interpretive Guidance on the Notion of Direct Participation in Hostilities Under International Humanitarian Law 61–62 (2009).

[65] Protocol Additional to the Geneva Conventions of 12 August 1949, and Relating to the Protection of Victims of Non-International Armed Conflicts, June 8, 1977, 1125 U.N.T.S. 609, art. 13.

[66] Rome Statute of the International Criminal Court, July 17, 1998, U.N. Doc. A/CONF.183/9, art. 8(2)(b)(i).

gun, fire it, and engage in combat, then the civilian is acting like—and should be treated like—a combatant.[67] If he walks, talks, and acts like a duck, he *is* a duck. This insight was translated into a legal rule that allows civilians to be attacked during an armed conflict for such time as they "directly participate in hostilities," in the words of Additional Protocol I to the Geneva Conventions.[68] If this rule didn't exist, civilians could participate in hostilities and get a free pass—they would fight in war and not themselves be subject to attack. If this were allowed, armies would have no incentive to configure themselves as armies; instead, they would fight as civilians. To close this loophole, the "directly participating in hostilities" rule was born.[69]

The question for US government lawyers was whether Awlaki was directly participating in hostilities or not. Several government lawyers weighed in on this question, including lawyers from the Justice Department's Office of Legal Counsel (OLC). Lawyers for OLC drafted a thirty-one-page legal memorandum studying whether Awlaki could be targeted and killed, eventually concluding that it was lawful to do so.[70] The memorandum was withheld from the public and remained classified until a redacted version was released in 2014.[71] The released version contains the legal analysis but blacks out part of the application of that analysis to Awlaki, presumably because this evidence remained classified. The memo concluded that "the facts represented to us indicate that al-Aulaqi has been involved, through his operational and leadership roles within AQAP, in an abortive attack within the United States and continues to plot attacks intended to kill Americans from his base of operations in Yemen."[72]

On the basis of this legal analysis, President Obama made the decision to place Awlaki on a list of terrorists subject to lethal targeting by US military forces. At the time, US military operations in Yemen were officially unacknowledged by the US government, presumably because American forces were operating in Yemen with the consent of the Yemeni government, but that consent came with strings attached—the United States would need to operate

[67] *See* Melzer, *supra* note 64.

[68] *Id.*

[69] W. Hays Parks, *Part IX of the ICRC "Direct Participation in Hostilities" Study: No Mandate, No Expertise, and Legally Incorrect*, 42 N.Y.U. J. Int'l L. & Pol. 769, 779 (2010) ("If the civilian's activities are determined by the enemy to constitute taking a 'direct part in hostilities,' the civilian relinquishes his or her immunity from direct attack.").

[70] US Department of Justice, Office of Legal Counsel, "Memorandum for the Attorney General, Re: Applicability of Federal Criminal Laws and the Constitution to Contemplated Lethal Operations Against Shaykh Anwar al-Aulaqi" (July 16, 2010).

[71] *Id.*

[72] *Id.* 21.

covertly.[73] The CIA was involved in these operations, not just the Department of Defense.[74]

Around this time, Awlaki's father, Nasser, learned of his son's placement on the targeting list, and filed suit against the US government in a federal district court.[75] His lawsuit named as defendants President Obama, Defense Secretary Robert Gates, and CIA Director Leon Panetta.[76] Drone opponents had high hopes for the lawsuit and predicted that a federal judge could be convinced to intervene against the executive branch. Nasser's lawsuit asserted several intuitive claims that corresponded with objections that were voiced by many regular citizens. First, Nasser's lawsuit asserted that his son's killing would violate the Fifth Amendment because the killing would take place without due process of law and would also constitute an unreasonable seizure under the Fourth Amendment.[77] He also asserted a separate due process claim on the basis that the *criteria* for inclusion on the targeting list was secret, which violated the concept of fair notice.[78] Underlying all of these claims was an implicit presumption: that the killing of Awlaki, when it occurred, should be evaluated under a domestic law enforcement paradigm. And the argument for this claim was relatively straightforward. Nasser claimed that the United States was not at war in Yemen. And how could it be? The United States was not killing thousands of people in Yemen. It was killing a few people here and there—one or two or three at a time—with drone strikes. That does not look like war. It looks like law enforcement. It looks like extraterritorial policing.

There was something deeply compelling and heartfelt about Nasser's plea for his son's life. Here was a father desperately trying to protect his son from the most awesome state power: the power to decide who lives and who dies. Nasser had made the United States his adoptive home and had brought his son into the world on American soil. And now he sought from the court that most American of promises—protection from arbitrary abuse of power. But the court declined to extend it. Why?

In a lengthy opinion, Judge Bates punted on the most pressing questions, calling them political questions that ought to be resolved by and through the political branches.[79] Judge Bates' hostility to Nasser's claim ran deep. He was not just saying that matters of national security, and the president's power therein, must be decided by the political branches. Indeed, if that were *always* the case, then the US Supreme Court would have no reason to intervene in these disputes.

[73] Corri Zoli, *The Changing Role of Law in Security Governance: Post-9/11 'Gray Zones' and Strategic Impacts*, 67 Syracuse L. Rev. 613, 641(2017).

[74] Robert Chesney, *Military-Intelligence Convergence and the Law of the Title 10/title 50 Debate*, 5 J. Nat'l Sec. L. & Pol'y 539, 617 (2012) (referring to "a combination of CIA and military drones operating under the CIA's Title 50 authority").

[75] Al-Aulaqi v. Obama, 727 F. Supp. 2d 1, 18 (D. D.C. 2010).

[76] *Id.*

[77] *Id.*

[78] *Id.*

[79] *Id.* 46–53.

In point of fact, though, the Supreme Court has intervened several times in national security policy in the crucial years since 9/11, ruling, among other things, that Guantánamo Bay detainees have the right to contest their detention before a neutral decision maker, and also ruling that the president must consult congress before creating a system of military commissions.[80]

In contrast, Judge Bates' determination that Nasser's case was beyond judicial review spoke more specifically to the type of judicial review that he was seeking:

> The type of relief that plaintiff seeks only underscores the impropriety of judicial review here. Plaintiff requests both a declaration setting forth the standard under which the United States can select individuals for targeted killing as well as an injunction prohibiting defendants from intentionally killing Anwar Al–Aulaqi unless he meets that standard—i.e., unless he "presents a concrete, specific, and imminent threat to life or physical safety, and there are no means other than lethal force that could reasonably be employed to neutralize the threat." Yet plaintiff concedes that the "imminence' requirement" of his proffered legal standard would render any "real-time judicial review" of targeting decisions "infeasible," and he therefore urges this Court to issue his requested preliminary injunction and then enforce the injunction "through an after-the-fact contempt motion or an after-the-fact damages action." But as the D.C. Circuit has explained, "[i]t is not the role of judges to second-guess, with the benefit of hindsight, another branch's determination that the interests of the United States call for military action." Such military determinations are textually committed to the political branches.[81]

Essentially, Nasser requested a level of judicial review that is fundamentally inconsistent with the conduct of military hostilities during an armed conflict. The fact of the matter is that *no one* has the right to judicial review of targeting during a war. So why would Nasser think that his son was entitled to such a thing? And why did so many people agree with Nasser? And why did the court disagree?

The answer lies in the fact that the government was engaged not in a wholesale military campaign, but rather an isolated killing—a *targeted* killing.[82] Since the government only killed Awlaki and his fellow passengers, the attack did not look warlike at all.[83] It looked more like an extrajudicial assassination authorized by the president and carried out by the CIA. That is why Nasser was pleading

[80] Hamdan v. Rumsfeld, 548 US 557, 594 (2006).

[81] Al-Aulaqi v. Obama, 727 F. Supp. 2d 1, 47–48 (D. D.C. 2010).

[82] Waldron & Meisels, *supra* note 30.

[83] *Id.* (noting that "I am told by defenders of targeted killing that tracking down and killing combatants in this way is a perfectly familiar aspect of modern warfare" and concluding flatly that "[i]t is not").

for some judicial involvement in the decision. Because when you decide the fate of a single individual, then a court should be involved in making a decision. Anything less is trial by combat.

The United States was trying to reduce its military footprint in Yemen by picking out specific targets—such as Awlaki—who are most responsible for planning and perpetrating attacks by AQAP against the United States. In an older era, such attacks would have been carried out against a wider set of targets—perhaps decimating an entire village or geographical area where the group is located. But such widespread destruction involves a large number of collateral damage, and it is also involves killing a large number of essentially fungible combatants—foot soldiers who are legally targetable during war but whose deaths do not necessarily increase the likelihood of victory. They are just more bodies. So the United States wanted to take a more targeted and surgical approach. It crafted a list.

V. Paradoxically, Discriminating Force Triggers Greater Legal Scrutiny

The existence of a list makes us uneasy, as it should. Something about the list *looks* like it should require more due process. After all, the intelligence community constructed the list without any meaningful opportunity for Awlaki—or his father—to contest his inclusion on the list. Moreover, the list was constructed in secret.[84] No one outside of the government knew the full scope of evidence that led the government to place him on the list. Sure, the conclusion of that process was identified—he crossed the line from propagandist to operational planner—but the underlying information was not publicly disclosed at the time of his targeting.[85] Now, years later, some of that information has been released in dribs and drabs. Some of it came from documents seized during the Navy Seals raid against Osama bin Laden's compound in Pakistan. After Awlaki was killed, Obama declared at the White House that Awlaki "took the lead in planning and directing efforts to murder innocent Americans . . . and he repeatedly called on individuals in the United States and around the globe to kill innocent men, women and children to advance a murderous agenda . . . And going forward, we will remain vigilant against any threats to the United States, or our allies and partners. But make no mistake: This is further

[84] Jameel Jaffer, *Known Unknowns*, 48 Harv. CR-CL L. Rev. 457, 464 (2013) (stating that "the government's official position is that the CIA's role in carrying out targeted killings cannot be confirmed or denied").

[85] *See* Jane Y. Chong, *Targeting the Twenty-First-Century Outlaw*, 122 Yale L.J. 724, 740 (2012).

proof that Al-Qaeda and its affiliates will find no safe haven anywhere in the world."[86]

The irony, of course, is that we only expect more due process because the CIA killed a small number of people. If the government had deployed a greater number of Defense Department forces—resulting in far more casualties—then the engagement would have been evaluated under the rules of warfare, which permit widespread destruction against legitimate military targets in pursuit of victory. Awlaki's complaint would not have gained the same level of traction if it were made during the course of a massive military engagement. In that situation, it would be impracticable to offer every member of the enemy group the right to contest their targeting in a judicial forum before a neutral decision maker, such as a judge or jury. But strangely enough, because the United States declined to kill every member of Al Qaeda in sight—and instead focused on Awlaki as an individual—the targeting is supposedly evaluated under criminal law enforcement principles.

There is one additional angle to consider. Nasser argued that Obama's targeting of Awlaki violated his right to due process because Awlaki was an American citizen. He was born in the United States. And so, recognizing Awlaki's asserted right to due process does not necessarily entail recognizing a right of due process for every enemy killed during an armed conflict. It only requires the recognition of some additional due process constraints on the targeting of *Americans* during armed conflict.[87]

The law on this question is sparse, in part because the issue rarely arises. The Supreme Court considered the relevance of citizenship for detention and ruled in 2004 that Yaser Hamdi, an American citizen captured on the battlefields of Afghanistan, was entitled under the US Constitution to contest his detention before a neutral decision maker.[88] But the question of targeting Americans does not occur often. To be sure, there were dual citizens who fought for the Axis powers in battle during World War II.[89] They were killed or captured just like any other enemy soldier. American GIs were not required to convene a trial in the midst of the Normandy Invasion before shooting a Nazi soldier who just happened to carry an American passport.

[86] The White House Office of the Press Secretary, "Remarks by the President at the Change of Office' Chairman of the Joint Chiefs of Staff Ceremony" (Sept. 30, 2011).

[87] For an argument that these targeted killings violate the US Constitution, *see* Benjamin McKelvey, *Due Process Rights and the Targeted Killing of Suspected Terrorists: The Unconstitutional Scope of Executive Killing Power*, 44 Vand. J. Transnat'l L. 1353, 1369 (2011) (suggesting that "[d]espite the fact that Aulaqi was hiding in Yemen, the Fifth Amendment still protected him").

[88] Hamdi v. Rumsfeld, 542 US 507, 533 (2004) ("We therefore hold that a citizen-detainee seeking to challenge his classification as an enemy combatant must receive notice of the factual basis for his classification, and a fair opportunity to rebut the Government's factual assertions before a neutral decisionmaker.").

[89] *Id.* 524 (discussing member of the Italian Army).

But that does not end the inquiry. A targeted killing is not Normandy, and some due process protections are feasible in this context even though they were not feasible during World War II. In theory, it would be possible to require more process for an American like Awlaki before he is placed on the administration's targeting list. For example, it is not absurd to require judicial preapproval before the executive branch places an American on this list.

There are two possibilities for how judicial preapproval might work.[90] One could require the government to petition to the court before adding a name to the list. Or, in the alternative, one could allow the government to unilaterally allow the government to construct the list but allow courts to entertain objections from targeted individuals who wish to be removed from the list.[91] The question is who would ever file such a petition? It is unlikely that an enemy combatant would have access to—or the incentive to access—a federal court to contest their inclusion on a list. Someone else could raise the due process claim on his or her behalf, which is exactly what Nasser did for his son. However, Judge Bates rejected the lawsuit on standing grounds—concluding that Nasser was not permitted to assert a claim on his son's behalf. Indeed, if Awlaki wanted to contest his inclusion on the targeted list, he should do so personally, Judge Bates ruled, because "there is nothing preventing him from peacefully presenting himself at the US Embassy in Yemen and expressing a desire to vindicate his constitutional rights in US courts."[92] This statement was greeted with raised eyebrows all around, because while literally true, everyone knows that neither Awlaki nor any other suspected terrorist is likely to vindicate their constitutional rights in this manner.

Let us assume for the moment that Awlaki had personally contested his inclusion on the targeted list. Call it a thought experiment. Then what? Would the Constitution's Due Process Clause allow or perhaps even require a court to make a judicial determination before allowing the targeting to proceed?[93] The Obama administration said little about this issue, though in a few speeches, administration officials insisted that they protected the due process rights of Americans targeted during armed conflict.[94]

[90] David W. Opderbeck, *Drone Courts*, 44 RUTGERS L.J. 413, 469 (2014) (concluding that "[c]urrent proposals for a drone court that would utilize a warrant process similar to that employed under the Foreign Intelligence Surveillance Act are a good start").

[91] For a critique of the idea of a "drone court," *see* Joshua Andresen, *Due Process of War in the Age of Drones*, 41 YALE J. INT'L L. 155, 158 (2016).

[92] Al-Aulaqi v. Obama, 727 F. Supp. 2d 1, 17 (D. D.C. 2010).

[93] Matthew Craig, *Targeted Killing, Procedure, and False Legitimation*, 35 CARDOZO L. REV. 2349, 2379 (2014).

[94] Attorney General Eric Holder, "Speech at Northwestern University School of Law," Chicago, Ill. (Mar. 5, 2012).

In a speech before students and faculty at Northwestern Law School, Attorney General Eric Holder argued that the administration fully respects the due process rights of Americans killed in drone strikes.[95] He concluded:

> Let me be clear: an operation using lethal force in a foreign country, targeted against a U.S. citizen who is a senior operational leader of al Qaeda or associated forces, and who is actively engaged in planning to kill Americans, would be lawful at least in the following circumstances: First, the U.S. government has determined, after a thorough and careful review, that the individual poses an imminent threat of violent attack against the United States; second, capture is not feasible; and third, the operation would be conducted in a manner consistent with applicable law of war principles.[96]

The problem here is that the process of making these determinations takes place entirely within the executive branch of the government: the CIA, the Department of Defense, the Justice Department, and ultimately, the White House. But there is no judicial review of the decision. And usually we think of "due process" as inherently involving some form of judicial review.[97] The whole point of due process is that some neutral arbiter looks at the evidence and makes a determination. That is what makes due process such an important element of the rule of law.

But not so, according to Holder. In his speech, Holder distinguished between due process and judicial process, arguing that the two concepts are not one and the same, "particularly when it comes to national security," and concluding that the Constitution guarantees the former but not the latter.[98] In other words, the US government's rigorous process for determining the targetability of every American on the administration's secret kill list ensures that these due process rights are protected. To critics of the US drone policy, this statement was laughable.[99] It cannot be the case that an internal decision-making process can satisfy the demands of due process. But then again, the demand for a judicial process is only made because the government insisted on targeting a single American individual in the first. And this triggers a system of perverse incentives. The government could have mollified the critics by simply targeting *more* individuals, and then the killing would no longer have seemed extrajudicial. It would have seemed

[95] *Id.*
[96] *Id.*
[97] *Id.*
[98] *Id.*
[99] Shirin Sinnar, *Rule of Law Tropes in National Security*, 129 Harv. L. Rev. 1566, 1573 (2016) (noting that "[t]he due process Holder cited, of course, consisted of a purely executive deliberative process based on executive-made rules" and concluding that "[w]ith courts and Congress unwilling to decide the permissibility of targeted killings, the only rules are those the Executive has chosen for itself").

like war. But that surely would have been morally worse, not better. Perhaps for these reasons, the OLC substantially de-emphasized Awlaki's citizenship, concluding that it did not provide "a basis for concluding that he is immune from a use of force abroad that the AUMF otherwise authorizes."[100]

Was Awlaki's killing truly necessary at the moment in time when the Hellfire missile was fired from the Predator drone, shortly after Awlaki and his fellow travelers stopped for breakfast? Under the constitutional rules that apply to police officers, deadly force is only legitimate if the police officer reasonably believes that either the officer or the public faces an imminent threat from a fleeing suspect.[101] In other words, the police are only supposed to kill a suspect if they identify an imminent or immediate danger.[102] If they can wait, they have to wait. Otherwise, the deadly force is not truly necessary.

A similar rule applies in the law of war, but only in a special sense. At the collective level, when one country goes to war against another country, the decision to resort to military force in self-defense is only appropriate if the country faces an imminent threat. It is not enough to perceive a hypothetical threat far in the future. The threat has to be on the horizon. One can debate about what it means for an attack to be imminent—the term is a bit vague—but the undeniable conclusion is that national self-defense is only appropriate in the face of an imminent and unjustified attack.[103]

Once an armed conflict is triggered, though, the rules are quite different for soldiers exercising individual force. Generally speaking, soldiers are entitled to kill enemy soldiers and do not have to wait to be attacked first.[104] If American soldiers came across a group of Nazi soldiers having lunch in a field, they were entitled to kill them even if the Nazis were not preparing an imminent attack. The rule exists because even if the Nazis are not particularly dangerous at that moment in time, their very existence contributes to the overall capacity of the Germans to fight and win the war.[105] So the rule in warfare is that soldiers are targetable as long as they are not outside the "zone

[100] Office of Legal Counsel, Memorandum, *supra* note 70.

[101] Tennessee v. Garner, 471 US 1, 11 (1985) ("Where the suspect poses no immediate threat to the officer and no threat to others, the harm resulting from failing to apprehend him does not justify the use of deadly force to do so.").

[102] *Id.*

[103] These requirements are arguably implicit in Article 51 of the UN Charter, which governs the resort to force in national self-defense.

[104] Thomas Michael McDonnell, *Rule of Law in the Age of the Drone: Requiring Transparency and Disqualifying Clandestine Actors—The CIA and the Joint Special Operations Command*, 72 U. Miami L. Rev. 34, 74 (2017) (noting that "[i]n an armed conflict, international humanitarian law generally permits the combatants on one side to attack the opposite side's combatants and other military targets without warning").

[105] This conceptual justification is discussed in May & Ohlin, *supra* note 19.

of combat"—the technical phrase is hors de combat—such as captured or injured or in a hospital.[106]

Was Awlaki participating in an imminent terrorist attack when the Hellfire missile obliterated his vehicle? Again, it depends on what you mean by imminent. He certainly was not holding a bomb with his hand on the trigger. He was not even on his way to detonate a bomb—or at the very least there is no publicly available, nonclassified evidence that he was in the process of launching an attack in a matter of minutes. But the administration argued that this did not matter. According to Holder, imminence does not necessarily mean that the terrorist attack is about to happen, despite the common sense, dictionary definition of the term. Holder said that the "evaluation of whether an individual presents an 'imminent threat' incorporates considerations of the relevant window of opportunity to act, the possible harm that missing the window would cause to civilians, and the likelihood of heading off future disastrous attacks against the United States."[107] Some critics have called the Obama administration's approach an example of "elongated imminence" because it strays from more traditional understandings of imminence.[108] Regardless of what term you use, the US government believes that it has the power to kill an American terrorist during that last opportunity to act, even if the coming terrorist attack is some distance in the future. The CIA believed that Awlaki might recede into the shadows again, hiding in safe houses and behind the anonymity of the internet. There might not be another opportunity to kill him, so US forces took the shot.

After the missile hit, the vehicle was decimated and what remained was a mass of smoldering metal. Awlaki's father traveled from his home and identified his son. His son's body was badly damaged, but apparently Nasser recognized his son's dagger lying nearby.[109] There was no doubt. Awlaki was dead.

While his body was buried, and his family in Yemen mourned his death, the reaction in the United States was divided. Many cheered the demise of Al Qaeda's most forceful and charismatic cleric. But others were far more critical. Senator Rand Paul sharply criticized the attacks and found a golden opportunity to make his message heard loud and clear. President Obama had recently nominated Harvard Law School Professor David Barron to the First Circuit US Court of Appeals. Before rejoining Harvard's faculty, Barron was in charge of the Justice Department's Office of Legal Counsel—the office that had produced the controversial memorandum concluding that the president had the constitutional

[106] Geneva Convention Relative to the Treatment of Prisoners of War, Aug. 12, 1949, [1955], art. 3(1), 6 U.S.T. 3316, 3318–20.

[107] Holder, *supra* note 94.

[108] This issue is discussed in Samuel Issacharoff & Richard H. Pildes, *Targeted Warfare: Individuating Enemy Responsibility*, 88 N.Y.U. L. Rev. 1521, 1599 (2013).

[109] *Yemen al Qaeda Wing Confirms Death of U.S.-born Cleric*, Reuters, Oct. 10, 2011.

authority to kill Awlaki in Yemen. Barron required Senate Confirmation before he could be seated on the First Circuit. Rand Paul responded with a filibuster, which included a direct attack on Obama's authority to kill Awlaki.[110] Barron was caught in the middle because he had authored the memo that made it all possible. Paul's filibuster of Barron echoed many of the themes he had explored during his previous marathon filibuster protesting the nomination of John Brennan, in which Paul had said: "The Fifth Amendment protects you, it protects you from a king placing you in the tower . . . but it also should protect you from a President that might kill you with a drone. We were granted due process."[111]

A few months after Awlaki was killed, his son Abdulrahman met a similar fate.[112] Abdulrahman was only a teenager, not even old enough to vote in the United States. He was allegedly seventeen years old. He was also an American.

At first, the White House refused to confirm that Awlaki's son had been killed in a drone strike. The entire Yemen campaign was conducted under a cloak of covert action, and the government was not in the habit of acknowledging its use of force there. The lack of transparency was especially problematic because the administration refused to clarify whether they had targeted Abdulrahman on purpose, like his father, or whether he was collateral damage in an attack against another target. Or perhaps it was neither and he was targeted in a so-called "signature strike"—an attack against a camp or other location that bears the signature of a terrorist encampment based on the behavior of its occupants. Either way, the administration said nothing.

The fact that Obama's drones killed two generations of the Awlaki family only added fuel to the criticism. Senator Paul refused to let through the Barron nomination. He was particularly incensed that an Obama advisor—under intense questioning from an anti-drone activist—made a clunky and ill-advised argument suggesting that Anwar Awlaki was responsible for his son's death because he became a terrorist instead of being a good father.[113] Paul stated that he was not going to let David Barron get onto the Court of Appeals without first drawing attention to Obama's extrajudicial killings.

In the end, a compromise was reached. Paul ended his filibuster; Barron got his vote and was eventually confirmed to the First Circuit. For its part, the administration agreed to release the Barron memorandum that provided the legal foundation for Awlaki's killing.[114] Although that ended the immediate dispute—the filibuster over the nomination—it hardly ended the underlying controversy

[110] Benjamin Wittes, *Rand Paul Announces Filibuster of David Barron*, LAWFARE, May 15, 2014.

[111] Rand Paul, Transcript of Remarks in US Senate, Mar. 7, 2013.

[112] Nasser al-Awlaki, *The Drone That Killed My Grandson*, N.Y. TIMES, July 17, 2013.

[113] Conor Friedersdorf, *How Team Obama Justifies the Killing of a 16-Year-Old American*, THE ATLANTIC, Oct. 24, 2012.

[114] Burgess Everett, *Barron Leads to Shorter Rand Stand*" POLITICO, May 21, 2014.

over the killing of an American citizen. Once the OLC memo was made public, criticisms of the administration's policy of targeted killings only intensified.

VI. Conclusion

One of the frequent claims made after the Awlaki strike is that a drone attack is ineffective at best, counterproductive at worst. This intuition stems from the fact that even if Awlaki did have some operational role in AQAP, approving or endorsing specific targets, his ideological support for a particular vision of jihad was far more consequential. And the Hellfire missile could not so easily silence that contribution. Indeed, Awlaki's sermons live on through the internet and through the Al Qaeda magazine *Inspire*, which continues to be true to its name—inspiring generations of "students" to follow a similar extremist path. Some go further and suggest that the strike was operationally counterproductive.[115] Each time the United States kills a member of Al Qaeda, it inspires a dozen more radical followers to take up the cause, ultimately amplifying rather than dampening Awlaki's extremist message. This is especially true when a minor like Abdulrahman is killed. It allegedly ends up producing more anger and makes America less—not more—safe. Whether this claim is true or not is difficult to assess, in part because it requires a counterfactual determination of whether the new recruits would have joined the cause in the absence of American military involvement and drone strikes. There are reasons to be skeptical. Some jihadist organizations target America not because of its involvement in the region but because at least some jihadists embrace a theistic worldview and reject the religious and cultural pluralism at the heart of American democracy.[116]

Setting the legalities aside for the moment, what is most striking about the negative reaction to the Awlaki strike is the intractable nature of the dispute. Some protested it, while others celebrated it. Even after debate, people rarely change their minds. Why? Because the background framework determines the reaction against which the strike is evaluated. Viewed through the lens of armed conflict, Awlaki's killing was far more humane than any military engagement that would have occurred during World War II or Vietnam. But when viewed through the lens of criminal law enforcement, the killing was brutal—a monarchical fiat fit for a tyrant. It is a Rorschach test. As the US government seeks to make law more and more humane, as force becomes more discriminating and based on individual determinations of threat and culpability,[117] the military force impinges

[115] Yasir Qadhi, *An Illegal and Counterproductive Assassination*, N.Y. Times, Oct. 1, 2011.

[116] *See* Haider Ala Hamoudi, *"Lone Wolf" Terrorism and the Classical Jihad: On the Contingencies of Violent Islamic Extremism*, 11 F.I.U. L. Rev. 19, 23 (2015) (explaining the difference between classical understandings of jihad and modern extremist interpretations of the concept).

[117] Issacharoff & Pildes, *supra* note 108, at 1578 (describing the "novel role of individuation").

on the conceptual ground once exclusively occupied by the criminal law. When this happens, the rules regarding the use of force become more rather than less restrictive. Unfortunately, this state of affairs gives states a legal incentive to use more force in order to bootstrap their way into the permissive legal regime of the law of war.

4

Fighting Terrorism under All Applicable Law

Joshua Andresen

I. Introduction

Four successive US administrations have waged counterterrorism operations under the aegis of the law of war. However, the question of which body of law properly governs the full range of operations has yet to be resolved. Although major counterterrorism operations after September 11, 2001 began as military operations and in some cases continue as pitched battles against groups like ISIS, the diffuse nature of most terrorist organizations has brought military force[1] far beyond active battlefields. While the war against terrorism has advanced the law on the question of whom may be targeted, it has not advanced on the question of the circumstances under which a legitimate target can be attacked with military force. The circumstances and context in which military force is permitted should be the critical focus in the war against terrorism. The central issue haunting this war is the use of lethal military force in populated areas where civilian death and injury, and destruction of the community's infrastructure, are expected. As senior government officials, including President Barack Obama, explicitly recognized, terrorist targets are frequently "hiding among civilian populations."[2] The crucial question then is what law should govern the use of force in populated areas away from active combat zones. While several commentators have argued that force used outside of an already existing armed conflict must be governed by

[1] Although "military force" can involve a broad range of activity including detention, I am using "military force" throughout this chapter only in the narrow sense of the use of arms generally and air power in particular.

[2] Harold Hongju Koh, Legal Advisor, US Dep't of State, "Remarks at Annual Meeting of the American Society of International Law in Washington, D.C.: The Obama Administration and International Law" (Mar. 25, 2010) ("this is a conflict with an organized terrorist enemy that does not have conventional forces, but that plans and executes its attacks against us and our allies while hiding among civilian populations.") https://2009-2017.state.gov/s/l/releases/remarks/139119.htm. President Barack Obama, "Remarks at the National Defense University" (May 23, 2013) ("by narrowly targeting our action against those who want to kill us, and not the people they hide among, we are choosing the course of action least likely to result in the loss of innocent life"), https://www.whitehouse.gov/the-press-office/2013/05/23/remarks-President-national-defense-university.

Joshua Andresen, *Fighting Terrorism under All Applicable Law* In: *Between Crime and War.* Edited by: Claire Finkelstein, Christopher Fuller, Jens David Ohlin, Mitt Regan, Oxford University Press. DOI: 10.1093/oso/9780197638798.003.0005

the international human rights law appropriate for law enforcement operations,[3] states like the United States and the United Kingdom continue to insist on a right to use military force in self-defense governed solely by the law of armed conflict (LOAC).[4] To its credit, the Obama administration developed policy guidance for the use of force outside areas of active hostilities that modulated the more permissive LOAC with law enforcement considerations.[5] However, because the Obama administration opted for policy guidance over a legal development of the rules governing the use of force in populated areas, those guidelines were rejected and circumvented by the Trump administration.[6] This chapter shows that rather than loosening restrictions on the use of force outside active war zones, we should embrace a more measured approach not only on legal grounds but also for our national security.

The claim that a more restrictive approach to the use of force is in our national security interest may strike some as Pollyannaish. After all, even political leaders who take very seriously the civilian deaths that result from counterterrorism operations insist that

> [they] must weigh these heartbreaking tragedies against the alternatives. To do nothing in the face of terrorist networks would invite far more civilian casualties—not just in our cities at home and facilities abroad, but also in the very places—like Sana'a and Kabul and Mogadishu—where terrorists seek a foothold.[7]

Deploying airstrikes in populated areas is not, however, the only alternative to doing nothing. Not only are limited military operations that conform more

[3] *See, e.g.*, John C. Dehn & Kevin Jon Heller, *Debate: Targeted Killing: The Case of Anwar Al-Aulaqi*, 159 U. Pa. L.R. Online 175, 183 (2010), https://www.pennlawreview.com/online/159-U-Pa-L-Rev-PENNumbra-175.pdf; Noam Lubell & Nathan Derejko, *A Global Battlefield?*, 11 J. Int'l Criminal Justice 87 (2013); Christof Heyns et al.,, *The International Law Framework Regulating the Use of Armed Drones*, 65 Int'l & Comp. L.Q. 791, 814 (2016).

[4] *See, e.g.*, Joint Committee on Human Rights, "The Government's policy on the use of drones for targeted killing: Government Response to the Committee's Second Report of Session 2015–16" (fourth report Oct. 19, 2016, HL 49, HC 747), 17; U.S. Department of State, "Fourth Periodic Report of the United States of America to the United Nations Committee on Human Rights Concerning the International Covenant on Civil and Political Rights" (Dec. 30, 2011), § 505.

[5] A redacted version of the Presidential Policy Guidance, "Procedures for Approving Direct Action Against Terrorist Targets Located Outside the United States and Areas of Active Hostilities," was recently released as a result of a lawsuit by the ACLU, https://www.aclu.org/foia-document/presidential-policy-guidance.

[6] *See, e.g.*, Charlie Savage & Eric Schmitt, *Trump Poised to Drop Some Limits on Drone Strikes and Commando Raids*, N.Y. Times, Sept. 21, 2017, https://www.nytimes.com/2017/09/21/us/politics/trump-drone-strikes-commando-raids-rules.html; Charlie Savage & Eric Schmitt, *Trump Eases Combat Rules in Somalia Intended to Protect Civilians*, N.Y. Times, Mar. 30, 2017, https://www.nytimes.com/2017/03/30/world/africa/trump-is-said-to-ease-combat-rules-in-somalia-designed-to-protect-civilians.html.

[7] Obama, "Remarks," *supra* note 2.

closely to international human rights law a clear alternative. They will often be more effective at disrupting terrorist operations outside active war zones. This chapter thus seeks to show that the frequently cast opposition between doves and realists presents a false dichotomy. The former Legal Adviser of the UK Foreign & Commonwealth Office, Sir Daniel Bethlehem, characterized the debate as one between "those who favor a restrictive approach to the law on self-defense and those who take the view that the credibility of the law depends ultimately upon its ability to address effectively the realities of contemporary threats."[8] *Pace* Bethlehem, a restrictive approach to the law governing the use of force against terrorist threats is the most effective way to address the reality of those threats. An increasing number of empirical studies show that more force, particularly in the form of airstrikes, increases terrorist violence and recruitment while increasing popular support for terrorist groups. A more liberal approach to using force against the threats we face is thus consistent with increasing, rather than decreasing, those threats. While individual strikes may temporarily weaken capacity or disrupt terrorist operations, after more than twenty years of military operations, we have still failed to restore our peace and security.

In addition to security reasons for restricting the use of lethal force in counterterrorism operations, a legal analysis of the use of force in civilian areas also speaks for a more restrictive approach. Although some have suggested that terrorist threats may be targeted "wherever and whoever they are,"[9] "whether on the battlefield or outside of it,"[10] and "at all times,"[11] such an approach conflates the conditions that would make an individual a valid military objective with an analysis of the conditions in which military force may be used in the first place. A state's choice to use military force does not automatically entitle it to law of war *permissions*, though it does thereby subject itself to law of war *restrictions* and *obligations*.[12] Moreover,

[8] Daniel Bethlehem, *Principles Relevant to the Scope of a State's Right of Self-Defense against an Imminent or Actual Armed Attack by Nonstate Actors*, 106 AJIL 769, 773 (2012).

[9] United Kingdom, House of Lords, Statement by the Parliamentary Under-Secretary of State for Defence, *Hansard*, October 13, 2003, vol. 653, Debates, col. 600.

[10] Israel Military Advocate General Headquarters, "Laws of War in the Battlefield, Manual," 42 (1998).

[11] Germany, Lower House of Federal Parliament (*Bundestag*), Reply by the Federal Government to the Minor Interpellation by Members Jerzy Montag, Hans-Christian Ströbele, Omit Nouripour, further Members and the Parliamentary Group BÜNDIS 90/DIE GRÜNEN, *BT-Drs*. 17/3916 (Nov. 23, 2010), 6 ("[M]embers of the opposing armed forces (combatants) in international armed conflict and, in non-international armed conflict, members of organized armed groups exercising a continuous combat function may be lawfully targeted at all times as enemy fighters under international humanitarian law, including with the use of lethal force.").

[12] United States Department of Defense Office of the General Counsel, *Law of War Manual* (June 2015), § 3.4 ("the fact that *jus in bello* restrictions apply is not determinative of whether the permissions that are sometimes viewed as inherent in *jus in bello* rules may be relied upon by a State or non-State actor.").

even in circumstances where lethal military force may be justified and thus subject to international humanitarian law (IHL), the application of IHL does not displace international human rights law (IHRL). There are contexts, such as those outside active combat areas or in conditions of military occupation, where the use of force requires more restrictive law than what is provided by IHL. We need to determine where more restrictive rules for the use of force are required not only by looking at whether a target is a valid military objective, but more importantly, by looking at the circumstances ruling in the area in which an attack is contemplated. Where the area, for example, contains civilians and is not an active combat zone, neither self-defense nor a belligerent nexus between the target and an ongoing armed conflict will, by itself, be sufficient to license the exercise of lethal military force governed solely by IHL. As I will argue, IHRL restrictions against the arbitrary deprivation of life should only be fully read in terms of more permissive IHL rules in active combat areas away from civilians.

The second section of the chapter examines several recent empirical studies and media reports showing the extent to which the use of military force in general, and air power in particular, have led to an increase in terrorist violence, recruitment, and popular support. Having called into question the effectiveness of military force, the third section turns to the threshold question of what law should govern counterterrorism operations by examining how international tribunals have analyzed the relation between IHL and IHRL. I show that the view embraced by the United States and the United Kingdom, that IHL alone imposes legal restrictions on the use of military force, is increasingly an outlier in the international legal community. Building off the analysis of international jurisprudence, the fourth section of the chapter identifies seven key criteria that should be used to determine the relative application of IHL and IHRL to a particular use of military force. I argue that IHRL restrictions on the use of force should be applied on a sliding scale depending on a combined analysis of the seven factors. I also show how these factors should be applied to actual counterterrorism operations to determine our legal obligations. In the fifth section of the chapter, I argue that the debate between those arguing for a more restrictive or a more permissive approach to the law governing the use of military force should be recast. It is not sufficient to focus on when IHL does and does not apply. We must also focus on how precisely IHL and IHRL will interact to cabin the ravages of war. In conclusion, I argue that the empirical and legal analysis demonstrates that a more restrictive approach to the use of force is not only required to maintain civilian protections in counterterrorism operations but is also in our national security interest.

II. More Force Increases Terrorist Violence

Empirical studies, expert opinions, and anecdotal data have consistently shown that the increased use of military force by a state, especially in civilian populated areas, triggers higher levels of terrorist and insurgent violence, increases public support for those opposing the state forces, and subsequently improves recruitment for associated terrorist organizations. A recent Associated Press report links a surge in civilian casualties under the Trump administration directly to terrorist public relations campaigns, stating that ISIS and Al Qaeda "are quickly moving to drum up outrage over a sharp spike in civilian casualties said to have been caused by U.S. airstrikes in Iraq and Syria."[13] The United States' use of air power, and drone strikes in particular, has long been a tool of terrorist recruitment and a spur of popular resentment and opposition to the United States. Focusing on the drone campaign in Yemen, local writer Ibrahim Mothana reported that "[d]rone strikes are causing more and more Yemenis to hate America and join radical militants; they are not driven by ideology but rather by a sense of revenge and despair."[14] Mothana concluded that "America's counterterrorism policy here is not only making Yemen less safe by strengthening support for A.Q.A.P. [Al-Qaeda in the Arabian Peninsula], but it could also ultimately endanger the United States and the entire world."[15] Mothana's assessment of the effects of counterterrorism operations in Yemen fits a common narrative. Dennis C. Blair, retired admiral and former US Director of National Intelligence from 2009 to 2010, relates almost an identical report, but with respect to operations in Pakistan. Blair observed that "as the drone campaign wears on, hatred of America is increasing in Pakistan. . . . Our reliance on high-tech strikes that pose no risk to our soldiers is bitterly resented in a country that cannot duplicate such feats of warfare without cost to its own troops."[16]

The negative repercussions of heavy military force are not limited to the use of special weaponry or isolated to targeting mistakes or violations of the law of war. Jason Lyall, who has conducted one of the most systematic analyses of the

[13] Susannah George & Zeina Karam, *Civilian Casualties in Iraq, Syria Undercut US Victories*, AP News, Mar. 31, 2017, https://apnews.com/5bdf68e4f44044678d96a547e541e8b2. The article states that civilian casualties from coalition airstrikes in Syria have risen from an average of 30 per month from September 2014 through January 2017 to 56 in February and 198 in March.

[14] Ibrahim Mothana, *How Drones Help Al Qaeda*, N.Y. Times, June 13, 2012, https://www.nytimes.com/2012/06/14/opinion/how-drones-help-al-qaeda.html.

[15] *Id.*

[16] Dennis C. Blair, *Drones Alone Are Not the Answer*, N.Y. Times, Aug. 14, 2011, https://www.nytimes.com/2011/08/15/opinion/drones-alone-are-not-the-answer.html. The US Army similarly notes in their 2006 Counterinsurgency Field Manual that "killing every insurgent is normally impossible. Attempting to do so can also be counterproductive in some cases; it risks generating popular resentment, creating martyrs that motivate new recruits, and producing cycles of revenge." U.S. Dep't Of The Army, FM 3-24, COUNTERINSURGENCY para. 1-128 (2006).

use of airstrikes for counterinsurgency in Afghanistan, asserts that "[e]vidence consistently indicates that airstrikes markedly increase insurgent attacks relative to non-bombed locations for at least 90 days after a strike."[17] In what would seem counterintuitive to some, Lyall's detailed empirical study showed that "repeated bombing of insurgents . . . only backfire[s], multiplying grievances among civilian populations and leading to increased violence."[18] His analysis revealed that even repeated bombings of locations more than one hundred times did not lead to a "tipping point after which attrition leads to the degradation of insurgent capabilities."[19]

Quite apart from the impracticality of resorting to heavy military force[20] to defeat an enemy that lacks "the key assets—capital, infrastructure, and fielded forces—that must be threatened if airpower is to have a chance at being successful,"[21] reliance on such methods actually works against our military advantage by bolstering the very enemy we seek to defeat. As Lyall points out, "the returns for inflicting harm accrue disproportionately to the weaker side" in radically asymmetric wars. Moreover, as reflected in the Taliban's "well documented . . . use of airstrikes as a recruitment device,"[22] almost any harm inflicted against insurgents and terrorists can be manipulated by them into a heroic David and Goliath narrative. Although Lyall's studies do not show a particular link between civilian casualties and increased violence, he does note that "[n]o matter how precise, airstrikes will kill civilians, shifting support away from the counterinsurgent while creating new grievances that fuel insurgent recruitment."[23]

A recent Open Society Foundations report complements Lyall's study by focusing specifically on the strategic costs of civilian harm in Afghanistan and from counterterrorism operations elsewhere, including drone strikes in Yemen and Pakistan. With respect to the war in Afghanistan, the report assesses "with high confidence that civilian harm by U.S., international, and Afghan forces contributed significantly to the growth of the Taliban, weakened the legitimacy of the U.S. mission and the Afghan government, and undermined the war effort by straining U.S.-Afghan relations."[24] The report documents how civilian harm led

[17] Jason Lyall, "Bombing to Lose? Airpower, Civilian Casualties, and the Dynamics of Violence in Counterinsurgency Wars," 1, Mar. 27, 2015, https://www.du.edu/korbel/sie/media/documents/research_seminar_papers/lyall-airstrikes-apr2015.pdf.

[18] *Id.* 19–20.

[19] *Id.* 20.

[20] Here, I also include drones firing hellfire missiles. For a correction to the mistaken view that drones are effectively "aerial sniper rifles" that allow "the pinpoint application of deadly force," *see* Joshua Andresen, *Putting Lethal Force on the Table: How Drones Change the Alternative Space of War and Counterterrorism*, 8 HARV. NAT'L SEC. J. 445, 464–65 (2017).

[21] Lyall, *supra* note 17, at 3–4.

[22] *Id.* 28.

[23] *Id.* 4.

[24] C. KOLENDA ET AL., THE STRATEGIC COSTS OF CIVILIAN HARM 23 (2016).

to increased revenge-driven violence, loss of support for International Security Assistance Force (ISAF) troops, and increased support for the Taliban.[25] The report echoes Lyall's findings with respect to recruitment, finding that "[c]ivilian harm was easily exploited by the Taliban. Taliban publications, public communications, and propaganda routinely made use of incidents of civilian harm to paint U.S. forces as an indiscriminate, anti-Muslim occupation force."[26] Perhaps even more interestingly, Christopher Kolenda, one of the report's authors and former senior advisor on Afghanistan and Pakistan to the US Department of Defense notes that "the vast majority of ISAF-caused civilian harm occurred *while operating in accordance with the Law of Armed Conflict*" and was "far more frequent" than harm to civilians caused by violations of IHL.[27] Kolenda thus suggests that conducting counterinsurgency and counterterrorism operations in accordance with IHL is not sufficient. Increasing civilian protection beyond what is required by IHL may be essential to winning the war.

The fact that most civilian casualties in the fight against terrorist groups can be legally justified under IHL should not be surprising given the commitment of US and allied forces to using military force only within lawful limits. It should, however, show us that IHL is not well suited to many counterterrorism operations in which military force is thought to be necessary. The current state of the law fails to preserve civilian protections and fails to work to the military advantage of law-abiding forces. Contrary to what the Trump administration believes, the evidence reviewed here shows that a more permissive approach to the use of force will actually work against the United States' military advantage. Rather than continuing to insist that US counterterrorism operations abroad are governed only by IHL, the United States and its allies should consider whether our IHRL obligations also impose legal restrictions on counterterrorism operations that are in our national security interest.

III. Fighting Terrorism under IHL and IHRL

The assumption by the United States since September 11, 2001, is that international counterterrorism operations are governed by the law of war alone. For instance, during Harold Koh's 2010 address to the American Society of International Law, he repeatedly stated that "lethal operations . . . are conducted in accordance with *all applicable law*."[28] However, the only law mentioned as applicable to lethal operations was the "law of war." John Brennan's 2011 speech on

25 *Id.* 24–25.
26 *Id.* 25.
27 *Id.* 5 (emphasis in original).
28 Koh, "Remarks," *supra* note 2.

"Strengthening our Security by Adhering to our Values and Laws" also characterized the fight against terrorist threats, even when outside "hot battlefields," as bound only by the "laws of war."[29] Likewise, in his 2013 speech at the National Defense University, Obama never mentioned human rights, and targeting was cast only in law of war terms.[30] Although American political leaders have emphasized the appropriateness of using law enforcement authorities to incapacitate terrorist threats domestically,[31] there has been no suggestion that the United States may be bound by anything other than IHL when using military force to respond to threats internationally. The United States made its position explicit in its recent report to the UN Committee on Human Rights in which it stated its view that human rights obligations as contained in the International Covenant on Civil and Political Rights (ICCPR) "would apply only to individuals who were both within the territory of a State Party and within that State Party's jurisdiction."[32] Although the United States does note that "international human rights law and the law of armed conflict are in many respects complementary and mutually reinforcing,"[33] the United States nevertheless takes the view that IHRL imposes no obligations on states outside their own territory.[34]

The US view of the non-applicability of IHRL to military actions outside its territory is an outlier and stands in marked contrast to the views of many of its allies and a growing consensus of international court jurisprudence. A review of international jurisprudence on the application of IHRL to the use of military force shows that the United States' strict territorial view of the scope of IHRL obligations is legally unsound. The International Court of Justice (ICJ), the European Court of Human Rights (ECtHR), and UK domestic courts have long found that IHRL applies to the use of military force abroad. Although courts acknowledge that IHRL obligations are limited to a state's "jurisdiction," they reject a strictly territorial approach. Courts not only find jurisdiction, and thus the application of IHRL, in areas where states exercise effective control, such as in

[29] John O. Brennan, "Strengthening our Security by Adhering to our Values and Laws," Remarks at Harvard Law School (Sept. 16, 2011).

[30] Obama, "Remarks," *supra* note 2.

[31] United States Attorney General, Eric H. Holder, Jr. letter to Senator Rand Paul (Mar. 4, 2013) ("As a policy matter . . . we reject the use of military force where well-established law enforcement authorities in this country provide the best means for incapacitating a terrorist threat.").

[32] Fourth Periodic Report of the United States, *supra* note 4, at § 505.

[33] *Id.* § 507.

[34] A possible exception to this view is the Obama administration's acknowledgment that the Convention Against Torture applies extraterritorially "in places outside the United States that the U.S. government controls as a governmental authority." See Statement by NSC Spokesperson Bernadette Meehan on the U.S. Presentation to the Committee Against Torture (Nov. 12, 2014), https://obamawhitehouse.archives.gov/the-press-office/2014/11/12/statement-nsc-spokesperson-bernadette-meehan-us-presentation-committee-a; Sarah Cleveland, *The United States and the Torture Convention, Part I: Extraterritoriality*, Just Security, Nov. 14, 2014, https://www.justsecurity.org/17435/united-states-torture-convention-part-i-extraterritoriality/.

conditions of military occupation, but also when states exercise authority and control over individuals through the use of force outside combat areas.

A. The ICJ's Application of IHRL to Military Operations

The ICJ began to define the jurisprudence on the relation between IHRL and IHL in its Advisory Opinion on *The Legality of the Threat or Use of Nuclear Weapons*. There the Court considered the question of whether "the use of nuclear weapons by a State in an extreme circumstance of self-defence, in which its very survival would be at stake," could be legal under international law.[35] With reference to the possible application of IHRL to the matter, the Court observed that

> the protection of the International Covenant for the Protection of Civil and Political Rights does not cease in times of war, except by operation of Article 4 of the Covenant whereby certain provisions may be derogated from in a time of national emergency. Respect for the right to life, however, is not such a provision. In principle, the right not arbitrarily to be deprived of one's life applies also in hostilities.[36]

Although the ICCPR explicitly states that there could be no derogation from the right to life even in times of "public emergency which threatens the life of the nation,"[37] the ICJ's affirmation of IHRL's applicability in times of war ran contrary to the position of several states. These states held that IHRL was directed only to "the protection of human rights in peacetime," leaving "questions relating to unlawful loss of life in hostilities [to be] governed by the law applicable in armed conflict."[38] Perhaps as a compromise with such positions, the Court restricted the reach of IHRL, holding that

> [t]he test of what is an arbitrary deprivation of life, however, falls to be determined by the applicable *lex specialis*, namely, the law applicable in armed conflict which is designed to regulate the conduct of hostilities. Thus whether a particular loss of life, through the use of a certain weapon in warfare, is to be considered an arbitrary deprivation of life contrary to Article 6 of the Covenant, can only be decided by reference to the law applicable in armed conflict and not deduced from the terms of the Covenant itself.[39]

[35] *Legality of the Threat or Use of Nuclear Weapons*, Advisory Opinion of July 8, 1996, [1996] ICJ Rep. 263, § 97.
[36] *Nuclear Weapons Case*, *supra* note 35, at § 25.
[37] ICCPR, art. 4(1).
[38] *Nuclear Weapons Case*, *supra* note 35, at § 24.
[39] *Id.* § 25.

Here the Court underscored the applicability of IHRL, including the right to life, to military operations in the extreme case of using nuclear weapons in self-defense. At the same time, however, the Court held that the IHRL right to life would be adequately respected as long as *jus ad bellum* and *jus in bello* rules governing the use of force were satisfied.

Three aspects of the Courts reasoning are notable in the context of our discussion. First, while the Court found that the IHRL prohibition on the arbitrary deprivation of life needed to be applied through the lens of IHL, it nevertheless reserved a place for the application of IHRL in armed conflict. Second, the Court justified its overall reasoning with respect to the applicability of IHL and a right to self-defense on "the fundamental right of every State to survival."[40] The preference for IHL rules over IHRL rules was thus couched in terms of the extreme severity of the situation contemplated by the Court. Third, although the applicability of IHRL in general, and the provisions of the ICCPR in particular, are contingent upon a state's exercise of jurisdiction and control, and primarily applied within a state's own territory, the Court did not address the question of jurisdictional requirements for the application of IHRL at all. The Court instead implied that states have a responsibility to respect the right to life of those it affects through military operations irrespective of jurisdictional or territorial limitations.

The ICJ advanced its jurisprudence on the relation between IHL and IHRL and addressed the possible territorial and jurisdictional limits to IHRL obligations at length in the Advisory Opinion on *The Legal Consequences of the Construction of a Wall in the Occupied Palestinian Territory*. The Court's analysis of the territorial and jurisdictional limits of IHRL began with Article 2 of the ICCPR, which states that "[e]ach State Party to the present Covenant undertakes to respect and to ensure to all individuals within its territory and subject to its jurisdiction the rights recognized in the present Covenant."[41] The Court first considered the reading of Article 2 endorsed by the United States, that the Covenant only applies to "individuals who are both present within a State's territory and subject to that State's jurisdiction."[42] The ICJ rejected this interpretation in favor of a reading of Article 2 "covering both individuals present within a State's territory and those outside that territory but subject to that State's jurisdiction."[43] The Court reasoned that although a state's jurisdiction is primarily territorial, a state may occasionally exercise jurisdiction extraterritorially. Considering the object and purpose of the ICCPR, the Court found that "it would seem natural that, even when [states

[40] *Id.* § 96.

[41] ICCPR, art. 2(1).

[42] *Legal Consequences of the Construction of a Wall in the Occupied Palestinian Territory*, Advisory Opinion [2004] ICJ Rep. 136, § 108.

[43] *Id.* § 108.

exercise jurisdiction extraterritorially], States parties to the Covenant should be bound to comply with its provisions."[44] The Court supported its finding with the "constant practice of the Human Rights Committee," which has found the ICCPR applicable "where a state exercises its jurisdiction on foreign territory," such as the case of "arrests carried out by Uruguayan agents in Brazil or Argentina" and in the "confiscation of a passport by a Uruguayan consulate in Germany."[45] Reviewing the *travaux préparatoires* of the ICCPR, the Court concluded that

> the drafters of the Covenant did not intend to allow States to escape from their obligations when they exercise jurisdiction outside their national territory. They only intended to prevent persons residing abroad from asserting, vis-à-vis their State of origin, rights that do not fall within the competence of that State, but of that of the State of residence.[46]

The Court found that the drafters of the ICCPR only intended to exclude a state's extraterritorial IHRL obligations in a rather narrow set of circumstances. The facts under consideration in the *Wall Case* thus made it an "easy" case of extraterritorial jurisdiction since, as the Court noted in 2004, "the territories occupied by Israel have for over 37 years been subject to its territorial jurisdiction as the occupying Power."[47] Looking beyond the specific facts of the case, the Court's reasoning and the *travaux préparatoires* show that jurisdiction should be inferred whenever a state exercises effective control in an area where no other state exercises de facto control. Since Israel had been the only state with jurisdiction over the Occupied Palestinian Territories since 1967, the Court concluded that Israel is bound by IHRL obligations in the context of its armed conflict occupation.

Even when IHRL is found applicable in armed conflict, we saw in the *Nuclear Weapons Case* that much of its effectiveness may be watered down by limiting IHRL obligations to what is required under IHL. The *Wall Case*, however, moved beyond the view that limits human rights obligations to the requirements of IHL. The Court found that Israel's construction of the wall on occupied territory violated both their IHL obligations and their distinct IHRL obligations, including IHRL rights to liberty of movement, work, health, education, and an adequate standard of living.[48] The Court explicitly stated that "the protection offered by human rights conventions does not cease in case of armed conflict."[49]

44 *Id.* § 109.
45 *Id.* § 109.
46 *Id.* § 109.
47 *Id.* § 112.
48 *Wall Case*, *supra* note 42, at §§ 137, 134.
49 *Id.* § 106. The ICJ continues, "save through the effect of provisions for derogation of the kind to be found in Article 4 of the International Covenant on Civil and Political Rights." Article 4(2) of the ICCPR expressly rules out derogations from the right to life.

With respect to the relation between IHL and IHRL in armed conflict, the Court set out three possibilities: "some rights may be exclusively matters of international humanitarian law; others may be exclusively matters of human rights law; yet others may be matters of both these branches of international law."[50] Although the Court went on to repeat the proposition set out in the *Nuclear Weapons Case* that IHL applies as *lex specialis* where IHRL and IHL obligations overlap, its finding that the construction of the wall violated obligations under both IHL and IHRL demonstrates that, even under armed conflict conditions of occupation, IHRL applies as a distinct set of obligations and restrictions on state behavior.

The ICJ moved even further in its application of IHRL as an independent source of obligations and restrictions on state actions in the *Case Concerning Armed Activities on the Territory of the Congo*. As in the *Wall Case*, the Court found in the *Armed Activities Case* that a state can violate its IHRL obligations in armed conflict. The Court, however, left the *lex specialis* view of IHL behind, finding that IHRL obligations are neither displaced by nor to be read solely in terms of IHL obligations. Instead, IHRL obligations remain in place alongside IHL obligations and "both branches of international law, namely international human rights law and international humanitarian law, [need] to be taken into consideration" in order to assess the full range of violations of international legal obligations.[51] In addition to finding violations of IHL rules of distinction and precaution in attack, the Court also found violations of overlapping IHL and IHRL provisions, including the prohibition against the arbitrary deprivation of life and torture found in ICCPR Articles 6(1) and 7.[52]

As in the *Wall Case*, the ICJ's finding of IHRL violations in the *Armed Activities Case* was supported by a jurisdictional analysis that "international human rights instruments are applicable in respect of acts done by a State in the exercise of its jurisdiction outside its own territory, particularly in occupied territories."[53] The fact that Ugandan troops had occupied the territory in which they committed human rights violations made the jurisdictional finding uncontroversial for the Court. A finding of jurisdiction and the applicability of basic human rights obligations under conditions of military occupation is also reflected in recent US case law, including the rejection of the US government's argument in *Boumediene* "that *de jure* sovereignty is the touchstone of habeas corpus jurisdiction."[54] In

[50] *Wall Case*, *supra* note 42, at § 106.

[51] *Case Concerning Armed Activities on the Territory of the Congo* (Democratic Republic of the Congo v. Uganda) [2005] ICJ Rep. 168, § 216.

[52] *Id.* § 219. Murder and torture are also prohibited Geneva Convention Relative to the Protection of Civilian Persons in Time of War (Fourth Geneva Convention), Aug. 12, 1949, art. 32 and Protocol Additional (I) to the Geneva Convention of 12 August 1949, and relating to the Protection of Victims of International Armed Conflicts (Protocol I), June 8, 1977, art. 75.

[53] *Armed Activities Case*, *supra* note 51, at § 216 (internal quotation marks omitted).

[54] Boumediene v. Bush, 553 U.S. 723, 755 (2008).

addition to a developing consensus that conditions of military occupation may impose IHRL obligations on the occupying power, there is also an emerging norm that IHRL obligations apply to a wider range of military operations that do not include occupation, particularly in the jurisprudence of the ECtHR.

B. The Application of the ECHR to Military Operations

As we have seen with respect to the ICCPR, a jurisdictional analysis has also been essential to finding the European Convention on Human Rights (ECHR) applicable to armed conflict. While the ECtHR has consistently held that the jurisdictional application of the Convention is "primarily territorial," it has also found states exercising extraterritorial jurisdiction in a variety of "exceptional cases." Two such cases are when a state has effective control over foreign territory during military occupation or exercises public powers at the consent, invitation, or acquiescence of a foreign government in that foreign government's territory.[55] The ECtHR has also found extraterritorial jurisdiction when diplomatic or consular agents exert authority and control over others, as well as when states use force to bring individuals under their power and control, particularly when the state's power and control are "exclusive."[56] The latter has been particularly applied "where an individual is taken into the custody of state agents abroad," such as when a foreign civilian is taken into military detention.[57] The ECtHR has gone further still and found that authority and control, and thus jurisdiction, can exist even when a state has not taken custody of an individual. For example, the Court found jurisdiction at a checkpoint in southeastern Iraq "under the command and direct supervision of a Netherlands Royal Army officer," holding that the Netherlands was asserting authority and control over persons passing through the checkpoint.[58]

While the ECtHR has not made an explicit determination of jurisdiction on the basis of a use of military force alone, the Court in *Andreou v. Turkey* came very close to doing so by finding that

[55] Banković v. Belgium [2001] 11 BHRC 435, paras. 60, 61, 67, 69–71. *See also* Issa and Others v. Turkey (2004) 41 EHRR 567, para. 69.

[56] Al-Skeini v. United Kingdom (2011) 53 EHRR 18, paras. 133–36. *See also Issa and Others, supra* note 55, at ¶ 71; and Öcalan v. Turkey (2005) 41 EHRR 985, para. 91.

[57] *Al-Skeini, supra* note 56, at ¶ 136. *See also* Hassan v. United Kingdom [2014] ECHR 9936, paras. 76–80.

[58] Jaloud v. The Netherlands App. No. 47708/08 (ECtHR [GC] Nov. 20, 2014), para. 152. While the checkpoint was under the command of the Netherlands, it was manned by Iraqi soldiers and, at the time of the incident, a patrol of six Dutch soldiers. *Id.* paras. 10–12.

> even though the applicant had sustained her injuries in territory over which Turkey exercised no control, the opening of fire on the crowd from close range, which was the direct and immediate cause of those injuries, had been such that the applicant should be regarded as "within [the] jurisdiction" of Turkey within the meaning of Article 1 of the Convention.[59]

In *Andreou*, Turkish-Cypriot soldiers opened fire at Greek-Cypriot demonstrators in or close to the UN buffer zone separating the Turkish controlled part of Cyprus from the rest of the island. Even though Ms. Andreou was in Greek-Cypriot territory when she sustained her injuries, the ECtHR nevertheless found that Turkey, through its soldiers, exercised jurisdiction over Ms. Andreou when they opened fire on her.[60]

One case that has found jurisdiction, and thus the application of IHRL, explicitly on the basis of the use of lethal military force is the British High Court case of *Al-Saadoon v. Secretary of State for Defence*. There the High Court found for the application of human rights obligations "whenever and wherever a state . . . party to the [ECHR] purports to exercise legal authority or *uses physical force*."[61] In the *Al-Saadoon* case, the judge reasoned that it was

> impossible to say that shooting someone dead does not involve the exercise of physical power and control over that person. Using force to kill is indeed the ultimate exercise of physical control over another human being. Nor as it seems to me can a principled system of human rights law draw a distinction between killing an individual after arresting him and simply shooting him without arresting him first, such that in the first case there is an obligation to respect the person's right to life yet in the second case there is not.[62]

The High Court in *Al-Saadoon* thus found that jurisdiction arises in such cases "through the exercise of physical power and control over the individual who was shot and killed."[63]

As sound as the High Court's reasoning may appear, some limiting principle is needed. Finding jurisdiction and applying IHRL whenever a state uses lethal force would be overbroad, implying that IHRL would govern all uses of force in armed conflict, thus generally displacing IHL.[64] An appropriate limit can,

[59] Andreou v. Turkey [2009] ECHR 1663, para. 25.

[60] Andreou v. Turkey App. No. 45653/99 (Admissibility Decision) (ECHR June 3, 2008), 9–11.

[61] Al-Saadoon v. Secretary of State for Defence [2015] EWHC 715 (Admin.) (Mar. 17, 2015), para. 106 (emphasis added).

[62] *Id.* paras. 95, 117.

[63] *Id.* para. 118.

[64] While Mr. Justice Leggatt does propose excluding armed conflict and security maintenance in "dangerous and hostile conditions" from the application of IHRL (*Al-Saadoon* [2015], *supra* note 61,

however, be found in the ECtHR's application of IHRL in cases where states exercise public powers and when their control over individuals is "exclusive."[65] Following the ECtHR, we can immediately distinguish cases of active hostilities, where no power has exclusive control or can be said to be performing a public function, from cases in which a state uses force far from active hostilities explicitly because the de jure authority is "unable or unwilling" to handle a terrorist threat. In the latter cases, the attacking state is avowedly exercising a public security function that the de jure authority could not or would not perform itself. Moreover, it is precisely in these latter cases that the attacking state is the exclusive authority asserting power and control over the individuals against whom it is using force. In such circumstances, far from active hostilities and where the attacking force has unchallenged and exclusive control over the lives of those it is subjecting to lethal force, it is sensible to require a higher IHRL standard on the use of force. Despite support for the High Court's judgment and the availability of an appropriate limiting principle in the jurisprudence of the ECtHR, its jurisdictional finding based on the use of force alone was overturned on appeal.[66] The United Kingdom conceded jurisdiction only "where claimants were in the custody of agents of the United Kingdom."[67]

The UK Court of Appeal's finding that IHRL obligations apply under conditions of occupation or physical custody, but not when lethal military force is used against a person unfortunately fosters a perverse incentive to use lethal force rather than capture the enemy in order to avoid IHRL obligations. As the High Court found in *Al-Saadoon*, "drawing a line between cases where force is used to detain and cases where force is used to kill" does not seem to be legitimate once we find jurisdiction on the basis of a state's authority and control over a person.[68] Although the ICJ was not addressing this issue in the *Wall Case*, its conclusion that IHRL obligations should apply to the state with the competence to respect them dovetails nicely with the ECtHR's "authority and control" jurisdictional principle and provides a promising solution to the perverse incentive problem. If we consider which rights may fall within the competence of a state exercising military force against a terrorist threat in a nation unwilling or unable to deal with the threat, the only state capable of respecting the rights of those affected by its use of military force is the state deploying the military force. In such instances, the people affected are under the authority and control not of the state

at para. 111), such an exclusion would contradict many of the instances in which the ECtHR has applied IHRL, including the *Al-Skeini* case on which Leggatt most prominently relies.

65 *See, e.g.*, *Al-Skeini*, *supra* note 56, at para. 136.

66 Al-Saadoon v. Secretary of State for Defence and Rahmatullah v. Secretary of State for Defence [2016] EWCA Civ. 811 (Sept. 9, 2016), para. 69.

67 *Al-Saadoon* [2015], *supra* note 61, para. 93.

68 *Id.* para. 107.

in which they reside, but of the state using military force in their direct vicinity. By finding that IHRL applies when lethal force is used outside areas of active hostilities, as well as in cases of occupation or detention, the perverse incentive for states to prematurely rule out nonlethal options in favor of lethal force is avoided. A desire to avoid such perverse incentives in the law is an additional reason to recognize IHRL restrictions on uses of lethal military force in counterterrorism operations.

Perhaps surprisingly, the United States addressed the perverse incentive problem in the 2013 Presidential Policy Guidance (PPG) put in place by the Obama administration to regulate the use of lethal force outside areas of active hostilities. The PPG authorized the use of lethal force only after a determination that "capture is not feasible at the time of the operation."[69] The guidance also came close to recognizing IHRL obligations on the use of lethal military force. As noted earlier, the United States consistently maintains that the provisions of the ICCPR "would apply only to individuals who were both within the territory of a State Party and within that State Party's jurisdiction."[70] Nevertheless, when asked by the Human Rights Committee to "clarify how targeted killings conducted through drone attacks on the territory of other States, as well as collateral civilian casualties are in compliance with Covenant obligations," the United States responded by referring to the PPG.[71] The United States indicated that the PPG exceeded the requirements of IHL by requiring lethal force to be used "only to prevent or stop attacks against U.S. persons, and even then, only when capture is not feasible and no other reasonable alternatives exist to address the threat effectively."[72] The PPG also demanded "near certainty that non-combatants will not be injured or killed."[73] Despite encouraging restraint, the PPG did not go all the way to barring the use of lethal force except when necessary to stop an immediate threat, as would be required in a law enforcement context applying IHRL. Yet the guidance clearly went beyond both *jus ad bellum* and *jus in bello* requirements by limiting the use of military force in self-defense only to instances in which US persons are threatened and by making civilian casualties altogether unacceptable. In the context of its response to the Human Rights Committee, the United States' reference to the PPG suggests that it acknowledged some heightened

[69] Fact Sheet: U.S. Policy Standards and Procedures for the Use of Force in Counterterrorism Operations Outside the United States and Areas of Active Hostilities (May 23, 2013), http://www.whitehouse.gov/the-press-office/2013/05/23/fact-sheet-us-policy-standards-and-procedures-use-force-counterterrorism.

[70] Fourth Periodic Report of the United States, *supra* note 4, at § 505.

[71] United States Written Responses to Questions From the United Nations Human Rights Committee Concerning the Fourth Periodic Report (July 3, 2013), § 35.

[72] *Id.*

[73] *Id.*

duty—short of a legal obligation—to respect civilian life and restrict the use of military force outside areas of active hostilities.[74]

IV. How to Apply IHRL to Counterterrorism Operations

The Obama administration recognized the need to restrict the United States' use of military force in counterterrorism operations in a way that went beyond the minimum constraints demanded by IHL. However, it squandered the opportunity to commit itself to higher restrictions as binding legal obligations. As the review of international jurisprudence shows, the United States thus remains an outlier vis-à-vis the growing consensus that IHRL is legally binding on at least some uses of military force in counterterrorism operations. The chief question for the international community today is not whether IHRL applies to international military operations, but to what extent it imposes obligations or restrictions on said operations that go beyond those imposed by IHL. At one end of the spectrum is the view held by nations such as the United Kingdom, that IHRL can "impose no greater constraints on the effective pursuit of military activity than are clearly imposed by international humanitarian law."[75] At the other end of the spectrum are views that any military force used outside the context of an already existing armed conflict will be governed by IHRL alone.[76] Between these two extremes, this chapter defends the reasonable middle ground. The application of IHRL to armed conflict and counterterrorism operations should work on a sliding scale. In active combat conditions where civilians and combatants are clearly distinguishable, IHRL obligations should be viewed through the lens of overlapping IHL obligations. In conditions far from active battlefields where civilians and combatants are difficult or impossible to distinguish from one another, IHRL obligations should be applied in their full force over and above any overlapping IHL obligations. In mixed conditions, IHRL restrictions should work to temper IHL.

My position tracks the reasoning of the court cases discussed earlier, in particular the ICJ's advisory opinion in the *Nuclear Weapons Case*. There the ICJ

[74] Unfortunately, the Obama administration's use of policy guidance rather than legal determinations has made the eliminations of some of its constraints significantly easier for the Trump administration. *See supra* note 6.

[75] Joint Report October 2016, *supra* note 4, at 17. The UK government specifically addresses the applicability of the right to life in Article 2 of the ECHR to the use of force against threats from ISIL. Although the United Kingdom did state to the UN Human Rights Council in 2014 that "[i]f armed [drones] were to be used outside the scope of an armed conflict, their use must be in accordance with international human rights law" (cited in Joint Report October 2016, *supra* note 4, at 17), the government's later statement suggests that compliance with IHRL may be interpreted to impose no greater requirements than those imposed by IHL.

[76] *See, e.g.*, Dehn & Heller, *supra* note 3, at 183.

found that provisions of IHRL which overlap with IHL—such as the prohibition on arbitrary deprivation of life—can be expected to have minimal additional application "in an extreme circumstance of self-defence, in which the very survival of a State would be at stake."[77] In such instances, the IHRL prohibition against the arbitrary deprivation of life would be applied according to the *jus ad bellum* rule of self-defense and the *jus in bello* rules of military necessity, distinction, proportionality, and so forth. The position defended here also follows the UK High Court in *Al-Saadoon* when it noted that there are "strong reasons" for easing the application of IHRL to "military operations in the field, particularly where actual fighting is involved."[78] The High Court went on to suggest that in battlefield conditions or "when seeking to maintain security in dangerous and hostile conditions," IHRL obligations and restrictions should be interpreted as satisfied as long as they are consistent with IHL.[79] Following this line of reasoning, conventional armed conflict between pitched armies and volatile peacekeeping missions may also be contexts in which IHRL should be applied through the lens of IHL. However, this approach still leaves a great deal of room to distinguish how IHRL might apply on the battlefield from the way in which it should apply to lethal force deployed far from the heat of battle where military personnel are under no immediate threat of harm. As the threats faced by states become less existential, and military force is deployed away from active combat areas and with increasing proximity and danger to civilians, the obligations and restrictions of IHRL should be applied with greater compulsion. At the limit, the use of military force will have to be deployed in full conformity with IHRL and any non-overlapping IHL restrictions. On the sliding scale model this chapter proposes, once an attack is determined to be lawful under other relevant *jus ad bellum* and *jus in bello* constraints, the following criteria should be assessed to determine the relative application of IHRL and IHL: (A) the gravity of the threat faced, (B) whether operations are taking place in active combat areas, (C) whether civilians are absent or readily distinguishable from combatants, (D) whether decisions are being made in the heat of battle, (E) whether the state exercises effective control over the area where the use of force is contemplated, (F) whether the state exercises authority and control over the people subject to the use of force, and (G) the reliability of the information on which the use of force is predicated. I will now examine why each of these factors is integral to a determination of the relative application of IHRL and IHL and then show how they can be applied to actual counterterrorism operations.[80]

[77] *Nuclear Weapons Case*, *supra* note 35, at § 97.
[78] *Al-Saadoon* [2015], *supra* note 61, at para. 106.
[79] *Id.* para. 111.
[80] A simplified flow chart showing how to determine the relative application of IHRL and IHL to a use of military force is included in Figures 4.1 and 4.2 at the end of this chapter.

A. The Gravity of the Threat

As this chapter has shown, the *Nuclear Weapons Case* explicitly based its finding that IHRL obligations should be applied in terms of IHL obligations on the "extreme circumstance of self-defence, in which the very survival of a State would be at stake."[81] The gravity of the threat that a state faces is an important indicator of what law should regulate the state's use of force in response. To a significant extent, the international law of self-defense, which recognizes a right to respond to an "armed attack,"[82] modulates the use of force by imposing necessity and proportionality requirements on the resort to military force. Moreover, IHL proportionality places restrictions on acceptable civilian casualties when force is used. Thus the graver the threat faced the greater the force and risk of civilian casualties a state will be able to justify as proportionate in its self-defense.

At the other end of spectrum from the extreme case of nuclear attack are terrorist threats. Since the immediacy of a threat is one vector of its gravity, most terrorist threats are not only less grave because they pose no existential threat to a nation, they are also less grave because counterterrorism operations rarely confront immediate threats. While a terrorist threat that rises to the level of an "armed attack"[83] would rightfully trigger a response governed by IHL, a threat that is below that threshold or that is remote or only a potential threat would militate for a response governed by IHRL.[84]

B. Active Combat vs. Non-Combat Area

The relative application of IHRL and IHL should depend on the context in which force is used. If force is to be used in an active combat area where conflict is already ongoing, the overlapping provisions of IHRL and IHL, such as the rights to life and liberty, are more justifiably interpreted and applied in standard IHL

[81] *Nuclear Weapons Case*, *supra* note 35, at § 97.

[82] United Nations, Charter of the United Nations (Oct. 24, 1945), art. 51.

[83] As to the threshold of intensity that an attack by a non-state actor must reach for it to constitute an armed attack, the United Kingdom has stated that it would be the same threshold of violence that would make an attack perpetrated by a state count as an armed attack. Joint Report October 2016, *supra* note 4, at 5. The ICJ, in the *Nicaragua* case, suggested that only those uses of force that, in their "scale and effects," constituted the "most grave forms of the use of force" would count as armed attacks. *Case Concerning Military and Paramilitary Activities In and Against Nicaragua* (Nicaragua v. United States) [1986] ICJ Rep. 14, §§ 195, 191. *See also* the *Case Concerning Oil Platforms* (Iran v. US) [2003] ICJ Rep. 161, §51. The United States is an outlier among nations in having long held that "the inherent right of self-defense potentially applies against *any* illegal use of force." Harold Koh, *International Law in Cyberspace*, 54 Harv. Int'l L.J. Online 7 (Dec. 2012) (emphasis in original). *See also* US DoD, *Law of War Manual*, supra note 12, at § 1.11.5.2.

[84] *See, e.g.*, McCann and Others v. the United Kingdom, where the United Kingdom acknowledged that its soldiers were bound by IHRL during a counterterrorism operation in Gibraltar.

terms. This is true for several reasons: (1) IHL is the universally accepted law for the regulation of active combat;[85] (2) IHL was developed specifically for areas of active combat; (3) there is a greater likelihood that combatants and civilians will be separate from one another in active combat areas, thus enabling greater civilian protection; and (4) in areas of active combat, civilians and combatants are already on general notice of the dangers of hostilities.

IHRL restrictions on the use of force can readily give way in active combat areas in part because IHL is the established and universally accepted[86] body of law for regulating the use of force in situations of active combat. The nations of the world have accepted that war is an exceptional circumstance and have developed a special set of rules for that unique context. This is seen perhaps most clearly if we consider the rule of distinction that requires attacks to be aimed only at military objectives.[87] Distinction was designed to protect civilians against the effects of hostilities and is universally considered to be satisfied as long as a commander *intends* to target a military objective, such as enemy combatants or a weapons depot.[88] The effectiveness of distinction as a rule to protect civilians from harm depends, however, on the assumption that civilians and combatants will be generally separate and distinguishable from one another. For if civilians and combatants are thoroughly intermingled, such as in a crowded marketplace,[89] a rule requiring commanders merely to intend to target combatants will do nothing at all to protect civilians. In classic areas of active combat, it could be generally assumed that civilians and combatants would be separate from one another and civilian presence, if any, would be limited and incidental. In such a context, the common understanding of distinction is both sensible and an effective way to protect civilians from attack. However, in contemporary asymmetrical warfare, and particularly in areas outside of active hostilities, there can be no presumption that civilians and combatants will be either separate or

[85] *See, e.g.*, Hassan v. United Kingdom [2014] ECHR 9936, para. 104, where the ECtHR is willing to apply the ECHR Article 5 right to liberty in terms of IHL "only . . . in cases of international armed conflict, where the taking of prisoners of war and the detention of civilians who pose a threat to security are accepted features of international humanitarian law."

[86] All UN member and observer states are parties to the four Geneva Conventions of 1949. The First and Second Additional Protocols to the 1949 Geneva Conventions have been ratified by 174 and 168 states, respectively.

[87] Protocol Additional (I) to the Geneva Convention of 12 August 1949, and relating to the Protection of Victims of International Armed Conflicts (AP I), June 8, 1977, art. 48.

[88] I examine the rule of distinction at length and argue that it should be reformulated for the use of military force outside active hostilities in Joshua Andresen, *Putting Lethal Force on the Table: How Drones Change of the Alternative Space of War and Counterterrorism*, 8 Harv. Nat'l Sec. J. 454–60, 463–67 (2017).

[89] *See, e.g.*, Human Rights Watch, "Yemen: US Bombs Used in Deadliest Market Strike," Apr. 7, 2016, https://www.hrw.org/news/2016/04/07/yemen-us-bombs-used-deadliest-market-strike (Saudi Arabia–led coalition airstrikes on a crowded market in the village of Mastaba in northwestern Yemen on March 15, 2016, killed at least ninety-seven civilians, including twenty-five children. The two strikes are thought to have also killed about ten Houthi fighters.).

distinguishable from one another. In fact, as we see in many counterterrorism operations resulting in civilian casualties, the opposite is likely to be the case.[90] It is thus reasonably clear that distinction was developed for active war zones, but has little applicability to the use of military force away from active war zones where civilians and combatants will be intermingled. This is one illustration of how, outside of active combat areas, IHL does not serve as a satisfactory substitute for IHRL. Outside active combat areas where civilians and combatants are more likely to be intermingled, IHRL restrictions on the use of force are needed to maintain the protected status of civilians and should not give way to IHL in those areas.

Finally, when force is used within an active combat area, any civilians present are already on general notice of the dangers of remaining in the area. When combat is already ongoing, it is also more feasible to warn civilians before specific attacks. The general notice and specific warnings give civilians the chance, at least in principle, to evacuate the combat area and take cover elsewhere. By contrast, when lethal military force is deployed in non-combat areas there is no general notice of the dangers of war to put civilians on alert. Moreover, because surprise is often indispensable to the effective use of military force outside active combat areas, civilians will also not receive a specific warning of attack.[91] Because civilians will neither have the chance to flee or take cover when military force is deployed outside active war zones, the IHL baseline presumption of civilian protections is not realized. As a result, more restrictive IHRL rules are appropriate, not to give civilians extra protections than they would enjoy in combat areas, but simply to maintain the minimal level of civilian protection in armed conflict that depends on the possibility of civilians removing themselves from harm's way.

C. Are Civilians Absent or Distinguishable?

The presence or absence of civilians from the battlespace and the ability of targeting forces to readily distinguish them from combatants and avoid unintended casualties are additional variables to consider. As section II of this chapter demonstrated, airstrikes and civilian casualties serve to bolster terrorist violence, recruitment, and popular support. As a result, the presence of civilians in a

[90] *See, e.g.*, Eric Schmitt & David Sanger, *Raid in Yemen: Risky from the Start, Costly in the End*, N.Y. Times, Feb.1, 2017, https://.nytimes.com/2017/02/01/world/middleeast/donald-trump-yemen-commando-raid-questions.html; George & Karam, *supra* note 13.

[91] Article 57(2)(c) of AP I, *supra* note 87, imposes the conditional requirement that "effective advance warning shall be given of attacks which may affect the civilian population, *unless circumstances do not permit*." (emphasis added).

targeting area should lead an attacking force to impose restrictions on the use of force that go beyond the requirements of IHL. The negative secondary effects of increased terrorist violence and recruitment go beyond the "concrete and direct" effects of an attack that *jus in bello* proportionality requires an attacking force to consider.[92] Thus IHRL's requirement of "absolute necessity" for the use of lethal force should be used in order to restrict the use of force in civilian populated areas to those that have a military advantage that directly saves lives. By contrast, in contexts where there is no civilian presence, or where adequate precautions can be taken to avoid harming a readily distinguishable civilian presence, IHRL restrictions on the use of force can be read in terms of IHL.

D. The Heat of Battle

As seen in the High Court's judgment in *Al-Saadoon*, it is commonly and sensibly thought that the less restrictive rules of IHL should take precedence when soldiers are engaged in the heat of battle. When soldiers are themselves under fire and must make life-or-death decisions for themselves and others, they should have greater discretion to use force both in self-defense and to eliminate threats. The same is true of commanders directing air support to protect their troops under fire. In the heat of battle, soldiers are under an immediate threat and must react under tremendous time pressure, often spontaneously formulating their response to the threat and circumstances in which they happen to find themselves. In such circumstances it is reasonable to apply IHRL obligations through the lens of IHL. By contrast, when military personnel preplan attacks from the relative calm of a command center, they are under no immediate threat, time pressures are far more relaxed, and operations can be carried out with considerable planning. When attacks are commanded far from the heat of battle, we should expect a lower tolerance for civilian casualties and a greater ability to use military force while respecting IHRL obligations. As a result, in such circumstances it is reasonable to expect greater application of IHRL.

E. Does the State Exercise Effective Control?

The effective control of a state, for example, over an area that it occupies militarily, is relevant to whether it should be bound by IHRL obligations. By

[92] Article 51(5)(b) of AP I, *supra* note 87, prohibits "an attack which may be expected to cause incidental loss of civilian life, injury to civilians, damage to civilian objects, or a combination thereof, which would be excessive in relation to the concrete and direct military advantage anticipated."

assuming effective control over an area of foreign territory, a state thereby takes responsibility for the treatment and security of the inhabitants of that area. While there is certainly a range of conditions under which a state might exercise effective control, it generally entails the jurisdiction of an occupying power and thus IHRL obligations. Where, for example, effective control is long-standing and essentially equivalent to domestic peacetime control, IHRL obligations should be applied fully. By contrast, IHRL will be less applicable immediately following hostilities, where a state exercises diminished control over occupied foreign territory within which a portion of the local population may seek to violently undermine the newly emerging or recently established order. The same would be true of peace enforcement missions that have a mandate to maintain order over a volatile region subject to constant threats.[93] Given the range of effective control that a state may have in foreign territory, we can say that the relative applicability of IHL and IHRL should track the actual level of stability and control enjoyed by the occupying state. The more ordered the territory and more clearly hostilities have actually come to a close, the greater the application of IHRL rules should be. However, should the occupation resemble a state of rebellion bordering on collapse back into full-scale war, the occupying power will be less capable of fulfilling IHRL obligations, and thus more martial law may need to substitute for IHRL.

F. A State's Authority and Control over Persons

A distinct criterion from effective control is the authority or control that a state has over individuals when it uses military force. Consistent with the jurisprudence of the ECtHR we have reviewed earlier, if a state is exercising exclusive authority and control over a person, for example, by taking the person into custody or processing her through a military checkpoint, then the state will have a greater duty to respect IHRL obligations. This is true both because the state is exercising a public security function that would normally be exercised by the local authority and because, in such circumstances, the state has exclusive power over the individuals, thus leaving the well-being of those persons in the hands of the controlling state alone. As we saw in the *Andreou* and *Al-Saadoon* cases discussed earlier, the same principles can be extended to circumstances in which states exercise control over individuals through the use of lethal force without

[93] For example, the ICRC maintains that an international armed conflict should not be considered to have come to an end in the absence of "a degree of stability and permanence" in the actual cessation of hostilities. ICRC, Commentary on the First Geneva Convention: Convention (I) for the Amelioration of the Condition of the Wounded and Sick in Armed Forces in the Field 277 (2d ed. 2016).

taking those individuals into custody or even establishing a formal point of authority such as a military checkpoint. For instance, when a state justifies extraterritorial counterterrorism operations on the basis that the local authority is unable or unwilling to deal with the threat, the intervening state asserts a public security function and authority. It also asserts, at least for the time of its operation, that it is the exclusive authority over the persons to whom it subjects lethal military force. Because of the total and exclusive power exercised over individuals while performing a public security function, the state incurs responsibility to respect those individuals' human rights as governed by IHRL. By contrast, where a state lacks exclusive authority and control over individuals, it will not be in a position to fully implement or respect IHRL obligations. Paradigm cases of such situations are conditions of active conflict, which are defined by a lack of exclusive authority and control over enemy combatants and foreign civilians. In such contexts, the state's IHRL obligations should be applied in terms of IHL.

G. How Reliable Is the Information Supporting the Use of Force?

Finally, the reliability of the information on which the use of force is predicated bears directly on whether IHL or IHRL is applicable, with higher degrees of information uncertainty generally calling for greater application of IHRL. For example, when the information that forms the basis of an attack is less reliable because it is a partial mosaic of various intelligence sources, there will be less certainty of who and where the enemy is, increasing chances of accidental civilian casualties, and consequently a greater need for caution before resorting to lethal military force. As has been recently publicized, coalition airstrikes in Iraq and Syria have led to significant civilian casualties as a result of mistaken or old intelligence.[94] Thus, when there is an inability to corroborate intelligence information, or when the information is potentially outdated in relation to changing conditions on the ground, IHL's relatively permissive requirement that precautions in attack must be taken only to the extent that they are "feasible" may not be sufficient to curtail the misuse of force. Instead, IHRL's requirement of absolute necessity should control any strike that might kill innocent civilians. By contrast, when the information supporting a strike is highly reliable, because it is corroborated by several sources, including sources on the ground and in real time, there is more precise knowledge of who and where the enemy is located, less chance of accidental civilian casualties, and, all things being equal, less need

94 Azmat Khan & Anand Gopal, *The Uncounted*, N.Y. Times, Nov. 16, 2017, https://www.nytimes.com/interactive/2017/11/16/magazine/uncounted-civilian-casualties-iraq-airstrikes.html.

for rules more restrictive than IHL obligations. The reality of counterterrorism operations today, however, often involves significant informational uncertainly and thus a greater need to apply IHRL constraints to the use of force.

H. Applying the Criteria

Before considering how these criteria apply to actual counterterrorism operations, it is worth considering what is at stake in the distinction between IHL and IHRL. The considerations of areas of active combat and the heat-of-battle scenario assume that a conflict is already under way and that soldiers responding to life and death situations must do so in accordance with core IHL rules of necessity, distinction, proportionality, and precaution in attack. Thus, the heat-of-battle scenario is already close to satisfying an IHRL threat assessment for the use of force. By assumption, the use of force is absolutely necessary for self- and other defense, and nothing less than lethal force will be sufficient to avert the threat. Where IHL status–based rules are more permissive, however, is with respect to how much force may be used and how much civilian death and injury and damage to civilian objects are thought to be justifiable.

Contrary to what is allowed under IHRL, under IHL more force than is necessary to avert the threat at hand may be deployed. Soldiers under fire may not only incapacitate the enemy firing at them but also the enemy's co-combatants. Soldiers under fire may also call in airstrikes to destroy the enemy's weapons cache or cut off supply lines. All force that has a military advantage and is aimed at military objectives, whether or not those objectives are threatening or being used at the moment, is fair game. By contrast, under the usual understanding of IHRL in a law enforcement scenario, the use of force is limited to what is necessary to avert the threat at hand and must be aimed only at those actually posing the threat. Lethal force cannot be used in anticipation of possible future threats, nor against nonthreatening associates.

In addition to the important differences between the magnitude and scope of force allowed under IHL and IHRL, the contrast in justifiable civilian, or innocent bystander, death also sets IHL starkly apart from IHRL. When IHL proportionality is applied, anticipated civilian death and injury, and damage to civilian objects is justifiable as long as it is not "excessive" in relation to the anticipated concrete and direct military advantage of the attack.[95] Despite the lack of a precise way of comparing civilian death to military advantage,[96] suffice it to say

[95] AP I, *supra* note 87, at art. 51(5)(b).

[96] For a thorough discussion of how to balance civilian casualties against military advantage, *see*, Joshua Andresen, *Challenging the Perplexity over Jus in Bello Proportionality*, 7 EUR. J. LEGAL STUD. 19 (2014).

that IHL proportionality contemplates and permits significant civilian death as long as a legitimate military objective is being pursued.[97] By contrast, IHRL only allows as much force as is absolutely necessary to avert an immediate threat and generally does not contemplate or permit the death of innocent bystanders. New York City, for instance, specifically forbids police officers from using force that unnecessarily endangers innocent bystanders.[98] Such a rule would be subject to the standard criminal law necessity defense, which holds that force can be used that causes harm only if it is necessary to avoid a much greater harm.[99] The IHRL standard of justifiable civilian casualties thus essentially inverts the IHL standard. Whereas IHL will tolerate more harm to civilians than the expected positive outcome as long as it is not "excessive," IHRL requires significantly greater harm averted than harm inflicted.[100] In sum, a determination that IHL applies to a use of military force will mean that far more destruction and civilian deaths will be tolerated than if IHRL is applied to the same situation.

We are now in a position to consider how these criteria would apply to a range of scenarios from active combat, to military occupation, to a targeted strike away from active hostilities. In a situation of active combat, such as the Iraqi ground campaign to recapture Mosul, we can assume heat-of-battle conditions, no effective control over the area, no authority or control over individuals, and at least some reliable direct evidence of who the enemy is and where it is located. We can also assume that the gravity of the threat posed by occupation of sovereign territory by a terrorist group is very high. Under such circumstances, we would normally expect that IHRL rights to life and liberty would be applied in terms of IHL rules pertaining to the use of force and detention. The presence of hundreds of thousands of civilians in a large city like Mosul, many of whom are trapped and possibly being used as human shields, tips the scales back toward a consideration of IHRL, however. Normally a situation of active combat militates for the application of IHL because civilian presence in active combat areas is presumed to be limited and incidental. Here, however, the opposite is the case. A situation like

[97] *See, e.g.*, Germany, Federal Court of Justice, the Federal Prosecutor General, *Fuel Tankers* case, Decision, Apr. 16, 2010; and Final Report to the Prosecutor by the Committee Established to Review the NATO Bombing Campaign Against the Federal Republic of Yugoslavia.

[98] Johnson v. City of New York, 942 N.E. 2d 219, 221–22 (N.Y. 2010) ("Police officers shall not discharge their weapons when doing so will unnecessarily endanger innocent persons.").

[99] *See, e.g.*, Judith Jarvis Thomson, *Self-Defense*, 20 PHIL. & PUB. AFF. 309 (1991); JEFF MCMAHAN, KILLING IN WAR 114 (2009); Jonathan Quong, *Killing in Self-Defense*, 119 ETHICS 528 (2009); Seth Lazar, *Associative Duties and the Ethics of Killing in War*, 1 J. PRACTICAL ETHICS 19–20 (2013). While the necessity defense is generally not available for intentionally killing an innocent bystander, we might imagine that an exceedingly rare "ticking time bomb" scenario could be a good candidate for the necessity defense.

[100] *Cf.* Justice Aharon Barak's discussion of the necessity defense as a possible justification for torture in extraordinary circumstances. HCJ 5100/94 Public Committee against Torture v. State of Israel [1999] IsrSC 53(4), 817.

Mosul calls into question the effectiveness of IHL rules in protecting civilians from the harms of war and a more restrictive approximation of IHRL rules may be required. Limited real-time intelligence on the enemy's location and changing conditions on the ground poses additional difficulties for the accurate use of air power in such contexts and again militates in favor of tighter IHRL restrictions. It is worth noting that militaries routinely impose additional restrictions on IHL for given battlefield conditions through rules of engagement (ROE). While ROE are a policy imposition rather than evidence of a legal obligation, I am arguing that a legal analysis of a battlespace like Mosul should require more restrictive uses of force as a legal obligation flowing from the applicability of IHRL to combat operations and the insufficiency of IHL to serve its civilian-protecting purpose in such contexts.

An intermediary example would be a situation of military occupation immediately following the cessation of major combat operations, such as the situation in Iraq for allied forces beginning in May 2003. Applying the criteria put forward in this chapter, there would no longer be a situation of active combat and the occupying power would now have effective control over the territory. These two factors would tend to militate in favor of finding the applicability of IHRL obligations over and above IHL restrictions and obligations. However, as was the case in Iraq in the summer of 2003, a situation of armed occupation immediately following combat operations is likely to be highly volatile. Troops on patrol may routinely find themselves subject to attack and back in the heat of battle. Their military presence at checkpoints may be a form of authority and control over the individuals they encounter, but they may otherwise have little or no authority or control over the population generally. These factors militate in favor of reducing the application of IHRL in favor of IHL. Finally, the information available to the occupying force is likely to be far from complete or fully reliable, which will tend to speak for the need to apply IHRL precautions over and above IHL. The range of circumstances that present themselves in conditions of military occupation means that a precise determination of the relative application of IHL and IHRL will have to be made by looking at the specific conditions of each case. To take just two examples, where occupying forces find themselves in an ambush, they will be thrust back into the heat of battle requiring the greater degree of discretion allowed by IHL. Where, however, the occupying force is maintaining a detention facility after the cessation of hostilities, IHRL obligations vis-à-vis the detainees should be fully applied in addition to applicable IHL obligations.

Finally, we can consider the case of a remotely targeted strike away from active combat areas. Here most of the criteria militate for the greater application of IHRL: there is no active combat; those launching the attack are free from an immediate threat of harm; the attack will be launched on the basis of intelligence information that is necessarily incomplete and probabilistic in nature; and following the reasoning of the ECtHR in *Andreou* and the High Court in *Al-Saadoon*, the state contemplating the use of lethal force exercises exclusive authority and control over all those who will be directly affected by the strike, including civilians. We can also assume, for the sake of this example, that the threat triggering the military response either has a sufficient nexus to an ongoing armed conflict, or rises to the level of an armed attack that is "imminent," though perhaps not immediate. The one factor that militates against the full application of IHRL is the state's lack of effective control over the area of attack. If we assume that the lack of effective control is an indication that capture is not feasible under the circumstances, that may be a reason to believe that the use of lethal force against the target is justified. An attacking force would need more information, however, to be able to justify the killing of innocent bystanders. Given the balance of factors we have considered that speaks for the application of IHRL, it would be exceedingly difficult to justify killing the innocent bystanders in the absence of an immediate threat. If the situation presented were reasonably deemed to be a unique opportunity to eliminate an imminent threat of grave harm, the attack might be justified. However, even then the attack could be justified only if it were necessary to avoid a much greater harm than that which would be inflicted on the innocent bystanders. In situations outside of the heat of battle, where there is no direct threat and counter measures are not immediately necessary, we should expect a greater application of IHRL and a lower tolerance for innocent bystander casualties.

The approach I have proposed for determining the relative application of IHRL and IHL to uses of military force is a distinct departure from the usual terms of the debate between those who argue for a more permissive or a more restrictive approach to the use of force. As we have seen, several states hold that IHL necessarily applies to all military activity, while many commentators hold that IHL can only apply to force used within an armed conflict. Both sides of the debate also typically argue that international law in general, and IHL in particular, are sufficient as they now stand to adequately regulate the use of force. In contrast to both of these views, this chapter advocates a mixed application of IHL and IHRL to a range of contexts through a legal consideration of the criteria articulated here. I will now turn to examining why the current debate around the application of IHL to uses of military force has broken down and show how the discussion can be shifted onto the more productive ground of applying IHL and IHRL to actual circumstances. Only by doing so will we establish legal rules that both maintain civilian protections in war and serve our security interests.

V. Changing the Terms of the Debate

The debate over the application of IHL and IHRL to armed conflict has broken down in two primary places: the use of military force in self-defense against non-state actors and the geographical reach of IHL in the context of non-international armed conflicts (NIACs). An increasingly recognized right to use force in self-defense against non-state actors has emerged since the September 11, 2001 terrorist attacks in the United States. However, the pronouncement of a "global war on terror" in which military force could be used against any terrorist threat anywhere in the world has prompted many commentators to try to rein in the unbridled use of force by emphasizing the limited applicability of IHL to already existing armed conflicts. Despite IHL's limited scope of application, emphasizing it has not been an entirely effective strategy in restricting the use of military force. The United States, for example, has long insisted that it is in a NIAC with both those responsible for the September 11 attacks and their "associated forces." At the same time, the threat posed by non-state actors has prompted states to read the application of IHL in NIACs as broadly as possibly in order to facilitate counterterrorism operations. I submit that a significant cause of the impasse between those who would like to restrict and those who would like to extend the application of IHL lies in a failure to distinguish IHL *permissions* from IHL *restrictions* and *obligations*, particularly when applying the jurisprudence of ad hoc international criminal tribunals. Distinguishing between the restrictive and permissive aspects of IHL not only helps us resolve the impasses over uses of force in self-defense and the geographical scope of IHL. It also enables us to see how both IHL and IHRL need be applied across a range of contexts in which force is used.

Among commentators on IHL, there is near universal agreement that "IHL applies only where there is a situation of either international or non-international armed conflict."[101] While an international armed conflict exists whenever states resort to armed force in their dealings with one another, a non-international armed conflict (NIAC) is subject to more restrictive criteria. The most common reference for the necessary criteria of a NIAC comes from the International Criminal Tribunal for the former Yugoslavia's (ICTY) *Tadić* case. There the ICTY found that there must be "protracted armed violence between governmental authorities and organized armed groups or between such groups" for a NIAC to exist.[102] If we take the *Tadić* criteria of "the intensity of the conflict and the organisation of the parties to the conflict"[103] at face value, it would appear that

[101] Heyns et al., *supra* note 3, at 805.

[102] Prosecutor v. Tadić (Decision on the Defence Motion for Interlocutory Appeal on Jurisdiction) ICTY-94-1 (Oct. 2, 1995), § 70.

[103] Prosecutor v. Tadić (Trial Judgment) IT-94-1-T (May 7, 1997), § 562.

IHL would never apply to first strikes in NIACs. For example, notwithstanding all of their insightful analysis, when Lubell and Derejko consider a case in which a "drone strike is taking place against the military leadership of armed group X who are directing their operations via satellite radio" far from an active battlefield, they argue that for IHL to apply to the strike, "it would need to be concluded that the drone strike occurred within the context of an armed conflict."[104] If no armed conflict already exists, Lubell and Derejko conclude that "IHL will not apply, and the only remaining framework for regulating force will be that of law enforcement as found in international human rights law."[105] However, the inference from the nonexistence of an armed conflict to the non-applicability of IHL is too fast. There is at least one clear instance when IHL would govern the response, that is, when the state acts in self-defense before an armed attack that is determined to be imminent.[106] Although such cases of legitimate self-defense may be rare, to rule them out completely would be to claim either that states may not act in self-defense against imminent attacks by non-state actors, or that IHL simply does not apply to first strikes in armed conflict. However, the UN Security Council is widely understood to have recognized a right to self-defense against non-state actors following the September 11, 2001 attacks in UN Security Council Resolutions 1368 and 1373.[107] Increasing state practice, certainly by the United States, the United Kingdom, and coalition states, also supports the view that there is such a right. As for the proposition that IHL does control first strikes in armed conflict, not only does the state practice and manuals of major militaries support it,[108] the *Nuclear Weapons Case* examined earlier explicitly supports the proposition.[109] The International Law Commission also clearly indicates that IHL obligations apply to the use of force by states in self-defense.[110] To claim then that military action in self-defense against non-state actors outside the context of an already existing armed conflict is necessarily controlled only by IHRL rather than IHL faces substantial legal hurdles, not to mention extraordinary political pressure in states that increasingly face terrorist attacks. A more balanced approach would recognize that IHL *restrictions* do indeed

[104] Lubell & Derejko, *supra* note 3, at 80. The hypothetical scenario is set on a ship on the high seas in order to avoid sovereignty issues under *jus ad bellum*.

[105] Lubell & Derejko, *supra* note 3, at 87. *See also* Dehn & Heller, *supra* note 3, at 183.

[106] On the threshold of intensity that an attack by a non-state actor must reach for it to constitute an armed attack, *see supra* note 83.

[107] A right to self-defense against non-state actors also appears to be confirmed by the ICJ in the *Wall Case*, at least with respect to threats that emanate from territory not under the control of the threatened state. *See* the *Wall Case*, *supra* note 42, at §§ 138–139.

[108] *See, e.g.*, U.S. Air Force, *Targeting*, Air Force Doctrine Doc. 3-60, at 88.

[109] *Nuclear Weapons Case* (n 35) §§ 95–97.

[110] International Law Commission, "Commentary to art 21, Articles on Responsibility of States for Wrongful Acts," UNYBILC vol. II (2001), Pt. Two. ("As to obligations under international humanitarian law and in relation to non-derogable human rights provisions, self-defence does not preclude the wrongfulness of conduct.").

apply to military force used in self-defense against non-state actors even outside the context of an already existing armed conflict.[111] However, a recognition of IHL restrictions should be accompanied by an analysis of the criteria discussed earlier in order to determine the extent to which IHRL should impose further restrictions on the use of force.

Permissive arguments for the application of IHL to the use of force against non-state actors also suffer from a failure to distinguish IHL restrictions from IHL permissions. We have seen that it is untenable to reject out of hand the possibility that IHL could control at least some strikes in self-defense against non-state actors outside an already existing armed conflict. It is equally untenable to hold that IHL necessarily controls all uses of military force throughout the entire territory of any state involved in a NIAC. For example, with respect to the NIACs in Yemen and Afghanistan, Michael Schmitt maintains, "[a]ny operations therein would accordingly be governed by IHL, even if hostilities did not regularly occur there."[112] Without some further limiting principle, this proposition has absurd consequences for countries the size of Yemen, and more so for very large countries like the United States, Russia, or Canada. Even if we follow the ICTY, as Schmitt does, and further limit the applicable sphere of IHL to actions "closely related to the hostilities occurring in other parts of the territories controlled by the parties to the conflict,"[113] that still does not go far enough. For such a limiting principle would still be too expansive with respect to IHL *permissions*. It would imply that wartime rules of engagement and greatly diminished civilian protections would prevail even in peaceful areas where civilian institutions were still functioning. However, as far back as the US Civil War, the landmark case of *Ex parte Milligan* flatly contradicts the proposition that the law of war necessarily governs all acts related to a conflict simply because there is conflict ongoing in some other part of its territory.[114] To the extent that areas are not affected by hostilities, or peacetime institutions, such as police and courts, continue to function, IHRL law enforcement rules should govern. Indeed, with respect to the hostilities in Syria in 2012, the International Committee of the Red Cross (ICRC) specifically stated that "measures taken outside the areas affected by hostilities,

[111] On this understanding, the military force used in self-defense would prompt the beginning of a new armed conflict with the non-state actor.

[112] Michael Schmitt, *Charting the Legal Geography of Non-International Armed Conflict*, 90 INT'L L. STUD. 11 (2014).

[113] *Tadić*, Decision on the Defence Motion for Interlocutory Appeal on Jurisdiction, *supra* note 102, at § 70. It is noteworthy that the ICTY develops the "nexus" condition as part of its jurisdictional analysis over the war crimes in question, i.e., violations of IHL restrictions and obligations, not with respect IHL permissions. Schmitt endorses this condition, but reads it to apply equally to permissions, e.g., with respect to targeting. *See* Schmitt's discussion of the rules applicable to targeting a Danish soldier in Copenhagen and a member of the Taliban in Turkmenistan, Schmitt, *supra* note 112, at 16.

[114] *Ex parte Milligan*, 71 U.S. 2, 4 (1866).

including those against demonstrations with the purpose of restoring law and order, 'must respect international law and standards governing the use of force in law enforcement operations.'"[115] Thus we should think twice when authors boldly pronounce that "it is . . . well-settled that IHL applies throughout the territory of parties to a NIAC irrespective of where the hostilities are underway (or likely to occur)."[116] While it is sensible to follow the ICTY's more expansive application of IHL restrictions and obligations,[117] that does not imply that IHL permissions govern on an equally expansive basis. Following the ICRC's position on Syria in 2012, where there have been no protracted hostilities, IHRL should govern uses of force in those areas.

Simply determining whether an armed conflict exists is insufficient to establish what law should govern responses to terrorist threats. More importantly, such a determination does not tell us how the circumstances on the ground where the response is contemplated should inform the application of law to the use of force. An analysis of whether an armed conflict exists and if proposed targets have a sufficient nexus to that conflict or are posing an imminent threat of armed attack is, of course, necessary to justifying a use of military force, particularly if force is used far from any apparent conflict. A determination of whether a target is a legitimate military objective is, however, just the first step in determining what kind of force may be used in the circumstances ruling at the time. In addition to determining the legitimacy of applying IHL to target, it is necessary to consider the circumstances in which force will be used by applying the criteria introduced earlier. When the use of force is contemplated far from the heat of battle, under conditions of considerable information uncertainty, and with a significant impact on civilians, the context will dictate a greater application of IHRL to the use of force. When, however, a decision must be made in the heat of active battle, the context will dictate a very limited application of IHRL. Figures 4.1 and 4.2 at the end of this chapter give a simplified outline of both how targeting decisions should be made and, once the legitimacy of a target has been determined, how the appropriate rules governing the use of force should be applied.

VI. Conclusion

The evidence shows that the use of military force in counterterrorism operations has had negative repercussions on the United States' peace and security. Fighting

[115] Lubell & Derejko, *supra* note 3, at 73, citing ICRC Operational Update, "Syria: ICRC and Syrian Arab Red Crescent maintain aid effort amid increasing fighting," July 17, 2012.

[116] Schmitt, *supra* note 112, at 15.

[117] For even if military personnel are only permitted to use force under the tighter constraints of IHRL, they could still violate IHL constraints and be justly prosecuted for doing so.

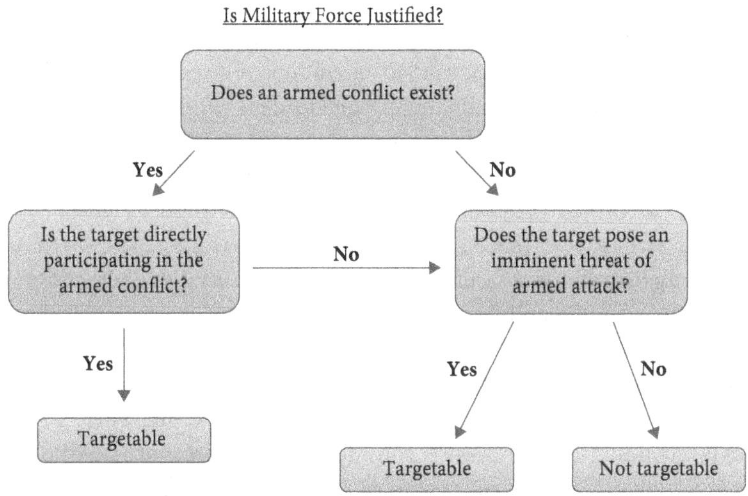

Figure 4.1 Is Military Force Justified?

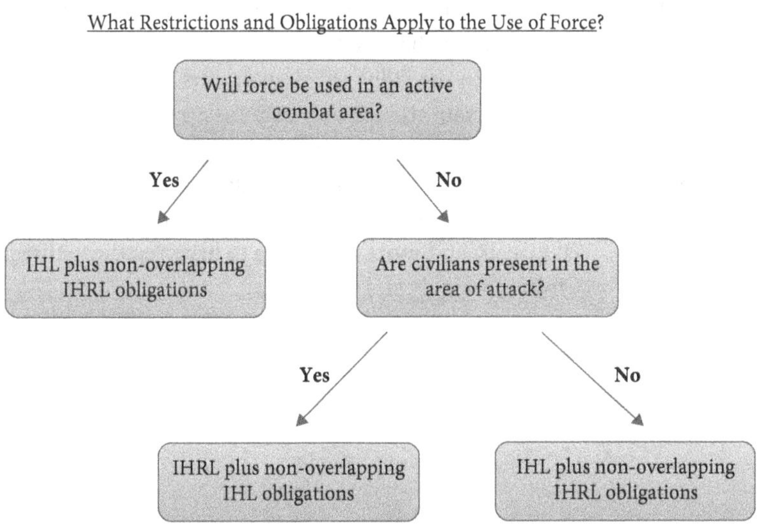

Figure 4.2 What Restrictions and Obligations Apply to the Use of Force?

ISIS, a group that has held and governed territory, may warrant and require a different approach than the fight against a more dispersed group like Al Qaeda that organizes and conducts operations from much smaller safe havens. It appears, however, that the model presented by ISIS is both exceptional and fleeting. As ISIS continues to be driven out of territory in Iraq and Syria it is expected that they will revert to the operational strategy of groups like Al Qaeda.[118] We can then anticipate that counterterrorism operations will continue to take place against limited numbers of individuals outside areas of active hostilities. While the United States and its allies have assumed that the use of military force is both required and justified to combat the terrorist threat, the number of terrorist attacks in the United States and Europe actually increased in recent years.[119] Moreover, we have seen that a growing body of empirical data shows that use of air power against terrorists and insurgents works to increase violent responses, while groups like ISIS and Al Qaeda actively exploit airstrikes and civilian casualties to bolster recruitment and local support for their cause.

The question of whether the use of lethal military force is an appropriate and effective response to terrorism is all the more urgent at a time when the United States is redefining areas previously considered outside areas of active hostilities, such as Somalia, as areas of active combat and rolling back the policy constraints placed on the use of military force by the Obama administration.[120] Despite the license to use lethal military force that the United States has assumed in broadening operations, a convincing analysis of the basis for doing so has yet to be delivered. The view that states should be licensed to use lethal military force to combat terrorist threats wherever they are found is neither legally well founded nor an effective approach given the failure of twenty years of combat to deliver peace and security. While certain threats may require an immediate response with lethal military force, in many instances an approach that applies IHRL restrictions on the use of force will be more legally sound and more effective. The framework that I have presented is legally well grounded, capable of responding to immediate terrorist threats, and more conducive to bringing those threats to an end by using force more sparingly and effectively.

[118] *See, e.g.*, Mara Revkin, *Brand Is Important, but ISIS's Territorial Sovereignty Is Integral to ISIS's Brand*, N.Y. Times, Oct. 21, 2016, https://www.nytimes.com/roomfordebate/2016/10/21/does-isis-need-territory-to-survive. Revkin argues "the ISIS 'brand' will survive in some form, even if it loses every square inch of its so-called caliphate." *See also* Eric Schmitt, *As ISIS Loses Land, It Gains Ground in Overseas Terror*, N.Y. Times, July 3, 2016, https://www.nytimes.com/2016/07/04/world/middleeast/isis-terrorism.html.

[119] Margot Sanger-Katz, *Is Terrorism Getting Worse? In the West, Yes. In the World, No*, N.Y. Times, Aug. 16, 2016, https://www.nytimes.com/2016/08/16/upshot/is-terrorism-getting-worse-in-the-west-yes-in-the-world-no.html.

[120] Savage & Schmitt, "Trump Poised to Drop Some Limits," *supra* note 6; Savage & Schmitt, "Trump Eases Combat Rules," *supra* note 6).

5

When Conflict Recurs

Classification of Conflict when Hostilities Break Out Anew

Laurie R. Blank[1]

International tribunals, regional courts, nongovernmental organizations, and scholars have devoted extensive analysis to the question of when armed conflict begins—as a legal matter, that moment marks the beginning of the applicability of the law of armed conflict and the transition from the legal regime applicable in peacetime to the law that governs during wartime. Recently, the question of how to identify the end of conflict, particularly non-international armed conflict, has garnered attention. These questions are essential for determining the application of the law of armed conflict and the concomitant protections for persons and obligations of the parties to the conflict or potential conflict. What happens, however, when a conflict ends or appears to end but then violence and hostilities bubble up again? The complexity of conflict identification and classification and the challenges of understanding and analyzing the facts and actors in such new rounds of violence raise interesting and often difficult questions regarding the appropriate approach in assessing whether such new violence constitutes an armed conflict and when.

Consider the conflict with ISIS in Iraq and Syria. Although it remains unclear at the time of this writing whether the conflict is actually over, notwithstanding statements by the Trump administration that ISIS has been defeated, we can envision a time when there will be a general consensus that the conflict has ended. If, at some point after that time, violence in that area or with the same or similar actors recurs, the question of conflict identification and classification will re-emerge—but this time with the backdrop of the previous conflict and its storyline and actors as a perhaps unavoidable ingredient in any discussion or analysis. For example, one might be quicker to identify the existence of an armed conflict if the same actors—states or armed groups, for example—are involved in

[1] Clinical Professor of Law; Director, Center for International and Comparative Law; Director, International Humanitarian Law Clinic, Emory University School of Law.

Laurie R. Blank, *When Conflict Recurs* In: *Between Crime and War*. Edited by: Claire Finkelstein, Christopher Fuller, Jens David Ohlin, Mitt Regan, Oxford University Press. © Claire Finkelstein, Christopher Fuller, Jens David Ohlin, Mitt Regan 2023. DOI: 10.1093/oso/9780197638798.003.0006

the new round of violence. Whether the legal framework accounts for or allows such a determination or other similar considerations is, however, unclear.

The law of armed conflict (LOAC), otherwise known as international humanitarian law or the law of war, governs the conduct of both states and individuals during armed conflict and seeks to minimize suffering in war by protecting persons not participating in hostilities and by regulating the means and methods of warfare.[2] LOAC applies during all situations of armed conflict, with the full panoply of the Geneva Conventions and customary law applicable in international armed conflict and a more limited body of treaty-based and customary law applicable during non-international armed conflict. The 1949 Geneva Conventions endeavor to address all instances of armed conflict[3] and set forth two primary categories of armed conflict that trigger the application of LOAC: international armed conflict and non-international armed conflict. Common Article 2 of the 1949 Geneva Conventions states that the Conventions "shall apply to all cases of declared war or of any other armed conflict which may arise between two or more of the High Contracting Parties, even if the state of war is not recognized by one of them."[4] Common Article 3 of the 1949 Geneva Conventions sets forth minimum provisions applicable "in the case of armed conflict not of an international character occurring in the territory of one of the High Contracting Parties."[5]

Just as the existence of an armed conflict triggers the application of LOAC to govern the status of persons and the rights and obligations of parties to the

[2] *See* International Committee of the Red Cross, "International Humanitarian Law in Brief," July 2004, http://www.icrc.org/eng/war-and-law/. The law of armed conflict is set forth primarily in the four Geneva Conventions of August 14, 1949, and their Additional Protocols. *See* United Nations, "Protocol Additional to the Geneva Conventions of 12 August 1949 and Relating to the Protection of Victims of International Armed Conflicts (Protocol I), adopted 8 June 1977" (1979) 1125 United States Treaty Series 3; United Nations, "Protocol Additional to the Geneva Conventions of 12 August 1949, and Relating to the Protection of Victims of Non-International Armed Conflicts (Protocol II), adopted 8 June 1977" (1979) 1125 United States Treaty Series 609; "Geneva Convention for the Amelioration of the Condition of the Wounded and Sick in Armed Forces in the Field of August 12, 1949" (1950) 75 United Nations Treaty Series 31; United Nations, "Geneva Convention for the Amelioration of the Condition of Wounded, Sick and Shipwrecked Members of Armed Forces at Sea of August 12, 1949" (1950) 75 United Nations Treaties Series 85; United Nations, "Geneva Convention Relative to the Treatment of Prisoners of War of August 12, 1949" (1950) 75 United Nations Treaty Series 135; United Nations, "Geneva Convention Relative to the Protection of Civilian Persons in Time of War of August 12, 1949" (1950) 75 United Nations Treaty Series 287

[3] Oscar M. Uhler et al., IV Geneva Convention Relative to the Treatment of Prisoners of War: Commentary, vol. 4, at 26 (Roger Griffin & C.W. Dumbleton, trans., 1958). "Born on the battlefield, the Red Cross called into being the First Geneva Convention to protect wounded or sick military personnel. Extending its solicitude little by little over other categories of war victims, in logical application of its fundamental principle, it pointed the way, first to the revision of the original convention, and then to the extension of legal protection in turn to prisoners of war and civilians. The same logical process could not fail to lead to the idea of applying the principle in *all* cases of armed conflicts, including those of an internal character."

[4] *See* Common Article 2 to the four Geneva Conventions, *supra* note 2.

[5] *See* Common Article 3 to the four Geneva Conventions, *supra* note 2.

conflict, the nature of the conflict—whether international or non-international—determines the extent of the applicable law. International armed conflicts are subject to the full panoply of the Geneva Conventions and the customary laws of war.[6] Non-international armed conflicts are subject to the more limited legal regime of Common Article 3 and the steadily growing customary international law applicable in non-international armed conflict, including the principles of military necessity, humanity, distinction, and proportionality.[7]

This chapter analyzes the appropriate analytical tools and thresholds for identifying the existence of and characterizing conflict in the face of a resurgence of hostilities. For conflicts between two states, the threshold for such international armed conflict is quite low, such that it could be hard to envision a quicker identification of armed conflict when violence recurs in the aftermath of an inter-state conflict. However, such scenarios pose challenging questions of whether actions by a proxy group or other entity could constitute an international armed conflict and, if so, whether the threshold or standard for such determination might be easier to satisfy if a recent conflict between the two states forms the backdrop for that analysis. In the context of non-international armed conflicts, one overarching question is whether the now-classical *Tadić* test with the factors of intensity and organization is the right approach in such situations of violence recurring after conflict, or whether some lower threshold or "accelerated analysis" could be more appropriate in these situations. Similarly, the nature of the armed group engaged in the resurgence of hostilities may be consequential, such that the thresholds or framework for hostilities recurring with the same group may not be the same as that for new or reconstituted groups, as well as the location and nature of the conflict. After a brief discussion of the basis for this inquiry and an introduction to the basic legal framework for identification and classification of armed conflict in the first section, the second section explores how the specific

[6] *See* Common Article 2 to the four Geneva Conventions, *supra* note 2. *See also* Geoffrey S. Corn, *What Law Applies to the War on Terror?*, *in* The War on Terror and the Laws of War: A Military Perspective 1, 15 (Michael Lewis et al. eds., Terrorism and Global Justice Series 2009)

[7] *See* Prosecutor v. Tadić, Decision on Defence Motion for Interlocutory Appeal on Jurisdiction (Case No. IT-94-1-T, International Criminal Tribunal for the Former Yugoslavia, Oct. 2, 1995), paras. 100–27, highlighting the development and applicability of necessity, distinction, humanity, and proportionality to internal armed conflict. *See also* Lindsay Moir, The Law of Internal Armed Conflict 133–34 (2002); Geoffrey S. Corn & Eric T. Jensen, *Untying the Gordian Knot*, 81 Temple L. Rev. 787, 788, 827 (2008); Christopher Greenwood, *International Law and the Tadić Decision*, 7 Eur. J. Int'l L. 265, 275–78 (1996). *See* Abella v. Argentina, Report No. 55/97 (Case 11.137, Inter-American Commission on Human Rights 1997), paras. 176–177; Ian G. Corey, *The Fine Line between Policy and Custom: Prosecutor v. Tadić and the Customary International Law of Internal Armed Conflict*, 166 Military L. Rev. 145 (2000); Anthony Cullen, *Key Developments Affecting the Scope of Internal Armed Conflict in International Humanitarian Law*, 183 Military L. Rev. 66 (2005); William A. Schabas, *Punishment of Non-State Actors in Non-International Armed Conflict*, 26 Fordham Int'l L.J. 907 (2003).

problem of violence recurring after the end of armed conflict poses interesting and challenging questions for the conflict classification schematic.

I. Framing the Problem and the Legal Landscape

A. When Violence Recurs after Conflict

Consider the example of ISIS and renewed violence introduced previously. Or Iraq in 2013 and 2014 as ISIS—generally believed to be a reconstituted Al Qaeda in Iraq[8]—began launching attacks and taking control of cities and territory across much of the country. The conflict in Iraq had ended by 2011 when US forces pulled out at the end of the year. Although it was evident quickly that the situation in 2013-2014 constituted an armed conflict, if the attacks and violence had been more sporadic and scattered, the fact that ISIS was an updated and reformed version of Al Qaeda in Iraq may well have been a relevant factor in assessing whether the situation met the threshold for an armed conflict. In essence, such situations raise the question of whether "we've seen this story before" is a relevant or acceptable ingredient in the conflict classification analysis. Alternatively, consider Libya, where the initial conflict ended[9] and then the resulting instability arguably eventually led to new violence erupting and developing into a conflict.[10] Could the fact of the original conflict and its contribution as a source of the follow-up conflict affect—perhaps "speed up"—the classification of the follow-up violence as an armed conflict?

Although the question of when conflicts, specifically non-international armed conflicts, start has been exhaustively examined in books, articles, blog posts, and more over decades, the specific issue of how to undertake this fundamental analysis in the context of violence recurring after conflict has received little if any attention. And yet resurgence of violence, renewed conflict, and other similar situations are not uncommon—whether the re-emergence of conflict in Libya in 2014 only a few years after the 2011 conflict, or cycles of conflict

[8] *See* transcription of remarks, Benjamin Wittes, *President Obama Addresses the Nation on ISIS*, LAWFARE, Sept. 10, 2014, https://www.lawfareblog.com/president-obama-addresses-nation-isis.

[9] *See, e.g.*, noting the end of the armed conflict, United Nations Human Rights Council, "Report of the International Commission of Inquiry on Libya" (A/HRC/19/68, Mar. 2, 2012), 4

[10] International Committee of the Red Cross, "Libya: Migrants Suffer as Security Remains Poor," Operational Update, Nov. 12, 2013, https://www.icrc.org/en/doc/resources/documents/update/2013/11-12-libya-migrants.htm; International Committee of the Red Cross, "Libya" in *Annual Report* vol. 1 (2013), 164 https://www.icrc.org/en/doc/assets/files/annual-report/icrc-annual-report-2013.pdf; International Committee of the Red Cross, "Libya: Fighting Parties Must Spare the Wounded" (Jan. 28, 2014), https://www.icrc.org/en/doc/resources/documents/news-release/2014/01-28-libya-fighting.htm.

between long-term adversaries, flare-ups of long-simmering grievances thought to be resolved, or new bouts of violence spurred by reformed, reconstituted, or reinspired terrorist or insurgent groups. Classification of conflict is essential to determining the applicable law and therefore to the protections of persons and rights and obligations of warring parties—specifically with regard to the use of force and detention, where the difference between peacetime law and wartime law is literally life and death. As a result, if the nature of a situation is likely to alter how states or other actors will view the classification determination, understanding why and how is an important addition to the overall discussion of when and how conflicts start.

A look at how states commonly view situations of violence either within their own borders or with non-state groups in one or more locations outside their territory is instructive. Before 9/11, states rarely, if ever, acknowledged that they were engaged in a non-international armed conflict. Classifying a situation as a non-international armed conflict could be seen as recognition that the state lacked control over the situation and was not able to resolve the dispute or eliminate the opposition—an admission few if any states would willingly make.[11] Even after 9/11, with the exception of the conflict in Colombia, states rarely openly acknowledge the existence of a non-international armed conflict with an opposition group on their own territory. As discussed later, the classification of armed conflict rests solely on an objective determination of the facts on the ground and not the political statements or other rhetoric of the state or other actors involved.[12] However, one certainly could argue that a state's reluctance or refusal to acknowledge the existence of an armed conflict offers a more protective environment for individuals in the locality of the violence because if the state does not consider the situation an armed conflict, the state would not resort to the authorities available to it under LOAC but instead would—at least theoretically—remain within the parameters of the law enforcement paradigm. In effect, it is possible that states' reluctance to recognize the existence of a non-international armed conflict within their territory could act as some sort of constraint against more robust uses of force by incentivizing states to at least create the appearance of responding within the law enforcement paradigm rather than on a war footing. In many cases, of course, the facts on

[11] For example, the United Kingdom never identified the conflict in Northern Ireland as a non-international armed conflict, either in public statements or in the relevant law applied to the situation, even though the facts of the situation could easily satisfy the threshold for non-international armed conflict at various moments throughout the history of the conflict. *See* Steven Haines, *Northern Ireland 1968–1998*, *in* INTERNATIONAL LAW AND THE CLASSIFICATION OF CONFLICTS 117, 133–36 (Elizabeth Wilmhurst ed., 2012), explaining that although at various times the "hostilities [were] significant above the level that could be described uncontroversially as merely civil disturbances," the UK government "denied this for policy reasons," as well as any other reasons.

[12] Uhler et al., *supra* note 3, at 23. *See also* Al Warafi v. Obama, No. CV 09-2368 (RCL) 2015 WL 4600420 (US District Court, DC July 30, 2015), 1.

the ground do not support this conjecture as states simply fought an armed conflict while denying or failing to acknowledge the existence of such conflict, but the possibility is worth noting nonetheless.

Were similar violence to erupt within a short- or medium-term time frame after a conflict, however, the likelihood that the same state that would have been reluctant to recognize the existence of an armed conflict would exhibit that same hesitation in either word or deed is significantly lower. Apart from the legal analysis that could conceivably support such a change in position, which is the main thrust of this chapter, the starting point for this analysis is that such a change in approach is highly likely factually and as a matter of common sense. If so, then understanding what consequence that change could have for the law is important. One option is that the nature of the post-conflict recurrence of violence is different enough to merit or justify a different legal analysis, in which case understanding why helps to deepen our understanding of the law and how it works in varied and changing circumstances. Alternatively, if the application of conflict classification analysis to the specific facts of post-conflict recurrence of violence do not support a different analysis, it is equally critical to understand how the actions and rhetoric of states in the opposite direction put pressure on the law and what that pressure may mean for the development and implementation of the law going forward.

The possible effects on the legal analysis of conflict classification are also consequential with respect to the types of post-9/11 conflicts and violence in which—unlike the attitude of states regarding internal violence, particularly before 9/11—states have been quick, indeed eager, to identify and characterize situations of violence involving non-state armed groups outside their territory as armed conflict. Doing so has enabled states to harness the permissive authority of LOAC in both the use of force and detention arenas.[13] Here the potential risk posed in situations of violence or conflict emerging after a previous conflict is less likely to be a quicker characterization as conflict, partly because states are already taking that quick step. Rather, the possible risk is that states will simply ignore or whitewash what appeared to be the end of the previous conflict and treat both rounds of violence as one single ongoing conflict, leading to a seemingly endless conflict that begins to merge the conditions of war and peace into a comingled and uncertain mix.[14] The consequences of this uncertainty and ambiguity for the law, and for the protection of persons the law seeks to protect, are significant.

[13] Corn, "What Law Applies," *supra* note 6.

[14] Rosa Brooks, How Everything Became War and the Military Became Everything: Tales from the Pentagon (2017).

B. The Beginning and End of Conflict: Conflict Classification in Brief

Identifying the existence of and classifying the nature of armed conflict is the essential prerequisite to the application of LOAC. The four Geneva Conventions of 1949 eschewed the historical reliance on the notion of "war" as the trigger for the application of the law and created a framework based on an objective analysis of the relevant situation of violence based on the facts on the ground, not the declaration, rhetoric, or views of the parties to the conflict. To that end, the Geneva Conventions seek to address all instances of armed conflict and set forth two primary categories of armed conflict that trigger the application of LOAC: international armed conflict and non-international armed conflict. International armed conflict is conflict between or among two or more states; non-international armed conflict refers to conflicts between a state and one or more non-state armed groups or among such non-state groups. The definition of armed conflict for each type of conflict is not the same, creating different triggers for the application of LOAC. Similarly, the tools for identifying the end of armed conflict are also important for the instant discussion. Analyzing whether recurring violence is a new armed conflict rests, decisively, on a determination that the previous conflict had already ended—otherwise the seemingly recurring violence is, instead, continuing the previous and ongoing conflict and not a new conflict at all.

The definition of and threshold for international armed conflict is set forth in Common Article 2 to the four Geneva Conventions, which states that "the present Convention shall apply to all cases of declared war or of any other armed conflict which may arise between two or more of the High Contracting Parties, even if the state of war is not recognized by one of them."[15] Although Common Article 2 does not specifically define the term "armed conflict," it is understood to apply to any situation in which the armed forces of two states engage with each other. No matter how short-lived or minor, any hostilities between the armed forces of two or more states constitute an international armed conflict, even if one or both states deny the existence of an armed conflict.[16] This threshold for international armed conflict is deliberately set quite low in order to maximize LOAC's protective purposes. The Commentary therefore explains that "it makes no difference how long the conflict lasts, how much slaughter takes place or how numerous are the participating forces; it suffices for the armed forces of one Power to have captured adversaries falling within the scope of Article 4 [of

[15] Geneva Convention I, *supra* note 2, at art. 2; Geneva Convention II, *supra* note 2, at art. 2; Geneva Convention III, *supra* note 2, at art. 2; Geneva Convention IV, *supra* note 2, at art. 2.

[16] Uhler et al., *supra* note 3, at 23, "[e]ven in that event it would not appear that they could, by tacit agreement, prevent the Conventions from applying. It must not be forgotten that the Conventions have been drawn up first and foremost to protect individuals, and not to serve State interests."

the Third Geneva Convention]."[17] Although some argue that the definition of international armed conflict requires some level of intensity to trigger LOAC, thus seeking to distinguish mere "border incidents" or "skirmishes" from armed conflict,[18] neither the treaty language, the Commentary, nor the jurisprudence of the international criminal tribunals supports such an analysis. Such an intensity threshold for international armed conflict would effectively exclude situations where LOAC's protective purposes are in demand, narrowing LOAC's application and ability to fulfill its goals. For example, if two states detain members of each other's armed forces, although no shots are fired, it is an international armed conflict and LOAC applies: the soldiers are in the hands of an adverse party, and the law mandates humane treatment and other protections. Indeed, LOAC "will apply immediately, since no other legal system can provide adequate protection given the clash of two domestic systems."[19]

With regard to the end of international armed conflict, the Geneva Conventions reference the end of international armed conflict with phrases such as "cessation of active hostilities"[20] and "general close of military operations."[21] At the time the conventions were drafted, the "general close of military operations" was considered to be "when the last shot has been fired."[22] This notion of the general close of military operations serves as an objective criterion to determine when the facts on the ground demonstrate that the conflict is over. In particular, clarity with respect to the end of hostilities is important; to that end, the International Criminal Tribunal for the former Yugoslavia (ICTY) emphasized that the central question was "whether at any point . . . the international armed conflict had found a sufficiently general, definitive and effective termination so

[17] *Id.*; *see also* Hans Peter Gasser, *International Humanitarian Law: An Introduction*, *in* HANS HAUG, HUMANITY FOR ALL: THE INTERNATIONAL COMMITTEE OF THE RED CROSS AND RED CRESCENT MOVEMENT 24 (1993), "[a]s soon as the armed forces of one State find themselves with wounded or surrendering members of the armed forces of another State on their hands, as soon as they detain prisoners or have actual control over a part of the territory of the enemy State, then they must comply with the relevant convention."

[18] *See, e.g.*, International Law Association, "Final Report on the Meaning of Armed Conflict in International Law," 3 (2010), https://www.rulac.org/assets/downloads/ILA_report_armed_conflict_2010.pdf.

[19] Andreas Paulus, *Non International Armed Conflict Under Common Article 3*, *in* PROCEEDINGS OF THE BRUGES COLLOQUIUM, ARMED CONFLICTS AND PARTIES TO ARMED CONFLICTS UNDER IHL: CONFRONTING LEGAL CATEGORIES TO CONTEMPORARY REALITIES 30 (No. 40, Autumn 2010).

[20] United Nations, "Geneva Convention Relative to the Treatment of Prisoners of War of August 12, 1949" (1950) 75 United Nations Treaty Series 135, referring to the release and repatriation of prisoners of war.

[21] United Nations, "Convention Relative to the Protection of Civilian Persons in Time of War of August 12, 1949" (1950) 75 United Nations Treaty Series 287, end of application of the Fourth Geneva Convention in the territory of parties to the conflict upon the general close of military operations. *See also* United Nations, "Protocol Additional to the Geneva Conventions of 12 August 1949, and Relating to the Protection of Victims of International Armed Conflicts (Protocol I) . . . Adopted at Geneva on 8 June 1977" (1979) 1125 United Nations Treaty Series 3, 8.

[22] *Final Record of the Diplomatic Conference of Geneva of 1949*, vol. IIa (Federal Political Department, Berne 1963), 815.

as to end the applicability of the law of armed conflict."[23] Traditionally, international armed conflicts ended based on a peace treaty, mutual consent, armistice, capitulation, surrender, or unilateral declaration.[24] However, contemporary conflicts have added another layer of complexity, with peace treaties becoming less common and international armed conflicts more "often characterized by unstable ceasefires, a slow and progressive decrease in intensity, or the intervention of peacekeepers."[25]

In contrast to the clearly stated—if not necessarily clear in practice or interpretation—markers for the beginning and end of international armed conflict, non-international armed conflict remains considerably murkier on both counts. For conflicts between a state and an armed group or between armed groups, i.e., conflicts that do not fall within the definition of international armed conflict, Common Article 3 sets forth a fundamental baseline of protection—prohibition on violence to life, torture, degrading treatment, and arbitrary detention for all persons not taking an active part in hostilities, including those who are *hors de combat*. This extension of LOAC to conflicts that are not between two states was enormously consequential for the application and enforcement of LOAC, as the work of international organizations, nongovernmental organizations, and tribunals has demonstrated over the past several decades. However, recognizing that LOAC does not apply to situations not rising to the level of an armed conflict is equally important. Thus, "not all forms of armed violence are considered as 'armed conflicts' under international humanitarian law."[26] Internal disturbances and tensions—such as riots, looting and "act[s] of banditry"[27]—do not constitute armed conflict and therefore do not trigger the application of LOAC. As a result, identifying the threshold for non-international armed conflict remains an important issue at both the operational level and in the accountability phase: LOAC obligations are triggered by the existence of a conflict, so parties need to have guidance for identifying that trigger; and LOAC violations

[23] Prosecutor v. Gotovina, Judgment (Case No. IT-06-90-T, International Criminal Tribunal for the Former Yugoslavia, July 15, 2011), para. 1694.

[24] *See* UK Ministry of Defence, "The Joint Service Manual of the Law of Armed Conflict" (Joint Service Publication 383, 2004), in particular, sections 10.13–10.32, https://assets.publishing.service.gov.uk/government/uploads/system/uploads/attachment_data/file/27874/JSP3832004Edition.pdf; Yoram Dinstein, *The Initiation, Suspension, and Termination of War*, 75 INT'L L. STUD. 131, 135 (2000); YORAM DINSTEIN, WAR, AGGRESSION AND SELF-DEFENCE 42–50 (5th ed. 2012).

[25] International Committee of the Red Cross, "Commentary of 2016, Article 3: Conflicts Not of an International Character" (2016), para. 276, https://ihl-databases.icrc.org/applic/ihl/ihl.nsf/Comment.xsp?action=openDocument&documentId=59F6CDFA490736C1C1257F7D004BA0EC.

[26] Arne Willy Dahl & Magnus Sandbu, *The Threshold of Armed Conflict*, 45 MILITARY L. & L. OF WAR REV. 369, 370 (2006)

[27] Uhler et al., *supra* note 3, at 36. *See also* International Criminal Court, "Rome Statute of the International Criminal Court" (A/Conf. 183/9, July 17, 1998), arts. 8(2)(d), 8(2)(f); *Tadić*, *supra* note 7, at para. 562.

can only be prosecuted if committed during armed conflict, so accountability will often rest on the existence of a conflict.

Common Article 3 does not provide a definition of or threshold for non-international armed conflict; rather, the drafters settled on a broad approach that would maximize the law's protective function and ability to achieve the underlying humanitarian objectives of Common Article 3. In the absence of a specific definition of armed conflict in the Geneva Conventions, the Appeals Chamber of the ICTY has provided the most common and oft-cited contemporary definition of armed conflict. In *Prosecutor v. Tadić*, the tribunal declared that an armed conflict exists whenever "there is a resort to armed force between States or protracted armed violence between governmental authorities and organized armed groups or between such groups within a State."[28] This definition has not only been the driving factor in the ICTY's jurisprudence, but was also adopted by the drafters of the Rome Statute establishing the International Criminal Court[29] and by the International Criminal Tribunal for Rwanda (ICTR).[30] Expounding on this definition in the merits phase of *Tadić*, the Trial Chamber elaborated on the broad guidelines in the definition above as follows:

> The test applied by the Appeals Chamber to the existence of an armed conflict for the purposes of the rules contained in Common Article 3 focuses on two aspects of a conflict; the intensity of the conflict and the organization of the parties to the conflict. In an armed conflict of an internal or mixed character, these closely related criteria are used solely for the purpose, as a minimum, of distinguishing an armed conflict from banditry, unorganized and short-lived insurrections, or terrorist activities, which are not subject to international humanitarian law.[31]

These two factors—intensity and organization—have over time become the international community's foundational framework for analyzing the existence of non-international armed conflict.[32]

[28] *Tadić*, *supra* note 7, at para. 70. *See also* International Law Association, *supra* note 18, noting that the *Tadić* decision is "widely cited for its description of the characteristics of armed conflict." *See also* Anthony Cullen, *Key Developments Affecting the Scope of Internal Armed Conflict in International Humanitarian Law*, 183 Military L. Rev. 66, 98 (2005).

[29] Rome Statute, *supra* note 27, at art. 8(2)(f), defining non-international armed conflicts as conflicts "that take place in the territory of a State when there is protracted armed conflict between governmental authorities and organized armed groups or between such groups."

[30] *See* Prosecutor v. Akayesu, Judgment (Case No. ICTR-96-4-T, Sept. 2, 1998), paras. 619–20, citing the *Tadić* criteria for determining the existence of an armed conflict.

[31] *Tadić*, *supra* note 7, at para. 562.

[32] *See, e.g.*, International Law Association, *supra* note 18, at 1–2, "[a]t least two characteristics are found with respect to all armed conflict: 1. The existence of organized armed groups; 2. Engaged in fighting of some intensity . . . For non-state actors to move from chaotic violence to being able to challenge the armed forces of a state requires organization, meaning a command structure, training, recruiting ability, communications, and logistical capacity. Such organized forces are only recognized

Although intensity and organization are fact-driven inquiries specific to the circumstances of each situation, the jurisprudence of the international tribunals and the broader discourse among states, international organizations and the advocacy and academic communities have highlighted some key considerations that help demonstrate a sufficient degree of intensity and organization in a particular situation. Information that helps to demonstrate the intensity of the violence, for example, can include "the seriousness of attacks and potential increase in armed clashes, their spread over territory and over a period of time, the increase in the number of government forces, the mobilisation and the distribution of weapons among both parties to the conflict, as well as whether the conflict has attracted the attention of the United Nations Security Council, and if so whether any resolutions on the matter have been passed."[33] With regard to organization, the presence of "some degree of organization"[34] or "a minimum amount of organization"[35] is required to characterize a situation as an armed conflict. More detailed examinations, primarily in cases before the ICTY, have highlighted a range of information about the groups involved in the conflict, such as a hierarchical structure; territorial control and administration; the ability to recruit and train combatants; the ability to launch operations using military tactics; the ability to enter peace or ceasefire agreements; the ability to issue internal regulations; and the ability to coordinate and launch attacks with multiple units.[36]

A formalistic and formulaic application of the intensity and organization factors can undermine effective conflict recognition, as the lengthy process of—and debates about—the nature of the conflict in Syria aptly demonstrated.[37] Nonetheless, the *Tadić* framework offers a useful analytical starting point for

as engaged in armed conflict when fighting between them is more than a minimal engagement or incident."

[33] Prosecutor v. Mrkšić, Judgment (Case No. IT-95-13/1-T, International Criminal Tribunal for the Former Yugoslavia, Sept. 27, 2007), para. 407. *See also* Prosecutor v. Haradinaj, Judgment (Case No. IT-04-84-T, International Criminal Tribunal for the Former Yugoslavia, Apr. 3, 2008), para. 49; Prosecutor v. Limaj, Judgment (Case No. IT-03-66-T, International Criminal Tribunal for the Former Yugoslavia, Nov. 30, 2005), paras. 135–143; *Tadić, supra* note 7, at paras. 564–65.

[34] *Limaj, supra* note 33, at para. 89, referring to a 1999 ICRC Working Paper submitted to the Preparatory Commission for the establishment of the elements of crimes for the International Criminal Court, which stated that armed conflict involves hostilities between armed forces that are organized to a greater or lesser extent.

[35] International Committee of the Red Cross, "How Is the Term 'Armed Conflict' Defined in International Humanitarian Law?," Opinion Paper, 2008, 5, http://www.icrc.org/eng/assets/files/other/opinion-paper-armed-conflict.pdf.

[36] *See, e.g.*, Prosecutor v. Lukić, Judgment (Case No. IT-98-32/1-T, International Criminal Tribunal for the Former Yugoslavia July 20, 2009), para. 884; *Haradinaj, supra* note 32, at para. 60; *Limaj, supra* note 33, at paras. 95–109.

[37] *See* Laurie R. Blank & Geoffrey S. Corn, *Losing the Forest for the Trees: Syria, Law and the Pragmatics of Conflict Recognition*, 46 Vand. J. Transnat'l L. 693 (2013), arguing that the strict and formulaic application of the so-called "elements test" undermines the original objectives of Common Article 3.

identifying the existence of a non-international armed conflict. Section II's examination of how classification of conflict analysis might unfurl in situations of recurring violence after a conflict thus relies, in significant part, on the intensity and organization factors to explore how states and other actors might approach such an analysis.

Identifying the end of non-international armed conflict is also an important building block for the instant discussion—the end of the previous conflict is, of course, a prerequisite for any questions regarding how violence recurring after a previous conflict can or should be characterized. However, LOAC provides little, if any, guidance in this regard. Common Article 3 has no language regarding the end of non-international armed conflict and although Additional Protocol II references the end of conflict with respect to protections for persons detained due to the conflict, it does not provide any rules or other information for identifying the end of conflict. The *Tadić* judgment includes a general statement that "[i]nternational humanitarian law applies from the initiation of such armed conflicts and extends beyond the cessation of hostilities until . . . , in the case of internal conflicts, a peaceful settlement is achieved,"[38] but precisely what such a peaceful settlement looks like remains unclear. Some non-international armed conflicts do end with a peace agreement, such as the 1998 agreement between the Philippines and the National Democratic Front of the Philippines,[39] the 1999 peace agreement between Sierra Leone and the Revolutionary United Front,[40] or, most recently, the agreement signed between Colombia and the Revolutionary Armed Forces of Colombia (FARC) in 2016,[41] but formal peace agreements are rarely the norm in non-international armed conflicts. In some cases, a conflict ends when the state has defeated the non-state armed group, such as in Sri Lanka, but identifying what "defeat" means in a conflict with a terrorist or insurgent group can be extraordinarily challenging.[42]

These challenges are particularly acute in non-international armed conflicts in which the state is using force outside its territory, such as spillover conflicts, cross-border conflicts, or conflicts between a state and transnational terrorist group or armed group that take place in or across multiple states.[43] In 2012,

[38] *Tadić*, *supra* note 7, at para. 70.

[39] "Comprehensive Agreement on Respect for Human Rights and International Humanitarian Law," Mar. 15, 1998, https://peacemaker.un.org/philippines-agreement-human-rights98.

[40] "Peace Agreement Between the Government of Sierra Leone and the Revolutionary United Front of Sierra Leone," July 12, 1999.

[41] "Final Agreement to End the Armed Conflict and Build a Stable and Lasting Peace," Mar. 24, 2017.

[42] For an extensive analysis of this question, *see* Blank, *supra* note 13.

[43] *See* International Committee of the Red Cross, "International Humanitarian Law and the Challenges of Contemporary Conflict" (EN 31IC/11/5.1.2, Oct. 2011), 9–11.

then-US Department of Defense General Counsel Jeh Johnson proposed the idea of

> a tipping point at which so many of the leaders and operatives of al Qaeda and its affiliates have been killed or captured, and the group is no longer able to attempt or launch a strategic attack against the United States, such that al Qaeda as we know it, the organization that our Congress authorized the military to pursue in 2001, has been effectively destroyed.[44]

More commonly, non-international armed conflicts may wane or peter out, when "one of the Parties ceases to exist," or in light of a "lasting cessation of armed confrontations without real risk of resumption," as the 2016 Commentary to the First Geneva Convention explains.[45] One way to identify the end point of such a conflict is to "reverse engineer" the *Tadić* test of intensity and organization for identifying the start of non-international armed conflict, such that when either the intensity of the violence or the level of organization of the non-state group drops below the threshold of "protracted armed violence" set forth in *Tadić*, the conflict has ended.[46] These questions regarding how and when conflict ends not only help frame the space for the instant discussion, by identifying the starting point for thinking about violence and conflict classification after a previous conflict, but also reappear throughout the conflict classification analysis of such recurring violence as constant source of uncertainty about whether such classification analysis is even appropriate—that is, whether the recurring violence is a new conflict or whether, with hindsight, the original conflict actually never ended.

[44] *See* transcription of remarks, Benjamin Wittes, *Jeh Johnson Speech at the Oxford Union*, LAWFARE, Nov. 30, 2012, https://www.lawfareblog.com/2012/11/jeh-johnson-speech-at-the-oxford-union/#_ftn11.

[45] International Committee of the Red Cross, "Commentary of 2016: Geneva Convention I for the Amelioration of the Condition of the Wounded and Sick in the Armed Forces in the Field (2016), paras. 489–491, https://ihl-databases.icrc.org/ihl/full/GCI-commentary. *See also* Rogier Bartels, *The End of Non-International Armed Conflicts and the Application of IHL*, ARMED GROUPS AND INTERNATIONAL LAW, Feb. 19, 2014, https://armedgroups-internationallaw.org/2014/02/19/the-end-of-non-international-armed-conflicts-and-the-application-of-ihl/, noting that fighting has continued in South Sudan notwithstanding various ceasefire agreements.

[46] Marko Milanovic, *The End of Application of International Humanitarian Law*, 96 INT'L REV. RED CROSS 96 (2014), 163, 180 (2014). *See also* Rogier Bartels, *From Jus in Bello to Jus Post Bellum: When Do Non-International Armed Conflicts End?*, *in* JUS POST BELLUM: MAPPING THE NORMATIVE FOUNDATIONS 297 (Carster Stahn, Jennifer S. Easterday, & Jens Iverson eds., 2014), proposing a framework for identifying when fighting has dropped below the *Tadić* threshold so as to end a non-international armed conflict. *See also* Dustin Lewis, Gabriella Blum, & Naz K. Modirzadeh, "Indefinite War: Unsettled International Law on the End of Conflict," Harvard Law School Program on International Law and Armed Conflict, Legal Briefing, Feb. 2017, https://pilac.law.harvard.edu/indefinite-war, using the notion of a "two-way ratchet theory" for this reverse *Tadić* approach.

II. Classifying Conflict After Conflict

As some of the preceding examples illustrate, certain situations of renewed violence after a previous conflict offer a particularly compelling story to showcase issues of classification of conflict after conflict. Imagine two parallel situations: in one, a state suffers a bombing or other isolated act of violence; in the other, a state that recently defeated, reached a peace settlement or otherwise ended a conflict with a non-state armed group suffers a bombing or other isolated act of violence. It is not inconceivable or even unreasonable that the state in the second example would view the question of "what law applies to the response to and operations against this group" differently than the state in the first example. At the same time, it is axiomatic that identification and classification of armed conflict rests on an objective analysis of the facts on the ground, not on the views, goals or rhetoric of the parties involved. And yet, if the difference between the perspectives in these two examples is reasonable, then either the fact of the previous conflict must be relevant to the objective facts on the ground or, in situations of violence recurring after a conflict, some greater weight given to the views and goals of the parties to the conflict may be appropriate. The former possibility fits within the general framework of LOAC's conflict classification scheme; the latter poses a substantial threat to the common understanding and implementation of that scheme and therefore demands careful consideration. Although these questions are more likely to arise in greater complexity in the context of a non-international armed conflict, and perhaps specifically an extraterritorial non-international armed conflict, they remain relevant with respect to all types of armed conflict.

A. International Armed Conflict

The low threshold for the international armed conflict trigger suggests that, in most cases, the analytical approach to violence recurring after a previous conflict will follow the same framework as the ordinary process of identifying the existence of an international armed conflict. If a single exchange of fire, targeting of enemy forces or facilities, or detention of enemy military personnel triggers the law of armed conflict, then envisioning a quicker or easier path to identifying an international armed conflict based on the fact of a previous conflict between the same two states is unlikely because, in essence, the threshold is already so low. Thus, neither the threshold itself nor the interpretation or application of that threshold should be any different between an "ordinary" situation of armed conflict between two states and a situation that follows on a previous conflict. Although their position is not generally accepted, for the minority who argue for an intensity threshold of some sort for international armed conflict,[47] the fact of a previous conflict could potentially contribute to the perception of intensity, as discussed later with regard to non-international armed conflict.

In one particular context, however, the fact of a previous conflict could be consequential in implementing and interpreting the threshold for international armed conflict when the two relevant states have already fought an armed conflict in the past—the use by one or both states of proxy forces to engage in violence against their adversary. In essence, the memory of the previous conflict could significantly affect how that adversary views the nature of the proxy force, the connection between the state and the proxy force, and the attribution of the proxy's acts to the state, with respect to the trigger for an international armed conflict between two states or the internationalization of a non-international armed conflict based on one state's overall control of the non-state party in that non-international armed conflict.

LOAC, and international law more generally, offers little if any guidance regarding the start of an international armed conflict through the actions of a non-state armed group functioning as a proxy for one of the states involved in the putative conflict. Nearly all discussions of proxy groups and international armed conflict focus instead on the internationalization of an already ongoing non-international armed conflict, as discussed below. With regard to an international armed conflict starting based on the actions of a proxy group, consider the basic interpretation of the threshold for international armed conflict: "any difference arising between states and leading to the intervention of members of the armed forces."[48] That simple but axiomatic statement would require that the relationship between a state and a non-state armed group functioning as its proxy be sufficiently direct such that the group's actions manifest a dispute between the two states—and not merely between the state and the armed group—and the group can be understood as a reasonable substitution for the state's armed forces. For this reason, an international armed conflict starting as the result of the actions of a proxy group is rare at best and has received little attention in the international law discourse, although the actions of Kataib Hezbollah and the US strike on General Qasem Soleimani in late 2019 and early 2020 did raise questions about such possibilities. Unlike the longer and more varied relationship of control one might examine in the internationalization context, the immediate nature of the start of international armed conflict seems to require a heightened level of control over the proxy's action. Such a proposed threshold of "strict control" thus rests on the notion that the relationship between and level of control exercised by the state over the non-state armed group must be assessed with respect to

[47] International Law Association, *supra* note 18.
[48] Uhler et al., *supra* note 3, at 23.

"the particular use of force that will lead to the emergence of an IAC"[49] because it is that particular use of force that starts the conflict. Given that a determination that an international armed conflict exists has enormous and significant consequences for the relations between the two states and the legal authorities and obligations of those two states, an extremely narrow space in which an international armed conflict can start based on the actions of a proxy group—rather than those actions being considered as pieces of a non-international armed conflict analysis—is appropriate.

However, imagine that same set of considerations when two states have fought a conflict with each other and then, at some point after the end of that conflict, a non-state armed group engages in one or more acts of violence against one of the states, and that victim state believes that the non-state group has some relationship with or is acting on behalf of the other state in some manner. Even with this type of strict control test in mind, a state might reasonably consider the fact of the past conflict, regardless of whether that non-state armed group existed at the time of or fought in the conflict, to be relevant in assessing the acts of the proxy group and its relationship to the state. In effect, the victim state may be primed to consider actions by or attributable to the other state as threatening, in light of the previous conflict, and may also be quicker to see a relationship of control between the state and the proxy group because of concerns about that threat.

With regard to internationalization of non-international armed conflict based on one state's overall control of a non-state armed group fighting against another state in that conflict,[50] most determinations will be made by a court, tribunal, international organization or other external observer, which would not likely be influenced by the fact of a previous conflict. However, for the state considering the nature of the conflict in which it is involved and whether another state is a party to that conflict—thus determining the law applicable to actions by and against that state—the fact of a previous conflict between those two states could well alter or quicken the march toward classification of the conflict as international from the state's perspective. The central consideration in this analysis is "the attribution of the actions of the organized armed group to a State."[51] As set forth in Article 8 of the Draft Articles on Responsibility of States for Internationally Wrongful Acts, the necessary level of control for the purposes of attribution requires that "the person or group of persons is in fact acting on the instructions of, or under the direction or control, of that State in carrying

[49] Djemila Carron, *When Is a Conflict International? Time for New Control Tests in IHL*, 98 Int'l Rev. Red Cross 1019, 1029 (2016).

[50] *Tadić*, *supra* note 7, at para. 122.

[51] Robert Heinsch, *Conflict Classification in Ukraine: The Return of the "Proxy War"?*, 91 Int'l L. Stud. 323, 346–47 (2015).

out the conduct."[52] Although the precise meaning of "on the instructions of" and "under the direction or control" remain subject to debate, the state's view of the actions of the organized armed group it is fighting and its relationship with another state—a state the first state fought in a previous conflict—could well be colored by the fact of the previous conflict and whether the other state is viewed as a threat and to what extent. Overall, however, internationalization of a non-international armed conflict is the least likely situation in which classification is likely to be affected by the fact of a previous conflict. It is important to emphasize that the state's perspective or perception of a quicker route to conflict does not mean that the law has changed or should change, or that the application or interpretation of the law should change. Recognizing how facts and perceptions may place pressure on that interpretation, however, is equally important.

B. Non-International Armed Conflict

Non-international armed conflict, in contrast, offers a rich arena of possibilities for a previous conflict between the state and one or more organized armed groups to color, affect, or even drive the identification of a situation of violence as a non-international armed conflict. Several considerations influence how the two *Tadić* factors of intensity and organization could be analyzed. One important aspect is the location of the violence—whether it is occurring inside the state or originating from or occurring predominantly outside the state's borders. The application of the intensity and organization factors to "internal" non-international armed conflict is the more classic story of non-international armed conflict: a state faces internal disturbances or other domestic unrest, responds with ordinary law enforcement measures to restore and maintain public order and security, the unrest increases and at some point, the military is called upon to counter the continued threat from the uprising. As clashes between the non-state forces and the military continue and develop in degree and frequency, we reach the threshold of non-international armed conflict.

When the non-state actors are located outside the state, however, the story often unfolds differently. Intensity and organization remain the main tools for analysis, but the implicit notion that the state will first use law enforcement to respond to the attack and to restore public order and security may simply not be relevant. Instead, the state will likely need to rely on its military to stop the attack and deter the attackers from continuing their operations as a first step, because

[52] United Nations, "Draft Articles on Responsibility of States for Internationally Wrongful Acts with Commentaries" (Adopted, International Law Commission, 53rd Session, 2001), https://legal.un.org/ilc/texts/instruments/english/commentaries/9_6_2001.pdf.

there would be no law enforcement option outside its borders. In either of these scenarios—internal or external non-international armed conflict—the fact of a previous conflict will almost ineluctably affect the analysis.

Second, the identity and nature of the organized armed group and its relationship to the group engaged in the previous conflict with the state is highly consequential. For example, is the group involved in the situation of violence the same group as in the previous conflict? A follow-on or successor group? A new group entirely, but perhaps with the same ideology or similar members or leaders? Each of these possibilities can lead to the fact of the previous conflicting affect the conflict identification and classification analysis in different ways. This section analyzes these possibilities within the framework of intensity and organization to explore how violence recurring after a previous conflict might be characterized through this mainstream approach.

Finally, it is important to note that the state involved will have different stressors and a different time frame, naturally, than an external observer seeking to identify the existence of non-international armed conflict. The state is primarily making operational decisions regarding how to respond to the violence or other threats and, at the same time, assessing how both its actions and the actions of the adversary group are determining the applicable law and any changes to that legal framework. "Pragmatically, threat and the concomitant need to respond to that threat will always be the primary consideration driving the strategic, operational, and tactical calculus."[53] As a result, the fact of the previous conflict will influence the state's assessment of the nature of the threat it faces more obviously than its assessment the relevant legal framework, but the state's actions and perspective inherently drive its legal analysis as well. The instant discussion therefore considers either or both types of influence on the analysis.

1. Intensity

The indicators of intensity are well-known and thoroughly examined in the jurisprudence of the ICTY, the International Criminal Court, commissions of inquiry, and many other sources, as detailed previously in brief. For any of these indicia, whether the number and frequency of attacks, the types of weapons used, or the number of deaths or amount of destruction of property, the specific question is whether the fact—and nature—of the previous conflict affects the analysis or understanding of intensity. In effect, if some degree of one or more of the

[53] Laurie R. Blank, *Learning to Live with (a Little) Uncertainty: The Operational Aspects and Consequences of the Geography of Conflict Debate*, 161 U. Pa. L. Rev. Online 347, 355 (2013); *see also* Geoffrey S. Corn, *Geography of Armed Conflict: Why It Is a Mistake to Fish for the Red Herring*, 89 Int'l L. Stud. 77, 82 (2013), "[a]rmed conflict is a threat-driven concept, arising when the threat necessitates resort to combat power, and extending to wherever the operational and tactical opportunity to produce a militarily valuable effect on the enemy arises."

indicia is ordinarily considered a manifestation of the requisite degree of intensity, consider now a state that is seeing such indicia with the backdrop of a recent conflict coloring all of its reactions and analyses, or a tribunal or other external observer that similarly analyzes such indicia in that context. As a starting point, this type of scenario poses an inherent challenge for LOAC's conflict classification scheme: although the Commentary to Common Article 3 affirms that "the scope of application of the article must be as wide as possible,"[54] the fundamental premise of the threshold for non-international armed conflict is to distinguish situations of armed conflict from riots, internal disturbances, and other low-level tensions and violence. This balance, between broad application of Common Article 3 and a threshold that recognizes the sovereign space for the state to manage unrest, requires an understanding of situations that may tip or alter that balance, either in the immediate term or the more longer-term evolution of the law. In effect, if the fact of a previous conflict is likely to—whether appropriately or not—speed the path to characterization of a situation as a non-international armed conflict, recognizing that divergence from the ordinary methodology is important in order to forestall it or, if appropriate, accommodate it.

Three variations of violence after a previous conflict introduce different ways in which assessment of intensity may differ. First, consider a state that fought a conflict with an organized armed group within its own territory and now, at some point after that conflict has ended, faces violence by the same group—whether the group remained in existence or disbanded and then reformed as the same group. Ordinarily, the conflict classification analysis would look to the various markers of intensity and seek a particular level, amount or spread of such markers before finding sufficient intensity. Now imagine that the state is trying to determine the law applicable to its actions in response to this renewed violence: there can be little doubt that the previous conflict will affect how the state views the group's acts and the threat they pose. In colloquial terms, the view of state officials will be akin to "I know what this looks like" or "I've seen this movie before," leading them to imbue any given indicia of intensity with greater meaning or force. The effect: the requisite level of intensity is achieved or identified more quickly than if the same acts of violence and situation were occurring without the backdrop of the previous conflict. Although an external observer, such as a commission of inquiry, a tribunal, or an international or nongovernmental organization, may be less influenced by that backdrop, the connection between the past conflict and the current violence would likely still be relevant at least in some implicit manner, if not overtly. For example, the February 2016 Office of the UN High Commissioner for Human Rights on Libya report begins its discussion of the armed groups involved in the new conflict in Libya by noting

[54] Uhler et al., *supra* note 3, at 36.

that any assessment of "[t]he current situation should be considered against the background of the rise of 'revolutionary' armed groups during the 2011 armed conflict."[55] In effect, the previous conflict forms, at a minimum, the setting for any discussion of the current violence.

The nature of the group might also play a role in the analysis, by suggesting—for either the state or external observers—that the only option in response to that type of group is violence at the level of armed conflict. An obvious example would be a terrorist group, whose only modus operandi and means of interaction with the state to achieve its goals is the use of violence against civilians.[56] Believing that such a group would not engage in negotiation or reconciliation of any kind, the state's view of the intensity component of the analysis may well be colored by its belief that the only option is to fight and win a conflict against the group, effectively adding a patina of additional intensity to each occurrence or engagement.

Second, if the new violence is perpetrated by a different group, the past conflict will infiltrate into the analysis in a different manner, primarily based on the relationship or affiliation between the group that fought in the past conflict and the new group. To the extent the state views the new group as simply an updated version of the group it fought in the last conflict, as the United States asserts with respect to ISIS and its predecessor, Al Qaeda in Iraq,[57] its reactions and analyses will be similar to those suggested in the preceding paragraph. But beyond such direct reconstitution or re-emergence, a critical component will be the nature of the linkages between the original group and this new group. If violence by the same group accelerates the intensity assessment, then a key question becomes how similar, and in what ways, must the new group be to the original group to have a similar type of "intensity boost." For example, relevant considerations might include whether the group is an offshoot of the earlier group, such as Al Qaeda in the Arabian

[55] United Nations, Human Rights Council, "Investigation by the Office of the United Nations High Commissioner for Human Rights on Libya: Report of the Office of the United Nations High Commissioner for Human Rights" (A/HRC/31/47, Feb. 15, 2016), para. 12, http://www.ohchr.org/Documents/Countries/LY/A_HRC_31_47_E.pdf.

[56] Such conduct is the essence of a terrorist group. *See* U.S. Department of Defense, "Antiterrorism" (Joint Publication 3-07.2, Nov. 24, 2010), https://www.hsdl.org/?abstract&did=753152, defining terrorism as "the unlawful use of violence or threat of violence to instill fear and coerce governments or societies"; United Nations, Security Council, "Resolution 1566" (S/RES/1566, Oct. 8, 2004), https://www.un.org/ruleoflaw/files/n0454282.pdf, defining terrorism as "criminal acts, including against civilians, committed with the intent to cause death or serious bodily injury, or taking of hostages, with the purpose to provoke a state of terror in the general public or in a group of persons or particular persons, intimidate a population or compel a government or an international organization to do or to abstain from doing any act." *See also* North Atlantic Treaty Organization, Glossary of Terms and Definitions (2013), "[t]he unlawful use or threatened use of force or violence against individuals or property in an attempt to coerce or intimidate governments or societies to achieve political, religious or ideological objectives."

[57] *See* Wittes, *supra* note 7.

Peninsula,[58] is comprised of members or leaders of the earlier group, as believed to be the case with the Khorasan Group,[59] or is acting in allegiance to or otherwise in operational connection with the earlier group, such as al-Shabaab in Somalia or other groups at times with respect to Al Qaeda or other groups with respect to ISIS.[60] Although each of these types of connections or affiliations might add some, even minimal, acceleration to the assessment of intensity from the state's perspective, they would be unlikely to grab the attention of an external observer in the same manner because external analyses do not occur within the scope of the same threat assessment. For looser types of affiliation, such as if the new group is motivated by the same ideology or is launching attacks in the style of the earlier group to gain adherents and attention as a result, it is unlikely that either the state or any external observers would find that such attenuated connections boost the intensity analysis.

Third, the location of the violence could affect how renewed violence is perceived in the context of the intensity analysis. One could imagine a variety of ways in which the location of the renewed violence, as well as the location of the previous conflict, might affect how the state or even the external observer considers the type, degree and extent of the new violence. For example, if the previous conflict took place within the territory of the state and the renewed violence also occurs domestically, the state might consider the violence a sign that conflict is returning, thus instinctively seeing greater intensity—even though the basic premise of the non-international armed conflict classification framework is that the state will take action to protect and restore law and order through the peacetime paradigm until the situation appears to have risen above the threshold for armed conflict. At the same time, the state in such a situation might consider that it has sufficient intelligence and resources in that area, precisely because of the previous conflict, that it does not need to react as vigorously as in the past, thus essentially putting an "intensity dampener" on its assessment of the events. Similarly, other alternatives of renewed violence outside the territory after a conflict inside the territory, or violence inside or outside the territory after a conflict outside the territory, could affect the state's calculus of both the threat and the intensity of the violence. For example, if the violence outside the territory after a conflict that was outside the territory is in the same location as that previous

58 Council on Foreign Relations, "Backgrounder: Al-Qaeda in the Arabian Peninsula," June 19, 2015, https://www.cfr.org/backgrounder/al-qaeda-arabian-peninsula-aqap.

59 Holly Yan, *Terrorist Leader Killed in Drone Strike—But What Is the Khorasan Group?*," CNN, July 22, 2015, referring to the Khorasan Group as a "collection of senior al Qaeda members who moved into Syria."

60 Claire Felter, Jonathan Masters, & Mohammed Aly Sergie, "Backgrounder: Al-Shabab," Council on Foreign Relations, Jan. 10, 2020, https://www.cfr.org/backgrounder/al-shabab; *Nigeria's Boko Haram Pledges Allegiance to Islamic State*, BBC NEWS, Mar. 7, 2015, https://www.bbc.com/news/world-africa-31784538.

conflict, the effect on the state's perception, and therefore the state's determination of the applicable law, could be similar to that noted previously.

2. Organization

In any armed conflict, the fundamental principles and obligations of LOAC rest on the basic premise that the conflict is being fought between two armed forces, whether two states, a state and non-state armed group, or two or more such non-state groups. Implementing distinction, proportionality, and precautions depends on the ability to differentiate between members of the enemy armed forces and civilians—in essence, on the fact that there is a collective enemy as opposed to random and disaggregated acts of violence. It is precisely because the organization factor in non-international armed conflict classification is a critical feature of assessing a situation of violence that understanding how the fact of a previous conflict may influence or color any analysis of the non-state group's organization or lack thereof is highly relevant. Insurgent and terrorist groups frequently morph, splinter, and reconfigure, or lie dormant after what appears to be a defeat, waiting until the next opportunity to pursue their agenda. As a result, it is not uncommon for new violence after a previous conflict to involve a group, or at least individuals, who were involved in that past conflict. How that group or those individuals relate to the group or groups involved in the previous conflict can play a significant role in how a state or an external observer views the nature and level of organization for purposes of conflict classification, even using the traditional and less formulaic understandings of "some degree of organization"[61] or "a minimum amount of organization,"[62] rather than the heavily factor-oriented approach in the jurisprudence of the ICTY.[63] On some level, the organization prong of the analysis poses greater challenges to—or offers more opportunity to affect—the analysis than the intensity prong because information about the nature of an insurgent or terrorist group can be difficult to gather and assess, providing a greater role for perception and conjecture.

As a starting point, consider a situation in which a state fought a conflict against a non-state armed group, the conflict ended, and then the same group begins fomenting violence and engaging in attacks at some point in the future. Given that the group manifested a sufficient degree of organization during the original conflict—as is evident from the fact that it was an armed conflict—an immediate question is whether the same or at least sufficient level of organization can now be presumed during this new phase of violence. A starting

[61] *Limaj*, *supra* note 33, para. 89.

[62] International Committee of the Red Cross, "How Is the Term 'Armed Conflict' Defined in International Humanitarian Law?," 5, Opinion Paper, Mar. 2008, http://www.icrc.org/eng/assets/files/other/opinion-paper-armed-conflict.pdf.

[63] *Limaj*, *supra* note 33, at paras. 95–109; *Haradinaj*, *supra* note 32, at para. 60.

presumption that the group does exhibit sufficient organization may not seem to be problematic, because non-international armed conflict requires both intensity and organization.[64] However, some type of sliding scale of organization and intensity in which lower levels of one factor are nonetheless sufficient when paired with higher levels of the other, is neither uncommon nor unreasonable.[65] If so, then an accelerated path to non-international armed conflict classification, and the concomitant legal authorities regarding the use of force and detention, is not hard to envision. The simple fact that the group involved in the new violence is the same as the previous group cannot therefore be sufficient to check the organization "box." Rather, a careful assessment must examine how the previous conflict ended and how that end to the conflict affected the existence, composition, and nature of the group. For example, if the conflict ended with a peace settlement between the state and the armed group, such that the armed group agreed to an end to the conflict but did not necessarily dissolve, such as in Colombia,[66] one would expect that a determination that sufficient organization exists would be straightforward. In contrast, if the previous conflict ended when the state thoroughly defeated the armed group, such that its fighters were killed or captured and the group was otherwise dissolved or disbanded, then the reappearance and violent activities of the same group months or years after the end of the conflict should still merit a full consideration of the organization prong of the analysis. At the same time, in considering not only how the law should apply but how it is likely to be applied, one can expect that the presence of the same group—regardless of how the previous conflict with it ended—would create at least a perception, if not a presumption, of organization.

A frequent scenario is that the group involved in the renewed violence is a follow-on or successor group to the group involved in the earlier conflict, such as the example of ISIS and Al Qaeda in Iraq. Although nearly all discussions of the Al Qaeda in Iraq as a predecessor to ISIS occur in the context of whether the US use of force against ISIS fell within an existing domestic authorization for the use of force,[67] the same information would be equally relevant if questions existed

[64] *See, e.g.*, United Nations, Human Rights Council, "Report of the Independent International Commission of Inquiry on the Syrian Arab Republic" (A/HRC/19/69, Feb. 22, 2012), https://undocs.org/A/HRC/19/69, finding sufficient intensity but declining to characterize the situation as an armed conflict for lack of sufficient organization.

[65] Blank & Corn, *supra* note 37.

[66] "Final Agreement to End The Armed Conflict and Build a Stable and Lasting Peace," Nov. 24, 2016, http://especiales.presidencia.gov.co/Documents/20170620-dejacion-armas/acuerdos/acuerdo-final-ingles.pdf; *Former Farc Rebels Take Seats in Colombia Congress*, BBC News, July 21, 2018, https://www.bbc.com/news/world-latin-america-44909273.

[67] *See, e.g.*, Patricia Stottlemyer, *Doe v Mattis: Is the War on ISIS Legal?*, JustSecurity, Feb. 23, 2018, https://www.justsecurity.org/52896/doe-v-mattis-war-isis-legal/, for a thorough discussion of the arguments regarding domestic authorization for the use of force against ISIS.

about the nature of the situation and whether it constituted an armed conflict at all. In addition to these questions regarding how the previous conflict ended and the nature of the disposition of the earlier group, this type of scenario adds questions regarding how the successor group formed and how that might affect the perception or actual nature of the organization of the group at the time of the renewed violence. For example, if the successor group is merely the same group with a new name, the actual analysis and the perceptions would be similar to those above-mentioned if the group were the very same group. If the successor group is comprised of many of the same members and leaders with a similar structure, one might also take a similar approach. But if the successor group has the same leaders with a mostly new membership of fighters, or perhaps the same general membership with new leaders, one could expect less automatic carry-over of organization from the earlier group and a greater need for examination of the nature of the group.

Finally, consider an entirely new group that adheres to a similar ideology, uses similar tactics, or professes the same goals or objectives, in which some or many individuals who fought in the earlier group are now participating. This situation offers little basis to presume that the organization prong is automatically satisfied, effectively only because there was a previous conflict. Even though the organization component of the *Tadić* framework is not a particularly high bar, it cannot be an automatic assumption driven solely by the fact of a previous conflict.

III. Conclusion

The fact of a previous conflict, whether between the same two parties, in the same location, or other variation, does not alter the legal threshold for either international armed conflict or non-international armed conflict. The former remains a dispute between states that leads to "the intervention of members of the armed forces,"[68] and the latter threshold continues to be "protracted armed violence between governmental authorities and organized armed groups or between such groups within a State."[69] Just as the type of dispute, the size of the states, the location of the violence, the motivation for the conflict, or any other factors do not alter the basic thresholds and tests for armed conflict, so the fact that one or more parties involved in the situation also fought in a previous conflict does not change the basic legal threshold or framework. However, the threshold itself is not the full story—the interpretation and implementation

[68] Uhler et al., *supra* note 3, at 23.
[69] *Tadić*, *supra* note 7, at 70.

of the framework is equally important in understanding how and when the law will be applied and how it might evolve over time. Recognizing and preparing for how situations might affect the implementation of the legal framework is essential to protect and preserve the law's ability to carry out its core objectives.

PART II

WAR AS CRIMINAL ENFORCEMENT

6

Fighting State Actors with the Tools of Hybridized Warfare

Can the Law of Armed Conflict be Saved?[1]

Claire Finkelstein

I. Introduction

With the extrajudicial killing of Qasem Soleimani, an Iranian major general in the Islamic Revolutionary Guard Corps and the commander of Iran's Quds Force, the United States ushered in a new era in the extended war on terror: the use of targeted killing against state actors outside the context of war. The Trump administration at first attempted to justify the killing in the language of international law and the law of armed conflict (LOAC). The explanations offered, however, were inconsistent and contradictory.[2] Former Secretary of State Mike Pompeo first tweeted that the killing was "in response to imminent threats to American lives." But the administration never produced any evidence of, or specifics regarding, the imminent attack it anticipated. Indeed, Pompeo himself admitted that "we don't know precisely when and we don't know precisely where," though President Donald Trump claimed in a news conference that "they were looking to blow up our embassy."[3] And later he claimed: "I think it could have been four embassies. Could have been military bases, could have been a lot of other things too. But it was imminent."[4] Former Chairman of the Joint Chiefs of Staff, General Mark Milley, maintained that he never saw evidence of a planned attack on our embassies, and thereafter the talk of imminence as a justification died away .

While no longer in the administration at the time of the Soleimani strike, former National Security Advisor General H.R. McMaster's remarks on this

[1] An earlier version of this article was published under the title "Restoring the Rule of Law to US Targeted Killing Operations in The Vanderbild Journal of Transnational Law, Vol. 53, No. 4 (2022). It is reprinted here, with modiications, by permission.

[2] Chris Cameron & Helene Cooper, *The Trump Administration's Fluctuating Explanations for the Soleimani Strikes*, N.Y. Times, Jan. 12, 2020. *The Trump Administration's Fluctuating Explanations for the Soleimani Strike*, N.Y. Times, https://nytimes.com.

[3] *Id.*

[4] *Id.*

Claire Finkelstein, *Fighting State Actors with the Tools of Hybridized Warfare* In: *Between Crime and War*. Edited by: Claire Finkelstein, Christopher Fuller, Jens David Ohlin, Mitt Regan, Oxford University Press. DOI: 10.1093/oso/9780197638798.003.0007

topic may have been a more forthright reflection of the Trump administration's thinking, which is that imminence is not necessary to justify such a strike. McMaster argued that the killing of Soleimani was justified because it was "the righteous use of violence."[5] But he also quipped that he did not care whether the killing violated international law. And thus far scholars and public policy experts have failed to offer any sort of explanation that would justify the killing under international law.[6] Since the Soleimani killing, there have been other strikes on state actors. In November 2020, Iran's top nuclear scientist, Mohsen Fakhrizadeh, was killed in an ambush widely attributed to Israel.[7] According to current intelligence reports, Fakhrizadeh was killed with the use of an autonomous machine gun that fired at his vehicle from another car. Reports later emerged that top U.S. officials participated in meetings with Israeli officials in the runup to the assassination.[8]

Unless the United States had a basis for going to war with Iran, attacking a high-ranking military official of a foreign country with which the United States is not at war is a clear violation of international law. How did we come to think such an action justified? The seeds of this unilateral act of war were sown almost two decades earlier in the approach taken by G.W. Bush administration lawyers and military and intelligence officials to a different problem: the status of violent non-state actors in Iraq and Afghanistan who had formed highly militarized terrorist organizations. Instead of classifying them as either combatants or civilians, as the traditional law of war dictates, the Bush administration created a sui generis category variously called "unlawful combatants," "enemy combatants," "unprivileged belligerents," and so forth, often changing names deliberately in order to create confusion and obscure the legal sleight of hand in which it was engaged. Obama and then Trump administration lawyers largely maintained this same legal structure, presumably in order to bolster the legal justification of targeted killing without a prior need to attempt capture. So-called unlawful combatants, however, were deemed to have none of the rights that attach to combatants under the laws of war. Operating in this "no man's land" between two legal regimes—the laws of war and the criminal law—has spawned confusion and damaged the rule of law.

This chapter will focus on the transition from the Bush-era concept of unlawful combatancy, which served to justify the torture of detainees captured in Iraq and Afghanistan, through to its role in justifying targeted killing against

[5] *"I don't really care what international law said": H.R. McMaster Debates Soleimani Killing, Iran*, The Stanford Daily.

[6] *Assassination of an Iranian Nuclear Scientist Raises New Questions*, CSMonitor.com.

[7] *State Media Says Iran's Top Nuclear Scientist Killed in Ambush*, N.Y. Times, https://nytimes.com.

[8] Ronen Bergman and Farnaz Fassihi, "The Scientist and the A.I.-Assisted, Remote-Control Killing Machine, *New York Times*, Oct. 26, 2021.

non-state actors under Presidents Barack Obama and Donald Trump. Now, as we transition from the war on terror involving non-state actors to a focus on states that commit acts of terror or sponsor terrorism by providing material support, we find the same techniques that were justified on the faulty premise of the notion of unlawful combatancy coming back around to be used against state actors, such as Qasem Soleimani. The absence of a clear legal framework for the use of targeted killing, particularly remote killing by unmanned aerial vehicles, has left the United States and its allies largely at sea with regard to the legality of targeted killing operations more generally, and this has carried over to state actors as the formerly clear understandings of the legality of such operations are increasingly subject to confusion. This problem is particularly grave given the dramatic increase in the number of targeted killings across the past three administrations. Overall, since 2010, the United States has killed upward of 16,900 people by drone strike, of which at least 2,200 people were civilians.[9] Amazingly, despite the fact that lethal drone technology has been in use almost since 9/11, the United States still has not fully articulated a legal framework for assessing the conformity of drone strikes to the confines of international humanitarian law (IHL).

Legal ambiguity is a threat to national security and to the rule of law. When the law is diluted or attenuated in one domain, there will be erosion of legal norms in adjacent areas of practice. In this case, the worry is not just that we have effaced the distinction between war and crime and have thereby weakened the laws of war. If we continue down this path, we will ultimately weaken not only the law of war but also the constitutional guarantees protecting domestic criminal suspects.

Despite modifications along the way, the United States is still fundamentally operating within the Bush-era framework regarding the categorization of non-state actors engaged in terror overseas. It is now time to rethink that legal framework from the immediate post-9/11 period and seek to harmonize the U.S. approach with basic principles of the law of war, on the one hand, and principles of domestic criminal law, on the other. It is critical that we undertake this work now, before the next significant foreign or domestic threat emerges, as normative questions relating to military engagement or law enforcement cannot be undertaken in the heat of battle. At a moment when our military presence overseas is greatly reduced and most national security threats from foreign nations are nonkinetic, we can afford to reconsider the legal framework we use to justify military engagement with violent foreign extremists. If we fail to engage in this necessary clarification of the legal basis for the targeted killing program, we will find the techniques we have used increasingly against suspected terrorists abroad

[9] *Targeted Killings*, CQR, https://cqpress.com.

becoming hard to contain. We may find that techniques adopted in one context morph and are adapted for use in another.

Moreover, the Russian war of aggression against Ukraine has reminded the international community of the critical role that adherence to the Law of Armed conflict plays in safeguarding democratic governance and the armed forces fighting to preserve their country's sovereignty. As Russian troops target civilians and civilian infrastructure, in flagrant violation of the law of war, it is difficult not to wonder whether U.S. indifference or even outright defiance of those same laws does not weaken the impact of Western denunciation of Russian war crimes.

What approach might the United States have taken in the wake of the 9/11 attacks to protect the country against the profound threat posed by violent non-state actors consistent with existing legal frameworks? Surveying the available options, there are three frameworks the Bush administration might have adopted for this purpose. On one end of what we might think of as a "combatancy scale," there is the possibility of according full combatancy status, such as would normally attach to members of a government-controlled state military. On the other end of the scale, we have domestic criminals, who are normally protected from wrongful deprivations of life and liberty through the constitutional guarantee of due process in US courts. In between we have a series of hybrid options, of which the Bush "unlawful combatancy" doctrine is one, but which may or may not comply with established legal frameworks.

This chapter argues in favor of a hybrid approach that is quite different from the problematic doctrine of unlawful combatancy, one that resides closer to the civilian criminal law model of responsibility. This position would differentiate clearly between state and non-state actors, and thus would do more to preserve the distinction between war and crime. On the model we will consider, non-state military operations, whether in or out of armed conflict, can be considered international criminal conspiracies, bringing the status of violent non-state actors more into line with the way we regard drug lords and other illegal international traffickers. The implications of this approach would be to help distinguish a non-state actor like Anwar al-Awlaki—a U.S. citizen targeted in Yemen because of his role in the broader Al Qaeda network--from a state actor like Qasem Soleimani, since non-state actors would be assessed according to a largely civilian legal framework and state actors like Soleimani would be immune unless they were combatants in the traditional sense within armed conflict. Under the approach this chapter proposes, the Anwar al-Awlakis of this world have more in common with agents of domestic terror than they would with members of state military organizations, such as Iran's Quds Forces, despite the fact their methods and the scale of their operations necessitate a military-level response.

II. The Traditional Notion of Combatancy

Traditionally armed conflict took place uniquely between the militaries of different international states, with soldiers wearing identifiable uniforms, on a clearly demarcated battlefield, and carrying their arms openly. In recent years, the traditional parameters of armed conflict have changed dramatically. At least until the Russian invasion of Ukraine in February of 2022, Most of the wars of the twenty-first century were fought not between one state and another, but between states and violent non-state actors. From the standpoint of the traditional law of war, it is difficult to characterize the operations of such terrorist organizations. How should sovereign nations approach violent non-state militias, and what legal frameworks should govern their treatment? Critically, for present purposes, how do we draw the line between state and non-state actors, and what consequences does this distinction have for LOAC and US policy? The answer we chose to that question in the immediate aftermath of 9/11 has had a profound impact on U.S. adherence to the law of war, including with regard to state actors and the perceived permissibility of extrajudicial killing.

Prior to 9/11, the assumption had always been that anyone connected in the right way with a state military operation would fall under the Geneva Conventions, and thus be guaranteed humane treatment in case of capture. If they were members of a foreign governmental military organization, they were "combatants," and their treatment was governed by the LOAC, or IHL as it is known outside the United States.

Much of the law of war was based originally on the concept of reciprocity, a notion that is often referred to the just war literature under the heading of "the moral equality of combatants," or "the moral equality thesis." This thesis maintains that all individuals having the status of combatants in an armed conflict possess an equal right to kill. This is so regardless of the justice of the cause for which they are fighting. A German soldier fighting for Hitler's army during the Second World War has the same right to kill a French soldier that the latter has to kill him, despite the fact that the Frenchman, whose country is under unlawful occupation, is fighting a just war, and the German, whose country is unlawfully occupying other sovereign nations, is not. The fact that Germany is in violation of international law does not mean that the German soldier is himself violating the laws of war. In invading France, the German soldier participates in an action that is illegal under international law, yet despite that fact, he is within his rights as a combatant when he kills. What gives the soldier "combatant immunity" is the fact that he acts on behalf of a state, from which he derives his authority and his orders. Unlike orders from a criminal organization, however, the orders from his military superiors immunize him in most cases from liability.

This question of who is a combatant is one of the most critical under LOAC. It is one that defines the application of the most important of the principles of the law of war, namely, the principle of distinction. Because the principle of distinction maintains that combatants may be targeted at any time but that civilians may never be targeted, unless they are actively lending assistance to enemy forces, the permissibility of the use of force in armed conflict will depend on our ability to identify clearly the parameters of combatancy and to articulate its implications.

The traditional elements of combatancy are generally summarized as follows: (1) combatants must be commanded by a responsible person who wields authority over his subordinates; (2) they must have a fixed distinctive emblem recognizable at a distance; (3) they must carry their arms openly; and (4) they must conduct their operations in accordance with the laws and customs of war.[10] These principles should best be understood as indications of combatancy, rather than conditions by which combatancy can be established. That is, they are indications that a person is a true combatant, but the *fact* of combatancy has traditionally only been established by an individual's bearing a certain relationship to the state. Thus the command structure mentioned in the first of these four elements can only be established by the relevant state authority. The significance of the uniform, then, is that it indicates membership in the state's command structure.

Combatancy status has depended traditionally on rather clear lines of demarcation between war and not-war: the ability to distinguish combatants from civilians depends on a prior ability to identify a battlefield, as well as to know temporally when wars begin and when they end. In contemporary armed conflict, where the geographical location of war is ill-defined, and the temporal identity of war seems to be attenuated as well, it is difficult to demarcate wars temporally and geographically. Accordingly, identifying who counts as a combatant is a task beset with this same ambiguity, and though the category remains hazy in contemporary conflict, we must work hard to articulate defining principles to govern the notion of armed conflict.

Most state actors, even those who resort to violence outside the context of war, satisfy at least the first three of the previously mentioned four indices of combatancy. Violent non-state actors, however, do not usually fit these criteria, since they do not operate according to a state-based command structure. They usually do not wear a uniform or other distinctive insignia or carry arms openly,

[10] Convention (ii) with Respect to the Laws and Customs of War on Land and its annex: Regulations concerning the Laws and Customs of War of Land. The Hague, July 29, 1899 (hereinafter Hague Convention 1899), *available at* http://www.icrc.org/applic/ihl/ihl.nsf/Article.xsp?action=openDocument&documentId=9FE084CDAC63D10FC12563CD00515C4D. *See also* Christopher Kutz, *The Difference that Uniforms Make*, 33 PHIL. & PUB. AFF., no. 2, 148–80 (2005).

and they do not typically conduct their operations in accordance with the laws and customs of war.

Despite the claims of members of the Bush administration that the legal status of violent non-state actors was novel and required the invention of unprecedented legal concepts, the subject of the relationship of non-state actors to traditional combatants has a rich history. The United States confronted this very question with respect to the Vietcong during the Vietnam War. Trained and funded by the North Vietnamese government, the Vietcong were technically non-state actors who engaged in terroristic acts outside the normal framework of war. Unlike Al Qaeda, however, they fought alongside and on behalf of a state entity. And indeed the American Civil War posed similar questions. The question is whether it was necessary to invent a new hybrid category, or whether the traditional concepts of "combatant" and "civilian" might not have accommodated the range of roles we need to take cognizance of in identifying rights and responsibilities within armed conflict.

III. Unlawful Combatancy and the Bush Doctrine

Domestically, the Bush administration was able to claim broad authority for the arrest and detention of members of the Taliban and Al Qaeda under the 2001 and 2002 Authorizations for the Use of Military Force (AUMFs), legislation that was a blank check for Congress, both with regard to time and with regard to geography.[11] The first public departure from the norms and traditions of war came in 2002, when then-Defense Secretary Donald Rumsfeld announced that captured members of the Taliban and Al Qaeda would henceforth be considered "unlawful combatants," and that as such they were not entitled to prisoner of war status or other privileges under Common Article III of the Geneva Conventions. POW status would have meant that the detainees had the right to refuse to answer questions, the right to counsel of their choosing, and the right to repatriation following the cessation of hostilities, all entitlements we saw as threatening our efforts to win the war on terror.

As later emerged, the Bush administration was increasingly seeking a way to justify the use of torture and the application of other harsh techniques in interrogation in the application of what was known as the Rendition, Detention, and

[11] The broadest grant of authority took place under the "associated forces" doctrine in the 2001 AUMF, a phrase that has been used to extend Congressional authorization from Al Qaeda and the Taliban to ISIS, many years after it was written and to broaden the administration's military mandate from the original domain of Afghanistan to Syria, Yemen, and other surrounding areas. Some scholars have argued, however, that Congress never intended this phrase to import such a broad grant of authority and that the authorization was always intended to be limited to the original terror groups the United States undertook to fight in the immediate aftermath of 9/11.

Interrogation (RDI) program. Justifying such techniques from a legal standpoint posed a profound challenge, given the numerous sources of law, both domestic and international, under which the RDI program was clearly illegal. According members of Al Qaeda and the Taliban full combatant status would have made the application of harsh interrogation techniques illegal under international law, under both the Geneva Conventions and the Convention on Torture. Even more worrisome for the Bush administration, however, was the existence of domestic federal law that would potentially provide a basis for subjecting all those involved in the RDI program to criminal liability.[12] The concept of "unlawful combatancy" was intended to situate the RDI program firmly on the war powers side of the war/crime distinction, which would give the administration both greater latitude and greater secrecy with regard to the treatment of detainees. But this strategy ran a risk on the other side, namely that there would be pressure to apply the traditional concept of combatancy and that the RDI program would be seen as a war crime. Thus the Bush administration had the complex task of fending off civil law-enforcement protections and protocol on the one hand, at the same time that it needed to keep law of war concepts at bay.

While there was a general consensus that members of terrorist organizations like Al Qaeda, arguably the Taliban, and later ISIS were not combatants in the traditional sense, there was no general agreement among experts about their status as "unlawful combatants" or what that label should be taken to mean precisely. Although the question of the status of violent nonstate actors had arisen before, the Bush administration's particular use of the expression "unlawful combatancy" was without precedent. The Bush administration nevertheless drew support from a World War II–era case, namely *Ex Parte Quirin*,[13] involving non-uniformed German U-boat operators who turned up off the coast of Long Island in submarines. Despite the fact that two of the defendants were U.S. citizens, the Supreme Court denied the defendants the right to criminal trials, but it also denied them the right to POW status, on the ground that as spies they were illicit saboteurs who were violating the laws of war, rather than privileged combatants. All eight defendants were convicted of treason and espionage, and six out of the eight were executed.[14] The case was controversial at the time, given its use of the "unlawful combatancy" title, but its impact was limited to the fairly specialized circumstances under which the arrests took place. The label "unlawful enemy combatant" did not reappear after that until the announcement of

[12] For a more detailed discussion of accountability for torture, *see* Claire Finkelstein & Stephen Xenakis, *Repairing the Damage from Illegal Acts of State: The Costs of Failed Accountability for Torture*, *in* Interrogation and Torture: Integrating Efficacy with Law and Morality (Steven Barela et al., eds., 2020).

[13] 317 U.S. 1 (1942).

[14] Nazi Saboteurs Trial, https://loc.gov.

Donald Rumsfeld in 2002 that it was adopting that same label for Al Qaeda and Taliban fighters.

Unlike in 1942, the Bush administration's use of the unlawful combatancy designation took root in common parlance and official legal reasoning about the legality of our practices, and despite criticism of many aspects of Bush-era counterterrorism policy, few commentators seriously questioned its usage in that post-9/11 environment. Echoing the infamous August 1, 2002, OLC memo, the public appears to have accepted the view that the laws of war are not binding when dealing with an enemy who himself refuses to be bound by the laws of war. The argument pressed by Bush administration lawyers was that since the enemy is totally uncivilized, one that knows no law of any sort, the United States is legally and morally permitted to ignore the law of war itself in conducting its defensive campaign against them. As then-Vice President Cheney said in 2005, "We also have to work, though, sort of the dark side, if you will. We've got to spend time in the shadows in the intelligence world. A lot of what needs to be done here will have to be done quietly, without any discussion, using sources and methods that are available to our intelligence agencies, if we're going to be successful. That's the world these folks operate in, and so it's going to be vital for us to use any means at our disposal, basically, to achieve our objective."[15] Self-restraint in the name of legality is for suckers, this theory holds, when dealing with an enemy who himself uses illegal tactics. All claim of right is therefore forfeit. This chapter will accordingly call this the "Forfeiture Theory" of common international legal obligations.

The Forfeiture Theory reflects a combination of realism in international relations, legal realism about jurisprudential concepts, and an unrelentingly skeptical view of the provisions of international law. A sustained defense of the latter position appears in a work by Jack Goldsmith and Eric Posner, entitled *The Limits of International Law* (2005). On this view, international law is a coordination game which each state enters into for the sake of maximizing its own welfare. Unlike domestic law, the lack of robust enforcement in international law means that the only true obligations nations have towards one another are those that are self-imposed for mutual gain. This skeptical view rejects the idea of jus cogens as a basis for duties under international law—namely, duties that apply regardless of whether they are voluntarily accepted by treaty or other vehicle that is subject to agreement. Only if one adopts this highly skeptical view of LOAC does the Forfeiture Theory make sense.[16]

[15] Dan Froomkin, *Cheney's "Dark Side" Is Showing*, WASH. POST, Nov. 7, 2005.

[16] It is important to distinguish here between the Geneva Conventions and the traditional law of armed conflict. The former is, of course, a treaty and as such is not binding unless it is specifically accepted and ratified. The latter, however, contains provisions that rest on an even more secure foundation than the Geneva Conventions, which, in principle, is a set of universally binding doctrines that

If one rejects skepticism about international law, it is easy to see why the duty to abide by the law of war is nonreciprocal, meaning that it is *not* dependent on the willingness of other states to abide by the laws of war themselves. While reciprocity may account for the origins of just war theory—namely, that it is mutually beneficial for all parties if states abide by the law of war generally—it is a great leap from that to the conclusion that if a state fails to follow the laws of war, other states are thereby excused from doing so. The Forfeiture Theory arguably depends on a confusion of level: from the fact that a practice emerged because participants in the practice saw themselves as better off under the mutually applicable rules of the practice, it does not follow that a state can exempt itself from its obligations under the practice in the future.

The Bush administration was never willing to pronounce allegiance to the applicability of Geneva as applied to detainees from the war on terror, and the Obama administration brought about only slight improvements with regard to targeted killing policy and compliance with international law. Unfortunately, the Obama administration retained the problematic concept of unlawful combatancy, even while seeming to dispense with it by eliminating the expression and distancing itself from the Bush-era associations of it with the RDI program. The failure on the part of the Obama administration to repudiate and dismantle the legal structure that had been used to justify torture, however, set the United States on a profoundly destructive path with regard to the rule of law in war. The lack of clarity in this area of the law, combined with a dangerous expansion of presidential war-making authority in the United States, has resulted in the near complete disregard of legal constraints when it comes to fighting terrorists abroad Yet the United States and other Western nations still hope to constrain Russia through threats to prosecute Russian leaders and troops for their commission of war crimes in Ukraine, a stance we are somewhat ill-equipped to take at present.

IV. The Obama Doctrine and the Targeted Killing of Non-State Actors

Under the Obama administration, the forfeiture theory morphed into a somewhat more moderate hybrid approach for dealing with violent non-state actors, one that, at least in theory, had greater resonance with international law. The general approach to the question of combatancy, however, remained largely the same, with only slight modification. In a 2009 Department of Justice (DOJ)

do not require agreement or ratification to impose obligations on all nations. It is these nondelegable aspects of the law of armed conflict that renders the Forfeiture Theory inapplicable.

memo discussing several habeas petitions that had been filed by Guantánamo prisoners, the DOJ rejected the term "enemy combatant" and all preceding variants of that expression, and in addition restricted detention of members of Al Qaeda and the Taliban to those who had given "substantial" support to the belligerency.[17] In addition, there was a shift of rationale: the new account did not rely on the president's commander-in-chief authority, independent of congressional authorization, but rather it relied entirely on the 2001 AUMF.[18] The government's reply brief stated:

> The President has the authority to detain persons that the President determines planned, authorized, committed, or aided the terrorist attacks that occurred on September 11, 2001, and persons who harbored those responsible for those attacks. The President also has the authority to detain persons who were part of, or substantially supported, Taliban or al-Qaida forces or associated forces that are engaged in hostilities against the United States or its coalition partners, including any person who has committed a belligerent act, or has directly supported hostilities, in aid of such enemy armed forces.[19]

The DOJ also maintained that "the particular facts and circumstances justifying detention will vary from case to case and may require the identification and analysis of various analogues from traditional international armed conflicts."[20] In other words, the Obama administration at least early on resisted all efforts to systematize its legal approach in this area and insisted on approaching matters on a case-by-case basis, presumably to leave the administration maximum latitude in dealing with non-state actors.

Of particular relevance is the Obama DOJ's rejection of the defendant's position in the above brief that the Guantánamo defendants should be treated as "civilians directly participating in hostilities" and that the United States may only detain individuals who belong to that category.[21] The government argued that under the law of war, the United States was not limited to that category of persons and that "a contrary conclusion would improperly reward an enemy that violates the laws of war by operating as a loose network and camouflaging its forces as

[17] Department of Justice Withdraws "Enemy Combatant" Definition for Guantanamo Detainees | OPA | Department of Justice; *Respondents' Memorandum Regarding the Government's Detention Authority Relative to Detainees Held at Guantanamo Bay*, in the United States District Court for the District of Columbia, Filed 3/13/2009, Misc. No. 08-442 (TFH).

[18] *DOJ Withdraws "Enemy Combatant" Definition*, POLITICO.

[19] United States, "The Obama Administration's Internment Standards | How Does Law Protect in War?," Online Casebook, https://icrc.org.

[20] *Id.*

[21] *Respondents' Memorandum Regarding the Government's Detention Authority Relative to Detainees Held at Guantanamo Bay*, in the United States District Court for the District of Columbia, Filed 3/13/2009, Misc. No. 08-442 (TFH) at 8.

civilians."[22] As this chapter explains later, it is not clear that relying on the "direct participation" standard would have reduced the Obama Administration's authority to pursue Al Qaeda and the Taliban significantly, and meanwhile it would have helped to protect the integrity of the law of war, as well as guarded against detainee mistreatment.

Under both the Bush and the Obama administrations' approach to violent non-state actors, the United States saw itself as involved in an armed conflict with highly organized, nongovernmental forces that controlled significant territory from which they were able to carry out sustained military operations. They distinguished military operations in these area from operations in places like Yemen, Syria, and Somalia, where many of the more controversial targeted killing strikes were carried out. Recognizing this distinction, the Obama administration regarded the latter areas as governed not by the LOAC, strictly speaking, but rather by the Presidential Policy Guidance (PPG), which assesses the permissibility of using lethal force according to roughly a civilian law-enforcement model. And thus they resisted any characterization of individuals within the zone of armed conflict as "civilians."

In cases in which violent non-state actors can be understood as sufficiently organized and the level of violence sufficiently intense, non-state actors can be understood as "civilians directly participating" at the same time that the conflict in which they are engaged in a non-international armed conflict (NIAC).[23] Their detainability and targetability would seem to follow, which still leaves them protected under international law against inhumane treatment. They would not be subject to the requirement that they be captured prior to targeting, since their conduct would allow us to say that they are serving a "continuous combat function," as the International Committee of the Red Cross recommends, and hence that they are targetable continuously as well.

Outside the zone of armed conflict, however, matters would be different, and here the Obama administration recognized that different by promulgating the PPG. Under the PPG, targeted killing is only permissible when capture is not feasible and there is "near certainty" that no civilians will be harmed.[24] Unlike a law of war framework, which makes it permissible to target combatants 24/7 based on their status and imposes no duty to attempt capture, non-state actors under the PPG are treated roughly as civilians who are assisting in the violent operations of their military counterparts within zones of armed conflict. The test for targetability is thus close to what would be used in a civilian law-enforcement model, namely, whether the individual in question poses an imminent risk of

[22] *Id.*

[23] *See* Additional Protocols of June 8, 1977 to the Geneva Conventions of Aug. 12, 1949.

[24] *See* Heather Brandon, *Will Obama's Targeted Killing Policy Say What "Areas of Active Hostilities" Means?*, LAWFARE, May 5, 2016.

harm based on his current or anticipated activity. When this standard was actually operationalized, however, the treatment of non-state actors in the domain of the PPG did not match the theory terribly well, and the resulting military or intelligence operations ended up looking a great deal more like the former Bush unlawful combatancy standard.

Consider the case of Anwar al-Awlaki, the American citizens who was killed by a US drone strike in Yemen, a country with which we were not at war. Al-Awlaki was a member of Al Qaeda in the Arabian Peninsula (AQAP), rather than Al Qaeda proper, and was in theory entitled to treatment under the PPG according to the civilian framework appropriate for law enforcement. Yet the formal parameters established by the PPG were left to interpretation by the Office of Legal Counsel,[25] which issued a confusing memo maintaining that the operation against al-Awlaki in Yemen was "part of the non-international armed conflict with al-Qaida."[26] Nevertheless, the OLC memo concluded that the targeted killing of al-Awlaki would fall within the armed conflict recognized by the *Hamdan* Court, and that therefore it would also be covered by the "public authority" justification for intentional targeting of an American citizen. Under the OLC memo, in other words, the strike on al-Awlaki was treated as an extension of the NIAC in Iraq and Afghanistan, which made al-Awlaki targetable as though we were situated in a combat zone, namely without prior attempt to capture.

In a gesture to the PPG, the OLC memo briefly dealt with the duty to capture by saying that both the Department of Defense and the CIA, which were to conduct the operation, "represented that they intend to capture rather than target al-Aulaqi if feasible; yet we also understand that an operation by either agency to capture al-Aulaqi in Yemen would be infeasible at this time."[27] In this way, the Obama administration essentially continued the "unlawful combatancy" framework established by the Bush administration by another name: instead of calling violent non-state actors "unlawful combatants," they paid lip service to the distinction between combatants and civilians, but ended up with the same conclusion by treating non-state actors as part of a NIAC, even if they were outside the formal areas of hostilities, as well as by declaring capture "infeasible."[28]

This was a profoundly problematic approach with regard to PPG-controlled territory. The basic distinction between war and not-war is no longer maintained if we treat individuals outside of zones of armed conflict as targetable without

[25] Office of Legal Counsel, U.S. Department of Justice, "Memorandum for the Attorney General Re: Applicability of Federal Criminal Laws and the Constitution to Contemplated Lethal Operations Against Shaykh Anwar al-Aulaqi," July 16, 2010.

[26] *Id.* at 24.

[27] *Id.* at 40.

[28] The OLC memo also used an expanded conception of "imminence" in order to reach the conclusion that Anwar al-Awlaki posed an "imminent" threat of harm, and that therefore the United States could not safely wait for an opportune moment to effectuate capture.

prior attempts at capture and an opportunity to surrender. The only justification for targeted killing outside of war can be self-defense, whether national self-defense under Article 51 of the UN Charter or individual self-defense based on a threat to an individual in the territory from which the threat emanates. Whenever legal distinctions are effaced, the result is lack of clarity on both sides of the line: in this case not only were the rules for civilian capture and the use of legal force outside of war damaged, but the rule of war would ultimately be effaced as well.

On the approach for which this chapter argues, by contrast, we should regard violent, non-state actors as criminal civilians outside of designated zones of armed conflict, and regard them as civilians engaged in a NIAC who thereby acquire an activity-based combatant status within domains of active hostilities. Section VI will explore this suggestion in greater detail. Let us first turn, however, to the next chapter in the war on terror, namely, the use of targeted killing by the Trump administration, particularly as exemplified in the Soleimani killing.

V. Trump and the Extrajudicial Killing of State Actors

The use of targeted killing reached a fever pitch under the Trump administration. In Somalia alone, the Trump administration engaged in 192 drone strikes, a significant increase from the Obama Administration's 43 in the same region. However until the killing of Qasem Soleimani, the Trump administration appeared to be simply continuing the pattern Obama more or less began. The Soleimani killing took us to a new level.

Long considered dangerous to US forces abroad and part of the Iranian mechanism for state-sponsored terrorism, Soleimani had been in the sights of both the Obama and Bush administrations, but foreign policy and military experts from those administrations had uniformly agreed that a strike on Soleimani would represent a dangerous escalation and was unacceptably risky, despite the fact that the two administrations had very different approaches towards Iran. Both previous administrations, however, understood that taking out a high-ranking military leader might be regarded as an act of war and might entitle Iran to retaliate in self-defense. Needless to say, neither administration had asked Congress for authorization to engage in targeted killing operations, even when these occur outside of zones of armed conflict, though much of the targeted killing in the war on terror was justified by the administration under the "associated forces" doctrine of the 2001 AUMF.

History bears witness to the fact that a single assassination of a state actor can precipitate an international armed conflict (IAC). The killing of Archduke Franz Ferdinand and his wife in 1914, for example, was the spark that ignited the First

World War, given that the Austro-Hungarian Empire blamed the killing on the Serbian government, and the complex network of alliances quickly produced a descent into international military conflict. Yet while the ingredients were present for Soleimani's killing to produce a comparable conflagration, the only immediate consequence was an Iranian attack on two US airbases in Iraq, resulting in brain injuries of over one hundred servicemen but no fatalities. Although Iran labeled the killing of Soleimani "an act of war," and other world leaders appeared to have sympathy with that perspective, still the United States did not thereby catapult itself, Iran, and their respective allies into an international conflagration. Unlike the response of the Austro-Hungarian Empire in 1914, Iran's response was ultimately tepid and the price the United States paid mostly diplomatic.

The critical question Trump introduced, and one that was not clearly answered after the Soleimani strike, is whether targeted killing of state actors is ever permissible outside a theater of war, and if so, under what theory it can be justified. From the previous discussion, it should be clear that where state agency exists, targeting is normally permissible only when in a state of armed conflict with the target nation. If no such state of war exists, there must be a legitimate casus belli to embark on military action, such as that the other country has engaged in a significant violation of the sovereignty rights of the country seeking to use force, or that there is a violation of the rights of a third-party nation the action would be defending. In short, the legality of the action must be judged by considerations drawn from the domain of the *jus ad bellum*. With the exception of the rare instances in which the use of preemptive force may be used in anticipation of imminent defensive action, a first strike on a sovereign nation is not permissible under international law.

We must then ask whether invocation of the doctrine of self-defense would have justified the strike on Soleimani. This raises the thorny question of the permissible scope of preemptive self-defense under the UN Charter, Article 51. On the face of that provision, it is not necessary for an actual kinetic strike to have occurred in order for the United States to invoke the self-defense doctrine. The concept of "anticipatory self-defense" goes back at least to 1837 and the *Caroline* Affair, which arguably established the doctrine of anticipatory self-defense in international law.[29] In an exchange of letters on the case, Daniel Webster and Alexander Baring appeared to agree that anticipatory self-defense is part of the law of self-defense. However, as Webster expressed it, self-defense could only be established if the state could show "a necessity of self-defense, instant, overwhelming, leaving no choice of means, and no moment for deliberation."[30] This

[29] The case arose when an expedition of Canadian militia crossed over the US shore and were quickly attacked by Canadian rebels fighting from the American side near to the US vessel the *Caroline*. The Canadian party lit the *Caroline* ablaze and untied it from its moorings, whereupon it was promptly lost when it went over Niagara Falls.

[30] See id.

was the first case to clearly state the need for states to satisfy the imminence requirement in the context of international relations and the law of armed conflict. But the case also had the effect of affirming the permissibility of preemptive self-defense in an international armed conflict.

This principle was confirmed in the landmark case of *Nicaragua v. United States*,[31] which came before the International Court of Justice (ICJ) in 1984 regarding military and paramilitary activities on the part of the United States in El Salvador to foment violence against Nicaragua. Without admitting to the alleged conduct, the United States claimed to be acting in defense of its right of "collective self-defense" on behalf of El Salvador, and thus to be asserting as third-party defense the right of El Salvador to act in anticipatory self-defense. The alleged activities involved in acting on this claim of self-defense were based on CIA covert operations in assistance of El Salvador, such as the mining of Nicaraguan harbors, attacks on Nicaraguan airports and shipping ports, attacks on oil storage facilities, as well as on helicopter and boats. The ICJ affirmed the principle of anticipatory self-defense but placed limits on the scope of that doctrine. It held in this case that the United States had exceeded the bounds of any reasonable right to self-defense, given the lack of imminence of El Salvador's asserted need to act in self-defense.

In Soleimani's case the public does not have access to the intelligence required to make a full assessment of the danger Soleimani posed and whether his killing would indeed forestall the risk of harm to US persons. While it cannot be doubted that Soleimani had hostile intentions toward the United States and had fomented violence over the years against Western powers, retribution for past wrongs is not a valid basis for exercising the *jus ad bellum* right to engage in a military strike against a foreign sovereignty. The question, therefore, must hinge entirely on the danger Soleimani posed prospectively, the imminence of that danger, and the effectiveness of the proposed military means of forestalling it. From the evidence presented before Congress and the American people, as well as the decision of the two previous administrations, one Democratic, one Republican, not to strike Soleimani, it seems most probable that the evidence would not support a claim of imminence.

An important argument was made in Soleimani's case, however, that insofar as he was planning terroristic actions against the United States, making use of his Quds Force and a network of terrorists with whom they are connected, he should be thought of as wearing two hats: he functions both as a state and a non-state actor, and as such, the analysis we use with respect to non-state actors generally

[31] Judgments | Military and Paramilitary Activities in and against Nicaragua (Nicaragua v. United States of America) | International Court of Justice, https://icj-cij.org.

can be applied here. The question then arises: How should international states treat individuals who occupy multiple categories in international law?

One of the arguments for "dual hattedness" goes back to the criteria for combatancy discussed in section II, namely, the condition that valid state combatants must respect the laws of war. Does failure to respect the laws of war then automatically mean that the individual can be considered a non-state actor for purposes of targetability? The argument would appear to be circular. For if an individual counts as a terrorist just by virtue of refusing to abide by the laws of war, that would suggest that no state could violate the laws of war, and therefore no legitimate basis can ever exist for exercising a first strike against another sovereign state .

This argument, however, would appear to prove too much. States can engage in illegal action just as individuals can. Therefore, rather than exempting Soleimani from the domain of state agency given his willingness to violate the terms of international law, the attribution should instead run the other way: insofar as Iran allowed Soleimani to retain his official position as leader of the Quds Force, as well as other official state functions, any actions in which he engaged that violated international law can in turn be attributed to the state. This is consistent, for example, with the *Tadic* case, in which the International Criminal Tribunal for the Former Yugoslavia (ICTY) held that it is permissible to ascribe the conduct of organized armed groups to states if that state exercises "overall control" over those groups. And that suggests that even in a NIAC, there is no reason to exempt the analysis of the threat posed by a state actor from the general laws of war and to treat them the same way we would treat violent non-state actors. Thus if Soleimani were to plan an unprovoked attack against American citizens, and he does so repeatedly, then his actions can be attributed to the sovereign nation of Iran, and Iran must in turn bear responsibility for his actions.

While the logic of the dual-hatted argument is clear, it cannot be used to justify a kinetic strike against a state actor, since state actor status must override non-state actor status under IHL. Moreover, the dual-hatted argument is a dangerous one to make. The argument would contribute most significantly to the erosion of the rule of law the law of in armed conflict, as it would permit a host country like Iran to avoid responsibility for the acts of its officials and to intentionally disclaim its duty to discipline Soleimani on the grounds that he does not speak or act in his official capacity when he foments or plans violence against other nations.

This approach clearly poses a significant obstacle to the use of force against a state actor, insofar as it requires any attack on such an individual to be justified under the *jus ad bellum* doctrine of LOAC. But the hurdle is a fully appropriate, even a desirable one. It should not be easy to justify the use of force against a leader of a foreign sovereign nation, but if a state actor does engage or is about to engage in a kinetic strike on US persons, the state must bear the responsibility for his actions in most instances. And indeed, when we consider the official Section 1264 report to Congress regarding the Soleimani strike, he is described as the "leader of Iran's Islamic Revolutionary Guard Corps-Quds Force," and the purpose of the strike "to deter Iran," "degrade Iran's and Quds Force-based militias' ability to conduct attacks," and "end Iran's strategic escalation of attacks," thus implying that the target was, from the start, conceived as the independent sovereign nation of Iran.

VI. Preserving the Distinction between War and Crime

The nature of warfare has changed dramatically over the course of the past fifty years, starting at least with Vietnam, and continuing with the war on terror launched after the 9/11 attacks by the Bush administration. The evolving nature of warfare, however, does not require a wholesale revision of the legal concepts we use to understand war and to establish rules for the treatment of both combatants and civilians within it. The biggest legal challenge post 9/11 has been determining the status of violent non-state actors organized into large militia-like hierarchies, yet unlike traditional combatants, they are lacking governmental involvement. The challenge we face is distinguishing state from non-state actors in conflict without effacing the line between armed conflict and civilian law enforcement. We have, in effect four categories that emerge from these two critical distinctions, as shown in Table 6.1.

Since 9/11, the most important and yet the most difficult domain to categorize is the lower left box in of Table 6.1, namely, the category of violent non-state actors who are engaged in a military-style conflict of high intensity with a hierarchically organized group possessing a command and control structure. This

Table 6.1

	Armed Conflict	Law Enforcement
State Actor	Full-Scale Status-based Combatancy IHL/LOAC POW status if captured	International Cooperation/Immunity Criminal Heads of State—governed by the *jus ad bellum*
Non-State Actor	Civilian Immunity/Civilian Engaged in Hostilities/NIAC No POW status Activity-based on status-based?	Domestic Criminal Law/Extradition/Capture Mission/Targeting in Self-Defense if Capture Infeasible (al-Awlaki) Activity-based assessment

is the group that the Bush administration dubbed "unlawful combatants," thus using a kind of hybrid categorization to justify indefinite detention and interrogation without extending POW status. This chapter has made clear that this solution does not work.

A number of commentators have suggested that this group should be treated as "functionally" equivalent to traditional combatants, as a way of resurrecting the idea of a status-based assessment of the targeting decision within this category. Jens Ohlin, for example, argues that if someone functions within an organization in the way that traditional combatants do in the state military hierarchy, they should count as a full-blown combatant for purposes of armed conflict. He writes: "The functional equivalent in cases of targeted killings would link the individual to the collective terrorist group if the individual is a card-carrying member of a terrorist organization or a self-declared enemy of the United States."[32] Ohlin goes on to explain that an individual terrorist bears the right relationship to the terrorist organization for purposes of combatancy if the organization is hierarchically organized, the individual in question is given orders or instructions to act on behalf of that organization, and there is a common ideology or group that unites the members of that organization and makes them into a single entity.

The Obama administration appears to have taken a functional approach at times as well, such as in its response to the habeas petitions which it filed in 2009. As the government wrote:

> *Under a functional analysis*, individuals who provide substantial support to al-Qaida forces in other parts of the world may properly be deemed part of al-Qaida itself. Such activities may also constitute the type of substantial support that, in analogous circumstances in a traditional international armed conflict, is sufficient to justify detention.[33]

But the government's brief does not explain why the fact that serving the same function in an IAC would justify the parallel conclusion with regard to Al Qaeda in this context—namely, that an individual who rendered material support is a member of Al Qaeda and thus counts as a combatant. The missing analysis seems particularly important given that the status of Al Qaeda is itself unclear under LOAC. Thus establishing membership in Al Qaeda on the basis of material support may not justify the conclusion that such individuals should count as

[32] Jen Ohlin, Targeting Co-Belligerents, Targeted Killings in Asymmetrical War (Claire Finkelstein, Jens Ohlin, & Andrew Altman eds., 2012).

[33] *See Respondents' Memorandum Regarding the Government's Detention Authority Relative to Detainees Held at Guantanamo Bay*, in the United States District Court for the District of Columbia, Filed 3/13/2009, Misc. No. 08-442 (TFH), at 7.

"combatants" in the same way that establishing material support for an enemy military may warrant the conclusion that the civilian rendering assistance has become a combatant.

Convenient as a middle ground would be for the ability of the law of war to absorb the non-state terrorist into its jurisprudence, the functionalist approach arguably misses the point of the traditional concept of combatancy, which has to do with the identity of the *state* as the organization to which the combatant is attached. The point is not that the concept of combatancy identifies individuals who act as part of a group, any group, as long as that group is sufficiently large, hierarchically organized and the actions of its members reflect the ideology of the group. If this were the criteria for combatancy, we would be unable to distinguish drug lords from foreign militaries, and the meaning of the combatant status would be significantly altered.

Instead, there is a way to bring the view of the Obama administration—namely, that violent non-state actors are targetable within traditional zones of hostility because they are combatants but must be captured unless infeasible outside those zones—within the fold of the traditional law of war, without necessitating the turn to the Bush category of "unlawful combatancy" or defining civilian terrorists as "combatants" on some sort of functional ground. This would be to say that members of Al Qaeda and the Taliban, and later ISIS, are "civilians directly participating in hostilities," a traditional hybrid category that has existed under LOAC for many years. It might then be argued that in Northern Iraq and Afghanistan, the level of intensity of the fighting was so great that such civilians "directly participating" can be considered civilian-combatants under international law, given that they serve what the International Committee of the Red Cross (ICRC) has called "a continuous combat function." In other words, within zones of armed combat, such as in Northern Iraq and Afghanistan, civilians directly participating in hostilities might be thought of as participants in a NIAC, namely, an armed conflict between one or more non-state armed groups and a state military, yet these same individuals revert to their civilian status outside this context.

Is it a contradiction in terms to say that non-state actors are both "civilians" and that they are "directly participating in hostilities?" Arguably it is not, given that so-called "combatants" in a NIAC have a somewhat different status under international law from participants in an IAC. In theory, to say someone is a participant in an IAC means he is a state actor, and that automatically makes him a combatant in the full, status-based sense of the term. It also means he has combatant immunity, and that if captured, he has full POW status under the Geneva Conventions. Participants in a NIAC, by contrast, do not have the same status, and if captured they do not have full POW protection. Participants in a NIAC are targetable, however, but we need not see their targetability as based on status, as both the Bush and Obama administrations did,[34] but rather on the dangerousness of their activities. For non-state actors to be continuously targetable, however, hostilities must reach a certain level of intensity and the nongovernmental armed forces involved must be hierarchically organized according to a formal command structure.[35]

With regard to detention and POW status, both combatants and civilians receive greater protection in an IAC than they do in a NIAC. Combatants in an IAC are protected not only by Common Articles 3 and 4 of the Geneva Conventions; they are also protected by Additional Protocol I.[36] For example, combatant protection for POWs is clearly articulated under Article 44 of the Additional Protocol I, which extends protection even to those who have violated some of the rules of international law in armed conflict under most conditions.[37] Additional Protocol I provides that those who fall captive while failing to observe the obligation to wear arms openly "shall, nevertheless, be given protections equivalent in all respects to those accorded to prisoners of war by the Third Convention and by this Protocol." In other words, even those who, like members of Al Qaeda and the Taliban, violate the most basic laws of war must be treated as humanely as official POWs.

The position for which this chapter has argued appears to be the rough position of the Israeli Supreme Court, which articulated a framework based on a more traditional model of civilians engaging in hostilities. The Court vigorously rejected the Bush administration's device of calling violent non-state actors "unlawful combatants," and it maintained that this category has not been recognized in customary international law.[38] Chief Justice Barak found that the Palestinian militants targeted by Israel were not combatants of any sort, but rather civilians who had in some cases forfeited their protected status by choosing to take part in hostilities. The Court found support for its approach in IHL under Article 51(3) of Additional Protocol I, which provides that "Civilians shall enjoy the protection afforded by this Section, unless and for such time as they take a direct part in hostilities," a position that the Court recognized as consistent with customary international law. The question, then, becomes: Under what conditions can a civilian be considered to have "directly participated in hostilities"? How far back do we trace the engagement of those who organize and support an attack behind the scenes? The Court took a reasonably broad view of this question, against the

34 *See* Hamdan v. Rumsfeld, 548 U.S. 557, 62–31 (2006).

35 *See* "Non-international Armed Conflict | How Does Law Protect in War?," Online Casebook, https://icrc.org.

36 Protocol Additional to the Geneva Conventions of Aug. 12, 1949, and Relating to the Protection of Victims of International Armed Conflicts (Protocol I), of June 8, 1977.

37 Additional Protocol I identifies as an exception an individual who fails to carry his arms openly during military engagements.

38 PCATI (2006) HCJ 769/02, [21] (President Barak), at 28.

position of the plaintiffs who argued for a narrow approach, meaning that the Court thought those who finance and support those in active hostilities could be considered civilians directly participating.

For present purposes, the exact line of demarcation between protected civilians and civilians engaging in hostilities is not what is most critical, though that is a question that must be solved in a fuller account of this type of approach. What is of greater importance is whether a hybrid approach can be integrated into the traditional law of war. Treating violent non-state actors as civilians seems like the right approach, but this is also an approach that requires an account of how and when such civilians make themselves targetable. The general approach of the Israeli Supreme Court is to regard civilians as targetable when they engage in conduct that would trigger the right of self-defense under Article 51 of the UN Charter on the part of the state actors. Once civilians conduct themselves in ways that threaten the lives of state actors, they forfeit their protected status.

Normally civilians who become targetable would regain that protection as soon as they cease to pose a threat. The Israeli Supreme Court, however, said that a civilian who is a member of a terrorist organization and whose role is to regularly participates in a chain of hostilities, "with short periods of rest between them," effectively may be targeted at any time, since "the rest between hostilities is nothing other than preparation for the next hostility." This person is not a combatant, but the requirement under Additional Protocol I that they may be targeted "for such time" as they are engaged in hostilities is applicable to them. The ICRC reaches a comparable conclusion, but characterizes such a person as a non-state combatant. It says that once that conduct amounts to a sufficiently high level of intensity, it is reasonable to think the non-state actors are serving a "continuous combat function," which means that we can treat them as targetable continuously, thus mimicking the liability of state actors who are targetable on the basis of status. This may seem to be a distinction without a difference, if it results in the same permissibility of targeting that a combatant approach would produce. However, there is a significant difference in the rationale for targeting state and non-state actors in that the status of non-state combatant, unlike state combatants, is dependent on conduct. This difference alters a number of aspects of the interaction in the treatment of non-state actors, as well as the conditions under which the actors may be targeted.

First, in the case of civilians directly engaging in hostilities, the permissibility of targeting will depend on the self-defense framework that applies in the context of law enforcement. Thus in order for it to be permissible to target a civilian, even one engaged in hostilities, that person must pose a threat of imminent harm, or, alternatively, it must be "immediately necessary" to act preemptively to forestall the harm, even if the harm itself is not imminent. While there are different approaches to both personal and national self-defense on the question of imminence, the general pattern is consistent: the justification for engaging in lethal force depends on the immediacy of the threat that needs to be forestalled or the urgency of acting to forestall it. This is entirely different from a status based justification for killing that usually accompanies the LOAC as applied to combatants. However, it fits reasonably well with the traditional treatment of civilians directly engaged in hostilities, and thus it seems unnecessary to create a new legal framework that makes use of hybrid categories like "unlawful combatancy" in order to articulate a coherent framework for dealing with violent non-state actors.

Once it is determined that the enemy belligerent poses a grave risk of harm and that it is necessary to act immediately to forestall that harm, the question is whether it is feasible to capture and detain that individual or whether capture is in fact in feasible. In a law of war framework, of course, it is not necessary to attempt capture prior to killing. But in a civilian framework, even when the threat is imminent, it is necessary to attempt capture prior to making use of lethal force provided that capture is feasible. If capture is infeasible, there is no obligation to attempt it, and the target may be killed directly assuming the other conditions of self-defense obtain.

Of course the meaning of "feasibility" in this context is complex. The question usually boils down to what degree of risk to combatants it is necessary to take before capture is declared infeasible. Particularly with the advent of drones, capturing a suspect requires confronting much greater risk than is involved in killing him, given that capture operations must be conduced up close and in person. The killing of Osama bin Laden, for example, was from all appearances a targeted killing operation. The question arises, however, whether there was any attempt to capture bin Laden before using lethal force against him. Immediately following the announcement of the bin Laden strike, President Obama delivered remarks in which he said that he had directed Leon Panetta, the director of the CIA, "to make the killing or capture of bin Laden the top priority of our war against al Qaeda," and that, at his direction, the United States "launched a targeted operation against [bin Laden's] compound in Abbattabad, Pakistan."[39] That statement did not clarify whether the operation was a targeted killing operation or whether it was originally a capture mission, but there were no statements to the effect that the United States intended to capture bin Laden and bring him back to the United States to stand trial.

Finally, once the threat posed by the non-state actor has been determined to be imminent or the use of force against him requires the immediate use of force, and the suspect's capture has been determined to be infeasible, the question arises whether it is permissible to breach the sovereignty of the host country where the

[39] "Osama Bin Laden Dead," https://whitehouse.gov (archives.gov).

suspected terrorist resides. Normally, international law would dictate that it is not. The autonomy of each nation normally overrules the need of an aggrieved country to demand access to a suspected terrorist who has performed acts of violence against it. In the case of Osama bin Laden, for example, Pakistan in theory had the right to refuse to turn bin Laden over to the Americans. However, a doctrine known as the "unable or unwilling" doctrine maintains that if a country is harboring a criminal (or suspected terrorist), and that person poses a continuing danger yet the host country is unwilling to turn that person over to stand trial or to otherwise eliminate the danger, the aggrieved country may take matters into its own hands and act against him. While it was widely suspected that Pakistan probably did covertly extend permission to the Americans to conduct its raid on the bin Laden compound, arguably if it had not granted that permission, the United States might have been entitled to act to defend itself in any event. If Pakistan harbors a terrorist and refuses to take steps to protect other nations from the harm he poses, then other countries can consider Pakistan either "unable" or "unwilling" to neutralize the danger and they can then take matters into their own hands.

Needless to say, no comparable doctrine exists in the law of war. If an enemy belligerent escapes from a zone of armed conflict and crosses the border into a neighboring country, the United States as pursuing country is not permitted to breach the sovereignty of the nonbelligerent nation under most circumstances. To proceed with a strike in such a case would be tantamount to an act of hostility against the harboring nation and could lead to drawing that country into war. Consider, for example, a fanciful case in which Hitler had fled Germany toward the end of the war and escaped to Switzerland. Imagine the United States had stopped pursuing him at the Swiss border and had then demanded permission of the Swiss to enter Switzerland to target Hitler. If Switzerland had refused such a request and the United States proceeded nevertheless, US military action inside Switzerland could well be considered an attack on Switzerland itself, despite the fact that US actions would be directed against a German citizen and a member of the German military. The "unable or unwilling" doctrine would not give the United States leave to ignore Swiss sovereignty.

The line between combatants and civilians, even civilians directly participating in hostilities, is thus of the utmost importance for establishing the legal framework in which kill or capture operations take place. Once again, a fuller treatment of this topic would be necessary to clarify the meaning of "direct participation in hostilities," and where to draw the line between that category and civilians who are not sufficiently involved to count as "direct participants." But for present purposes, our focus is only on establishing the correct framework for determining the status of violent non-state actors. The framework set out above makes clear that there is a perfectly viable way to understand violent non-state actors based on the traditional law of war categories, and that it is therefore unnecessary to establish new categories such as "unlawful combatancy" in order to determine the treatment to which such individuals may be subjected.

VII. The Importance of the State in Combatancy

Stepping back from these details, however, the question arises: What the basis is for distinguishing violent non-state actors from violent state actors, where the latter's methods are as brutal and threatening as the former? What is significant about the fact that a combatant acts in the name of a state in the traditional account is that it is a *politically recognized*, autonomous, and sovereign entity, one that possesses the same rights and entitlements as other sovereign entities with whom it might have disagreements. In the traditional approach to the law of war, states are special, and different from other organizations in multiple ways, but one of particularly great importance is the concept of state sovereignty. Since states do not rule each other, and there is little in the way of common law that governs relations among states, war is the last resort for autonomous entities that have no common judge or other sovereign to whom they can appeal to settle their differences. Within a given state, the matter is entirely different: where, as Hobbes would say, there is "a common power to keep men in awe," there is no need in theory to resort to war. The law, as implemented by the sovereign under whose power it falls, provides the answers, and any resort to force in that context is usually not an act of war but a *crime*.

Accounts that attempt to find a middle ground between combatancy and criminal responsibility, or more particularly attempts to bring terrorism within the fold of combatancy by revising the definition of the latter, create the risk of weakening the limits on war, as well as the prerogatives of civil authority within a given legal regime. The concept of combatancy is integrally linked to the concept of "armed conflict." When there is armed conflict there are combatants, and without that designation of their activities, we cannot say there are belligerents. Thus the functionalist view of combatancy, insofar as it broadens that concept, also broadens the concept of armed conflict. There are grave risks, however, involved in expanding that notion, despite the fact that it is already one that has lost its boundaries. Partly this has occurred because of the unbounded nature of war: military confrontations tend now to have no distinct beginning, middle, or end, as well as no clear location. With a further loosening of the criteria for what counts as armed conflict, we risk losing the distinctiveness of war, with its distinct rules and norms, entirely, a state of affairs the famous theorist of war, Von Clausewitz, described as a hellish descent into "absolute war."[40]

[40] *See* CARL VON CLAUSEWITZ, ON WAR 529 (1976).

On the alternative view suggested here, violent non-state actors are civilians, albeit civilians engaged in militaristic activity that may amount to a NIAC. Below the level of intensity of a NIAC, we might think of violent non-state actors as highly dangerous members of an illegal criminal conspiracy, precisely on a par with violent members of drug cartels, comparable to the FARC, one of the largest organized crime syndicates in history.[41] Below the level of armed conflict, we might consider efforts to combat such groups as lying within the ambit of law enforcement practices, and international efforts to fight political terrorism as coordinated law enforcement operations among sovereign nations with a stake in the outcome. While such an approach may appear to tie the hands of our military and our ability to defend ourselves from terrorism, this is not in fact the case, as military tools and methods can be deployed to fight civilian threats. Indeed, the civil law enforcement model possesses great advantages, both for the rule of law and for national security efforts in fighting terrorism.

First, and most notably, there is a legal advantage in approaching members of terrorist organizations as members of a criminal conspiracy, which is that mere membership in the relevant organization is per se *illegal*. Under the armed conflict approach that has dominated since 9/11, since terrorists are combatants, there is nothing wrong with being a member of Al Qaeda or ISIS. The concept of "combatancy," after all, in theory affords as much protection and entitlement as it does targetability. There is no reason, however, to dignify membership in Al Qaeda or ISIS with the protection and status that state military organization possess. The latter are legitimate because sovereign states are entitled to defend their existence, but Al Qaeda and ISIS deserve no such protection. The organizations themselves are illegal and as such mere membership should be illegal.

The question we must consider carefully, however, is the extent to which the civilian law enforcement model applies within armed conflict—that is, to a high intensity battle with non-state actors where we can classify the civilians in question as serving "a continuous combat function." Under Additional Protocol I, individuals fighting for self-determination, for example, against colonial rule, would be engaged in "armed conflict" and would have the protections of the Geneva Conventions despite not being full combatants in the sense intended under Common Article III. Article 43 of Additional Protocol I says that the armed forces of a party "consist of all organized armed forces, groups and units which are under a command responsible to that Party for the conduct of its subordinates." And it maintains that all members of the armed forces of a party to a conflict "are combatants, that is to say, they have the right to participate directly in hostilities." Moreover, Additional Protocol I, Article 44, treats any combatant

[41] *See* Jeremy McDermott, *The Changing Face of Colombian Organized Crime*, Perspectivas, Sept. 2014.

who falls into the power of an adverse party as a "prisoner of war," and Article 44(3) extends certain traditional combatancy requirements to such individuals, such as the requirement that they carry their arms openly.

The question we are considering with regard to Al Qaeda and ISIS, then, seems to boil down to this provision in the Additional Protocol I: Given that the members of the terrorist organizations in question did not follow carry their arms openly and also did not follow the laws of war, should they still be treated according to the combatancy model suggested in Geneva for combatants in a NIAC? Or should they be treated instead according to the civilian law enforcement model we discussed earlier? Additional Protocol I supports the view that violent non-state actors should be thought of as on a par with civilians taking part in hostilities. Although the Additional Protocol does not specifically articulate such a conception, on this view, non-state combatants would be targetable on an activity-based theory, rather than a purely status-based account. In the case of the high-intensity conflict, such as we saw in Afghanistan and Iraq, state actors can target non-state combatants in a continuous fashion because the threat they pose is continuous and the activity in which they are engaged is hostile. As the level of threat diminishes, however, activity-based targeting would require a greater demonstration of threat. Such would be the case outside the zone of armed conflict, in which members of terrorist organizations are not presenting a continuous threat.

What this means for all intents and purposes is that once we are talking about Al Qaeda or ISIS in areas outside the zone of active hostilities, for example those areas covered by Obama's PPG, such individuals are not serving a continuous combat function and thus are not targetable in the first instance unless they pose an imminent danger of harm. Like Anwar al-Awlaki, they must be arrested, not summarily executed, unless the threat they pose warrants the immediate use of lethal force based on the need to forestall an imminent danger. On this view it is problematic to target someone from a distance, such as with a drone, unless they pose an imminent threat or their apprehension is "immediately necessary" and there is no way to apprehend them. However, the use of drones against civilians participating in hostilities may well be permissible within the formal zone of armed conflict, given that the intensity of conflict and the high level of danger in effect creates an activity-based justification for making the enemy continuously targetable.

Outside a zone of armed conflict, the civilian model must actually prevail in practice over the military model, and individuals targeted cannot be thought of as combatants in any sense, with the exception of the self-defense based killing that applies to every civilian. A common point of agreement must be that members of Al Qaeda who are outside former zones of hostilities must be considered civilians, plain and simple. It is also clear that this implies that they cannot just be targeted without an antecedent attempt to capture, and a determination that capture is "infeasible," as we discussed earlier. It is only by massaging the nature of the feasibility and imminence determinations that we have seemingly arrived at the conclusion that non-state actors can be directly targeted under the PPG.

Moreover, these areas are still considered sovereign nations, and as such it is not permissible under LOAC to conduct targeted killings against enemy belligerents in those areas without permission of the host nation. In theory, permission to carry out such operations is necessary from the host country, and if we proceed without such permission, we are effectively declaring war.[42] This once again helps to distinguish conflict in outlying areas, at the periphery of the conflict, from a situation that would quality as a NIAC, in which sovereignty considerations would not impede military engagement.

VIII. Conclusion

This chapter has argued in favor of the traditional position that the notion of combatancy is fundamentally tied to the concept of the state and the idea of state agency. Because of this, the chapter has also argued that violent non-state actors are essentially criminal civilians, rather than combatants, based on the fact that they are non-state actors. In the case of high-intensity conflict, such civilians may become continuously targetable based on their levels of activity and the threat they pose. This is what leads IHL, specifically Additional Protocol I, to treat such non-state actors as "combatants" and to distinguish them from civilians as though the traditional principle of distinction applied. On the view defended here, the label "combatant" in a NIAC is only a rough approximation: individuals are combatants only in the sense that they are targetable and that they must be treated on a par with formal POW's, despite the fact that they lack the state-based identity that provided the true basis for both combatant POW protections and for targetability based on status.

The insistence on state agency as a feature of combatant identity connects that concept with the deeper justification for permitting armed combat, namely, that states have equal autonomy, and so there is no power over them to resolve disputes between them. A non-state actor who wages "war" does not in

[42] In May 2016, the United States targeted and killed Mullah Akhtar Muhammad Mansour in the Pakistani province of Baluchistan. For the first time the Pakistanis were notified of the strike only after it occurred, signaling a change in US policy with respect to Pakistani sovereignty. This action is legal conduct for a strike within the zone of hostilities. In theory, neither the duty to capture before killing nor the deference to another state's sovereignty were observed in this case. *See* Mujib Mashal, "Taliban Chief Targeted by Drone Strike in Pakistan, Signaling a U.S. Shift, N.Y. Times, May 22, 2016. http://www.nytimes.com/2016/05/23/world/asia/afghanistan-taliban-leader-mullah-mansour.html?_r=0.

fact possess that justification for resolving differences through combat. Instead of supplying a military justification for acting, he has acted on a principle that lends itself to resolution within the context of existing state or inter-state political and legal frameworks. To proceed as though he possessed the same justification as a traditional state actor is to confuse structure or function with normative principle.

The concept of a NIAC suggests that there is a form of warfare that is asymmetric, in that it pits an international state against a large and highly organized militant organization. When this occurs, the UN Charter suggests that the LOAC will broadly speaking apply, though the basis for this is not fully present. This, then, underscores the flaw in the Forfeiture theory of compliance with international norms: the fact that Al Qaeda does not follow international law does not release us from the duty to follow those same norms, since the source of authority of the norms in question is not the compliance of the other party.

With regard to Qasem Soleimani and other state actors, there is no avoiding the full panoply of rules of the LOAC. Despite Soleimani's potentially terroristic activities, his status as a state actor must take precedence over his non-state actions. The "dual-hatted" theory does not work as a justification for extrajudicial killing. Nor, from what we know of the facts, does the rationale of self-defense, which requires an imminent threat to the country or to an individual state actor. Once the limitations on the moves that can legitimately be made in this space become clear, it is quite a bit easier to justify those targeted killings that are legitimate, and also easier to protect the boundaries that demarcate domestic criminal law. The more we efface the distinction between the law of war and the law of crime, the greater the erosion we will encounter in our constitutional principles like due process, rights that require constant vigilance to safeguard and protect.

Polarization and even radicalization of the US population has created a grave risk that the norms of war will seep into domestic law enforcement practices as we battle increasingly extreme divisions in American society. Previously clear legal distinctions between the domestic law of crimes and the law of war have become difficult to maintain. As a result, other distinctions that are neighboring concepts in our rule of law traditions, such as that between state and non-state actors or that between foreign and domestic criminals, are also becoming eroded. We have seen the effects of such erosion in other countries, where illiberal regimes do not hesitate to turn deadly force on their own populations as a method of political control. Political assassinations have been a particularly preferred method of maintaining political control on the part of the Russians.[43] We

[43] *See* Richard W. Painter & Peter Golenbock, American Nero: The History of the Destruction of the Rule of Law and Why Trump Is the Worst Offender 243–44 (2020).

have seen the same thing in North Korea, in China, in Saudi Arabia, in Chile, and in many other places around the globe.

The legal confusion we have brought to this area and the weakening of formerly clear legal principles may ultimately open the door to domestic abuse of the technologies of war. As a result, there is a risk that the practices we render commonplace abroad may not stay on foreign soil when the conditions for their use are ill-defined. We face increasing militarization of domestic law enforcement, aided by a set of legal norms that knows fewer and fewer distinctions between the law of war and the law of crimes. While it is commonplace to suppose that extrajudicial killings, particularly those involving drone technology, could not occur on US soil, drone technology is already in use by federal law enforcement for surveillance purposes, and that practice will surely because increasingly commonplace. When these technological advances are combined with the significant development of growing violent extremism in the US population, not unlike that which we confronted in Iraq and Afghanistan at the beginning of the war on terror, the erosion of of the war/crime distinction presents a significant threat to the rule of law in the United States.

7
Urban Warfare
Policing Conflict

Kenneth Watkin

> *[I]n the 23 cases in which police or paramilitaries were not ineffective, COIN [counterinsurgency] forces won 69 percent of the time.*[1]

I. Introduction

Twenty-first-century conflict presents a number of significant challenges for international lawyers and security professionals who view armed conflict as the exclusive purview of military forces. These challenges arise as a result of the proliferation of a diverse range of non-state actor threats, the involvement of those actors in criminal activity in addition to terrorism and insurgency, and the increased tendency for such conflict to occur within heavily populated urban areas. The unique nature of contemporary conflict is captured in Rupert Smith's reference to conflict with non-state actor as fighting "amongst the people."[2] Inevitably armed conflict among the people must be reconciled with the broader responsibilities of the state for policing, which ultimately involves "the prevention and detection of crime and the maintenance of public order."[3] Policing roles, even in the context of military operations, can include controlling public demonstrations, suppressing crime, responding to crimes against individuals and property, and disarming persons.[4] A key issue is how the legal paradigm

[1] Christopher Paul et al., Paths to Victory, at xxviii (2013).

[2] Rupert Smith, The Utility of Force: The Art of War in the Modern World 3 (Penguin Books, Ltd., 2005).

[3] Oxford Dictionaries, <https://en.oxforddictionaries.com/definition/police> ("'Police' is defined as the civil force of a state, responsible for *the prevention and detection of crime and the maintenance of public order*.") (emphasis added).

[4] Timothy McCormack & Bruce M. Oswald, *The Maintenance of Law and Order in Military Operations*, *in* The Handbook of the International Law of Military Operations 444, para. 1 (Terry Gill & Dieter Fleck eds., Oxford University Press, 2010).

Kenneth Watkin, *Urban Warfare* In: *Between Crime and War*. Edited by: Claire Finkelstein, Christopher Fuller, Jens David Ohlin, Mitt Regan, Oxford University Press. © Claire Finkelstein, Christopher Fuller, Jens David Ohlin, Mitt Regan 2023. DOI: 10.1093/oso/9780197638798.003.0008

governing policing (i.e., human rights law) is impacted by the involvement of these state agencies in armed conflict.

This chapter will explore how law enforcement, which relies on a human rights based approach, is reconciled with conduct of hostilities based operations that have dominated much of the contemporary dialogue about defeating terrorist groups such as the Islamic State and even Al Qaeda (e.g., Damascus, Raqqa, Mosul, and Fallujah). The importance of incorporating a policing response into urban operations will be outlined in five sections. First, there is the growing challenge of an increasingly urbanized population and challenges to governance. Secondly, the nature of the contemporary security threats will be assessed to highlight the role that law enforcement can perform in preventing, containing, and ultimately defeating terrorist and insurgent activity in cities. This includes looking at the "police primacy" approach to counterinsurgency, which is not altered by the fact such operations occur in cities and towns. Next, an assessment of the human rights legal frameworks governing the law enforcement and its interface with more traditional applications of the law governing hostilities will be provided. The focus of this section is twofold. There will be an outline of the human rights based authority to use force that ordinarily applies to policing. This will highlight the interface and overlap of the two bodies of law governing the use of force: humanitarian law and human rights law. The analysis then turns to the impact of the criminalization of terrorist and insurgent acts, which helps makes the policing role key in bringing its perpetrators to justice. The fifth section will discuss the pressures that an insurgency place on police forces. The types and roles of police forces will be outlined to highlight how police can be employed to react to an insurgency threat. This will help identify policing options for states and their military commanders when seeking to counter terrorist and insurgent violence.

II. Urbanization and Challenges to Governance

The increasing urbanization of the world population is having a particular impact on how states respond to contemporary security threats. By 2000, the percentage of the world population living in cities "had reached at least 45 percent."[5] Fifty percent of the population lived in cities by 2008.[6] Further, it has been noted "of the four hundred-plus cities with over one million inhabitants, over 60 percent are in the Third World."[7] In Africa, it is predicted "that in 2030, Lagos, Cairo

[5] ANTHONY JAMES JOES, URBAN GUERRILLA WARFARE 6 (The University Press of Kentucky, 2007).
[6] *Id.* 1–2.
[7] *Id.* 2.

and Kinshasa will each have to cater for over 20 million people, while Luanda, Dar es Salaam and Johannesburg will have crossed the 10 million mark."[8] By 2035, Lagos could reach thirty million inhabitants, and a third of Africa's urban population will be living in West Africa.[9] An estimated 66 percent of the world's population will live in cities by 2050.[10] Further, this population is largely littoral, with 75 percent of the world's cities located on a coast and 80 percent of its population living within 60 miles of the sea.[11] The threat posed to urban areas in littoral regions was graphically demonstrated during the 2008 attack by LeT terrorists in Mumbai.[12] The threat of terrorism and insurgency in cities means that security cannot be the responsibility of military forces alone but rather must include the police and other law enforcement agencies (e.g., the coast guard).

The migration of populations to urban areas and the creation of megacities raise questions about how effectively they will be governed. This is particularly the case because most urbanization will occur in the poorest, less developed areas of the world. Large portions of that population live in "sprawling shantytowns, without streets or street addresses."[13] Weak governance in cities raises not only issues of rising crime levels but also terrorism and insurgencies. For much of the world, the violence associated with contemporary armed groups such as Al Qaeda and the Islamic State is looked at through the lens of terrorism. This includes transnational attacks occurring in cities such as Paris, New York, Ankara, Ottawa, Brussels, Mumbai, and Nairobi. However, the threat is also from groups such as those that seek to seize and hold urban territory. In other words, insurgents.

A particular challenge when addressing this threat is that there is no widely accepted definition of "terrorism" or "insurgency." Associated in the 1970s and 1980s with small groups focused on politically related violence and viewed almost exclusively as criminal activity, terrorism underwent a significant change at the end of the twentieth century in terms of levels of violence.[14] Insurgency has been rather loosely defined as occurring when "the rebelling faction being

[8] "Africa's Future Is Urban," Institute for Security Studies, Dec. 2, 2016, <https://issafrica.org/iss-today/africas-future-is-urban>.

[9] *Id.*

[10] United Nations, Department of Economic and Social Affairs, Population Division, "World Urbanization Prospects, the 2014 Revision: Highlights" (2014), <https://esa.un.org/unpd/wup/Publications/Files/WUP2014-Highlights.pdf>.

[11] David Kilcullen, Out of the Mountains: The Coming of Age of the Urban Guerrilla 30 (Oxford University Press, 2013).

[12] *Id.* 52–60.

[13] Joes, *supra* note 5, at 2.

[14] J. Paul de B. Taillon, Hijacking and Hostages: Government Responses to Terrorism 61 (Praeger, 2002) ("we are experiencing what has been described as hyperterrorism, superterrorism and megaterrorism.").

sufficiently organised to mount a credible threat to the government."[15] The difference between terrorism and insurgency is often assessed according to the scale of the violence, the ability to take and hold territory, and the goal of the group in displacing state authorities. The attacks of 9/11, which were directed at centers of economic and political power inevitably located in urban areas, highlighted that "terrorist" groups were capable of levels of violence long associated with armed conflict. There are groups that exclusively engage in terrorism. However, it is also clear that many insurgent groups use terrorism as part of their strategy to displace existing state governments. It is not uncommon to have those groups engaged in an insurgency, including ones that are transnational in nature (e.g., Al Qaeda, the Islamic State), also designated as terrorist groups.

The question of whether urban violence can rise to the level of an insurgency is not new. It was raised in the 1960s in Latin America with Carlos Marighella's theory of urban *focoists* (small armed bands carrying out attacks that provide the "focus" for the revolution), which had developed from a shift in population from rural to urban areas.[16] Due to the type of violence, and the cellular nature of the groups involved, urban insurgency was largely seen at that time as a form of terrorism. The term "urban insurgency" was itself referred to by one commentator as a "misnomer,"[17] and the concept as "terrorism in a new dress."[18] At best, it was seen as "an alternative to or in conjunction with guerrilla warfare."[19] However, this skeptical view of urban insurgency has undergone change in the past quarter century.

Ultimately, those seeking to govern territory must also control the cities.[20] Groups challenging the state have become increasingly focused on urban warfare and capable of fighting in that environment. In the late 1990s, Chechen warriors demonstrated they were "extremely adroit at innovating and extending the fight to the cities—a new operational environment for them. They adapted their small-team approach—ambushes, hit-and-run tactics, surprise attacks, and quick withdrawals—to the capital city of Grozny with lethal efficiency."[21] Further, insurgent forces in locations such as Iraq, Syria, Somalia, and the

[15] Lindsay Moir, *The Historical Development of the Application of Humanitarian Law in Non-International Armed Conflicts to 1949*, 47 INTERNATIONAL AND COMPARATIVE LAW QUARTERLY 337, 338 (1998).

[16] IAN F.W. BECKETT, MODERN INSURGENCIES AND COUNTER-INSURGENCIES: GUERRILLAS AND THEIR OPPONENTS SINCE 1750 174–75 (Routledge, 2001).

[17] Joes, *supra* note 5, at 7.

[18] WALTER LAQUEUR, GUERRILLA WARFARE: A HISTORICAL AND CRITICAL STUDY, at xix (Transaction Publishers, 2006).

[19] *Id.*

[20] LOUIS DIMARCO, CONCRETE HELL: URBAN WARFARE FROM STALINGRAD TO IRAQ 2 (Osprey Publishing, 2012).

[21] RICHARD H. SHULTZ & ANDREA J. DEW, INSURGENTS, TERRORISTS AND MILITIAS: WARRIORS OF CONTEMPORARY COMBAT 265 (Columbia University Press, 2006).

Occupied Territories have all demonstrated an ability to operate effectively in an urban environment.[22] Notably, a key Salafi jihadist doctrinal document, *The Management of Savagery: The Most Critical Stage Through Which the Umma Will Pass*,[23] followed by groups such as Al Qaeda and the Islamic State,[24] have identified "regions of savagery" to include "a city, or a village, or two cities, or a district, or part of a large city."[25] Jihadists have fought vicious battles in cities such as Fallujah, Mosul, and Raqqa. In this respect, US military operations in Iraq between 2003 and 2011 were "conducted almost entirely within Iraq's largest cities."[26] This is a trend that will continue.

The transnational threat posed by Salafi jihadists has dominated the security dialogue of the twenty-first century, although as David Kilcullen has noted more generally:

> [T]he main cluster of threats, both for individuals (sometimes known as threats to human security) and from a collective standpoint (threats to public safety or national security), will come from the environment itself [collapsing, overwhelmed urban infrastructure], not from any one group in it.[27]

However, "at least for the immediate future term, the future belongs to urban guerrilla warfare."[28] Attempts by insurgents to seize and hold urban areas have not ultimately proven successful.[29] As has been noted in respect of Syria and Iraq, "[o]utright victory against jihadis is difficult to achieve, but militant organisations targeted by the west are usually forced at the very least to abandon territorial gains, particularly urban centres."[30]

These conflicts have taken a tremendous toll on the civilian population and civilian infrastructure. This has been evident in recent clashes in

[22] *Id.* 265–66; James Fergusson, The World's Most Dangerous Place: Inside the Outlaw State of Somalia 18 (Da Capo Press, 2013).

[23] Abu Bakr Naji, The Management of Savagery: The Most Critical Stage Through Which the Umma Will Pass, [16] (William McCants trans., 2006), <https://azelin.files.wordpress.com/2010/08/abu-bakr-naji-the-management-of-savagery-the-most-critical-stage-through-which-the-umma-will-pass.pdf>. *See also* William McCants, The ISIS Apocalypse: The History, Strategy, and Doomsday Vision of the Islamic State 84 (St. Martin's Press, 2015) ("Today seasoned jihadists in the Islamic State study Naji's book in their camps. Online Islamic fanboys also celebrate the manual.").

[24] Ali Soufan, Anatomy of Terror: From the Death of bin Laden to the Rise of the Islamic State 260 (W.W. Norton & Company, 2017); Michael W.S. Ryan, Decoding Al-Qaeda's Strategy: The Deep Battle Against America 143 (Columbia University Press, 2013).

[25] Naji, *supra* note 23, at [16].

[26] DiMarco, *supra* note 20, at 213.

[27] Kilcullen, *supra* note 11, at 30.

[28] Joes, *supra* note 5, at 2.

[29] *Id.* 7.

[30] Jason Burke, *Rise and Fall of Isis: Its Dream of a Caliphate Is Over, So What Now?*, The Guardian, Oct. 21, 2017, <https://www.theguardian.com/world/2017/oct/21/isis-caliphate-islamic-state-raqqa-iraq-islamist>.

Damascus, Mosul, and Raqqa. For example, in December 2017, it was estimated that in the nine-month battle for Mosul, one million persons were displaced, 60,000 homes became inhabitable, and at least 20,000 commercial and government buildings were destroyed.[31] Some two years after Ramadi "was retaken from ISIS, more than 70 percent of the city remains damaged or destroyed."[32]

While insurgency and terrorism present unique challenges to state security forces it is also true that, ultimately, "war is war."[33] It involves death and destruction, which even in an insurgency context can involve the attributes of attritional conventional conflict. Not surprisingly, assaults on insurgent held cities and other "regions of savagery" have proven to be exceptionally destructive. Although the focus of humanitarian and human rights groups has largely been on restricting the use of such weapons in urban conflict,[34] the International Committee of the Red Cross has recognized that "explosive weapons—like bombs, rockets and shells—are not prohibited as such under humanitarian law."[35] As important as this issue is, there is a danger that concentration on the effects of aerial or artillery delivered ordnance is far too limiting an approach. Effectively countering the terrorism and insurgent violence associated with contemporary urban combat, and providing humanitarian protection to the civilian population, demands a more holistic response centered on the performance of a policing function contemporaneously with the conduct of more traditional military operations. This in turn requires a broader discussion of the levels of force to be applied in securing cities, the role of police forces in doing so, and how traditional notions of human rights law based policing can be reconciled with the conduct of hostilities. That dialogue must start with an analysis of a security challenge that presents an almost inseparable mélange of criminal violence and armed conflict.

[31] Margaret Coker, *After Fall of ISIS, Iraq's Second-Largest City Picks Up the Pieces*, N.Y. Times, Dec. 10, 2017, <https://www.nytimes.com/2017/12/10/world/middleeast/iraq-isis-mosul.html?_r=0>.

[32] Susannah George & Lori Hinnant, *Few Ready to Pay to Rebuild Iraq after the Islamic State Group Defeat*, Military Times, Dec. 28, 2017, <https://www.militarytimes.com/flashpoints/2017/12/28/few-ready-to-pay-to-rebuild-iraq-after-islamic-state-group-defeat/?utm_source=Sailthru&utm_medium=email&utm_campaign=EBB%2012.29.17&utm_term=Editorial%20-%20Early%20Bird%20Brief>.

[33] Hew Strachan, The Direction of War 207–09 (Cambridge University Press, 2013) (outlining the importance of a unitary vision of war).

[34] *See, e.g., ICRC Q&A on the Issue of Explosive Weapons In Populated Areas*, 98 International Review of the Red Cross 97 (2016).

[35] Vincent Bernard, *War in the Cities: The Spectre of Total War*, 98 International Review of the Red Cross 1, 7–8 (2016).

III. The Urban Threat and Policing Responses

A. Governance, Crime, and Threats to Security

While the 2016–2017 urban battles against the Islamic State in Iraq and Syria have created an enduring image of almost World War II Stalingrad-type street-by-street battles, the threat posed by non-state actors in the world's cities spans a much wider range of conflict. It has been indicated that "there are five major levels of insecurity that may be encountered in stability operations": war, insurgency, subversion, disorder, and "[n]ormal crime, including organized crime."[36] The contemporary threat posed to states involves an almost intimate intertwining of crime, terrorism, and insurgency. As will be discussed in this section, these threats favor a policing response for a number of reasons. First, there is the degree to which criminal activity thrives in situations of instability and poor governance. Secondly, non-state actors rely on crime and criminal elements to fund and support their activities. Thirdly, jihadist doctrine recognizes and even institutionalizes an approach that sees criminal activity, and at times low-level attacks, as part of how it conducts warfare. Fourthly, an effective counterinsurgency strategy prioritizes a "police primacy" approach.

Crime, terrorism, and insurgency are inevitably interrelated. There is an almost symbiotic relationship between instability and these activities. As has been noted by Bernard Fall, "[w]hen a country is being subverted it isn't being outfought; it's being out-governed."[37] The failure to govern adequately is typically a generator of criminal activity. Organized crime and insurgency "sprout from common roots: ineffective governance, systemic weakness and pathology, and a culture or tradition of clandestine activity."[38] Ungoverned spaces can lead to a proliferation of warlords and powerful criminal gangs that can establish themselves in an urban environment. In this respect, "leaders/warlords sometimes capture the city, sometimes just move in, but are always attracted by the city because of its importance as a transport hub, as a financial and services center and because of its prestige."[39]

In some cases, criminal activity alone can lead to what has been described as a criminal insurgency. This has occurred in Central and South America with

[36] David H. Bayley & Robert M. Perito, The Police in War: Fighting Insurgency, Terrorism, and Violent Crime 72 (Lynne Rienner Publishers, 2010).

[37] Bernard Fall, *The Theory and Practice of Insurgency and Counterinsurgency*, Naval College Review 21, 34.

[38] Steven Metz, Rethinking Insurgency 29 (2007), <http://ssi.armywarcollege.edu/pdffiles/pub790.pdf>.

[39] Antonio Giustozzi, Empires of Mud: Wars and Warlords in Afghanistan 21 (Hurst & Company, 2009).

the proliferation of drug cartels and other transnational criminal groups.[40] With parts of cities like Rio de Janeiro, Brazil, being almost impassable to police forces with significant military assistance,[41] and with an estimated two hundred thousand people killed in Mexico between 2006 and 2017,[42] the international community has struggled with the question of whether this violence constitutes an armed conflict.[43] States such as Mexico have focused on law enforcement based responses; however, the distinction between other contemporary insurgencies and a crime-based one can be exceedingly subtle.[44]

Criminal gangs and groups threatening the state often share "common origins based on tribalism, and therefore, it is expected that they will exhibit similar structures and behaviors."[45] As happened in Algiers in the 1950s, members of the insurgent organization may be recruited "from the seamier elements of the city, delinquents or habitual criminals."[46] This is evident in the contemporary recruiting of Islamic State fighters from the West, including for terrorist attacks in Europe and elsewhere.[47] Criminals, insurgents, tribal authorities, business networks, and government can be integrated to the extent that "the same individuals play multiple roles in multiple hierarchies."[48] The complex relationship between criminal gangs and insurgent groups was experienced in Iraq where it was often difficult to separate when kidnapping was being carried out by criminal gangs for purely economic motives or for political purposes.[49] It is also evident in

[40] Ioan Grillo, Gangster Warlords: Drug Dollars, Killing Fields, and the New Politics of Latin America 6 (Bloomsbury Press, 2016) ("the cartels spent their billions building armies of assassins who carry out massacres comparable to those in war zones and outgun police. They have diversified from drugs to a portfolio of crimes including extortion, kidnapping, theft of crude oil, and even wildcat mining. And they have grown to control the governments of entire cities and states in Latin America.").

[41] Dom Phillips, *Rio Police Hail Arrest of Drug Kingpin in 3,000-strong Favela Operation*, The Guardian, Dec. 6, 2017, <https://www.theguardian.com/world/2017/dec/06/most-wanted-trafficker-brazil-rogerio-da-silva-in-rio-arrested-3000-strong-operation>.

[42] *Mexico Violence: Six Bodies Found Hanging from Bridges near Resort*, BBC News, Dec. 21, 2017, <http://www.bbc.com/news/world-latin-america-42439421>.

[43] Emily Crawford, Identifying the Enemy: Civilian Participation in Armed Conflict 180–89 (Oxford University Press, 2015). *See also* The War Report: Armed Conflicts in 2017 83 (2018), <https://www.geneva-academy.ch/joomlatools-files/docman-files/The%20War%20Report%202017.pdf > ("In 2017, Mexico's security forces were arguably engaged in non-international armed conflicts with at least the Sinaloa Cartel and the Jalisco Cartel New Generation. It is important to note that this classification is controversial.").

[44] Kenneth Watkin, Fighting at the Legal Boundaries: Controlling the Use of Force in Contemporary Conflict 178–79 (Oxford University Press, 2016).

[45] John P. Sullivan & Robert J. Bunker, *Iraq and the Americas: 3 Gen Gangs Lessons and Prospects*, *in* Mexico's Criminal Insurgency 1 (John P. Sullivan & Robert J. Bunker eds., iUniverse.com, 2012).

[46] Roger Triquinier, Modern Warfare: A French View of Counterinsurgency 11 (Praeger Security International, 2006).

[47] Burke, *supra* note 30.

[48] Kilcullen, *supra* note 11, at 128.

[49] Paul Williams, Criminals, Militia, and Insurgents: Organized Crime in Iraq 129–34 (Books Express Publishing, 2009).

respect of the drug trade in Afghanistan[50] and the refinement and smuggling of oil in Iraq and Syria.[51]

The environment in which terrorism and insurgency develop has a definite impact on how such groups organize themselves and operate. In this respect, many of these groups adopt a cellular organization or have their roots in a noncentralized command relationship. While terrorists are most often associated with a cellular network, insurgencies may also adopt this structure depending upon the degree of insecurity they are experiencing[52] and where they are operating. It is a structure that is reflected in the improvised explosive device and suicide bombing cells of contemporary conflict.[53] Like criminal gangs, the urban environment has long forced those seeking to challenge the state to adopt a cellular approach in order to survive. One Al Qaeda doctrine writer, 'Adb Al-'Aziz Al-Muqrin, suggests that "[u]rban operations require small independent units whose number of personnel usually does not exceed four."[54] It is the networked structure of these organizations that makes police forces, and in particular their criminal intelligence expertise, an extremely valuable asset for engaging and defeating such groups.[55] Ultimately, these police based intelligence capabilities offer a key force multiplier for military commanders operating in an urban environment. The challenge is that military commanders frequently fail to recognize or fully take advantage of this capability.

While insurgent groups may adopt a cellular network in cities, they can also maintain a more traditional guerrilla, or military organization in rural areas. On other occasions, such as in Fallujah in 2004, the displacement of government authorities may permit an insurgent group to defend a city in street battles reminiscent of hostilities involving conventional armies.[56] In this respect, "[m]ilitary experts compare the assaults on Mosul and ISIS-held Raqqa in Syria to the devastating 1968 battle for the Vietnamese city of Hue."[57] It has been suggested that "[t]he late 20th century and first decade of the 21st century highlighted a

50 Abdel Bari Atwan, After bin Laden: Al Qaeda, the Next Generation 147 (The New Press, 2012).

51 Keith Johnson, *The Islamic State Is the New Petrostate*, Foreign Policy, July 28, 2014, <http://foreignpolicy.com/2014/07/28/the-islamic-state-is-the-newest-petrostate/>; Max Boot, Invisible Armies: An Epic History of Guerrilla Warfare from Ancient Times to the Present 532 (W.W. Norton & Company, 2013) ("[b]y its peak in 2005–2006 AQI was raising nearly $4.5 million a year, primarily from criminal rackets such as gasoline smuggling, car theft, and extortion.").

52 Abdulkader H. Sinno, Organizations at War in Afghanistan and Beyond 17 (Cornell University Press, 2008).

53 Ahmed S. Hashim, Insurgency and Counter-Insurgency in Iraq 60–62 (Cornell University Press, 2006).

54 Norman Cigar, Al-Qa'ida's Doctrine for Insurgency 120 (Potomic Books, Inc., 2009).

55 Randall Wilson, Blue Fish in a Dark Sea: Police Intelligence in a Counterinsurgency 147–50 (The University of Buckingham Press, 2013) (discussing this issue in respect of insurgencies). *See also* Williams, *supra* note 49, at 263–65.

56 Jason Burke, The 9/11 Wars 173 (Penguin Books, 2011).

57 George & Hinnant, *supra* note 32.

hybrid type of urban warfare that lies somewhere between intense conventional combat and low-intensity internal security operations."[58] When control of a city is exercised by a non-state actor, the violence inevitably requires the use of many of the traditional weapons of war to displace that group, including the use of air-power and artillery. However, security also ultimately depends on addressing the lower level and more indirect forms of warfare associated with insurgency and the criminal activity that frequently fuels it.

B. Funding Terrorism and Insurgency

The link between criminal gangs and terrorist and insurgent groups is not simply one of a common origin or similar organization. Participation in criminal activity has long been used by terrorist groups to alienate recruits from the government and the local population.[59] Importantly, proceeds from crime provide essential funding for groups challenging the state. As Paul Williams notes in his work on organized crime in Iraq, criminal activity undermines the security of the state and also provides "a funding mechanism for a variety of violent nonstate armed groups."[60] Such criminal acts go far beyond the traditional notion of terrorist groups robbing banks to support their activities,[61] although considerable wealth has been gained from looting banks by groups such as the Islamic State.[62] It can include insurgents smuggling of various goods (e.g., drugs, oil, charcoal, cigarettes), extortion, arms trafficking, human trafficking, counterfeiting, money laundering, fraud, intellectual property piracy, illegal trade in ivory, and the expropriation of humanitarian assistance funds.[63] For example, in Iraqi city of Kahlidiya [population 25,000] insurgent agents were selling black market oil, and "[t]he profiteers had a huge incentive to pay $100 to each digger who would plant a mine to prevent the Snake Eaters [Iraqi battalion advised by a US military advisory team] from gaining control of the streets—and of the fuel business."[64]

58 DiMarco, *supra* note 20, at 212.

59 Kilcullen, *supra* note 11, at 128.

60 Williams, *supra* note 49, at 269.

61 Carlos Marighella, Minimanual of the Urban Guerrilla 25–26 (Red and Black Publishers, 2008) (1972).

62 Matthew Rosenburg, Helen Cooper, & Nicholas Kulish, *U.S. Military Campaign Takes Toll on ISIS' Cash Flow*, N.Y. Times, Apr. 12, 2016, <https://www.nytimes.com/2016/04/13/world/middleeast/isis-iraq-syria.html?_r=0>.

63 *See* Juan C. Zarate, Treasury's War: Unleashing of a New Era of Financial Warfare 23 (Public Affairs, 2013); Matthew Levitt, Hezbollah: The Global Footprint of Lebanon's Part of God 13 (Georgetown University Press, 2013); David Smith, *Al-Shabaab Rebuilds Forces in Somalia as African Union Campaign Stalls*, The Guardian, Oct. 28, 2013, <https://www.theguardian.com/world/2013/oct/28/al-shabaab-somalia-african-union>; Johnson, *supra* note 51.

64 Owen West, The Snake Eaters: An Unlikely Band of Brothers and the Battle for the Soul of Iraq 267 (Free Press, 2012).

Hostage-taking is a significant source of income for jihadist groups with the Islamic State having earned millions ransoming Western hostages.[65] It is an activity that forms part of their widely adopted doctrine.[66] Kidnapping, either insurgent- or criminal-based, has been a common occurrence in various conflict zones such as Iraq, Columbia, the Philippines, Nigeria, and the African Sahel and Maghreb. In Iraq, kidnapping was very profitable, with many more Iraqis being kidnapped than foreigners[67] and with hostages being taken for both economic and political reasons.[68] Some entities used organized criminal activities as a means of furthering their political goals.[69] It proved extremely difficult to ascertain the motives of many groups, which included former regime elements, former convicts, unemployed youths and men, opportunistic amateurs, insurgents and militia groups, as well as militias and militia factions.[70] The failure to understand the relationship between the violence in Iraq and organized crime has been described as a "strategic surprise," with criminality adding "to the hybrid quality of the anti-coalition violence."[71] This is an area where a focus on law enforcement, rather than armed conflict, can degrade the ability of a non-state actor to carry out its political agenda.

Coalition armed forces have not entirely ignored the link between criminal activity and the insurgencies in Afghanistan, Iraq, and Syria. The United States has been a strong proponent of kinetically attacking drug production and distribution in Afghanistan[72] and the illicit refinement and smuggling of oil in Iraq and Syria under the theory that such activity is "war sustaining."[73] In effect, the proceeds from the smuggling of drugs and oil are fueling the insurgencies. Such targeting has also been extended to money-storage sites. It should come as no surprise that such sites would be located in an urban environment where governance structures are concentrated.[74] There is evidence that such action has impacted on the financial capacity of the Islamic State to carry out its operations, although its overall impact on bringing about the collapse of that group in its

[65] Jessica Stern & J.M. Berger, ISIS: The State of Terror 46 (HarperCollins Publishers, 2015).
[66] Naji, *supra* note 23, at [33].
[67] Williams, *supra* note 49, at 146.
[68] *Id.* 109–11.
[69] *Id.* 14.
[70] *Id.* 113–15.
[71] *Id.* 16.
[72] Ryan Browne, *US Conducts Airstrikes on Afghanistan Opium Labs*, CNN, Nov. 20, 2017, <http://www.cnn.com/2017/11/20/politics/us-afghanistan-airstrikes-drug-processing/index.html>.
[73] Ryan Goodman, *The Obama Administration and Targeting 'War-Sustaining' Objects in Noninternational Armed Conflict*, 110 Am. J. Int'l L. 663 (2016).
[74] Daphené Richemond-Barak, *Is Money a Legitimate Target*, Just Security, Feb. 10, 2016, <https://www.justsecurity.org/29255/money-legitimate-target/>; *"Millions" in Isis Cash Destroyed in Airstrike on Storage Site in Mosul*, The Guardian, Jan. 12, 2016, <https://www.theguardian.com/world/2016/jan/12/us-led-coalition-air-strike-destroys-islamic-state-cash-storage-site-in-mosul>.

ability to hold and control territory is less clear.[75] The legal interpretation underpinning such strikes has proven to be controversial with Additional Protocol I being widely seen as providing a more limited right to target military objectives based on their effective contribution to "military action."[76] Further, given the scale of this criminal activity, it is unlikely that airstrikes alone can address this threat.

One of the challenges this kinetic approach presents is the increased likelihood of collateral civilian casualties and damage and with it the alienation of the civilian population. These airstrikes are directed at an activity that predated the rise of the Islamic State, and which appears to be a part of criminal activity endemic to the region.[77] The potential targeting of sites in urban areas compounds collateral damage concerns. There is also the question of the degree to which those engaged are direct participants in hostilities (i.e., therefore lawful targets) or must be considered to be the equivalent of nontargetable "factory workers," albeit engaged in criminal activity. In this respect, many participants in this illicit trade are not necessarily members of the jihadist armed groups, may have been coerced, or could have simply partnered with the non-state actors involved without actually engaging in hostilities.

While those conducting airstrikes have taken steps to limit the collateral effects of the strikes, there remains the issue of whether other less kinetic means might offer an effective alternate approach.[78] For example, this might have included more effective border enforcement at the Turkish/Syrian border to limit oil smuggling.[79] Notwithstanding the championing of this kinetic option against "terrorists," it should be noted that in Afghanistan, security forces continue to conduct ground operations to counter Taliban-led drug activities.[80] It also raises fundamental legal questions regarding the impact on any future inter-state

[75] Mathew Reed, *Blowing Up the Islamic State's Oil Company*, Foreign Policy, Oct. 26, 2016, <http://foreignpolicy.com/2016/10/26/blowing-up-the-islamic-states-oil-company-isis-abu-sayyaf/>.

[76] Protocol Additional to the Geneva Conventions of 12 August 1949, and Relating to the Protection of Victims of International Armed Conflicts, opened for signature 12 December 1977, 1125 UNTS 3, art. 52(2) (Additional Protocol I [AP I]). *See also* Kenneth Watkin, *Targeting "Islamic State" Oil Facilities*, 90 Internationall Law Studies 499 (2014); Michael N. Schmitt, *Targeting Narcoinsurgents in Afghanistan: The Limits of International Humanitarian Law*, 12 Year Book of International Humanitarian Law 6 (2009).

[77] Williams, *supra* note 49, at 63–93.

[78] Beth Van Schaack, *Targeting Tankers—And Their Drivers—Under the Law of War (Part 2)*, Just Security, Dec. 3, 2015, <https://www.justsecurity.org/28071/targeting-tankers-drivers-law-war-part-2/>.

[79] Fehim Taştekin, *Turkish Villages Smuggle IS Oil through Makeshift Pipelines*, Al-Monitor: The Pulse of the Middle East, Sept. 15, 2014, <https://www.al-monitor.com/pulse/originals/2014/09/turkey-syria-iraq-illegal-oil-pipeline.html>.

[80] Kyle Remptor, *Commandos Raid "Red Unit" in Ongoing Campaign against Taliban Financial Network*, Military Times, Jan. 4, 2018, <https://www.militarytimes.com/flashpoints/2018/01/04/commandos-raid-red-unit-in-ongoing-campaign-against-taliban-financial-network/>.

warfare regarding such a broad claim for a humanitarian law–based targeting authority. Further, there are human rights concerns, moral issues and questions of public policy regarding the use of airstrikes when what is fundamentally criminal activity cannot be controlled through police action. This is an issue that has arisen in other contexts regarding piracy in Somalia,[81] illegal immigration in the Mediterranean,[82] and drug smuggling in South America.[83]

C. The Jihadist "Way of War"

The strategic approach of the jihadist movement toward the conduct of hostilities also increases the likelihood that police forces will be engaged in countering their efforts to overthrow existing states in order to install a caliphate. One of the most important of their doctrine writers has been Abu Mus'Ab al-Suri, and "[l]ike Naji, al-Qurashi, al-Muqrin, and other Al Qaeda strategists, al-Suri subscribes to a classic three-stage guerrilla war strategy loosely following the Maoist model."[84] Under Mao's model, the displacement of local governments was seen as an integral part of revolutionary warfare.[85] His three phases of warfare involved the organization, consolidation, and preservation of a base area with "agitators and propagandists set forth, individually or in groups of two or three" to persuade or convince inhabitants to support the cause;[86] then a second phase involving acts of sabotage and terrorism, attacks made on "vulnerable military and police outposts" with an overall focus on improving guerrilla force capabilities, and the establishment of expanding liberated areas;[87] and finally "the enemy's destruction by orthodox military operations which do not necessarily deny guerrilla operations but place them in a subsidiary role."[88]

Much of the jihadist doctrine adopts a theme of proceeding in three phases. Al-Suri's doctrine, set out in 2005 work, *The Military Theory of the Global Islamic*

[81] *EU Naval Force Delivers Blow against Somali Pirates on Shoreline*, EU NAVFOR Somalia, May 15, 2012, <http://eunavfor.eu/eu-naval-force-delivers-blow-against-somali-pirates-on-shoreline/>.

[82] *Stop the Boats*, The Economist, May 19, 2015, <https://www.economist.com/news/europe/21651693-european-union-ministers-are-turning-their-navies-mediterranean-migrant-traffickers-stop>.

[83] Christopher Woody, *"Better to Be Belligerent than Innovative": Argentina's New Approach to Fighting Drugs Is Stoking Concern*, Business Insider, Nov. 2, 2016, <http://www.businessinsider.com/argentina-police-militarization-drug-war-2016-11>; Sam Tabory, *Peru Revives Controversial Drug Plane Shoot-Down Law*, InSight Crime, Aug. 21, 2015, <https://www.insightcrime.org/news/brief/peru-revives-controversial-shoot-down-law-for-narco-planes/>.

[84] Ryan, *supra* note 24, at 230. *See also* Cigar, *supra* note 54, at 12.

[85] Samuel B. Griffith II, *Introduction*, *in* Mao Tse-tung, On Guerrilla Warfare 27 (first published 1961, Samuel B. Griffth, trans., University of Illinois Press, 2000).

[86] *Id.* 20.

[87] *Id.* 21.

[88] Robert B. Asprey, War in the Shadows: The Guerrilla in History 255 (William Morrow and Company, Inc., 1994).

Resistance Call, sets out three stages of conflict: the stage of exhaustion (small guerrilla and limited terrorist warfare), the stage of equilibrium (large, strategic attacks "in which guerrillas will carry out operations in which they will temporarily control some areas"), and the liberation stage ("the guerrillas enter operations that are semi-regular and other that are regular, and they control some areas").[89] The triumvirate nature of jihadist thinking is also reflected in the three "schools of jihad" identified as having been followed prior to September 2001: "secret military organizations (regional—secret—hierarchical)," "open fronts and overt confrontations," and "individual jihad and small cell terrorism."[90] In al-Suri's view, it was the latter form of operations that the jihadist movement was forced to undertake as a result of post-9/11 attacks by coalition forces.[91] It "*paves the way for the other kind (Open Front Jihad), aids and supports it.*"[92] Individual and small-cell terrorism has particular relevance to the call by the Islamic State for "lone wolf" participants to carry out attacks in Europe, North America, and elsewhere. Notably, the previously mentioned *Management of Savagery* also adopts a three-phased approach:

> Phase one involves creating and exploiting chaos, or "savagery." Phase two entails building popular support for Salafi-jihadi rule. Not until phase three do we reach the establishment of a permanent Islamic state.[93]

This is not to suggest that all jihadist groups follow the same trajectory in seeking the goal of establishing a caliphate with the Islamic State rushing to do so, and Al Qaeda adopting a more long-term approach.[94] Mao's theory favored operations in rural and mountainous areas. However, as has been noted regarding the *Management of Savagery*, the jihadist approach anticipates operating within cities.[95] Similarly, Al-Muqrin specifically addresses the challenges of urban operations in his work, *A Practical Course for Guerrilla War*.[96] In 2004, Abu Musab al-Zarqawi, the leader of the Islamic State in Iraq, sought to establish Fallujah as a safe haven.[97] This ultimately led to significant combat as primarily US forces fought to liberate the city in November of that year.

89 Brynjar Lia, Architect of Global Jihad: The Life of Al-Qaida Strategist Abu Mus'ab Al-Suri 471–72 (Columbia University Press, 2008).

90 *Id.* 352–68.

91 *Id.* 362.

92 *Id.* 371.

93 Soufan, *supra* note 24, at 184. *See also id.* 185 (where it is noted the *Management of Savagery* and the *Call of the Global Islamic Resistance* remain popular amongst jihadists, but there is also another book called *Al-Zarqawi: The Second Generation of al-Qaeda*, which "presents an ambitious, seven-stage, two-decade strategy for reestablishing the caliphate").

94 McCants, *supra* note 23, at 15.

95 Naji, *supra* note 23, at [16].

96 Cigar, *supra* note 54, at 120–25.

97 Soufan, *supra* note 24, at 134.

A key element of this phased approach is that groups may advance to or slip back from one phase to another depending upon the success of their operations. That can often happen where the guerrilla organization attempts to transition to a more conventional mode of operations that can make the group an easier and more traditional target for State armed forces. In this respect, "[t]he fighting around Kandahar in 2006 could be seen as a confirmation that some Maoist concepts of guerrilla warfare seem to have made it into the mindset of Taliban commanders."[98] However, it appears to have been a premature move,[99] with Taliban efforts to move on the city being blocked by Canadian and other coalition forces.[100] The transit between phases can be seen most recently with the dismantling of the declared "caliphate" in Syria and Iraq. The Iraqi government claimed victory in its territory in December 2017.[101] It is evident that the Islamic State insurgents have withdrawn to more rural and desert areas and adopted a more traditional guerrilla mode of operations.[102] While this is a traditional response by insurgent groups confronted with overwhelming state action, it does not mean conflict in the urban environments is over. For example, one report notes that attacks have continued in the cities of Iraq and Syria long after their "liberation" was declared.[103] Further, as happened in Kandahar in 2011, when insurgents are subject to a "military onslaught" in rural areas, they may make a deliberate decision to focus their attacks in cities.[104]

The challenge for the state armed forces will be altering their approach from the more conventional style of fighting that has most recently occurred in urban areas to one focused more on guerrilla-based counterinsurgency. Success will ultimately depend upon how well the states involved treat the civilian population as they reassert their governance role. That includes policing, fair treatment of the population, and the establishment of an effective justice-based response. In Iraq, the tensions between the Shia-dominated government and the predominantly Sunni population, the desire for revenge by members of the state

[98] ANTONIO GIUSTOZZI, KORAN, KALASHNIKOV AND LAPTOP: THE NEO-TALIBAN INSURGENCY IN AFGHANISTAN 128–29 (Columbia University Press, 2008).

[99] *Id.* 129.

[100] Bill Roggio, *NATO Led Forces Kill 200 Taliban in Operation Medusa*, LONG WAR JOURNAL, Sept. 3, 2006, <https://www.longwarjournal.org/archives/2006/09/nato_led_forces_kill.php>.

[101] Ahmed Aboulenein, *Iraq Holds Victory Para Islamic State*, REUTERS, Dec. 10, 2017, <https://www.reuters.com/article/us-mideast-crisis-iraq-parade/iraq-holds-victory-parade-after-defeating-islamic-state-idUSKBN1E407Z>.

[102] Jeremy Berke, *ISIS' Loss of Its Caliphate Signals the End of One Type of ISIS—And the Beginning of a New One*, BUSINESS INSIDER, Oct. 18, 2017, <http://www.businessinsider.com/isis-defeated-in-raqqa-syria-2017-10>.

[103] DANIEL MILTON & MUHAMMAD AL-'UBAYDI, THE FIGHT GOES ON: THE ISLAMIC STATE'S CONTINUING MILITARY EFFORTS IN LIBERATED CITIES (June 2017), <https://ctc.usma.edu/app/uploads/2017/07/The-Fight-Goes-On.pdf>.

[104] BERND HORN, NO ORDINARY MEN: SPECIAL OPERATIONS FORCES MISSIONS IN AFGHANISTAN 225 (Dundurn, 2016).

security services[105] and courts meeting out "fast-tracked executions"[106] in a system viewed as being unable or unwilling to provide fair trials suggest this will be a significant challenge.[107] Ultimately, "[t]he fear is that if Sunni populations feel they've been abandoned and left to fend for themselves in shattered cities, the resentment will feed the next generation of militants.[108] As the Salafi jihadists have done in the past, as those cities are once again made inhabitable, those militants will inevitably migrate to that urban environment.[109]

As has been noted, this phased "way of war" and its associated organizational structure (e.g., cellular, semiregular, conventional) is not unique to the jihadist cause. In this respect, "revolutionaries adopt organization strategies across ideological divides."[110] In terms of policing, it is clear that the cauldron of instability, criminal action, and terrorism from which insurgency is generated demands good governance, including effective law enforcement in order to avoid advancement to the elevated phases of conflict. That is necessary whether the threat arises from within or outside an urban environment. Setting aside the issue of engagement in the higher intensity urban battles that have successfully wrestled control of cities (e.g., Mosul, Raqqa) from non-state armed groups, the involvement of policing agencies is key in the aftermath of those conflicts. Effective police forces help ensure that the operational capability of the insurgent forces is further degraded. In effect, the threat is reduced from one based on guerrilla tactics to one more readily dealt with as ordinary crime. It is this role, what is described as a "police primary" approach to counterinsurgency, that will now be addressed.

D. "Police Primacy" and Counterinsurgency

It has been increasingly recognized that a military dominant approach, which often relies significantly on the use of kinetic force, is not the most effective way

[105] Alice Fordham, *When Mosul's Cops Return, Will They Seek Reconciliation or Revenge?*, NPR, Oct. 21, 2016, <https://www.npr.org/sections/parallels/2016/10/21/498721966/when-mosuls-cops-return-will-they-seek-reconciliation-or-revenge>.

[106] Tamar El-Ghobashy & Mustafa Salim, *Iraq's Rapid-Fire Trials Send Alleged ISIS Members—Including Foreigners—To the Gallows*, Wash. Post, Dec. 28, 2017, <https://www.washingtonpost.com/world/iraqs-rapid-fire-trials-send-alleged-isis-members--including-foreigners--to-the-gallows/2017/12/22/b65d903a-e598-11e7-9ec2-518810e7d44d_story.html?utm_term=.463a95606df4>.

[107] Tamar El-Ghobashy, *Iraq Declares Complete Victory in the War against Islamic State*" Wash. Post, Dec. 9, 2017, <https://www.washingtonpost.com/world/iraq-declares-complete-victory-in-the-war-against-islamic-state/2017/12/09/9a0c5ea6-dce3-11e7-8e5f-ccc94e22b133_story.html?tid=a_inl&utm_term=.ddd355be0344>.

[108] George & Hinnant, *supra* note 32.

[109] Michael Petrou, *Defeating the Islamic State in Mosul Is a Victory for Iraq. The Challenge Will Be in Making It Last*, CBC News, July 13, 2017, <http://www.cbc.ca/news/opinion/defeat-of-isis-1.4201961>.

[110] Sinno, *supra* note 52, at 302.

to defeat an insurgency. Rather there has developed a greater reliance on making police forces the lead rather than privileging the military option.[111] One often cited example is the decision by the British government in the 1970s to change its approach toward the Irish Republican Army from a militarily dominant one to one that was intelligence led and with an emphasis on the primacy of policing.[112] The reliance on a "police primacy" approach is entirely consistent with the aforementioned theory that the state being subverted is being outgoverned.[113] In this respect, "[e]ffective, legitimate policing is at the core of democratic nation building."[114] A key element in creating a self-sustaining legitimate government is policing.[115]

This does not mean that the use of military force will not be essential to defeating an insurgency. There remains a requirement for counterinsurgency (COIN) forces to overmatch an insurgent force in order to win.[116] Further, the security situation may significantly impact on the ability of police forces to operate in a given area, at least not without military support. As occurred in Khalidiya, Iraq, the police are often the first target of insurgent forces:

> [Lieutenant-Colonel] Zientek was convinced that a local police force was needed to crack the insurgency in Khalidiya, but they had been driven out in the fall of 2003, when the police chief was assassinated and a car bomb leveled the Khalidiya station on Market Street, killing twenty-three cops and civilians.[117]

The security situation was ultimately turned around by a joint effort of US military, Iraqi military, police, and local inhabitants. The military forces involved were able to "put a lid on the local insurgency in Khalidiya. But its defeat depended on the people who had enabled the insurgency for years."[118]

After more than sixteen years of war against terrorist and insurgent groups, the United States and other Western powers are now reluctant to engage in what has been described as "nation building." Instead, they largely prefer to provide air and artillery support (e.g., enablers) to territorial state security forces and other militias, give training, facilitate logistics, and carry out their own air strikes and special forces raids against high-value targets. However,

[111] *See, e.g.*, THE U.S. ARMY, MARINE CORPS, COUNTERINSURGENCY FIELD MANUAL 229, paras. 6–90 (2007).
[112] Asprey, *supra* note 88, at 1130.
[113] Fall, *supra* note 36.
[114] Bayley & Perito, *supra* note 36, at 67.
[115] *Id.* 68.
[116] Paul et al., *supra* note 1, at xxviii.
[117] West, *supra* note 64, at 188.
[118] *Id.* 306.

there remains a requirement for the territorial state's security forces to engage in police-led counterinsurgency operations. Crucially, an "iron fist path" that has "a focus preponderantly (and often almost exclusively) on eliminating the insurgent threat" has failed to win significantly more often than "the motive-focused path, with primary or at least balanced attention to addressing the motives for beginning and sustaining the insurgency."[119] Further the "iron fist" approach has frequently involved significant human right abuses.[120] Described by Martin Wayne as a top-down, rather than a bottom-up approach toward counterterrorism and counterinsurgency, "it is only when the evolving and social nature of warfare is taken seriously, as advocated by a bottom-up approach, can insurgency be defeated."[121] Policing is an integral part of that bottom-up approach.

Given the tremendous humanitarian crisis that is caused by large scale combat in many of the cities in Syria and Iraq, it is understandable that the international humanitarian and human rights community has focused on this more intense level of urban warfare involving more conventional operations. However, as has been indicated, the link between terrorist and insurgent groups and crime; a way of warfare that relies on initial phases with lower but an increasing level of violence; the need to operate integrally "amongst the people" in order to prevent, contain, and ultimately win a counterinsurgency; and the requirement to return society back to a "normal" existence all point to the essential role policing performs. It is a role that transcends the conflict spectrum.

Ultimately, throughout the life of an insurgency there must be a balancing of military and police units engaged in counterinsurgency operations. The challenge is that "[i]nsurgent violence is both the problem police may help to solve and the major impediment to police."[122] That said, the need to integrate within the population being protected to root out the threat and restore a territory or city to a sense of "normalcy" ultimately favors a policing approach. It has been suggested that the police primacy principle means "that insurgency should be controlled as much as possible by personnel deployed singly or in pairs among the population, visibly distinguishable from soldiers, trained to minimize the use of force, and capable of making decisions on their own."[123] Restoring public order during an insurgency "invariably involves careful and sustained police

[119] Paul et al., *supra* note 1, at 180 ("COIN forces following the iron fist path won only 32 percent of the time, while those on the motive-focused or mixed path won 73 percent of the time.").

[120] *Id.*

[121] Martin I. Wayne, China's War on Terrorism: Counter-Insurgency, Politics and Internal Security 145 (Routledge, 2008).

[122] Bayley & Perito, *supra* note 36, at 67.

[123] *Id.* 68.

work" regardless of whether that occurs in rural areas, towns, other urban areas, or the megacities of the twenty-first century.[124]

A 2007 discussion that a senior Royal Canadian Mounted Police officer had with Canadian generals in Khandahar, Afghanistan, regarding the US approach toward viewing the Afghan police as an auxiliary to the Afghan National Army reflects the challenge. The view expressed was that the majority of the equipment and training had gone to the army, and the Afghan military approach of riding in closed military vehicles and using firepower to kill would not allow them to develop the informants necessary to gather the information required to defeat the insurgency.[125] As was noted:

> "Police are the key to fighting an insurgency," [Superintendent] McAllister wrote home in an email. "The Coalition can clear any place they want pretty much at will; it's the hold portion that we haven't been able to expand on because we need indigenous police for that."[126]

It has been also noted that if the Afghan city of Khandahar was to be cleared of Taliban influence, it would not be an army or air force that did it. Rather "[i]t would be a civilian police force living among the population who knew what went on in their own warren of neighbourhoods."[127]

IV. Legal Frameworks and Policing.

A. Policing and the Use of Force

The two international law frameworks associated with maintaining order in society, human rights law and humanitarian law, have a significant impact on policing and its role in countering terrorist and insurgent threats in an urban environment. The first issue that will be addressed is the authority to use force and the interaction between the two legal paradigms, while the second relates to the effect of the broad criminalization of those seeking to violently challenge state authority and a resulting emphasis on the application of human rights norms.

Policing is primarily associated with a human rights legal framework. As the eminent historian John Keegan noted, "[t]he civilized societies in which we best

[124] C. Christine Fair & Sumit Ganguly, *Introduction: The Police in Counterinsurgency Operations*, *in* POLICING INSURGENCIES: COPS AS COUNTERINSURGENTS 1 (C. Christine Fair & Sumit Ganguly eds., Oxford University Press, 2014).

[125] TERRY GOULD, WORTH DYING FOR: CANADA'S MISSION TO TRAIN POLICE IN THE WORLD'S FAILING STATES 44 (Random House Canada, 2014).

[126] *Id.*

[127] *Id.* 43.

like to live are governed by law, which means they are policed, and policing is a function of coercion."[128] Human rights does authorize the use of force to maintain order in society. However, it does so in a manner, and to a degree that is different than the law governing the conduct of hostilities.[129] The force used under the human rights paradigm is governed by the principles of minimum force, necessity, and proportionality. In this context, proportionality refers to the level of force in relation to the threat being posed, as opposed to the humanitarian law–based proportionality concept relating to collateral civilian casualties and damage. Traditionally, human rights law abhors any degree of collateral injury or death. Deadly force is only permitted where it is strictly unavoidable. A "shoot to kill" policy is not permitted. The emphasis is on capture rather than kill,[130] and there is a strict accountability regime focused on investigating every use of force leading to death or injury.

In contrast, humanitarian law relies on different principles, even if the same terminology as human rights law is sometimes applied. A key principle is that of distinction, which requires that only those taking a direct part in hostilities, and other military objectives may be targeted. In the context of a non-international armed conflict against non-state actors, this would include members of organized armed groups and individual civilians directly participating in hostilities.[131] Contrary to human rights law, the law governing the conduct of hostilities in such conflict permits "status" targeting, unless the person is especially protected (e.g., medical personnel), or is hors de combat, with a frequent issue being the criteria applied to identify someone as a direct participant in hostilities. Further, unlike human rights law, consideration of capture before killing an enemy is not a legal requirement.[132] Notably, under the humanitarian law concept of proportionality, civilians may be lawfully collaterally killed or injured, and civilian property may be destroyed or damaged as long as those casualties are not excessive in relation

[128] John Keegan, A History of Warfare 386 (Vintage Books, 1993).

[129] *See generally* Watkin, *supra* note 44, at 131–33.

[130] David Jens Ohlin, *The Duty to Capture*, Minnesota Law Review 1268, 1270 (2013).

[131] Interpretive Guidance on the Notion of Direct Participation in Hostilities Under International Humanitarian Law 80–81 (Nils Melzer ed., 2009). The ICRC interpretation of "direct participation in hostilities" has been criticized on a number of bases. *See* Michael N. Schmitt, *Deconstructing Direct Participation in Hostilities*, 42 New York University Journal of International Law and Politics 697 (2010); Bill Boothby, *"And For Such Time As": The Time Dimension to Direct Participation in Hostilities*, 42 New York University Journal of International Law and Politics 741 (2010); W. Hays Parks, *Part IX of the ICRC "Direct Participation in Hostilities Study": No Mandate, No Expertise, and Legally Incorrect*, 42 New York University Journal of International Law and Politics 769 (2010); Kenneth Watkin, *Opportunity Lost: Organized Armed Groups and the ICRC "Direct Participation in Hostilities" Interpretive Guidance*, 42 New York University Journal of International Law and Politics 641 (2010).

[132] W. Hays Parks, *Memorandum of Law: Executive Order 12333 and Assassination*, The Army Lawyer, no. 6, 7 (1989), <https://www.loc.gov/rr/frd/Military_Law/pdf/12-1989.pdf>.

to the concrete and direct anticipated military advantage.[133] Accountability is also an important part of humanitarian law, although it does not require an investigation every time someone is killed or injured. Such an investigation is only required, at law, if there is a suspicion that a person had been unlawfully targeted, or excessive collateral injury, death, or destruction has occurred.

While these two bodies of law are often presented in terms of their differences, in reality they are far more intertwined, both at law and operationally, than is often discussed. This reality has a significant impact on how the policing function, and as a result human rights–based standards are integrated into military operations. Perhaps Richard Baxter said it best when he noted, "humanitarian law of war is a form of human rights law operating for the protection of those who cannot be properly safeguarded by the country to which they belong."[134] The law governing armed conflict includes human rights norms. For example, Additional Protocols I (AP I) Article 75 and Additional Protocol II (AP II) Article 4 reflect human rights law provisions. Geneva Convention IV has been referred to as a bill of rights for the occupied population.[135] To the extent these treaty rights may not apply as a matter of law to a particular conflict, there is increasing recognition that such rights are part of customary international humanitarian law.[136]

In any event, in certain circumstances state armed forces must apply human rights–based norms during armed conflict. For example, there is the requirement to deal with ordinary civilians or even those who may provide support to a terrorist or insurgent group but who cannot be targeted. An authority to detain, the standards of treatment, and possible criminal action are founded on human rights norms. This different approach to the use of force was summed up by one Israeli paratrooper operating a Palestinian neighborhood in Gaza in 2009 as "Police Mode," where "we functioned much more like an American SWAT team and did our best to capture and interrogate. We assumed that human contact was civilian until proven to be a threat."[137] Further, there may be a requirement to deal with a civilian population in terms of evacuating it from an urban area of combat, or otherwise providing humanitarian relief should they shelter in

[133] AP I, art. 57(2)(a)(iii).

[134] Richard Baxter, *Human Rights in War*, *in* Humanizing the Laws of War: Selected Writings of Richard Baxter 341, 346 (Detlev F. Vagts et al., eds., Oxford University Press, 2013).

[135] Eyal Benvenisti, The International Law of Occupation 105 (Princeton University Press, 1993).

[136] *See* Watkin, *supra* note 44, at 147–149 (for a discussion of the Obama administration application of the AP I, art. 75 principles out of a sense of "legal obligation" to the treatment of detainees). *See also* Hamdan v. Rumsfeld, 45 I.L.M. 1130, 1155 (2006) (US Supreme Court 2006) (A plurality of the court ruled that, as a matter of customary international law, Article 75 of Additional Protocol I applied to the armed conflict with Al Qaeda.).

[137] Yared M. Ben-Caro, Dreidel Full of LEAD: From the Wild West to the Streets of Gaza 222 (Futility Press LLC., 2015).

place during the hostilities. The maintenance of law and order in these contexts must be based on human rights norms found either in humanitarian or human rights law.

While the "special law" principle (*lex specialis derogate lex generali*—the *lex specialis*) is frequently applied by proponents of the human rights and humanitarian law paradigms, respectively, to exclude the application of the other body of law, the reality is that both legal frameworks can apply simultaneously. As was determined in *Legal Consequences Of The Construction Of A Wall In The Occupied Palestinian Territory*,

> some rights may be exclusively matters of international humanitarian law; others may be exclusively matters of human rights law; *yet others may be matters of both these branches of international law.*[138]

In any event, by virtue of the integration of human rights standards into humanitarian law (e.g., AP I, Article 75), those norms continue to apply even when that body of law is viewed as being applicable.

In a counterterrorism and counterinsurgency context, these bodies of law not only frequently have simultaneous application but can also overlap. This leaves the state in a position of being able to, and ultimately having to, choose which body of law to apply. In this regard, territorial states are normally very reluctant to admit their governance is threatened to the point that an armed conflict can be said to be in existence. In legal terms this is reflected in the historical resistance by states to admit that international humanitarian law applies to internal conflicts. Almost by default the preference from a governance perspective is to apply a human rights based policing approach particularly within a state's own territory. In cases where an armed conflict is occurring there is often political pressure within states to not acknowledge that is the case.[139]

The result is that security forces deal with an insurgency under a law enforcement paradigm or attempt to mask humanitarian based uses of force under a policing mandate. Significantly, the extension of human rights law–based policing to counterterrorism and counterinsurgency operations may also occur as a result of legal interpretation. For example, the European Court of Human Rights has viewed such conflict occurring within the jurisdiction of the member states of the European Convention on Human Rights exclusively through a

[138] *Legal Consequences Of The Construction Of A Wall In The Occupied Palestinian Territory* (Advisory Opinion) 2004 ICJ 178, para. 106 (emphasis added).

[139] *See, e.g.*, Felicity Szesnat & Annie R. Bird, *Columbia*, *in* International Law and the Classification of Conflicts 203, 214–15 (Elizabeth Wilmhurst ed., Oxford University Press, 2012) (where it is noted President Santos reclassified the conflict with the FARC to an armed conflict, while his predecessor had viewed the conflict as "terrorism" and did not view it as either an armed conflict or civil war).

human rights lens. That Court has distinguished between "routine police operations" and "situations of large-scale anti-terrorist operations," with the latter frequently involving the employment of military forces.[140] Regardless, the approach has been adopted that both types of operations are governed by human rights law. Although military units, including airpower and artillery, have been used against the "terrorist" groups, the European Court has treated the security forces as a "law enforcement body in a democratic society" and assessed their actions against a "normal legal background."[141] This was done even though the Court recognized the need for exceptional measures "to suppress the illegal *armed insurgency*."[142]

Traditionally, human rights law is not designed to deal with the increased levels of violence or the collateral casualties and damage than can be expected from the use of these weapon systems in what is factually, and can be argued legally, an armed conflict. The Court has done so by importing conduct of hostilities wording into its human rights analysis, such as taking "all feasible precautions in the choice of means and methods of a security operation mounted against an opposing group with a view to avoiding and, in any event, minimising, incidental loss of civilian life."[143] However, even though humanitarian-based concepts were imported, the Court also applied human rights law principles of a strict and compelling test of necessity, using no more force than absolutely necessary and the requirement that the force used is strictly proportionate to the permitted aims to overall establish a more restrictive approach to the use of force than might ordinarily be allowed by the law governing armed conflict.[144] The result appears to have been a blending of human rights and humanitarian law principles.

Similarly, the European Court of Human Rights has accepted significant levels of collateral casualties (i.e., 129 hostages) arising during the 2002 Moscow theater hostage rescue incident,[145] albeit while suggesting this situation was different than the use of "bombs or air missiles."[146] Perhaps it was in terms of means, but it is difficult to suggest that it was regarding the ultimate effect of the use of force. The Court has also imported humanitarian law concept of indiscriminate weapons into a 2016 human rights analysis of the 2004 Beslan school siege.[147]

[140] Tagayeva v. Russia App. No. 26562/07 and 6 other applications (ECtHR, 2017), paras. 594–96, 139–40. *See also* for reference to operating under a "normal legal background."

[141] Kerimova v. Russia App. Nos. 17170/04, 20792/04, 22448/04, 23360/04, 5681/05, and 5684/05 (ECtHR, May 3, 2011), para. 254.

[142] *Id.* para. 246 (emphasis added).

[143] Isayeva v. Russian II App. No. 57950/00 (ECtHR, 2005), para. 176 <http://www.refworld.org/cases,ECHR,4223422f6.html>.

[144] *Id.* para. 238.

[145] Finogenov v. Russia (VI ECtHR, 2011) 409, para. 236 (extracts).

[146] *Id.* 408, para. 232.

[147] Tagayeva v. Russia App. No. 26562/07 and 6 other applications (ECtHR, 2017) 144, para. 609, <http://hudoc.echr.coe.int/eng?i=001-172660>.

Previously, the jurisprudence arising out of the Northern Ireland "Troubles" had focused on a "shoot to kill" policy having breached human rights law.[148] The Court's later Russia decisions appear to represent a marked departure in terms of its willingness to have human rights law expanded to accept elevated uses of force in the context of a counterterrorism response. This blending of legal paradigms might be said to represent a "militarization" of human rights law, which like the controversy surrounding the militarization of the police raises concerns whether this approach will result in a more aggressive use of force by state authorities in ordinary policing situations. It highlights a problem with viewing terrorism almost exclusively through a law enforcement lens. Human rights law is asked to regulate violence far beyond that associated with ordinary crime. Serious questions need to be asked as to what the outer limits of the effectiveness of a human rights legal regime are, and whether it should apply humanitarian law principles in an effort to exert greater judicial control of state action.

Another legal issue that can impact on the degree to which human rights law must be used to counter terrorist and insurgent violence and the requirement to resolve the interface with humanitarian law is the threshold for determining an armed conflict is in existence. It is widely recognized that humanitarian law does "not apply to situations of internal disturbances and tensions, such as riots, isolated and sporadic acts of violence and other acts of a similar nature."[149] Applying the high threshold of the *Prosecutor v. Tadić* criteria for determining the existence of such a conflict: the intensity of violence (protracted armed violence) occurring between a state and organized armed groups limits when humanitarian law can be applied.[150]

This has particularly been an issue regarding what appear or are interpreted to be "one off" attacks by terrorist groups.

However, as is reflected in the 2016 International Committee of the Red Cross *Updated Commentaries*, there has been a recognition that " 'the requisite degree of intensity may be met "when hostilities are of a collective character or when the government is obliged to use military force against the insurgents, instead of mere police forces.' "[151] The increasingly accepted theory that the "totality of the circumstances" must be considered also suggests a more flexible standard

[148] *See, e.g.*, McCann v. United Kingdom App. No. 18984/91 (ECtHR, Judgment, 1995), para. 118, <http://hudoc.echr.coe.int/sites/eng/pages/search.aspx?i=001-57943>.

[149] AP II, art. 1(2).

[150] Prosecutor v. Tadić (Decision on the Defence Motion for Interlocutory Appeal on Jurisdiction) IT-94-1-A, para. 70 (ICTY, 1995), <http://www.icty.org/x/cases/tadic/acdec/en/51002.htm>.

[151] Commentary on the First Geneva Convention: Convention (I) for the Amelioration of the Condition of the Wounded and Sick in Armed Forced in the Field (2d ed. 2016), para. 431, <https://www.icrc.org/applic/ihl/ihl.nsf/Treaty.xsp?action=openDocument&documentId=4825657B0C7E6BF0C12563CD002D6B0B>(quoting an ICRC opinion paper, *How is the Term 'Armed Conflict' Defined in International Humanitarian Law?*, 2008, p. 3.).

for determining the existence of an armed conflict.[152] That said, states may never overtly acknowledge what legal paradigm they are operating under, and the violence may be such that there is a mixed military and police-based response. This latter situation was evident in the 2008 Mumbai attack where the National Security Guard (a joint military/police counterterrorism unit), India's military Marine Commando counterterrorism force (the MARCOs), the Maharashtra State Anti-Terrorism Squad, as well as local police were deployed to counter the highly destructive terrorist attack on that city.[153]

The nature of a counterinsurgency inevitably requires a nuanced application of the legal frameworks governing the use of force. At the strategic level, as a form of conflict, it is unlike traditional international armed conflict between states. Not only does an insurgency require a different government response focused on reinforcing and applying all the mechanisms of good governance (e.g., military, police, prisons, courts, social-economic ministries), success is ultimately measured in terms of gaining the support of the government efforts from the population. The killing of civilians, even lawfully (i.e., applying the international humanitarian law version of proportionality) can be extremely counterproductive. Even "[t]he death of an insurgent can create many more insurgents from his family and friends."[154] Further, the political audiences interpreting the success of action by security forces can extend beyond the borders of that state.[155]

The goal of maintaining the support of the population, and frequently an international audience, factors into how operations are conducted, and force is used. Whether instituted because of a belief that strategic counterinsurgency goals change the acceptability of collateral casualties and damage as a matter of law,[156] or simply as a result of operational choice,[157] the end result is normally privileging the capture rather than killing of terrorists. Further, restrictions can be placed on the use of high-explosive ordnance, such as that delivered by airpower and artillery, with a desired outcome of having limited or even no

[152] *See* Prosecutor v. Boškoski (Judgment) IT-04-82-T 90, para. 257 (ICTY, 2008) (for reference to the "totality of circumstances"); Laurie R. Blank & Geoffrey S. Corn, *Losing the Forest for the Trees: Syria, Law, and the Pragmatics of Conflict Recognition*, 46 Vanderbilt Journals of Transnational Law 693, 731–45 (2013); Watkin, *supra* note 44, at 375–78; Geoffrey S. Corn, *Legal Classification of Military Operations*, *in* U.S. Military Operations: Law Policy, and Practice 67, 74–75 (Geoffrey S. Corn, Rachel E. Vanlandingham, & Shane R. Reeves eds., Oxford University Press, 2016).

[153] Kilcullen, *supra* note 11, at 57–60.

[154] Emile Simpson, War from the Ground Up: Twenty-First Century Combat as Politics 73 (Oxford University Press, 2012).

[155] *Id.*

[156] Kenneth Watkin, *Military Advantage: A Matter of "Value, Strategy and Tactics*, 277 International Year Book of Humanitarian Law 350–56 (2014).

[157] Michael Schmitt, *Targeting and International Humanitarian Law in Afghanistan*, 85 International Law Studies 307, 323 (2009).

collateral civilian casualties.[158] In an environment focused on restoring the rule of law, the use of the term "arrest" has increasingly entered the lexicon of military commanders.[159] Yet another area of interface is what this author has described elsewhere as the narrowing operational and normative gap. For example, military units engaged in hostage rescue frequently adopt tactics approximating a law enforcement approach, while threat posed by improvised explosive devices and suicide vests force the police to use force approaching that of a first resort to deadly force, which is ordinarily associated with humanitarian law.[160]

Another factor that must be considered is that the type of units involved does not necessarily reflect whether a law enforcement– or hostilities-based approach is being applied by state security forces. For example, military units regularly become involved in a policing role. Even in international armed conflict there is an obligation on an occupying power to maintain order.[161] Perhaps the classic example of failure to do so is the US decision to disband the Iraqi Army and other interior security forces, and then not adequately provide for the maintenance of law and order once the Iraqi police largely dissolved.[162] The resulting situation of unlawfulness was closely related to a growing insurgency. With increasing levels of insecurity there can be a greater number of policing functions that the foreign military forces are required to perform.[163] This can include vital point security, manning checkpoints, and detaining suspects.[164] This was a role Coalition forces were ill-equipped to do.[165] However, involvement by military forces in policing is not limited to those situations. The US military commanders found themselves asking for increased numbers of military police to fill the void as the operational center of gravity shifted from kinetic action to law enforcement.[166] As the US Counterinsurgency Manual notes, counterinsurgency operations more closely resemble policing than traditional combat.[167] What this means for military forces is that they must be trained to apply a human rights–based approach toward the use of force.[168] Even countries with traditionally stable internal security

[158] Daniel P. Bolger, Why We Lost: A General's Inside Account of the Iraq and Afghanistan Wars 305 (Hartland Mifflin Harcourt Publishing Company, 2014).

[159] Stanley McChrystal, My Share of the Task: A Memoire 229 (Penguin, 2013)(for a reference to arresting anyone who escaped from the blast site at which al-Zarqawi was killed in Iraq).

[160] Watkin, *supra* note 44, at 483–533.

[161] *1907 Hague Land Warfare Regulations*, art. 43, and GC IV art. 64.

[162] Matt Sherman & Josh Paul, "The Role of Police in Counterinsurgency Operations in Iraq, 2003–2006," in *Policing Insurgencies*, *supra* note 124, at 230.

[163] Bayley & Perito, *supra* note 36, at 80.

[164] *Id.*

[165] Robert M. Perito, Where Is the Lone Ranger When We Need Him: America's Search for a Postconflict Stability Force 311–15 (The United States Institute of Peace Press, 2004).

[166] Gordon Cucullu & Chris Fontana, Warrior Police 188 (St. Martin's Press, 2011).

[167] *The Counterinsurgency Manual*, *supra* note 111, at 247, paras. 7–29.

[168] Matthew R. Modarelli, *Military Police Operations and Counterinsurgency*, Small Wars Journal, 2008, <http://smallwarsjournal.com/jrnl/art/military-police-operations-and-counterinsurgency>.

situations may declare an emergency, or call out military forces to patrol urban environments as has occurred in France[169] and the United Kingdom[170] following terrorist attacks.

Conversely, during armed conflict, police units may directly engage in combat. This can result simply from the fact that they are the public face of the government and often relatively easy targets for insurgent groups. Police units may be designed to combat insurgents. In Iraq the units liberating Mosul from ISIS in street-to-street fighting included the federal police "mechanized infantry unit: thousands of men in dark blue camouflage with Humvees and machine guns. Accompanying them is another elite unit called the ERD, or Emergency Response Division."[171] In 2007, "it was estimated that 70 per cent of Afghan National Police (ANP) time was spent fighting the insurgency as opposed to law and order tasks."[172] Afghanistan's most effective paramilitary police unit, "[t]he Crisis Response Unit, also known as the 222, is often the first to arrive and neutralize high-profile attacks—such as in March, when militants dressed in lab coats opened fire inside Kabul's main military hospital, killing 50 people."[173] These and other Special Weapons and Tactics (SWAT) units "conduct so-called 'high risk arrests' and *provide police rapid response to insurgent action*."[174] Similarly, in May 2011, it was the Afghan Special Police Unit, the Provincial Response Company-Kandahar (PRC-K), being mentored by Canadian Special Operations Task Force personnel, that responded to counter a major Taliban assault on numerous objectives in Kandahar City.[175]

Some police units receive no or little police training. Rather they are used as crowd-control, commando, or special forces units. For example, in Iraq, Civil Intervention Force and Public Order Battalions were created "to fill the gap between the crowd-control capabilities of the Iraqi army and the ordinary police."[176] However, while "titled and uniformed as 'police'", their "personnel training did not cover criminal justice issues, and the units lacked formal legal

[169] *French Emergency Terror Powers Enshrined in Law*, Fin. Times, Oct. 3, 2017, <https://www.ft.com/content/6b68aa54-a850-11e7-93c5-648314d2c72c>.

[170] *Critical Threat Level: Who Made the Decision and What Does It Mean?*, The Guardian, May 24, 2017, <https://www.theguardian.com/politics/2017/may/23/raise-terror-level-critical-5000-troops-streets-operation-temperer>.

[171] Seth J. Frantzman, *On the Ground in Mosul: The Face of a New Iraqi Military, Forged in War*, The Jerusalem Post, Apr. 5, 2017, <http://www.jpost.com/Middle-East/On-the-ground-in-Mosul-The-face-of-a-new-Iraqi-military-forged-in-war-486112.

[172] Antonio Giustozzi & Mohammed Isaqzadeh, Policing Afghanistan 41 (Columbia University Press, 2012).

[173] Shashank Bengali, *These Are Afghanistan's Best Troops. The U.S. Is Backing a Plan to Create Many More of Them*, L.A. Times, Dec. 10, 2017, <http://www.latimes.com/world/asia/la-fg-afghanistan-special-operations-20171209-htmlstory.html>.

[174] Austin Long, "The Police in Afghanistan, 2002–11," in *Policing Insurgencies*, *supra* note 124, at 203, 210 (emphasis added).

[175] Horn, *supra* note 104, at 219–243.

[176] Sherman & Paul, *supra* note 162, at 236.

powers of arrest and detention."[177] Nor was the emphasis on military training limited to special forces trained units. As one Canadian civilian police woman reported, in Afghanistan "the [US] MPs were mainly training the ANP [Afghan National Police] to set up fighting positions that could withstand frontal assault, and not how to police communities."[178] Part of this training was undoubtedly out of necessity; however, it has also been noted, "it is easier to train local police as 'little soldiers.'"[179] This raises fundamental questions regarding what is a proper policing role when police units are employed in a counterterrorism or counter-insurgency role.

B. The Criminalization of Non-State Actors

Human rights–based law enforcement has an enhanced profile in the present security environment by virtue of the criminalization of terrorism and insurgency. This can lead to a policy of privileging a law enforcement response. The 2016 UN Security Council Resolution 2322 notes "that terrorism in all its forms and manifestations constitutes one of the most serious threats to peace and security and that *any acts of terrorism* are criminal and unjustifiable regardless of their motivations, whenever, wherever, and by whomsoever committed."[180] While the international community has struggled to find a common definition of terrorism, states tend to enact criminal terrorism related offenses under their domestic law, some of which are very broadly worded. For example, the "material support or resources to a foreign terrorist organization" offense found in US law[181] that extends to any property or tangible or intangible service.[182]

A similar issue arises in respect to insurgents. As participants in non-international armed conflict, they are not entitled to either prisoner of war (POW) status or the combatant's privilege of not being prosecuted for hostile acts. During international armed conflict, members of organized armed groups who are not entitled to POW status are treated as "unprivileged belligerents" subject to prosecution in the domestic courts of the capturing state. The term "unprivileged belligerent" has also been adopted in a non-international armed conflict context, as evidenced by the Military Commission Act of 2009, which includes among those who can be tried as an "enemy unprivileged belligerent" an

[177] *Id.*

[178] Gould, *supra* note 125, at 100.

[179] Bayley & Perito, *supra* note 36, at 76.

[180] UNSC Res. 2322 (Dec. 12, 2016) UN Doc. S/RES/2322, para. 3 <http://www.un.org/en/ga/search/view_doc.asp?symbol=S/RES/2322%282016%29&referer=/english/&Lang=E> (emphasis added).

[181] 18 U.S.C. §2339B(a)(1).

[182] *See* Holder v. Humanitarian Law Project, 130 S. Ct. 2705, 2708 (2010).

individual "who has purposefully and *materially supported* hostilities against the United States or its coalition partners."[183]

In addition to the breadth of terrorism offenses there is a tendency for states to rely on the criminal justice system, rather than an administrative security detention regime to deal with terrorists, insurgents, and those offering support. This in turn creates considerable pressure to provide evidence to the domestic criminal justice system upon which detention, charges, and ultimately a trial can be based. Failure to provide adequate evidence may result in the release of the detainee. This situation can be compounded by the reality that despite existing rhetoric states cannot kill their way to victory. Frequently, their security forces detain far more suspects than can be proven to be engaged in insurgent or terrorist activity.[184] As a result, the gathering of evidence on the battlefield has taken on a greater profile in respect of contemporary operations against terrorist and insurgent groups. At the same time the investigatory and forensic skills provided by the police have been found to be extremely useful in an intelligence context in dealing with the improvised explosive device and suicide bomber threat.

The result has been increased deployment of police on military operations where they can use their investigative skills. Conversely, military personnel have been provided investigatory and forensic training to be able to carry out that function. This can be seen in examples such as the deployment of FBI Hostage Rescue Team members on special forces raids to detain or arrest suspects,[185] and the use of Canadian military police and bomb disposal personnel in improvised explosive device incident site exploitation.[186] There have been accused brought to trial in the United Kingdom and the United States based on forensic evidence obtained on the battlefield.[187] This is an issue that has gained even greater

183 Military Commission Act of 2009, Pub. L. No. 111-84, § 948(a)(7)(B), 123 Stat. 2190 (codified at 10 U.S.C 47A (2006)) (emphasis added).

184 Ameh Comrade Godwin, *Boko Haram: Bama Women Cry to Buhari over Detained 1,300 Suspected Terrorists*, NIGERIA DAILY POST, Mar. 9, 2018, <http://dailypost.ng/2018/03/09/boko-haram-bama-women-cry-buhari-detained-1300-suspected-terrorists/> (outlining allegations of improper detention in Nigeria); Gareth Porter, *Ninety Percent of Petraeus's Captured "Taliban" Were Civilians*, IPS, June 12, 2011, <http://www.ipsnews.net/2011/06/ninety-percent-of-petraeuss-captured-taliban-were-civilians/>; Horn, *supra* note 104, at 95 (where it is indicated that forty-five individuals were detained on one operation; however, "the next day they were all released, since they did not meet the criteria established for detention.").

185 Adam Goldman & Julie Tate, *Inside the FBI's Secret Relationship with the Military's Special Operations*, WASH. POST, Apr. 10, 2014, <https://www.washingtonpost.com/world/national-security/inside-the-fbis-secret-relationship-with-the-militarys-special-operations/2014/04/10/dcca3460-be84-11e3-b195-dd0c1174052c_story.html?utm_term=.f4f780e1a4a1>.

186 Tu Thanh Ha, *Canadian Forces Bring Forensics to the Battlefield*, THE GLOBE AND MAIL, Aug. 5, 2011, <https://beta.theglobeandmail.com/news/national/canadian-forces-bring-forensics-to-the-battlefield/article4181923/?ref=http://www.theglobeandmail.com&>.

187 *See* Haroon Siddique, *London Cab Driver Jailed for Life for Making Bombs to Kill US Soldiers in Iraq*, THE GUARDIAN, May 22, 2015, <https://www.theguardian.com/uk-news/2015/may/22/london-cab-driver-anis-abid-sardar-jailed-bombs-kill-us-soldiers-iraq>; Tom Hays, *Jury Hears Openings at Trial of American Terror Suspect*, U.S. NEWS, Sept. 12, 2017, <https://www.usnews.com/news/best-states/new-york/articles/2017-09-12/fingerprints-on-bomb-central-to-terror-trial-of-us-citizen>.

prominence with the transnational activities of foreign terrorist fighters who have traveled to Syria and Iraq to fight with the Islamic State. Their return to the states of which they are nationals, or to third states, has raised concerns about whether there is sufficient evidence available to carry out prosecutions.[188] Once again the unique threat of terrorism and insurgency engages legal issues that inevitably result in police carrying out an essential function in the context of an armed conflict. It also forces states to address the humanitarian law and human rights law interface.

V. Policing Challenges in Unstable Security Environments

A. The Policing, Terrorism, and Insurgency Interface

The threat of terrorism and insurgency present significant challenges for states. In addressing these challenges, the issue of effective policing transcends the potential spectrum of conflict. Not only does policing provide an essential prevention role, the ability of police forces to integrate within society means they can perform an important intelligence-gathering function given the relationship between crime, gangs, instability, terrorism, and insecurity. However, it is clear that in many instances the response by states has primarily been a military one. Much of the literature and focus of study has been on the role of military forces and "[w]hen the police are mentioned, it is largely in the context of a supportive and adjunctive role to the efforts of more traditional military operations."[189] Unfortunately, this has frequently overshadowed the requirement for effective policing, and it can be argued has ultimately hampered the return to "normalcy," which may be the only true reflection of success for states when countering these threats.[190] Indeed, fundamental questions may be asked whether the terrorist and insurgent threats of this century can ever be won with an emphasis on a military response. The prospects for ending the potential "forever war"[191] of the 9/11 period will ultimately be related to good governance. Given the extensive migration of populations toward cities, twenty-first-century "good governance"

[188] Bibi van Ginkel & Christophe Paulussen, *The Role of the Military in Securing Suspects and Evidence in the Prosecution of Terrorism Cases before Civilian Courts: Legal and Practical Challenges*, ICCT, May 2015, 9, para. 4.2, < https://www.icct.nl/wp-content/uploads/2015/05/ICCT-Van-Ginkel-Paulussen-The-Role-Of-The-Military-In-Securing-Suspects-And-Evidence-In-The-Prosecution-Of-Terrorism-Cases-Before-Civilian-Courts.pdf>.

[189] Wilson, *supra* note 55, at 2; C. Christine Fair & Sumit Ganguly, "Introduction: The Police in Counterinsurgency Operations," in *Policing Insurgencies*, *supra* note 124, at 1.

[190] Watkin, *supra* note 44, at 610–16.

[191] Taken from the title of Dexter Filkins, The Forever War (Alfred A. Knopf, 2008).

increasingly means effective policing in an urban environment even when it is experiencing armed conflict.

As an essential part of the state security apparatus, police forces face a number of significant challenges from terrorism and insurgency that require careful consideration when developing a response to those threats. As David Fidler has noted, police forces are not the primary cause of insurgency, which arise for various "political, economic, and social fissures that stimulate efforts to overthrow governments."[192] However, police weakness can be destabilizing and help fuel the insurgency. In this respect, "[d]ysfunctional police contribute to insurgency momentum, the perception of government venality and weakness, and the militarization of COIN responses."[193] One of the challenges in crafting a response to the threat, which ultimately requires reform of the existing police capability, is that "the role of the police in any given society reflects dominant governing principles and how state actors implement those principles through policy and government sanctioned coercion."[194] It is no coincidence that terrorism and insurgency particularly take hold in failed or failing states. The police can be both part of the problem and a critical part of the cure.

The task of reforming the police agencies of a state and deciding how to employ them in response to these security threats is not an easy one. Afghanistan stands out as an example where it is difficult to claim success as "[t]he ANP [Afghan National Police] remains focused on the front lines, combating the Taliban-led insurgency, with professionalization as a secondary objective."[195] Part of the challenge is that for numerous historical, societal, and legal reasons, the role and type of police forces vary worldwide. Differences in approaches can be seen even in highly functioning societies with the existence of paramilitary police, or "constabulary" units in parts of Europe and elsewhere. These units have been described as "a significant unit of a police force charged with paramilitary duties or a separate para-military organization."[196] The use of the term "paramilitary" in this context is potentially misleading since it can be interpreted broadly enough to encompass groups that include "nonstate, illegitimate, poorly trained, lightly armed, highly fragmented, and politically motivated" armed

[192] David P. Fidler, "Police in Counterinsurgency: The Challenge of Comprehensive Reformation," in *Policing Insurgencies*, *supra* note 124, at 320.

[193] *Id.* 320–21.

[194] *Id.* 323.

[195] Special Inspector General for Afghan Reconstruction, "Reconstructing the Afghan National Defense and Security Forces: Lessons from the U.S. Experience in Afghanistan" (Sept. 2017), 123 <https://www.sigar.mil/pdf/lessonslearned/SIGAR-17-62-LL.pdf> ("In many cases, the police still suffer from poor leadership, are under-equipped, under-trained, and subsequently incapable of effectively executing their mission, leading to the reported abandonment of 112 police checkpoints in late 2016.").

[196] Grant Wardlaw, Political Terrorism 97 (2d ed., Cambridge University Press, 1990).

groups such as "the Yugoslav Interior Ministry's Special Police Units . . . Haiti's Tontons Macoutes, and the Irish Republican Army."[197]

This has led to one commentator preferring to use the term "constabulary" forces, which are viewed as having "both military capabilities and police powers," and "in democratic countries are trained and tasked with performing policing functions such as traffic control, criminal investigations and public security."[198] They can serve as border guards, customs officers, and in riot squads, and frequently operate as part of the military.[199] Constabulary forces are "trained to operate as mobile light infantry and to perform military police duties such as handling prisoners, directing vehicle traffic, and policing the battlefield." As members of international peacekeeping forces, they have performed "both military and police functions and can be assigned in either a military or civilian capacity."[200] In this respect, they operate as a form of "third force," intended to conduct policing operations during periods of insecurity and instability.[201] Nations with constabulary or paramilitary police units include France (i.e., National Gendarmarie[202]), Italy (i.e., Carabinieri[203]), the Netherlands (i.e., Marechausse[204]), Spain (i.e., Guarda Civil[205]), Turkey (i.e., Gendarmarie of the Turkish Republic[206]), Jordan (i.e., the General Directorate of the Gendarmarie of Jordan[207]), and Argentina (Argentine National Gendarmarie).[208] The constabulary approach has a number of advantages, including relying on an organization

[197] Perito, *supra* note 165, at 34. *See also* Filip Rudic & Die Morina, *Kosovo Massacre Survivor Slams Serbian Perpetrator's Release*, BALKANINSIGHT, Apr. 25, 2018, <http://www.balkaninsight.com/en/article/kosovo-victim-condemns-scorpions-member-s-early-release-04-25-2018> (for reference to a 1999 massacre conducted by the Serbian "Scorpions" unit).

[198] Perito, *supra* note 165, at 46.

[199] *Id.* 46–47.

[200] *Id.* 47.

[201] Wardlaw, *supra* note 196, at 91, 97–100.

[202] "Gendarmarie Nationale," International Association of Gendarmeries and Police Forces with Military Statues, <http://www.fiep.org/member-forces/french-national-gendarmerie/>; Perito, *supra* note 165, at 37–39.

[203] "Carabinieri," International Association of Gendarmeries and Police Forces with Military Statues, <http://www.fiep.org/member-forces/italian-carabinieri/>; Perito, *supra* note 165, at 39–40.

[204] "Marechausse," International Association of Gendarmeries and Police Forces with Military Statues, <http://www.fiep.org/member-forces/royal-netherlands-marechaussee/>; Perito, *supra* note 165, at 40–42.

[205] "Guarda Civil," International Association of Gendarmeries and Police Forces with Military Statues, <http://www.fiep.org/member-forces/spanish-guardia-civil/>; Perito, *supra* note 165, at 42–44.

[206] "Gendarmarie of the Turkish Republic," International Association of Gendarmeries and Police Forces with Military Statues, <http://www.fiep.org/member-forces/turkish-gendarmerie/>.

[207] "General Directorate of the Gendarmarie of Jordan," International Association of Gendarmeries and Police Forces with Military Statues, <http://www.fiep.org/member-forces/darak-forces-jordan/>.

[208] "Argentine National Gendarmarie," International Association of Gendarmeries and Police Forces with Military Statues, <http://www.fiep.org/associated-forces/argentinian-national-gendarmerie/>; Perito, *supra* note 165, at 44–46.

that is "especially trained to deal with difficult decisions such as riots, terrorist incidents, or insurrections."[209]

However, the constabulary model of policing has also been suggested to be anathema to British common law–based policing, in part, because paramilitary police in Europe have historically been tied to public order duties, with specialized units having more "overtly political functions."[210] The common law–based model of policing is frequently viewed as relying on police forces applying a more individualized approach, and its focus, according to Sir Robert Peel's 1829 Principles, is on the police securing "the willing cooperation of the public in voluntary observance of the law to be able to secure and maintain the respect of the public."[211]

However, this difference in policing approach, and as a result the units engaged in counterterrorism and counterinsurgency, is not as stark as the contrast between paramilitary stabilization units and common law–based policing might suggest. Historically, the British have not necessarily followed the "traditional model of 'bobby'" when dealing with the governance of external territories (e.g., Malaysia, Palestine, Rhodesia).[212] Neither has the United States, which has at various points in its history relied on constabulary forces (e.g., Cuba, Haiti, Nicaragua, and post–World War II Germany and Japan).[213] Further, in common law–based countries, long before the 9/11 attacks questions were being raised about whether police forces were becoming too militarized in the quest to counter the threat of counterterrorism.[214] This is an issue that has gained considerable prominence since that time, particularly in the United States.[215] At the heart of this issue is the question of what the proper role of the police and the military is respectively in addressing terrorist threats and in times of instability.

There is an unclear interface between military and police roles in state practice pointing to no one perfect answer. This is evidenced by the development in of counterterrorist hostage rescue paramilitary police units, such as Germany's Border Protection Group 9 (GSG-9)[216] and France's National Gendarmerie Intervention Group (GIGN),[217] while in other countries the same function is

209 Wardlaw, *supra* note 196, at 98.

210 *Id.* 99.

211 *Sir Robert Peel's Nine Principles of Policing*, N.Y. Times, Apr. 15, 2014, <https://www.nytimes.com/2014/04/16/nyregion/sir-robert-peels-nine-principles-of-policing.html> (quote of Principle 3).

212 Wardlaw, *supra* note 196, at 100.

213 Perito, *supra* note 165, at 51–71.

214 Grant Wardlaw, Political Terrorism 91–97 (Cambridge University Press, 1982) (where this issue was addressed in the first edition of Grant Wardlaw's book).

215 Radley Balko, Rise of the Warrior Cop: The Militarization of America's Police Forces 333–36 (Public Affairs, 2013).

216 Chris NcNabb, Storming Flight 181: GSG 9 and the Mogadishu Hijack 11–12 (Osprey Publishing Ltd., 2011).

217 Martin C. Arostegui, Twilight Warriors: Inside the World's Specific Forces 82–90 (22 Books, 1996).

performed by specialist military units such as Britain's Special Air Service or Canada's JTF 2.[218] Some countries, such as Israel, maintain both high-end police (e.g., Yaman) and military units (i.e., Sayaret Maktal),[219] while, as has been noted, India has developed a composite police/military unit in the form of the National Security Guard (the Black Cats).[220]

There are fundamental questions for states and their police and military commanders engaged in counterterrorism/counterinsurgency, which center on the degree to which reliance should be placed on police integrated into the community, on more offensively equipped police and paramilitary units targeting terrorist/insurgent groups, or military units performing specialized tasks. A decision has to be made whether the policing response to insecurity will involve a "police service" or a "police force."[221] This also engages the issue of what types of policing units are available or should be developed to counter terrorism and insurgency, and importantly, what legal authority to use force they should apply. Further, the use of paramilitary and SWAT-style police units in what might be viewed as an offensive capacity needs to be reconciled with the role performed by military units in combating these threats.

B. Policing and Applying the Legal Frameworks

Police roles have been identified as: uniformed general duties police; nonuniformed criminal investigators; stability police units; armed units for "offensive operations against insurgents, terrorists, criminal gangs, and violent criminals"; covert intelligence agents; and border police.[222] With integration within the community being a key aspect of "police primacy" based counterinsurgency, what has been described as "core police" (i.e., the uniformed police and nonuniformed criminal investigators) appear to be best situated to demonstrate that "government can provide security and justice in response to the needs of individuals."[223] They are also the most likely, by training and circumstance, to respond uniquely within the confines of the minimum force human rights–based paradigm.

The challenge is that core police require a relatively benign security environment within which to perform their traditional policing function. As the situation

[218] Horn, *supra* note 104, at 59–62 (outlining the history of JTF2 and its taking over of the hostage rescue role from the RMCP in 1993).

[219] Or Heller, *Rescuing Hostages*, Israel Defence, Aug. 24, 2013, <http://www.israeldefense.co.il/en/content/rescuing-hostages>.

[220] "History of the National Security Guard," <http://www.nsg.gov.in/about-us/history-nsg>.

[221] Fidler, *supra* note 192, at 323.

[222] Bayley & Perito, *supra* note 36, at 73.

[223] *Id.* 74.

deteriorates, it becomes increasingly difficult for traditional community-based police functions to be performed. This raises the possibility of providing more robust support to these police from two sources: either constabulary-style formed police units capable of operations in more insecure environments, or military units assigned to secure an area. As has been noted, in the absence of functioning police, the military may have to take over the policing role.

There is a range of possible police units that can provide greater security. Post conflict stability operations in the Balkans have been performed by Multinational Specialist Units based on Carabinieri and other traditional constabulary forces,[224] and also in the case of Kosovo, Special Police Units (SPUs) modeled on the French Gendarmerie. The SPUs were recruited "from existing constabulary forces or from regular police units" and specially trained to perform their role.[225] An example of the potential interface and even overlap of roles within police forces has been the suggestion that a US civilian constabulary force for stability operations might be created using police SWAT teams and special operations units.[226] The range of police units does not stop there because there has also been the development of separate offensive armed units (e.g., police commandoes).

An important question is the difference between constabulary units and offensive armed police units regarding how they are situated on the force continuum. In this respect, constabulary forces (e.g., gendarmerie) are normally more directly associated by training and organization for "tasks such as crowd management, where discipline and hierarchy have to take over once disorder has broken out."[227] They have a hierarchical structure, military discipline, an investigative ability, and can have armored vehicles and military assault weapons.[228] However, a key function is that they can perform a policing function. Further along the spectrum, in the form of offensively armed police, are the "little soldiers" such as those established in Iraq and Afghanistan and mentored largely by military forces.

It appears there are a number of factors that will impact on the development of the policing response in failed or failing states. First, are the security situation and the type of units, armament, and training necessary to effectively operate in the territory. Secondly, whether police training is being established and carried out by military, or civilian police authorities. Thirdly, whether those assisting authorities come from a background that relies more heavily on policing integrated within a community or are used to a "third force" concept of policing,

[224] Perito, *supra* note 165, at 153–82, 184–89.
[225] *Id.* 195.
[226] Perito, *supra* note 165, at 330.
[227] Giustozzi & Isaqzadeh, *supra* note 172, at 5.
[228] *Id.* 4.

Fourthly, the political structure of the territorial state and its historical approach toward policing will also affect what police forces are developed.

It has been suggested that there should be no offensive counterinsurgency role for police forces. In this model, paramilitary police should be used for "the maintenance of public order, including riot control" and what are effectively defensive duties such as "VIP protection, convoy escorts, and guarding of facilities."[229] Any offensive role would be performed by military units.[230] While such a distinction has considerable value in terms of clarity, practice has proven it is extremely difficult to maintain. Indeed, looking at the use of specialized counterterrorism forces in Europe, North American, and elsewhere, it seems that a clear separation is not always possible even in relatively benign security situations. The development of offensively minded police units is a common aspect of contemporary counterterrorism. These forces have undoubtedly been developed out of need.

An additional challenge is how well European models of policing can be introduced into a state that is not only undergoing significant challenges to its governance but can also be lacking a history or culture of effective rights-based policing. Models that work in stable states may not transfer well to those that have relied historically on militia and more informal policing arrangements. The types of police units that are developed may differ depending upon location and the ability of the government to centrally administer those forces. A tension can develop between centrally controlled forces and police that are village-based. This was evident in Afghanistan with the "[s]uccessive experiments with local police forces (Auxiliary Police, Afghan Public Protection Force, Afghan Local Police)."[231] One critical assessment has suggested that the European models of policing had some scope for application in cities, however, the countryside required more "down-to-earth" approaches. There had to be engagement with "the armed groups roaming the countryside."[232] A "stronger focus on a viable form of paramilitary policing could have helped the reformers at the MoI [Ministry of the Interior] approach armed groups in the villages from a position of greater strength and extract a better compromise."[233] While a successful "police primacy" counterinsurgency ultimately depends more upon a police service type approach, getting to that stage can be a complex process. The state, its commanders, and its foreign allies may have to manage a variety of police actors, many of whom may have overlapping roles with army units.

What cannot happen is for military commanders to automatically believe that a unit with "police" in its title is capable, equipped, or trained to conduct the

229 Bayley & Perito, *supra* note 36, at 78.
230 *Id.* 77.
231 Giustozzi & Isaqzadeh, *supra* note 172, at 62.
232 *Id.* 186.
233 *Id.*

type of local core policing that ultimately underpins true security in urban areas. Neither is it guaranteed they will have any training in human rights–based law enforcement. There must be an awareness by military forces of the true nature and capability of the police units they are supporting or operating alongside of during an insurgency. As was evidenced in the Balkans, there has also frequently been a fundamental misunderstanding, not only by military commanders but also by police commanders from countries that do not use constabulary forces, of the role those units can perform.[234] This can lead to their underutilization by both military and police authorities.[235] The failure to develop "core police" or an effective policing model at the local level that operates within a functioning justice system does not bode well for a successful urban counterterrorism or counterinsurgency campaign.

Even though non-state actor groups may lose individual battles against military forces and even be forced to flee or go underground, this does not ultimately guarantee success. Ultimately, cities have to be effectively policed. States should make a conscious choice to separate policing from the conduct of hostilities, in effect emphasizing the importance of a "police service" approach and its related application of human rights norms. First, in order to limit confusion as to when a policing or military response is being applied, a line should be drawn regarding police and military roles. Emphasis should be placed on ensuring that while the police may be forced by a terrorist or insurgent threat to respond under a hostilities paradigm, their operations should not focus on mirroring or displacing more traditional military capabilities and functions.

With absent or weak military forces, the existence of militarized police forces, and with the military units themselves frequently engaging in policing roles, it will not always be straightforward to determine where that line concerning the role of policing units should be drawn. However, a distinction should be made that focuses on police carrying out non-offensive roles. One example favoring a less offensive police capability can be found in Northern Ireland where, following a 1982 controversial shooting of three terrorists, Royal Ulster Constabulary special units had their role changed from directly confronting terrorists to supporting the British Special Air Service.[236] While in one way this signaled a limit to the police primacy approach by uniquely retaining this aspect of counterterrorism in the hands of the military, it also reinforced a less aggressive policing role that underpins the counterinsurgency concept of police primacy. In that context, the line had appeared to be crossed when questions began to be asked whether the security forces were adopting an aggressive "shoot to kill"

234 Perito, *supra* note 165, at 330.

235 *Id.* 219–22 (outlining why the Kosovo Special Police Units were not used to their full potential).

236 Mark Urban, Big Boy Rules 160 (Faber and Faber, 1992).

policy, rather than applying the more restrained force options associated with human rights–based policing.[237] It was not ultimately established that a "shoot to kill" policy was in existence, but the association of police units with that possibility appears to have highlighted how far their role had progressed beyond an accepted policing function.

Secondly, states and courts should be wary of adopting a blended approach toward the application of human rights law. There is a significant advantage, both legally and operationally, in maintaining a separation of humanitarian and human rights law. It is the latter body of law that represents normalcy and contains the standards that the public will most readily support. Ultimately, there needs to be careful consideration of the emphasis that will be placed on how and which of the legal frameworks should govern police and military operations. As these frameworks frequently overlap, states telegraph the relative importance they place on each body of law by the choices they make. The application of human rights norms, whether applied under humanitarian or human rights law, should take precedence. In many situations, those norms must be applied (e.g., the absence of an armed conflict, dealing with situations of ordinary crime, maintaining order among supporters of the terrorists or insurgents who are not taking a direct part in hostilities). In others, the choice should be based on whether a human rights approach effectively addresses the threat. This includes a strategic assessment of the impact of force on the population from which the state is seeking support. Favoring a less violent approach that emphasizes the use of minimum force makes more strategic, operational, and tactical sense when operating in the exceptionally crowded urban environments of the twenty-first century. It is important to keep human rights–based policing as a concept separate from the law governing the conduct of hostilities, just as it is important to avoid militarizing either the police or the law governing their activities.

VI. Conclusion

Conflict in the twenty-first century will inevitably be centered on urban populations that are not only growing to almost unfathomable levels but which also will present significant governance challenges for states. Among those challenges will be groups seeking to usurp government authority by gaining control of urban areas. In order to counter the terrorist and insurgent threats arising in those overcrowded environs, states cannot rely solely on military force. The maintenance of order is simply too fundamental a concept of governance for that to be the case. These threats rely heavily on criminal activity, and as a result

[237] *Id.* 159–60.

policing cannot be ignored. Criminal activity not only funds and supports terrorist and insurgent action, it exists in a strata of society that can provide a form of safe haven from which threats to the government can spring but also retreat should the security situation warrant it.

If the conflicts of the first two decades of this century are any indication, states will not only have to rely heavily on police forces but will likely will also have to develop new units or reform existing police agencies. In doing so, conscious decisions have to made regarding the type of policing to be applied by states. In this respect, it is a police service approach that ultimately favors success during counterinsurgency. While states may have to develop more offensively minded police units at various points in the conflict, there remains a significant advantage in adopting an approach that emphasizes core policing. Similarly, states inevitably have choices to make in terms of what legal regime to emphasize in countering the threats posed by these terrorist and insurgent groups. As with policing, it is the traditional employment of human rights–based policing that is most likely to lead to success. The goal is to establish normalcy in cities and other urban areas. The application of human rights–based policing represents the societies that function best, and as John Keegan noted, the ones where we do want to live.[238] Reliance on such policing cannot end when hostilities in urban centers escalate, or wait for hostilities to end before it and human rights norms are applied to address the contemporary security challenges.

[238] Keegan, *supra* note 128, at 386.

8

Ratchet Down or Ramp Up?

Contemporary Threats, Armed Conflict, and Tailored Authority

Geoffrey S. Corn[*]

Since the United States initiated its military response to the terrorist attacks of September 11, 2001, "conflict characterization" has become a central theme of legal and policy discourse.[1] This discourse normally focuses on the conditions that justify characterizing a military operation as an "armed conflict," thereby resulting in applicability of the law of armed conflict (LOAC). Additionally, and to a lesser extent, the discourse seeks to identify the demarcation point between non-international and international armed conflicts, with the accordant impact on legal authority and regulation (most notably related to the status of captured enemy belligerent personnel).[2]

The discussion about conflict characterization has played an important role in clarifying where, when, and how a state may employ military forces and invoke the expansive response authorities, inherent in a situation of armed conflict, to address non-state security threats. Central to this clarification was the assertion that military operations, directed against a transnational non-state organized armed group, may qualify as an armed conflict.[3] This theory of armed

[*] Vinson and Elkins Professor of Law, South Texas College of Law Houston; Lieutenant Colonel, US Army (Retired) and former Special Assistant for Law of War Matters and Chief of the Law of War Branch, Office of the Judge Advocate General, US Army; Chief of International Law for US Army Europe; Professor of International and National Security Law at the US Army Judge Advocate General's School. Special thanks to my research assistants John Wooldridge and Kyle Moore.

[1] International Committee of the Red Cross, "Commentary of 2016: Geneva Convention I for the Amelioration of the Condition of the Wounded and Sick in the Armed Forces in the Field" (2016). *See also* Sandesh Sivakumaran, The Law of Non-International Armed Conflict 192 (2012); Yoram Dinstein, Non-International Armed Conflict in International Law the Law of Non-International Armed Conflict (2014).

[2] International Committee of the Red Cross, *supra* note 1. *See generally* Geoffrey S. Corn, *Hamdan, Lebanon, and the Regulation of Hostilities: The Need to Recognize a Hybrid Category of Armed Conflict*, 40 Vand. J. Transnat'l L. 295, 303 (2006), noting that although there is no single factor to establish a demarcation line, the key concern addressed by the ICRC Commentary when determining the existence of non-international armed conflict was to draw the line between internal/domestic disturbances and military conflict.

[3] *Id.* at 319.

Geoffrey S. Corn, *Ratchet Down or Ramp Up?* In: *Between Crime and War.* Edited by: Claire Finkelstein, Christopher Fuller, Jens David Ohlin, Mitt Regan, Oxford University Press. © Claire Finkelstein, Christopher Fuller, Jens David Ohlin, Mitt Regan 2023. DOI: 10.1093/oso/9780197638798.003.0009

conflict has, however, also elevated the critical question of properly/legally identifying the conditions that justify treating such a threat as an armed conflict, rather than a threat warranting only non-conflict response authority consistent with international human rights law (IHRL).[4] This, in turn, implicates the complex relationship between the LOAC and IHRL in this nebulous new zone of military operations. This new zone is what Brigadier General Kenneth Watkin calls "fighting in the grey zone" in his award-winning book, *Fighting at the Legal Boundaries: Controlling the Use of Force in Contemporary Conflict*.[5] Although the two bodies of law are fundamentally different, a "grey zone" within the "legal boundary" occurs, in large part, because the similarities and considerable overlap between the two creates a mischaracterization.[6]

It is fair to say that early in the evolution of this new conception of non-international armed conflicts (NIACs)—armed conflicts between states and organized armed groups operating transnationally[7]—this relationship was viewed through a conflict of laws lens—a binary "applicable law" equation.[8] Under this view, IHRL applied until the situation evolved into an armed conflict; at which point the LOAC displaced IHRL.[9] This binary conception of law applicability has itself evolved substantially, with widespread recognition that these two branches of international law need not be understood as applying exclusively.[10]

Instead, a complementarity approach will become increasingly dominant, recognizing that IHRL continues to play an important regulatory role, especially in a NIAC context.[11] However, this complementarity approach has also created many subsequent questions that had, prior to the notion of a "transnational" NIAC, been functionally nullified by the assumption that only host-nation law

[4] KENNETH WATKIN, FIGHTING AT THE LEGAL BOUNDARIES: CONTROLLING THE USE OF FORCE IN CONTEMPORARY CONFLICT 328–29 (2016).

[5] *Id.*

[6] *Id.* at 130–31.

[7] United Nations, "Geneva Convention for the Amelioration of the Condition of the Wounded and Sick in Armed Forces in the Field of August 12, 1949," (1950) 75 United Nations Treaty Series 31, 970; United Nations, "Geneva Convention for the Amelioration of the Condition of Wounded, Sick and Shipwrecked Members of Armed Forces at Sea of August 12, 1949," (1950) 75 United Nations Treaties Series 85, 971; United Nations, "Geneva Convention Relative to the Treatment of Prisoners of War of August 12, 1949," (1950) 75 United Nations Treaty Series 135, 972; United Nations, "Geneva Convention Relative to the Protection of Civilian Persons in Time of War of August 12, 1949," (1950) 75 United Nations Treaty Series 287.

[8] Laurie R. Blank & Geoffrey S. Corn, *Losing the Forest for the Trees: Syria, Law, and the Pragmatics of Conflict Recognition*, 46 VAND. J. TRANSNAT'L L. 693 (2013).

[9] UNITED STATES DEPARTMENT OF DEFENSE, LAW OF WAR MANUAL (Dec. 2016), secs. III, XVII.

[10] *See generally* Geoffrey S. Corn & Eric T. Jensen, *Transnational Armed Conflict: A 'Principled' Approach to the Regulation of Counter-Terror Combat Operations*, 42 ISRAEL L. REV., no. 1, 43–44 (2009), discussing how the continued evolution of TAC, or the acts of "war" carried out by states that attack non-state targets outside of their boundaries, must preserve "the fundamental balance between authority and obligations that lies at the core of the LOAC" to preserve its legitimacy as it becomes more common.

[11] Eric T. Jensen, *Combat Status: It Is Time for Intermediate Levels of Recognition for Partial Compliance*, 46 VAND. J. TRANSNAT'L L. 209 (2005).

and IHRL would apply to any extraterritorial military operation that did not qualify as an international armed conflict (IAC).[12]

Identifying the point, or points, at which the LOAC provides the exclusive source of regulatory authority, in relation to the conduct of operations during a NIAC, is an increasingly complex question. One response—the response that has defined US military operations—is that once the line between "peace" and "armed conflict" is crossed, the LOAC applies to all aspects of these operations.[13] It is at this point that the US armed forces are provided broad authority to disrupt or disable the "enemy" (i.e., transnational non-state threat).[14] While policy considerations may frequently lead to the implementation of rules of engagement (ROE) that "ratchet down" this authority,[15] or other policy directives that impose limits on the full extent of LOAC authority, the nation retains the prerogative to invoke that broad authority when it deems necessary and appropriate.

This approach may be operationally appealing because it clarifies, through policy, operational authority. Indeed, for the operational commander, it is common to look to the ROE as *the only* source of authority, with little concern over the extent to which that authority is coextensive with or more restrictive than the LOAC itself. However, this tendency to rely solely on ROE to clarify operational authority does not negate the underlying legal consequence of characterizing the struggle against these transnational organized armed groups as an armed conflict. This may inevitably create a consequential operational option to "ratchet up" authority to the maximum level consistent with the LOAC. Inherent in this consequence is the risk of authority overbreadth: permitting operational forces to exercise authority permitted by the LOAC in situations where the nature of the threat does not credibly necessitate such authority. Of course, there may also be times and places where such authority is necessary, which will often be dictated by the threat and not based on some arbitrary temporal or geographic factor.[16] But a binary approach to operational authority, that allows for

[12] Dinstein, *supra* note 1, at 32–33.

[13] Corn, *supra* note 2, at 325–26.

[14] *See* The White House, "National Security Strategy" (May 2010), <https://obamawhitehouse.archives.gov/sites/default/files/rss_viewer/national_security_strategy.pdf; *see also* Greg Jaffe, *How Obama's Nobel Prize Speech Became a Guide to His Wartime Decision-Making*, WASH. POST, June 3, 2016, <https://www.washingtonpost.com/graphics/national/obama-legacy/nobel-peace-prize-oslo-2009-speech.html;; *see also* John O. Brennan, "Strengthening our Security by Adhering to our Values and Laws," Harvard Law School, Program on Law and Security, Sept. 16, 2011, < https://obamawhitehouse.archives.gov/the-press-office/2011/09/16/remarks-john-o-brennan-strengthening-our-security-adhering-our-values-an. *See also* Eric Holder, "Remarks," Northwestern University School of Law, Mar. 5, 2012, < https://www.justice.gov/opa/speech/attorney-general-eric-holder-speaks-northwestern-university-school-law; Ryan J. Vogel, *Drone Warfare and the Law of Armed Conflict*, 39 DEN. J. INT'L L. & POL'Y 101, 108 (2010).

[15] INTERNATIONAL AND OPERATIONAL LAW DEPARTMENT, OPERATIONAL LAW HANDBOOK (16th ed. 2016).

[16] *See* Geoffrey S. Corn, *Geography of Armed Conflict: Why It Is a Mistake to Fish for the Red Herring*, 89 INT'L L. STUD. 77, 13 (2013).

a per se use of LOAC compliant operations, seems ill-suited to the hybrid nature of these threats. Many have considered this to create a risk of unjustified human suffering, as well as creating an inherent incentive for an overzealous armed conflict characterization.[17]

It is unrealistic, however, to expect that a state will adopt a response governed exclusively by IHRL when it is confronted with the types of threats exemplified by transnational terrorism. This is primarily because of the general understanding that IHRL does not provide states with a scope of response authority even close to that derived from the LOAC, especially in relation to the use of force.[18] While Watkin challenges the assumption that conduct of hostilities-type rules can never be squared with a IHRL,[19] his interpretation of IHRL security response authority is unconventional. In fact, there seems to be a significant delta between Watkin's theory to expand IHRL security response authority and the dominant approach to this challenge, most notably among states, that this framework allows only security measures consistent with normal law enforcement authority.[20] This, in large measure, explains why states, like the United States, adopt the armed conflict characterization to respond to these "hybrid" transnational threats.[21]

Watkin also acknowledges, in my view appropriately, that it is ultimately the nature of an organized armed threat that must dictate the point at which state response authority moves from one based exclusively on IHRL, to one based on the LOAC.[22] However, as Watkin explains in great detail, the nature of these threats routinely straddles the line between ordinary criminal activity and the type of threat associated with organized armed groups.[23] Indeed, Watkin devotes substantial space to explaining how the modern transnational non-state enemy functions in many ways like the types of insurgencies that animated the development of the LOAC applicable to NIACs.[24] The point is not to simply justify a LOAC-based response framework but to highlight that, consistent with classic Maoist insurgency doctrine, the nature of the threat posed by such groups is rarely unitary.[25] Instead, the threat ebbs and flows between low-level criminal

[17] Watkin, *supra* note 4, at 337.

[18] *Id.* 484; *see also* United Nations, "Basic Principles on the Use of Force and Firearms by Law Enforcement Officials" (Sept. 7, 1990), para. 4.

[19] Watkin, *supra* note 4, at 337.

[20] International Committee of the Red Cross, "What Is the difference between IHL and Human Rights Law?," Jan. 22, 2015, <https://www.icrc.org/en/document/what-difference-between-ihl-and-human-rights-law; *see generally* Gary P. Corn, "Should the Best Offense Ever Be a Good Defense," Strategy Research Project, United States Army War College, 2014.

[21] *See* Brennan, *supra* note 14. *See also* Benjamin Wittes, *State Department Legal Advisor Brian Egan's Speech at ASIL*, LAWFARE, Apr. 8, 2016, <https://www.lawfareblog.com/state-department-legal-adviser-brian-egans-speech-asil.

[22] Watkin, *supra* note 4, at 532.

[23] *Id.* 196.

[24] *Id.* 604.

[25] *Id.* 204.

violence to much more dangerous organized armed operations, which seek to exploit any space they find available and to use any tactic that offsets the normal superior capabilities of their state opponents.[26] Thus, even when capable of fielding organized military-type forces, to engage in isolated "peer-to-peer"[27] conflict with state armed forces, these groups will continue to conduct many activities that fall outside that characterization and are completely amenable to traditional law enforcement responses.

The transnational terrorist organizations the United States considers itself to be in an armed conflict against—Al Qaeda and associated forces such as ISIS[28]—arguably provide ideal examples of this hybrid or fluid threat dynamic. These groups often present the type of operational challenge that necessitates resort to LOAC-based authority to achieve the goal of disrupting or disabling their capability.[29] However, they also engage in a range of activities that are, by any rational assessment, criminal activities that do not take the form of military-type threats.[30] A strategic dilemma results from such threats that are arguably a much more common modus operandi than the military-type activities.[31] While the low-level threat, associated with criminal-type activities, might justify abandoning the armed conflict characterization, it would also divest the state of the response flexibility to address those situations where law enforcement rules are assessed as too restrictive to respond to the threat. However, characterizing the threat as an armed conflict results in the perception that all aspects of the

[26] *Id.* 160–61.

[27] *See* Thomas Donnelly, "Peers, Near-Peers, and Partial Peers: Making Sense of America's Balance-of-Power Interest," American Enterprise Institute, Feb. 16, 2017, < https://www.aei.org/wp-content/uploads/2017/02/Reshaping-the-US-Military_Donnelly-testimony.pdf?x91208.

[28] *See* Mary L. Kelly, *When the U.S. Military Strikes, White House Points to a 2001 Measure*, ALL THINGS CONSIDERED, Sept. 6, 2016, https://www.npr.org/sections/parallels/2016/09/06/492857888/when-the-u-s-military-strikes-white-house-points-to-a-2001-measure; Rita Siemion, *Trump Administration Says Its Broad Powers Under the 2001 AUMF Are Plenty*, JUST SECURITY, Aug.2, 2017, <https://www.justsecurity.org/43831/trump-administration-broad-powers-2001-aumf-plenty/; Charlie Savage, Eric Schmitt, & Mark Mazzetti, *Obama Expands War with Al Qaeda to Include Shabab in Somalia*, N.Y. TIMES, Nov. 27, 2016, <https://www.nytimes.com/2016/11/27/us/politics/obama-expands-war-with-al-qaeda-to-include-shabab-in-somalia.html. *See also* Patricia Zengerle & Idrees Ali, *Trump Administration Does Not Want Limits on War Authorization*, REUTERS, Oct. 30, 2017, <https://www.reuters.com/article/us-usa-defense-authorization/trump-administration-does-not-want-limits-on-war-authorization-idUSKBN1CZ0CC

[29] Geoffrey S. Corn & Eric T. Jensen, *Transnational Armed Conflict: A "Principled" Approach to the Regulation of Counter-Terror Combat Operations*, 42 ISRAEL L. REV. 45 (2009)

[30] *See generally* Watkin, *supra* note 4, at 329, demonstrating the complexity in identifying a non-state actor conflict that results in correspondingly different normative rules that apply when non-state actors qualify as international in character, while others situations are not.

[31] Clayton Thomas, "Al Qaeda and U.S. Policy: Middle East and Africa," Congressional Research Service, Feb. 5, 2018, <https://fas.org/sgp/crs/mideast/R43756.pdf; *see also* Kenneth Katzman, "Al Qaeda: Profile and Threat Assessment," Congressional Research Service, Aug. 17, 2005, < https://fas.org/sgp/crs/terror/RL33038.pdf; Kim Cragin & Sara A. Daly, "The Dynamic Terrorist Threat: An Assessment of Group Motivations and Capabilities in a Changing World," RAND Project Air Force, 2004, <https://www.rand.org/content/dam/rand/pubs/monograph_reports/2005/MR1782.pdf.

responsive security operation should be addressed through measures based on the LOAC—creating the proverbial hammer that leads to viewing the entire problem as a nail. Accordingly, while the armed conflict characterization may be perceived as a strategic necessity, there will be many situations at the level of operational execution where the threat will resemble the type of threat addressed through law enforcement–based responses.[32]

A binary approach to the authority to respond to these threats is operationally problematic because it creates a genuine risk of overbreadth or underinclusiveness.[33] Addressing these threats through a pure law enforcement framework ignores the occasional drifting of the operational situation into one more appropriate for LOAC authorities. But, as noted above, treating all aspects of the threat as falling within that LOAC framework creates a risk that operational authority will be pragmatically overbroad to deal with aspects of the threat that are amenable to law enforcement–type response authorities.[34]

What is required is a more nuanced understanding of how these two regulatory regimes should influence the development and implementation of operational authority.[35] Clearly, this will not be satisfied by simply rejecting a US-type *lex specialis* approach, which does not recognize any applicability of IHRL in the context of armed conflict.[36] Moreover, acknowledging a complementary application of these two bodies of law is an insufficient first step.[37] Instead, what is needed, especially at the operational level, is a rational approach to determine when it is appropriate to rely on expansive LOAC authorities instead of the more restrictive IHRL regime.

My emphasis on the operational level of command is deliberate. Unlike my friend Kenneth Watkin, I am not yet convinced that states dealing with these type of hybrid threats are willing to accept, at least at the strategic level, the constraining effect of a pure IHRL legal response framework.[38] Instead, as I have explained in prior articles,[39] the NIAC characterization is influenced

[32] David Glazier, *Playing by the Rules: Combating Al Qaeda Within the Law of War*, 51 Wm. & Mary L. Rev. 957, 1018 (2009).

[33] Watkin, *supra* note 4, at 575.

[34] *Id.* 444.

[35] *Id.* 574, explaining that operational law developed because of the need to resolve the simultaneous application, interaction, and overlap between the various bodies of law.

[36] United States Department of Defense, *supra* note 9, at 8–11; *see also* Nancie Prud'homme, *Lex Specialis: Oversimplifying a More Complex and Mutlifaceted Relationship?*, 40 Israel L. Rev. 356 (2007)

[37] *Id.* 11; *see also* Martti Koskenniemi, "Fragmentation of International Law: Difficulties Arising from the Diversification and Expansion of International Law" (International Law Commission, United Nations General Assembly, A/CN.4/L.682, Apr. 13, 2006), https://legal.un.org/ilc/documentation/english/a_cn4_l682.pdf.

[38] Watkin, *supra* note 4, at 329, establishing the criteria of applying the "totality of the circumstances approach" to armed conflict when there is a presence of intense violence and group organization.

[39] Geoffrey S. Corn, *Regulating Hostilities in Non-International Armed Conflicts: Thoughts on Bridging the Divide between Tadic Aspiration and Conflict Realities*, 91 Int'l L. Stud. 281 (2015);

substantially by that advancement of national security interests triggered by a credible assessment of these types of threats that impose a response framework that provides the flexibility to utilize both law enforcement– *and* LOAC-based measures. Watkin makes a compelling case that there are a range of security situations that necessitate a more nuanced understanding of the relationship between IHL and IHRL. Some situations, like the ongoing hostilities against Al Qaeda and ISIS, qualify as ongoing armed conflicts. But, as Watkin notes, it may be more credible to apply an IHRL security response approach to many aspects of such armed conflicts, with the necessary space to address periodic "flare ups" of threat capability through the IHL lens. Thus, even in the context of an ongoing armed conflict, the use of LOAC-based response measures should be carefully limited to only those aspects of the threat that exceed the efficacy of more restrained IHRL measures.[40] In contrast, there are short-duration or "springing" armed conflicts: armed conflicts that arise in the midst of an ongoing law enforcement–based security operation. Watkin uses the British military action in Sierra Leone[41] and the Argentine Abella[42] incident as examples of this type of "micro" or "pop up" NIAC.[43] This "pop up" or springing armed conflict approach presents its own challenges, especially at the strategic level. To be effective, states would have to identify the point at which an ongoing threat, that is generally not yet characterized as an armed conflict, periodically progresses into that realm of legal regulation. Perhaps an even more complicated judgment is when a state would also be expected to revert back to a pure IHRL response framework in response to a reduced threat level. This complication is illustrated by the reticence of the United States to revise its assessment of the Al Qaeda threat. Assuming *arguendo* that characterizing the response to that transnational terrorist threat as a NIAC was justified when invoked, at what point is this characterization no longer valid? And how should the United States indicate a reversion to a pure IHRL/law enforcement response framework?

Geoffrey S. Corn & Tanweer Kaleemullah, *The Military Response to Criminal Violent Extremist Groups: Aligning Use of Force Presumptions with Threat Reality*, 47 ISRAEL L. REV. 253 (2014); *see also* Corn, *supra* note 2.

40 Kenneth Watkin, *Humanitarian Law and 21st-Century Conflict: Three Block Wars, Terrorism, and Complex Security Situations*, *in* TESTING THE BOUNDARIES OF INTERNATIONAL HUMANITARIAN LAW (Susan C. Breau & Agnieszka Jachec-Neale eds., 2006).

41 RICHARD CONNAUGHTON MODERN WARFARE: THE TRUE STORY OF CONFLICT FROM THE FALKLANDS TO AFGHANISTAN 283 (2008).

42 Abella v. Argentina, Comission Report 55/97 (Case 11.137, Inter-American Commission on Human Rights, 1997), http://hrlibrary.umn.edu/cases/1997/argentina55-97a.html; International Law Association, "Final Report of the Use of Force Committee: The Meaning of Armed Conflict" (Aug. 2010), 30, http://ww.ila-hq.org/en/committees/index.cfm/cid/1022, where reliance is placed on the *Abella* case in reaching the conclusion "[t]he two concepts, intensity, and protraction, are linked and a lesser level of duration may satisfy the criterion if the intensity level is high."

43 Watkin, *supra* note 4, at 412.

In my view, it is at the *operational* level where Watkin's proposal holds the greatest promise. At that level, military forces are tasked with the mission of implementing the nation's strategic objective of defeating or disrupting these transnational non-state threats.[44] That *mission*, in contrast to the overall strategic objective, will often require the type of nuanced or hybrid approach to operational regulation.[45] Watkin highlights a critical operational law question: What should be considered the "presumptive" regulatory framework applicable to extraterritorial military operations against hybrid threats?[46] This question is based on an important premise: it is operationally and tactically shortsighted to assume that at the level where strategy is implemented, the strategic NIAC characterization demands a binary approach to *operational* authority. Indeed, this is the consistent theme that runs through Watkin's work. Answering this question will contribute to an analysis of what conditions justify providing for an expanded operational and tactical authority derived from the LOAC when forces are engaged in these operations.

I believe Watkin has offered a compelling justification for seeking a more rational alignment between operational response authority with the varying nature of security threats confronted *within* the context of an ongoing armed conflict. Central to this alignment is the recognition that law enforcement–type authority consistent with IHRL will often be the optimum use of force framework for dealing with these threats.[47] However, because operations are in fact conducted in the context of a NIAC, it is equally necessary to recognize that there will be situations where the nature of the threat exceeds the IHRL/law enforcement response capabilities, making it appropriate to utilize expanded LOAC measures.[48]

Accordingly, this chapter proposes that treating the IHRL response framework as a presumptive limit on military authority will contribute to mitigating the risks of operational overbreadth or underinclusiveness. Whether dealing with an internal or external non-state threat, this presumptive limitation should provide guidance to the ROE and other tactical and operational measures based on the IHRL model. By treating this model as presumptive, even in the broader context of a NIAC, operational commanders will be compelled to identify necessity-based justifications for authorizing use of the more expansive LOAC

[44] *See, e.g.*, United States Department of the Army, "Field Manual 3-0 Operations" (Feb. 22, 2011).

[45] *See, e.g.*, International Security Assistance Force, "Tactical Directive" (NATO/ISAF UNCLASS memorandum, July 6, 2009), <https://www.nato.int/isaf/docu/official_texts/Tactical_Directive_090706.pdf; Watkin, *supra* note 4, at 258.

[46] Dinstein, *supra* note 1, at paras. 720, 742, defining operations known as "extraterritorial law enforcement."

[47] Watkin, *supra* note 4, at 350–51.

[48] *See generally* Commentary on the HPCR Manual of International Law Applicable to Air and Missile Warfare (2010), suggesting that "[a]s the 2001 terrorist attacks against the Twin Towers in New York City show, highjacked civilian airliners may also be used as means of warfare in flagrant violation of the law of international armed conflict."

derived authority.[49] This presumption is based on the premise that armed conflict, and the LOAC authority it permits, is an exceptional situation; and that IHRL is the normal legal framework for responding to the type of threats that dominate the contemporary strategic environment.[50] Equally important, however, is the recognition that this is a rebuttable presumption, and that when and where the nature of such a threat renders it pragmatically beyond the disabling reach of law enforcement authority, the measures pursuant to the LOAC will be justified.[51]

The value of this operational-level presumption is obviously debatable. Ultimately, the goal of this approach is to better align operational practice with Watkin's compelling argument that when engaging "legal boundary" threats, treating IHRL as the primary response framework will advance both operational and strategic objectives.[52] However, this operational-level presumption also seeks to bypass the complexity of the strategic level debate over whether response to such threats justify a NIAC characterization.[53] Ultimately, the goal is to temper the tendency to view operational execution of a state response to such threats through a binary lens. Instead, even in the context of an ongoing NIAC, states should consistently assess if, and when, "ratcheting down" the security response modality so that it aligns more closely with law enforcement principles serves to achieve the *strategic* objective. Such an approach will preserve a necessity-based invocation of the more permissive LOAC response authority while still providing a constant gravitational pull back to the IHRL law enforcement framework.

To be clear, I recognize that such an approach cannot be characterized as an obligation derived from *lex lata*. Nor am I so naïve as to consider such an approach a panacea for the many complexities associated with responding to non-state threats that operate at that "legal boundary," particularly with military capabilities. Instead, this proposal is pragmatic in nature, seeking to accommodate what must be recognized as two important state objectives: the interest in effective response to non-state threats *and* the interest in preserving legitimacy by avoiding the perception of overzealous and operationally unnecessary assertions

[49] Geoffrey S. Corn, *Regulating Hostilities in Non-International Armed Conflicts: Thoughts on Bridging the Divide between the Tadic Aspiration and Conflict Realities*, 91 INT'L L. STUD. 281, 309 (2015), emphasizing that commanders and other operational decision makers will be pressured to employ systems in response to the perceived operational necessity.

[50] Watkin, *supra* note 4, at 583, this approach means that the state response to many contemporary non-state actor attacks will occur in the context of armed conflict, while those not rising to the legal and factual level of such a conflict must be addressed as a human rights–based law enforcement matter.

[51] *Id.* 582.

[52] *Id.* 3.

[53] *Id.* 30–31; *see also* Geoffrey S. Corn, *Taking the Bitter with the Sweet: A "Full and Fair" Critique of the Military Commissions*, 35 STETSON L. REV. 811 (2006).

of authority.[54] Thus, this "presumptive" operational framework approach is proposed as a best practice when operating in this realm of legal complexity. Recognizing a legal framework that dictates the scope of a military operational response to these "legal boundary" threats can ebb and flow just as the nature of the threat ebbs and flows between criminal and military capabilities,[55] will provide for a more rational balance between power and restraint—a balance central to strategic legitimacy.

I. Non-International Armed Conflict: The Exigency Assumption

No single development in the regulation of armed conflict has arguably been more complex than extending the scope of NIACs to non-state threats operating extraterritorially.[56] Extensive effort has been devoted to important questions central to the relationship between military operations and this theory of NIAC. The effort has focused primarily on the legitimacy of recognizing a "transnational" NIAC, and the conditions that bring such a threat into existence.[57] Less effort has been devoted to what may, today, be an even more important question: operational implementation of the strategic mission to address these transnational threats.[58]

If, as is increasingly accepted, state response to transnational non-state threats may qualify as a NIAC, this question is vitally important to ensure operationally rational limits on what might otherwise be overbroad assertions of the extraordinary state response powers. Unfortunately, the "foundational" source of authority for the notion of NIAC itself is Common Article 3 of the four 1949 Geneva Conventions.[59] Common Article 3 offers nothing that addresses when, where, and how a state should employ force or exercise other authorities (like detention) in the context of a NIAC. Nor does Common Article 3 address the equally significant question of when such a NIAC terminates.[60] This temporal

[54] Watkin, *supra* note 4, at 337.

[55] As an example, Watkin, *supra* note 4, at 590–91, discussion of an organized criminal gang taking advantage of a situation of insecurity within the context of an ongoing armed conflict. If a military commander were compelled to address the security threat posed by such a gang, the mission would be law enforcement in nature as the gang's activities are not related to the armed conflict.

[56] Corn, *supra* note 2; Watkin, *supra* note 4, at 150–51.

[57] *Id.*

[58] This strategic objective is the principal focus of Watkin, *Fighting at the Legal Boundaries*, *supra* note 4.

[59] *See* Common Article 3 of the Geneva Conventions, *supra* note 7).

[60] *See, e.g.*, United Nations, "Protection of Civilian Persons in Time of War," *supra* note 7, at art. 3, and United Nations, "Protocol Additional to the Geneva Conventions of 12 August 1949, and Relating to the Protection of Victims of Non-International Armed Conflicts (Protocol II)" (June 8, 1977), art. 3, neither the four Common Article 3 provisions nor the two Additional Protocols,

scope question could, to some extent, mitigate concerns over operational overbreadth by establishing the point at which LOAC-derived authorities terminate. However, because there is nothing close to a consensus on how to determine when a transnational NIAC terminates,[61] much less whether a situation can legitimately vacillate between periods of armed conflict and periods of operations falling below that threshold, it is unlikely that focusing on temporal limits will produce this outcome. More significantly, even if there was widespread consensus as to when a transnational NIAC terminates, the issue of operational overbreadth will remain significant prior to that termination point.

What Common Article 3 does suggest, however, at least when considered in the context in which it was adopted, is that the existence of a NIAC need not automatically justify dispensing with the use of law enforcement–type operational measures.[62] Instead, the entire notion of NIAC that emerged from the development of Common Article 3 is linked to the objective "exigency" necessitating deviation from the norm of an exclusive criminal response paradigm.[63] While this conclusion is not explicitly laid out in the article, the Commentary provides compelling support.[64] What can best be understood as the conflict identification portion of the Commentary focused on the conditions that justify the determination that a situation of internal instability justifies the armed conflict determination.[65] However, because this determination was presupposed to be made in the context of violence internal to the responding state, it was arguably also

developed in 1977 to update the Geneva Conventions, extended any form of legitimacy to non-state actors. International Committee of the Red Cross, *supra* note 1; *see also* Blank & Corn, *supra* note 8.

[61] Blank & Corn, *supra* note 8.

[62] *See* United Nations, the four Geneva Conventions, *supra* note 7; International Committee of the Red Cross, Commentary on the First Geneva Convention (2016), art. 3, sec. 1A(2). By including Common Article 3 in the revision of the Geneva Convention in 1949, it represented the first interjection by treaty of international humanitarian regulation into the realm of NIAC. According to the Commentary:

> This Article is common to all four of the Geneva Conventions of 1949, and is one of their most important Articles. It marks a new step forward in the unceasing development of the idea on which the Red Cross is based, and in the embodiment of that idea in the form of international obligations. It is an almost unhoped for extension of Article 2 above. Born on the battlefield, the Red Cross called into being the First Geneva Convention to protect wounded or sick military personnel. Extending its solicitude little by little to other categories of war victims, in logical application of its fundamental principle, it pointed the way, first to the revision of the original Convention, and then to the extension of legal protection in turn to prisoners of war and civilians. The same logical process could not fail to lead to the idea of applying the principle to all cases of armed conflicts, including those of an internal character.

[63] *Id.* 28–35 (expressing the explicit indication that Common Article 3 substantive protection are applicable to all non-international armed conflict.); *see also* Sivakumaran, *supra* note 1; Dinstein, *supra* note 1.

[64] Blank & Corn, *supra* note 8, at 49.

[65] Watkin, *supra* note 4, at 354.

presupposed that the state would be responding to a threat that continued to present itself on both sides of the law enforcement/armed conflict dividing line.

Indeed, the entire thrust of this portion of the Commentary was distinguishing the "normal" situation of relying on law enforcement to respond to internal instability from the point at which a situation necessitated resort to *regular* armed forces to address the threat.[66] The term "regular" was likely emphasized because it seems relatively apparent that the states that adopted Common Article 3 recognized that armed forces are often used to aid in peacetime law enforcement activities, and that this use alone was not dispositive of the nature of the situation.[67] This is reflected by the fact that the nature of the state forces is only one factor in a totality analysis proposed by the Commentary. As an indicia of armed conflict, the term "regular" (as opposed to "irregular" or "paramilitary") was likely intended to connote the use of armed forces to perform combat-type missions; missions that ipso facto reflect the existence of an armed conflict.[68] What is clear is that it is not the use of armed forces for security operations that indicate the existence of an armed conflict; it is the nature of the threat and the accordant military response that compels that conclusion.[69] Accordingly, what the Commentary sought to highlight was the distinction between situations where state armed forces were utilized to supplement law enforcement operations, as opposed to the use of these armed forces in a combat or wartime capacity.

Unfortunately, a combination of this dichotomy and the insignificance of the nature of the military missions assigned to such forces contributed to a binary understanding of legal response authority. When security forces performed internal security law enforcement–type missions, their operations were subject to the IHRL/law enforcement paradigm.[70] But once the nature of the threat necessitated a wartime or combat-type "regular armed forces" mission, the LOAC

[66] *See* International Committee of the Red Cross, *supra* note 62, at 49; *see also* United Nations, "Additional Protocol," *supra* note 60, at art. 1(2), excluding from scope of Protocol "situations of internal disturbances and tensions, such as riots, isolated and sporadic acts of violence and other acts of similar nature," since these are not considered armed conflicts.

[67] *See* Red Cross, 2016 Commentary, *supra* note 1.

[68] *Id.*

[69] *Id.*

[70] *See* Jeff A. Bovarnick et al., Law of War Workshop Handbook 25–34 (Brian J. Bill ed., 2004); *see also The Joint Service Manual of the Law of Armed Conflict* (Joint Service Publication 383, The Joint Doctrine & Concepts Centre, 2004), para. 3.1; International Committee of the Red Cross, "What Is International Humanitarian Law?," Advisory Service on International Humanitarian Law, July 2004, 1, <https://www.icrc.org/en/doc/assets/files/other/what_is_ihl.pdf. The fact sheet reflects the international or internal evolution of the triggering paradigm as follows:

> International humanitarian law distinguishes between international and non-international armed conflict. International armed conflicts are those in which at least two States are involved. They are subject to a wide range of rules, including those set out in the four Geneva Conventions and Additional Protocol I.
>
> Non-international armed conflicts are those restricted to the territory of a single State, involving either regular armed forces fighting groups of armed dissidents, or armed groups fighting each other. A more limited range of rules apply to internal armed conflicts and are

became the controlling source of response authority. What Common Article 3 did not address, however, is whether a situation of armed conflict justified complete suspension or abandonment of the law enforcement response paradigm. This could be because Common Article 3 was never conceived as a source of treaty-based *authority* for armed forces engaged in such missions. Instead, it seems clear from the text, and the Commentary, that it was exclusively humanitarian in nature, intended to impose minimum humanitarian obligations to situations of de facto armed conflict.[71] Nonetheless, these obligations were responsive to the underlying assumption that the state would be employing measures based on its determination that it was engaged in an armed conflict, which is consistent with how the understanding of NIAC evolved since 1949.[72] Today, Common Article 3, and its associated Commentary, remain a primary source of authority for assessing the existence of a NIAC—an assessment that is understood to bring into force both humanitarian obligations *and* LOAC authorities.

But how should crossing this threshold influence the assessment of where and when a LOAC authority is justifiably utilized, and where and when it should ratcheted back? In the internal or more traditional type of NIAC, it may be that the drafters of Common Article 3 assumed that states would instinctively revert to law enforcement authority when the internal threat was sufficiently disabled to allow for a restoration of government authority.[73] While armed forces would likely continue to play a security role at that point, the perception of state authority would naturally be enhanced by demonstrating a return to "normal" governing modalities. After all, the ostensible objective of state use of military force in the internal NIAC context is to restore the government's control and authority in response to an organized armed threat. Accordingly, in the traditional internal NIAC context, this interest creates an incentive for reverting to a law enforcement response framework whenever operationally feasible. This necessity-focused approach, which in this context is well aligned with state strategic interests, is arguably reflected in the history of internal armed conflicts.[74] In short, just as a threat situation may necessitate the use of military forces to perform "combat

laid down in Article 3 common to the four Geneva Conventions as well as in Additional Protocol II. *See also* Watkin, *supra* note 4, at 480.

[71] *See* ICRC Commentary, *supra* note 62, at 32, the term "armed conflict" was intended to apply to de facto hostilities no matter how brief or non-destructive they might be.

[72] Sivakumaran, *supra* note 1, at 192; Geoffrey Corn & Eric Talbot Jensen, *Transnational Armed Conflict: A "Principled" Approach to the Regulation of Counter-Terror Combat Operations*, 42 Israel L. Rev. 1 (2009). *See also* Geoffrey S. Corn, *Hamdan, Lebanon, and the Regulation of Hostilities: The Need to Recognize a Hybrid Category of Armed Conflict*, 40 Vand. J. Transnat'l L. 1 (2007); Anthony Cullen, The Concept of Non-International Armed Conflict in International Humanitarian Law 60 (2010), noting that Common Article 3 was initially interpreted as applying only to civil wars, much as is the case with Additional Protocol II currently.

[73] Sivakumaran, *supra* note 1, at 192.

[74] Watkin, *supra* note 4, at 536–50.

type" missions, when the necessity for such measures subsides, it is appropriate to implement a mission shift by those armed forces. At that point, while there may still be necessity to supplement law enforcement capabilities with military forces, the function of those forces becomes constabulary in nature to support the government objective to restore normalcy.

This does not, however, suggest that the *legal* determination that a NIAC has terminated is simple. To the contrary, while states may through policy restrictions ratchet back operational use of force authority as an internal security threat stabilizes, the nature of such threats warrants caution over that ultimate legal determination. The reality that non-state groups rarely progress or recede on a straight-line trajectory, nor do they constantly take the same form in all areas impacted by their efforts, must also factor into both the legal and operational response equation. Indeed, as Watkin explains, these threats routinely fluctuate between a character primarily amenable to law enforcement–type responses and a character that renders such measures insufficient. Furthermore, these different threat characteristics may exist at the same time in different areas of operations.

The risk that the apparent recession of a threat may be temporary, and that it may or will likely escalate, is almost certainly a disincentive for a state to make some type of formal announcement that a NIAC has terminated. The insurgent doctrine actually seeks to exploit opportunities presented by such state constraint by resurrecting more aggressive activities. This dynamic may also influence a decision by a state to impose even operational level restraints on its armed forces because of concern that doing so will undermine the credibility of asserting the existence of an ongoing NIAC. This latter impact is unfortunate, because when coupled with the perceived need to preserve strategic response flexibility, it is a recipe for operational overbreadth.

Acknowledging the credibility of an operational framework that seeks to produce a highly contextual alignment between threat driven necessity and the scope of response authority will ideally mitigate this risk by encouraging states to approach the *operational* domain of authority with much greater nuance. In short, endorsing a policy that presumes operational authority aligned with IHRL principles *within* the context of an ongoing NIAC will offset the potential authority overbreadth resulting from the uncertainty as to when a NIAC terminates. Such an approach will serve the interests of the state, especially in the internal or traditional NIAC situation, as well as contribute to the state's interest in demonstrating a return to civil normalcy.

The influences and incentives related to identifying the appropriate strategic and operational framework when responding to *transnational* non-state threats are substantially different. Like so many other complexities created by the evolution of NIAC to apply to this transnational threat context, the likelihood that a state engaged in such an armed conflict will perceive a significant benefit by demonstrating that it considers the threat to have receded to a law enforcement level is substantially diminished. Unlike the internal NIAC context, where reversion to the normalcy reflected by a law enforcement response serves important state interests, the state's strategic interest may be substantially compromised by such an approach. The following excerpt from my chapter in Jens Ohlin's book titled *Research Handbook on Remote Warfare*[75] seeks to explain this phenomenon:

> The assertion of transnational NIAC was significantly influenced by a number of factors. First among these was the assessment of the non-State threat capability and the resulting conclusion that law enforcement authority and capability was insufficient to effectively address this threat. This led to the conclusion that only an expanded invocation of the nation's military power would be effective in addressing this threat. Reliance on law enforcement authority would not allow these forces to fully leverage their combat power, power that could only be employed within an armed conflict legal framework. And, while there was tremendous uncertainty at the inception of these operations as to the true nature of the applicable legal authority, over time the proverbial legal dust settled to reveal an unavoidable conclusion: the US viewed the struggle against Al Qaeda as an armed conflict.
>
> The authority to employ lethal combat power as a measure of first resort—quite often through an armed drone—is perhaps the most significant consequence of this armed conflict determination. Drones were and are certainly not the only tool for employing such power, but they are often considered ideal, for all the reasons discussed above. The rapid evolution of lethal drone capability in many ways complemented, or perhaps responded to, the assertion of transnational NIAC. And this dual evolution has produced both an expanded scope of legal authority to attack non-State opponents and an expanded capability to do so.
>
> The international legal standards for assessing the existence of armed conflict is not generally understood as a constraint on the state's authority to engage in armed conflict, but rather as addressing the distinct question of the law applicable to such conflicts. From inception, the law of NIAC and the "test" for assessing the existence of a NIAC has had a constraining effect, if not de jure, then at least de facto. This de facto constraint flowed from the perceived second and third-order consequences of treating an internal threat to state authority as an "enemy" in an armed conflict. As noted above, states have been and remain reticent to acknowledge the existence of internal NIAC based on these concerns, which inevitably constrain the invocation of armed conflict authority to address internal threats.

75 Jens D. Ohlin, Research Handbook on Remote Warfare (2017).

> The de facto consequence of the transnational NIAC interpretation is arguably the exact opposite. Unlike an internal domestic threat, what the US response to Al Qaeda indicates is that states may often perceive a powerful political benefit from asserting a more aggressive response to transnational non-State threats. Confining responses to such threats to the more limited authority permitted outside the context of armed conflict risks a perception of national weakness. Indeed, in the realm of US political and policy discourse, even strategically and operationally motivated restrictions on armed conflict authority in the form of rules of engagement are condemned as manifestations of national weakness.
>
> Thus, when confronting an external non-State threat, the state will not perceive recognition of armed conflict as an indication of national weakness, but instead one of national strength. And because of the NIAC classification, the responding state is much less constrained by jus ad bellum considerations; the NIAC classification allows the state to disavow any intention to act aggressively against another state. Instead, by invoking "failed state" or "unable or unwilling" theories, the state using force against the transnational non-State opponent minimizes concerns related to jus ad bellum constraints.

Ultimately, unlike in the domestic context, there seems to be powerful incentives for an aggressive assertion of transnational NIAC, with few disincentives.[76]

From a tactical and operational perspective, the transnational NIAC classification opens the door to assert otherwise unavailable national military powers: the power to kill as a measure of first resort;[77] the power to detain preventively without charge or trial;[78] and the power to use extraordinary criminal tribunals to punish captives.[79] Furthermore, this characterization may facilitate a use of national military power consistent with an assessment that the non-state action qualified as an armed attack within the meaning of the *jus ad bellum*

[76] The US response to the September 11 attacks arguably illustrates this incentives equation. The attacks were met with an expansive assertion of transnational armed conflict justifying a robust military response, but the response did not include domestic security operations. Response measures in the domestic context continued to treat internal security as a law enforcement problem. For example, when the FBI discovered what was believed to be an Al Qaeda cell in Lakawana, New York, the attorney general resisted proposals by the vice president to utilize military special operations forces to attack the safe house, opting instead to use law enforcement resources. *See* Mark Mazzetti & David Johnston, *Bush Weighed Using Military in Arrests*, N.Y. TIMES, July 24, 2009, <https://www.nytimes.com/2009/07/25/us/25detain.html. A similar approach seems reflected in the French response to the 2015 Paris attacks. The French president announced a more aggressive extraterritorial use of military assets in response, while the domestic response remained constabulary in nature. *See Paris Attacks: Hollande Blames Islamic State for "Act of War,"* BBC, Nov. 14, 2015, <https://www.bbc.com/news/world-europe-34820016.

[77] Geoffrey S. Corn, Laurie R. Blank, & Chris Jenks, *Belligerent Targeting and the Invalidity to of a Least Harmful Means Rule*, 89 INT'L L. STUD. 536 (2013).

[78] Hamdi v. Rumsfeld, 542 U.S. 507 (2004).

[79] Hamdan v. Rumsfeld, 548 U.S. 557 (2006).

(although acting in self-defense is not necessarily synonymous with the existence of an armed conflict).[80] But perhaps most significant is the political incentive inherent in signaling a message of strength and resolve in response to such threats. Thus the political consequence of pushing the proverbial NIAC envelope is the inverse of those inherent in the internal NIAC context: restricting the response to cooperative international law enforcement efforts creates a perception of weakness whereas invoking "wartime" response authorities creates a perception of power.[81]

It is difficult to deny the existence of this powerful incentive to maximize the perception of effective military action, with virtually no risk that an aggressive use of military force will undermine the domestic credibility of state authority. In this sense, the considerations that arguably incentivize a state reticence to assert the existence of an internal NIAC, and once having done so seek to demonstrate restoration of normalcy through a reversion to a peacetime security posture as soon as operationally practicable, are simply inapposite to the transnational NIAC context. In fact, in that context, reversion to a pure law enforcement response framework may be perceived as politically detrimental as an indication of weakness in the face of the threat. In contrast, both asserting the existence of a NIAC *and* an aggressive invocation of LOAC authorities may be perceived as politically advantageous.

When coupled with the fact that the notion of transnational NIAC is increasingly accepted, this inverse incentive equation creates an obvious risk: that states will leverage the extraordinary authority inherent in a situation of armed conflict beyond the point where use of such authority is objectively justified. A prime example of this risk, according to numerous critics, is the US approach to its struggle with Al Qaeda. While the initial assertion of a extraterritorial or transnational NIAC was certainly controversial, the magnitude of the attack that produced that characterization seemed to temper this criticism, at least during the early stages of the US military response. Furthermore, those operations were

[80] Brian Egan, *International Law, Legal Diplomacy, and the Counter-ISIL Campaign: Some Observations*, 92 INT'L L. STUD. 235, 237–41 (2016); *see also* Ashley S. Deeks, *"Unwilling or Unable": Toward a Normative Framework of Extraterritorial Self-Defense*, 52 VA. J. INT'L L., no. 3, 483 (2012). *See also* Watkin, *supra* note 4, at 83–86, noting that conflict characterization is not the only factor, as the constraints of the *jus ad bellum* are context-dependent and lessen as the conflict expands and lengthens.

[81] It is interesting to consider whether the reticence on the part of many traditional US allies to embrace an expansive notion of transnational armed conflict indicates they consider an IHL-based response as a sign of weakness and not strength. This debate has been ongoing since the initial response to the September 11 attacks. In my view, this reticence may be motivated by many other factors, including the far more extensive role of IHRL in the policymaking equation for many of these states, and perhaps even the opportunity to benefit from a more aggressive US position without having to endorse it. For an excellent discussion on the latter influence, *see* Robert Kagan, *Power & Weakness*, HOOVER INSTITUTION POL'Y REV., June/July 2002, <https://www.hoover.org/research/power-and-weakness.

directed primarily at Al Qaeda's capabilities in Afghanistan, where members of this terrorist group functioned in a manner more aligned with an organized military threat than a dispersed criminal threat.[82] However, as months dragged into years, and years into almost two decades, criticism shifted to what was perceived as an unjustified perpetuation of what should be considered an extraordinary situation.[83] Many of these critics hoped that President Barack Obama would declare an end to the armed conflict, especially after he announced the end of active hostilities involving US forces in Afghanistan.[84] Even after no such declaration was made, any hope to end the armed conflict evaporated with the election of Donald Trump, as the forty-fifth president of the United States.

Another recent illustration of the perceived risk of overbreadth emerged from the clashes between Palestinians and Israel Defense Forces (IDF) along the security barrier between Israel and Gaza.[85] Much of the criticism directed toward Israel, as the result of the deaths and injuries resulting from military action to prevent breach of that barrier, was based on the assumption that Israel unjustifiably employed military force against civilian protesters.[86] For Israel, however, these events occurred in the context of an ongoing NIAC with Hamas, the terrorist organization in control of Gaza.[87] This armed conflict has, as Watkin points out is the norm for such conflicts, ebbed and flowed between periods of intense combat operations and much longer periods of no hostilities.[88] And the hybrid-type threat situation was also apparent, as there is substantial information that indicates Hamas belligerent operatives were using the civilian protesters as cover for their infiltration efforts.[89] Nonetheless, the vast majority of people engaged in

[82] *See* Watkin, *supra* note 4, at 46. As seen in the cases of Iraq and Afghanistan, the situation may occur where an international armed conflict transforms into a non-international one; *see also* Yoram Dinstein, *Terrorism and Afghanistan*, 85 Int'l L. Stud. 43, 51 (2008), stating that notwithstanding the perspective that the post-9/11 Afghan conflict was an inter-state war, the International Committee of the Red Cross took the view that the conflict had changed from an international armed conflict to one of non-international character.

[83] *See* Rosa E. Brooks, *War Everywhere: Rights, National Security Law, and the Law of Armed Conflict in the Age of Terror*, 153 U. Pa. L. Rev. 675–761 (2004).

[84] *See generally* Paul D. Shinkman, *Obama: "Global War on Terror" Is Over*, U.S. News, May 23, 2013, <https://www.usnews.com/news/articles/2013/05/23/obama-global-war-on-terror-is-over.

[85] Megan Specia & Rick Gladston, *What Is the Gaza Fence and Why Has It Set Off Protests Against Israel?*, N.Y. Times, May 16, 2018, <https://www.nytimes.com/2018/05/16/world/middleeast/israel-gaza-fence.html

[86] Hannes Jöbstl, *Lost Between Law Enforcement and Active Hostilities: A First Glance at the Israeli Supreme Court Judgment on the Use of Lethal Force During the Gaza Border Demonstrations*, EJIL: Talk, June 4, 2018, <https://www.ejiltalk.org/lost-between-law-enforcement-and-active-hostilities-a-first-glance-at-the-israeli-supreme-court-judgment-on-the-use-of-lethal-force-during-the-gaza-border-demonstrations/.

[87] Elena Chachko & Yuval Shany, *The Supreme Court of Israel Dismisses a Petition Against Gaza Rules of Engagement*, Lawfare, May 26, 2018, <https://www.lawfareblog.com/supreme-court-israel-dismisses-petition-against-gaza-rules-engagement.

[88] *See* Watkin, *supra* note 4, at 367–68.

[89] Geoffrey S. Corn & Peter Margulies, *Use of Force at the Gaza Border: A Hybrid Approach to Tactical Challenges*, Lawfare, June 20, 2018, <https://www.lawfareblog.com/use-force-gaza-border-hybrid-approach-tactical-challenges.

these protests were civilians. Because of the mixed nature of those involved in the breach efforts, denying that the situation fell within the broader strategic context of an ongoing NIAC would have been unrealistic, as the prior periods of relative lulls in confrontations in no way suggested Hamas had abandoned its strategic goals that include launching attacks against Israel. But it was equally clear that the IDF engaged in these operations could not justifiably operate pursuant to an exclusive LOAC use of force paradigm. Indeed, as the Israeli government explained during the litigation over the IDF procedures for authorizing use of deadly force, their operational response was quite nuanced. Contrary to widespread assumptions, their ROE were premised on a blended application of both LOAC conduct of hostilities rules and IHRL law enforcement rules.[90]

A number of pragmatic considerations almost certainly influence the positions of the United States and Israel. For instance, despite periodic lulls in violent activity, their respective armed conflicts against terrorist organizations are still ongoing. Most importantly, the ongoing nature of these respective security challenges preserves the strategic flexibility to utilize the full range of military response capabilities to disrupt or defeat "enemy" efforts when such measures are necessitated by the nature the threat. For the United States, another important consideration is preserving the legal foundation for the ongoing "belligerent" detention of captives previously designated as unprivileged belligerents.[91] With the combination of legislative restrictions on transferring these individuals to civilian custody for domestic criminal prosecution,[92] the snail-pace progress of prosecutions before the military[93] operating pursuant to the Military Commissions Act of 2006,[94] and the determination that they represented a continued threat necessitating detention, means there is no real alternative to deal with these captives. As a result, declaring an end to the armed conflict with Al Qaeda and associated forces would create a genuine dilemma, as it would nullify the principal authority for their continued detention. The ascendance of ISIS exacerbated the significance of these considerations, as it created a renewed

[90] Eliav Lieblich, *Collectivizing Threat: An Analysis of Israel's Legal Claims for Resort to Force on the Gaza Border*, JUST SECURITY, May 16, 2018, <https://www.justsecurity.org/56346/collectivizing-threat-analysis-israels-legal-claims-resort-force-gaza-border/.

[91] Boumediene v. Bush, 553 U.S. 723 (2008); Hamdi v. Rumsfeld, *supra* note 78; *see also* National Defense Authorization Act for Fiscal Year 2014, Pub. L. 113-66, 127 Stat. 672, sec. 1037; Jennifer K. Elsea & Michael J Garcia, "Wartime Detention Provisions in Recent Defense Authorization Legislation," Congressional Research Service, Mar. 14, 2016, <https://fas.org/sgp/crs/natsec/R42143.pdf.

[92] David M. Herszenhorn, *Senate Passes Military Bill that Bans Transfers of Guantanamo Detainees*, N.Y. TIMES, Nov. 10, 2015, <https://www.nytimes.com/2015/11/11/us/politics/senate-passes-military-bill-that-bars-transfers-of-guantanamo-detainees.html.

[93] Steve Vladeck, *Why Aren't the Military Commissions Working? Look No Further Than Al-Nashiri*, LAWFARE, May 21, 2018, <https://www.lawfareblog.com/why-arent-military-commissions-working-look-no-further-al-nashiri.

[94] Military Commissions Act of 2006, Pub. L. 109-366, 120 Stat. 2600.

necessity to employ force pursuant to LOAC conduct of hostilities rules,[95] and the potential need to subject a new category of captives to "law of war" detention. Furthermore, because the post–September 11, 2001, Authorization for the Use of Military Force[96] provides the *domestic* legal basis for combat operations against ISIS, the government need to avoid any indication that this authority is no longer valid seems obvious.

The credibility of these ongoing transnational NIAC assertions is certainly vulnerable to substantial criticism.[97] However, for purposes of this chapter, it is important to accept two assumptions related to this legal position: first, the United States does in fact consider itself engaged in an ongoing transnational NIAC with Al Qaeda (and associated forces);[98] second, this characterization is unlikely to change in the foreseeable future. Watkin makes a compelling case for why such an approach to dealing with a threat, like Al Qaeda, may lead to authority overbreadth in the conduct of operations under the overall armed conflict umbrella, and in turn how an inflexible default to IHL authority in situations amenable to a more restrained approach risks undermining strategic legitimacy. This is precisely why he advocates addressing many transnational security threats pursuant to the IHRL framework even in the context of an ongoing armed conflict.[99] Such an approach would certainly mitigate authority overbreadth, but, for the reasons addressed above, it seems unlikely that this proposal will gain substantial traction. Nonetheless, the concern Watkin highlights that a broad conception of ongoing transnational NIAC may result in a troubling gap between operational necessity and authority is significant.

As noted above, states, like the United States, have a powerful interest in preserving strategic flexibility that allows for periodic invocation of LOAC

[95] Mary L. Kelly, *When the U.S. Military Strikes, White House Points to a 2001 Measure*, All Things Considered, Sept. 6, 2016, <https://www.npr.org/sections/parallels/2016/09/06/492857888/when-the-u-s-military-strikes-white-house-points-to-a-2001-measure; *see also* Derek Tsang, *To Justify ISIS Airstrikes, Obama Using Legislation He Wants Repealed*, Politifact, Sept. 18, 2014, <https://www.politifact.com/punditfact/statements/2014/sep/18/julie-pace/justify-airstrikes-against-islamic-state-obama-usi/.

[96] Authorization for the Use of Military Force, Pub. L. 107-40, 115 Stat. 224.

[97] Massimo Calabresi, *Obama's Anti-ISIS War in Syria May Be Illegal*, Time, Sept. 11, 2014, <http://time.com/3328080/isis-syria-aumf-obama-law/. *See also* Marco Sassòli, "Transnational Armed Groups and International Humanitarian Law," HPCR Occasional Paper Series, Winter 2006, <https://www.uio.no/studier/emner/jus/humanrights/HUMR5503/h09/undervisningsmateriale/sassoli_transnational_armed_groups_and_ihl.pdf; Dustin A. Lewis, Gabriella Blum, & Naz K. Modirzadeh, *Section 7—International Law and the End of the United States' War on Terror*, *in* Indefinite War: Unsettled International Law on the End of Armed Conflict (Feb. 2017),< http://blogs.harvard.edu/pilac/files/2017/03/Indefinite-War-February-2017-HLS-PILAC.pdf.

[98] Brian Egan, "International Law, Legal Diplomacy, and the Counter-ISIL Campaign," Remarks, American Society of International Law, Apr. 8, 2016, <https://www.lawfareblog.com/state-department-legal-adviser-brian-egans-speech-asil.

[99] Watkin, *supra* note 4, at 365–67, noting that the intensity criterion could include an assessment of factors such as the duration, the number of deaths, injuries, damage to property, and the magnitude or scale of the violence.

authorities. These authorities enable the United States to attack, capture, and punish groups of operatives that pose a security threat in a manner that would be difficult to justify, if not outright impermissible, outside the context of an armed conflict. This interest is, of course, not inconsistent with Watkin's IHRL primacy approach. Importantly, nor is what is likely perceived by states like the United States as a significant strategic imperative: facilitating a pragmatic and flexible scope of response measures to address these threats. The ease of tailoring operational authority to threat imperatives might be undermined by a state acknowledgment that an armed conflict is not ongoing but instead an isolated and short-term situation, arising periodically for very limited periods of time. In other words, the notion that a struggle against a transnational security threat may vacillate between periods of peacetime legal authorities and situations of armed conflict seems incompatible with the interest in retaining strategic flexibility.

These *strategic* concerns do not, however, necessitate a binary approach to *operational* authority. It is at this intersection where a more carefully tailored approach to operational authority aligns with Watkin's view that states must preserve operational flexibility to respond to the evolving and devolving nature of contemporary security threats. As Watkin notes, the multifaceted nature of these threats necessitates a recognition that the legal response framework cannot be compartmentalized. Instead, different legal frameworks, most notably the LOAC and IHRL, will often overlap—applying in different places and times to operations against the same opponent.[100] More specifically:

> The result may be that in order to effectively regulate what are proving to be novel and dangerous security threats, extraordinary efforts and new approaches will be needed to address the concerns of both camps [international law traditionalists and operational pragmatists]. This assessment of the unfolding legal struggle suggests the real challenge for the broader international community will not be in considering whether the integration of legal regimes is necessary. Rather it will be to consider what policy choices need to be made in the privileging of one regime over another at the overlap between the various bodies of law is acknowledged and dealt with. Suggesting by rote that one body of law (i.e., international humanitarian law) is special and therefore displaces the other (i.e., human rights law) will not provide the answer.[101]

Watkin then asserts that it is IHRL and not the LOAC (IHL) that must earn this "privileged" position.[102]

[100] *Id.* 330.
[101] *Id.* 23.
[102] *Id.* 30.

Watkin uses the phrase "privileged" to suggest a rule of presumption: when engaged with hybrid non-state threats whose activities straddle the line between crime and armed conflict, military forces tasked with disabling or disrupting these threats should view IHRL as the presumptively applicable operational legal framework. Like most presumptions, however, this presumption must be understood as rebuttable, and when and where rebutted, the broader authority derived from the LOAC comes into force. Consistent with Watkin's thesis, a threat situation that exceeds the response capabilities inherent in a law enforcement/constabulary authority should be understood as the necessity-based justification for the use of such expanded authority.

This latter aspect of a presumptive IHRL equation is obviously complex. Perhaps more importantly, its efficacy will inevitably depend on the good faith commitment of states to prevent the LOAC exception from swallowing the IHRL rule. And this is certainly not a given: states engaged in what they characterize as transnational NIACs are routinely criticized for measures their critics assert reflect overzealous assertions of LOAC authority.[103] Accordingly, it is essential that any such presumptive threat response framework be linked to strategic and operational benefit. Watkin understands this, and notes that if states implement this privileged or presumptive IHRL primacy, it will contribute to both operational and strategic success. This argument is most compelling at the point where military forces operationally implement security strategy. At that level, relying on a presumptive IHRL response framework will contribute to a more effective alignment of military power with operational necessity, and in so doing mitigate the risk of alienating the civilian population. This more restrained military response to hybrid non-state security threats will ideally enhance the legitimacy of the counterinsurgency or counterterrorism efforts.[104]

Interestingly, the operational response framework to address this type of security threats may actually be evolving in just such a direction, not as the result of top-down directives but as military doctrine has evolved for centuries: from the ground up. As Watkin notes, while major state players in the counterinsurgency/counterterrorism game may not have formally embraced his IHRL primacy proposal, the practices of their armed forces seem to increasingly indicate that this is exactly how military operations are framed.

Perhaps instead of thinking in terms of "springing" armed conflicts, a more effective approach to bridge the delta between strategic and operational interests

[103] Charlie Savage, *U.N. Report Highly Critical of U.S. Drone Attacks*, N.Y. Times, June 2, 2010, https://www.nytimes.com/2010/06/03/world/03drones.html;; *see also* Mary E. O'Connell, *Drones Are Illegal Beyond the Battlefield*, N.Y. Times, Apr. 24, 2015, https://www.nytimes.com/roomfordebate/2015/04/24/should-a-court-approve-all-drone-strikes/drones-are-illegal-beyond-the-battlefield; *see also* Mary E. O'Connell, *Game of Drones*, 109 Am. J. Int'l L. 889 (2015).

[104] Watkin, *supra* note 4, at 163.

would be to focus on "springing" operational authority. At the operational level, this springing authority will arise in situations that indicate operational necessity to utilize more permissive LOAC-derived measures in order to respond to situations where a law enforcement–type response is simply too restrained to effectively deal with a threat. While this might seem somewhat simple conceptually, there are three main challenges that would have to be addressed for this to become a viable approach for addressing the concerns central to Watkin's IHRL primacy proposal.

First, states must be willing to reconsider the formalistic approach to assessing the existence of a NIAC. This view is generally understood as necessitating hostilities of significant *duration* involving a non-state party with military-type *organization*. However, as Watkin goes to great lengths to explain, the very nature of unconventional insurgency-type threats is that they defy traditional conceptions of military organization.[105] More importantly, the duration of hostilities associated with such threats routinely spikes in an opportunistic manner, defying a formalistic notion of hostilities of substantial duration. This, as Watkin notes, is the very essence of Maoist insurgent strategy.[106] This necessitates a more flexible approach to operational authority that is responsive to the true nature of an ongoing armed conflict. Ultimately, it should be the periodic intensity of the threat, and not necessarily military organization or duration of hostilities, that dictates operational authority.

The second challenge is that states will need to acknowledge that this periodic ramping-up of operational authority must be narrowly tailored to the generating necessity. States will need to develop a methodology that limits the invocation of LOAC authority to the challenge that necessitates the invocation. In most situations, this means the armed conflict authority will be primarily focused on uses of force, and therefore should recede when the necessity for more aggressive use of force ROE dissipates. Other issues, such as detention and criminal sanction, could still fall within the scope of the presumptive IHRL framework, although there may be situations where necessity dictates reliance on LOAC-based authorities. Ideally, this type of more nuanced and integrated application of various legal response mechanisms—what Watkin calls a "hybrid" legal response—will become increasingly natural for armed forces.

The third issue that favors an operational, as opposed to legal primacy approach, is belligerent detention. Certainly for the United States (and perhaps also for Israel), the NIAC characterization for its operations against transnational terrorist groups is the foundation for the authority to indefinitely detain captives it

[105] Watkin, *supra* note 4, at 160.
[106] *Id.* 164.

determines are members of Al Qaida, the Taliban, or associated forces.[107] Other states have approached this problem differently, relying on criminal process as the authority for such detentions.[108] But even for the majority of states that approach such detention through the IHRL lens, there may be situations where the IHL belligerent detention approach could be perceived as necessary. In US practice, because the United States considers the situation with Al Qaeda an ongoing armed conflict, the question of detention authority (as opposed to process) is relatively settled. The armed conflict characterization enabled the use of LOAC-based belligerent detention,[109] which is functionally indefinite, based on the assertion that hostilities with these groups are themselves indefinite.[110] While the government has been compelled to respond to judicial challenges to this detention system, in truth they have amounted primarily to a nuisance.[111] Since 2004, when the US Supreme Court upheld this detention program in *Hamdi v. Rumsfeld*,[112] the basic legal premise for belligerent detention has never been seriously questioned.

Nonetheless, the continued detention of a small number of individuals captured and designated as unprivileged belligerents is prime evidence for many critics who believe the continuing armed conflict theory is legally and functionally overbroad.[113] Obviously, treating IHRL as the exclusive source of *legal* authority to respond to these threats, while recognizing periodic "pop up" armed conflicts, would seriously undermine the legal foundation for this type of ongoing detention regime. In this regard, it is important to note that Watkin does not advocate such an approach, and instead asserts operations against Al Qaeda and ISIS qualify as ongoing armed conflicts. His primary emphasis is on the scope of use of force authority, which he asserts should be more carefully aligned with highly contextual threat realities *within* these ongoing armed conflicts. But

[107] Hamdi v. Rumsfeld, *supra* note 78; United States Department of Defense, "Military Commission Order No. 1" (U05204-02, Mar. 21, 2002), < https://biotech.law.lsu.edu/blaw/dodd/corres/mco/mco1.pdf. *See also* Dvir Saar & Ben Wahlhaus, *Preventive Detention for National Security Purposes in Israel*, 9 J. Nat'l Sec. L. & Pol'y 413 (2018), discussing "Israel's three different frameworks of preventive detention, each individually designed so as to contend with the specific challenges stemming from the different contexts in which such a measure may be required, and each of which corresponds with a different legal regime under international law."

[108] *See* Watkin, *supra* note 4, at 97–99, discussing impact of the proper authority principle and noting that war crimes are generally addressed through penal sanctions under domestic criminal law.

[109] Hamdi v. Rumsfeld, *supra* note 78, at 548–49; *see also* Jennifer K. Elsea, "Detention of U.S. Person as Enemy Belligerents," Congressional Research Service, Jan. 23, 2014, <https://fas.org/sgp/crs/natsec/R42337.pdf.

[110] *See* Boumediene v. Bush, *supra* note 91, at 785, identifying the risk that "detention . . . may last a generation or more."

[111] *See generally* Lakhdar Boumediene, *My Guantanamo Nightmare*, N.Y. Times, Jan. 7, 2012, <https://www.nytimes.com/2012/01/08/opinion/sunday/my-guantanamo-nightmare.html.

[112] Hamdi v. Rumsfeld, *supra* note 78.

[113] *UN Body Terms Pakistani's Detention at Gitmo Illegal*, Dawn, Mar. 1, 2018, <https://www.dawn.com/news/1392455; *see also Guantanamo Bay: 14 Years of Injustice*, Amnesty International UK, Jan. 12, 2018, <https://www.amnesty.org.uk/guantanamo-bay-human-rights.

this also warrants caution against confusing what is essentially a policy-based constraint on IHL authority with a legally mandated constraint suggesting a very limited temporal scope of these armed conflicts. How long could an individual captured during a period of armed conflict that recedes to IHRL primacy be detained? Would prosecution or release be mandated by such recession? Would trial by military tribunal for alleged war crimes occurring in the context of the "springing" armed conflict be permissible? These challenges all reflect an almost unavoidable reality: there is no neat alignment between strategic and operational interests related to an ongoing armed conflict legal characterization for threats that vacillate between periods of armed conflict "type" hostilities and more traditional law enforcement threats. This divergence of interests does not, however, invalidate the Watkin IHRL primacy theory. Instead, by adopting a more nuanced approach to the *operational* authority used to deal with transnational non-state threats, the United States might contribute to a positive evolution toward the type of approach Watkin advocates. Interestingly, the foundational US doctrine for use of force authorizations, the Chairman of the Joint Chiefs of Staff Instructions on Rules of Engagement,[114] suggests that this "presumptive IHRL/springing LOAC" authority approach may already be central to US military operations.[115]

II. Human Rights Primacy, Use of Force, and the Standing Rules of Engagement

Watkin provides several examples of US counterinsurgency operations to support his thesis is that an IHRL primacy approach is already evolving from the ground up.[116] These examples reflect the use of policy-based constraints and limitations on the otherwise broad scope of LOAC. This process of tailoring actual operational authority with mission requirements is central to the process whereby US forces are granted use of force authority on a mission-by-mission basis through the Standing Rules of Engagement (SROE), the most important source of operational authority in US practice. Indeed, among operational forces, the term "ROE" is almost always used as a synonym for the LOAC authority. While this is legally imprecise,[117] it reflects the centrality of ROE to mission

[114] Chairman of the Joint Chiefs of Staff, "Standing Rules of Engagement/Standing Rules for the Use of Force for US Forces" (Instrument 3121.01B, June 13, 2005), encl. A, paras. 1–4.

[115] International and Operational Law Department, *supra* note 15.

[116] *See* Watkin, *supra* note 4, at 478, noting the jihadist insurgents in Fallujah as an example.

[117] *See* Corn, *supra* note 29, at 354. While ROE often incorporates LOAC obligations and authorities, it should be noted that each are independent and distinct sources of operational regulation.

accomplishment authority, which for the average operational commander or staff officer *is* the LOAC, whether expansive or restrictive.[118]

Much of the SROE is classified, but the unclassified portion provides enough information to glean why, in practice, use of force authority will frequently reflect a springing LOAC authority methodology. First, the standing use of force authority—which is really the presumptive primary authority—tracks an IHRL default concept: force is authorized only in situations of actual or imminent threat implicating individual or collective unit self-defense.[119] And, pursuant to this default rule, forces invoking this authority are obligated to employ a gradual escalation of force, resorting to deadly force only as a measure of last resort. Thus, the SROE default is aligned with IHRL/law enforcement authority.

Of course, there will be situations requiring more expansive use of force authority. The SROE relies on supplemental measures to address these requirements. However, what is important for purposes of this chapter is that these measures are designed to be mission-specific, driven by the mission and threat situation. Procedurally, subordinate commanders are expected to carefully assess the mission accomplishment requirements, and then request such measures to tailor the scope of use of force authority to anticipated operational demands.[120] And, if the mission evolves in ways that necessitate different authorities, they will submit supplemental requests accordingly. In other words, the process for requesting and granting supplemental measures reflects a necessity-based exception to the standing presumption of IHRL-type use of force authority, even in the context of an ongoing NIAC. Furthermore, even when a SROE supplemental measure authorizes all measures consistent with the LOAC, subordinate commanders routinely impose their own command directed limitations on that broad authority tailored to the unique aspects of the mission at their level of operations.[121] This process of tailoring a mission-specific use of force reinforces the notion that, even in the context of an ongoing armed conflict, there is always a risk of use of force overbreadth inherent in a binary legal authority framework.

Even when issuing more narrowly tailored mission-specific ROE, the existence of an armed conflict is an essential legal predicate for authorizing any use of force measures that would be incompatible with determination that the operations did not qualify as armed conflicts. Thus, a situation of ongoing armed

[118] Geoffrey S. Corn & Eric Talbot Jensen, *Untying the Gordian Knot: A Proposal for Determining Applicability of the Laws of War to the War on Terror*, 81 Temple L. Rev. 787, 809 (2008).

[119] Watkin, *supra* note 4, at 605. An operational law process establishes key decision points, with a particular emphasis being placed on defaulting on the application of human rights–based law enforcement when it provides an effective means of dealing with the threat.

[120] *See generally* Geoffrey S. Corn et al., The Law of Military Operations (2015), ch. 7. *See also* International and Operational Law Department, *supra* note 15, at para. A-3.

[121] *See* Watkin, *supra* note 4, at 595, stating for "example, under the ROE doctrine, commanders may have a discretionary authority to further restrict the authority to use force that they are provided."

conflict provides maximum operational flexibility to rapidly implement tailored mission-specific measures derived from the LOAC when necessary. Treating IHRL primacy as a legal construct would complicate this tailoring process, as each decision to ramp up authority would necessitate a strategic determination that an armed conflict has emerged. Nonetheless, practice suggests that developing mission-specific ROE based on a foundation derived from IHRL principles may provide significant operational advantages while avoiding the constraining effect of defaulting to an IHRL framework as a matter of law.[122]

Adopting, as Watkin suggests, an IHRL primacy approach to use of force authority during NIAC will align strategic and operational interests when dealing with hybrid threats. This alignment, and the flexibility to tailor authority to threat necessity, is also why I believe this approach is more viable than the alternative suggestion of expanded use of force framework within a pure IHRL framework. As Watkin notes, some contemporary human rights jurisprudence may be contributing to an expansive interpretation of use of force authority within a pure IHRL legal framework, allowing what is in essence IHL conduct of hostilities rules to be utilized to address significant security threats.[123] Watkin cites the Russian theater as an example of how this trend creates a risk of corrupting the logic of IHRL.[124] But this conception of an IHRL-based use of force expansion is nascent at best, and seems difficult to reconcile with the fundamental IHRL principle that use of force should always be treated as an extraordinary measure justified only by actual cause and necessity.[125] This puts states in a dilemma: Should they press the bounds of IHRL authority to avoid characterizing a hybrid security threat as an armed conflict and avoid the perception and reality of authority overbreadth? Or should they make more aggressive assertions that the responses to such threats qualify as armed conflicts, and then use ROE and other policy-based control measures to "ratchet down" the expanded authority triggered by such legal characterizations?[126]

The ROE methodology utilized by the United States seems to point to support for the latter approach. As noted above, any "mission accomplishment" SROE supplemental measure must be based on the underlying determination that the

[122] Interestingly, there is also an inverse correlation between ROE supplemental measures and assessing the existence of an armed conflict. As proposed in an article, co-authored with my colleague Eric Jensen, the issuance of mission specific ROE that reflects LOAC-based use of force authorities provides one of the most important indicia that the United States (or any other state) considers a situation to qualify as an armed conflict. *See* Corn & Jensen, *supra* note 10, at 78.

[123] Watkin, *supra* note 4, at 552–59.

[124] *Id.* 452–54, 498–99.

[125] Geoffrey S. Corn & Tanweer Kaleemullah, *The Military Response to Criminal Violent Extremist Groups: Aligning Use of Force Presumptions with Threat Reality*, 47 Israel L. Rev. 253 (2013); *see also* Carina Bergal, *The Mexican Drug War: The Case for a Non-International Armed Conflict Classification*, 34 Fordham Int'l L.J. 1042 (2001).

[126] Corn & Kaleemullah, *supra* note 39, at 123.

mission will be conducted in the context of an armed conflict. However, the tailoring of ROE authority to align with the operational mission reflects the type of IHRL primacy methodology Watkin advocates.[127] More importantly, this reflects an important strategic/operational distinction in relation to the assertion of armed conflict with transnational non-state threats: an expansive strategic level assertion to preserve national response flexibility, coupled with a more narrowly tailored operational implementation ostensibly intended to offset the tendency toward operational overbreadth. Thus, at the operational level, the essential *authority* derived from a situation of armed conflict is rarely treated as a constant but will instead spring periodically in response to operational and tactical necessity.

Of course, this approach is not characterized as a springing armed conflict, and indeed such a characterization finds no real authority in *lex lata*. But perhaps, as Watkin notes, this methodology could provide a credible approach to balancing state interests and humanitarian considerations in the context of military operations against the type of hybrid non-state threats that defy simple classification. By preserving the strategic flexibility to ratchet up response authority when operationally necessary, this approach advances operational *and* strategic imperatives of tailoring use of force authority to the threat situation, and in so doing advances the benefits of the Watkin IHRL primacy during security operations along "legal boundaries." Only when a threat situation exceeds the capability of the type of restrictive self-defense ROE would operational forces be armed with more permissive mission accomplishment supplement authority, with that authority reverting back to the IHRL framework when that necessity dissipates.

Interestingly, other scholars seem to be exploring paths to an analogous outcome. As already noted, Watkin suggests that evolving IHRL interpretations may be creating an expectation, albeit problematic, that security forces may ratchet up threat response authority beyond what is normally tolerated within the IHRL law enforcement framework.[128] In the *Isayeva* case, the court chose not to condemn a use of tactical measures that could hardly be reconciled with normal self-defense-type law enforcement rules. Monika Hakimi has also proposed a more pragmatic approach to the challenge of dealing with unconventional security threats, arguing that the legal formalism exemplified by the IHRL/IHL applicability debate has undermined the search for rational and pragmatic solutions to this challenge.[129] Her alternative proposal actually seems somewhat aligned with

[127] Watkin, *supra* note 4, at 569.

[128] *See* Isayeva v. Russia I, App. Nos. 57947/00, 57948/00, 57949/00 (ECtHR, 2005), para. 29, <http://hudoc.echr.coe.int/sites/eng/pages/search.aspx?i=001-68381; Isayeva v. Russian II, App. No. 57950/00 (ECtHR, 2005), para. 176, <http://www.refworld.org/cases,ECHR,4223422f6.html.

[129] Monica Hakimi, *The Theory and Practice at the Intersection Between Human Rights and Humanitarian Law*, 4 Am. J. Int'l L. 1011, 1063–74 (2018).

an "SROE principles" approach, as she suggests that the nature of the threat and the necessary response should define the response authority, which will often reflect a blending of IHRL and IHL principles. For Hakimi, the angst over which of these legal frameworks must apply to every situation contributes little to the application of carefully regulated state power in response to security threats.

These approaches all share a common thread: it is the nature of the threat, and not a formalistic interpretation of IHL or IHRL, that must dictate the scope of state military response authority.[130] They also all implicitly acknowledge the inherent risk of authority overbreadth that can result from a generalized application of LOAC to a threat situation more aligned with organized criminal activity. For Watkin, one solution to this overbreadth risk is to press the limits of IHRL security response authority;[131] for Hakimi, it is to discard what are increasingly exposed as arbitrary distinctions between the two branches of international law. Both these approaches have merit. But if the "ground up" approach to addressing such threats is probative of how strategic and operational considerations are actually being reconciled, it suggests there is merit in the SROE methodology so routinely relied upon by US commanders. And, the central premise of this methodology aligns with the approach proposed by both Watkin and Hakimi: that even in the context of an ongoing armed conflict, the scope of use of force authority should be understood as presumptively restrictive, springing beyond that presumption only when necessitated by the threat.

III. IHRL Primacy and Additional Impacts

One consideration that must be contemplated in relation to this IHRL primacy theory is how it might contribute to an unrealistically broad conception of self-defense authority: relying on self-defense as a fig leaf for what is in fact conduct of hostilities-type use of force rules.[132] Some recent operations suggest US forces invoke self-defense ROE authority to utilize measures that are in effect mission accomplishment in nature, such as pre-attack strikes, indirect fire preparation of objectives, and a generalized definition of enemy threat that allows for what is in essence status-based targeting.

Examples of this trend to stretch SROE self-defense authority into the realm of mission accomplishment ROE can be found in the unclassified US Central Command investigation into the US attack on the Kunduz Treatment Facility

[130] Watkin, *supra* note 4, at 616, stating that, given the nature of the threat, the ultimate goal should be to reduce the challenges to state authority to a level where they can be dealt with accordingly.
[131] *Id.* 552–59.
[132] *Id.* 388, citing to Dinstein, *supra* note 1, at 256; *see, e.g.*, CENTCOM Kunduz Investigation (illustrating that forces were compelled to engage in hostilities under self-defense ROE).

(KTF) run by Doctors without Borders.[133] The Report of Investigation (ROI) indicates that US forces were operating pursuant to self-defense ROE throughout that mission (authority to use force in self-defense or in defense of Afghan partner forces). In one statement, a member of a US special operations team explains how an AC-130 aerial gunship (the same platform used to attack the KTF) was used to conduct fires against "suspected" enemy ambush sites along the route that was used to move into Kunduz. How such strikes were justified as actions in self-defense is difficult to understand, even under the traditionally broad notion of imminence utilized by US forces.[134] A "suspected" ambush site does not even indicate a determination of the presence of enemy personnel. Instead, the statement suggests something much more akin to "templated" fires—the use of fires to attack anticipated enemy locations based on analysis of the terrain and enemy doctrine. Such fires are doctrinally integrated into combat operations against a declared hostile enemy force, normally in the context of an international armed conflict. But in that context, the declaration of a hostile force indicates an authorization to use all force permitted by the LOAC, which is a far cry from self-defense ROE.

Even the unclassified information in the ROI related to the actual attack on the KTF reflects what appears to be an expansive notion of self-defense as a substitute for mission accomplishment ROE—a notion even broader than that found in the SROE.[135] When the Joint Terminal Air Controller (JTAC) located with the US force commander on the ground called for fire against the KTF, the sensor operators on the AC-130 raised concerns with the aircraft commander because when they scanned the target they were unable to identify any muzzle flashes indicating that Afghan partner forces were under attack from *that* facility. At that point, the aircraft commander asked the JTAC to clarify the ROE authority he was relying on. The response was "self-defense." Unfortunately, the dialogue never progressed to an exchange on what the JTAC or his commander, *were at that moment observing*, that triggered this self-defense authority (which would have almost certainly have exposed the conflict between the ground and

[133] United States Central Command, "Investigation Report of the Airstrike on the Medecins Sans Frontieres/Doctors without Borders Trauma Center in Kunduz, Afghanistan on 3 October 2015" (2015), <https://info.publicintelligence.net/CENTCOM-KunduzHospitalAttack.pdf.

[134] *See generally* Gary P. Corn, *Should the Best Offense Ever Be a Good Defense? The Public Authority to Use Force in Military Operations: Recalibrating the Use of Force Rules in the Standing Rules of Engagement*, 49 Vand. J. Transnat'l L. 1 (2016).

[135] *See* Chairman of the Joint Chiefs of Staff, *supra* note 114, defining "Self-Defense" as "all appropriate action in self-defense of the unit, including other U.S. forces in the vicinity," and subdividing the definition into "Inherent Right of Self-Defense," defined as "individual self-defense in response to a hostile act or demonstrated hostile intent," "National Self-Defense," defined as "[t]he act of defending the United States, U.S. forces, and in certain circumstances, U.S. citizens and their property and/or U.S. commercial assets, from a hostile act, demonstrated hostile intent, or declared hostile force," and "Collective Self-Defense," defined as "[t]he act of defending designated non-U.S. citizens, forces, property, and interests from a hostile act or demonstrated hostile intent.").

air perceptions of the threat). Unfortunately, it was erroneously assumed that the KTF was the location of that engagement. While the ROE authorized the use of AC-130 fires to defend these partner forces, the attack decision was ultimately based on this flawed assumption. What is so revealing about this incident is the talismanic function of the phrase "self-defense." Once this phrase was relayed back to the aircraft commander, the assumption was that the attack was justified, despite the conflicting sensor indications.

This is, of course, only one episode in almost two decades of an ongoing NIAC. But this concern—that the notion of self-defense is being stretched beyond rational limits to provide a pretext for measures that are not authorized by mission accomplishment supplemental measures—has been raised by other experts.[136] And, ironically, this trend may be the result of what could be called strategic schizophrenia—a strategic assertion of the existence of an ongoing NIAC coupled with ROE that simply do not allow for the use of force authority necessary for operational mission accomplishment. This certainly seems to have been a major influence in the KTF debacle, where US forces were tasked with the mission of ensuring Kunduz did not fall under Taliban control by using the force needed to support Afghan partner forces, but were expected to do so within the framework of self-defense ROE.[137]

How did US forces find themselves in this predicament, where the nature of their operational and tactical mission was fundamentally inconsistent with their authorized use of force? The answer most likely derives from the *strategic*-level interest in signaling an end of active combat in Afghanistan.[138] That strategic policy interest led to inversed authority schizophrenia: an ongoing NIAC could not be disavowed because of the need to preserve strategic response flexibility against Al Qaeda and associated forces. However, the mission transition in Afghanistan led to a predominately self-defense ROE paradigm for US forces in that theater of operations. All of this would be consistent with the Watkin IHRL presumption, but for the fact that there seemed to be little tolerance for those forces to periodically invoke LOAC-type conduct of hostilities/mission accomplishment authority, a consequence of a presumed IHRL approach that Watkin clearly rejects. Indeed, his discussion of *operational* choices emphasizes why it is so important to retain the flexibility to utilize IHL conduct of hostilities rules when doing so is dictated by the nature of the threat.[139]

[136] Randall Bagwell & Molly Kovite, *It is Not Self-Defense: Direct Participation in Hostilities Authority at the Tactical Level*, 224 MILITARY L. REV. 1 (2015); *see also* Gary P. Corn, *Authority to Use Force in Military Operations: Recalibrating the Use of Force Rules in Standing Rules of Engagement*, 49 VAND. J. TRANSNAT'L L. 1 (2016).

[137] United States Central Command, *supra* note 133.

[138] *See* Kevin Liptak, *Obama Marks End of Combat in Afghanistan*, CNN, Dec. 28, 2014, <https://www.cnn.com/2014/12/28/politics/obama-afghanistan-end-of-combat/.

[139] Watkin, *supra* note 4, at 228–37.

It is probably impossible to identify a completely accurate explanation for this reticence to allow commanders to empower their forces with the authority dictated by the nature of the mission, but the most likely answer is that there was a strategic-level assumption that permitting such authority would be incompatible with the message the United States sought to signal: that US forces were no longer engaged in active combat in Afghanistan.

All of this points to a problematic consequence of viewing operational mission authority through the binary legal methodology that Watkin and Hakimi condemn. The application of a law enforcement framework within the broader context of armed conflict, especially NIACs, is not itself problematic, a point that is central to Watkin's thesis. What is problematic, however, is the difficulty in facilitating the movement between these two frameworks at the operational level. Unless use of force authority decisions are based on the pragmatic, mission-driven considerations related to security operations against hybrid threats, operational forces may find themselves in a "mission-to-authority mismatch." And importantly, that mismatch can operate in both directions. Watkin's main concern is authority overbreadth, where military forces operate pursuant to conduct of hostilities rules in situations that do not justify such robust use of force authority, with the accordant risks to human rights and compromising the essential objective of enhancing legitimacy and avoiding alienation of a local population. But the KTF incident also reveals that the mismatch can work in the opposite direction, when military forces are tasked with missions that pragmatically necessitate conduct of hostilities rules but struggle to conduct those operations within a self-defense authority framework due to the strategic aversion to acknowledging the true nature of the threat situation.

In my view, embracing the type of rebuttable IHRL presumption will go a long way to averting this type of mission/authority schizophrenia. Such an approach enables states, like the United States, to assert that the overall nature of a hybrid threat justifies a LOAC-based military response. However, it will also compel them to recognize that many aspects of that threat will fall on the law enforcement side of the response spectrum. In those situations, the military response can be executed pursuant to standing ROE reflecting self-defense and defense of other authority. In this regard, it is especially important to recognize that this authority may be extended to partner forces, enabling the use of military forces to provide essential support to their law enforcement–based security operations. This support, as Watkin notes, may at times involve levels of combat power not normally associated with law enforcement activities due to the nature of the hybrid threat.

This of course is no panacea, and complicated questions will arise even when applying this methodology. The first, and most obvious, is what justifies rebutting the presumptive IHRL/law enforcement framework? To say that only pragmatic considerations of operational necessity will suffice leaves as potentially broad a margin of appreciation as is central to the circular debates over what justifies classifying a strategic response to a hybrid threat as an armed conflict. But if nothing else, the notion of a presumptive response authority ought to at least produce a practical reticence toward overzealous assertions of expanded LOAC authority. Of equal importance, it will contribute to the development of a methodology within the military culture and an accordant instinct reflecting the inherent limits of authority in most operations against hybrid threats. This will in turn impose a burden on commanders to demand operationally logical justifications for expanding authority beyond the IHRL norm.[140] Watkin makes much of this burden, arguing that states should be forthcoming in providing the justification for moving from the IHRL framework to the armed conflict framework. I am less optimistic that such a trend will evolve. It is also debatable whether the transparency Watkin advocates would be reasonably expected at the operational level, when a command decided it was necessary to authorize mission accomplishment ROE. However, Watkin's other point should be more persuasive in compelling commanders to give genuine meaning to the presumption: the risk of undermining the mission by allowing for overzealous operational measures.

Another question that this presumptively restrained approach raises is whether it will cede a windfall to the hybrid enemy. Armed conflict between organized belligerent groups, or parties to the conflict, involve fundamentally different use of force equations than law enforcement–type security operations. The ultimate objective in armed conflict is not to reduce threats on an individualized basis but to bring the "enemy," in the collective sense, into submission.[141] Individual members of organized armed groups are not autonomous actors; instead they are agents of the enemy group. Watkin makes a compelling point that in many situations, the threat posed by these agents will straddle the line between a law enforcement–type threat and the threat traditionally associated with conventional armed forces.[142] Indeed, this is the central characteristic of the hybrid nature of such threats. However, as Watkin also notes, the nature of these hybrid threats will vacillate between these two sides of the threat divide, thereby periodically justifying conduct of hostilities use of force authority drawn from the LOAC.

[140] *See, e.g.*, DICK CAMP, OPERATION PHANTOM FURY: THE ASSAULT AND CAPTURE OF FALLUJAH, IRAQ 150–51 (2009). In the November 2004 Fallujah battle, the exercise of discretion regarding what legal principles will be applied to control force was often made at higher levels of military command.

[141] Geoffrey S. Corn et al., *Belligerent Targeting and the Invalidity of a Least Harmful Means Rule*, 89 INT'L L. STUD. 536 (2013).

[142] Watkin, *supra* note 4, at 54, arguing that the dividing line between the two frameworks can be seen in Article I(2) of Additional Protocol II, which does not apply "to situations of internal disturbances and tensions, such as riots, isolated and sporadic acts of violence and other acts of similar nature, as not being armed conflicts."

As I have argued in several previous articles,[143] one of the most important justifications for the LOAC's expanded use of force authority is that, unlike a law enforcement operation, force is not employed to address individualized threats. Instead, in the context of armed conflict, force is employed to bring the "enemy," in the collective sense, into submission.[144] Limiting military response to presumptive law enforcement authority seems inconsistent with this objective because the essence of law enforcement use of force authority is that it is responsive to individual and actual threats: only when the individual manifests an actual or imminent threat to a protected person is the use of force justified.[145] Furthermore, because the exclusive objective of using force in this context is to reduce the threat, the object of state violence is protected by a proportionality limitation: only the force necessary to reduce the threat may be employed. By contrast, use of force against an individual reasonably assessed as falling into the category of enemy belligerent does not require an analogous cause-based individualized threat assessment. Instead, the fact that the individual is an agent of the enemy leadership triggers a threat presumption, which provides the basis for status-based targeting. Unless and until the enemy belligerent is rendered *hors de combat*, that status alone justifies use of force.[146] And, unlike use of force pursuant to law enforcement authority to reduce an individual threat, the enemy belligerent is not protected by a proportionality limitation: use of deadly force as a measure of first resort is permissible.

Calibrating use of force authority to the nature of the threat is logical, but the devil is in the details. An overemphasis on an IHRL presumption will dilute authority state forces may utilize to disrupt or disable the enemy. This risk does not necessarily invalidate the logic of the restrictive force presumption, but it does indicate that the criteria for deviating from this presumption must turn on more than simply the combat capability of a given threat. Instead, it is the combination of threat capability, the intended *effects* on the hybrid enemy organization, and the anticipated efficacy of restrictive measures to achieve those effects that should provide the pillars to a totality assessment of when expanded use of force

[143] Geoffrey S. Corn, *Mixing Apples and Hand Grenades: The Logical Limit of Applying Human Rights Norms to Armed Conflict*, 1 J. INT'L HUMANITARIAN LEGAL STUD. 52 (2010); Geoffrey S. Corn et al., *Belligerent Targeting and the Invalidity of the Least Harmful Means Rule*, 89 INT'L L. STUD. 536 (2013).

[144] *Id.*

[145] For a discussion regarding the controversy over use of force authority associated with security options in Northern Ireland, *see* Watkin, *supra* note 4, at 536–52.

[146] *See* Corn, *supra* note 2, at 346, "the employment of combat forces by the state in response to a threat and the authorization for these forces to engage an enemy not exclusively in response to hostile act or intent, but based on status identification—provides an effective means of determining the existence of any armed conflict." *See also id.* at 314 (Common Article 3's substantive mandate is focused only on the treatment of persons placed *hors de combat* and not on the regulation of combat operations producing such a consequence).

should be authorized. Ultimately, the scope of authority for the conduct of operations in the context of an ongoing NIAC must account for the legitimate collective nature of the enemy and allow for use of force that strikes at the enemy's center of gravity.[147] While in some cases law enforcement–type authority may contribute to this objective, an overly restrictive approach to operational authority risks ceding initiative to the enemy and disabling the effectiveness of friendly operations.

IV. The Broader Impact of an "IHRL Policy Presumption"

At the operational level of command, use of force authority is probably the most acute issue impacted by the presumptive application of IHRL-derived law enforcement-based policies within the broader context of an armed conflict. However, it is also worth considering how such an approach might impact other measures used to incapacitate these enemies, most notably detention and the use of military tribunals to impose post-capture criminal sanction.

The US belligerent detention regime has been one of the most controversial consequences of the armed conflict characterization of operations against Al Qaeda and associated forces. While it is beyond the scope of this chapter to review these criticisms, the common thread that runs through them is the aversion to justifying what Justice Kennedy characterized as "generational detention"[148] through reliance on LOAC authority. Issues related to the legitimacy of invoking this authority, the definition of enemy belligerent, the procedures needed to establish that status, and review procedures are all derived from this common concern.

Extending an IHRL presumption to the detention context might contribute to a more rational disposition of individuals detained in the context of this ongoing "legal boundary" armed conflict. Applying an IHRL presumption would require reliance on criminal process to incapacitate captives whenever feasible. This might be implemented through a mandatory review procedure which would authorize deviation from this presumption only pursuant to findings that evidentiary or procedural impediments render criminal prosecution nonfeasible. At that point, an alternative review process would apply to the captive to assess not

[147] *See* Corn, *supra* note 16, at 85, stating that a central theme of authority overreach is that the nature of the struggle justifies invoking and applying LOAC-based authority, while at the same time the dispersed and unconventional nature of the "enemy" necessitates taking the fight to where the attack opportunity arises.

[148] *See* Boumediene v. Bush, *supra* note 91, identifying the risk that "detention . . . may last a generation or more"; *see also* Geoffrey S. Corn & Peter A. Chickris, *Unprivileged Belligerents, Preventive Detention, and Fundamental Fairness: Rethinking the Review Tribunal Representation Model*, 11 Santa Clara J. Int'l L. 99 (2012).

only the individual's status as a member of an enemy belligerent group but also the risk that the individual will return to belligerent activities if released.

Of course, such a standard for authorizing detention would straddle the line between status-based belligerent detention and conduct-based civilian security internment. But, as Watkin argues, the hybrid nature of contemporary threats provides a credible justification for developing hybrid legal response. If this is true at the operational level, there is no theoretical reason why it should not also influence long-term detention policies. Indeed, the current detention model already reflects a hybrid between these two sources of authority. First, the initial detention decisions based on status determinations, followed by periodic review more akin to civilian internment "risk of release" assessments.[149]

Indeed, there is little doubt that IHRL principles have already influenced the US belligerent detention process. Acknowledging that this administrative detention is a necessity-based exception to the norm of criminal prosecution might further influence the nature of process provided to validate detainable status. That process has concededly evolved positively and substantially since 2001, to include both an initial and periodic review of the need for detention. However, perhaps something more akin to the process endorsed by the Supreme Court in *United States v. Salerno*[150] provides a template for the adequacy of procedures to subject an individual to a nonpunitive alternative detention. *Salerno* reviewed the constitutionality of the administrative "preventive" detention authorized by the Bail Reform Act of 1984.[151] In rejecting the procedural due process challenge to the act, the Supreme Court emphasized the nature of the process Congress required to justify detention based on a finding that an individual pending trial represented a serious threat of further criminal activity if released.[152] Essential aspects of that process included a clear and convincing burden of proof, a contested hearing with assistance of counsel, an independent Article III judge, and a prompt opportunity for appellate review of a finding of detainability.[153]

These procedures could be integrated into the existing detainee review process: a clear and convincing burden to justify detention and use of military judges as hearing officers. Of course, *Salerno* did not contemplate years or decades of detention, which is a major concern with the current detention regime. And, while all belligerent detention is inherently indefinite, the prospect of LOAC-based

[149] United States Department of Defense, "The Periodic Review Board" (Periodic Review Secretariat), http://www.prs.mil/About-the-PRB/; *see also* Human Rights First, "Guantanamo Periodic Review Boards," Apr. 9, 2018, <https://www.humanrightsfirst.org/resource/guantanamo-periodic-review-boards; Adam R. Pearlman, *Meaningful Review and Process Due: How Guantanamo Detention is Changing the Battlefield*, 6 Harv. Nat'l Sec. J. 255 (2015).

[150] United States v. Salerno, 481 U.S. 739 (1987).

[151] 18 U.S.C. sec. 3142 (2008).

[152] United States v. Salerno, *supra* note 150, at 743.

[153] *Id.* 751–52.

detention that persists for decades, if not a lifetime, is by all accounts aberrational outside this "war on terror" context. Accordingly, an additional safeguard that could be implemented is a presumptive termination of detention authority, perhaps ten or fifteen years after the initial decision. At that point, the burden to justify continued security-based detention would increase to proof beyond a reasonable doubt. Absent such proof, the detainee would be released.

A similar presumptive approach might also substantially limit the use of military tribunals to subject captives to criminal trial for pre-capture misconduct. An IHRL-based presumption would restrict use of military tribunals to only those offenses that share broad consensus as genuine war crimes. For all other alleged offenses, such as material support to terrorism or conspiracy to engage in terrorism, the presumption would mandate normal criminal process.

In November 2001, President George W. Bush directed the secretary of defense to establish a military commission to try captured Al Qaeda and Taliban personnel for violations of the laws and customs of war.[154] Because the United States determined that its struggle with Al Qaeda qualified as an armed conflict, this order was certainly not unprecedented; military commissions had been used by the United States throughout its history to try captured enemy personnel for such war crimes.[155] Of course, the armed conflict characterization itself was and remains controversial, although, interestingly enough, when the use of military commissions was challenged before the Supreme Court,[156] it appears the petitioner chose not to contest this characterization. Instead, the focal point of the challenge was the procedural rules adopted for the commission, and to a lesser extent the scope of subject-matter jurisdiction.[157]

Military Commission Order Number 1 required the secretary of defense to provide for a "full and fair" criminal trial.[158] The procedures, ultimately implemented through Department of Defense regulation, subsequently became a focal point of criticism. This criticism was rooted in the fact that these procedures were simply antiquated: they mirrored procedures used by US courts-martial and military commissions prior to the substantial reforms adopted by

[154] Military Order of November 13, 2001: Detention, Treatment, and Trial of Certain Non-Citizens in the War Against Terrorism, 66 Fed. Reg. 57831 (2001), which establishes "military commissions to try alien unlawful enemy combatants for offenses triable by military commission as provided in chapter 47A of title 10." This order was superseded by Executive Order 13425 Trial of Unlawful Enemy Combatants by Military Commission, 72 Fed. Reg. 7737 (February 14, 2007).

[155] *See generally* Timothy C. MacDonnell, *Military Commissions and Court-Martial: A Brief Discussion of the Constitutional and Jurisdictional Distinction Between the Two Courts*, The Army Lawyer 19, 19 (Mar. 2002).

[156] Hamdan v. Rumsfeld, *supra* note 79.

[157] *Id.*

[158] United States Department of Defense, "Military Commission Order No. 1" (March 21, 2002), para. 6(b), <http://www.esd.whs.mil/Portals/54/Documents/FOID/Reading%20Room/Detainne_Related/10-F-0341_Doc_1.pdf.

Congress in 1950 in the Uniform Code of Military Justice (UCMJ) and its subsequent amendments.[159] This law, the law by which all US military personnel are subject to military criminal jurisdiction, was intended to bring rules of procedure and evidence for military trials generally in line with those for civilian trials in the United States.[160] Because the procedural and evidentiary rules, originally adopted for the military commission, were virtually identical to those of military commissions conducted after World War II and before these reforms, there was a palpable delta between the rights provided for trial by military court to enemy belligerent defendants and those afforded to US military personnel.[161]

This defect in the military commission process was essentially cured by Congress following the Supreme Court's holding[162] that at least one of the procedures violated Common Article 3 of the Geneva Conventions and the UCMJ.[163] The Military Commission Act (MCA) of 2006, as amended in 2009, generally aligned military commission procedural and evidentiary rules with those for trials by courts-martial.[164] The minor deviations come nowhere near the major differences that existed prior to the enactment of that law. The MCA also codified the subject-matter jurisdiction of the military commission by incorporating, for the first time in US history, enumerated offenses subject to trial by military commission.[165]

In some ways, this enumeration was a welcome development. Up to that point, charges referred for trial by military commission were derived from what the Supreme Court called the "common law of war,"[166] providing the government tremendous latitude in deciding what it considered to be a war crime subject to military commission jurisdiction. While most of the offenses enumerated in Part IV of the Military Commission Act reflect well-established war crimes—offenses legitimately derived from the laws and customs of war—Congress also included several offenses that, at best, straddle the line between war crimes and ordinary civilian crimes, and in the view of many fall outside the category of war crimes.[167]

[159] 10 USC secs. 801–950 (2008).

[160] Uniform Code of Military Justice, art. 37.

[161] Hamdan v. Rumsfeld, *supra* note 79.

[162] *Id.*

[163] *Id.*

[164] Military Commissions Act, Pub. L. 109-366, 120 Stat. 2600 (2006) sec. 9450(p), stating purpose as to "codify offenses that have traditionally be triable by military commissions." *See also* Geoffrey S. Corn, *Questioning the Jurisdictional Moorings of the MCA*, 43 TEX. INT'L L.J. 29 (2007–2008), stating that the most significant change reflected in the MCA is the creation of a judiciary with guarantees of independence analogous to that of the traditional military justice system.

[165] *See* Military Commissions Act, *supra* note 164, Subchapter VII, Punitive Matters; *see also* Section 948(d), providing that "a military commission under this chapter shall have jurisdiction to try any offense made punishable by this chapter or the law of war when committed by an alien unlawful enemy combatant before, on, or after September 11, 2001"; *see generally* Department of Defense, Manual for Military Commissions, Part IV (2007).

[166] *Ex parte Quirin* 317 US 1 (1942); Hamdan v. Rumsfeld, *supra* note 79.

[167] Stephen I. Vladeck, *Military Courts and Article III*, 103 GEO. L.J. 933 (2015).

Challenges to the validity of this subject-matter jurisdiction have become the primary focal point of post-MCA litigation.[168] While decisions by the District of Colombia Court of Appeals have been favorable to the government,[169] subjecting captives to trial before a "war crimes" court for these offenses remains highly controversial. Foremost among this criticism is the argument that there is no legitimate justification for deviating from the norm of civilian trials for these offenses. Indeed, unlike traditionally accepted war crimes, it is difficult to understand why a military tribunal would have special competence over such offenses, or how trial by military tribunal would substantially enhance deterrence of future *battlefield* misconduct.

When the foundation for these criticisms is considered, it is apparent that at the core of the debate over the use of military commissions is not that they are inherently invalid; their use throughout history rebuts this inference. Instead, the true focal point is the legitimacy of subject-matter jurisdiction that includes offenses that are fundamentally indistinguishable from civilian terrorism offenses, and why deviation from the civilian criminal prosecution norm is justified. Thus, in a very real sense, an IHRL presumption is at the core of the military commission debate: Is the United States justified in deviating from the presumptive reliance on normal law enforcement modalities to prosecute and punish captured non-state operatives?

Choosing the forum for prosecution of crimes that fall within the scope of both civilian and military jurisdiction unquestionably falls within the scope of executive discretion.[170] Congress, by including terrorism-type offenses in those enumerated within the MCA, essentially affirmed the president's authority to choose between federal civilian prosecution or military commission prosecution for individuals who fall under the MCA's personal jurisdiction provisions.[171] But this discretion need not mean that reliance on military criminal jurisdiction should be the norm when seeking to hold captured non-state operatives accountable for alleged pre-capture misconduct.[172] Instead, the exercise of this discretion could be guided by presumptive reliance on civilian criminal process, rebutted only for offenses that fall into a category of well-established war crimes.[173]

[168] Al Bahlul v. United States, 840 F.3d 757 (D.C. Cir. Oct. 20, 2016) (en banc); Hamdan v. United States, 696 F.3d 1238 (D.C. Cir. 2012).

[169] *Id.*

[170] Corn, *supra* note 53, at 827, noting that the president is vested with the authority under both domestic law (i.e., the US Constitution) and international law to convene such a tribunal to enforce the law of war.

[171] *Id.*

[172] Geoffrey S. Corn, *Taking the Bitter with the Sweet: A Law of War Based Analysis of the Military Commission*, 35 Stetson L. Rev. 811, 826 (2006).

[173] *Id.*

Although not related to a presumptive IHRL response approach, this is an argument I offered early in the military commission debate in an article[174] that was completed prior to the Supreme Court's decision in *Hamdan v. Rumsfeld*.[175] Since the decision to invoke military commission jurisdiction to prosecute captured alleged war criminals, the expanding conception of what falls within that jurisdiction has been troubling. Equally troubling, however, has been the assertion that such jurisdiction is never valid. In my view, a military tribunal may serve a legitimate and important role in demonstrating US commitment to holding enemy personnel accountable for violations of the laws and customs of war.[176] But if that is, as I believe (and as was suggested by the Supreme Court in *Hamdan*) the principal justification for invoking this jurisdiction, the exercise of this jurisdiction should be narrowly tailored to this justification.

When the nature of alleged pre-capture misconduct is essentially indistinguishable from federal terrorism offenses, requiring no nexus to an armed conflict, reliance on civilian criminal process should be the norm.[177] Extending IHRL primacy to this aspect of an armed conflict would advance this goal. Might there be some cases where military commission jurisdiction might nonetheless be utilized? So long as these "cross-over" offenses remain part of the MCA, the answer must be yes. Perhaps, for example, considerations related to joinder of offenses or offenders might justify the trial of such offenses by military commission. But if deviation from the civilian prosecution is treated as a rare exception, as opposed to the norm based on the captives designation as an enemy belligerent, it will enhance the credibility of the military commission process and will also align the reliance on tribunals to hold captives accountable with the special competence of military personnel to sit in judgment of genuine war crimes. In short, a presumptive reliance on civilian criminal process will produce a more credible alignment between the rationale of military tribunals and the exercise of jurisdictional discretion.

V. Conclusion

As Kenneth Watkin explains so effectively in his book, complex operational situations necessitate a more nuanced and wholistic approach to the challenge of legal regulation. His proposal of an IHRL/law enforcement policy "primacy" is

[174] Corn, *supra* note 172.
[175] Hamdan v. Rumsfeld, *supra* note 79.
[176] *See generally* Corn, *supra* note 2.
[177] Noting that both Common Article 3 and Additional Protocol II reflect a clear presumption: any assertion of criminal responsibility for the decision to participate in a NIAC is a matter of domestic law, and not international law.

appealing on many levels. However, it is important to recognize that at the core of his proposal is that this should be more of an *operational*, as opposed to a legal presumption; a position I fully agree with. As noted herein, I believe it unlikely that states are willing or perhaps even able to adopt a legal construction that vacillates between periods of pure IHRL applicability and periodic armed conflict when dealing with the same threat. The impact of a vacillating legal authority on issues such as detention and criminal sanction of captured opponents make such an approach difficult to reconcile with the interests of strategic response flexibility.

However, Watkin's premise, that addressing contemporary security challenges that straddle the line between crime and armed conflict through a binary legal lens results in detrimental consequences, has merit. These detrimental consequences are most likely to arise in relation to use of force authority, the authority granted to armed forces and other state security forces to use force against these threats. Accordingly, Watkin's IHRL "primacy" logic is most compelling at the operational and tactical domains of security operations. Indeed, as he notes, a nuanced and generally restrained approach to actual mission authority seems to be the norm in such operations, even when operating within a broad armed conflict framework.

This all points to the need to consider the wisdom of adopting this IHRL primacy approach not as a legal construct but as an operational framework within the context of ongoing armed conflicts against these "legal boundary" threats. Such an approach is actually consistent with the ROE methodology currently used by US armed forces, pursuant to which the "standing" or default use of force authority is self-defense-based, with "conduct of hostilities" authority normally tailored to mission-specific needs. In other words, the ongoing situation of armed conflict provides the strategic and operational "maneuver space" to shift between a presumptive IHRL/self-defense use of force paradigm to periodic "conduct of hostilities" authority when needed. This approach preserves the ability for commanders to "ramp up" authority when the threat situation so dictates, while ensuring the overall nature of operations is conducted in a manner that mitigates risk of alienating civilian populations and coalition partners due to a perception of operational overbreadth. Furthermore, an analogous IHRL primacy or presumption, if extended to other aspects of operations such as detention and criminal sanction of captives, would better align state practice with expectations related to logical limits on state security authority.

There is, of course, no talisman that will simplify the inherently complex task of what Watkin calls "fighting at the legal boundary." But if the best doctrine evolves from the ground up, there is great merit in heeding the experience of the past seventeen years of US and coalition operations in this realm of conflict. The message that seems to resonate from this experience is that even within the context of an ongoing armed conflict, strategic legitimacy and operational success will often be advanced by a restrained approach to mission execution. So long as commanders are able to shift authority in response to the shifting nature of the threats they must contend with, a presumptive notion of operational restraint is both logical and strategically beneficial.

9

Using Law as a Weapon against Nuclear Proliferation and Terrorism*

The US Government's Financial Lawfare against Iran

Orde F. Kittrie

The Treasury "has opened up a new battlefield for the United States."
—US Treasury Secretary Jacob J. Lew

During the Obama administration's multiyear campaign to halt Iran's nuclear weapons program without bombing it, "Treasury's undersecretary for terrorism and financial intelligence [was] sometimes described within the administration as President Obama's favorite combatant commander,"[1] said the *New York Times*. According to Treasury Secretary Jacob J. Lew, Treasury "opened up a new battlefield for the United States."[2] "In a dingy suite of offices, in a Treasury Department annex, the troops . . . blast out advisories ordering banks to block targeted people, then threaten them with consequences—fines that can range into millions of dollars—if they do not," said the *Times*, stating that "today, this is how the Obama Administration goes to war."[3]

At a peak in the campaign, Iranian President Mahmoud Ahmadinejad complained bitterly of how "the enemy has banned Iran's oil sales and banking transactions so Iran is not able to transfer or spend money," referring to it as a "hidden war . . . on a far-reaching global scale . . . a kind of war through which the enemy assumes it can defeat the Iranian nation."[4] "What's increasingly clear,"

* This chapter is an updated version of Chapter 3 in ORDE KITTRIE, LAWFARE: LAW AS A WEAPON OF WAR (OXFORD UNIVERSITY PRESS, 2016).

1 Annie Lowrey, *Aiming Financial Weapons from Treasury War Room*, N.Y. TIMES, June 3, 2014, https://www.nytimes.com/2014/06/04/business/aiming-financial-weapons-from-war-room-at-treasury.html?_r=0.

2 *Id.*

3 *Id.*

4 *Ahmadinejad: Hidden War on Global Scale Waged Against Iran's Oil Sector*, IRAN DAILY BRIEF, Oct. 8, 2012, http://www.irandailybrief.com/2012/10/08/ahmadinejad-hidden-war-on-global-scale-waged-against-irans-oil-sector/, quoted in part in JUAN ZARATE, TREASURY'S WAR: THE UNLEASHING OF A NEW ERA OF FINANCIAL WARFARE, at ix (2013).

Orde F. Kittrie, *Using Law as a Weapon against Nuclear Proliferation and Terrorism* In: *Between Crime and War*. Edited by: Claire Finkelstein, Christopher Fuller, Jens David Ohlin, Mitt Regan, Oxford University Press. DOI: 10.1093/oso/9780197638798.003.0010

wrote *Washington Post* columnist David Ignatius about US policy toward Iran in 2011, "is that low-key weapons—covert sabotage and economic sanctions—are accomplishing many of the benefits of military action, without the costs."[5]

"Fifteen years ago, the idea that the Treasury Department would be at the center of our national security would have been inconceivable," said Daniel Glaser, who served from 2011 to 2017 as the Treasury Department's Assistant Secretary for Terrorist Financing.[6] "But," explains Glaser, "we have developed a whole new set of tools to put at the President's disposal."[7]

When Russia invaded Ukraine in 2014, it was no surprise that the US response relied heavily on the Treasury Department "using financial weaponry to hit carefully chosen targets" linked to the Russian government.[8] When the Islamic State rose to prominence that same year, the *New York Times* called Treasury the "first line of attack against ISIS" and said Treasury's financial lawfare "may be more important in the fight against the Islamic State than the Tomahawks fired off American warships or the bombs dropped from F-16s."[9] "This is the 21st century version of waging war," said Judith Lee, chair of the international trade group at the law firm of Gibson, Dunn and Crutcher.[10] *Newsweek* asserted that, for the United States at least, "the first salvo in modern warfare is likely to be financial—and the result is increasingly effective."[11]

This chapter will describe and analyze how US financial lawfare works and how it differs from the imposition of traditional economic sanctions. The chapter will also describe and analyze the strengths and weaknesses of US financial lawfare and assess what its future may hold.

The chapter will do so largely by focusing on the preeminent and most sophisticated US financial lawfare campaign completed thus far: the US financial lawfare, designed to halt Iran's nuclear weapons program and state sponsorship of terrorism,[12] which resulted in the Joint Comprehensive Plan of Action

[5] David Ignatius, *Buying Time with Iran*, WASH. POST, Jan. 9, 2011, https://www.washingtonpost.com/wp-dyn/content/article/2011/01/07/AR2011010703149.html.

[6] Leah McGrath Goodman & Lynnley Browning, *The Art of Financial Warfare: How the West Is Pushing Putin's Buttons*, NEWSWEEK, Apr. 24, 2012, https://www.newsweek.com/2014/05/02/art-financial-warfare-how-west-pushing-putins-buttons-248424.html.

[7] *Id.*

[8] *Id.*

[9] Julie Hirschfeld Davis, *Enforcer at Treasury Is First Line of Attack Against ISIS*, N.Y. TIMES, Oct. 21, 2014, http://www.nytimes.com/2014/10/22/business/international/enforcer-at-treasury-is-first-line-of-attack-against-isis.html?_r=0.

[10] Goodman & Browning, *supra* note 6.

[11] *Id.*

[12] In doing so, this chapter draws heavily on several previous works by the author, including especially ORDE F. KITTRIE, LAWFARE: LAW AS A WEAPON OF WAR (2016); Orde F. Kittrie, *Lawfare and US National Security*, 43 CASE W. RES. J. INT'L L. 393 (2011), http://law.case.edu/journals/JIL/Documents/43_Kittrie.pdf; and Orde F. Kittrie, *New Sanctions for a New Century: Treasury's Innovative Use of Financial Sanctions*, 30 U. PA. J. INT'L L. 789 (2009), http://scholarship.law.upenn.edu/cgi/viewcontent.cgi?article=1149&context=jil.

(JCPOA). The Obama administration joined Iran and the P-5 + 1 (the UN Security Council's five permanent members plus Germany) in announcing the JCPOA in July 2015.[13]

The JCPOA provided for the lifting of most nuclear-related sanctions on Iran in exchange for various constraints on Iran's nuclear program. On JCPOA "Implementation Day," January 16, 2016, the International Atomic Energy Agency verified that Iran had implemented key nuclear-related measures as described in the JCPOA.[14] As a result, the United States lifted various nuclear-related sanctions on Iran, as specified in the JCPOA.[15]

The JCPOA did not commit the United States to suspend US sanctions on Iran for its involvement with terrorism, or lift Iran's designation as a state sponsor of terrorism.[16] Officials in the Obama administration Treasury Department insisted that they planned to continue to vigorously engage in financial lawfare against Iran for its terrorism-supporting activities. For example, Adam Szubin, the Acting Under Secretary of the Treasury for Terrorism and Financial Intelligence, testified before Congress on August 5, 2015, that notwithstanding the JCPOA, "the United States will maintain and continue to vigorously enforce our powerful sanctions targeting Iran's backing for terrorist groups such as Hizballah."[17] However, in a July 22, 2015, hearing before the House Financial Services Committee, Steven Perles, a leading private sector counterterrorism litigator, asserted that various US "administrative agencies have made recent decisions that raise concerns about their continuing willingness to carry out their legal obligations to enforce antiterrorism sanctions against Iran after nuclear sanctions are removed."[18]

Such criticisms were leveled at the Obama administration for the remainder of its term in office, with some expressing concern that the administration softened its approach to Iran on non-nuclear sanctions out of fear that aggressive implementation of such measures might discourage Iran from continuing to

[13] Joint Comprehensive Plan of Action, July 14, 2015, http://eeas.europa.eu/statements-eeas/docs/iran_agreement/iran_joint-comprehensive-plan-of-action_en.pdf.

[14] "Statement Relating to the Joint Comprehensive Plan of Action Implementation Day of January 16 2016," US Dep't of the Treasury, Jan. 16, 2016, https://www.treasury.gov/resource-center/sanctions/Programs/Pages/iran.aspx.

[15] *Id.*

[16] Kenneth Katzman & Paul K. Kerr, "R4333, Iran Nuclear Agreement," Congressional Research Service, July 30, 2015, https://fas.org/sgp/crs/nuke/R43333.pdf.

[17] Written testimony of Adam Szubin, Acting Under Secretary of Treasury for Terrorism and Financial Intelligence, "The Implications of Sanctions Relief Under the Iran Agreement" (Hearing Before the S. Comm. On Banking, Housing, and Urban Affairs, Aug. 5, 2015), https://www.banking.senate.gov/public/index.cfm?FuseAction=Files.View&FileStore_id=267050cd-f198-4bbe-8f23-4b9aed9110e4.

[18] Statement of Steven R. Perles before the Task Force to Investigate Terrorism Financing of the H. Comm. On Financial Services, July 22, 2015, http://financialservices.house.gov/uploadedfiles/hhrg-114-ba00-wstate-sperles-20150722.pdf.

abide by the JCPOA.[19] In addition, concerns were raised that the efficacy of any US financial pressure on Iran to halt its state sponsorship of terrorism would be impacted by factors including the lessening of nuclear-related sanctions on Iran and the resulting release of tens of billions of dollars of Iranian assets from its blocked accounts in Europe and Asia.[20]

On May 8, 2018, President Donald Trump announced that the United States would withdraw from the JCPOA and reimpose the sanctions it imposed on Iran before the deal.[21] As of that date, Iran had, by most accounts, largely complied with its obligations under the JCPOA since the deal was announced three years before. In April and July 2017, the Trump administration itself certified to Congress that Iran had not materially breached the JCPOA.[22]

However, Iran had not significantly reduced its state sponsorship of terrorism.[23] Some analysts argued that the release of Iranian assets as a result of the lessening of nuclear sanctions and associated concessions had enabled Iran to increase its sponsorship of terrorism.[24] Even Secretary of State John Kerry, who participated in negotiating the JCPOA, acknowledged that some money from Iran's sanctions relief "will end up in the hands of the IRCG or other entities, some of which are labeled terrorists," referring to the Iran Revolutionary Guard Corps.[25]

Notwithstanding the Trump administration's eventual withdrawal from the JCPOA, the financial lawfare waged by the US government against Iran in the

19 *See, e.g.*, Benny Avni, *The Coming US Crackdown on Iran*, N.Y. Post, April 25, 2017, http://nypost.com/2017/04/25/the-coming-us-crackdown-on-iran/>; Jenna Lifhits, *Senate Democrats Open to New Sanctions on Iran After Latest Missile Test*, The Weekly Standard, Jan. 31, 2017, https://www.weeklystandard.com/senate-democrats-open-to-new-sanctions-on-iran-after-latest-missile-test/article/2006592.

20 *See, e.g.*, Statement of Matthew Levitt, "The Implications of Sanctions Relief Under the Iran Agreement" (Hearing Before the S. Comm. On Banking, Housing, and Urban Affairs, Aug. 5, 2015), https://www.banking.senate.gov/public/index.cfm?FuseAction=Files.View&FileStore_id=f311b065-a725-442a-bb39-613d5c81ac0d; Jonathan Schanzer & Mark Dubowitz, *It Just Got Easier for Iran to Fund Terrorism*, Foreign Policy, July 17, 2015, http://foreignpolicy.com/2015/07/17/it-just-got-easier-for-iran-to-fund-terrorism-swift-bank/.

21 Mark Landler, *Trump Abandons Iran Nuclear Deal He Long Scorned*, N.Y. Times, May 8, 2018, https://www.nytimes.com/2018/05/08/world/middleeast/trump-iran-nuclear-deal.html.

22 Peter Baker, *Trump Recertifies Nuclear Deal, But Only Reluctantly*, N.Y. Times, July 17, 2017, https://www.nytimes.com/2017/07/17/us/politics/trump-iran-nuclear-deal-recertify.html?_r=0.

23 *See, e.g.*, Nicole Gaouette, *Iran Remains Top Terror Sponsor as Global Atttacks Decline*, CNN, July 19. 2017, https://www.cnn.com/2017/07/19/politics/state-country-terror-report/index.html>; Daniel Byman, *Iran's Support for Terrorist Groups*, Lawfare, May 25, 2017, https://www.lawfareblog.com/irans-support-terrorist-groups>; Matthew Levitt, "Iran's Support for Terrorism Under the JCPOA," The Washington Institute for Near East Policy July 8, 2016, https://www.washingtoninstitute.org/policy-analysis/view/irans-support-for-terrorism-under-the-jcpoa.

24 *See, e.g.*, Statement of Mark Dubowitz, Executive Director, Foundation for Defense of Democracies, "Fueling Terror, The Dangers of Ransom Payments to Iran" (Hearing Before the Subcomm. On Oversight and Investigations of the H. Comm. on Financial Services, Sept. 8, 2016), https://financialservices.house.gov/uploadedfiles/hhrg-114-ba09-wstate-mdubowitz-20160908.pdf.

25 Rebecca Kheel, *Kerry: Some Iran Sanctions Relief Will Go to Terrorists*, The Hill, Jan. 21, 2016, http://thehill.com/policy/defense/266619-kerry-some-iran-sanctions-relief-will-go-to-terrorists.

nine years before the JCPOA is an exceptionally worthwhile subject of study. Both leading US supporters and leading US opponents of the JCPOA credited that US financial lawfare with providing the United States with considerable leverage over Iran. The various innovations of pre-JCPOA US financial lawfare against Iran will remain tested options for lawfare practitioners to draw from in future such campaigns.

In describing and analyzing the US financial lawfare campaign against Iran, this chapter will briefly reference other very significant US financial lawfare campaigns, including those against North Korea and on Russia in response to its occupation of Crimea. This chapter will also briefly reference some of the US economic lawfare campaigns in other sectors that have been heavily influenced by lessons learned from US financial lawfare against Iran. That includes the US energy lawfare campaign against Iran, US insurance lawfare, and the US lawfare campaign against suppliers to Iran's nuclear program.

Section I of this chapter discusses the pre-JCPOA US financial lawfare against Iran in conceptual context. Section II describes and analyzes the key nexus between US financial lawfare and Iran's nuclear weapons program and state sponsorship of terrorism: Iran's use of the international financial system to advance those objectives. Section III provides an overview of key innovative elements of the pre-JCPOA US financial lawfare against Iran. Section IV describes and analyzes the impact that this US financial lawfare had against Iran. Section V systematically describes and analyzes how the US government implemented this financial lawfare against Iran.

Section VI discusses lessons learned. It concludes that the effects of the various lawfare deployments described in this chapter indicate that lawfare, deployed in a more coordinated and systematic manner, could likely save US and foreign lives, and US taxpayer dollars, by supplementing or replacing kinetic warfare as a tool for achieving some significant US military objectives.

I. US Financial Lawfare against Iran in Conceptual Context

Each of the major categories of US governmental economic lawfare against Iran that are discussed in this chapter differs significantly from traditional economic sanctions. Traditional economic sanctions broadly and bluntly embargo trade between the imposing country (e.g., the United States) and the target country (e.g., Iran). As of spring 2015, just before the JCPOA was announced, nearly all US trade with Iran had been prohibited for some twenty years (since 1995).[26] With such embargoes, the focus tends to be relatively straightforward: prohibiting persons in the United States from engaging in all or some trade

[26] Kenneth Katzman, "RS20871 Iran Sanctions," Congressional Research Service, June 17, 2015, https://www.hsdl.org/?view&did=767891.

with an entire foreign country, and then policing US persons and patrolling US borders to ensure compliance.

The focus of pre-JCPOA US governmental economic lawfare against Iran was instead on halting some or all commerce between Iran and foreign persons and entities located in third countries. While curtailing such international commerce has traditionally been attempted through quarantines imposed by force of arms, economic lawfare principally accomplishes this objective through the creative, dynamic, and aggressive leveraging of US law and jurisdiction to pressure foreign companies that engage in commerce with particular Iranian bad actors. Both US financial and US energy lawfare against Iran involved an implied or explicit threat of legal action pursuant to US federal law, delivered to the foreign company by US federal officials, which persuaded the foreign company to stop doing business with the targets, even though such business may not have been prohibited by the government of the country in which the foreign company is headquartered.

It is in light of these characteristics that this chapter refers to these US economic measures against Iran as economic lawfare. These measures have thus far been more typically referred to in the media as sanctions or "smart sanctions." However, Major General Charles W. Dunlap, Jr., who first coined the term "lawfare" to describe the use of law as a weapon of war, included financial warfare within the ambit of lawfare. For example, Dunlap referred to "the use of legal processes to deconstruct terrorist financing" as a type of lawfare[27] and explained that while attacking the funding of terrorist groups "may be called 'financial warfare' rather than 'lawfare'" by some, "it nevertheless depends upon legal instruments and methodologies."[28]

Juan Zarate, a leading architect of these measures during his service as a senior Treasury and White House official, referred to US financial measures against Iran as "financial warfare" in his magisterial book, *Treasury's War: The Unleashing of a New Era of Financial Warfare*.[29] It is this chapter's hypothesis that, consistent with Dunlap's view, these financial measures are also a salient, and indeed paradigmatic, example of lawfare. As this chapter will demonstrate, analyzing Treasury's war from the perspective of lawfare helps in understanding both Treasury's war and the broader power and potential of lawfare.

The pivotal actions undertaken by the officers in Treasury's war involved drafting and enacting innovative laws, innovatively threatening to enforce those

[27] Charles J. Dunlap, Jr., *Lawfare Today. . . and Tomorrow*, *in* International Law and the Changing Character of War (Raul A. Pedrozo & Daria P. Wollschlaeger eds., 2011), http://scholarship.law.duke.edu/faculty_scholarship/2465/.

[28] Charles J. Dunlap, Jr., *Does Lawfare Need an Apologia?*, 43 Case W. Res. J. Int'l L. 121, 124 n.16 (2010).

[29] Juan Zarate, Treasury's War: The Unleashing of a New Era of Financial Warfare (2013).

laws in scores of meetings directly with foreign private banks, and enforcing those laws with dramatically escalating and eventually unprecedented penalties imposed through settlements or convictions within the US domestic legal system. The law-centered nature of Treasury's war is not surprising, as each of the five Treasury policymakers who were its leading architects and implementers—David Cohen, Daniel Glaser, Stuart Levey, Adam Szubin, and Juan Zarate—were lawyers rather than, for example, bankers.

While Treasury's war reflected a new approach to using US financial muscle to achieve national security objectives, it was equally innovative in its aggressive, impact-focused, yet carefully targeted and calibrated use of law to achieve national security objectives. Many of its legal innovations were not unique to finance but could and would be subsequently applied to the US government's energy, insurance, and weapons-of-mass-destruction (WMD)–supply lawfare against Iran, and could in the future be applied to lawfare against other targets in other economic sectors. In addition, the financial lawfare measures undertaken by the US government against Iran in several ways provided critical legal underpinnings for private civil litigation and other nongovernmental US lawfare against Iran.

The US Treasury Department's war against Iran took off in 2006 under the George W. Bush administration. It lasted until the end of the Bush administration, continued (and indeed increased in firepower) under the Obama administration, and was generally credited with helping convince Iran to negotiate seriously regarding its nuclear program. As discussed earlier in this chapter, the resulting negotiations resulted in the JCPOA, pursuant to which most nuclear-related sanctions on Iran were to be lifted in exchange for various constraints on Iran's nuclear program.

In a tribute to the bipartisan appeal of Treasury's war against Iran, the Obama administration made the extraordinary decision to retain in place Stuart Levey, the Bush-appointed Under Secretary of the Treasury who was principally known as the leading architect of this financial lawfare.[30] Levey served for the first two years of the Obama administration, until he resigned and was replaced by his deputy, David Cohen.[31] After Cohen left to become Deputy Director of the CIA,[32] Obama nominated Adam Szubin to replace him.[33] Szubin had previously served

[30] *See, e.g.*, Paul Richter, *Obama Administration Keeps Bush Official Involved with Iran Sanctions*, L.A. TIMES, Feb. 3, 2009, http://articles.latimes.com/2009/feb/03/world/fg-usiran3.

[31] Samuel Rubenfeld, *White House Nominates David Cohen as Sanctions Point Man*, WALL ST. J., Jan. 25, 2011, http://blogs.wsj.com/corruption-currents/2011/01/25/white-house-nominates-david-cohen-as-sanctions-point-man/.

[32] "President Obama Announces More Key Administration Posts," Press Release, The White House, Jan. 9, 2015, https://www.whitehouse.gov/the-press-office/2015/01/09/president-obama-announces-more-key-administration-posts.

[33] "President Obama Announces More Key Administration Posts," Press Release, The White House, Apr. 16, 2015, https://www.whitehouse.gov/the-press-office/2015/04/16/president-obama-announces-more-key-administration-posts.

as director of Treasury's Office of Foreign Assets Control, in which capacity he had played a key role in Treasury's war against Iran since its beginning.[34]

During the first six years or so of the Obama administration, the primary objective of US financial lawfare against Iran was halting Iran's nuclear weapons program. The Obama administration's nuclear negotiations with Iran from 2012 to 2015, in which it largely subordinated concerns about Iran's state sponsorship of terrorism in order to focus on Iran's nuclear program, reflect the preeminence which the administration gave to the nuclear issue.

President Obama explained his concerns about Iran's nuclear program in a 2012 speech as follows:

> [The] entire world has an interest in preventing Iran from acquiring a nuclear weapon. A nuclear-armed Iran would thoroughly undermine the non-proliferation regime that we've done so much to build. There are risks that an Iranian nuclear weapon could fall into the hands of a terrorist organization. It is almost certain that others in the region would feel compelled to get their own nuclear weapon, triggering an arms race in one of the world's most volatile regions. It would embolden a regime that has brutalized its own people, and it would embolden Iran's proxies, who have carried out terrorist attacks from the Levant to southwest Asia. And that is why, four years ago, I made a commitment to the American people, and said that we would use all elements of American power to pressure Iran and prevent it from acquiring a nuclear weapon. And that is what we have done.[35]

US economic lawfare, and especially the financial lawfare led by the US Treasury Department, also targeted Iran's state sponsorship of terrorism. Iran was first designated as a state sponsor of terrorism by the US government in 1984, and remained designated as such until at least February 2022.[36] In March 2014, the year before the JCPOA was announced, the Treasury Department stated, "Iran remains the world's most active state sponsor of terrorism, planning terrorist attacks, providing lethal aid, and delivering hundreds of millions of dollars per year in support to extremist groups across the globe."[37]

[34] *Id.*

[35] "Remarks by the President at AIPAC Policy Conference," Press Release, The White House, Mar. 4, 2012, https://www.whitehouse.gov/the-press-office/2012/03/04/remarks-president-aipac-policy-conference-0.

[36] "State Sponsors of Terrorism," US Department of State, https://www.state.gov/j/ct/list/c14151.htm.

[37] "Remarks of Under Secretary for Terrorism and Financial Intelligence David Cohen Before the Center for a New American Security on 'Confronting New Threats in Terrorist Financing,'" Press Release, US Dep't of the Treasury, Mar. 4, 2014, https://www.treasury.gov/press-center/press-releases/Pages/jl2308.aspx.

In order to advance its primary objective of halting Iran's nuclear weapons program and secondary objective of halting Iran's state sponsorship of terrorism, US financial lawfare (as well as energy lawfare) against Iran employed two principal means of leverage: coercion and constraint.[38] Treasury Under Secretary Stuart Levey described both aspects of the Obama administration's financial measures against Iran. The coercive aspect was "to sharpen the choice for Iran's leaders between integration with the international community, predicated on fulfilling their international obligations, and the hardship of further isolation."[39] Levey explained that "[b]y dramatically isolating Iran financially and commercially and by capitalizing on Iran's existing vulnerabilities, we can impact Iran's calculations" so as to "create crucial leverage for our diplomacy."[40] The second, constraining aspect was described by Levey, in the nuclear context, as designed to "make it harder for Iran to pursue international procurement for its nuclear and military programs."[41]

Coercing the target (in this case, Iran) into halting its illegal behavior succeeds if the costs of the behavior (in this case proceeding with the nuclear weapons program or state sponsorship of terrorism) come to be perceived by the target as outweighing the benefits to the target of proceeding with the behavior.[42] For example, coercion will succeed if all US and allied responses to the nuclear weapons program, including economic lawfare, cost the Iranian regime more than the nuclear program is worth to it. The costs might, for example, include endangering the regime's control over the Iranian people. In contrast, *constraining* the target from engaging in illegal behavior succeeds if all US and allied responses to the nuclear weapons program, including economic lawfare, so materially reduce the target's supply of assets necessary to engage in the illegal behavior that the target is no longer able to engage in some or all of the illegal behavior.

As mentioned previously, Iran is not the only target against which US government entities have waged financial lawfare. Al Qaeda, Hezbollah, North Korea, Russia, Serbia, Syria, and various narcotics traffickers have also been major targets. However, Iran provides an exceptionally useful case study, because the financial lawfare against Iran was particularly sustained, systematic, creative, and

[38] "Remarks at the Center for Strategic and International Studies by Treasury Under Secretary for Terrorism and Financial Intelligence Stuart Levey," Press Release, US Dep't of the Treasury, Sept. 20, 2010, https://www.ustreas.gov/press/releases/tg862.htm.

[39] *Id.*

[40] *Id.*

[41] *Id.*

[42] *See* Kimberly Ann Elliott, *Analyzing the Effects of Targeted Sanctions*, *in* SMART SANCTIONS: TARGETING ECONOMIC STATECRAFT (David Cortright & George A. Lopez eds., 2002). This paragraph draws heavily from Orde F. Kittrie, *Averting Catastrophe: Why the Nuclear Nonproliferation Treaty Is Losing Its Deterrence Capacity and How to Restore It*, 28 MICH. J. INT'L L. 337, 354–60 (2007), http://ssrn.com/abstract=996953>.

intensive, and was publicly discussed and explained in extraordinary detail by US officials.

Lawfare was an apt response to Iran in part because in pursuing its nuclear weapons program and state sponsorship of terrorism, the Iranian government egregiously violated international law. For example, Iran for years violated legally binding UN Security Council resolutions ordering it to suspend its nuclear enrichment, reprocessing, and heavy water–related activities.[43] In a series of periodic reports, the Director General of the International Atomic Energy Agency determined again and again that "contrary to the relevant resolutions of the Board of Governors and the Security Council, Iran has not suspended all of its enrichment related activities" and "has not suspended work on all heavy water related projects."[44]

Iran also persisted in providing destabilizing support to terrorist groups,[45] including by supplying them with arms in violation of UN Security Council Resolutions 1701 and 1747.[46] In addition, Iran chose to violate numerous other

[43] S.C. Res. 1737, para. 2, U.N. Doc. S/RES/1737 (Dec. 27, 2006); *see also* S.C. Res. 1747, paras. 12–13, U.N. Doc. S/RES/1747 (2007) (Mar. 24, 2007) (reaffirming Resolution 1737); S.C. Res. 1803, paras. 1, 14, 18–19, U.N. Doc. S/RES/1803 (2008) (Mar. 3, 2008) (reaffirming Resolutions 1737 and 1747); S.C. Res. 1929, paras. 1–2, 36–37, U.N. Doc. S/RES/1929 (2010) (June 9, 2010) (affirming Iran's noncompliance with Resolutions 1737, 1747, and 1803 and reaffirming Resolution 1737).

[44] *See, e.g.*, "Implementation of the NPT Safeguards Agreement and Relevant Provisions of Security Council Resolutions in the Islamic Republic of Iran," Int'l Atomic Energy Agency [IAEA]' 4, 8 (IAEA Doc. GOV/2015/15, Feb. 19, 2015), https://www.iaea.org/sites/default/files/gov2015-15.pdf>; "Implementation of the NPT Safeguards Agreement and Relevant Provisions of Security Council Resolutions in the Islamic Republic of Iran," Int'l Atomic Energy Agency [IAEA] 4 (IAEA Doc. GOV/2014/28, May 23, 2014), https://www.iaea.org/Publications/Documents/Board/2014/gov2014-28.pdf> "Implementation of the NPT Safeguards Agreement and Relevant Provisions of Security Council Resolutions in the Islamic Republic of Iran," Int'l Atomic Energy Agency [IAEA], 11 (IAEA Doc. GOV/2010/46, Sept. 6, 2010), https://www.iaea.org/Publications/Documents/Board/2010/gov2010-46.pdf (similar language).

[45] *See, e.g.*, "Country Reports on Terrorism," US Dept. of State, 2013, https://www.state.gov/j/ct/rls/crt/2013/225328.htm. (Iran "continued to provide arms" to the Assad regime, "assisted in rearming Hizballah," and "attempted to smuggle arms to Houthi separatists in Yemen and Shia oppositionists in Bahrain." Iran has also "provided weapons, training, and funding to Hamas and other Palestinian terrorist groups," and "has provided hundreds of millions of dollars in support of Hizballah.").

[46] For example, Iranian arms transfers to Syria's Assad government and to Hamas violated UN Security Council Resolution 1747, which ordered that "Iran shall not supply, sell or transfer directly or indirectly from its territory or by its nationals or using its flag vessels or aircraft any arms or related materiel." Jay Solomon, *US, Israel Fear Pickup in Iranian Support of Hamas*, Wall St. J., July 30, 2014, http://blogs.wsj.com/washwire/2014/07/30/u-s-israel-fear-pickup-in-iranian-support-of-hamas/>; Anne Barnard, Michael R. Gordon, & Jodi Rudoren, *Israel Targeted Iranian Missiles in Syria Attack*, N.Y. Times, May 4, 2013, https://www.nytimes.com/2013/05/05/world/middleeast/israel-syria.html?pagewanted=all>; Joe Vaccarello, *Iran Sending Banned Weapons to Syria, UN Report Says*, CNN, May 12, 2011, https://www.cnn.com/2011/WORLD/meast/05/12/un.syria.iran.weapons/>; S.C. Res. 1747, *supra* note 34, at para. 5. Iranian arms transfers to Hezbollah violate Resolution 1747 as well as Resolution 1701, which ordered all States to "prevent . . . the sale or supply to any entity or individual in Lebanon of arms and related materiel of all types." Adam Entous, Charles Levinson, & Julian E. Barnes, *Hezbollah Upgrades Missile Threat to Israel*, Wall St. J., Jan. 2, 2014, http://online.wsj.com/news/articles/SB10001424052702304361604579290613920542386>; S.C. Res. 1701, para. 15, U.N. Doc. S/RES/1701 (2006) (Aug. 11, 2006).

international legal obligations. For example, Iran's brutal response to its opposition Green Movement contravened its human rights obligations under international law, including the legally binding International Covenant on Civil and Political Rights.[47]

II. Iran's Use of the International Financial System to Accomplish Its Nuclear and Terrorism Sponsorship Objectives

Iran for over a decade utilized the international financial system to accomplish both its nuclear and its terrorism sponsorship objectives.[48] Iran's integration into the international financial system both provided the Iranian government with the global financial capability to support its nuclear and terrorism sponsorship activities and exposed elements of the international financial system to a risk of facilitating these activities.[49]

"Iran uses various techniques to engage in seemingly legitimate commercial transactions that are actually related to its nuclear and missile programs," said Daniel Glaser, Deputy Assistant Secretary of the Treasury for Terrorist Financing and Financial Crimes, in a 2008 congressional hearing.[50] "This deceptive behavior," said Glaser, "coupled with Iran's access to the global economy, gives the Iranian regime the financial capability to support its activities."[51] "All of this adds up to enormous risks for the international financial system," added Glaser.[52]

One might expect that Iran would have avoided the formal financial system and relied instead on moving money using such methods as *hawala* that can be effectuated without the creation of official financial records. However, Treasury

[47] G.A. Res. 2200A (XXI), U.N. GAOR, 21st Sess., Supp. No. 16, U.N. Doc. A/6316, at 52–60, International Covenant on Civil and Political Rights (Dec. 16, 1966), http://www.ohchr.org/Documents/ProfessionalInterest/ccpr.pdf; International Covenant on Civil and Political Rights, Dec. 16, 1966, S. Treaty Doc. 95-20, 999 UNTS 171.

[48] Statement of Daniel Glaser, Deputy Assistant Secretary for Terrorist Financing and Financial Crimes, US Dep't of Treasury, "Between Feckless and Reckless: US Policy Options to Prevent a Nuclear Iran" (Joint Hearing Before the Subcomm. on the Middle East and South Asia, and the Subcomm. on Terrorism, Nonproliferation and Trade of the H. Comm. on Foreign Affairs, 110th Cong. 24, 2008), https://www.gpo.gov/fdsys/pkg/CHRG-110hhrg41849/pdf/CHRG-110hhrg41849.pdf.

[49] This and the other paragraphs in this section draw heavily from Orde F. Kittrie, *New Sanctions for a New Century: Treasury's Innovative Use of Financial Sanctions*, 30 U. Pa. J. Int'l L. 789 (2009), http://ssrn.com/abstract=1402265.

[50] Glaser, *supra* note 48.

[51] *Id.*

[52] *Id.*

has found that for rogue actors, there is sometimes "no good alternative and, in many cases, no alternative at all" to the formal international financial system.[53]

Proliferation networks, for example, turn out to require letters of credit and other types of financing for many of their purchases.[54] Such networks often depend heavily on generally legitimate businessmen or manufacturers who will supply a proliferation-sensitive item because of profit rather than ideology. Such suppliers may find it harder to turn a blind eye or may be otherwise discomfited by a transaction that avoids the formal financial system. In addition, rogue states, including Iran, themselves depend on the global financial system for such functions as holding reserves and financing both their revenue-earning exports and their imports of such strategic commodities as gasoline.

In order to avoid suspicion and minimize the risk of detection, Iran's state-owned banks and other entities used an array of deceptive practices when employing their global financial ties to advance Iran's nuclear program and sponsorship of terrorism.[55] For example, Iran used front companies and intermediaries to surreptitiously purchase technology and materials for its nuclear and missile programs from countries that would prohibit such exports to Iran.[56]

In addition, Iranian banks asked other financial institutions to remove the Iranian banks' names when processing their transactions through the international financial system.[57] The goal was to allow Iranian banks to remain undetected as they moved money through the international financial system to pay for the Iranian government's nuclear- and missile-related purchases and to fund terrorism.[58] The name-removal tactic was intended to evade the controls put in place by responsible financial institutions further down the line and had the effect of potentially involving those institutions in transactions that were illegal, that placed their reputations at risk, and that they might never have engaged in if they knew who was really involved.[59]

Iran's reliance on deceptive financial transactions to support its nuclear and terrorism sponsorship activities contributed to its persistent unwillingness to meet international standards for the development and implementation of laws

[53] "Remarks by Treasury Secretary Paulson on Targeted Financial Measures to Protect Our National Security" (Press Release, US Dep't of the Treasury, June 14, 2007), https://www.treasury.gov/press-center/press-releases/Pages/hp457.aspx.

[54] *Id.*

[55] Glaser, *supra* note 48.

[56] *See, e.g.*, Final Report of the Panel of Experts Established Pursuant to Resolution 1929 (2010), at 23, 26–27, June 5, 2014, UN Security Council, contained in S/2014/394, June 11, 2014, https://www.un.org/ga/search/view_doc.asp?symbol=S/2014/394.

[57] *See, e.g.*, Deferred Prosecution Agreement, US v. Standard Chartered Bank, US District Court for the District of Columbia, Dec. 10, 2012, at 8, https://www.mainjustice.com/wp-admin/documents-databases/114-1-Standard-Chartered-Bank-DPA.pdf; Glaser, *supra* note 48.

[58] Glaser, *supra* note 48.

[59] "Remarks by Treasury Secretary Paulson," *supra* note 53.

and enforcement capabilities that would detect and prevent money laundering or terrorist financing. In February 2015, the Financial Action Task Force (FATF), an intergovernmental body that sets standards for anti-money-laundering (AML) and combating the financing of terrorism (CFT), stated that "[t]he FATF remains particularly and exceptionally concerned about Iran's failure to address the risk of terrorist financing and the serious threat this poses to the integrity of the international financial system. . . . The FATF urges Iran to immediately and meaningfully address its AML/CTF deficiencies."[60]

III. Innovative Design of US Financial Lawfare against Iran

The US government's multifaceted financial lawfare campaign against Iran relied heavily on the primacy in international finance of US dollars, the preferred currency of international trade. As of 2012, the US dollar was involved in some 87 percent of the world's foreign-exchange transactions and was the leading global reserve currency.[61] (The dollar retained this preeminence over the decade, with involvement in 88 percent of foreign-exchange market transactions in 2019.[62]) In leveraging the dollar's primacy, the US financial lawfare strategy deployed several key innovations that will be described in detail in this and subsequent sections. The innovations include: direct outreach to individual foreign private financial institutions, aggressive use of financial regulatory authorities to pursue political goals, effective development and harnessing of intelligence about global financial transactions, a focus on the illicit conduct of lawfare targets, and an eye for deterring transactions beyond what is explicitly prohibited.

In developing and implementing its multifaceted financial lawfare campaign, the United States used the UN Security Council or partnered with allies where possible, but also found effective ways to operate outside of such cooperative arrangements. To maximize its effectiveness, the United States worked to convince not only individual foreign governments but also individual non-American companies to join the effort. Identifying ways to persuade such non-American companies was "a particularly daunting challenge given the limits of US jurisdiction over foreign entities."[63]

However, once private sector financial institutions are persuaded to act, they are "able to act much more quickly than governments who often lack the

[60] "FATF Public Statement," Financial Action Task Force, Feb. 27, 2015, https://www.fatf-gafi.org/documents/documents/public-statement-february-2015.html.

[61] Goodman & Browning, *supra* note 6; Zarate, *supra* note 29.

[62] "Market Share of Leading Foreign Exchange Currencies in 2019, By Value of Turnover," Statista, https://www.statista.com/statistics/247362/global-foreign-exchange-market-turnover-by-currency/.

[63] Michael Jacobson, *Sanctions Against Iran: A Promising Struggle*, 31 WASH. Q. 69 (2008).

necessary authority or the political will to take action on their own"[64] or who may face cumbersome bureaucratic procedures for exercising whatever relevant authority they do have. The US financial lawfare campaign's focus on directly persuading such non-American companies to curtail financial transactions with Iran, and its success in doing so—both described and analyzed in detail in section V.C of this chapter—were among the campaign's most significant innovations.

Another of the campaign's most innovative aspects was its use of the US Treasury Department's financial authorities to pursue national security objectives. Treasury had, from time to time, used its financial authorities to pursue criminal justice policy objectives. For example, Al Capone famously received his career-ending jail sentence not for his suspected involvement in dozens of murders (which apparently could not be proven) but for tax evasion—running afoul of the Treasury Department's Internal Revenue Service, which subjected him to a nonrandom audit.[65]

National security policy objectives had, however, long remained off limits. "Years ago," recalled Robert Einhorn, the State Department's former Assistant Secretary for Nonproliferation, "people at State would go to Treasury and say, 'We've got a lot of financial muscle, we should use it to pursue political goals,' but Treasury would always say it didn't want to mess around with the international financial system."[66]

Indicative of the novel approach taken by the architects of US financial lawfare against Iran was the statement of Henry Paulson, Treasury Secretary under George W. Bush, that he and his finance ministry counterparts around the world had a responsibility "to broaden our role beyond economic stewardship and become valuable contributors to help ensure our countries' and our citizens' security."[67] James Wilkinson, chief of staff of the Bush Treasury Department, noted that "[o]ur financial tools are sometimes the most powerful weapons our government has to help change behavior."[68]

Economic sanctions had previously focused largely on transnational trade in goods. Treasury's willingness to use its financial muscle to pursue national security objectives was particularly and increasingly important because "[g]lobal financial flows are growing rapidly and greatly exceed the trade in goods and services."[69]

64 "Remarks by Treasury Secretary Paulson," *supra* note 53.

65 "Famous Cases & Criminals: Al Capone," FBI, https://www.fbi.gov/about-us/history/famous-cases/al-capone>; *In re* Alphonse Capone, Memorandum from the Internal Revenue Service Intelligence Unit of Chicago, Illinois (July 8, 1931), https://www.irs.gov/pub/irs-utl/file-1-letter-dated-07081931-in-re-alphonse-capone.pdf>; Douglas O. Linder, Al *Capone Trial (1931): An Account*, LAW2, 2011, http://law2.umkc.edu/faculty/projects/ftrials/capone/caponeaccount.html.

66 Bay Fang (quoting Robert Einhorn), *Treasury Wields Financial Sanctions: US Strategy Straddles the Line Between Diplomacy, Military Might*, CHICAGO TRIBUTE, Apr. 23, 2007.

67 "Remarks by Treasury Secretary Paulson," *supra* note 53.

68 Steven R. Weisman, *The Ripples of Punishing One Bank*, N.Y. TIMES, July 3, 2007.

69 "Remarks by Treasury Secretary Paulson," *supra* note 53.

A third major innovation contributing to the success of US financial lawfare against Iran was Treasury's systematic development and harnessing of intelligence regarding global financial transactions. In 2004, the US Treasury Department became the world's first finance ministry to develop in-house expertise in the collection and analysis of such intelligence.[70] In an era of globalization, such intelligence is increasingly available because "technology and integration have made it more difficult for anyone using the financial system to hide."[71] In order to be useful for purposes of financial lawfare, the financial intelligence must of course be accurate. It also must be shareable, in a way that traditional national security intelligence, which depends heavily on sources and methods that are themselves secret, is often not. Fortuitously, transactions using the international financial system "typically leave a trail of detailed information. . . . Opening an account or initiating a funds transfer requires a name, an address, a phone number" that is collected and stored by a financial institution.[72] Treasury used such information to identify and target key actors and their networks.[73]

Intelligence about specific financial transactions enabled Treasury to present its financial lawfare as "specifically targeted against those individuals or entities engaging in illicit conduct."[74] In other words, Treasury could assert that the Iranian individuals or entities with whom commerce was being targeted were not targeted simply because they were Iranian but because they had engaged in specific proliferation, terrorism support, deceptive financial, or other illicit activity.

Once sanctions were in place against a particular Iranian entity or individual, efforts by that entity or individual to use deception in an effort to evade the sanctions (for example, by fraudulently hiding their engagement in a transaction) could become another reason to sanction that entity or individual. In that case, the illicit "behavior of the actors themselves as they try to access the international financial system" provided a rationale for their isolation.[75]

Deception by the targeted nation's entities and individuals is one of several factors that can result in a chilling effect on transactions beyond what is explicitly prohibited by US law. Although Treasury presented its financial lawfare as targeted against only Iranian bad actors, and US law required foreign financial institutions to halt their transactions only with those bad actors, some foreign financial institutions ultimately halted all business with Iran. In June 2007, within two years of the lawfare campaign's launch, Treasury Secretary Paulson announced that "most of the world's top financial institutions have now

[70] *Id.*
[71] *Id.*
[72] *Id.*
[73] *Id.*
[74] *Id.*
[75] Zarate, *supra* note 29, at 9–10.

dramatically reduced their Iranian business or stopped it altogether."[76] In doing so, Paulson noted that "for the most part, they are not legally required to take these steps but have decided, as a matter of prudence and integrity, that they do not want to be the bankers for such a regime."[77]

It is unclear to what extent the initial goal of US financial lawfare against Iran was in fact to halt Iran's general commercial connectivity with the rest of the world while purporting to be targeting only bad actors. However, this appears to have become the goal by the fall of 2009, after the failure of President Obama's initial outreach to Iran. As Juan Zarate described in his book, *Treasury's War: The Unleashing of a New Era of Financial Lawfare*, a meeting hosted by President Obama in the White House in the fall of 2009 involved then Under Secretary Levey laying out a plan to "cripple Iran's ability to engage in international commerce."[78] The plan, implemented over the next year, constituted "a financial pressure campaign premised on attacking the enablers of Iran's connectivity to the rest of the world."[79]

In addition to the risk of unwitting engagement in a transaction with a bad actor, the sheer complexity of Treasury's financial sanctions, combined with the aggressiveness with which they were enforced, also had a chilling effect on transactions beyond the scope of what was explicitly prohibited. A detailed examination of financial sanctions by *Newsweek* reported that "a number of lawyers and executives from big banks and multinationals privately told Newsweek that their confusion over how to apply the sanctions is only exceeded by their fear of violating them."[80] *Newsweek* asserted that "Treasury does not provide exact guidance on how to apply sanctions to third parties and leaves much up to the guesswork of banks while also 'reserving the right to fine the banks if they happen to guess wrong.'"[81]

In an article published in October 2012, Sean Thornton, who had served from 2005 to early 2012 as chief counsel for Treasury's Office of Foreign Assets Control (OFAC), acknowledged widespread "confusion about what US secondary sanctions actually target," resulting in part from the existence of "so many different legal authorities, which overlap and occasionally contradict themselves."[82] In the article, Thornton discussed one of the key terms in US sanctions laws,

[76] "Remarks by Treasury Secretary Paulson," *supra* note 53.

[77] *Id.*

[78] Zarate, *supra* note 29, at 329.

[79] *Id.*

[80] Leah McGrath Goodman & Lynnley Browning, *Sanctions Land Like a Bomb in Corporate Suites*, Newsweek, May 2, 2014, https://www.newsweek.com/sanctions-land-bomb-corporate-suites-248608.

[81] *Id.*

[82] Sean M. Thornton, *Iran, Non-US Banks and Secondary Sanctions: Understanding the Trends*, Skadden.com, Oct. 24, 2012, https://www.skadden.com/insights/iran-non-us-banks-and-secondary-sanctions-understanding-trends.

"control," and noted that "control is not defined, and US authorities seem likely to keep the concept vague."[83] "Because these lines seem almost purposefully confusing," said Thornton, "many non-US financial institutions . . . steer well clear of the line."[84]

Whether or not Treasury intentionally left their sanctions more confusing than necessary,[85] they were exceptionally complex, leading to the already mentioned chilling effect on transactions beyond the scope of what was explicitly prohibited. Such a chilling effect is heightened when the fines imposed for violations are of the magnitude of the fines, in the hundreds of millions and even billions of dollars, that are described later in this chapter.

IV. Impact of US Financial Lawfare against Iran

As a result of these innovations, Treasury's financial lawfare differed not only in design but also, ultimately, in result from traditional economic sanctions, which have the reputation of being ineffective in pressuring rogue actors, disproportionately harmful to innocent persons, and riddled with unaddressed cheating by private businesses that evade sanctions while their governments turn a blind eye.[86] In sharp contrast with the reputation of traditional economic sanctions, many key foreign banks, in an abundance of caution, reportedly eventually went even beyond the letter of the law in implementing financial measures against Iranian individuals and entities.[87]

In part because so many banks were so responsive, the financial lawfare had an impact on the Iranian economy that was both significant and relatively quick in getting started. The retreat of major global banks from the Iranian market soon disrupted key Iranian trading relationships, including in its vital energy sector.[88]

[83] *Id.*

[84] *Id.*

[85] This author has no knowledge that Treasury intentionally leaves their sanctions more confusing than necessary in order to increase their chilling effect. However, he has firsthand knowledge of other agencies having done so with regard to other sanctions.

[86] "Remarks by Treasury Secretary Paulson," *supra* note 53.

[87] *See, e.g.*, Maria Tadeo, *Paying the Price for Sanctions: The Customers with Iranian Links Being Ditched by British Banks*, THE INDEPENDENT, Aug. 19, 2014, https://www.independent.co.uk/news/business/analysis-and-features/paying-the-price-for-sanctions-the-customers-with-iranian-links-being-ditched-by-british-banks-9679692.html; Steve Slater & Michelle Price, *Bruised and Grumbling, Foreign Banks Bend to US Rules*, CHICAGO TRIBUNE, July 13, 2014, http://articles.chicagotribune.com/2014 07 13/business/sns-rt-us-banks-sanctions-20140713 1 u-s-sanctions-foreign-banks-british-bankers.

[88] *See, e.g.*, *Bank Jitters Hit Iran Fuel Imports*, PETROLEUM ECONOMIST, Feb. 2008, at 28 (concluding that, due to US-led sanctions, "Iran is starting to feel the effect of international sanctions on its domestic energy sector"); Paul Sampson, *Iran: Products in Flux*, ENERGY COMPASS, Feb. 8, 2008, at 1 (stating that due to the "US-led squeeze on Iran" many financial institutions have ceased to provide credit to Iranian companies); Mark Trevelyan, *More Companies Suspend Business with Iran*,

As a result of the financial lawfare, by January 2008, it had reportedly become almost impossible in Europe to arrange for transactions involving Iranian companies using a letter of credit, the standard payment guarantee used in international trade.[89]

By October 2008, the *New York Times* was reporting that "ordinary businesses" had been "hard hit" by Treasury's "financial squeeze on Iran," with both "big companies and small *bazaaris*—as traditional merchants are called in Iran . . . increasingly forced to pay for imports in advance, in cash."[90]

The financial measures also affected Iran's ability to finance petroleum development projects, with Iran's oil minister admitting in March 2007 that "overseas banks and financiers have decreased their cooperation" on such projects.[91] Within just two years, US financial lawfare reportedly increased the cost of imports to Iran by some 20 to 30 percent.[92]

In November 2008, sixty leading Iranian economists called in an open letter for the regime to drastically change course, saying that Iran's " 'tension-creating' foreign policy has 'scared off foreign investment and inflicted heavy damage' on the economy."[93] The economists said that the US measures had cost Iran "many billions of dollars" by forcing a "large part" of its imports and exports to be "carried out through middlemen."[94]

It seems evident that by 2008, US financial lawfare was already costing the Iranian regime funds that might otherwise have gone toward furthering its nuclear ambitions or supporting terrorism. This constraining effect was significant.[95] However, it took several more years before the financial lawfare—sustained over several years and combined with US energy sector lawfare—contributed to

Int'l Herald Tribune, Jan.17, 2008, at 15 (discussing the effects of sanctions on "Iran's oil-based economy").

[89] Trevelyan, *supra* note 88, at 15 (quoting a senior German banking and finance consultant as stating that "[i]t is today impossible more or less in Europe, with a couple of exceptions, to get a letter of credit" for trade with Iran); *No Letters of Credit, No Steel for Iranian Importers, Say Traders*, Metal Bulletin Weekly, Sept. 13, 2010, https://www.metalbulletin.co.uk/Article/2675316/No-letters-of-credit-no-steel-for-Iranian-importers-say-traders.html.

[90] Robin Wright, *Stuart Levey's War*, N.Y. Times, Oct. 31, 2008, https://www.nytimes.com/2008/11/02/magazine/02IRAN-t.html?pagewanted=all.

[91] Robin Wright, *Iran Feels Pinch as Major Banks Curtail Business: US Campaign Urges Firms to Cut Ties*, Wash. Post, Mar. 26, 2007, at A10, (quoting Iranian Oil Minister Kazem Vaziri Hamaneh).

[92] *See* David Blair, *Banks Recruited to Wage Financial War on Teheran*, Daily Telegraph, Sept. 18, 2007, at 17 ("One Teheran newspaper recently reported that Iranian companies had seen their import costs rise by 20 or 30 per cent because they had to employ middlemen to evade financial restrictions.").

[93] Borzou Daragahi, *Economists in Iran Criticize Ahmadinejad*, L.A. Times, Nov. 10, 2008, at A3.

[94] "Sixty Iranian Economists Write Open Letter to President," *BBC*, November 14, 2008, at 3.

[95] "Remarks of Under Secretary for Terrorism and Financial Intelligence David Cohen Before the Center for a New American Security on 'Confronting New Threats in Terrorist Financing'" (Press Release, US Dep't of the Treasury, March 4, 2014), https://www.treasury.gov/press-center/press-releases/Pages/jl2308.aspx.

a coercive effect on Iranian decision-making, and then only with regard to Iran's nuclear program.

In November 2011, Iran's President Mahmoud Ahmadinejad, who had previously been dismissive of the sanctions, admitted: "Our banks cannot make international transactions anymore."[96] By 2012 and 2013, the financial lawfare had "cut off Iran's access to most of its hard currency held outside the country,"[97] with estimates that as much as $80 billion out of Iran's total $100 billion in hard currency reserves could not be repatriated due to compliance with US measures by foreign financial institutions.[98]

The contemporaneous implementation of US, UN, and EU financial and nonfinancial measures during the period from 2010 to early 2013 makes it difficult to attribute a specific outcome to a particular measure, unless, as with the transactions hindrances and asset repatriation difficulties, a particular measure is the major one that would be likely to have had that outcome.[99] In addition to financial lawfare, energy lawfare also clearly contributed to a 60 percent reduction in Iranian crude oil sales from 2011 to 2013; the combination reduced Iran's revenue from crude oil sales from $100 billion in 2011 to about $35 billion in 2013.[100] Iran's revenue from crude oil sales fell even further after the worldwide price of crude oil started to slump in June 2014 after remaining stable for nearly five years.[101]

By July 2012, the combination of financial and economic lawfare had reduced Iran's total foreign currency reserves by as much as $110 billion,[102] and the value of Iran's currency, the rial, had dropped by 80 percent.[103] In 2013, Iran's gross domestic product dropped about 5 percent (its first drop in two decades).[104] Under Secretary of the Treasury David Cohen testified before the Senate in January 2015 that Iran's economy was at that point 15 to 20 percent "smaller than it would have been had sanctions not been imposed."[105]

Particularly hard hit was Iran's manufacturing sector, which relied heavily on foreign parts.[106] Many Iranian manufacturers were unable to obtain credit and

[96] Indira A.R. Lakshmanan, *Iran Is Seen Suffering Crippling Effect of Sanctions on Oil Trade, Banking*, Bloomberg News, Feb. 29, 2012, https://www.bloomberg.com/news/2012-02-29/iran-is-seen-suffering-crippling-effect-of-sanctions-on-oil-trade-banking.html.

[97] Kenneth Katzman, "RS20871, Iran Sanctions," Congressional Research Service, Oct. 23, 2014, https://www.hsdl.org/?view&did=759207> (quoted language is in summary page).

[98] *Id.* 53.

[99] "US and International Sanctions have Adversely Affected the Iranian Economy" (GAO-13-326, Accountability Office, 2013), http://gao.gov/assets/660/652314.pdf.

[100] Katzman, *supra* note 16.

[101] *Why the Oil Price Is Falling*, The Economist, Dec. 8, 2014, https://www.economist.com/blogs/economist-explains/2014/12/economist-explains-4.

[102] Zarate, *supra* note 29, at 340.

[103] *Id.* 340.

[104] Katzman, *supra* note 16.

[105] *Id.*

[106] *Id.* 52.

had to pay in advance, often through complex and costly mechanisms, to obtain parts from abroad.[107] Iran's production of cars fell by about 40 percent from 2011 to 2013.[108]

In the June 2013 Iranian presidential election, Hassan Rouhani ran on a platform of ending Iran's international isolation and easing sanctions.[109] Economic pressure was widely regarded as the major reason Iran, in the wake of Rouhani's election, came to the negotiating table in 2013 and 2014 to discuss and, at least for an interim period, limit its nuclear program.[110] In April 2015, CIA Director John Brennan stated in public remarks that Iran's Supreme Leader, Ayatollah Khamenei, had become more flexible in negotiations with the West because Rouhani had persuaded Khamenei that "six years of sanctions had really hit," and Iran's economy was "destined to go down" unless a deal was reached with the West and sanctions were lifted.[111]

On July 14, 2015, the P-5 + 1 announced that they had agreed with Iran on the JCPOA to address Iran's nuclear program.[112] The JCPOA provided for the lifting of most nuclear-related sanctions on Iran in exchange for various constraints on Iran's nuclear program. In his July 14, 2015, and August 5, 2015, statements praising the JCPOA, President Obama attributed the Iranian concessions to "the sanctions that have proven so effective,"[113] that "were put in place precisely to get Iran to agree to constraints on its program."[114]

Many commentators, and many members of Congress from both parties, criticized the JCPOA's curtailments of Iran's nuclear program for being insufficiently long-term and verifiable.[115] Some commentators suggested that the deal could have been more favorable to the United States if the economic pressure had been

[107] *Id.*

[108] *Id.* 51.

[109] *Id.* 48.

[110] *See, e.g.*, Katzman, *supra* note 16.

[111] David E. Sanger, *CIA Director Says Iran's Economic Peril Helped Drive Nuclear Deal*, N.Y. Times, Apr. 8, 2015, http://mobile.nytimes.com/2015/04/09/world/middleeast/cia-director-says-irans-economic-peril-helped-drive-nuclear-deal.html?_r=0&referrer=.

[112] Joint Comprehensive Plan of Action, July 14, 2015, http://eeas.europa.eu/statements-eeas/docs/iran_agreement/iran_joint-comprehensive-plan-of-action_en.pdf.

[113] "Statement by the President on Iran," The White House, July 14, 2015, https://www.whitehouse.gov/the-press-office/2015/07/14/statement-president-iran.

[114] President Barack Obama, "Remarks by the President on the Iran Nuclear Deal," The White House, Aug. 5, 2015, https://www.whitehouse.gov/the-press-office/2015/08/05/remarks-president-iran-nuclear-deal.

[115] *See, e.g.*, United States Senator Charles E. Schumer, "My Position on the Iran Deal" (Press Release, Aug. 6, 2015), https://www.schumer.senate.gov/newsroom/press-releases/my-position-on-the-iran-deal (Schumer was at the time the third ranking Democrat in the Senate); Congressman Eliot L. Engel, "Engel Statement on Iran Deal" (Press Release, Aug. 6, 2015), http://engel.house.gov/latest-news1/engel-statement-on-iran-deal (Engel was at the time the ranking Democrat on the House Committee on Foreign Affairs); Lauren Fox, *Sen. Bob Corker Rails Against the Iran Deal*, National Journal, July 23, 2015, https://www.nationaljournal.com/congress/sen-bob-corker-rails-against-the-iran-deal-20150723 (Corker, a Republican, was at the time the chairman of the Senate Foreign Relations Committee).

stronger. For example, in announcing in early August 2015 that he would "vote to disapprove the agreement," Senator Charles Schumer (D-NY) said that it would be "better to keep US sanctions in place, strengthen them, enforce secondary sanctions on other nations, and pursue the hard-trodden path of diplomacy once more, difficult as it may be."[116] Other commentators suggested that the US negotiating position could also have been strengthened if economic pressure had been supplemented with a more credible threat to halt Iran's nuclear weapons program by force of arms if all other options failed.[117]

Although they were divided on the sufficiency of the JCPOA, most, if not all, key supporters and opponents of the JCPOA seemed to agree that the US economic lawfare campaign had proven a valuable weapon against Iran's nuclear weapons program. They all seemed to credit the economic lawfare campaign with achieving significant (albeit to some, insufficient) curtailment of an Iranian nuclear program that otherwise might only have been curtailed by kinetic means.

V. Implementation of US Financial Lawfare against Iran

The US government implemented its financial lawfare campaign against Iran through the following three interrelated initiatives: (1) imposition by the United States of unilateral financial restrictions targeting Iran's nuclear and terrorism sponsorship activities; (2) promoting financial measures against Iran by key international organizations and foreign governments; and (3) direct outreach to key foreign financial institutions.

A. US Imposition of Unilateral Financial Restrictions Targeting Iran's Nuclear and Terrorism Sponsorship Activities

1. US Executive Orders and Designations

US financial lawfare against Iran relied heavily on two executive orders: Executive Order 13224 and Executive Order 13382. The key statutory authority for both executive orders was the International Emergency Economic Powers Act (IEEPA), a little-known statute that provides the president with extraordinarily powerful

[116] Schumer, *supra* note 115.

[117] *See, e.g.*, William B. Caldwell IV & Charles Wald, *Remind Iran of US Military Option*, NEWSDAY, July 11, 2015 (Caldwell and Ward were both retired generals in the US armed forces); "Expert Opinions on the Extension of Negotiations," Harvard Belfer Center, July 22, 2014, http://iranmatters.belfercenter.org/blog/expert-opinions-extension-negotiations (mini essay by Orde Kittrie); David Albright et al., "US Nonproliferation Strategy for the Changing Middle East," 58–62 (2013), http://isis-online.org/uploads/isis-reports/documents/FinalReport.pdf.

authority "to deal with any unusual and extraordinary threat, which has its source in whole or substantial part outside the United States, to the national security, foreign policy, or economy of the United States, if the President declares a national emergency with respect to such threat."[118]

Once the president has declared such a national emergency, he has the authority, pursuant to IEEPA, to prohibit the following with respect to "any person, or with respect to any property, subject to the jurisdiction of the United States": "transfers of credit or payments between, by, through, or to any banking institution, to the extent that such transfers or payments involve any interest of any foreign country or a national thereof."[119] Once such a national emergency has been declared, the president may also, pursuant to IEEPA, block, "nullify, void, prevent or prohibit, any acquisition, holding, withholding, use, transfer, withdrawal, transportation, importation or exportation of, or dealing in, or exercising any right, power, or privilege with respect to, or transactions involving, any property in which any foreign country or a national thereof has any interest by any person, or with respect to any property, subject to the jurisdiction of the United States."[120]

Executive Order 13224, issued pursuant to IEEPA by President Bush on September 23, 2001 (and still in effect as of February 2022), authorized the Treasury Department to designate, and block the assets of, foreign persons determined "to have committed, or to pose a significant risk of committing, acts of terrorism that threaten the security of US nationals or the national security, foreign policy, or economy of the United States."[121] In addition, the executive order authorized Treasury to block the assets of persons that provide support, services, or assistance to, or are "otherwise associated with" terrorists and terrorist organizations designated under the order.[122]

Blocking (sometimes also referred to as "freezing") assets is a principal tool deployed by Treasury in its financial lawfare against Iran and other targets. When an asset is blocked, the title to it remains with the targeted person or entity. However, the exercise of the powers and privileges normally associated with ownership, including transfers or transactions of any kind, is prohibited without authorization from Treasury's Office of Foreign Assets Control.[123]

The entities designated under Executive Order 13224 included, for example, Iran's state-owned Bank Saderat.[124] Bank Saderat was designated in October 2007

[118] International Emergency Economic Powers Act, 50 U.S.C. paras. 1701–1707 (2006).

[119] *Id.* sec. 1702(a)(1)(A)(ii).

[120] *Id.* sec. 1702(a)(1)(B).

[121] Exec. Order No. 13,224, 66 Fed. Reg. 49,079 (Sept. 23, 2001).

[122] *Id.* 49,080.

[123] US Gov't Accountability Office GAO-13-326, *supra* note 20.

[124] "Fact Sheet: Designation of Iranian Entities and Individuals for Proliferation Activities and Support for Terrorism," Press Release, US Dep't. of the Treasury, Oct. 25, 2007, https://www.treasury.gov/press-center/press-releases/Pages/hp644.aspx.

for being "used by the Government of Iran to channel funds to terrorist organizations, including Hizballah and EU-designated terrorist groups Hamas, PFLP-GC, and Palestinian Islamic Jihad."[125] In designating Bank Saderat, Treasury noted that "from 2001 to 2006, Bank Saderat transferred $50 million from the Central Bank of Iran through its subsidiary in London to its branch in Beirut for the benefit of Hizballah fronts in Lebanon that support acts of violence," that Hamas has "had substantial assets deposited in Bank Saderat," and that "in the past year, Bank Saderat has transferred several million dollars to Hamas."[126]

Executive Order 13382,[127] issued pursuant to IEEPA by President Bush in June 2005 (and still in effect as of February 2022), provided for blocking the assets of designated persons engaged in proliferation of weapons of mass destruction, as well as the support networks of such persons. Designations under Executive Order 13382 prohibited all transactions between the designees and any US person, and froze any assets the designees might have under US jurisdiction. The executive order delegated to the Treasury and State Departments the authority to designate WMD proliferators and their supporters, and they designated scores of Iran-related individuals and entities under this authority.

Iranian entities designated for their direct involvement in production of weapons of mass destruction and their delivery systems included the Atomic Energy Organization of Iran, Iran's Aerospace Industries Organization, Iran's Islamic Revolutionary Guard Corps (IRGC), and Iran's Ministry of Defense and Armed Forces Logistics.[128] The designation of the IRGC, which explicitly included a list of companies owned or controlled by the IRGC and its leaders, had a particularly strong impact on the Iranian economy because, as Treasury noted, the "IRGC has significant political and economic power in Iran, with ties to companies controlling billions of dollars in business and construction and a growing presence in Iran's financial and commercial sectors."[129] "The IRGC," Treasury noted, "is involved in a diverse array of activities, including petroleum production and major construction projects across the country."[130]

The designees under Executive Order 13382 also included some two dozen Iranian banks.[131] For example, Bank Melli, Iran's largest bank, was designated in October 2007 for providing a range of "banking services to entities involved in Iran's nuclear and ballistic missile programs, including entities listed by the UN

[125] *Id.*
[126] *Id.*
[127] Exec. Order No. 13,382, 70 Fed. Reg. 38,567 (July 1, 2005).
[128] "Fact Sheet" (Press Release, US Dep't of the Treasury), *supra* note 124.
[129] *Id.*
[130] *Id.*
[131] "Fact Sheet: Overview of Iranian-Linked Financial Institutions Designated by the United States," US Dep't of the Treasury, https://www.treasury.gov/press-center/press-releases/Documents/012312_Fact_Sheet_-_Designated_Iranian_Financial%20Institutions.pdf.

for their involvement in those programs."[132] Bank Melli "facilitated numerous purchases of sensitive materials for Iran's nuclear and missile programs."[133] In the process of "handling financial transactions on behalf of the IRGC, Bank Melli . . . employed deceptive banking practices," such as requesting that its name be removed from financial transactions, to hide its involvement from the international banking system.[134]

Several other executive orders played a narrower role in US financial lawfare against Iran. For example, Executive Order 13622, issued by President Obama on July 30, 2012 (and revoked in January 2016 in implementation of the JCPOA),[135] was designed to help constrict Iranian oil export revenues by deterring foreign financial institutions from conducting business with Iran's energy sector.[136] The executive order principally authorized sanctions against foreign banks found to have knowingly conducted or facilitated significant transactions for the purchase of petroleum from Iran.[137] The sanctions included being prohibited from opening or maintaining correspondent or payable-through accounts in the United States.[138]

As of January 2013, Treasury had—under the various Iran-related executive orders—designated more than 360 individuals and entities linked to Iran's WMD programs and support for terrorism.[139]

In addition to executive orders, and the designations pursuant to them, several other executive branch steps played key roles in the campaign of financial lawfare against Iran. For example, in November 2008, the United States revoked authorization for so-called "u-turn" transactions with Iran.[140] The "u-turn" authorization had allowed foreign transactions with Iran, which originated and terminated outside the United States, to transit the US financial system just long enough to be converted into dollars, and then be sent back out of the country.[141] Revocation of the authorization meant that foreign banks and institutions facilitating the financing for Iranian oil and other transactions were no longer permitted to "use their American correspondent relationships" to dollarize their transactions.[142]

[132] "Fact Sheet" (Press Release, US Dep't of the Treasury), *supra* note 124.
[133] *Id.*
[134] *Id.*
[135] Exec. Order No. 13,716 of January 16, 2016, 81 Fed. Reg. 3,693 (Jan. 21, 2016).
[136] Exec. Order No. 13,622 of July 30, 2012, 77 Fed. Reg. 45,897 (Aug. 2, 2012).
[137] *Id.*
[138] *Id.*
[139] US Gov't Accountability Office, GAO-13-326, *supra* note 20.
[140] Iranian Transactions Regulations, 73 Fed. Reg. 66541 (Nov. 10, 2008) (to be codified at 13 C.F.R. pt. 560), https://www.treasury.gov/resource-center/sanctions/Documents/fr73_66541.pdf.
[141] Zarate, *supra* note 29.
[142] *Id.*

Another key executive branch step in its campaign of financial lawfare against Iran was the November 2011 finding that the entire Islamic Republic of Iran was a jurisdiction of "primary money laundering concern" under Section 311 of the USA PATRIOT Act.[143] In issuing the finding, the US government stated that it was thereby identifying "the entire Iranian financial sector, including Iran's Central Bank . . . as posing illicit risks for the global financial system."[144] According to Juan Zarate, this step made it clear that the goal of Treasury's financial lawfare against Iran was "intended as a full financial strangulation."[145]

The US executive orders restricting foreign banks in the US financial system from engaging in particular transactions with Iran were supplemented with several statutory measures, which are described in the following subsection 2. Violations of these restrictions by various foreign banks were then aggressively enforced, as described later in section C.

2. Statutory Measures

Between 2010 and 2013, Congress passed, and the president signed, several new laws enhancing US financial lawfare against Iran. These laws typically reflected compromises between Congress and the administration. While key members of Congress tended to want "more pressure, faster" against Iran, the administration took a more gradualist approach, for fear of harming the overall international financial system or causing "allies in Europe and Asia to resist further cooperation because of perceived American threats or overreach."[146] The following are the key provisions of these laws.

a. Section 104 of the Comprehensive Iran Sanctions, Accountability, and Divestment Act

Section 104 of the Comprehensive Iran Sanctions, Accountability, and Divestment Act of 2010 (CISADA), signed into law in July 2010, required the Secretary of the Treasury to "prohibit, or impose strict conditions on, the opening or maintaining in the United States of a correspondent account or a payable-through account by a foreign financial institution" that knowingly engaged in activities including one or more of the following: facilitating the WMD program or terrorism support efforts of the Iranian government, or "facilitat[ing] a significant transaction or transactions or provid[ing] significant financial services for"

[143] "New Sanctions on Iran: Fact Sheet" (Press Release, US Dep't of State, Nov. 21, 2011), https://www.state.gov/r/pa/prs/ps/2011/11/177609.htm.

[144] *Id.*

[145] Zarate, *supra* note 29, at 333.

[146] *Id.* 336.

the IRCG or any of its agents or affiliates, or any financial institution designated pursuant to Executive Order 13224 or 13382.[147]

The reference to engagement with any financial institution designated pursuant to the two executive orders "gave the Secretary of the Treasury the authority for the first time to require US banks to terminate correspondent banking relationships with foreign banks that knowingly engaged in significant transactions with designated Iranian banks."[148] According to then Under Secretary of the Treasury David Cohen, this was a "particularly powerful provision."[149]

Foreign financial institutions that do not have their own operations in the United States typically access the US financial system by establishing correspondent accounts or payable-through accounts with US banks.[150] Such access to US-based banks is "critically important" to the ability of these foreign banks to offer dollar-denominated services to their clients.[151] "This is new in the sense that it puts at risk something that's very important to every financial institution, namely their access to the United States," said then Under Secretary of the Treasury Stuart Levey in discussing the provision shortly after its enactment.[152]

Cohen said that after the provision's enactment, he and his colleagues "fanned out around the globe to explain the new law, visiting or talking to government counterparts in over 50 countries and representatives from more than 150 foreign financial institutions."[153] The Treasury officials explained that "CISADA offered foreign banks a choice: they could do business with banks in the US, or they could do business with designated Iranian banks."[154] "But," emphasized Cohen, "they could not do both."[155]

While Section 104 was CISADA's most important provision from a financial perspective, the new law also contained several other key measures, particularly in relation to Iran's energy sector. Several of CISADA's key measures had an impact on Iran even while the legislation was making its way through Congress.

[147] Comprehensive Iran Sanctions, Accountability, and Divestment Act of 2010, para. 104, 22 U.S.C. sec. 8513 (2010), https://www.treasury.gov/resource-center/sanctions/Documents/hr2194.pdf.

[148] "Remarks of Under Secretary for Terrorism and Financial Intelligence David Cohen Before the New York University School of Law on 'The Law and Policy of Iran Sanctions'" (Press Release, US Dep't of the Treasury, Sept. 12, 2012), https://www.treasury.gov/press-center/press-releases/Pages/tg1706.aspx.

[149] *Id.*

[150] Kenneth Katzman, "Iran Sanctions" (Congressional Research Service, June 17, 2015), https://www.hsdl.org/?view&did=767891.

[151] "Remarks of David Cohen," (Press Release, US Dep't of the Treasury), *supra* note 148.

[152] Michael Rothfeld, *Barclays to Pay $298 Million for Evading US Economic Sanctions*, Wall St. J., Aug. 17, 2010, http://blogs.wsj.com/law/2010/08/17/barclays-to-pay-298-million-for-evading-us-economic-sanctions/.

[153] "Remarks of David Cohen" (Press Release, US Dep't of the Treasury), *supra* note 148.

[154] *Id.*

[155] *Id.*

Seeing the writing on the wall, some foreign banks and energy companies halted business with Iran as soon as they saw it would be proscribed, without waiting for CISADA to be passed and signed into law.[156]

b. Section 1245 of the Fiscal Year 2012 National Defense Authorization Act

Section 1245 of the fiscal year 2012 National Defense Authorization Act (NDAA), signed into law in December 2011, targeted the involvement of the Central Bank of Iran (CBI) in the international financial system. It did so by requiring the president to prevent a foreign financial institution from opening a correspondent or payable-through account in the United States, and to impose strict limitations on a foreign financial institution's existing such accounts, if that financial institution knowingly conducted or facilitated any significant transaction with the CBI or any other designated Iranian financial institution.[157]

Foreign financial institutions could be granted an exemption from these restrictions if the president determined that the parent country of the financial institution had "significantly reduced" its crude oil purchases from Iran during a specified period.[158] In other words, under this provision, "foreign banks involved in significant transactions with the CBI—including making payments for Iranian oil—can be cut off from the United States banking system unless their home jurisdiction has significantly reduced its oil imports from Iran."[159]

Section 1245 used financial lawfare to reduce Iran's oil exports by, to an extent, holding foreign banks hostage to the level of Iranian oil imports of their home jurisdictions.[160] Then Under Secretary Cohen explained that the provision "leverages foreign banks' desire to have access to the US financial system to drive down Iran's oil revenues."[161] Countries that import oil from Iran were provided a "powerful incentive" to reduce those imports, said Cohen, "namely, if they significantly reduce their Iranian oil imports, their banks will be protected, for a period of time, against the possibility of sanctions for transactions with the CBI."[162]

Following enactment of Section 1245, Cohen and his colleagues embarked on a campaign to explain the provision to foreign governments and businesses and "encourage importers of Iranian oil to protect their banks from sanctions by significantly reducing their imports."[163] According to Cohen, the response was "quite positive," with "every country that imported oil from Iran" taking "steps to

156 Zarate, *supra* note 29.

157 National Defense Authorization Act for Fiscal Year 2012, para. 1245, 22 USC, para. 8513a (2011), https://www.treasury.gov/resource-center/sanctions/Programs/Documents/ndaa_pub law.pdf.

158 *Id.*

159 "Remarks of David Cohen" (Press Release, US Dep't of the Treasury), *supra* note 148.

160 *Id.*

161 *Id.*

162 *Id.*

163 *Id.*

significantly reduce the volume of their Iranian oil imports—driving down Iran's oil revenues."[164]

In June 2015, the Congressional Research Service published a chart showing major reductions in various countries' crude oil imports from Iran between 2011 (at the end of which Section 1245 went into effect) and implementation in January 2014 of the Joint Plan of Action (JPA), an interim deal between Iran and the P-5 + 1 that laid the foundation for the more comprehensive JCPOA.[165] For example, prior to JPA implementation, China reduced its purchases from 550,000 to 410,000 barrels per day; Japan reduced its purchases from 325,000 to 190,000 barrels per day; and India reduced its purchases from 320,000 to 190,000 barrels per day.[166] Pursuant to the JPA, the president waived Section 1245 in January 2014, meaning that Iran's oil customers would not be required to further reduce oil purchases from Iran while the JPA remained in effect.[167]

c. Sections 302 and 504 of the Iran Threat Reduction and Syria Human Rights Act

Section 302 of the Iran Threat Reduction and Syria Human Rights Act of 2012, signed into law in August 2012, required imposition of at least five out of a menu of twelve listed sanctions on entities that knowingly materially assisted, or provided financing or other support for, the IRGC.[168] The sanctions menu included a prohibition on US government procurement from the entity, a prohibition on transactions in foreign exchange by the entity, exclusion from the United States of corporate officers, blocking of the sanctioned entity's US-based assets, and a prohibition on any credit or payments between the entity and any US financial institution.[169]

Section 504 of the Iran Threat Reduction and Syria Human Rights Act of 2012 amended Section 1245 of the fiscal year 2012 NDAA by requiring that any funds owed to Iran as a result of exempted transactions (e.g., purchases of Iranian oil) be credited to an account located in the country with primary jurisdiction over the foreign bank making the transaction.[170] This had the effect of preventing Iran from bringing earned hard currency back to Iran, leading it to instead either use the funds to buy products from the customer countries[171] or have the funds remain in those countries. According to then Under Secretary Cohen, "because almost all of the countries that purchase oil from Iran run a significant trade

[164] *Id.*
[165] Katzman, *supra* note 150.
[166] *Id.*
[167] *Id.* 20.
[168] Iran Threat Reduction and Syria Human Rights Act of 2012, para. 302, 22 USC, para. 8742 (2012), https://beta.congress.gov/112/plaws/publ158/PLAW-112publ158.pdf.
[169] Id.
[170] Id.
[171] Katzman, *supra* note 16.

deficit—that is, they import more from Iran than they sell to Iran—this provision should 'lock up' a significant portion of Iran's earnings in each of these countries."[172] Pursuant to the JPA, the president issued a waiver applicable to Section 504 in January 2014 "to allow Iran to receive some hard currency from ongoing oil sales" in installments while the JPA remained in effect.[173]

B. Promoting Financial Measures against Iran by Key International Organizations and Foreign Countries

Recognizing that economic restrictions, including those in the financial arena, are almost always more effective when they are multilateral, the US government's financial lawfare campaign against Iran placed considerable emphasis on, where possible, promoting financial measures against Iran by key international organizations and foreign countries. These efforts focused on: (1) including financial components in UN Security Council resolutions addressing Iran, (2) working through the Financial Action Task Force, and (3) direct outreach to key foreign governments.

1. Including Financial Components in Security Council Resolutions

Prior to the JCPOA, the four principal UN Security Council resolutions imposing sanctions on Iran were Resolution 1737 of December 23, 2006; Resolution 1747 of March 24, 2007; Resolution 1803 of March 3, 2008; and Resolution 1929 of June 9, 2010 (the Iran sanctions resolutions). On July 20, 2015, six days after the P-5 + 1 and Iran announced the JCPOA, the Security Council passed Resolution 2231.[174]

Resolution 2231 provided that the Iran sanctions resolutions were to be terminated upon receipt by the Security Council of a report from the IAEA confirming that Iran had taken various actions specified in the JCPOA.[175] On JCPOA "Implementation Day," January 16, 2016, the International Atomic Energy Agency verified that Iran had implemented key nuclear-related measures as described in the JCPOA.[176] As a result, the United States lifted various nuclear-related sanctions on Iran, as specified in the JCPOA.[177]

172 "Remarks of Under Secretary for Terrorism and Financial Intelligence David Cohen Before the New York University School of Law on 'The Law and Policy of Iran Sanctions'" (Press Release, US Dep't of the Treasury, Sept. 12, 2012), https://www.treasury.gov/press-center/press-releases/Pages/tg1706.aspx.

173 Katzman, *supra* note 16.

174 S.C. Res. 2231, U.N. Doc. S/RES/2231 (July 20, 2015).

175 *Id.* paras. 5, 7.

176 "Statement Relating to the Joint Comprehensive Plan of Action Implementation Day of January 16, 2016" (Statement, US Dep't of the Treasury, Jan. 16, 2016), https://www.treasury.gov/resource-center/sanctions/Programs/Pages/iran.aspx.

177 *Id.*

Resolution 2231 also included a procedure pursuant to which the Iran sanctions resolutions could be reimplemented if a JCPOA participant state were to notify the Council of "an issue that the JCPOA participant State believes constitutes significant non-performance of commitments under the JCPOA."[178] In September 2020, Secretary of State Mike Pompeo, based on steps taken in August 2020, asserted that the United States had utilized this procedure to re-instate the Iran sanctions resolutions.[179] However, the United Kingdom, France, and Germany, among others, opined that the US action was devoid of legal effect and the status of the sanctions was thus unchanged.[180]

Even if the Iran sanctions resolutions remain in abeyance, the various innovations contained in them will remain tested options for lawfare practitioners to draw from in a future campaign against another US adversary.

The Iran sanctions resolutions contained the following principal provisions related to financial measures:

a. legally binding requirements that member states freeze the assets of, and block commerce with their jurisdiction by, specified persons or entities associated with Iranian nuclear and missile programs, as well as persons or entities owned or controlled by them or acting on their behalf or at their direction;[181]
b. legally binding requirements that member states prohibit resource transfers and other financial activities relating to Iran's nuclear and missile programs;[182]
c. a legally binding requirement that all states require persons or firms subject to their jurisdiction "to exercise vigilance when doing business with entities incorporated in Iran or subject to Iran's jurisdiction" and any individuals or entities acting on their behalf or at their direction "if they have information that provides reasonable grounds to believe that such business could contribute to Iran's proliferation-sensitive nuclear activities or the development of nuclear weapon delivery systems";[183]
d. a nonbinding call upon member states to "exercise vigilance over the activities of financial institutions in their territories with all banks domiciled in Iran";[184]

[178] S.C. Res. 2231, para. 11, para. 12, U.N. Doc. S/RES/2231 (July 20, 2015).

[179] "Iran's Nuclear Program and UN. Sanctions Reimposition," Congressional Research Service Oct. 29, 2020, https://fas.org/sgp/crs/nuke/IF11583.pdf.

[180] "UN Ban on Iran Arms Transfers and Sanctions Snapback," Congressional Research Service, Oct. 16, 2020, https://fas.org/sgp/crs/mideast/IF11429.pdf.

[181] S.C. Res. 1737, para. 12, U.N. Doc. S/RES/1737 (Dec. 23, 2006).

[182] S.C. Res. 1737, para. 6, U.N. Doc. S/RES/1737 (Dec. 23, 2006).

[183] S.C. Res. 1929, para. 22, U.N. Doc. S/RES/1929 (June 9, 2010).

[184] S.C. Res. 1803, para. 10, U.N. Doc. S/RES/1803 (Mar. 3, 2008).

e. a nonbinding preambular reference to "the potential connection between Iran's revenues derived from its energy sector and the funding of Iran's proliferation-sensitive nuclear activities";[185] and
f. in Resolution 1929, nonbinding calls upon member states to prevent or prohibit various activities "if they have information that provides reasonable grounds to believe that such [activities] could contribute to Iran's proliferation-sensitive nuclear activities or the development of nuclear weapon delivery systems," including:
   - to prevent the provision of financial services or assets or other resources if they have such information;[186]
   - to prohibit in their territories the opening of "new offices of Iranian banks," or other activities by Iranian banks including "establishing or maintaining correspondent relationships," if they have such information;[187] and
   - to prohibit financial institutions within their jurisdiction from opening offices or subsidiaries or "banking accounts in Iran," if they have such information.[188]

Key Iranian entities specifically targeted by these resolutions included the Atomic Energy Organization of Iran, the Islamic Revolutionary Guard Corps, the Islamic Republic of Iran Shipping Lines, and three Iranian banks: Bank Sepah, Bank Melli, and First East Export Bank. Since each of these targets had previously been designated by the US government under Executive Order 13382, the Security Council resolution listings had the effect of multilateralizing aspects of Treasury's unilateral actions against Iran's proliferation infrastructure.

While the resolutions' legally binding requirements most directly contributed to this multilateralization, the nonbinding "calls-upon" and even preambular provisions also contributed, including by providing multilateral reinforcement of Treasury's warnings to foreign governments and banks. For example, the US Department of the Treasury deemed the "all-banks-domiciled-in-Iran" provision of Security Council Resolution 1803 to be of "critical importance" as it "significantly reinforces the concerns Treasury has expressed for many months."[189] The nonbinding "calls-upon" provisions also contributed by providing "hooks" for action by individual states, as described later in subsection 3.

[185] S.C. Res. 1929, Preamble, U.N. Doc. S/RES/1929 (June 9, 2010).
[186] S.C. Res. 1929, para. 21, U.N. Doc. S/RES/1929 (June 9, 2010).
[187] *Id.* para. 23.
[188] *Id.* para. 24.
[189] Glaser, *supra* note 48.

2. Working through the Financial Action Task Force

The Financial Action Task Force (FATF) is an intergovernmental body that as of summer 2015 had thirty-six members including the five permanent members of the UN Security Council, the European Commission, India, Japan, South Korea, and Turkey.[190] The FATF's stated objectives were "to set standards and promote effective implementation of legal, regulatory and operational measures for combating money laundering, terrorist financing and other related threats to the integrity of the international financial system."[191]

The FATF promulgated a series of "Recommendations," recognized as "the international standard for combating of money laundering and the financing of terrorism and proliferation of weapons of mass destruction."[192] The FATF's standards were endorsed by the World Bank, the International Monetary Fund, and the United Nations and recognized by more than 175 countries.[193]

While the FATF focused for many years on anti-money laundering and combating the financing of terrorism (which it sometimes referred to as AML/CFT), in February 2012, the FATF formally agreed that "the proliferation of weapons of mass destruction is a significant security concern, and financial measures can be an effective way to combat this threat," and adopted a new recommendation aimed at ensuring consistent and effective implementation of targeted financial sanctions related to proliferation when the UN Security Council calls for them.[194] The proliferation recommendation was adopted as part of the FATF's newly renamed International Standards on Combating Money Laundering and the Financing of Terrorism & Proliferation.[195]

In addition to setting standards for countering money laundering and terrorist and proliferation finance, the FATF also singles out jurisdictions with serious vulnerabilities in their relevant legal frameworks. In October 2007, the FATF issued a public statement expressing its concern that Iran's "lack of a comprehensive anti-money laundering/combating the financing of terrorism (AML/CFT) regime represents a significant vulnerability within the international financial system."[196] FATF noted that its "members are advising their financial institutions to take the risk arising from the deficiencies in Iran's AML/CFT regime into

[190] "FATF Members and Observers," Financial Action Task Force, May 10, 2015, https://www.fatf-gafi.org/pages/aboutus/membersandobservers/.

[191] "Who We Are," Financial Action Task Force, May 10, 2015, https://www.fatf-gafi.org/pages/aboutus/.

[192] *Id.*

[193] Glaser, *supra* note 48.

[194] "FATF Recommendations 2012—Press Handout," Financial Action Task Force, Feb. 16, 2012, https://www.fatf-gafi.org/media/fatf/documents/Press%20handout%20FATF%20Recommendations%202012.pdf.

[195] *Id.*

[196] "FATF Statement on Iran," Financial Action Task Force, Oct. 11, 2007, https://www.fatf-gafi.org/dataoecd/1/2/39481684.pdf.

account for enhanced due diligence."[197] Iran thereafter adopted an AML law.[198] However, the FATF concluded that Iran's AML/CFT regime remained deficient and issued statements of concern about Iran in both February 2008 and October 2008.[199]

The October 2008 FATF statement noted Iran's steps toward remedying its AML deficiencies and urged Iran to "address the remaining weaknesses."[200] In this October 2008 statement, the FATF expressed particular concern that Iran's "lack . . . of effort" to "address the risk of terrorist financing continues to pose a serious threat to the integrity of the international financial system" and declared that "urgent action to address this vulnerability is necessary."[201] The FATF called on its members, and urged all jurisdictions, to "strengthen preventive measures to protect their financial sectors from this risk."[202] In response to these warnings, the governments of several major economic powers warned their financial institutions that choosing to do business with Iran would entail significant risks.[203]

As of February 2015, the FATF remained dissatisfied with Iran's financial system and continued to warn its members about the risks posed by transactions with Iran. "The FATF remains particularly and exceptionally concerned about Iran's failure to address the risk of terrorist financing and the serious threat this poses to the integrity of the international financial system. . . . The FATF urges Iran to immediately and meaningfully address its AML/CTF deficiencies," said the FATF.[204] The FATF also said that it "reaffirms its call on members, and urges all jurisdictions, to advise their financial institutions to give special attention to business relationships and transactions with Iran, including Iranian companies and financial institutions."[205] The FATF also urged "all jurisdictions to apply effective counter-measures to protect their financial sectors from money laundering and financing of terrorism (ML/FT) risks emanating from Iran."[206]

In addition to its broader warnings about Iran's financial system, the FATF also played a significant role in promoting effective implementation by its members of the specific financial measures contained in the Security Council

197 *Id.*

198 Glaser, *supra* note 48.

199 "FATF Statement," Financial Action Task Force, Feb. 28, 2008, https://www.fatf-gafi.org/topics/high-riskandnon-cooperativejurisdictions/documents/fatfstatement-28february2008.html; "FATF Statement," Financial Action Task Force, Oct. 16, 2008, https://www.fatf-gafi.org/topics/high-riskandnon cooperativejurisdictions/documents/fatfstatement-16october2008.html.

200 "FATF Statement," Financial Action Task Force, *id.*

201 *Id.*

202 *Id.*

203 Glaser, *supra* note 48.

204 "FATF Public Statement," Financial Action Task Force, Feb. 27, 2015, https://www.fatf-gafi.org/documents/documents/public-statement-february-2015.html.

205 *Id.*

206 *Id.*

resolutions targeting Iran. For example, the FATF issued guidance in June 2007,[207] September 2007,[208] and October 2007[209] on implementation of these measures. This FATF work was recognized in Security Council Resolution 1803, which explicitly welcomed the guidance issued by FATF to assist states in implementing their Security Council obligations. Then, once the FATF formally adopted a proliferation finance recommendation, it issued a document containing guidance addressing all of the relevant financial provisions of Security Council resolutions countering the proliferation of weapons of mass destruction.[210] Such detailed guidance is particularly important in light of the typically brief and ambiguous phrasing of requirements as they are set forth in Security Council resolutions.

3. Direct Outreach to Key Foreign Governments

Treasury Department officials built upon the Security Council resolution financial provisions and the FATF guidance with intensive outreach to foreign governments. Such outreach was essential because many national governments have a poor record of implementing even the mandatory requirements of Security Council resolutions. The outreach was also vital because the resolutions, including especially Resolution 1929, additionally contained very significant nonbinding "calls-upon" recommendations that the US government hoped foreign governments would choose to implement.

In order to take financial measures against Iran of the type Treasury was requesting, many foreign governments needed or preferred, for domestic legal or political reasons, an international law requirement or at least a "hook."[211] A legally binding requirement contained in a treaty or UN Security Council resolution can, of course, serve as a basis for action; indeed, it obligates the government to take the specified action. However, in many countries, a "calls-upon" provision

[207] "Guidance Regarding the Implementation of Financial Provisions of United Nations Security Council Resolutions to Counter the Proliferation of Weapons of Mass Destruction," Financial Action Task Force, June 29, 2007, https://www.fatf-gafi.org/dataoecd/28/62/38902632.pdf. This June 2007 guidance addressed not only the financial measures contained in Resolutions 1737 and 1747 regarding Iran but also the financial measures contained in Resolutions 1695 and 1718 regarding North Korea's WMD and missile programs.

[208] "Annex: Financial Sanctions Against a Financial Institution Designated Under United Nations Security Council Resolutions Relating to Prevention of WMD Proliferation, Financial Action Task Force" (Sept. 5, 2007), https://www.fatf-gafi.org/dataoecd/23/16/39318680.pdf.

[209] "Guidance Regarding the Implementation of Activity-Based Financial Prohibitions of United Nations Security Council Resolution 1737, Financial Action Task Force" (Oct. 12, 2007), https://www.fatf-gafi.org/dataoecd/43/17/39494050.pdf.

[210] "FATF Guidance: The Implementation of Financial Provisions of United Nations Security Council Resolutions to Counter the Proliferation of Weapons of Mass Destruction," Financial Action Task Force, June 2013, https://www.fatf-gafi.org/media/fatf/documents/recommendations/Guidance-UNSCRS-Prolif-WMD.pdf.

[211] Zarate, *supra* note 29, at 330.

of a UN Security Council resolution can be a sufficient "hook" for action,[212] if the government chooses to use it.

The nonbinding "calls-upon" provisions in Security Council resolutions provided "hooks" for many UN member states to impose their own legally binding restrictions on transactions with Iran.[213] According to David Cohen, then Treasury's Under Secretary for Terrorism and Financial Intelligence, the "hooks" in Resolution 1929 were particularly useful to such governments because their evidentiary standard—"reasonable grounds to believe" that these activities "could contribute" to Iran's nuclear or missile programs—was relatively easy to meet, and Treasury "had a wealth of information" demonstrating how Iranian banks used deceptive practices to facilitate Iran's proliferation activities.[214] According to Cohen, these "hooks" in Resolution 1929 contributed in the summer and fall of 2010 to the European Union, the United Kingdom, Japan, South Korea, Canada, Australia, Norway, and Switzerland taking "robust action to restrict Iran's banking activities."[215]

In 2012, the European Union took further steps to restrict Iran's banking activities. These included financial sanctions against the Central Bank of Iran[216] and a prohibition restricting the provision of specialized financial messaging services to persons and entities designated by the United Nations or the European Union or otherwise associated with Iran's nuclear weapons and missile programs.[217]

C. Direct Outreach to Key Foreign Financial Institutions

1. Warning Meetings with Key Foreign Banks

From early in the financial lawfare initiative against Iran, senior Treasury Department officials engaged in an unprecedented campaign of outreach to the international financial private sector. Following Secretary Paulson's initiation of this outreach in the fall of 2006, Treasury met, over the next eighteen months,

[212] *See, e.g.*, Neil MacFarquhar, *UN Approves New Sanctions to Deter Iran*, N.Y. TIMES, June 9, 2010, https://www.nytimes.com/2010/06/10/world/middleeast/10sanctions.html?pagewanted=print; "Remarks of Under Secretary for Terrorism and Financial Intelligence David Cohen Before the New York University School of Law on 'The Law and Policy of Iran Sanctions'" (Press Release, US Dep't of the Treasury, Sept. 12, 2012), https://www.treasury.gov/press-center/press-releases/Pages/tg1706.aspx.

[213] *See, e.g.*, MacFarquhar, *supra* note 212; "Remarks of David Cohen" (Press Release, US Dep't of the Treasury), *supra* note _148.

[214] "Remarks of David Cohen" (Press Release, US Dep't of the Treasury), *supra* note 148.

[215] *Id.*

[216] Council Decision 2012/35/CFSP, 2012 O.J. (L 19) 22.

[217] Council Decision 2012/152/CFSP, 2012 O.J. (L77) 18.

"with more than 40 banks worldwide to discuss the threat Iran poses to the international financial system."[218]

According to then Secretary Paulson, within the first nine months of the campaign, "most of the world's top financial institutions" either committed to Treasury officials that they would halt or scale back their business with Iran, or simply did halt or scale back their transactions.[219] By fall 2008, Stuart Levey, the Under Secretary of the Treasury for Terrorism and Financial Intelligence, had made more than eighty foreign visits of his own to talk to more than sixty banks.[220] By then, more than eighty banks had curtailed their business with Iran.[221] While some committed to Treasury that they would do so, others simply curtailed their business. "We haven't had Chinese banks tell me that they won't do deals with Iran . . . they just stop," said Levey in October 2008.[222]

While some of the commitments could, of course, have been less than genuine, there is open-source evidence that many of the banks kept their word. One indication is the campaign's swift impact on Iran's trading relationships, which is described in section IV of this chapter.

Another window into banks' actual behavior during this time period is provided by the US government's forfeiture agreements, for illicit transactions with Iran, with several of the world's largest non-US banks. It is interesting to note that only two of these banks appear to have engaged in illicit transactions with Iran after 2008, and only one of those appears to have engaged in illicit transactions with Iran after 2009. Based on the agreements, several of the other banks appear to have stopped by 2008. For example, in June 2012, ING, a Dutch bank, agreed to forfeit $619 million to the United States and New York State for illicit transactions, on behalf of Iranian and other clients, that continued until 2007.[223] In December 2012, HSBC, a UK bank which was the largest in Europe,[224] forfeited $1.256 billion and agreed to pay an additional $665 million in penalties for various violations of sanctions laws,[225] including illicit transactions with Iran that lasted until the end of 2006.[226]

218 Glaser, *supra* note 48.

219 "Remarks by Treasury Secretary Paulson on Targeted Financial Measures to Protect Our National Security" (Press Release, US Dep't of the Treasury, June 14, 2007), https://www.treasury.gov/press-center/press-releases/Pages/hp457.aspx.

220 Wright, *supra* note 90.

221 *Id.*

222 *Id.*

223 "ING Bank N.V. Agrees to Forfeit $619 Million for Illegal Transactions with Cuban and Iranian Entities" (Press Release, US Dep't of Justice, June 12, 2012), https://www.justice.gov/opa/pr/2012/June/12-crm-742.html.

224 *HSBC to Pay $1.9bn in US Money Laundering Penalties*, BBC, Dec. 11, 2012, https://www.bbc.com/news/business-20673466.

225 "HSBC Holdings PLC and HSBC Bank USA N.A. Admit to Anti-Money Laundering and Sanctions Violations, Forfeit $1.256 Billion in Deferred Prosecution Agreement" (Press Release, US Dep't of Justice, Dec. 11, 2012), https://www.justice.gov/opa/pr/2012/December/12-crm-1478.html.

226 *Id.*

The one bank that continued to engage in illicit transactions with Iran after 2009 was BNP Paribas, which ultimately admitted that from 2004 to 2012, it "knowingly and willfully moved more than $8.8 billion through the US financial system on behalf of Sudanese, Iranian, and Cuban sanctioned entities," according to a Department of Justice press release.[227] At least in part because of the dates on which it was continuing to engage in illicit transactions, BNP Paribas's penalty was by far the largest of any of the banks—$8.9736 billion (including an $8.8336 billion forfeiture and a $140 million fine).[228] Thus, it appears that BNP Paribas was an outlier, and at least several of the world's largest non-US banks largely or entirely halted their illicit transactions with Iran in response to Treasury's outreach campaign between fall 2006 and the end of 2008.

The momentum of Treasury's campaign to persuade foreign banks to curtail their business with Iran slowed somewhat during 2009, while the newly inaugurated President Obama focused on diplomatic outreach to Iran.[229] However, during the subsequent three years, Treasury officials "conducted outreach to more than 145 foreign financial institutions in more than 60 countries,"[230] including many banks outside the ranks of the world's largest.

As described in detail in section IV of this chapter, Treasury's financial lawfare against Iran had an impact that was more powerful and quicker than that typically caused by traditional economic sanctions. The strength and speed of Treasury's financial lawfare stemmed largely from its direct outreach to foreign banks. Rather than relying, for example, on asking the Swiss government to halt Swiss banks from conducting proliferation- or terrorism-related business with Iran, Treasury officials went directly to the Swiss banks. Treasury officials found that their unprecedented direct outreach to a country's key private financial institutions could yield results much more quickly than could outreach to that same country's government.[231]

[227] "BNP Paribas Agrees to Plead Guilty and to Pay $8.9 Billion for Illegally Processing Financial Transactions for Countries Subject to US Economic Sanctions" (Press Release, US Dep't of Justice, June 30, 2014), https://www.justice.gov/opa/pr/2014/June/14-ag-686.html.

[228] "BNP Paribas Sentenced for Conspiring to Violate the International Emergency Economic Powers Act and the Trading with the Enemy Act" (Press Release, US Dep't of Justice, May 1, 2015), https://www.justice.gov/opa/pr/bnp-paribas-sentenced-conspiring-violate-international-emergency-economic-powers-act-and; "BNP Paribas Agrees to Plead Guilty" (Press Release, US Dep't of Justice), *supra* note 227.

[229] *See, e.g.*, Tony Karon, *Stalemate: How Obama's Iran Outreach Failed*, TIME, Dec. 22, 2009, http://content.time.com/time/world/article/0,8599,1949265,00.html; Zarate, *supra* note 29, at 322, 324 ("Levey was instructed to hold his powder dry while the administration attempted to reach out to the regime in Tehran. Meetings with bankers, designations of Iranian entities, and enlistment of partners to isolate Iranian financial activity stopped.").

[230] "GAO-13-326, US and International Sanctions Have Adversely Affected the Iranian Economy," US Gov't Accountability Office (2013), http://gao.gov/assets/660/652314.pdf.

[231] "Remarks by Treasury Secretary Paulson on Targeted Financial Measures to Protect Our National Security" (Press Release, US Dep't of the Treasury, June 14, 2007), https://www.treasury.gov/press-center/press-releases/Pages/hp457.aspx.

Once a foreign private bank decides to halt business with entities or individuals of concern, the bank's competitors have an increased risk of harming their reputations if they continue doing such business. After all, the last Swiss bank still transacting with designated Iranian banks will look shady to upstanding customers.

In addition, those banks that halted some or all business with Iran often preferred to see their competitors also lose out on that market, and certainly did not want to see their competitors pick up the Iranian business they lost. Thus, foreign banks that exited the Iranian market would often quietly cooperate with the United States in putting pressure on those who had not yet done so,[232] including by providing US officials with evidence of their competitors' continued transactions. In light of the quality of competitive intelligence banks are able to collect, this cooperation was often very valuable. As a result of the reputational and competitor cooperation factors, the exit of one bank from a country often soon led to the exit of others.[233]

Such private sector decisions could, in turn, make it more politically feasible for foreign governments to impose restrictions, because some or all of the major relevant companies in their jurisdiction had already forgone the business.[234] Treasury's financial measures were also seen as more palatable because, unlike sanctions of the past that targeted entire countries and were criticized as harming innocent people, Treasury's measures were perceived as more targeted.[235]

What specifically did Treasury officials say to the foreign banks to get them to curtail business with Iran? As Daniel Glaser, who served beginning in 2004 as Deputy Assistant Secretary and then Assistant Secretary of the Treasury for Terrorist Financing, described it, in their meetings with foreign bankers, Treasury officials largely "shared information about Iran's deceptive financial behavior and raised awareness about the high financial and reputational risk associated with doing business with Iran."[236] Treasury officials attributed the success of their outreach efforts to their emphasis on Iran being "demonstrably engaged" in illicit financial conduct and to the sensitivity of the international financial private sector to reputational and business risk.[237] In their outreach to both foreign governments and international private financial institutions, Treasury officials

232 *Id.*
233 *Id.*
234 Glaser, *supra* note 48.
235 Bay Fang, *Treasury Wields Financial Sanctions: US Strategy Straddles the Line Between Diplomacy, Military Might*, CHICAGO TRIBUNE, Apr. 23, 2007.
236 Glaser, *supra* note 48.
237 *Id.*

emphasized that the issue is not just "conduct that the US doesn't like politically, but conduct that's contrary to international law or international standards and norms."[238]

Treasury officials also raised the prospect that doing even prima facie licit business with Iran posed a significant risk of inadvertently doing business with proscribed Iranian entities. For example, Treasury Secretary Paulson cautioned business executives that in light of Iran's deceptive financial practices, including its use of front companies, and since "[t]he IRGC is so deeply entrenched in Iran's economy and commercial enterprises, it is increasingly likely that if you are doing business with Iran, you are somehow doing business with the IRGC."[239] Similarly, Under Secretary of the Treasury Stuart Levey said he told foreign firms that "if they're dealing with Iran it's nearly impossible to protect themselves from being entangled in that country's illicit conduct."[240]

For international private financial institutions, this was reputationally daunting given the IRGC's leading role in Iran's terrorism and proliferation activities.[241] It was also legally daunting for them in light of the Treasury Department's designation of the IRGC under Executive Order 13382 and the Security Council's requirement that member states freeze the assets of, and block commerce with their jurisdictions by, the IRGC and "any individuals or entities acting on their behalf or at their direction," as well as "entities owned or controlled by them."[242]

Such warnings had an impact. As Stuart Levey noted, "[f]inancial institutions want to identify and avoid dangerous or risky customers who could harm their reputations and business."[243] Accordingly, "[r]ather than comply with just the letter of the law, we have seen many in the banking industry voluntarily go beyond their legal requirements because they do not want to handle illicit business," said Daniel Glaser.[244]

[238] Fang, *supra* note _235_ (quoting Adam Szubin, director of Treasury's Office of Foreign Assets Control).

[239] "Remarks by Treasury Secretary Paulson on Targeted Financial Measures to Protect Our National Security" (Press Release, US Dep't of the Treasury, June 14, 2007), https://www.treasury.gov/press-center/press-releases/Pages/hp457.aspx.

[240] Michael Hirsh, *Obama Prepares to Get Tough on Iran*, NEWSWEEK, Dec. 11, 2009, https://www.newsweek.com/obama-prepares-get-tough-iran-75581.

[241] For example, Treasury Secretary Paulson accused the IRGC of being "directly involved in the planning and support of terrorist acts." "Remarks by Treasury Secretary Paulson," *supra* note 53.

[242] S.C. Res. 1929, para. 12, U.N. Doc. S/RES/1929 (June 9, 2010).

[243] "Minimizing Potential Threats from Iran: Assessing the Effectiveness of Current US Sanctions on Iran: Hearing Before the Senate Committee on Banking, Housing and Urban Affairs," 110th Congress (2007) (statement of Stuart Levey, Under Secretary for Terrorism and Financial Intelligence).

[244] Glaser, *supra* note 48

Consistent with Glaser's assessment, many banks around the world decided to screen their customers against Treasury's list of designees, even when they were not required to do so by the laws of the country in which the bank was domiciled.[245] Major US and foreign banks became so cognizant of the risks posed to them by the infiltration of illicit money that many of them hired large numbers of staff dedicated to protecting against such infiltration. For example, HSBC reportedly had 7,000 people, about 10 percent of its employees worldwide, working on risk and compliance issues at the end of 2014 (a fourfold increase from before its $1.9 billion settlement with Treasury in 2012 for illicit transactions with Iranian and other proscribed entities).[246] Citigroup, which had also been penalized for illicit transactions with Iran, had nearly 30,000 employees working on regulatory and compliance issues at the end of 2014, 13 percent of the bank's total 244,000 employees.[247] Meanwhile, J.P. Morgan Chase & Co. said that it would hire 13,000 new staff in compliance, audit, and other areas during 2014, after being the subject of fines for various non-Iran-related compliance problems. Treasury's designations helped advise such compliance officers as to "who they need to protect against."[248]

At least while they were in office, the Treasury officials leading the campaign tended to characterize their Iran-related financial outreach as educating rather than threatening banks. For example, in describing Treasury's outreach campaign, George W. Bush administration Treasury Secretary Paulson said: "We never threaten. . . . We talk about how important it is not to violate the rules and engage in illicit transactions."[249]

Despite Treasury officials' tendency to downplay it, foreign banks clearly curtailed Iran-related business in response to Treasury's outreach principally because those banks were concerned that continued transactions with Iran could result in US regulatory penalties, such as fines or even loss of access to the US market. According to Juan Zarate, bank executives often understood individualized briefings by Treasury officials to be "not-so-subtle threats of sanctions and enforcement to come" if they didn't halt business with the target country.[250]

The following subsection describes the major enforcement actions taken by Treasury and other US government agencies between 2004 and 2014 against

[245] "Remarks by Treasury Secretary Paulson," *supra* note 53.

[246] Sarah Butcher, *HSBC's Compliance Binge and How You Can Get a 6 Figure Compliance Job*, Financial Careers, Nov. 3, 2014, http://news.efinancialcareers.com/us-en/189083/hsbcs-compliance-binge-can-get-6-figure-compliance-job/.

[247] Sital S. Patel, *Citi Will Have Almost 30,000 Employees in Compliance by Year-End*, Marketwatch, July 14, 2014, http://blogs.marketwatch.com/thetell/2014/07/14/citi-will-have-almost-30000-employees-in-compliance-by-year-end/.

[248] "Remarks by Treasury Secretary Paulson," *supra* note 53.

[249] Wright, *supra* note 90.

[250] Zarate, *supra* note 29.

foreign banks that engaged in illicit transactions with Iran. The fines were remarkably large. In addition, the size of the US market and the primacy of the dollar and of US banks in the international financial system naturally made many banks leery of putting their access to the US banking system at risk for the sake of maintaining financial ties to terrorists, proliferators, or even benign actors in Iran.

2. Prosecuting Banks

At the height of its financial lawfare against Iran, the US government entered into massive forfeiture agreements, for illicit transactions with Iran, with several of the world's largest non-US banks. These included UBS ($100 million),[251] ABN Amro ($80 million),[252] Lloyds TSB ($350 million),[253] Credit Suisse ($536 million),[254] Barclays PLC ($298 million),[255] ING ($619 million to US and to New York),[256] Standard Chartered ($327 million),[257] HSBC ($1.9 billion),[258] and BNP Paribas ($8.9736 billion).[259] The fines and other punishments were typically (but not always) imposed as part of deferred prosecution agreements, described in this context as agreements pursuant to which "corporate defendants pay fines, don't dispute they've done wrong, and promise to reform—all with the threat looming of a potential future criminal indictment" if they don't follow through on their promise to reform.[260]

[251] John D. McKinnon & Marcus Walker, *Fed Fines UBS $100 Million for Money-Transfer Violations*, Wall St. J., May 11, 2004, http://online.wsj.com/news/articles/SB108419978061306718.

[252] Barnaby J. Feder, *ABN to Pay $80 Million for Violations*, N.Y. Times, Dec. 20, 2005, https://www.nytimes.com/2005/12/20/business/worldbusiness/20bank.html?_r=0.

[253] "Lloyds TSB Bank PLC Agrees to Forfeit $350 Million in Connection with Violations of the International Emergency Economic Powers Act" (Press Release, US Dep't of Justice, Jan. 9, 2009), https://www.justice.gov/opa/pr/2009/January/09-crm-023.html.

[254] "US Treasury Department Announces Joint $536 Million Settlement with Credit Suisse AG" (Press Release, US Dep't of the Treasury, December 16, 2009), https://www.treasury.gov/press-center/press-releases/Pages/tg452.aspx.

[255] "Barclays Bank PLC Agrees to Forfeit $298 Million in Connection with Violations of the International Emergency Economic Powers Act and the Trading with the Enemy Act Press Release," US Dep't of Justice, Aug. 18, 2010, https://www.justice.gov/opa/pr/2010/August/10-crm-933.html.

[256] "ING Bank NV Agrees to Forfeit $619 Million for Illegal Transactions with Cuban and Iranian Entities" (Press Release, US Dep't of Justice, June 12, 2012), https://www.justice.gov/opa/pr/2012/June/12-crm-742.html.

[257] "Standard Chartered Bank Agrees to Forfeit $227 Million for Illegal Transactions with Iran, Sudan, Libya, and Burma" (Press Release, US Dep't of Justice, Dec. 10, 2012), https://www.justice.gov/opa/pr/2012/December/12-crm-1467.html.

[258] "HSBC Holdings PLC and HSBC Bank USA N.A. Admit to Anti-Money Laundering and Sanctions Violations, Forfeit $1.256 Billion in Deferred Prosecution Agreement" (Press Release, US Dep't of Justice, Dec. 11, 2012), justice.gov/opa/pr/2012/December/12-crm-1478.html.

[259] "BNP Paribas Agrees to Plead Guilty and to Pay $8.9 Billion for Illegally Processing Financial Transactions for Countries Subject to US Economic Sanctions" (Press Release, US Dep't of Justice, June 30, 2014), https://www.justice.gov/opa/pr/2014/June/14-ag-686.html.

[260] Paul M. Barrett, *Can Banks Be Held Liable for Terrorism?*, Bloomberg Businessweek, Mar. 18, 2015, http://businessweekme.com/Bloomberg/newsmid/190/newsid/479#cnttop.

VI. Lessons Learned and the Future of US Financial Lawfare

A. Incomplete Success

US financial lawfare against Iran was clearly very successful in hindering Iranian financial transactions. The significant impact on Iranian transactions that was seen as early as 2007 and 2008 had reached a new, even higher level of impact by 2014. By 2014, major international banks were taking quick action in response to changes to Treasury's list of designated entities, and designated entities were finding it harder and harder to find any bank with which to do business. "The biggest, most sophisticated banks have it built into their filters and start screening out potential transactions within minutes," said then OFAC Director Adam Szubin in April 2014.[261] "Once you're on an OFAC list, no bank anywhere will deal with you," said Judith Lee, chair of the international trade group at the law firm of Gibson, Dunn and Crutcher.[262]

This impact on Iranian transactions in turn greatly weakened the Iranian economy. In August 5, 2015, Congressional testimony, Szubin, then serving as Acting Under Secretary of the Treasury for Terrorism and Financial Intelligence, detailed the effect on the Iranian economy of the US financial lawfare against Iran in the years preceding the July 14, 2015, JCPOA announcement.[263] "The powerful set of US and international sanctions on Iran . . . effectively isolated Iran from the world economy," said Szubin.[264]

Szubin provided several metrics of "the impact of the sanctions campaign."[265] He said that "today, the Iranian economy is estimated to be only 80 percent the size that it would have been . . . absent our sanctions."[266] In addition, "Iran has foregone approximately $160 billion in oil revenue alone since 2012, after our sanctions reduced Iran's oil exports by 60 percent."[267] Szubin added that the Iranian currency had also "declined by more than 50 percent."[268]

Assessing the extent to which US financial lawfare had succeeded by 2015 in achieving its ultimate objectives of halting Iran's nuclear weapons program and state sponsorship of terrorism was more complicated. With regard to the secondary objective, Iran's state sponsorship of terrorism, the bottom line was

[261] Goodman & Browning, *supra* note 6.

[262] *Id.*

[263] "Written Testimony of Adam J. Szubin, Acting Under Secretary of Treasury for Terrorism and Financial Intelligence, before the S. Comm. on Banking, Housing, and Urban Affairs" (Press Release, US Dep't of Treasury, Aug. 5, 2015), https://www.treasury.gov/press-center/press-releases/Pages/jl0144.aspx.

[264] *Id.*

[265] *Id.*

[266] *Id.*

[267] *Id.*

[268] *Id.*

that Iran's sponsorship continued unabated. For example, the State Department asserted in its report on state sponsorship of terrorism during 2012 that Iran's sponsorship of terrorism underwent "a marked resurgence" that year, reaching levels not seen in twenty years.[269] The State Department's reports on state sponsorship of terrorism during 2013 and 2014 asserted that "Iran continued its terrorist-related activity" during those years and provided extensive descriptions of such activity.[270] The report covering 2014 was released in June 2015. In a June 19, 2015, news article about the report's release, the *New York Times* stated: "Although the report covers 2014, American officials said the Iranian policies described in it had continued this year."[271]

The pre-JCPOA US financial lawfare clearly failed to coerce Iran into halting its state sponsorship of terrorism. In addition, while US financial lawfare had undoubtedly increased the cost to Iran of its sponsorship of terrorism, the constraining effect of the US campaign was apparently insufficient to cause Iran to reduce its support for its terrorist allies.

In contrast, US financial lawfare (combined with US energy and insurance lawfare) was generally credited with helping coerce Iran to negotiate more seriously about its nuclear weapons program. For example, as mentioned previously, in April 2015, CIA Director John Brennan stated that Iran's Supreme Leader, Ayatollah Khamenei, had become more flexible in negotiations with the West because Rouhani had persuaded Khamenei that "six years of sanctions had really hit," and Iran's economy was "destined to go down" unless a deal was reached with the West and sanctions were lifted.[272]

The negotiations culminated in the announcement, on July 14, 2015, that the P-5 + 1 and Iran had agreed on the JCPOA to address Iran's nuclear program.[273] As mentioned previously, the JCPOA provided for most nuclear-related sanctions on Iran to be lifted in exchange for various constraints on Iran's nuclear program.

In his August 5, 2015, Congressional testimony, Adam Szubin, then Acting Under Secretary of the Treasury for Terrorism and Financial Intelligence,

[269] Warren Strobel, *Iran's Sponsorship of Terrorism Sees "Marked Resurgence,"* REUTERS, May 30, 2013, https://www.reuters.com/article/2013/05/30/us-usa-terrorism-idUSBRE94T16Y20130530.

[270] "Chapter 3: State Sponsors of Terrorism Overview," Country Reports on Terrorism, US Dept. of State, 2013, https://www.state.gov/j/ct/rls/crt/2013/224826.htm; "Chapter 3: State Sponsors of Terrorism Overview," Country Reports on Terrorism, US Dept. of State, 2014, https://www.state.gov/j/ct/rls/crt/2014/239410.htm.

[271] Michael R. Gordon & Eric Schmitt, *Iran Still Aids Terrorism and Bolsters Syria's President, State Department Finds*" N.Y. TIMES, June 19, 2015, https://www.nytimes.com/2015/06/20/world/middleeast/state-department-terrorism-report-iran-syria.html.

[272] David E. Sanger, *CIA Director Says Iran's Economic Peril Helped Drive Nuclear Deal*, N.Y. TIMES, Apr. 8, 2015. http://mobile.nytimes.com/2015/04/09/world/middleeast/cia-director-says-irans-economic-peril-helped-drive-nuclear-deal.html?_r=0&referrer=.

[273] Joint Comprehensive Plan of Action (July 14, 2015), http://eeas.europa.eu/statements-eeas/docs/iran_agreement/iran_joint-comprehensive-plan-of-action_en.pdf.

attributed the newly agreed constraints on Iran's nuclear program to "the global sanctions coalition built and led by the United States that gave us the leverage necessary to secure unprecedented nuclear concessions from Iran."[274] "The point of these efforts was clear: to change Iran's nuclear behavior, while holding out the prospect of relief if Iran addressed the world's concerns about its nuclear program," said Szubin.[275] "This campaign yielded results," asserted Szubin, explaining that "after years of intransigence, Iran came to the table prepared to negotiate seriously over its nuclear program."[276]

Former Senator Joseph Lieberman, chair of United Against Nuclear Iran, a nongovernmental organization critical of the JCPOA for containing insufficient constraints on Iran's nuclear program,[277] put it very similarly. "It was only because of the sanctions adopted by Congress, and ultimately signed by President Obama," said Lieberman, "that sufficient economic pressure was put on the Iranian government that its leaders came to the negotiating table."[278]

In the wake of the announcement of the JCPOA, commentators and members of Congress were divided over whether the JCPOA's curtailments of Iran's nuclear program were sufficiently long-term and verifiable.[279] Some suggested that the deal could have been more favorable to the United States if the economic pressure had been stronger. For example, in announcing in August 2015 that he would "vote to disapprove the agreement," Senator Schumer said that it would be "better to keep US sanctions in place, strengthen them, enforce secondary sanctions on other nations, and pursue the hard-trodden path of diplomacy once more, difficult as it may be."[280] Other commentators suggested that the US negotiating position could also have been strengthened if economic pressure had

[274] "Written Testimony of Adam J. Szubin, Acting Under Secretary of Treasury for Terrorism and Financial Intelligence, before the S. Comm. on Banking, Housing, and Urban Affairs" (Press Release, US Dep't of Treasury, Aug. 5, 2015), https://www.treasury.gov/press-center/press-releases/Pages/jl0144.aspx.

[275] *Id.*

[276] *Id.*

[277] Julian Hattem, *Ex-Sen. Lieberman Takes Reins of Anti-Iran Deal Group*, THE HILL, Aug. 11, 2015, http://thehill.com/policy/national-security/250808-ex-sen-lieberman-takes-reins-on-anti-iran-deal-group.

[278] Joseph I. Lieberman, *Congress Should Step Up to Block the Terrible Iran Agreement*, WASH. POST, Aug. 14, 2015, https://www.washingtonpost.com/opinions/congress-should-step-up-to-block-the-terrible-iran-agreement/2015/08/14/57629e4c-41ce-11e5-8e7d-9c033e6745d8_story.html.

[279] *See, e.g.*, "My Position on the Iran Deal, United States Senator Charles E. Schumer" (Press Release, Aug. 6, 2015), https://www.schumer.senate.gov/newsroom/press-releases/my-position-on-the-iran-deal (Schumer was at the time the third ranking Democrat in the Senate); "Engel Statement on Iran Deal, Congressman Eliot L. Engel" (Press Release, Aug. 6, 2015), http://engel.house.gov/latest-news1/engel-statement-on-iran-deal1/ (Engel was at the time the ranking Democrat on the House Committee on Foreign Affairs); Lauren Fox, *Sen. Bob Corker Rails Against the Iran Deal*, NATIONAL JOURNAL, July 23, 2015, https://www.nationaljournal.com/congress/sen-bob-corker-rails-against-the-iran-deal-20150723 (Corker, a Republican, was at the time the chairman of the Senate Foreign Relations Committee).

[280] Schumer, *supra* note 115.

been supplemented with a more credible threat to halt Iran's nuclear weapons program by force of arms if all other options failed.[281]

Although they were divided on the sufficiency of the JCPOA, most, if not all, key supporters and opponents of the JCPOA seemed to agree that the US economic lawfare campaign had proven a valuable weapon against Iran's nuclear weapons program. They all seemed to credit the economic lawfare campaign with achieving significant (albeit to some, insufficient) curtailment of an Iranian nuclear program that otherwise might only have been curtailed by kinetic means.

B. Concerns about Collateral Damage

Aside from the question of whether and how US lawfare could generate sufficient leverage to achieve particular US objectives vis-à-vis Iran's nuclear weapons program, the deployment of US financial lawfare against Iran also raised concerns as to possible collateral damage. For example, the Iranian government and others blamed Western sanctions for making it difficult to import medicine and other humanitarian goods.[282]

However, the humanitarian impact of US economic lawfare against Iran appeared to be minimal, especially when compared with the reportedly grave humanitarian impact of the broader US sanctions on Iraq during the 1990s. This was due to the fact that US lawfare against Iran was specifically designed not to hinder Iranian acquisition of food and medicine, and was repeatedly adjusted to ensure that it did not have that effect.[283] Indeed, even US legal restrictions on exports from the United States to Iran (let alone US measures against third-country companies) excluded food, medicine, and medical devices,[284] and such exports from the United States to Iran remained substantial even at the height of US lawfare against Iran.[285]

Concerns were also raised as to the potential impact of US financial lawfare on the dollar's primacy in the international financial system. The dollar's primacy

[281] *See, e.g.*, Caldwell & Wald, *supra* note 117 (Caldwell and Ward were both retired generals in the US armed forces); "Expert Opinions on the Extension of Negotiations," Harvard Belfer Center, July 22, 2014, http://iranmatters.belfercenter.org/blog/expert-opinions-extension-negotiations (mini essay by Orde Kittrie); Albright et al., *supra* note 117, at 58–62.

[282] *See, e.g.*, Golnaz Esfandiari, Iranian Media Say Sanctions Taking Toll on Seriously Ill Patients, Radio Free Europe/Radio Liberty, Oct. 15, 2012, https://www.rferl.org/content/iran-media-say-sanctions-taking-toll-seriously-ill-patients/24740542.html.

[283] *See, e.g.*, Benoit Faucon, *EU Firms Join Debate over US Sanctions on Iran*, Wall St. J., Aug. 15, 2012, https://www.wsj.com/articles/SB10000872396390444233104577591311307733418.

[284] The Trade Sanctions Reform and Export Enforcement Act of 2000, Title IX of Pub. L. 106-387 (Oct. 28, 2000).

[285] *See, e.g.*, Arshad Mohammed, *US Exports to Iran Rise Nearly One-Third Despite Sanctions*, Reuters, Oct. 15, 2012, https://www.reuters.com/article/2012/10/15/us-iran-usa-exports-idUSBRE89E04L20121015. This issue is addressed in more detail in Albright et al., *supra* note 117, at 43–44.

in the international financial system has long served various US interests. For example, it allows the United States to borrow and spend more than it might otherwise. In addition, US financial lawfare depends largely on the dollar's primacy in the international financial system. As Treasury Secretary Paulson stated: "Treasury can effectively use these tools largely because the US is the key hub of the global financial system."[286]

Should the dollar's primacy wane, either because financial lawfare deters dollar usage or because the US economy declines in relative influence, the United States' ability to wage financial lawfare will likely wane along with it. US rivals, including China and Russia, have, for a variety of reasons, periodically tried to bypass the US dollar.[287] This is a significant concern for the United States, which should give strong consideration as to how to design future financial lawfare so as to minimize its risk to the dollar's primacy. One way of minimizing the risk to the dollar's primacy is, to the extent possible, to implement financial lawfare jointly with the issuers of key alternative currencies. One of the numerous benefits of partnering with the European Union on many of the financial measures against Iran was that waging financial lawfare against Iran with the dollar, euro, and pound sterling left the dollar less exposed.

C. The Challenges of Unwinding Financial Lawfare

The US financial lawfare campaign against Iran demonstrates the challenge of unwinding financial lawfare if the objective is met (or a decision is otherwise made by the US federal government to curtail the lawfare, for example, as part of a deal with the adversary that addresses some but not all of the objectives). The potential challenges of unwinding US and allied economic lawfare against Iran were the subject of considerable discussion as the nuclear negotiations proceeded.[288] One set of challenges had to do with the complex and intertwined provisions, and varying suspension and termination criteria, of the relevant US laws. For example, some provisions could be waived, but not terminated, by the administration without new congressional legislation.[289] This reduced the

[286] "Remarks by Treasury Secretary Paulson on Targeted Financial Measures to Protect Our National Security" (Press Release, US Dep't of the Treasury, June 14, 2007), https://www.treasury.gov/press-center/press-releases/Pages/hp457.aspx.

[287] Michael Pizzi, *Russia, China Sign Deal to Bypass US Dollar*, Al Jazeera America, May 20, 2014), http://america.aljazeera.com/articles/2014/5/20/russia-china-bankdeal.html.

[288] *See, e.g.*, "Spider Web: The Making and Unmaking of Iran Sanctions," International Crisis Group, Feb. 25, 2013, https://www.crisisgroup.org/~/media/Files/Middle%20East%20North%20Africa/Iran%20Gulf/Iran/138-spider-web-the-making-and-unmaking-of-iran-sanctions.pdf.

[289] *See, e.g.*, "Kenneth Katzman, Easing US Sanctions on Iran," Atlantic Council, June 2014, https://www.atlanticcouncil.org/images/publications/Easing_US_Sanctions_on_Iran.pdf.

magnitude of the incentives that US executive branch negotiators could guarantee Iran in exchange for Iranian nuclear concessions.

Another challenge posed by curtailing financial lawfare against Iran in implementation of the JCPOA was the risk that curtailing financial measures against Iran solely in exchange for nuclear concessions by Iran could undermine the credibility of the stated reason for Iran's financial isolation—to protect the international financial system against Iran's illicit financial activities. Such harm to the credibility of financial measures could undercut their future use against both other adversaries and Iran (for example, in response to Iranian noncompliance with the JCPOA or continued Iranian sponsorship of terrorism).

Juan Zarate and others raised such concerns in response to the planned lifting of financial and other economic measures in exchange for Iran's nuclear concessions in the JCPOA (which included no financial integrity concessions by Iran).[290] For example, in congressional testimony on July 30, 2015, Zarate said that "the JCPOA sanctions unwinding framework does damage to the conduct-based sanctions and measures that have been so effective and driven most of the listings and designations by the United States and the international community."[291] Zarate provided as an example the JCPOA "allowing most of the Iranian banks back into the international financial order without dealing with their underlying conduct or controls."[292]

Another set of challenges posed by curtailing financial lawfare against Iran in implementation of the JCPOA had to do both with financial lawfare's dependence on market sentiment and also its variety of practitioners. Much as extra-legal factors, including reputational risk, contributed to some banks voluntarily forgoing licit business with Iran at the height of US financial lawfare against Tehran, there was no guarantee that all banks would choose to re-enter the Iranian market once US federal legal restrictions were withdrawn. In addition, as demonstrated by the separate punishments of some banks by the New York State Department of Financial Services and planned lawsuits against some such banks by private sector litigators on behalf of terrorism victims, the US federal government did not even necessarily control all of the relevant US legal levers over financial transactions with Iran. Both the dependence on market sentiment and the variety of practitioners posed the potential risk that Iran might not receive some of the economic relief it was expecting even if it complied with its

[290] *See, e.g.*, Jonathan Schanzer & Mark Dubowitz, *It Just Got Easier for Iran to Fund Terrorism*, FOREIGN POLICY, July 17, 2015, http://foreignpolicy.com/2015/07/17/it just got easier-for-iran-to-fund-terrorism-swift-bank/.

[291] "Sanctions and the JCPOA: Hearing Before the S. Comm. on Foreign Relations," 12 (July 30, 2015) (statement of Juan Zarate), https://www.foreign.senate.gov/imo/media/doc/07-30-15%20ZarateTestimony.pdf.

[292] *Id.* 14.

commitments under the JCPOA and the US federal government wanted it to receive that relief.

This is one way in which ending financial lawfare can be more complicated than ending kinetic lawfare. In this era of modern telecommunications, when a president orders troops to stop bombing an adversary and orders US diplomats to return to the adversary's capital, the bombing stops and the diplomats return. In contrast, when a president orders the executive branch to stop waging financial lawfare against an adversary, state officials and private sector litigators may find ways of continuing the war, and private sector banks may for that or their own reasons not choose to resume business with the adversary.

D. US Financial Lawfare's Role in US Strategy Going Forward

The impact of the US government's pre-JCPOA financial lawfare on Iran—which cost the Iranian regime tens of billions of dollars without causing disproportionate humanitarian damage—calls into question the accuracy of the dominant paradigm in the scholarly literature regarding sanctions, which derides unilateral sanctions as inevitably ineffective in a globalized economy. To the extent US economic lawfare failed to achieve its ultimate objectives with regard to Iran's nuclear weapons program and state sponsorship of terrorism, the result might well have been different if the lawfare had been more vigorous and combined with a more credible threat to halt Iran's nuclear weapons program by force of arms if all other options failed.[293] The considerable economic impact of the US government's financial lawfare against Iran, in addition to the considerable impacts of several of the other lawfare deployments described in this book, provide support for the proposition that lawfare, deployed systematically and effectively, may be able to save US and foreign lives by supplementing or replacing kinetic warfare as a tool for achieving some significant US military objectives.

The relative success of US government financial lawfare against Iran soon inspired imitation. As mentioned earlier, the United States applied a similar approach with regard to Iran's energy trade and insurance sector. The United States also drew from the Iran model in waging vigorous financial lawfare against Russia[294] and the Islamic State.[295]

Treasury seems certain to continue to wage financial lawfare against US adversaries. It will do so not only against new targets but also in new ways. Treasury

[293] Albright et al., *supra* note 117, at 58–62.
[294] Goodman & Browning, *supra* note 6.
[295] Julie Hirschfeld Davis, *Enforcer at Treasury Is First Line of Attack Against ISIS*, N.Y. Times, Oct. 21, 2014, https://www.nytimes.com/2014/10/22/business/international/enforcer-at-treasury-is-first-line-of-attack-against-isis.html?_r=0.

officials' experience and creativity, new evasive maneuvers by US adversaries, the differing economies of US adversaries, and changes in the financial markets and regulatory regimes will lead Treasury to enhance and refine the financial lawfare tools described in this chapter.

Meanwhile, the innovative components of Treasury's financial lawfare against Iran seem highly likely to continue to influence the design of US economic lawfare against other targets. These innovations include the previously referenced direct outreach to individual foreign private companies, aggressive use of US regulatory authorities to pursue traditionally military objectives, and effective development and harnessing of intelligence about global private sector business transactions.

Globalization has inevitably increased the business interests in the United States of many leading foreign companies, leaving them subject to US government regulation and leverage and reliant on the goodwill of the US government and consumers. As a result, major foreign companies in sectors beyond finance, energy, and insurance may also be susceptible to US government economic lawfare. Foreign companies in exceptionally globalized, strategic, regulated, and information-rich sectors such as mobile telecommunications, the internet, aviation, and shipping could be next in line.

Before the US government expands its economic lawfare into additional sectors, it will want to analyze and weigh both the risk posed by such US lawfare to US economic and regulatory preeminence in those sectors and the risk that such lawfare might set problematic precedents that could be used against the US by current or future adversaries. However, given US economic lawfare's proven efficacy (against target economies if not target policies), the lack in many situations of usable kinetic or other alternative weapons, and policymakers' tendency to discount future risks, the expansion of US government economic lawfare into additional sectors seems highly likely. Overall, the addition of economic lawfare to the US government's arsenal is a welcome development. As this chapter has demonstrated, lawfare waged by the US government has tremendous potential for achieving US objectives with less loss of life and at reduced expenditure of taxpayer dollars.

10
Human Rights Law as an Alternative to *Jus in Bello*

Christopher J. Fuller

> No nation could preserve its freedom in the midst of continual warfare.
>
> James Madison
>
> *Our systematic effort to dismantle terrorist organizations must continue. But this war, like all wars, must end. That's what history advises. That's what our democracy demands.*
>
> Barack Obama

The United Kingdom has long clung to the notion that it has a "special relationship" with the United States—that the two nations are closer in global vision and action than any other. While it is arguable that this is more rhetorical than functional in most spheres, and is deeply asymmetric in terms of power, when it comes to post-9/11 counterterrorism the two nations do indeed remain very close allies—at least when it comes to foreign policy. Following the attacks upon the American homeland, British elites, expertly flattered and manipulated by platitudes of the nation's historical place alongside the United States, standing ovations in Congress, and sharing a similar overconfidence in the power of military force and nation building to enable successful regime change, made the error of supporting the United States' poorly executed mission in Afghanistan and ill thought out invasion of Iraq. As the calamitous fallout of both wars have proven, being the closest ally should not translate into following a partner wherever they lead, especially when that partner's leadership is as self-destructive and counterproductive as the wars which formed the core of the United States post-9/11 counterterrorism approach.

Fortunately for the United Kingdom, on the domestic front its counterterrorism diverted from that of its close ally, with the British government purposefully rejecting the United States' militaristic response of launching a preemptive global killing campaign via drone strikes as a way of securing the homeland. Instead, the British government adopted an approach more akin to that of the

Christopher J. Fuller, *Human Rights Law as an Alternative to* Jus in Bello In: *Between Crime and War*. Edited by: Claire Finkelstein, Christopher Fuller, Jens David Ohlin, Mitt Regan, Oxford University Press. © Claire Finkelstein, Christopher Fuller, Jens David Ohlin, Mitt Regan 2023. DOI: 10.1093/oso/9780197638798.003.0011

famous World War II poster which urged citizens to "Keep calm and carry on" in the face of the pending Nazi threat, as the country retained a crime paradigm, treating terrorists as criminals, and the protection of the nation as a matter of law enforcement, not warfare. Since 2015 however, the seductive nature of remote killing has gradually seen America's style of drone warfare creep into British counterterrorism policy. The "special relationship" has always ensured the roots of this policy shift have been present. The United States supplies the United Kingdom with cutting-edge armed drone technology courtesy of an exclusive Defense Security Cooperation agreement. The Royal Air Force's (RAF) pilots train alongside their terrorist-hunting American counterparts of 432d Wing. And the intelligence which drives the strikes is the product of one of the closest collaborations in modern history. But despite the shared capabilities, British policymakers did not use these weapons in a similar manner to that employed by their American counterparts until the rise of the Islamic State of Iraq and Syria (ISIS) and the persistent threat which followed, first from attacks coordinated from the group's safe haven across Iraq and Syria, and then from the phenomenon of its dispersed foreign fighters following the collapse of the group's territorial holdings. The 2015 Defense Review, a precedent-setting strike in the same year, increasingly aggressive ministerial intentions in 2017, and new defense spending plans in 2020 have all reflected the gradual adoption and normalization of lethal drone strikes as a tool of British counterterrorism. This aping of questionable US methods has been a much slower corruption than Britain's disastrous support of America's post-9/11 wars, but is a shift which, if continued, will likely have equally significant and problematic consequences for both the country and its long-term counterterrorism objectives.

Addressing the United Kingdom's troubling slide to adoption of targeted killing by drone, this chapter begins by examining the domestic costs of America's application of a war paradigm in its counterterrorism efforts, comparing it unfavorably over the past two decades to the United Kingdom's less disruptive retention of a crime paradigm. It then demonstrates the ways in which the British government has gradually begun to adopt aspects of America's approach, including a reliance upon the laws of war to justify lethal action against terrorist targets abroad. Finally, the chapter challenges this shift toward the use of a war paradigm to defend the UK homeland by urging that Britain retain its recognition of terrorists as criminals not combatants, instead utilizing human rights law, in particular Article 6 of the International Covenant on Civil and Political Rights (ICCPR) and Article 2 of the European Convention on Human Rights (ECHR), to provide an adequate and less domestically fractious model for the application of lethal force when absolutely necessary against terrorists plotting imminent attacks from foreign safe havens.

I. "Our War on Terror Begins with Al-Qaeda, but It Does Not End There"

Establishing the correct paradigm through which a nation will confront terrorism—as a criminal enterprise or an act of war—is vital in ensuring the state has access to the necessary tools, resources, and legislation to protect itself, while safeguarding against the overextension of its authority, which may imperil the human rights integral to healthy democracies and undermine international legal norms. Despite the importance of making this distinction, there is no formal checklist within international law by which to determine the approach that ought to be applied. This situation has been further complicated by the extent to which increasingly well resourced, organized, and violent jihadist groups have blurred the lines between a war in a traditional sense, and criminal acts of terrorism.

In declaring a global War on Terror, President George W. Bush gained access to unprecedented powers and military tools to assault Al Qaeda and their affiliates. By transforming Islamic extremist terrorists from criminals to enemies, the United States ensured that the laws of war, not domestic laws and their entangling constitutional rights, or international laws with their associated human rights protections, would apply to America's counterterrorism actions abroad. In theory, this empowered the executive, enabling the commander in chief to unleash the US military, while the associated rhetoric expressed resolve and rallied the nation behind the cause. In reality, the adoption of the war paradigm has constrained the government, setting unrealistic and unachievable goals, and locking presidents into the need to secure "wins" against the perennial notion of "terror." While traditional measures of warfare have been applied to the struggle with Islamic extremism, with tactical engagements, kills, and the control of territory being used as determinants of success, the past two decades have confirmed that killing terrorists does not get rid of terrorism.

The global commitment to eliminate Islamic extremism has its roots in a post–Cold War misconception. First presented by Under Secretary of Defense Paul Wolfowitz, and his deputy Irv Lewis Libby in the 1992 Defense Planning Guidance proposal, then later enshrined in the Bush administration's National Security Strategy of 2002, the idea stemmed from an overconfidence in how changes in the nature of war had granted the United States unmatched military superiority. In theory, this preeminence, if assertively applied, could be used to overcome any foe and reshape the international order in America's favor. Thoroughly tested in Afghanistan, Iraq, and over twenty years of combat against non-state terrorist groups, this supposition has been proven utterly false. The United States has spent over $6 trillion waging its War on Terror; it is engaged in counterterrorism activities in eighty countries, and over 335,000 civilians have died because of the fighting associated with the conflict.[1] Yet the enemy has persevered. Even with the advances in the tools at America's disposal; mass electronic surveillance; drones and precision-guided munitions, and a dramatically expanded and battle-hardened special forces capability, the asymmetric nature of the conflict with non-state terrorist groups has enabled them to survive in the face of America's overwhelming martial superiority. "The use of the term 'war,'" RAND's Brian Jenkins reflects, "created unrealistic expectations," with the American public seeing warfare as a "finite undertaking," whereas counterterrorism campaigns are typically better characterized as decades-long struggles.[2] While the American public have become frustrated and disillusioned over the protracted conflict—a fact borne out by a range of opinion polling, alongside the popularity of Donald Trump's 2016 campaign promises to scale back conflicts and bring troops home—the United States' enemies have relished engaging in a battle they seek to drag out indefinitely.[3] Individuals who embrace the jihadist ideologies promoted by groups such as Al Qaeda and ISIS see themselves as contributing to a struggle which has played out for centuries, and will continue until Judgment Day. Furthermore, bleeding out the American economy has been a core jihadist strategy since Al Qaeda first declared its jihad, and little depletes a nation's treasure faster than war.[4] Thus, rather than a conclusive military victory, a familiar pattern has emerged where in one theater after another, fighting erupts, ebbs, flows, and eventually settles into an ambiguous status quo with no clear conclusion. Rather than demonstrating that America can shape the world with its unmatched military power, the lesson of waging a war against terror has been that defeating an abstraction is inherently unachievable.

It is easy to understand the temptation of seeing non-state terror groups such as Al Qaeda and ISIS as dependent upon a hierarchal command-and-control structure—it provides something which can be tracked, targeted, and eliminated.

[1] "Costs of War," Watson Institute, Brown University, https://watson.brown.edu/costsofwar/.

[2] Brian Jenkins, "Fifteen Years On, Where Are We in the War on Terror?," RAND, Sept. 7, 2016, <https://www.rand.org/blog/2016/09/fifteen-years-on-where-are-we-in-the-war-on-terror.html>.

[3] Ruth Igielnik & Kim Parker, "Majority of US Veterans, Public Say the Wars in Iraq and Afghanistan Were Not Worth Fighting," Pew, July 10, 2019, <https://www.pewresearch.org/fact-tank/2019/07/10/majorities-of-u-s-veterans-public-say-the-wars-in-iraq-and-afghanistan-were-not-worth-fighting/>; John Mueller & Mark G. Stewart, *Trends in Public Opinion on Terrorism*, POLITICAL SCIENCE May 14, 2020, <https://politicalscience.osu.edu/faculty/jmueller/terrorpolls.pdf>; Douglas Kriner & Francis Shen, "Battlefield Casualties and Ballot Box Defeat: Did the Bush-Obama Wars Cost Clinton the White House," Social Science Research Network, June 19, 2017, <https://papers.ssrn.com/sol3/papers.cfm?abstract_id=2989040>; Dan Lamothe, How Swing-State Military Veterans Played a Key Role in Donald Trump Winning the White House, WASH. POST, Nov. 10, 2016, <https://www.washingtonpost.com/news/checkpoint/wp/2016/11/10/how-swing-state-veterans-played-a-key-role-in-donald-trump-winning-the-white-house/>; Nicholas Confessore, *Veterans, Feeling Abandonment, Stand by Donald Trump*, N.Y. TIMES, Nov. 2, 2016, <https://www.nytimes.com/2016/11/03/us/politics/donald-trump-veterans.html>.

[4] Al-Qurashi Abu-Ubayd, *A Lesson in War*, AL-ANSAR, Dec. 19, 2002, quoted in MICHAEL SCHEUER, IMPERIAL HUBRIS: WHY THE WEST IS LOSING THE WAR ON TERROR 101 (2007).

Indeed, following its formation in 1988, Al Qaeda had a physical infrastructure, constituting brigades of fighters, arms dumps, and training camps dotted across Afghanistan. There was also a clear command structure, with Osama bin Laden and Ayman al-Zawahiri personally involved in the running of the organization. But following the overthrow of their Taliban hosts in late 2001, this formal structure was swiftly dismantled, with the group evolving into a dispersed franchise operation, exploiting ungoverned territories around the globe.[5] Although a decade of drone warfare succeeded in containing and withering Al Qaeda's remaining core leadership in the tribal regions of Pakistan, the franchise has proven remarkably survivable precisely because it does not rely upon centralized command. Similarly, ISIS has already devolved from a hierarchal local government back to the covert terrorist group it started as once before, and has shown itself capable of doing so again following the sustained US-led campaign against it, keeping its ideological base alive, even as its territorial holdings were stripped away.[6] The names Al Qaeda and Islamic State are rallying calls, representing a core set of extremist Islamic beliefs, centered on the desire to undertake a defensive jihad to drive the "crusader-Zionist alliance" out of the "lands of Islam," replacing political institutions and heretical man-made laws with the literal implementation of sharia law. Thus, unlike traditional wars, in the modern conflict against terrorists, nothing really ends. "It's about ideology," notes terrorism expert John Mueller, "You can't extinguish it."[7]

Despite compelling evidence that the war paradigm was adopted through misplaced hubris, it has remained central to American counterterrorism policy. The Obama administration rejected the rhetorical aspects of the War on Terror, reduced the conflict's conventional footprint, and sought to place United States' counterterrorism policies more in line, although not wholly within, the limits of international law.[8] However, the maintenance of the state of emergency enacted following 9/11 and the decision to retain of the Laws of War as the legal yardstick against which the conduct of America's global campaign would be measured revealed the continuation of the warfare ethos which had underscored the predecessor's counterterrorism approach.[9] And despite Trump's 2016 campaign

[5] Patrick Cockburn, The Rise of Islamic State: ISIS and the New Sunni Revolution 52–55 (2015).

[6] "Letter from the Chair of the Security Council Committee pursuant to resolutions 1267 (1999) 1989 (2011) and 2253 (2015) concerning Islamic State in Iraq and the Levant (Da'esh), Al-Qaida and associated individuals, groups, undertakings and entities addressed to the President of the Security Council" (United Nations Security Council, Jan. 20 2020), <https://undocs.org/S/2020/53>.

[7] John Mueller & Mark Stewart, Chasing Ghosts: The Policing of Terrorism (2016).

[8] Michelle Bentley, *Ending the Unendable: The Rhetorical Legacy of the War on Terror*, *in* The Obama Doctrine: A Legacy of Continuity in US Foreign Policy? 57–69, 57 (Michelle Bentley & Jack Holland eds., 2017); Colin Dueck, The Obama Doctrine: American Grand Strategy Today 131–32 (2015).

[9] Michelle Bentley, *Continuity We Can Believe In: Escaping the War on Terror*, *in* Obama's Foreign Policy: Ending the War on Terror (Michelle Bentley & Jack Holland eds., 2014)

rhetoric referring to a drawdown of US foreign interventions, withdrawals from some areas of conflict have been countered with escalations in other regions.[10] Resultantly, US forces have become more or less permanently engaged in ongoing hostilities, as the global commitment to fight and defeat Islamic extremists has turned the world into a battlefield. As if on autopilot, the Pentagon retained its commitments in Afghanistan and Iraq even after the United States had officially withdrawn, while accruing new obligations from Yemen to Somalia, Libya to Syria. Policymakers have seemed oblivious to the lack of progress toward anything resembling a victory, or the possibility that in some parts of the world, US forces may no longer be needed for the protection of American interests, whereas in others, their presence for counterterrorism purposes may in fact be detrimental to America's global standing and long-term interests.[11]

II. "No Nation Can Preserve Its Freedom in the Midst of Continual Warfare"

"No nation can preserve its freedom in the midst of continual warfare," warned James Madison. True to his admonition, the maintenance of a war footing has had a detrimental effect upon the United States, leading to the erosion of important norms and values, and the fraying of the very social fabric of the country. The first consequence of willfully engaging in an unwinnable conflict has been the gradual attrition of the public's faith in the ability of the government to keep them safe. Following the 1995 Oklahoma City bombing, which killed 168 people, pollsters asked a sample of Americans if they were worried that they or a member of their family would become victims of terrorism. In the immediate aftermath, 42 percent responded that they were indeed concerned. Over the next five years however, despite several international terrorist attacks, including Al Qaeda's 1998 bombing of two US embassies in Africa and a suicide attack upon the USS *Cole* in Yemen's port of Aden, the American public's fear of terrorism dissipated, with just 24 percent professing to being concerned by mid-2001. In the wake of 9/11, fear of terrorism among American's understandably increased: the combined scale, spectacle, and domestic nature of the attack causing 58 percent of those polled to acknowledge their concerns that they or a family member could become a future victim of terrorism. Over the subsequent month as the anticipated

91–107, 91; "Continuation of the National Emergency with Respect to Certain Terrorist Attacks," White House, Aug. 30, 2016, <https://www.whitehouse.gov/the-press-office/2016/08/30/notice-continuation-national-emergency-respect-certain-terrorist-attacks> accessed September 10 2016.

10 Peter Neumann, Bluster: Donald Trump's War on Terror 108–12 (2019).

11 Andrew J. Bacevich, *Ending Endless War*, Foreign Aff. 34 (Sept.–Oct. 2016).

follow-up attacks failed to materialize—or in the case of Richard Reid's attempted bombing of American Airlines Flight 63, were thwarted—anxiety levels once more began to dissipate. But as George W. Bush committed the United States to a conflict which would "not end until every terrorist group of global reach has been found, stopped and defeated," the return to normalcy was halted. As America's state of emergency was extended indefinitely, so too was the public's fear of terrorism, which has remained elevated ever since. Bearing little reality to the relative safety of the American homeland from acts of terror, polling over the past two decades has consistently revealed that approximately three quarters of all Americans questioned continue to rate terrorism as the primary threat facing the United States, with almost half of those citizens believing that they or a close family member are at risk of becoming victims of terrorism.[12]

Not only have a large section of the American public maintained an unduly elevated fear of terrorism but further polling has revealed that fear to be predominantly of some form of large-casualty event in the vein of 9/11. The years since September 11, 2001, have revealed that Al Qaeda's largest assault was, as Mueller puts it, "an aberration, and not a harbinger."[13] Countered by a combination of enhanced homeland security and the disruption of Al Qaeda's networks abroad, subsequent terror attacks killed 221 US citizens worldwide in the fifteen years since September 2001—a figure the White House put into some context by comparing it to the 406,496 Americans who had died in domestic gun violence between 2001 and 2013.[14] Despite this, the percentage of American's fearful of a large-casualty terrorist attack occurring in the near future has remained as high as 70 to 80 percent. This figure did briefly drop to 65 percent following the killing of bin Laden, but when that event failed to signal the end of the War on Terror, anxiety quickly rose again, actually exceeding immediate post-9/11 levels after ISIS's attack upon Paris in 2015.[15] The dissonance between the public's fear and actual threat posed is extremely problematic and reveals a symptom of the United States being involved in an open-ended, unwinnable war. As long as the

[12] Alvin Chang, *Amercans' Sustained Fear From 9/11 Has Turned into Something More Dangerous*, Vox, Sept. 11, 2017, <https://www.vox.com/2016/9/9/12852226/fear-witches-terrorists>; Jacob Poushter & Moira Fagan, "Americans See Spread of Diseases as Top International Threat, Along with Terrorism, Nuclear Weapons, Cyberattacks," Pew, Apr. 13, 2020, <https://www.pewresearch.org/global/2020/04/13/americans-see-spread-of-disease-as-top-international-threat-along-with-terrorism-nuclear-weapons-cyberattacks/>.

[13] John Mueller, *Harbinger or Aberration: A 9/11 Provocation*, National Interest, Fall 2002, <http://nationalinterest.org/article/harbinger-or-aberration-a-911-provocation-521>.

[14] "American Deaths in Terrorist Attacks," START Global Terrorism Database, <https://www.start.umd.edu/pubs/START_AmericanTerrorismDeaths_FactSheet_Oct2015.pdf>; "Number of Deaths Caused by Terrorism vs. Gun Violence," Centres for Disease Control and Prevention, US State Department, in *CNN*, Dec. 30, 2015, http://edition.cnn.com/2015/10/02/us/oregon-shooting-terrorism-gun-violence/>.

[15] Alvin Chang, *Amercans' Sustained Fear From 9/11 Has Turned into Something More Dangerous*, Vox, Sept. 11, 2017, <https://www.vox.com/2016/9/9/12852226/fear-witches-terrorists>

government maintains the war footing and state of emergency, a significant portion of the American public will retain their belief that they are engaged in an existential conflict with enemies who seek the destruction of the United States—enemies seemingly powerful and numerous enough that the armed forces of the world's leading military power have been unable to defeat them in twenty years of warfare.

Since the attacks of September 11, the United States has made significant advances in securing both the homeland and American interests abroad. Yet the domestic public's sustained fear of terrorism has led Americans to harbor unrealistic demands for near-complete security. In turn, this has forced the government into what Colonel Mark Maxwell dubbed the "whack-a-mole cycle," which has shaped counterterrorism policy around short-term tactics to disrupt plots, such as targeted killings by drone, over a focus upon longer-term strategy.[16] A more strategic approach may, in its pursuit of significant change, temporarily leave the nation more vulnerable to small-scale attacks as resources are diverted from the tactical military interventions. As Audrey Cronin argued in her analysis of what "winning" the War on Terror might entail, this means there is a need for the American people to build a "psychological resilience" to terrorism before any significant change in policy direction can occur. The former Head of the National Counterterrorism Center, Michael Leiter, echoed this position, warning that in order to see progress in counterterrorism, "the American people do need to understand that at least the smaller-scale terrorist attacks are with us for the foreseeable future."[17] The hard truth is, it is extremely difficult to stop groups who are prepared to use extreme violence in the pursuit of an ideological end, and whose members are willing to die for its cause. Al Qaeda, ISIS, and whatever foreign-based extremist groups may emerge in the future will be able to kill Americans. For an open society which plays a leading role on the global stage, zero risk is an impossibility. Yet as tragic as victims from any terrorist event are, the United States can, and must, learn to absorb the kind of small-scale attacks these groups have been limited to organizing, or indirectly inspiring. While not to be dismissed, such occurrences do not pose an existential threat to the nation, and accordingly do not require a continued state of war and emergency in response.

As in any democracy, the public's perception plays an important role in determining how the American government responds to terrorism. If citizens believe

[16] Colonel Mark Maxwell, *Rebutting The Civilian Presumption: Playing Whack-A-Mole Without a Mallet*, *in* TARGETED KILLINGS: LAW AND MORALITY IN AN ASYMMETRICAL WORLD (Claire Finkelstein et al., eds., 2012); Jenna Jordan, *Attacking the Leader, Missing the Mark: Why Terrorist Groups Survive Decapitation Strikes*, 38 INT'L SEC., no. 4, 7 (2014).

[17] Audrey Cronin, *The "War on Terrorism": What Does It Mean to Win?*, 37 J. STRATEGIC STUD., no. 2, 174, 191 (2013).

the threat necessitates the application of military force, but the government responds purely with law enforcement techniques, it risks being seen as weak, especially should a significant terrorist attack occur. The government plays a part in shaping the public's perception of the threat posed by terrorists, as does the nation's media. Unfortunately, due to what Martha Crenshaw labeled the "aura of perversely tragic glamour" which accompanies acts of terrorism, America's news media have been all too willing to stoke the fears terrorists seek to engender for the ratings bump such events generate.[18] ISIS, for example, through the spectacle of extreme violence promoted via social media platforms, were able to form a narrative, amplified by US news media, which dramatically skewed the public's perception of the threat they posed, manipulating citizens through the spread of fear and anxiety, and subsequently limiting the government's policy options.[19] In a clumsy effort to counter this manipulation, President Obama infamously described the Islamic State as the "jayvee team" to Al Qaeda.[20] Such language was at odds with the American public's perception, which, heavily influenced by the group's propaganda machine and skillful media manipulation, saw ISIS as a major domestic threat. Facing a backlash, the Obama administration was forced to engage in a large-scale publicity campaign to promote their strategy against the group and to reassure the public that the appropriate level of force was being applied to secure the homeland.[21]

Correctly distinguishing enemy from criminal is not just a matter for the security of the state but also its political and social well-being. Disagreements over the nature and identity of the enemy are a tension which can pull at the social fabric of a nation. The sustained rise in Islamophobia across the United States, which manifests itself in verbal and physical assaults against Muslims, attacks upon mosques, and armed anti-Muslim demonstrations, and even the introduction of laws which have been specifically identified as anti-Muslim, can be linked to America's post-9/11 state of perpetual warfare.[22] While criminals are regarded within the law as individuals, a war's enemy is instead defined by their membership to a specific state organization, or with regard to non-state terrorists, a particular group. This broad-stroke labeling is necessary in warfare, where combat is

[18] Martha Crenshaw, *Thoughts on Relating Terrorism to Historical Contexts*, *in* TERRORISM IN CONTEXT 12 (Martha Crenshaw ed. 1995); John Koblin, *Coverage of Paris Terror Attacks Lifts Network News Ratings*, N.Y. TIMES, Nov. 24, 2015, <https://www.nytimes.com/2015/11/25/business/media/coverage-of-paris-terror-attacks-lifts-network-news-ratings.html?_r=1>.

[19] J.M. BERGER & JESSICA STERN, ISIS: THE STATE OF TERROR 130–38 (2015).

[20] David Remnick, *Going the Distance: On and Off the Road with Barack Obama*, NEW YORKER, Jan. 27, 2014, <https://www.newyorker.com/magazine/2014/01/27/going-the-distance-david-remnick>.

[21] Barack Obama, "Statement by the President on ISIL," White House Sept. 10, 2014, <https://www.whitehouse.gov/the-press-office/2014/09/10/statement-president-isil-1>.

[22] "Islamaphobia and its impact in the United States," Council on American-Islamic Relations, 2016, <http://islamophobia.org/images/ConfrontingFear/Final-Report.pdf>.

between large bodies of forces. But an indirect consequence of America's labeling of Islamic extremists as enemies has been the removal of the individual from the equation, allowing sweeping statements and false assumptions about Islam and Muslims to garner greater domestic resonance.[23] This generalization, combined with the American public's elevated fear of terrorism and frustration at the protracted war have been carefully manipulated by extremists who purposefully wrap themselves in a bastardization of Islam to fuel the rise of the very inter-religious tensions they have sought to stoke since their emergence, in an effort to eliminate what they dub the "grayzone" of cohabitation between Muslims and Western societies.[24]

As well as contributing to growing social discord and ugly public discourse about the place of Muslims in American society, the United States' constant war footing has also distorted other fundamental aspects of the nation's domestic environment. Narratives spun by political leaders to enable domestic support for foreign policies do not exist in isolation, but wash back over the domestic audience, shaping attitudes and influencing behavior. Harry S. Truman's warnings of the covert Soviet menace undermining European institutions won the support necessary for the adoption of the policy of containment, but also ushered in an era of domestic fear and paranoia, culminating in a second "Red Scare" and McCarthyism. Similarly, Dwight Eisenhower's extensive reliance upon covert CIA operations in the 1950s enabled America to shape the foreign landscape, but the undermining of the rule of law and democratic principles abroad eventually blew back onto the United States itself. Described by Malcom X as the "chickens coming home to roost," a spate of assassinations, including John F. Kennedy, Martin Luther King Jr., Bobby Kennedy, and Malcolm X himself, eventually led to the Senate's Church Committee "condemn[ing] the use of assassination as a tool of foreign policy," an action which, in Senator Church's words, "violate[d] moral precepts fundamental to [the American] way of life."[25] This pattern can be seen to have repeated itself post-9/11, where an increased sense of violence and militarism has gripped the American people. There is a myriad of factors which have contributed to the rise in mass shootings across multiple US states, the increasingly forceful and all too frequent lethal conduct of an overly militarized police force against the citizens they are charged to protect and serve, and the hostile political rhetoric which often descends into Islamophobia.[26] It would be

[23] Neumann, *supra* note 10, at 59–68.

[24] "The Extinction of the Grayzone," *Dabiq*, no. 7, in Clarion Project, 54–66, <http://media.clarionproject.org/files/islamic-state/islamic-state-dabiq-magazine-issue-7-from-hypocrisy-to-apostasy.pdf>.

[25] "Alleged Assassination Plots Involving Foreign Leaders," Church Committee Interim Report (Congress 1975) 257, in Assassination Archives and Research Center, <https://www.aarclibrary.org/publib/church/reports/ir/html/ChurchIR_0136a.htm>.

[26] Mohsin Hassan Khan et al., *A Critical Discourse Analysis of Anti-Muslim Rhetoric in Donald Trump's Historic 2016 AIPIC Policy Speech*, J. Muslim Minority Aff. 543 (Oct. 2020), <https://www.

naïve, however, for policymakers to ignore the impact the United States' current lethal conduct abroad is having on the domestic front; hardening attitudes and challenging long-held beliefs on life, death, justice, humanity, and innocence.[27] Just as America has eroded the sanctity of the civilian abroad for the sake of expediency in the pursuit of its terrorist enemies, so too has it eroded its own citizens' sanctity at home.

While America's counterterrorism approach may have demonstrated the risks of an overreliance upon a war paradigm to fight something as interminable as terrorism, events in France exhibited the shortcomings of the crime paradigm. The French state was specifically targeted by ISIS for a number of reasons: first, proportionately, it has the largest Muslim population in Western Europe, with 7.5 percent of its citizens following the faith; more significantly, a large portion of that community, which by median age is markedly younger than the religiously unaffiliated citizens of the state, are located in poorer, underdeveloped districts of France.[28] Furthermore, the fiercely secular republic has a long-running history of tension between its efforts to uphold this ethos while recognizing the desire of some among its Muslim community to emphasize their faith, be it through worship, conduct, or dress.[29] Such tensions have fed into a polarized situation, where the more assertive Islamic voices have found their echo on the far right, with an active political grouping centered around the openly anti-Islamic Front National party, seeing the two strands feeding off one another.[30] A further challenge to the stability of the nation comes from its place in the Schengen area of the European Union, meaning the country shares open borders with the rest of the continent, making the movement of individuals and weapons much harder to control.

tandfonline.com/doi/abs/10.1080/13602004.2020.1828507>; Sarah Aziza, *The 2018 Midterm Cycle Could Be the Most Islamophobic US Election Ever*, The Intercept, Oct. 22, 2018, <https://theintercept.com/2018/10/22/2018-midterms-muslim-candidates-islamophobia/>.

[27] Jessica Katzenstein, *The Wars Are Here: How the United States' Post-9/11 Wars Helped Militarize US Police*, Costs of War, Sept. 16, 2020, <https://watson.brown.edu/costsofwar/files/cow/imce/papers/2020/Police%20Militarization_Costs%20of%20War_Sept%2016%202020.pdf>.

[28] Conrad Hackett, "5 facts about the Muslim population in Europe," Pew, July 19, 2016, <https://www.pewresearch.org/fact-tank/2016/07/19/5-facts-about-the-muslim-population-in-europe/>; *Why France Is So Vulnerable to Islamist Terrorism*, Telegraph, Aug. 1, 2016, <https://www.telegraph.co.uk/news/2016/08/01/analysis-why-france-is-so-vulnerable-to-islamist-terrorism/>.

[29] Joan Wallach Scott, The Politics of the Veil 40 (2007).

[30] Lowell Turner, "Marine Le Pen, Islamophobia, and the Polarization of French Society," Cornell School of Industrial and Labor Relations, May 9, 2017, <https://www.ilr.cornell.edu/post/marine-le-pen-islamophobia-and-polarization-french-society>; Nicolas Lebourg, *Islamophobia in France*, Hal archives-ouvertes, Feb. 2, 2018, <https://halshs.archives-ouvertes.fr/halshs-01696784/file/Islamophobia_in_France.pdf>; Catherine Fieschi, *Muslims and the Secular City: How Right-Wing Populists Shape the French Debate over Islam*, Brookings, Feb. 20, 2020, <https://www.brookings.edu/research/muslims-and-the-secular-city-how-right-wing-populists-shape-the-french-debate-over-islam/>.

Despite its vulnerabilities and ISIS's declared interest in taking a match to these combustible conditions, France's security response was poor. Even with heavy constraints designed to protect the civil liberties which are regarded as fundamental to French democracy, the nation's intelligence services are generally well respected. But with a 2015 budget of just €208 million per year ($232 million) and a greater number of French citizens than those of any other European nation having migrated to Syria, the country's security services were overwhelmed. Following the attack upon Paris in 2015, in which 130 were killed and hundreds more injured by jihadists trained and dispatched by ISIS, President François Hollande enacted a state of emergency and declared that France was at war. However, unlike America's post-9/11 shift to a war footing, Hollande's call was largely rhetorical. The government introduced a drive to expand its security services—a lengthy process which has taken years to deliver active agents—but beyond retaliatory airstrikes in Syria (part of the US-led campaign in which France was already engaged), there were no fundamental changes. The French government continued to rely upon its own and the wider European crime fighting structures—institutions which, given the nature of the threat, had been repeatedly found wanting. This was cruelly underscored in July 2016 when, days before the government planned to repeal the state of emergency, a truck was driven along the busy Nice promenade by an ISIS sympathizer, killing eighty-seven and injuring hundreds more. The symbolism was particularly poignant, the attack having occurred during the Bastille Day celebrations, an event which marks the very essence of the secular French state. A poorly considered ban upon burkini beachwear swiftly followed, leading to images of French police officers forcing a Muslim woman to remove the garment on a beach in the same city the attack had occurred in. Although the ban was swiftly struck down by France's supreme court, the pictures had already been seen worldwide, further stoking the tensions which had attracted ISIS to France in the first place. These tragic events and the far-right's anti-Islamic response led Patrick Calvar, the head of France's domestic intelligence service, to warn French politicians that the state was being driven to "the brink of civil war."[31] ISIS's temporary decline following the dismantling of their self-declared caliphate across Iraq and Syria bought the French state a reprieve from the intense pressure its security services were under, but continued incidents of smaller-scale but high-profile jihadist violence, including the live-streamed murder of a police officer and his wife in their home in 2016, the decapitation of a teacher for discussing images of Muhammad in 2020, and

[31] Quoted in Jason Burke, *Why Does France Keep Getting Attacked?*, GUARDIAN, July 15, 2016, <https://www.theguardian.com/world/2016/jul/15/why-does-france-keep-getting-attacked>.

the stabbing of churchgoers just weeks later reveal the continued divisions and vulnerability over France's secular identity.[32]

III. "Keep Calm and Carry On"

As a nation with extensive experience in combating protracted terrorist campaigns, there are valuable lessons to be learned from the United Kingdom's approach to jihadist violence, which for most of the past two decades has sought to strike a balance between America's hyperactivity and France's comparative complacency. While not to the same degree as their American counterparts, the 9/11 attacks shocked British society and its policymakers. Sixty-seven UK citizens died on September 11, the largest single loss of British life in a terrorist attack. At first glance, Britain's initial response was similar to that of the United States: substantial forces were dispatched to fight alongside their American allies in Afghanistan to oust the Taliban and remove Al Qaeda's safe haven. Furthermore, British Prime Minister Tony Blair committed the country to supporting the Bush administration's plans for regime change in Iraq in early 2002, convinced of the benefits and stability such a course of action could bring to the Middle East.[33] Yet despite unity in the major set pieces of the War on Terror, the British government's domestic counterterrorism policy quickly diverged from the approach adopted by the United States. As the White House pivoted to a war paradigm, the British government introduced its CONTEST strategy, developed by the Home Office in 2003 with the stated aim of reducing "the risk to the UK and its interests overseas from terrorism, so that people can go about their lives freely and with confidence."[34] In contrast to the dramatic American paradigm shift which embedded previously hardline measures as new norms, the British government sought to reassure its populace and tourists, encourage investment, and stabilize markets by emphasizing the resumption and continuity of ordinary life. Like the motivational poster produced by the government on the eve of the Second World War evoking the public to "Keep Calm and Carry On," the United Kingdom's response channeled the Victorian-era belief in British stoicism—the sense of the stiff upper lip and unflappable fortitude in the

[32] *France Calls for "Rapid and Coordinated" European Front Against Terrorism*, FRANCE24, Nov. 10, 2020, <https://www.france24.com/en/europe/20201110-france-calls-for-rapid-and-coordinated-european-front-against-terrorism>.

[33] Christoph Bluth, *The British Road to War: Blair, Bush and the Decision to Invade Iraq*, 80 INT'L AFF., no. 5, 871, 885 (Oct. 2004), <https://www.jstor.org/stable/3569476>; Nick Hopkins, *When Blair Met Bush: How the UK Went to War in Iraq*, GUARDIAN, July 9, 2016, <https://www.theguardian.com/uk-news/2016/jul/09/iraq-war-after-blair-and-bush-met-the-tempo-changed>.

[34] "CONTEST: The United Kingdom's Strategy for Countering Terrorism," HM Government, July 2011, <https://www.gov.uk/government/uploads/system/uploads/attachment_data/file/97994/contest-summary.pdf>.

face of adversity. Terrorists were to remain as criminals, dealt with through the United Kingdom's courts and legal systems, denying them their self-conferred status as soldiers in a war of their own declaration. While abroad Britain went to war, in the homeland the goal was, on the surface at least, business as usual.

In the two decades which have followed the introduction of the CONTEST strategy, the United Kingdom's security services—which function with an annual budget of approximately £1.9 billion ($2.4bn), prevented over forty serious Al Qaeda and ISIS plots against the homeland.[35] Through well-coordinated cooperation between Britain's intelligence agencies and police forces, as well as collaboration and intelligence sharing with allied nations such as the United States, the European Union's counterterrorism coordinator, and close Arab allies such as Saudi Arabia, the United Kingdom had arrested 7,309 individuals on terrorism-related offences as of December 2019. Of those, 2,061 were charged, and 614 convicted.[36] During this period, there have been two successful jihadist bombings: the first an attack upon London's public transport system on July 7, 2005, which killed fifty-two people, and the second, the bombing of a music concert held at the Manchester Arena on May 22, 2017, which resulted in twenty-two fatalities.[37] In addition to these complex set-piece attacks, in May 2013, a forerunner of what would become a common terrorism technique encouraged by ISIS saw a single British citizen, the soldier Fusilier Lee Rigby, stabbed to death on a London street outside his barracks by two individuals who were known to the security services. A government investigation later cleared UK intelligence, instead blaming Facebook for failing to provide the police with details of a revealing exchange between the killers which would have tipped officers off to the men's motives.[38] This style of attack, particularly difficult to prevent but mercifully limited in terms of scale and victims, has occurred on a number of occasions in London, with an attack in Westminster in March 2017 claiming the lives of four, and two attacks on London bridge, in June 2017 and November 2019, seeing a further six people killed. Given the significant number of terrorism-related arrests, convictions, and subsequent foiled plots, the United Kingdom's security services have done well in protecting the nation against what

[35] Patrick Worrall, *FactCheck: How Many Terror Plots Have Been Busted Since the 7/7 Bombings?*, Channel 4 News, July 7, 2015, <http://blogs.channel4.com/factcheck/factcheck-terror-plots-busted-77/21225>.

[36] "Operation of police powers under the Terrorism Act of 2000 and subsequent legislation: Arrests, outcomes, and stop and search," Home Office, Dec. 2019, <https://assets.publishing.service.gov.uk/government/uploads/system/uploads/attachment_data/file/869780/police-powers-terrorism-dec2019-hosb0720.pdf>.

[37] David Omand, *Keeping Europe Safe: Counterterrorism for the Continent*, Foreign Aff. 83, 87–88 (Sept.–Oct. 2016).

[38] "Report on the intelligence relating to the murder of Fusilier Lee Rigby," Intelligence and Security Committee of Parliament, Nov. 2014, at 7, <http://isc.independent.gov.uk/committee-reports/special-reports>.

has been a persistent jihadist threat, especially at the height of ISIS's self-declared caliphate, from where they sought to motivate frequent assaults against those countries engaged in the dismantling of their territorial holdings, of which the United Kingdom was a major actor. Arguably the most impressive aspect of the United Kingdom's relative preservation of its security in the face of such persistent threats is the fact that, for the majority of this time security has been maintained without significantly infringing upon domestic civil liberties or acting outside of European and wider international legal norms. One could point to the fact that the United Kingdom is one of the most watched societies in the world, with extensive CCTV networks. And as the Edward Snowden leaks revealed, there is a long history of extensive cooperation between Britain's GCHQ and America's NSA in the monitoring of citizens' electronic communications. But these are trade-offs the British public had already accepted well-before the events of 9/11 identified new targets to direct the state's surveillance capabilities toward, and frequent appeals and reviews have found the practices to be kept carefully within the bounds of the ECHR in terms of citizens' privacy.[39]

Considering the scale and persistence of the jihadist threat projected against them, both the United States and the United Kingdom have managed to protect their homelands to an impressive degree. The most significant separation between the two approaches lies in their wider societal impacts. While there is clear evidence that anti-Islamic sentiment in Britain has intensified since 9/11, the country has not seen the same level of hostility toward its Muslim communities as parts of the United States, with such extreme legislation as a ban on Muslim immigration entering the mainstream political domain.[40] Much of the antagonism toward Islam is the result of negative stereotypes, resulting in bias, discrimination, and the marginalization of Muslims in social, political, and civic life. However, in its research, Gallop found the most accurate description for Islamophobia to be "an exaggerated, usually inexplicable and illogical fear" of the faith and those who follow it.[41] The American public's illogical fear is linked to the ongoing struggle with Islamic extremists,

[39] Silkie Carlo, *Britain Has More Surveillance Camera Per Person Than Any Country Except China. That's a Massive Risk to Our Free Society*, TIME, May 17, 2019, <https://time.com/5590343/uk-facial-recognition-cameras-china/>. *GCHQ Does Not Breach Human Rights, Judges Rule*, BBC NEWS, Dec. 5, 2014, <https://www.bbc.co.uk/news/uk-30345801>; "List of judgements," Investigatory Powers Tribunal, Dec. 5, 2014, <https://web.archive.org/web/20150206211011/http://www.ipt-uk.com/section.aspx?pageid=8>; "Privacy International & others -v- Secretary of State for Foreign and Commonwealth Affairs & others," Investigatory Powers Tribunal, Aug. 10, 2020, <https://www.ipt-uk.com/judgments.asp>.

[40] President Donald Trump, Executive Order 13769 "Protecting the Nation from Foreign Terrorist Entry into the United States," White House, Jan. 27, 2017, <https://www.federalregister.gov/documents/2017/02/01/2017-02281/protecting-the-nation-from-foreign-terrorist-entry-into-the-united-states>.

[41] "Islamophobia: Understanding Anti-Muslim Sentiment in the West," Gallop, no date, <http://www.gallup.com/poll/157082/islamophobia-understanding-anti-muslim-sentiment-west.aspx>.

making the War on Terror a primary driver of this growing social discord. Rather than making the American public feel safer, the knowledge that their government has drones in the air above terrorist safe havens and special forces deployed around the world ready to strike at a moment's notice, accentuates the struggle against terrorism. It builds its proponents up from criminals to combatants, inflates terrorism's profile, and places it permanently on the political agenda and the public's mind. Polling carried out on both sides of the Atlantic in the aftermath of ISIS's 2015 Paris attack revealed that, despite the event occurring in a European capital, its effects were felt more deeply in the United States. Sixty-six percent of American's polled stated that they believed there was a real threat to their personal safety and security being violated, as opposed to 57 percent of British citizens.[42] The United Kingdom's emphasis on continuity and retaining normality in lieu of America's normalization of a state of emergency has enabled Britain and its citizens to largely eschew the war narrative extolled by the terrorists who target its institutions, avoiding the clash of civilizations characterization the terrorists have sought to promote. Accordingly, the British government has managed to sustain lower levels of fear among its citizens and limit the resultant Islamophobia, despite being connected by the Land Frontier of the Channel Tunnel to the primary European target of ISIS's exported terror attacks.

Perhaps the most significant difference between American and British counterterrorism policy is the added flexibility the criminal paradigm has afforded the United Kingdom's policymakers. While one can connect the events of 9/11 to the ongoing threat posed by Islamic extremism, by shunning the temptation to unleash the hounds of war, successive British governments have avoided locking themselves into an open-ended conflict. The public's expectation is security, but this is mitigated by an acceptance that criminals are an ever-present fact of life in modern society. The state has a responsibility to try to prevent criminal acts and to track down those who do perpetrate them and bring them to justice. But such a contract comes with an acceptance that pursuing criminals will not end crime but rather reduce its likelihood and impact. Thus, there is no overarching belief among the British public that terrorism will be eradicated, nor that the nation is engaged in some sort of existential battle with an enemy force which must be defeated. This narrative ensures Britain's parliamentarians, and the security services which serve them, are faced with significantly lower expectations, where ongoing security, not absolute victory, is the primary objective against which success will be measured.

42 "Immigration, Refugees & Security," Ipsos Public Affairs, Nov. 2015, <https://www.ipsos-mori.com/Assets/Docs/Polls/ipsos-global-@dvisor-nov-2015-immigration-refugees-and-security.pdf>.

IV. "A New Departure"

Despite lower levels of public fear and the more realistic overall objective produced by Britain's long-term strategy, the United Kingdom's national terrorism threat level has been set at either "Severe" or the highest category of "Critical" since August 2014.[43] Initial increase of the threat level was triggered by the danger posed by ISIS as it expanded its territorial hold across Iraq and Syria; its extensive resources, Western recruits, and an external operations branch dedicated to exporting attacks posing what the UN Security Council described as "an unprecedented threat."[44] In the face of this new challenge, the UK government quietly began to make controversial adjustments to its counterterrorism policy, adopting various aspects of the American model, in particular its use of lethal drone strikes as a form of preemptive self-defense. The 2015 National Security Strategy stated that Britain would utilize its unmanned systems to maintain a global strike capability, targeting those suspected of plotting attacks against the United Kingdom and its global interests from "beyond the reach of justice," namely, ISIS's strongholds in Syria or other terrorist safe havens around the world. The first example of this approach in action had actually occurred three months prior to the strategy's publication, when an RAF Reaper drone was deployed over Syria to kill Rayeed Khan, a British citizen linked by UK intelligence agencies to efforts to inspire attacks on Britain's streets. In its legal justification of the strike, the British government borrowed heavily from the American war paradigm, stating that the deed had been an act of self-defense under Article 51 of the UN Charter, executed in accordance with the Laws of War.[45] This decision was criticized by a range of observers, troubled that what Prime Minister David Cameron described as "a new departure" for the United Kingdom risked sucking the country into the sort of expansive targeted killing campaign that the United States has unleashed from the skies over Pakistan, Yemen, Somalia, and Syria.

Concerns over the United Kingdom's gradual slide toward the war paradigm were further realized as the RAF played an increasingly aggressive role in the coalition campaign against ISIS in Syria and Iraq, launching a total of 1,997 strikes between 2014 and 2019.[46] While many of these sorties can be chalked up as typical military operations aimed at destroying ISIS's infrastructure undertaken by

43 "MI5 Threat Levels" (MI5), <https://www.mi5.gov.uk/threat-levels>.

44 UNSC Resolution 2249, United Nations, Nov. 20, 2015, <https://www.securitycouncilreport.org/atf/cf/%7B65BFCF9B-6D27-4E9C-8CD3-CF6E4FF96FF9%7D/s_res_2249.pdf>.

45 Prime Minister's oral statement to Parliament, "Syria: refugees and counter-terrorism," UK Government, Sept. 7, 2015, <https://www.gov.uk/government/speeches/syria-refugees-and-counter-terrorism-prime-ministers-statement>.

46 "UK Air Operations in Iraq and Syria 2014—Dec 2019" (Drone Wars UK), <https://dronewars.net/uk-drone-strike-list-2/>.

a combination of Tornado, Typhoon, and F-35 aircraft, 472 of these strikes—one-fifth—were undertaken by RAF Reaper drones, the platform typically associated with precision strikes against individuals and groups, such as that launched against Khan. From 2018 onward, after the fall of ISIS's de facto capital of Raqqa and the collapse of the group's self-declared caliphate, the RAF's Reaper drone strikes were undertaken exclusively in Syria, with sixty-six in 2018 and eight in 2019.[47] Details of the targets of these strikes remain classified—a troubling marker of the emulation of the American approach to counterterrorism. But a series of statements from Britain's top military commander in the campaign against ISIS, Major General Rupert Jones, and then Minister of Defence, Gavin Williamson, provided further evidence of the militarization of the United Kingdom's counterterrorism policy. Speaking at a briefing on the coalition's military efforts against ISIS in March 2017, Jones warned British citizens: "If you are going to take up arms on behalf of Daesh [ISIS] and you are going to kill innocent civilians we will find you and we will kill you."[48] Nine months later Williamson echoed this position and revealed the Ministry of Defence's new hardline policy by declaring in an interview with the *Daily Mail* newspaper that "a dead terrorist can't cause any harm to Britain." Using the interview to set out how the government would respond to the threat posed by UK citizens who had traveled to Syria to join ISIS, Williamson stated that such individuals would be "hunted down" and "eliminated" to prevent them bringing "destruction, death and bloodshed" onto the streets of the United Kingdom. The timing of these statement was particular relevant, as it came shortly after the liberation of Raqqa—a significant victory against ISIS which had caused the terrorist organization's fighters to disperse across Syria, Iraq, and in many cases to seek to return to their countries of origin. "We should do everything we can do to destroy and eliminate that threat," concluded the minister, using a militaristic rhetoric previously eschewed by British politicians.[49]

Estimates in 2017 identified some 5,600 foreign fighters from across the world returning to their home nations following the collapse of ISIS's so-called caliphate. Of these, it was predicted that 1,200–2,000 were from the European Union, of which 800 from the United Kingdom, and that at least 400 of those were not accounted for. Such numbers put security services under unsustainable pressure unless steps are taken to intervene in the development of these threats

[47] *Id.*

[48] *"We Will Find You and We Will Kill You": Britain's Top Commander in War against ISIS Vows to Hunt Down and Wipe Out British Jihadis*, DAILY MAIL, Mar. 1, 2017, <https://www.dailymail.co.uk/news/article-4269480/Britain-s-commander-vows-wipe-British-jihadis.html>.

[49] *Defence Secretary Is Accused of Dreaming Up a Netflix-style Plot by Threatening to "Eliminate" UK Jihadis Before They Can Return to Britain*, DAILY MAIL, Dec. 6, 2017, <https://www.dailymail.co.uk/news/article-5153613/Gavin-Williamson-Brits-fighting-be.html>.

before they materialize into active plots.[50] As the Provisional Irish Republican Army (IRA) warned following a failed assassination attempt on British Prime Minister Margaret Thatcher in 1984, terrorists only have to be "lucky once," whereas security services "have to be lucky always."[51] Given the intensity of ISIS's efforts to export terror, combined with the group's significant numbers of foreign recruits that sought to return home, an overly defensive strategy in which the state does not seek to actively neutralize those plotting attacks against the homeland tempts fate. But while the nature of the safe havens exploited by the likes of ISIS makes it unrealistic to think that these interventions could come in the form of the criminal arrest and prosecution of all of those foreign fighters, it is equally unrealistic to think, as Jones and Williamson boasted, that all of these individuals could be hunted down and eliminated. Not only would doing so commit the United Kingdom to the exact open-ended conflict that has been pursued unsuccessful by the United States, but it would also signal a willingness for extrajudicial killings to form a part of the United Kingdom's security policy—an approach which would not only break the Geneva conventions and UK law but also undermine British society and how the government defends it. It is not the case, however, that there is only the binary solution of the United Kingdom either ignoring the threat posed by these safe havens and foreign fighters or embarking on an open ended and legally questionable war. Human rights law, while requiring higher applicable standards to govern the use of lethal force than those imposed by the laws of war, is adequate in this situation, granting the government the legal authority to employ the lethal force necessary to protect the United Kingdom from the non-state predators of the twenty-first century, while avoiding the pitfalls associated with waging a forever war against an abstraction.

V. "Rights versus Rights"

Within British counterterrorism circles there is a perception that the protection of the individual and preservation of life enshrined in human rights law is at odds with the state's efforts to maintain national security. The roots of this tension can be traced back to the controversial Operation Falvius, which took place in March 1988 in the United Kingdom's overseas territory of Gibraltar. British security services had intelligence that three members of the IRA were planning to detonate a car bomb targeting UK service personnel during a changing of the guard ceremony in the small country's central square. The known terrorists had

[50] *ISIS Foreign Fighters after the Fall of the Caliphate*, 6 Armed Conflict Survey, no. 1, 23 (2020), <doi = 10.1080/23740973.2020.1761611>.

[51] Adam Gabbatt, *The Brighton Bombing, 25 Years On*, Guardian, Oct. 13, 2009, <https://www.theguardian.com/uk/blog/2009/oct/13/brighton-bombing-magee>.

been identified crossing the border from Spain to Gibraltar and were kept under surveillance until the suspected car bomb was identified. When four members of the British Special Air Service moved in to arrest the terrorists, concern that they might have been equipped with remote detonators led the soldiers to controversially shoot and kill the unarmed IRA operatives. No radio detonators were discovered, and the suspect car was found to be empty. The investigation later uncovered a hire car leased to a member of the group containing Semtex and detonators over the border in Spain, leading to legal accusations from the deceased's families that, in the absence of an imminent threat, the British government had conspired to assassinate the three paramilitaries from the operation's conception.[52]

The UK High Court dismissed the terrorists' family members' case, and the Gibraltarian court ruled the killings had been legal. But when the families appealed to the European Commission of Human Rights, arguing that the operation had violated Article 2 (the right to life) of the ECHR, the panel upheld the criticism, referring the case to the European Court of Human Rights for a final ruling. The British government argued that the state had been permitted to derogate from Article 2's obligations under the convention that the killings had been "absolutely necessary" in order to protect the people of Gibraltar from unlawful violence, because the soldiers had genuinely believed the IRA members were capable of detonating the bomb at the moment they were shot. Although the court accepted it was not possible to find the soldiers guilty of a violation of Article 2 without placing an unrealistic burden upon law enforcement personnel to make on the spot judgments about the imminence of a threat, it was highly critical of the government's planning and control of the operation. The judges concluded that the decision not to arrest the suspects at the border, combined with the intelligence which was passed onto the special forces operatives, ensured that the use of lethal force was the only possible outcome, thus finding the United Kingdom guilty of a violation of Article 2.[53] The Court rejected the families' claims for damages, but in a decision which caused considerable consternation among British policymakers, ordered the United Kingdom pay their costs for the court's proceedings. The government initially declared it would not pay, and the ruling triggered a debate in Parliament over Britain's withdrawal from the ECHR. While Britain ultimately opted to retain the convention and paid the costs, significant damage was done to the United Kingdom's perception of the role of Europe's human rights legislation in counterterrorism. The legacy of this mistrust could still be seen in the Tory Party's 2015 manifesto, which promised

[52] McCann and Others v. United Kingdom [September 27 1995] European Court of Human Rights, <http://hudoc.echr.coe.int/eng?i=001-57943#{"itemid":["001-57943"]}>.
[53] *Id.*

to review the application of the ECHR to the operation of the United Kingdom's armed forces, and more fundamentally in the eventual result of Britain's 2016 referendum on EU membership.

Cases like that of Operation Flavius have served to distort the debate over the correct balance between the protection of individuals' liberties and the maintenance of national security. The prevailing sense of a contest, where efforts to protect human rights are in some way detrimental to national security, is misleading. It sets two sides seeking the same outcome—the protection of the state and its citizens—against one another. In reality, the safeguarding of the human right to life and protection of millions of citizens from potential violence and coercion is a central tenant of the contract between the modern state and its citizens, and thus is a matter of national security. Human rights legislation should not be regarded as something which impedes the government in its efforts to protect its citizens but rather as something which, when correctly employed, actually *compels* the state to defend against any violation of the individual human rights of its law-abiding citizens, using all available tools, including lethal force, if necessary.[54] With regard to Operation Flavius, it was not the killing of the IRA operatives that the European Court of Human Rights ruled against, but the fact that the planning meant that other, viable forms of nonlethal recourse were overlooked. Applied with careful planning and within an appropriate framework, human rights law is sufficient to authorize the state's use of lethal force against terrorists operating from safe havens outside of zones of armed conflict, preemptively before threats fully materialize.

A. The Legal Obligation to Use Lethal Force to Protect Life under Human Rights Law

The individual's right to life is widely recognized within both domestic and international law as the most fundamental of all human rights. The criminal offences of murder and manslaughter represent a core social contract of the state, ensuring that the government—under specific criteria—has the monopoly on the legitimate use of lethal force, thus bringing order to mankind's otherwise "short, brutish and violent" state of nature.[55] Beyond the borders of the state, this right is universalized through international law. Article 6 of the ICCPR rules against the arbitrary deprivation of life, noting that every human has the inherent right to life, while Article 2 of the ECHR both prohibits the state from intentionally

[54] Michael Arnheim, *The Problem with Human Rights Law*, CIVITAS, Mar. 2015, <https://www.civitas.org.uk/content/files/TheProblemwithHumanRightsLaw.pdf>.

[55] Max Weber, *Politics as a Vocation*, *in* FROM MAX WEBER: ESSAYS IN SOCIOLOGY (H.H. Gerth & C. Wright Mills eds., 1991).

killing and imposes an obligation to protect the right to life. The ECHR does, however, permit the use of lethal force if it is "no more than absolutely necessary" to avert an immediate threat of unlawful violence to other people.[56] In fact, not only does the Convention permit lethal force but should the government have intelligence indicating that there is a direct and imminent threat to citizens from a terrorist attack with no alternative to prevent it other than killing those responsible, it imposes a positive obligation upon the state to protect its citizens through such measures. The European Court of Human Rights clarified this in the 1998 case of *Osman v. UK*, in which it ruled that Article 2's obligation to protect life required the state to take preventive action, within the scope of its powers, where "the authorities knew or ought to have known at the time of the existence of a real and immediate risk to the life of an identified individual or individuals from the criminal acts of a third party."[57] Subsequently, the Court has expanded this obligation beyond individuals to the protection of the public at large. Thus, rather than shackling governments, the legislation's obligation to protect life is intrinsically valuable in efforts to neutralize terrorists plotting violence from safe havens beyond the reach of the legal system.

Similar to the requirements of proportionality within the laws of war, should lethal force be employed by the state under the auspices of the ECHR, it must be effectively regulated by a clear legal framework and, unlike Operation Flavius, the planning and control must be such as to minimize the risk of loss of life. Where ECHR-related actions differ from those undertaken utilizing the laws of war is Article 2's requirement that there be an official investigation into any deaths resulting from the state's use of force, or any situation where the state has failed to protect life. Such investigations must be promptly brought by the state on its own initiative, be independent of government influence, open to public scrutiny, and capable of leading to accountability for any unlawful deprivation of life.[58] Therefore, the applicable standards which govern the use of lethal force are higher than those imposed by the laws of war. However, the adoption of these standards would not necessarily be a hindrance to counterterrorism efforts. Research into the attitudes of those living under lethal drones and of citizens concerned with their use has revealed that greater transparency in how such weapons are employed would create confidence and win greater support for their deployment.[59] Even as the United Kingdom began its slide toward the adoption of

[56] Art. 15(1), European Convention on Human Rights.

[57] Osman v. UK, European Court of Human Rights (Oct. 28, 1998), <https://www.bailii.org/eu/cases/ECHR/1998/101.html>.

[58] Art. 2, European Convention on Human Rights, <https://www.liberty-human-rights.org.uk/human-rights/what-are-human-rights/human-rights-act/article-2-right-life>.

[59] C. Christine Fair et al., *Pakistani Opposition to American Drone Strikes*, 129 Pol. Sci. Q., no. 1 33 (Spring 2014); Stephen Ceccoli & John Bing, *Taking the Lead? Transatlantic Attitudes Towards Lethal Drone Strikes*, 16 J. Transatlantic Stud., no. 3, 247 (2018), <https://doi.org/10.1080/14794012.2018.1482711>.

the covert counterterrorism practices established by the United States, the White House was in the process of acting on the abundance of evidence which demonstrated that transparency and accountability are powerful drivers in ensuring that lethal operations are planned with the prevention of civilian casualties as the highest priority—an approach which brings both humanitarian and strategic benefits. Consistent pressure applied in mainstream press op-eds, by nongovernmental agency reports, and from human rights organizations contributed to the Obama administration's desire to leave behind a "playbook" to regulate future drone strikes.[60] President Obama's June 1, 2016, executive order channeled many of the requirements a human rights framework for drone strikes would require by formalizing the need for "near certainty" that civilians would not be harmed in any counterterrorism strike and committing future administrations to greater transparency by demanding the publication of official data related to targets and casualties, as well as implementing accountability mechanisms and reparations procedures for the families of victims who perish as a result of collateral damage from counterterrorism efforts.[61]

Despite the initial progress promised by the Obama administration's reforms on drone strike procedures, the choice to issue guidance in the form of an executive order and policy report, as opposed to overseeing the transition to a legally binding framework further highlighted the flaws of operating under a war paradigm when Obama's successor took office. Despite the apparent agreement with the principle of prioritizing civilian safety from President Trump's first Secretary of Defense General (Ret.) James Mattis, who stated in response to questioning regarding collateral damage during his preconfirmation hearing that the United States should do "everything humanly possible to prevent civilian deaths in war," the Trump administration promptly ignored the regulatory framework controlling drone strikes, instead adopting a much more aggressive and opaque approach while dramatically escalating attacks in Somalia and Yemen.[62] The administration eventually issued its own executive order revoking the standards and reporting measures introduced during the Obama administration. The counterproductive nature of excessive targeted killings has since been evidenced

[60] Josh Gerstein, *Obama Releases Drone Strike "Playbook*," POLITICO, Aug. 6, 2016, <https://www.politico.com/blogs/under-the-radar/2016/08/obama-releases-drone-strike-playbook-226760>; "Procedures for Approving Direct Action Against Terrorist Targets Located Outside the United states and Areas of Active Hostilities," US Justice Department White Paper, May 22, 2013, published by ACLU, <https://www.aclu.org/sites/default/files/field_document/presidential_policy_guidance.pdf>.

[61] President Obama, "Executive Order—Policy on Pre- and Post-Strike Measures to Address Civilian Casualties in US Operations Involving the Use of Force," White House, July 1, 2016, <https://www.whitehouse.gov/the-press-office/2016/07/01/executive-order-united-states-policy-pre-and-post-strike-measures>.

[62] "Covert Drone War," Bureau of Investigative Journalism, <https://www.thebureauinvestigates.com/projects/drone-war>.

in reporting which reveals that the Trump administration's erosion of transparency coincided with an increase in civilian casualties and hampered local efforts to control the very same militias the United States has been targeting.[63] This serves as a valuable lesson to the UK government regarding the risks a dependency upon a policy solution brings when implemented instead of a legal framework. The expansion of drone violence, with likely long-term negative effects to a counterterrorism agenda, would only ever be one decision away, and should a prime minister decide for the sake of political expediency or their own image that authorizing summary executions of British citizens by drone strike is the best way to remove a threat, they could do so. Thus the adoption of the ECHR's more stringent criteria regarding lethal operations not only promises the tactical and strategic benefits which come from restraint and precision in operations so often linked to the hearts and minds of those communities within which terrorist groups operate, but it would remove the temptation for future leaders to shift the parameters and thresholds for lethal action and the associated risk of civilian casualties, as has been the case with the United States.[64]

B. The Legal Use of Lethal Force outside of Armed Conflict under Human Rights Law

A further advantage of human rights law is its universality. The United States' and the United Kingdom's current reliance upon the laws of war creates a legal tension whereby both states must rely upon an argument that they are engaged in a global state of armed conflict with Islamic extremists in order to justify the use of lethal force. The United States and now Britain have had to turn the world into a battlefield to retain the freedom to use lethal force wherever threats may emerge. This not only locks both countries into the open-ended conflict discussed above but serves to reinforce the extremist narrative that the West is engaged in a global clash of civilizations with a legitimate enemy force, as opposed to a counterterrorism campaign against stateless criminals. Typically, jurisdiction under the ICCPR and the ECHR is territorial, but the legislation also has extraterritorial application in certain circumstances. As already mentioned, the ICCPR's right to life and ECHR's Article 2 create a legal obligation for the state to act "within the scope of its powers" to prevent the loss of life of its citizens.[65] The ability to

[63] Kelsey D. Atherton, *Trump Inherited the Drone War but Ditched Accountability*, Foreign Policy, May 22, 2020, <https://foreignpolicy.com/2020/05/22/obama-drones-trump-killings-count/>; *Eroding Transparency: Trump in Yemen*, Airwars, October 2020, at 14–19, 21–26, <https://airwars.org/report/eroding-transparency-trump-in-yemen/>.

[64] Stephen Ceccoli, *Taking the Lead? Transatlantic Attitudes Towards Lethal Drone Strikes*, 16 J. Transatlantic Stud., no. 3, (2018), <https://doi.org/10.1080/14794012.2018.1482711>.

[65] Art. 6, ICCPR, <https://www.ohchr.org/en/professionalinterest/pages/ccpr.aspx>.

launch precision strikes from drones has significantly increased the state's capability to defend its citizens by enabling it to project lethal force into areas beyond the reach of domestic or international law enforcement, and it has been argued in the British High Court case of *Al Sadoon v. Secretary of State for Defence* that an aerial assault involving UK Armed Forces (in that case over Iraq) falls within Britain's jurisdiction. Such a ruling means the capability to operate above otherwise inaccessible safe havens thus enables the state to exercise power and control over suspected terrorists, and accordingly to bring them under the remit of Human Rights Law.[66] Consequently, lethal action would be legally justified by the ICCPR's right to life and the ECHR's Article 2, and executed under the state's obligation to protect life from the violence of a third party. Such an approach would eliminate the need to rely upon an ongoing global state of armed conflict, while retaining the government's freedom to intervene wherever legitimate and pressing threats emerge. Operating within a human rights framework as opposed to the laws of war would necessitate strikes being executed under the more stringent accountability criteria discussed earlier, but in reality, the approach would not differ significantly from the standards the United States briefly committed itself to following at the tail end of the Obama administration. Strikes would still be taken on a case-by-case basis and judged against the likelihood of an attack depriving citizens of their right to life, the lack of any alternative non-lethal recourse, and the immediacy of the threat. But, critically, they would exist as individual applications of the state's duty to protect the lives of its citizens as opposed to part of an ongoing war—an important narrative shift both for the domestic audience, and wider community, and an added degree of oversight and bureaucracy which would encourage the use of force to only be applied for its absolute necessity as opposed to its ease.

C. Imminence under Human Rights Law

The most significant drawback with a reliance upon human rights law to justify lethal action as opposed to the current practice of drawing upon the laws of war relates to the different standards concerned with the imminence of the threat. Under the laws of war, imminence is a very flexible concept. When operating under typical rules of engagement, soldiers do not need to wait until their lives are imminently endangered before they are permitted to employ lethal force. By being engaged in an armed conflict, the enemy's intentions, regardless of time

[66] Mr. Justice Leggatt, "*Al Saadoon v Secretary of State for Defence*," High Court of Justice, Mar. 17, 2015, para. 95, <https://www.judiciary.gov.uk/wp-content/uploads/2015/12/r-al-saadoon-v-secretary-of-state-for-defence-2015-ewhc-715-admin.pdf>.

frame, are clear. An enemy combatant can be justifiably killed so long as there is sufficient evidence that they are indeed a combatant belonging to a nation or organization with which the state is engaged in armed hostilities. Such flexibility is well suited to counterterrorism, where the opponent claims the tactical advantage of invisibility, fluidity, and surprise to gain maximum shock value when targeting the static institutions of the state. Hence, under the modern interpretation of imminence applied by the United States and the United Kingdom, the decision to employ lethal force is based upon the *opportunity* to hit the target, as opposed to the specific imminence of the threat they are deemed to pose. "[T]he best defense," argued the former Bush administration lawyer John Yoo, "will be available only during a small window of opportunity when terrorist[s] become visible."[67] Hence, as an enemy combatant in an armed conflict, the terrorist can be killed at any time as an ongoing threat to the state, something which has allowed American drones, and now those of their British counterparts, to become opportunistic hunters, striking when a target can be eliminated with, in theory at least, the minimal collateral damage, as opposed to when the threat they pose is a certainty.

Over recent years, the UK government has followed the American lead in seeking to establish a new norm for the criteria of imminence. "Let no one be in doubt that the rules of the game are changing," warned Prime Minister Tony Blair following London's bombing in 2005.[68] In light of terrorist's utilization of encrypted Internet platforms as command and control hubs from which to inspire and direct strikes from abroad, the British Attorney General, speaking before the Justice Select Committee in September 2015, reiterated that imminence ought to be judged on more flexible criteria.[69] Three months later, the UK Defence Secretary Michael Fallon, speaking before the Joint Committee on Human Rights in relation to the killing of Rayeed Khan, maintained that "an imminent threat can presumably grow in immediacy. It may grow in seriousness. It may grow in likelihood. It may exist for some period of time."[70] This broader interpretation of imminence under which, as Fallon went on to argue, the potential risk and necessity to act should be judged on a case-by-case basis, had the implicit support of the UN Security Council, which urged

[67] John Yoo, *Assassination or Targeted Killing After 9/11*, 56 N.Y.L. Sch. Rev. 57, 73 (2011–12).

[68] Simon Jeffrey, *The Rules of the Game Are Changing*, Guardian, Aug. 5, 2005, <https://www.theguardian.com/uk/2005/aug/05/july7.uksecurity5>.

[69] Attorney General oral evidence before Justice Select Committee (HL, Sept. 15, 2015), <http://data.parliament.uk/writtenevidence/committeeevidence.svc/evidencedocument/justice-committee/the-work-of-the-attorney-general/oral/21698.pdf>.

[70] Secretary of Defence Michael Fallon, oral evidence before Joint Committee on Human Rights (HL May 10, 2016), 46, <https://www.publications.parliament.uk/pa/jt201516/jtselect/jtrights/574/574.pdf>.

members to do all in their power to prevent and suppress terror attacks by ISIS.[71]

Despite the general move toward a loosening of the criteria of imminence to address the evolving terror threat, the UK Parliament's Joint Human Rights Committee cautioned against an overly expansive interpretation. With extensive intelligence networks, unrivaled electronic surveillance, and the capability to project lethal force with precision, the United States—and to a lesser extent the United Kingdom—are uniquely placed to take advantage of a flexible interpretation of imminence to launch preemptive action against terrorists across the globe. But, unchecked by a strict legal architecture, these capabilities—as the War on Terror has demonstrated—lead to ever-growing kill lists and reinforce a state of perpetual warfare. The creation of the most sophisticated hunter-killer network in the world has not moved America toward the end of the War on Terror, rather it has become a self-generating enterprise. While greater freedom to act before the threat posed by a terrorist fully materializes offers clear security benefits, the costs of America's pursuit of total security demonstrates that there are also advantages to restraint.

The strict standards of the ICCPR and ECHR require that, outside the state of armed conflict, the right of self-defense can only be exercised if there is an *immediate* threat of unlawful violence to others which makes it "absolutely necessary" to employ lethal force to prevent it.[72] Rather than weakening British counter-terrorism efforts, this enforced restraint would serve to protect against the sort of hyperactivity which has dragged the United States into open-ended warfare in pursuit of unachievable levels of security, an aim which, ironically, has done more to stoke domestic tensions and generate fear among Americans than the nation's terrorist enemies ever could. Under a human rights framework, potential threats would need to be proven to be genuine before an independent body which oversees the application of lethal force. The British government would need to accept the burden of proving to the best degree they could that a covert plot was truly imminent and that the potential target of lethal action had both the capability and will to act. Such a process would require a degree of flexibility given the near impossibility of determining the exact intention of an opponent that relies upon surprise.[73] But while the more strict requirements would reduce the government's latitude to act, the greater insistence upon evidence of a genuine possibility of attack and the independent oversight of that decision would

71 UNSCR 2249, para. 5, Nov. 20, 2015, <https://www.securitycouncilreport.org/atf/cf/%7B65BFCF9B-6D27-4E9C-8CD3-CF6E4FF96FF9%7D/s_res_2249.pdf>.

72 ICCPR art. 12; ECHR, art. 2, 2.(a).

73 "Government's policy on the use of drones for targeted killing," UK Parliament Joint Committee on Human Rights, May 10, 2016, at 46–47, <https://www.publications.parliament.uk/pa/jt201516/jtselect/jtrights/574/574.pdf>.

reduce the temptation for policymakers to come to rely upon killing as the first option and reduce the risk of Britain's capabilities seeing it fall into an open-ended killing campaign.

VI. Conclusion

What this chapter has proposed—the adoption of a human rights framework to justify and regulate the United Kingdom's lethal drone strikes—requires a new interpretation of the geographical scope of application of the ECHR, and as such needs to be approached with caution. The use of human rights law for lethal drone strikes is an approach which is legally incomplete in terms of its exploration in law courts and academia and untested in its implementation. There remain core legal definitions and rulings which would need to be resolved, in particular what the threshold criterion would be for an individual targeted by a drone strike to fall within the jurisdiction of the United Kingdom when outside of the geographical sphere of a hot battlefield and in the territory of another state. As such the preceding serves as an introduction as to why this would be a good measure for the United Kingdom to pursue, and a warning of what the current alternative—Britain's slow adoption of an expansive war paradigm—would ultimately mean for the nation and its counterterrorism efforts.

While the full legal architecture for lethal drone strikes executed under a human rights framework remains to be resolved, what is known is that the adoption of human rights law as the primary vehicle through which lethal force would be employed in counterterrorism operations would be a way of ending a war which cannot be won in a traditional sense and shifting today's glorified enemy combatants back to the less glamorous status of criminals. The proposal to make this change does not reflect a naivety about the threat groups such as Al Qaeda and ISIS pose. The use of lethal force is, at times, entirely necessary in the defense of a modern, open, democratic state. What it does ensure is that the lethal force which is employed is used within the boundaries of international laws and norms, reducing the opportunities for other nations to challenge the existing global order, and removing accusations of hypocrisy. And while the United Kingdom's foray into the world of preemptive lethal strikes is still at an early stage compared to the United States' sustained killing campaigns, the British government would do well to take the initiative with adopting such a change, rather than waiting to gradually have the details of drone strikes and their associated casualties forced out through legal action, leaks, and pressure from external organizations. Doing so would not only serve the strategic benefits raised above but would also avoid eroding the public's trust and raising suspicion toward the government's counterterrorism activities, as has been the case with the American drone program.

The United States and the United Kingdom have two of the most capable counterterrorist systems in the world. While greater transparency may be unusual, and initially uncomfortable for security services used to functioning under the veil of secrecy, both nations should have the confidence to reveal their practices, assured in the knowledge that these quiet professionals do their utmost on a daily basis to protect their fellow citizens' intrinsic right to life, while upholding the values and standards espoused by the laws of both their state and the international order. While certain aspects of operations and intelligence gathering will need to remain classified, accessible only to a select few with the necessary security clearance, greater oversight and transparency will ultimately serve to increase trust in the mechanisms used by those charged with the responsibility to make life and death decisions. Parliamentary oversight should be welcomed not just as a measure to ensure best practice in counterterrorism activities but also as an essential check on executive action. As the United States' experience has shown, drone strikes are seductive to political leaders, offering a seemingly risk-free shortcut to what can only ever be a temporary state of security. Official monitoring of the use of such weapons is an important bulwark against their potentially corrupting influence.

Finally, shifting from a reliance upon the laws of war to human rights law signals the overdue renunciation of the preventive war doctrine which has become the American norm since 9/11, and has been gradually seducing the United Kingdom too. Despite a slide in its international standing, and a relative decline in wealth and power compared to its closest competitors, the United States remains the world's most influential nation. Where it leads, others follow, and its erosion of important norms, such as the principle of deterrence over force, the scope of imminence, and the expansive use of the laws of war, is ultimately undermining the global system it was the primary architect and beneficiary of. If we are to accept that there is such a thing as a "special relationship" between the United States and the United Kingdom, Britain's policymakers should take it as a responsibility to show its wayward ally that there is another way to balance the security of the homeland and the stability of the international order in the most British way possible. Rather than being seduced by capabilities and an apparent high-tech, low-risk solution to the terrorist threat, the United Kingdom's policymakers should remember the government's motivational words as a much more existential threat gathered over the Channel: "keep calm and carry on."

PART III

FIGHTING CRIME AS WAR

11

National Security Policymaking in the Shadow of International Law

Laura A. Dickinson

This chapter describes how the norms and values embedded in international human rights law (IHRL) can sometimes be adopted, if not as a matter of formal law at the international level, then as a matter of official policy and practice. In addition, it surveys the advantages and disadvantages of such an approach, using two different Obama administration counterterrorism policies as case studies. Ultimately, I argue that the emergence and persistence of such policies is evidence of international law's constraining impact. I also analyze the attributes of these policies, including their "legalistic" character, and the consequences of creating policies of this type. This analysis suggests that national security policymaking in the shadow of international law can be a pragmatic and effective alternative to formal international lawmaking, and it is a practice that human rights organizations, and administrative, constitutional, and international law scholars need to consider. In addition, the stickiness of such policymaking, even in subsequent administrations, illustrates the importance of institutional path dependence, the role of lawyers, the constraint of interoperability with key allies in multilateral military actions, and the way norms get embedded in government organizations.

The Obama administration sought to address a fundamental conflict between the United States and many of its allies over the appropriate international legal paradigm that should govern extraterritorial counterterrorism operations, such as those involving the use of lethal force or military detention. These counterterrorism operations have, in the years since the September 2001 attacks on the United States, stretched the boundaries of armed conflict both geographically and temporally.[1] The question therefore arose: Should government lawyers assess such operations under a war paradigm, governed by international humanitarian

[1] *See generally* Rosa Brooks, How Everything Became War and the Military Became Everything (2016); Charlie Savage, Power Wars: The Relentless Rise of Presidential Power and Secrecy (2015).

Laura A. Dickinson, *National Security Policymaking in the Shadow of International Law* In: *Between Crime and War.* Edited by: Claire Finkelstein, Christopher Fuller, Jens David Ohlin, Mitt Regan, Oxford University Press. DOI: 10.1093/oso/9780197638798.003.0012

law (IHL), sometimes called the law of armed conflict (LOAC)?[2] Or, by contrast, should they evaluate these counterterrorism operations abroad as law enforcement operations, which would generally be governed under the more restrictive regime of IHRL?[3] Or does some combination of these domains of international law form the governing legal framework?

This issue of the appropriate legal paradigm is not merely of technical, academic interest to lawyers toiling away at their desks in the bowels of the Pentagon, the State Department, and other government buildings. Rather, it has profound consequences for any proposed military operations to detain or kill terrorist targets abroad. For example, with respect to the use of lethal force, under a war paradigm targeted killing of an enemy is lawful unless it runs afoul of broad principles such as distinction (civilians[4] and civilian objects[5] must not be attacked) and proportionality (the expected military advantage of the action must exceed the expected harm to civilians and civilian objects).[6] But in peacetime, when IHRL generally governs, individuals cannot be killed except in much more limited circumstances, such as when capture is not feasible and the use of lethal force is absolutely necessary to defend oneself or others.[7]

[2] Central IHL/LOAC treaties include United Nations, "Convention (I) for the Amelioration of the Condition of the Wounded and Sick in Armed Forces in the Field of August 21 1949" (1950) 75 United Nations Treaty Series 31, art. 3; United Nations, "Convention (II) for the Amelioration of the Condition of Wounded, Sick and Shipwrecked Members of Armed Forces at Sea of 12 August 1949" (1950) United Nations Treaty Series 85, art. 3; United Nations, "Convention (III) Relative to the Treatment of Prisoners of War of 12 August 1949" (1950) 75 United Nations Treaty Series 135, art. 3; United Nations, "Convention (IV) Relative to the Protection of Civilian Persons in Time of War of 12 August 1949" (1950) 75 United States Treaty Series 287, art. 3; United Nations, "Protocol Additional to the Geneva Conventions of 12 August 1949, and relating to the Protection of Victims of International Armed Conflicts (Protocol I), 8 June 1977" (1979) 1125 United Nations Treaty Series 3; United Nations, "Protocol Additional to the Geneva Conventions of 12 August 1949, and relating to the Protection of Victims of Non-International Armed Conflicts (Protocol II), June 8, 1977" (1979) 1125 United Nations Treaty Series 609.

[3] Key human rights treaties potentially applicable to counter-terrorism operations include United Nations, "International Covenant on Civil and Political Rights, 19 December 1966" (1976) 999 United Nations Treaty Series 171; United Nations, "Convention Against Torture and Other Cruel, Inhuman or Degrading Treatment or Punishment, 10 December 1984" 1465 United Nations Treaty Series 85; United Nations, "Convention for the Protection of Human Rights and Fundamental Freedoms, 4 November 1950" (1955) 213 United Nations Treaty Series 222; "American Convention on Human Rights: Pact of San Jose, Costa Rica, 22 November 1969" (1979) 1144 United Nations Treaty Series 123; Organization of African Unity, "African Charter on Human and People's Rights, 27 June 1981" (1988) 1520 United Nations Treaties Series 217.

[4] United Nations, "Protocol Additional to the Geneva Conventions of 12 August 1949, and Relating to the Protection of Victims of International Armed Conflict (Protocol I) . . . Adopted at Geneva on 8 June 1977" (1979) 1125 United Nations Treaties Series 3 art. 51.2.

[5] *Id.* art. 52.1.

[6] *Id.* arts. 51.5(b), 57.2(a)(iii).

[7] *See, e.g.*, McCann and others v. United Kingdom, App. No. 18984/91 (ECtHR, Sept. 27, 1995) para. 200; Kakoulli v. Turkey, App. No. 38595/97 (ECtHR, Nov. 2005) para. 121. *See also* United Nations, Human Rights Committee, "General Comment 36, Article 6: Right to Life" (2018). For an overview of this legal framework, *see, e.g.*, Philip Alston, "Report of the Special Rapporteur on Extrajudicial, Summary, or Arbitrary Killings" (United Nations, Human Rights Council A/HRC/14/24/, 2010) para. 33; Marie Aronsson, Susan Breau, & Rachel Joyce, "Discussion Paper

Significantly, the Obama administration—like the Bush administration before it—took the position that, as a purely legal matter, IHL/LOAC rather than IHRL applies globally to US counterterrorism operations, at least as to certain terrorist organizations such as Al Qaeda.[8] Even outside zones widely recognized as embroiled in armed conflict, the United States has maintained that, with respect to certain hostile groups, a war is taking place. Accordingly, the law of war should govern. The Trump administration continued to embrace this view.[9] This interpretation of international law, however, contrasts with that of many US allies, who have maintained that IHL/LOAC does not necessarily apply globally to operations against terrorists such as Al Qaeda.[10] These states adopt a more fact-specific analysis of whether an armed conflict is actually occurring in the particular geographic location where operations are contemplated. If an armed conflict is not occurring, according to their analysis, the generally higher standards of IHRL applicable to the use of force and detention would likely govern.[11]

This conflict in legal approach is potentially quite significant. Many of the countries that adopt a more confined view of IHL/LOAC, such as the United Kingdom,[12] France, Germany,[13] and Canada, partner regularly with the United

2: Drone Attacks, International Law, and the Recording of Civilian Casualties" (June 2011); Mary Ellen O'Connell, *Lawful Use of Drones in* RISE OF THE DRONES II: EXAMINING THE LEGALITY OF UNMANNED TARGETING 20 (Hearing testimony, United States House of Representatives, Serial No 111-120, Apr. 28, 2010); KENNETH WATKIN, FIGHTING AT THE LEGAL BOUNDARIES: CONTROLLING THE USE OF FORCE IN CONTEMPORARY CONFLICT 287–300 (2016).

[8] *See, e.g.*, "Report on the Legal and Policy Frameworks Guiding the United States Use of Military Force and Related National Security Operations" (Dec. 2016).

[9] *See* Office of the White House, "Report on the Legal and Policy Frameworks Guiding the United States' Use of Military Force and Related National Security Operations" in Mathew Kahn, *Document: White House Legal and Policy Frameworks for Use of Military Force*, LAWFARE, Mar. 14, 2018, https://www.lawfareblog.com/document-white-house-legal-and-policy-frameworks-use-military-force.

[10] John O. Brennan, "Strengthening our Security by Adhering to our Values and Laws, Remarks at the Program on Law and Security," Harvard Law School, Sept. 16, 2011). *See also* Marco Sassoli, *The Role of Human Rights and International Humanitarian Law in New Types of Armed Conflicts*, *in* INTERNATIONAL HUMANITARIAN LAW AND INTERNATIONAL HUMAN RIGHTS 34, 56 (Orna Ben-Naftali ed., 2011) (stating that many US allies limit applicability of IHL/LOAC to hot battlefields such as Afghanistan). *See also* Nehal Bhuta & Hin-Yan Liu, "Policy Brief: Targeted Killing, Unmanned Aerial Vehicles and EU Policy" (Global Governance Programme, European University Institute, Mar. 2013), 1, 3, http://cadmus.eui.eu/bitstream/handle/1814/27737/2013-1-Policy%20Brief_RSCAS_GGP.PDF?sequence=1.

[11] *See, e.g.*, Watkin, *supra* note 7.

[12] *See* Joint Committee on Human Rights, "The Government's Policy on the Use of Drones for Targeted Killing (second report)" (2015-16, HL 141, HC 574), 50.

[13] *See* Leander Beinlich, *German and Its Involvement in the US Drone Programme before German Administrative Courts*, EJIL:TALK!, Apr. 8, 2019, <https://www.ejiltalk.org/germany-and-its-involvement-in-the-us-drone-programme-before-german-administrative-courts/; Jurgen Bering, "Legal Explainer: German Court Reins in Support for U.S. Drone Strikes," JUST SECURITY, Mar. 22, 2019, <https://www.justsecurity.org/63336/legal-explainer-german-court-reins-in-support-for-u-s-drone-strikes; Emma DiNapoli, *German Courts Weigh Legal Responsibility for U.S. Drone Strikes*,

States in counterterrorism operations around the globe. Thus, different views regarding the applicable legal regime present the specter of numerous so-called "interoperability"[14] challenges that could make it more difficult for these allies to co-operate with the United States.[15]

Enter what I am calling "legalistic" national security policies. In the face of these conflicting interpretations of applicable international law, the Obama administration crafted a number of national security policies that have imposed rules and standards that are more restrictive than the legal minimum, but they have done so as a matter of *policy* rather than as an interpretation of *international law requirements*. These policies, although they are merely policies at the international level, are often quite legalistic. They are written in a way that requires legal analysis and legalistic judgments, because they impose rules and standards that must be interpreted. Indeed, many of them impose legal obligations as a matter of domestic law. Yet because they are framed as policies, they allow the US government to formally retain its interpretation of the scope of IHL/LOAC and reject IHRL's applicability even as it adopts IHRL standards as a matter of practice.

In order to explore this sort of national security policymaking in the shadow of international law, this chapter describes two sets of these "legalistic" national security policies adopted by the Obama administration, one addressing operational rules for targeted killings of suspected terrorists abroad,[16] and the other pertaining to the procedures required to justify continued US detention of suspected terrorists.[17] Each of these policies includes norms and procedures that I contend bring US practice closer to the norms of IHRL, even as the United

LAWFARE, Apr. 4, 2019, <https://www.lawfareblog.com/german-courts-weigh-legal-responsibility-us-drone-strikes.

[14] "Interoperability" is not a term that appears within IHL/LOAC, but the North Atlantic Treaty Organization (NATO) defines the term as "the ability to act together coherently, effectively and efficiently to achieve Allied tactical, operational and strategic objectives." *See* "NATOTerm, Official NATO Terminology Database" (NSO), <https://nso.nato.int/natoterm>. As one commentator has noted, "Interoperability is necessary to ensure a coalition can function with unity of effort and unity of purpose. . . . It is indispensable to the implementation of a comprehensive approach to armed conflict operations." Blaise Cathcart, *Coalition Warfare and the Law of Armed Conflict in 2040*, *in* THE LAW OF ARMED CONFLICT AT 2040 (Mike Schmitt and Matt Waxman eds., 2020).

[15] *See* Cathcart, *supra* note 14. *See also* Kirby Abbott, *A Brief Overview of Legal Interoperability Challenges for NATO Arising from the Interrelationship Between IHL and IHRL in Light of the European Convention on Human Rights*, 96 INT'L REV. RED CROSS 107 (2014); Steven Hill, *The Role of NATO's Legal Adviser*, *in* THE ROLE OF LEGAL ADVISERS IN INTERNATIONAL LAW (Andraz Zidar & Jean-Pierre Gauci eds., 2016); Steven Hill & David Lemetayer, *Legal Issues of Multinational Military Operations: An Alliance Perspective*, 55 MILITARY L. & L. OF WAR REV. 13 (2016–17).

[16] Executive Office of the President, "Presidential Policy Guidance: Procedures for Approving Direct Action Against Terrorist Targets Located Outside the United States and Areas of Active Hostilities" (redacted May 23, 2013), https://www.justice.gov/oip/foia-library/procedures_for_approving_direct_action_against_terrorist_targets/download.

[17] Executive Office of the President, Executive Order No. 13567 "Periodic Review of Individuals Detained at Guantanamo Bay Naval Station Pursuant to Authorization to Use Military Force" (Mar. 10, 2011) 76(47) Federal Register 3277.

States has never accepted the applicability of IHRL to the counterterrorism operations that these policies govern. And both sets of policies have been surprisingly durable. Implemented during the Obama administration, each policy faced harsh political criticism by candidate Donald Trump on the campaign trail. Yet despite rolling back some aspects of these policies, the Trump administration preserved core elements of each.[18]

Having described these two policies, I turn to consider the implications of this "legalistic policy" path. By adopting these policies, the United States did not formally agree to be bound by IHRL in conducting extraterritorial counterterrorism operations. Yet these policies implement human rights values to some degree. Arising in an intergovernmental setting in which key US allies follow IHRL, interoperability benefits appear to have pushed the United States in a more human rights–oriented direction that has persisted across administrations to a surprising degree. IHRL, it seems, casts a long shadow, even in situations where governments are articulating discretionary policies, rather than formally binding legal interpretations.

To some human rights advocates, the Obama administration missed an opportunity to formally roll back the war paradigm and articulate a stronger role for IHRL as it applies to extraterritorial counterterrorism. And, to be sure, the costs of this approach are significant. On the other hand, the policy approach helped, as a practical matter, to move the United States toward greater alignment with human rights norms than might have otherwise been the case. Specifically, these policies helped mitigate the interoperability challenges involved when collaborating with allies on counterterrorism operations, smoothed over interagency disputes about the proper scope of IHRL in this area, and, as a procedural matter, preserved legalistic judgments (and a corresponding role for lawyers) even as formally these judgments remained outside the realm of IHRL. And, as mentioned at the outset, these policies have been surprisingly durable. Policy is, in theory, more variable from administration to administration. In practice, however, it tends to persist.

Thus, this chapter explores how national security policymaking plays a hitherto unrecognized role both in effectuating international law norms even in the absence of formal law and in advancing those norms in the face of conflicting interpretations about their content. In a rapidly changing domain of international affairs, such legalistic policies can serve an important bridging function that can further multilateral operations while preserving commitments to fundamental rule of law values. In addition, such policies can help address internal

[18] *See, e.g.*, Office of the Whitehouse, *supra* note 9; Executive Office of the President, Executive Order No. 13823 "Protecting America Through Lawful Detention of Terrorists" (Feb. 2, 2018) 83(23) Federal Register 4831.

differences within governments as well. At a minimum, the phenomenon of such legalistic policies, drafted in the shadow of international legal norms, is worthy of ongoing study and discussion.

I. Legalized Policies for Counterterrorism Operations

Although the United States has continued to embrace a war paradigm with respect to the international law regime governing its activities against certain terrorist organizations, it has nonetheless *as a matter of policy* at the international level imposed certain additional restrictions on its operations. These restrictions consist of rules that are more demanding than the minimum legal requirements the United States has said it is obligated to follow under international law. But they are policies that effectively reflect the very international human rights norms that the government formally says it is not required to obey.

This section examines two such policies. First, it discusses the Obama administration's policy for targeting terrorist suspects abroad, entitled the Presidential Policy Guidance on Procedures for Approving Direct Action Against Terrorist Targets Located Outside the United States and Areas of Active Hostilities (PPG).[19] Second, it describes the Periodic Review Board (PRB) process that has been instituted to address the ongoing detention of terrorism suspects at Guantánamo Bay naval base. In both cases, the policies include elements that exceed the legal minimum requirements imposed by IHL/LOAC and resemble, to some degree, elements of IHRL. Moreover, in both cases, although the Trump administration reportedly discarded some aspects of these policies, critical elements appear to have survived.

A. The PPG Framework

The PPG provides a detailed framework for using force against terrorists outside territories described as "areas of active hostilities."[20] Although the term "areas of active hostilities" does not correspond to any accepted legal category within IHL/LOAC, the term has been interpreted to refer to those zones that are unequivocally sites of armed conflict within existing IHL/LOAC tests.[21]

[19] *See* Executive Office of the President, *supra* note 16.

[20] *See* Executive Office of the President, *supra* note 16.

[21] In the Frameworks Report, the United States identified the specific places that it deemed at the time to be "areas of active hostilities." As of December 2016, the date of the Frameworks Report, those areas included Afghanistan, Iraq, Syria, designated areas in Libya, and US actions to defend US or partner interests outside the terrorism context, such as the 2016 US military strikes on radar facilities in Houthi-controlled territory in Yemen. Office of the White House 2016, *supra* note 8.

Outside these "areas of active hostilities," the PPG provides a detailed set of substantive and procedural rules for "direct action" against terrorist targets, including the use of lethal force and capture. With respect to substantive rules, the PPG requires that lethal force can only be used against a target that poses a "continuing, imminent threat" to US persons. In addition, the PPG mandates that, before lethal action can be taken, a determination must be made that there is (1) near certainty that the terrorist target is present and that non-combatants will not be injured or killed; (2) an assessment that capture is not feasible at the time of the operation; (3) an assessment that the relevant governmental authorities in the country where action is contemplated are unwilling/unable to effectively address the threat; and (4) an assessment that no other reasonable alternatives exist to effectively address the threat to US persons.[22]

In addition to these substantive rules, the PPG also imposes rigorous procedural requirements. For example, in most cases involving the use of lethal force, the PPG mandates that senior executive branch officials are required to review and approve the operation.[23]

The Trump administration reportedly retained some, but not all, of these requirements.[24] The new administration did not release a report of comparable detail outlining its policy, but it did acknowledge that "[t]he United States continues, as a matter of policy, to apply heightened targeting standards that are more protective of civilians than are required under the law of armed conflict."[25] Newspaper accounts supplied additional details, for example, that the Trump administration expanded the zones designated as areas of "active hostilities" to include Somalia.[26] With respect to the substantive rules specifically, journalistic accounts suggest that the administration reportedly dispensed with the rule that a terrorist target must pose a continuing, imminent threat to US persons and interests and that there must be a near certainty that the terrorist target is present—instead adopting a "reasonable certainty" test. But the Trump administration appears to have retained other elements found in the PPG, such as the requirement that there must be "near certainty" that civilians will not be harmed before lethal force may be used. With respect to the procedural elements, the

[22] *Id.*

[23] Executive Office of the President, *supra* note 16.

[24] *See, e.g.*, Charlie Savage & Eric Schmitt, *Trump Poised to Drop Some Limits on Drone Strikes and Commando Raids*, N.Y. Times, Sept. 21, 2017, https://www.nytimes.com/2017/09/21/us/politics/trump-drone-strikes-commando-raids-rules.html?smid=url-share.

[25] Office of the White House, *supra* note 9. The Trump administration follow-up report to the 2016 Frameworks Report is quite paltry, but it does acknowledge that there is a targeting policy that includes heightened standards above what IHL/LOAC requires.

[26] *See, e.g.*, Charlie Savage & Eric Schmitt, *Trump Eases Combat Rules in Somalia Intended to Protect Civilians*, N.Y. Times, Mar. 30, 2017, https://www.nytimes.com/2017/03/30/world/africa/trump-is-said-to-ease-combat-rules-in-somalia-designed-to-protect-civilians.html?smid=url-share.

Trump administration reportedly retained the basic idea that these sorts of operations required certain approvals, but permitted decision-making to take place at lower levels of command.

The elements of the PPG, and to a lesser extent the Trump administration successor policy, exceed the requirements of IHL/LOAC and, I would argue, at least move in the direction of IHRL. Both the substantive standards and the procedures set forth in these policies contain elements that resemble components of the IHRL framework for the use of lethal force. Although the terms used are not exactly the same, the concepts are similar.

For example, under the PPG, US authorities are required to determine that a terrorist target poses a "continuing, imminent threat" to US persons and interests before approving the use of lethal force. This standard far exceeds the targeting standards of IHL/LOAC. Rather, it looks more like the standard typically mandated by IHRL that authorities may not deploy lethal force except when "strictly" or "absolutely necessary," limiting the use of such force to circumstances such as when harm is "imminent."[27] Similarly, the PPG's preference for capture mirrors IHRL's rule that lethal force must be a last resort, with no other reasonable alternatives (such as capture). In addition, the PPG resembles IHRL in mandating that there must be "near certainty" civilians will not be harmed before lethal action may be taken. The IHL/LOAC proportionality rule does not even come close to dictating such certainty, but rather accepts the grim reality that civilian casualties are lawful within an armed conflict if expected casualties are proportionate to expected military advantage. IHRL, by contrast, requires under some formulations, "due regard" for harm to third parties, and in others, a degree of certainty that third parties will not be injured.[28]

The procedural aspects of the PPG also bear similarities to the obligations of IHRL and far exceed any procedural rules found in IHL/LOAC. IHRL formulations of the right to life encompass obligations on the part of the state to undertake certain procedures such as advance planning before conducting operations that entail the use of lethal force[29] as well as an obligation to investigate after the fact.[30] IHRL does not map out specific procedures per se, but a lack of adequate planning could trigger a violation. IHL/LOAC might be said to impose some procedural requirements, such as the obligation to take feasible precautions where possible to warn civilian populations before military

[27] *See, e.g.*, "General Comment No. 36," *supra* note 7; *see also* Alston, *supra* note 7.

[28] *See, e.g.*, Tagayeva and others v. Russia, App. No. 26562/07 (ECtHR, Apr. 13, 2017) para. 603; Ahmet Ozkan and others v. Turkey, App. No. 21689/93 (ECtHR, Apr. 6, 2004) para. 308.

[29] *See, e.g.*, *McCann*, *supra* note 7. *See also* Carandiru v. Brasil, Case 11.291 Inter. Am. Comm. HR No. 34/00 (2000) paras. 61, 66, 91.

[30] *See, e.g.*, Finogenov and others v. Russia, App. No. 18299/03 (ECtHR, Dec. 20, 2011) para. 282; Al-Skeini and others v. The United Kingdom, App. No. 55721/07 (ECtHR, July 7, 2011) para. 166; Cruz Sanchez et al. v. Peru, Inter-American Court of Human Rights Series C No. 292 (Apr. 17, 2015).

operations commence, but such obligations are less stringent and more flexible.[31] The PPG's rules about levels of authorization, and even the existence of the PPG itself, could be seen to implement the kind of procedural obligation that IHRL envisions.

The Trump administration successor policy, despite discarding some aspects of the PPG, nonetheless retained elements that exceed the requirements of IHL/LOAC and move in the direction of IHRL. In particular, the requirement that lethal force may only be used if there is a "near certainty" civilians will not be harmed went far beyond the IHL/LOAC proportionality rule. And although the Trump administration successor policy reportedly dispensed with rules mandating approval of operations by senior civilian officials, the continued existence of the policy itself was more than IHL/LOAC would demand. As in the case of the PPG, the successor policy also went some distance toward satisfying the kind of procedural planning obligations imposed by IHRL.

Thus, as a matter of policy, the PPG and the Trump administration successor policy could be seen to incorporate some elements of IHRL. To be sure, it is a little unclear precisely which legal categories the policies adopted. And the PPG (and presumably the Trump administration successor) did not specifically acknowledge that they were incorporating legal categories at all. But the bottom line is that the United States has adopted restrictive rules—both in the PPG and in the Trump administration successor policy—that are more akin to IHRL standards than to the IHL/LOAC standards that the United States continues to insist are the appropriate legal rules in this context.

B. The PRB Framework

As in the case of targeting, the United States has embraced a war paradigm for detention of terrorism suspects captured outside the United States and held in military detention, even far from conventional battlefields. Since 9/11, the United States has held thousands of persons in military detention extraterritorially, not only in Iraq and Afghanistan but also notably at Guantánamo Bay.[32] Across multiple administrations, the United States has consistently clung to the view that such extraterritorial detainees are war detainees and that the international legal requirements applicable to them are therefore those mandated by IHL/LOAC,[33] rather than the more restrictive rules of IHRL.[34] Yet, as in the case of the PPG,

[31] "Protocol Additional to the Geneva Conventions of 12 August 1949," *supra* note 4, at art. 57.

[32] *See* Laura A. Dickinson *Military Lawyers on the Battlefield: An Empirical Account of International Law Compliance*, 104 AM. J. INT'L L. 1 (2010).

[33] *Id.*, for a more detailed treatment of this issue.

[34] *Id.*

the United States has *as a matter of policy* adopted procedures and practices for these detainees that exceed the requirements of IHL/LOAC as the United States interprets it and move at least somewhat in the direction of IHRL. The most significant of these policies is the Periodic Review Board procedure (PRBs) for Guantánamo detainees adopted in the Obama administration and continued in the Trump administration.[35]

The PRBs emerged in 2011 when the Obama administration issued an executive order forming the boards to assess the status of Guantánamo detainees who had been designated for preventive detention under the laws of war or who had been referred for criminal prosecution but had not yet been charged.[36] The PRBs provided enhanced protections for detainees as compared to precursor procedures initiated in the Bush administration. Pursuant to the order, the PRBs' function was to evaluate whether the continued detention of a covered individual was warranted in order "to protect against a significant threat to the security of the United States." In cases where the PRB concluded that continued detention was not necessary, the secretaries of state and defense were designated responsible for making vigorous efforts to transfer such detainees outside the United States, consistent with national security interests. The executive order also mandated that the administration was to make PRB rules and procedures available to the public. Congress subsequently codified this executive order as part of the 2012 National Defense Authorization Act.[37]

The PRB procedures require an initial review as to whether the continued detention of each individual is necessary to prevent a security risk.[38] Each detainee, who is provided with a personal representative, has the opportunity to participate in a hearing before the PRB. In addition, detainees may hire lawyers to represent them at their own expense. At the hearing, the detainee and his representative can challenge the government's factual basis for ongoing detention and introduce evidence. After the initial review, officials must conduct a full review every three years, with interim reviews every six months.

The boards are composed of senior civilian officials from the Departments of Defense, Homeland Security, Justice, and State, members of the Office of the Director of National Intelligence, and officials from the Joint Chiefs of Staff. Each board has access to all government information relevant to the detainee being reviewed and considers this information alongside diplomatic considerations, security assurances, the detainee's mental and physical health, and any other

[35] The United States has adopted similar, though somewhat less stringent, policies for detainees held extraterritorially in locations other than Guantánamo, such as Afghanistan. For a more detailed account of these policies, *see* Dickinson, *supra* note 32.

[36] Executive Office of the President, Executive Order No. 13567, *supra* note 17.

[37] National Defense Authorization Act for Fiscal Year 2012 Pub. L. 112-81 sec. 1023, 125 Stat. 1564–65, codified at 10 USC sec. 801 note (2012) (US).

[38] *Id.*

mitigating information. The board may not rely on any information obtained through torture or cruel, inhuman, or degrading treatment. The recommendation of the board is submitted to cabinet-level officials at the represented departments and agencies, and these officials are allotted thirty days to object to the PRB's disposition of any given detainee. An objection triggers review by a committee of these agency principals. Once the decision is made, it is published on the review secretariat's website.[39]

Despite statements by President Trump suggesting that he would radically depart from the Obama administration approach to military detention at Guántanamo and elsewhere, the Trump administration largely continued the procedures established in the Obama administration to evaluate military detainees, including the PRBs. Indeed, an executive order issued fairly early in the Trump administration explicitly provided for the continued operation of the PRBs.[40] To be sure, federal law required the administration to continue with the PRBs because the PRBs were codified in the 2012 National Defense Appropriation Act.[41] But the order went further than the statute required, stating that such boards and their existing procedures (inherited from the Obama administration) would be used "to determine whether continued law of war detention is necessary to protect against a significant threat to the security of the United States."[42] Secretary of Defense James Mattis also issued implementing guidelines for the PRB process.[43] And in habeas proceedings initiated by Guantánamo detainees, Trump administration lawyers referred to the PRB proceedings as evidence of fairness in decision-making about ongoing detention.[44]

Like the PPG, the PRB procedure can be seen as a legalized policy that moves somewhat in the direction of IHRL. The US executive branch has never stated that the PRBs are required as a matter of international law—either IHRL or IHL/LOAC. Yet the board procedures come closer to the kinds of due process requirements of IHRL (and also the kind of procedures IHL/LOAC mandates for certain categories of detainees in international armed conflicts) than the pre-existing procedures from the Bush administration. The PRBs provided enhanced procedural protections, allowing detainees more opportunity to present and rebut evidence and entitling them to personal representatives to assist them. Though comprised entirely of executive branch officials and therefore

39 U.S. Department of Defense, "Periodic Review Secretariat," https://www.prs.mil/Review-Information.

40 *Id.*

41 National Defense Authorization Act, *supra* note 38 , at sec. 1023.

42 *Id.*

43 Secretary of Defense, "Memorandum from Patrick M. Shanahan, Secretary of Defense, Implementing Guidelines for Periodic Review of Detainees Held at Guantanamo Bay per Executive Order 13567" (Nov. 27, 2017).

44 Respondents' Opposition to Petitioners' Motion for Order Granting Writ of Habeas Corpus, Al-Bihani v. Trump, No. 04-cv-1194 (District Court, D.C. 2018).

not courts constituted within a separate branch of government, the boards bear some hallmarks of independence. For example, they are more independent than purely military tribunals, as members include career officials from multiple agencies. Moreover, the establishment and continuation of the PRBs via executive orders and the codification of key elements in US legislation increases the transparency and rationality of proceedings. Although the contents of many of the specific proceedings remain classified, the legal framework for the proceedings and its rules are clear and open to the public.

To be sure, PRB procedures still do not provide the kind of full-fledged judicial proceedings that would be required under IHRL when state agents detain criminal suspects in peacetime. IHRL mandates that detention must conform to rigorous standards, including minimum standards regarding the conditions of detention, as well as due process requirements regarding access to a lawyer, charges to be filed before an independent court within a specific period of time, notice of such charges to the detainee, and so on. Although the detainees have the benefit of assistance from a personal representative and may hire lawyers at their own expense, they are not entitled to legal representation. Hearsay is still permitted, and detainees are not necessarily entitled to view all of the evidence. And, of course, the PRBs are not independent courts.

Moreover, in practice, the PRBs have a mixed record. As a result of the PRB reviews, many of the Guantánamo detainees were deemed not to be a continuing threat and therefore were "eligible for transfer" to their home countries or third countries[45] (given that the US Congress prohibited transfer to the United States).[46] Although the initial executive order specified that all initial reviews would commence no later than one year from the date of the order, the hearings did not begin until 2013, and all initial hearings were not completed until September 2016.[47] To date, the PRBs have held 89 hearings, for 64 detainees. Of the 64 detainees who have received decisions, 38 were cleared for transfer, and 26 were recommended for continued detention. During the Obama administration, 36 of the 38 that were cleared for transfer were released from Guantánamo and transferred to their home countries or third countries.[48] Overall, the Obama administration transferred 144 Guantánamo detainees (some were transferred pursuant to procedures that predated the PRBs). But at the end of the Obama administration, 41 remained in detention, 26 of whom still had not been charged

[45] *See, e.g.*, Laura A Dickinson & James E Baker, "The U.S. Military Commissions: Looking Forward," Report, American Bar Association, Standing Committee on Law and National Security, May 2018, 25.

[46] National Defense Authorization Act, *supra* note 38, at sec. 1027.

[47] Human Rights First, "Guantanamo Periodic Review Boards" (Apr. 9, 2018), https://www.humanrightsfirst.org/resource/guantanamo-periodic-review-boards.

[48] *Id.*

with a crime but who had been recommended for continued detention. Those 26 did, however, remain subject to the PRB process.[49]

Furthermore, critics have suggested that, despite operating according to the same administrative framework, the work of the PRBs in practice under the Trump administration was deeply flawed.[50] In particular, critics cited long delays in the publication of PRB decisions as evidence of dysfunction and likely interference by senior political officials.[51] Over four years the boards conducted only four full reviews and fourteen subsequent reviews.[52] None of those proceedings resulted in approval to release and transfer any additional Guantánamo detainees. At least one commentator argued that the failure of the PRBs to recommend release or transfer in any case turned the review boards into a "one-way ratchet for justifying continued detention" and a "fig leaf."[53]

Despite their significant flaws, the boards nonetheless represent a middle ground between the kind of unchecked military detention established in the early Bush administration and the full-fledged judicial process that would be required for detainees in the civilian justice system. As such, they provide an example of the kind of policies that serve a variety of functions discussed below—bridging differences with US allies and internal critics who take a more constrained view of the war paradigm for extraterritorial counterterrorism.

C. Legalistic Nature of Policies

The two policies discussed here are distinctive in an important respect: they are what we might call "legalistic." Both in substance and in the procedures they set forth, each of the policies contains legalistic categories. Moreover, each demands a role for lawyers, even if that role is implicit. To implement the policies, agency and military officials must as a practical matter obtain advice from executive branch lawyers, both civilian and military.

With respect to substance, each of the policies includes categories that, if not directly imported from legal frameworks, bear at least some resemblance to such categories. For example, in the case of the PPG, the concept of "continuing, imminent threat" has analogs in both IHRL and the law of self-defense. And the term "near certainty" is the kind of term that is relevant in a variety of legal

[49] *See* Dickenson & Baker, *supra* note 46, at 25.

[50] *See, e.g.*, Benjamin Farley, *Who Broke Periodic Review at Guantanamo Bay*, LAWFARE, Oct. 15, 2018, https://www.lawfareblog.com/who-broke-periodic-review-guantanamo-bay.

[51] *Id.*

[52] U.S. Department of Defense, "Periodic Review Secretariat, Full Review," https://www.prs.mil/Review-Information/Full-Review; U.S. Department of Defense, "Periodic Review Secretariat, Subsequent Full Review," https://www.prs.mil/Review-Information/Subsequent-Full-Review.

[53] Farley, *supra* note 51.

analyses. Similarly, the PRB procedures require officials to evaluate whether a detainee poses a "continuing threat"—another term that could easily be lifted from another legal framework. And these policies, are, in any event, now codified as law at the domestic level even if not recognized as required by international law.

These policies are also legalistic in the procedures they establish. The PPG requires government officials at certain levels to assess operations. That requirement implies some type of formalized bureaucratic process. Much less is known about the details of the Trump administration successor targeting policy, though journalistic accounts suggest that it allowed decisions to be made by lower level officials.[54] It is not unreasonable to assume, however, that even here there was some type of formalized internal bureaucratic process to apply the rules set forth in the policy. The PRB policy is even more legalistic in the procedures it creates: effectively, it establishes a kind of administrative tribunal and review process.[55]

All of these policies imply a role for executive branch lawyers. Lawyers would appear to be necessary to interpret the terms of the targeting policy as it is applied. And executive branch lawyers are crucial to evaluating the terms of the PRB policy. Thus, although the United States has never acknowledged that these policies are required by international law, they establish an institutional role for lawyers.

II. International Law's Shadow and the Advantages and Disadvantages of the Policy Approach

By implementing these terrorism targeting and detention policies, the United States moved in the direction of IHRL even as it rejected the formal legal constraints of this body of law. Why did it do so? The context in which these policies emerged strongly suggests that interoperability—the ability to work with partners who follow IHRL—is a significant factor. Specifically, the multilateral dimension of counterterrorism operations requires the United States to take account of other countries' view of the law, leading to a ratcheting up in standards. Whether they are providing intelligence to the United States or offering consent to US operations on their territory, partner states that follow IHRL exert pressure on the United States to observe human rights principles.

In addition, when the United States adopts these policies, they acquire a "legalistic" valence that appears to exert a kind of binding force through internal organizational culture and practice. Lawyers help write the policies, using legal

[54] *See* Savage, *supra* note 1.

[55] *See* Dickinson, *supra* note 32.

terms that in turn require legal analysis. As a consequence, the process of approving military operations internally requires evaluation of these policies in the same manner as if they were international legal standards. The durability of these policies may stem, in part, from the way they become embedded in the national security bureaucracy. As in the case of the interoperability benefits, the organizational dimension of these policies could be tested in future empirical work.

The story of these policies therefore contributes an important new perspective to the long-running international law compliance debate. What we see is that even when international law does not exert binding force, its values can cast a long shadow that end up making a real (and possibly lasting) difference.

But that then raises the question: is it actually *better* for these international human rights norms to be effectuated through discretionary national security policymaking? Or would it have been preferable for the Obama administration to have produced a formal legal determination that counterterrorism operations outside the hot battlefield are legally bound by IHRL? In other words, what are the pros and cons of seeking international law compliance or addressing international law's ambiguities through policy rather than law?

From the perspective of US executive branch officials, it may be advantageous to embrace a legal paradigm that sets fewer minimum requirements and then adopts legalistic policies such as the PPG and the PRBs that exceed these minimum legal requirements. In the face of ambiguity about the scope of international law and the choice of the appropriate legal paradigm, this approach offers an attractive path forward for a variety of reasons. Indeed, it may often be easier for executive branch officials to adopt policies than to clarify the scope of the law or choose the more demanding legal paradigm.

First, policy is flexible. When executive branch officials assert only a minimalist view of legal requirements but then exceed those requirements as a matter of policy, officials maintain room to maneuver. In this sense, such an approach reflects a kind of pragmatism. It can be fine-tuned and calibrated to specific circumstances, and it preserves discretion for the executive branch.

This flexibility was likely an important consideration in adopting the PPG and the PRBs. Forcing governments to satisfy all the requirements of IHRL may make it difficult to counter threats quickly, particularly if the governments are always required to first demonstrate that the threat is imminent. The more minimalist rules of IHL/LOAC do not require strict necessity or imminence assessments before lethal force may be used. A state that embraces policies such as the PPG or PRB procedures therefore retains the discretion to choose standards that resemble those of IHRL when it is feasible to do so. But because the policy does not impose legal restraints at the international level, a state that has adopted such a policy may also *deviate* from the policy if circumstances dictate. The state thus preserves scope for a range of action while still emphasizing its commitment to follow international law.

Second, a policy approach serves to bridge different interpretations of international law held by different states. When one state believes that IHL/LOAC governs extraterritorial counterterrorism operations even outside traditional battlefields, and another asserts that the more demanding law of international human rights applies, a policy that incorporates elements of IHRL can minimize the impact of these contrasting views. If the state that adheres to the more permissive rules of IHL/LOAC implements practices that exceed those minimum rules, the practical impact of this state's contrasting legal approach will diminish. The conflict over legal paradigms thus may virtually disappear as a practical matter, at least at the operational level.

One could make the case that the PPG and the PRBs served this type of role. The PPG brought the United States closer—at least in practice—to the approach of many allies, international organizations, and civil society groups that take a more constrained view of the scope of armed conflicts with terrorist groups. The standards for direct action specified in the PPG, including for targeted killing and capture, approximate the rules of IHRL outside "areas of active hostilities." To be sure, these standards do not fully equal the stringent requirements of IHRL, and the terms of each do not fully map onto one another. Furthermore, the Trump administration successor policy moved back in the other direction, expanding the gap in approaches. But nonetheless, this policy still exceeds the minimum requirements of IHL/LOAC and thus still comes closer to an IHRL framework than a purely minimalist application of IHL/LOAC. Even under the Trump administration approach, outside areas of active hostilities the US military reportedly still was not authorized to use lethal force unless there was a near certainty that civilians would not be killed. Thus, even though US allies may still disagree with the US view of the appropriate legal paradigm for such operations, there are fewer practical disagreements with regard to the specific actions the United States actually undertakes during counterterrorism operations.

Similarly, the PRBs have brought the United States a few steps closer to a human rights paradigm for detention of terrorism suspects. Although the procedures do not fully embody human rights due process protections, they do provide more protections for detainees in the form of regularized administrative proceedings.

The PPG, and to a slightly lesser extent the Trump administration successor policy, along with the PRB procedures, also potentially reduced conflicts with the territorial states where the United States was taking direct action. By requiring US actors to ensure there is a near certainty that civilians will not be harmed during a direct action, the PPG and the Trump administration policy both minimized the extent to which host states could object to such action on their territory. And the operation of the PRBs potentially blunted criticisms of human rights–oriented US allies regarding the Guantánamo detainees.

By bridging these types of differences among states, legalized policies such as the PPG and the PRBs can reduce interoperability concerns of multilateral operations. Such interoperability needs could arise when, for example, US allies must consider whether to share intelligence that could be used in a US targeting or detention operation. Indeed, the 2016 Frameworks Report acknowledges that differences in legal interpretation among states can bring challenges to such operations.[56] The report notes that the United States regularly consults with allies to find pragmatic solutions in such situations—to find a way to work together. The PPG and the Trump administration successor policy, as well as the existence of the PRB procedures, can help with this effort.

Finally, a legalistic policy has the potential to bridge differences *within* a government. Executive branch officials may themselves disagree about the applicable legal framework for a particular operation or type of operation. When such disputes arise, a legalistic policy can smooth over such differences. It may be easier in many cases to achieve consensus to adopt such a policy than to resolve the dispute with a definitive decision about which legal regime should apply.

Accounts now public of debates within the Obama administration indicate that top administration lawyers were locked in heated discussions regarding contrasting paradigms under international law and the use of force, as well as the interpretation of the rules within those paradigms.[57] Against the backdrop of hard-fought contests over legal meaning, a policy approach such as the PPG or the PRB procedures would certainly seem attractive. Rather than hashing out freighted differences over legal restrictions on US action, executive branch officials crafting policy solutions can avoid such differences altogether. The choice of a legal paradigm and an explicit public acknowledgment of the applicability of that paradigm, particularly a restrictive one, has enormous consequences for a state that tries to hew faithfully to its international legal commitments. Policies such as the PPG and the PRB procedures circumvent this issue while advancing the underlying values of the human rights paradigm. For executive branch officials opposed to the human rights paradigm, the policy preserves the legal discretion of the United States. For executive branch officials who believe the human rights principles are important, the policy enables them to implement those principles in a pragmatic way. In this sense, such a policy is a win-win.

Despite these important advantages, there are reasons to be concerned about the policy approach. Indeed, even as they serve a bridging function among states, policy approaches may slow or impede the actual *resolution* of legal differences

[56] Office of the White House 2016, *supra* note 8, at 14.
[57] *See* Savage, *supra* note 1.

among such states. Such policies to some extent mask the legal dimensions of a problem and can interfere with the development of the law. For example, a state that only chooses to bind itself as a matter of policy might still want *other* states to similarly bind themselves, but it loses its ability to insist on such compliance if the issue is only treated as a matter of policy, not law.

The PPG and the PRB procedures offer examples of policies that, while potentially easing interoperability concerns among states with different legal views, mask the legal dimensions of the problem and potentially slow the development of customary international law. The PPG (and to a lesser degree the Trump administration successor policy), along with the PRB procedures, put the United States more on the same page—as a matter of practice—as those states that adopt a law-enforcement approach to extraterritorial counterterrorism operations. But in doing so, those policies obscure the differences among states about the appropriate international law paradigm that governs the extraterritorial use of force or detention with regard to such operations. The policies themselves do not refer to specific legal categories. Although the standards in the PPG and the PRB procedures resemble the categories of IHRL, the standards do not match these categories exactly. Indeed, the policies do not directly refer to IHRL at all and do not in any sense explicitly acknowledge the conflict in legal paradigms. Accordingly, with respect to extraterritorial direct action outside of "hot" battlefields, and extraterritorial military detention, the policies do nothing to advance greater harmonization of divergent legal perspectives—either in the direction of the more restrictive IHRL or the more minimalist IHL/LOAC approach.

The PPG and PRB procedures thus do not contribute to the development of customary international law in this area. Because the United States has embraced its practices as a matter of policy at the international level—not as actions taken due to a sense of legal obligation—it would be difficult to cite the PPG or PRB procedures as evidence to support the development of customary international law. One might argue that, to the extent that the policy is law at the domestic level, actions taken pursuant to the PPG and the PRB procedures should count as actions taken pursuant to a sense of legal obligation. Yet the notion that domestic legal obligations of this nature could satisfy the *opinio juris* element of customary international law is not universally accepted. Thus, operations conducted within the framework of the PPG or the PRB procedures would not clearly establish customary international law.

Likewise, because policy approaches paper over differences in legal interpretation internally within a state, the adoption of such policies block efforts to actually resolve those differences of legal interpretation. The policy decision can therefore lead to long-term inconsistency because it does not bind future administrations in the same way that legal interpretations do. And though of course even a legal interpretation can be revisited by a future administration, the process for doing so is far more difficult than simply changing a policy.

In the case of the PPG and the PRB procedures, the policy approach has led to just this sort of malleability. It did not resolve what may have been internal differences in legal views about extraterritorial direct action against terrorists. For example, as discussed earlier, one of the first initiatives the Trump administration reportedly took was to revise the PPG, even as it retained some of the policy's elements. And it is possible that future administrations could make further changes to the policy. As discussed previously, policies are stickier than we might assume, but there can be little doubt that they are at least somewhat easier to revise than are formal legal determinations.

Finally, the implementation of a legalistic policy may also spark confusion about whether the policy is evidence of customary international law. As discussed previously, the adoption of a policy should not establish customary international law because the states that embrace such policies are not doing so out of a sense of legal obligation. Nonetheless a variety of actors in the international community—including some states, international organizations, or nongovernmental organizations—may draw attention to a policy and assert that it is at least some evidence of customary international law. Even if the state adopting the policy would stand on strong legal ground in rejecting such assertions, these types of statements require executive branch time and attention. From an executive branch perspective, legalistic policies therefore carry the risk that other entities will misconstrue the legal dimension of state actions according to the policies.

This risk has arguably been borne out to some degree with respect to the PPG and the PRB procedures. Some entities have suggested that the PPG and the PRB procedures reflect legal, rather than policy, rules. To be sure, executive branch officials could mitigate this risk by repeatedly and transparently asserting that it is acting pursuant to policy. Indeed, if every time states adopt such policies an effort is made to infer that customary international law has been created, then states might stop adopting more restrictive policies altogether and might instead retreat to a more minimalist approach.

From a human rights perspective, these sorts of policies are a mixed bag. On the one hand, such policies have the practical impact of making the state more compliant with human rights norms in its day-to-day counterterrorism operations. This is a big plus from a human rights perspective, and it is possible that if the human rights community had pushed for a full-throated legal interpretation the effort would have failed. Thus, one might see the adoption of legalistic policies as an important, pragmatic human rights victory with very real positive consequences on the ground. Moreover, even though administrations can in theory change such policies, they are remarkably durable in practice.

In the case of the PPG and the PRB procedures, the human rights–protecting standards they imposed were a real win for the human rights community. Under the PPG, as a matter of policy, the United States agreed to adhere to human rights values in the use of force extraterritorially. Under the PRBs, the United States has provided more procedural protections for Guantánamo detainees. Furthermore, it is significant that some of these policies remained intact, even in the Trump administration. These policies are therefore evidence that published policy decisions can be sticky and lead to path dependence, even if not to the same extent as legal determinations.

On the other hand, as discussed previously, the adoption of legalistic policies can slow the development of the law. Thus, if a state opts to make policy rather than embrace a human rights–oriented view of the law, human rights groups may view this choice as a cop-out. And, as previously noted, a policy is more vulnerable to subsequent reinterpretation or case-by-case backsliding than a legal interpretation would be (though of course even a legal interpretation can be changed or withdrawn in a subsequent administration).

With respect to both the PPG and the PRBs, a fair case can be made that the Obama administration missed an opportunity to articulate a more human rights–oriented approach to counterterrorism. By adopting legalistic policies, it failed to articulate legal limitations beyond the minimum rules of IHL/LOAC with respect to extraterritorial counterterrorism operations outside of armed conflict. This failure made it easier for the Trump administration to reverse course. Of course, from a human rights perspective, adoption of the policies was still far preferable to a minimalist IHL/LOAC legal interpretation, so adoption of a potentially sticky policy was certainly better than no human rights regarding action at all.

Policy presents one final issue worth noting. From a human rights perspective, one might be worried that rules adopted as a matter of policy rather than legal obligation might diminish the role of lawyers in decision-making regarding counterterrorism operations. In general, decreasing the role of lawyers might give military officers a freer hand to make determinations that might be less human rights regarding. However, because the policies I have described are sufficiently legalistic, they actually still require a role for lawyers in interpreting them. Thus, it is not clear that the role of lawyers actually diminishes. Indeed, it may be that lawyers are *more* needed because the interaction of the underlying IHL/LOAC and the policy may actually make the rules more complicated to parse. Of course, one could also view the role of lawyers as a problem because legal vetting can delay the deployment of military operations or tie the military's hands.

In the case of the PPG and most likely its successor Trump administration policy, along with the PRB procedures, both military and civilian lawyers must engage at a variety of levels to assess the implementation of the policy. And, as

I have argued elsewhere, military lawyers often play a very real constraining role on military operations.[58] On the other hand, the role for lawyers imposes a greater complexity on operations and could in theory slow them down. Whether that is good or bad depends on whether you focus on the potential human rights value in increased deliberation or whether you think military operations will be unnecessarily delayed by needless red tape.

III. Conclusion

The story of the PPG and the PRB procedures highlights that one of the critical frontiers in thinking about international law compliance is the boundary between law and policy in the domain of extraterritorial counterterrorism operations. Although scholars and human rights observers who work in this domain tend to focus on legal rules, it turns out that executive branch policies can be a crucial aspect of compliance with the values underlying international legal regimes. Even if governments do not accept certain international legal regimes as binding at the international level, the policies they adopt may nonetheless embed aspects of those international legal categories.

And such policies may have important advantages, both for governments that seek consensus with other countries and within their own national security bureaucracy, as well as for human rights advocates who seek greater practical human rights compliance on a day-to-day level. Indeed, governments may be more willing to adopt robust human rights policies for many of their activities if they do not feel that doing so will bind them in all circumstances as a matter of law. On the other hand, when governments adopt policies, they miss important opportunities to clarify international law and incorporate core legal standards more forcefully into their military operations.

Thus, the decision whether to adopt policies rather than legal rules is a key issue for further study, and the advantages and disadvantages of policies versus legal interpretations is a fruitful area for continued investigation and debate. Comparative analysis may also reveal differences in decision-making processes in this area from country to country. And scholars of the sociology of institutions may provide insights regarding the impact of lawyers in interpreting these legalistic policies within governmental bureaucracies. Finally, it will be important to see the extent to which voluntary policies harden into customary law over time.

In any event, given that global counterterrorism operations are likely to continue for the foreseeable future, those interested in charting the path of international law compliance must pay attention not only to the formal categories

[58] *See generally* Dickinson, *supra* note 32.

of international law but also to the way different governments finesse those categories through the use of policy. Indeed, sometimes these policies may actually be more important in determining actual state practice on the ground than the official international law doctrines. Further, as a normative matter, scholars, nongovernmental organizations, and others must considers the advantages and disadvantages of a policy-oriented approach to international law compliance.

12
Emerging Transnational Self-Defense Norms and Unrealized Liberal Values

John C. Dehn[*]

This chapter critiques emerging norms surrounding the use of alleged defensive force by powerful states against violent non-state groups located in the territory of other states, here termed "transnational self-defense." Although international law and the contemporary international security system embrace basic liberal political principles of sovereignty, sovereign equality, and liberty/autonomy, not all states and peoples are treated equally in state practice.[1] This disparity likely stems from what I will call the Grotian tradition, wherein sovereignty and humanity were deemed equal only between so-called "civilized" nations and peoples. The rules and formalities limiting "public war" applied only between such entities. Other peoples and powers, including indigenous persons, were equated with pirates and others against whom the use of armed force to defend or to punish was much more freely permitted. There is abundant state practice confirming these aspects of the Grotian tradition.

The Charter of the United Nations and other treaties regulating wartime conduct and protecting fundamental individual rights are all significant steps in a centuries-long process of adopting and refining basic liberal principles and extending them to all societies and peoples. Now that basic liberal principles are universally recognized, at least formally, respect for sovereignty, human rights, and strict constraints on the resort to and use of armed force should guide state practice as well. Nevertheless, this chapter will show that emerging norms of transnational self-defense effectively perpetuate a system of de facto sovereign and human inequality traceable to the Grotian tradition. The use of war measures against "terrorist" non-state armed groups, including targeted killing in what is effectively preemptive or preventive self-defense, perpetuates a discriminatory international system of sovereignty and human rights "haves" and "have nots."

* The author thanks to Adil Haque, Joseph Ferguson, Barry Sullivan, and James Gathii for helpful discussions and comments on earlier drafts. Thanks also to Emily Binger, Amelia Parker, and Allyson Thompson for relevant research and editorial assistance.

1 *See* UN Charter arts. 1–2.

John C. Dehn, *Emerging Transnational Self-Defense Norms and Unrealized Liberal Values* In: *Between Crime and War.* Edited by: Claire Finkelstein, Christopher Fuller, Jens David Ohlin, Mitt Regan, Oxford University Press. © Claire Finkelstein, Christopher Fuller, Jens David Ohlin, Mitt Regan 2023. DOI: 10.1093/oso/9780197638798.003.0013

To better respect the basic liberal values that now inhere to all states and peoples, states should adopt a more circumscribed view of their right to engage in transnational self-defense when no relevant non-international armed conflict exists.[2] Properly understood, the self-defense principles of necessity and proportionality require that states: (1) resort to defensive measures only when necessary to protect lives and property from relatively certain, significant harm, and (2) use only the amount of force which is strictly necessary to neutralize the threat that is reasonably believed to exist at the time force is used. Because these self-defense principles should be understood to limit both the resort to force and the nature of any force used, this more constrained and humane approach does not implicate contested issues involving the extraterritorial application of human rights law.[3]

I. Liberal Values and the Use of Force

A. The Grotian Tradition

Basic liberal principles of sovereignty, sovereign equality, autonomy, and respect for the rights and liberty of other nations or "states" have long been an aspect of international legal theory and the international system.[4] In his seminal seventeenth-century work, *On the Law of War and Peace*, Hugo Grotius articulated principles applicable to the use of armed force by and against both states and "non-State" societies or peoples.[5] Although refined over several centuries, many of these principles continue to influence international law and state practice to this day. Reviewing key features of the Grotian tradition related to the use of armed force is therefore essential to examining contemporary self-defense norms.

Grotius theorized several conditions on the use of force between states. States may only use force against other states for a just cause, meaning in response to an injury already suffered (to recover or to punish) or about to be inflicted (in defense).[6] States had an obligation to resolve inter-state disputes peacefully if

[2] A "relevant" non-international armed conflict refers to a situation of protracted violence to which international humanitarian law applies in the context of which a defensive attack occurs.

[3] *See*, e.g., Oona A. Hathaway et al., *Human Rights Abroad: When do Human Rights Treaty Obligations Apply Extraterritorially*, 43 Ariz. St. LJ. 389 (2011).

[4] The intellectual origins of these principals are, at the very least, traceable to Grotius in the context of the territorial nation or state. *See, e.g.*, Richard Tuck, The Rights of War and Peace: Political Thought and the International Order from Grotius to Kant (2009 reprint) 108.

[5] *See* 1 Hugo Grotius, The Rights of War and Peace, ch. 1, para. 2.1 (Richard Tuck ed., 2005).

[6] *See* 2 Hugo Grotius, The Rights of War and Peace, ch. 1, pt. II (Richard Tuck ed., 2005). The rules were similar for non-states to justify private war.

possible.[7] "Public wars" occurred only between or among sovereign states and should commence only when decided upon by their sovereign civil authority after due deliberation, including the consideration of peaceful alternatives.[8] A sovereign wishing to use nondefensive force should issue a declaration of war to provide a final demand for redress and opportunity for the peaceful resolution of a dispute.[9] Once public war had commenced, the parties involved should observe certain constraints on their conduct.[10]

In the Grotian tradition, however, these rules and formalities applied only to "public" wars between entities deemed "civilized" states. In his preliminary discourse, Grotius clarified that he was expounding a law "common to many nations" with origins in either natural law, divine command, or custom and tacit consent.[11] A state or nation within this system had a sovereign civil authority, the power to wage war and make peace, and, as a general matter, denounced war against other states.[12] Even if such a state were to engage in clearly unjust behavior, Grotius averred that "a state is still a state so long as it has law and judgements and other means necessary for natives and strangers to preserve or recover their just rights."[13]

Grotius distinguished these so-called "civilized" nations from other peoples or powers that he labeled "the rest[, who] are but pirates, or robbers."[14] This distinction between "civilized" and "uncivilized" societies would persist. As Professor Antony Anghie has noted, the notion of sovereignty in international law entailed a determination of what entities could be regarded as sovereign, and ultimately excluded non-European, nonterritorial societies as "uncivilized."[15]

Grotius posited that any state can engage in war to punish pirates, hostile indigenous persons, and others who were thought to violate fundamental laws of nature.[16] As Professor Richard Tuck has observed, "[t]he idea that foreign rulers can punish tyrants, cannibals, pirates [and robbers], those who kill settlers, and those who are inhuman to their parents . . . legitimated a great deal of European action against native peoples around the world."[17] Grotius's views aligned with humanist jurists like Alberico Gentili rather than scholastic jurists like Vasquez

[7] *See* 3 HUGO GROTIUS, THE RIGHTS OF WAR AND PEACE, ch. 3, pts. V–VII (Richard Tuck ed., 2005).

[8] *See* 1 Grotius, *supra* note 5, at ch. 3, pt. I.

[9] *See* 3 Grotius, *supra* note 7, at ch. 3, pts. II, V.

[10] *Id.* chs. 1–2.

[11] 1 Grotius, *supra* note 5, at Preliminary Discourse, para. I. *See also id.*. ch. 3, pt. IV.

[12] *Id.*

[13] *See* 3 Grotius, *supra* note 7, at ch. 3, pt. II.

[14] *Id.* pt. I.

[15] ANTONY ANGHIE, IMPERIALISM, SOVEREIGNTY AND THE MAKING OF INTERNATIONAL LAW 56–62 (2007 reprint).

[16] *See* 2 Grotius, *supra* note 6, at ch. 20, pt. XL.

[17] *See* Tuck, *supra* note 4, at 102–03.

and Vittoria.[18] The latter believed such punishments could only be imposed by states that had been injured by a non-state entity or had civil authority over the offender.[19] Jurists from both traditions, however, acknowledged the right of a state to punish any non-state entity that had injured it in some way.

B. The Persistence of the Grotian Tradition

Although Western jurists through the nineteenth century disagreed about certain principles, many or most accepted the idea that basic liberal values inhered only to "civilized" states, as espoused by Grotius.[20] Illustrative is Swiss jurist Emmerich de Vattel, who explained that "nations or states are bodies politic" composed of people and therefore "a moral person . . . susceptible of obligations and rights"[21] and are therefore subject to the laws of nature.[22] "We must therefore apply to nations the rules of the law of nature, in order to discover what their obligations are, and what their rights."[23]

Vattel also posited basic liberal values among states, such as sovereign equality: "[s]ince men are naturally equal . . . [n]ations composed of men . . . are naturally equal."[24] He also explained the basic liberty of nations: "Nations being free and independent of each other, in the same manner as men are naturally free and independent . . . each nation should be left in the peaceable enjoyment of that liberty which she inherits from nature."[25] Additionally, just as the governments based upon liberal values derive their just powers from the consent of the governed,[26] nations, too, are governed in their mutual relations only by rules to which they consent.[27] Nations are to refrain from infringing upon the

[18] *See* 2 Grotius, *supra* note 6, at ch. 20, pt. XL (distinguishing Vitoria, Vasquez, and others).

[19] *See* Tuck, *supra* note 4, at 68–77 (examining disagreements among scholastic jurists on this issue).

[20] *See id.* 4, 140–65 (comparing theoretical assumptions and disagreements among jurists, primarily Grotius, Hobbes, and Pufendorf). *See also id.* 1–15 (briefly canvassing a broader range of jurists and intellectual thought).

[21] *See* Emmerich de Vattel, The Law of Nations, at preliminaries, 67, §§ 1–2 (Knud Haakonssen ed., Thomas Nugent tr., 2008).

[22] *Id.* 68, § 5.

[23] *Id.* 68, § 6.

[24] *Id.* 75, § 18.

[25] *Id.* 74, § 15.

[26] For example, as stated in the US Declaration of Independence, "We hold these truths to be self-evident, that all men are created equal; that they are endowed by their Creator with certain unalienable rights; that among these are life, liberty, and the pursuit of happiness; that, to secure these rights, governments are instituted among men, deriving their just powers from the consent of the governed." Declaration of Independence, para. 2 (US 1776).

[27] Vattel described the "necessary law of nations" as deriving from natural law and immutable but "internal," by which he meant binding only upon the "conscience" of states. Vattel, *supra* note 21, at 70, § 7. Only "external" rights and obligations were legally binding between or among nations. *Id.* 74, § 17. Vattel called these the "positive law of nations," and explained that they were created by presumed, express, or tacit (implied) consent. *Id.* 80, § 27.

"perfect rights" of other nations,[28] and may respond to infringements of their perfect rights with force when appropriate.[29]

Vattel also accepted Grotius's views regarding the use of force by "civilized" states or nations. Public war occurred only between nations or sovereigns.[30] States were obliged to resolve disputes peacefully if possible.[31] A state could only undertake public war as a last resort when supported by a just cause,[32] and preceded by a declaration—a final demand for redress before resort to arms.[33] Civilized states must observe certain limitations in wars with other sovereigns,[34] and in their internal, civil wars as well.[35]

Like Grotius, Vattel distinguished wars between "civilized" entities from those against a nation with a "savage disposition,"[36] as well as "illegitimate and informal wars" undertaken "without apparent cause" or "solely with a view to plunder."[37] He confirmed the right of nations to punish the peoples and powers that engage in the latter.[38] Vattel also accepted a state's right to wage more unrestrained wars against "savages" or "inhuman" enemies.[39]

Vattel defined the "law of nations" as a general "system of right and justice which ought to prevail between nations or sovereign states"[40] As this brief survey has shown, however, its more humane elements inhered only to purportedly "civilized" societies. As described by a recent commentator, the concept of international law "was born and developed in 17th century Europe," and "the process through which international law became global involved the expansion of European international law."[41] This law applied differently between "Western sovereigns under formal equality [and] . . . Western and non-Western polities under inequality, granting special privileges to the former."[42]

[28] *Id.* 74–75, §§ 17, 20.

[29] *Id.* 74–77, §§ 17, 20, 22–23.

[30] Vattel, *supra* note 21, at bk. 3, ch. 1, 469, § 2.

[31] *Id.* bk. 3, ch. IV, 500–03, §§ 51–56.

[32] *Id.* bk. 3, ch. III.

[33] *Id.* bk. 3, ch. IV, 501–02, §§ 52–54.

[34] *Id.* bk. 3, chs. VIII–X, 541–85.

[35] Vattel first distinguishes civil war from commotion, insurrection and sedition. *Id.* bk. 3, ch. XVIII, 641–42, 644–45, §§ 287–89, 292. He then asserts that parties to a true civil war must observe the "common laws of war—those maxims of humanity, moderation, and honour, which" he had detailed earlier. *Id.* bk. 3, ch. XVIII, 645–47, § 294.

[36] *Id.* bk. 3, ch. IV, 503, § 58.

[37] *Id.* 507–08, § 67.

[38] *Id.* bk. 3, ch. VIII, 544, § 141.

[39] *See* e.g., *Id.* 544–46, §§ 141–42 (reprisals and denial of quarter permitted against "inhuman" enemies); *id.* ch. IX, 570–72, §§ 167–68 (outlining relatively unrestrained war permitted against "an unjust and barbarous nation").

[40] *See id.* preface, 7.

[41] *See* Arnulf Becker Lorca, *Universal International Law: Nineteenth-Century Histories of Imposition and Appropriation*, 51 HARV. INT'L L.J. 475, 476 (2010).

[42] *Id.* 477. Professor Anghie appears to perceive the shift to a positivist view of international law emerged from European and "descendant" states in the nineteenth century. *See* Anghie, *supra* note

The belief that it was morally just to use armed force to punish non-state entities for their alleged depravity or violence has persisted for centuries in Western legal thought. A great deal of State practice rested on this view. To use the United States as an example, its Congressional Research Service has documented no less than thirty-eight instances of punitive US military actions or expeditions against pirates, robbers, indigenous peoples, and others between 1798 and 1945—some of which continued for months or years and involved multiple uses of armed force.[43]

C. The Propagation and Evolution of Liberal Values

The nations considered a formal member of this egalitarian international system varied over time but have steadily grown. States that committed to peacefully resolving disputes, to refraining from unnecessary war, and to observing humane limits on wartime conduct were deemed worthy of "civilized" status and, at least in theory, of reciprocal respect.[44] At the dawn of the twentieth century, treaties enshrining these obligations began determining the nations with equal status, at least nominally.

Several treaties committing to peaceful resolution of disputes and limiting the resort to war were adopted in this era. They included Hague Convention (I) of 1899, revised and readopted in 1907, in which parties agreed to settle disputes peacefully and created a Permanent Court of Arbitration to assist them in doing so.[45] Additionally, in Hague Convention (III) of 1907, states agreed to provide other parties to that treaty an explicit warning and opportunity to redress injuries prior to commencing war.

After World War I, nations attempted to strengthen commitments to avoid war by creating a League of Nations, including a Council and the Permanent Court of International Justice to assist in resolving international disputes.[46] The League was largely ineffective, and by 1928, fourteen nations—including

15, at 52–60. Professor Tuck reveals it had earlier intellectual origins in the Humanist tradition, later including Grotius, Vattel, and others. *See generally* Tuck, *supra* note 4.

[43] *See* Congressional Research Service, *Instances of Use of United States Armed Forces Abroad, 1798–2020*, at 2–10 (2020). *See also* (n 170–171).

[44] *See* Anghie, *supra* note 15, at 56–65 (discussing efforts to exclude non-European states from having status of equal sovereigns). *See also* Lorca, *supra* note 41, at 477–78 (arguing Western international legal system did not expand through inclusion by concession but rather through "the reinterpretation of rules by non-Western states" by "[s]emi-peripheral jurists [who] internalized European legal thought in order to change rules"). Lorca concludes that this resulted in "the inclusion of semi-peripheral states in the international community, where states are considered formally equal." *Id.* 478.

[45] *See* Pacific Settlement of International Disputes (Hague I) (July 29, 1899); Pacific Settlement of International Disputes (Hague I) (Oct. 18, 1907).

[46] *See* Covenant of the League of Nations (Apr. 28, 1919).

only European nations plus Canada, New Zealand, South America, the United States, and Japan—separately committed to resolving all disputes peacefully and declared "that they condemn recourse to war for the solution of international controversies, and renounce it, as an instrument of national policy in their relations with one another" in the Kellogg-Briand Pact.[47] Several other states later adhered to this Pact before its entry into force.[48] Although a right of self-defense was not explicitly mentioned in it, state parties believed that the right was so fundamental that it need not be explicitly stated to be preserved.[49] In the course of events leading to World War II, however, several states, including Germany and Japan, withdrew from or violated the Pact.[50]

In this same time frame, states engaged in similar efforts to enshrine humane constraints on wartime conduct. For example, fewer than thirty states initially agreed to observe specific constraints on their wartime conduct in Hague Convention (II) of 1899 and Hague Convention (IV) of 1907.[51] The nations whose views of proper wartime conduct were deemed most important is evidenced by what is known as the Martens Clause of Hague Convention (II) of 1899:

> Until a more complete code of the laws of war has been issued, the High Contracting Parties deem it expedient to declare that, in cases not included in the Regulations adopted by them, the inhabitants and the belligerents remain under the protection and the rule of the law of nations, *as they result from the usages established among civilized peoples*, from the laws of humanity and the dictates of public conscience.[52]

After World War I, states adopted additional treaties to codify rules related to various emerging technologies and other matters.[53]

[47] *See* Convention Providing for the Renunciation of War as an Instrument of National Policy (Kellogg-Briand Pact) (Aug. 27, 1928), arts. 1–2.

[48] A list of parties to this treaty, including ratification, accession and withdrawal dates, is available at <https://www.state.gov/wp-content/uploads/2020/02/249-Kellogg-Briand-Treaty.pdf>.

[49] *See* Terry D. Gill & Kinga Tabori-Szabó, *Twelve Key Questions on Self-Defense Against Non-State Actors*, 95 Int'l L. Stud. 467, 472–73 (2019).

[50] *See supra* note 45.

[51] *See* Convention with Respect to the Laws and Customs of War on Land (Hague II) (July 29, 1899) [Hague II (1899)]; Laws and Customs of War on Land (Hague IV) (Oct. 18, 1907) [Hague IV (1907)]. A complete list of signatories and parties for Hague Convention (II) of 1899 is available at <https://ihl-databases.icrc.org/applic/ihl/ihl.nsf/States.xsp?xp_viewStates=XPages_NORMStatesParties&xp_treatySelected=150>; and for Hague Convention (IV) of 1907 at <https://ihl-databases.icrc.org/applic/ihl/ihl.nsf/States.xsp?xp_viewStates=XPages_NORMStatesParties&xp_treatySelected=195>. Several other conventions addressing specific aspects of international law related to war were adopted at the 1899 and 1907 Hague Peace Conferences. A more complete list is available at <https://ihl-databases.icrc.org/applic/ihl/ihl.nsf/vwTreatiesByDate.xsp>.

[52] *See* Hague II (1899), preamble (emphasis added).

[53] *Id.* A chronological list of these treaties is available at <https://ihl-databases.icrc.org/applic/ihl/ihl.nsf/vwTreatiesHistoricalByDate.xsp> and includes a 1925 protocol on poisonous and

Because treaties formally bind only the parties to it,[54] they perform a sorting function, in this case, by identifying the nations that had agreed to observe "civilized" rules of warfare. Some pre–World War II treaties, however, further limited their application through general participation clauses. These clauses provided that in the event any party to an armed conflict was not a party to the relevant treaty, the treaty would not apply at all, not even between those that had joined it.[55] Put differently, states were required to observe the rules of "civilized warfare" only if all parties to a given armed conflict had agreed to them.

D. The UN Charter Era

World War II prompted a renewed international effort to expand and cement enforceable limits on war-making as well as to recognize and respect sovereign and human rights—to solidify and extend basic liberal values to societies and individuals. These efforts most prominently included the Charter of the United Nations, the Geneva Conventions of 1949 and their progeny, and various human rights instruments, beginning with the Universal Declaration of Human Rights.

The UN Charter created a collective security system to maintain international peace and security wherein all states possess formal sovereign equality.[56] At its inception, however, the UN Charter maintained the preexisting system of sovereignty "haves" and "have-nots." Only fifty-one states were original UN members.[57] Membership remains open "to all other peace-loving states which accept" the Charter's obligations and are "able and willing to carry out these obligations."[58] Members are to "refrain from the threat or use of force against the territorial integrity or political independence of *any [member or non-member] state*, or in any other manner inconsistent with the Purposes of the United Nations."[59] Article 51 preserved the inherent right of individual or collective self-defense if an armed attack occurs "against a Member of the United Nations,"[60] but not all societies were then states or members.

asphyxiating gases, and the 1929 Geneva Conventions related to the wounded, sick, and prisoners of war.

[54] Vienna Convention on the Law of Treaties (May 22, 1969) art. 26.

[55] *See,* e.g., Hague II (1899) art. 2 ("These provisions shall cease to be binding from the time when, in a war between Contracting Powers, a non-Contracting Power joins one of the belligerents."); Hague IV (1907) art. 2 (similar).

[56] *See* UN Charter art. 2 (1).

[57] The timeline of when states acquired or were granted UN membership is available at <https://www.un.org/en/sections/member-states/growth-united-nations-membership-1945-present/index.html>.

[58] *See* UN Charter art. 4.

[59] *Id.* art. 2(4) (emphasis added).

[60] *See* UN Charter art. 51.

Chapters 11–13 of the Charter preserved the "protectorate" or "mandate" system for "non-self-governing territories," wherein some societies, called "trust territories," were to remain subject to the control of other states.[61] A trust territory gained formal sovereign equality under the Charter only when it became a member of the United Nations.[62] Until then, it was subordinate to its trustee, which was to manage the territory in a way that benefited its inhabitants, maintained international peace and security, and promoted human rights.[63]

These aspects of the Charter and later geopolitical developments explain the growth of UN membership over time. Polities that were considered sufficiently developed, capable of self-governance, and therefore able to meet Charter obligations were admitted.[64] Admission to the United Nations became the new means by which "civilized" states would determine who should be counted among their number. Before state status and UN membership became universal, however, a mix of preexisting treaty and UN Charter obligations related to member states, non-member states, and non-self-governing territories created a patchwork of self-defense and use of force norms.[65] This complex legal and geopolitical history complicates the analysis of state practice and customary norms related to both inter-state self-defense and transnational self-defense.

New treaties regulating wartime conduct performed a similar sorting function. In 1949, several states adopted four Geneva Conventions that form the cornerstone of contemporary laws regulating warfare.[66] Participation in these treaties remained open to other states and, unlike the relevant Hague Conventions, compliance between the parties to them is always required.[67] Parties to these treaties

[61] *Id.* arts. 75–85.

[62] *Id.* art. 78.

[63] *Id.* art. 76. This system has been rightly criticized. *See generally* SIBA N'ZATIOULA GROVOGUI, SOVEREIGNS, QUASI-SOVEREIGNS, AND AFRICANS: RACE AND SELF-DETERMINATION IN INTERNATIONAL LAW (1996). The trust system had origins in the mandate system of the League of Nations. *See* Anghie, *supra* note 15, at 115–95 (reviewing origins and development of mandate system).

[64] For example, many African nations did not become UN members until the 1960s. Vietnam was not admitted until 1977. North and South Korea were not admitted until 1991. Several former Soviet republics were admitted—or readmitted with different names and/or territorial configurations—in the 1990s. Although Sudan was admitted in 1956, South Sudan obtained independence and, ultimately, UN member status in 2011. The list of UN member states and dates of membership is available at <https://www.un.org/en/sections/member-states/growth-united-nations-membership-1945-present/index.html>.

[65] *See* John Dehn, *The U.N. Charter's Original Effect on State Sovereignty and the Use of Force*, JUST SECURITY, Aug. 27, 2020, <https://www.justsecurity.org/72177/the-un-charters-original-effect-on-state-sovereignty-and-the-use-of-force/>.

[66] All adopted on August 12, 1949, these were: Geneva Convention (I) on Wounded and Sick in Armed Forces in the Field, Geneva Convention (II) on Wounded, Sick, and Shipwrecked Armed Forces at Sea, Geneva Convention (III) relative to the Treatment of Prisoners of War, and Geneva Convention (IV) relative to the Protection of Civilian Persons in Time of War.

[67] *See* Geneva Convention (I), *supra* note 66, at art. 60 (accession by non-parties); art. 2 ("Although one of the Powers in conflict may not be a party to the present Convention, the Powers who are parties thereto shall remain bound by it in their mutual relations."). Articles 1–3 are the same in all four treaties.

also agreed to observe minimal humane constraints in their internal armed conflicts, as Vattel had stated.[68] Widely adopted protocols refined and extended various protections in both international and non-international armed conflicts (international armed conflict (IAC) and non-international armed conflict (NIAC), respectively).[69] With a few exceptions, the International Committee of the Red Cross—a global nongovernmental organization that promotes respect for and facilitates development of rules regulating warfare—concludes states now accept that most rules regulating warfare are customary international law applicable in both IAC and NIAC.[70]

The United Nations also began efforts to universally extend liberal values to individuals. Among its purposes was "[t]o develop friendly relations among nations based on respect for the principle of equal rights and self-determination of peoples."[71] An important initial step toward this goal was the Universal Declaration of Human Rights, adopted by the UN General Assembly in 1948.[72] This effort was followed by regional and other human rights treaties,[73] and eventually, by the International Covenant on Civil and Political Rights, which, for example, obliges states to refrain from arbitrarily depriving individuals of life and liberty.[74] Some states, including the United States, assert that not all human rights obligations apply to extraterritorial state action.[75] This exacerbates the already-complicated situation regarding the norms applicable to transnational self-defense.[76]

Now that UN membership and human rights obligations formally span the globe, a state's ability to use armed force, especially lethal force, should be narrowly circumscribed. Unlike the norms of the pre-U.N. Grotian system, state sovereignty and individual rights to life and liberty must be globally and equally respected and protected. Authority to invade or abrogate these rights should be

[68] *See id.* art. 3.

[69] *See* Protocol Additional to the Geneva Conventions of 12 August 1949, and relation to the Protection of Victims of International Armed Conflict (Protocol I) (June 8, 1977); Protocol Additional to the Geneva Conventions of Aug. 12, 1949, and relation to the Protection of Victims of Non-International Armed Conflict (Protocol II) (June 8, 1977). More protocols have since been adopted. *See* "Treaties, States Parties and Commentaries," ICRC, <https://ihl-databases.icrc.org/applic/ihl/ihl.nsf/vwTreatiesByDate.xsp>.

[70] *See generally,* CUSTOMARY INTERNATIONAL HUMANITARIAN LAW: VOLUME I (Jean-Marie Henckaerts & Louise Doswald-Beck eds., 2009) [hereinafter Customary IHL Study].

[71] *See* UN Charter art. 1 (2).

[72] *See* GA Res. 217(III), UN GAOR, 3d Sess., Supp. No. 13, UN Doc. A/810 (1948) 71.

[73] *See* "Regional Human Rights Treaties," UN Hum. Rts., <https://www.ohchr.org/en/issues/escr/pages/regionalhrtreaties.aspx> (listing regional treaties); "Multilateral Treaties Deposited with the Secretary-General," UN Treaty Collection <http://treaties.un.org/pages/Treaties.aspx?id=4&subid=A&lang=en> (listing UN-sponsored treaties).

[74] *See* International Covenant on Civil and Political Rights (Dec. 16, 1966) arts. 6, 9.

[75] *See, e.g.*, Beth Van Schaack, *The United States' Position on the Extraterritorial Application of Human Rights Obligations: Now Is the Time for Change*, 90 INT'L L. STUD. 20 (2014).

[76] *See* Monaca Hakimi, *Defensive Force Against Non-State Actors: The State of Play*, 91 INT'L L. STUD. 1 (2015) (examining unsettled status of norms).

narrowly construed. Unfortunately, the legal arguments states make to support emerging transnational self-defense norms effectively perpetuates the pre–UN Charter, pre-human rights, international system.

II. Emerging Transnational Self-Defense Norms

Representative legal arguments supporting the emerging transnational self-defense norms are contained in a December 2016 report released by the Obama administration (Report).[77] Its purpose was to "enhance the public's understanding of the legal and policy principles that have guided U.S. national security operations."[78] In a foreword, President Obama claimed the Report "reinforce[s] the fact that we defend our interests at home and around the world in a manner consistent with the laws, values, and traditions that are the source of our greatest strength."[79]

The legal framework articulated in the Report, even when coupled with the 2013 Presidential Policy Guidance (PPG),[80] is inconsistent with both international law and universal respect for basic liberal values in two important ways.[81]

[77] *See* THE WHITE HOUSE, REPORT ON THE LEGAL AND POLICY FRAMEWORKS GUIDING THE UNITED STATES' USE OF MILITARY FORCE AND RELATED NATIONAL SECURITY OPERATIONS (2016) [hereinafter Obama Framework Report]. It cites an article by Daniel Bethlehem, a former principal legal advisor in the United Kingdom Foreign and Commonwealth Office. Daniel Bethlehem, *Self-Defense Against an Imminent or Actual Armed Attack by Nonstate Actors*, 106 AM. J. INT'L L. 769 (2012). International law "experts" have made similar assertions. *See, e.g.*, Jeremy Wright, A-G (Speech at the International Institute for Strategic Studies, UK, Jan. 11, 2017), <https://www.gov.uk/government/speeches/attorney-generals-speech-at-the-international-institute-for-strategic-studies> ("Like many other states, the long-standing UK view is that Article 51 of the UN Charter does not require a state passively to await an attack [. . .], but includes the 'inherent right'—as it's described in Article 51—to use force in self-defence against an 'imminent' armed attack, [. . .] any use of force in self-defence under Article 51 must be both necessary and proportionate to the threat. A part of the assessment of necessity, where an attack has not yet taken place, is that the attack must be imminent for states to take action."); ELIZABETH WILMHURST, PRINCIPLES OF INTERNATIONAL LAW ON THE USE OF FORCE BY STATES IN SELF-DEFENCE 2 (2005), <https://www.chathamhouse.org/sites/files/chathamhouse/public/Research/International%20Law/ilpforce.doc> (providing a set of Principles that the Internal Law Programme prepared to offer "a clear statement of the rules of international law governing the use of force by states in self-defence", and indicating that "the view that states have a right to act in self-defence in order to avert the threat of an *imminent* attack—often referred to as "anticipatory self-defence"—is widely, though not universally, accepted.").

[78] *Obama Framework Report*, *supra* note 77, at ii.

[79] *Id.*

[80] *See* US Dept. of Just., *Presidential Policy Guidance, Procedures for Approving Direct Action Against Terrorist Targets Located Outside the United States and Areas of Active Hostilities* (2013) (redacted) [hereinafter 2013 PPG], <https://www.aclu.org/foia-document/presidential-policy-guidance?redirect=node/58033>; *Obama Framework Report*, *supra* note 77, at 24–26 (summarizing *2013 PPG*).

[81] In fairness, "there was . . . never any single, authoritative version of liberalism, and recent scholarship has shown that many sources beyond the liberalism of [John] Locke contributed to early American political ideas." ROGERS M. SMITH, LIBERALISM AND AMERICAN CONSTITUTIONAL LAW (1988) 13. Of course, Locke "remains the most exemplary liberal theorist precisely because—as the founding generation recognized—he reveals most powerfully the fundamental ends that early

First, both documents permit the resort to lethal force in preemptive or "proactive" self-defense against a non-state armed group (NSAG) when not clearly necessary to neutralize an impending threat of harm. Second, the documents strongly imply that all defensive uses of force in transnational self-defense occur within the context of armed conflict regulated by international laws of warfare, known as the *jus in bello*, law of war, or international humanitarian law.[82] This assertion is clearly erroneous in some contexts: not all violence between states and NSAGs creates an armed conflict to which the law of war applies. The Report extends a war paradigm to attacks against alleged "associated forces" of NSAGs without clarifying the legal and factual basis for doing so.[83] When combined, these errors allow for abrogation of state sovereignty and the right to life more than is necessary to defend against a relatively specific, certain, and immediate threat of harm. This part will briefly examine each of these claims.

A. The Resort to Force

The Report advances normative claims that are either erroneous, doubtful, or ambiguous, as well as extraordinarily malleable in practice. Not only does it claim a right of preemptive self-defense against "ongoing," indefinite threats rather than specific, imminent threats, it also asserts the ability to exercise that right in response to vague threats to US citizens or government organs located anywhere in the world against non-state armed groups located anywhere in the world.

The Report first accurately states the accepted legal bases for the resort to armed force under the UN Charter. States may lawfully resort to armed force: (1) when "authorized by the Security Council acting under the authority of Chapter VII of the U.N. Charter"; (2) in self-defense; and (3) in "an otherwise lawful manner with the consent of the territorial State."[84] Regarding the inherent right of self-defense, the Report notes that states possess and may exercise it either individually or collectively and in response to armed attacks by both states and non-state actors.[85] They must also observe fundamental self-defense principles of necessity and

liberalism proposed for political life and that America's constitutionalists promoted." *Id.* 16. Others trace liberalism to more ancient philosophical roots. *See, e.g.*, John Finnis, *Liberalism and Natural Law Theory*, 45 Mercer L. Rev. 687 (1994) (tracing basic principles of liberalism to Aristotle and St. Thomas Aquinas); Tuck, *supra* note 4 (examining numerous prominent jurists).

[82] For example, the Report states, "all U.S. military operations involving the use of military force under any of the [international legal] justifications noted above are conducted consistent with the law of armed conflict, also known as the *jus in bello*." *Obama Framework Report, supra* note 77, at 8.

[83] *Id.* 4–5.

[84] *Id.* 8.

[85] *Id.* 9.

proportionality.[86]

There is some disagreement about whether a state's Article 51 inherent right of self-defense extends to armed attacks by NSAGs.[87] The International Court of Justice (ICJ) has suggested that it does not.[88] Additionally, the ICJ has implied that a state's right to engage in transnational self-defense is contingent upon its right to engage in self-defense against a state in which a threatening non-state actor is located, known as a territorial state.[89] The apparent views of UN member states undermine these ICJ assertions. For example, in response to the September 11, 2001, terrorist attacks on the United States, the UN Security Council unanimously passed a resolution recognizing each state's inherent right of individual and collective self-defense.[90] Indeed, long before the September 11, 2001, attacks, states engaged in acts self-defense or punitive reprisal against non-state actors in the territory of other states both before and after the adoption of the UN Charter.[91]

To support a long-standing right to engage in transnational self-defense against non-state actors, the Report cites "the oft-cited *Caroline* incident involv[ing] the use of force by the British in alleged transnational self-defense within the United States."[92] The *Caroline* incident involved a British attack against a private, US-flagged vessel in US territory that had ferried men and arms to support an insurrection in British-controlled Canada.[93] All diplomatic correspondence related to this incident, which section III of this chapter examines in more detail, accepted the basic proposition that a state's right of self-defense extends to hostile acts by a non-state actor located in another state's territory.

An additional concern is that the Report's approach to the temporal aspect of self-defense does not align with the predominant view of relevant international norms. Textually, Article 51 of the UN Charter preserves member states'

86 *Id.*

87 *See generally* Gill & Tabori-Szabó, *supra* note 49.

88 *See Legal Consequences of the Construction of a Wall in the Occupied Palestinian Territory* (Advisory Opinion) 2004 ICJ Rep. 136, para. 139 (July 9) (suggesting no right of self-defense against non-state actors under Article 51 of UN Charter).

89 *See Case Concerning Armed Activities on the Territory of the Congo* (Democratic Republic of the Congo v. Uganda) 2005 ICJ Rep. 168, paras. 146–47 (2019) (finding no right to act in self-defense against territorial state from which non-state actor attacked); *but see id.*. para. 147 ("[T]he Court has no need to [address] whether and under what conditions contemporary international law provides for a right of self-defense against large-scale attacks by irregular forces").

90 *See* UNSC Res. 1368 (Dec. 20, 2001).

91 *See, e.g.*, Gill & Tabori-Szabó, 49, at 470–71; Andrew W.R. Thompson, *Doctrine of the Protection of Nationals Abroad: Rise of the Non-Combatant Evacuation Operation*, 11 Wash. U. Global Stud. L. Rev. 627, 639–51 (2012); Thomas M. Franck, Recourse to Force: State Action Against Threats and Armed Attacks 53–68 (2002). *See also* Ian Brownlie, International Law and the Use of Force by States 289 (1963).

92 *See Obama Framework Report*, 77, at 9.

93 *See infra* section III for a more detailed description of the incident. At the time of the incident, the area was known as Upper Canada. It was joined with Lower Canada to form the Province of Canada by the time of the correspondence cited *infra*.

"inherent right" of self-defense only when an "armed attack occurs."[94] The Report asserts, however, that states may engage in defensive uses of force "not only in response to armed attacks that have already occurred, but also in response to *imminent* attacks immediately before they occur."[95] This statement is consistent with substantial state practice and commentary.[96]

Thereafter, however, the Report deviates from this practice and commentary by articulating a questionable view of imminence. Both states and commentators frequently trace the traditional understanding of imminence in self-defense to a letter by US Secretary of State Daniel Webster related to the *Caroline* incident. Webster asserted that there must be "a necessity of self-defence, instant, overwhelming, leaving no choice of means, and no moment for deliberation."[97] According to Professor Yoram Dinstein, this allows a state to intercept any attack that has already been launched.[98] The Report goes well beyond these concepts. When determining whether an attack is imminent, the Report asserts that states may consider

> the nature and immediacy of the threat; the probability of an attack; whether the anticipated attack is part of a concerted pattern of continuing armed activity; the likely scale of the attack and the injury, loss, or damage likely to result therefrom in the absence of mitigating action; and the likelihood that there will be other opportunities to undertake effective action in self-defense that may be expected to cause less serious collateral injury, loss, or damage.[99]

The Report further claims that "the absence of specific evidence of where an attack will take place or of the precise nature of an attack does not preclude a conclusion that an armed attack is imminent."[100]

This claim drains the term "imminence" of its traditional and logical meanings. If "immediacy," "the probability of the attack," and "the likelihood that there will be other opportunities to undertake effective action in self-defense" are only relevant factors,[101] then the Report's view of "imminence" has no connection to its

[94] *See* UN Charter art. 51.

[95] *See Obama Framework Report, supra* note 77, at 9.

[96] *See, e.g.*, Franck, *supra* note 91, at 97–108; Oscar Schachter, *The Right of States to Use Armed Force*, 82 Mich. L. Rev. 1620, 1633–35 (1984) (summarizing state practice and commentary).

[97] *See* Hunter Miller, Treaties and Other International Acts of the United States of American 449 (vol. IV, 1934) (discussing the *Caroline* case and providing a copy of the text of the *Caroline* Correspondence of Mr. Webster, Secretary of State, and Lord Ashburton, British plen.). Notably, the US Constitution similarly limited the rights of the several United States, prohibiting them from "engaging" in war "unless actually invaded, or in such imminent Danger as will not admit of delay." US Constitution, art. 1, § 10, cl. 3.

[98] *See* Yoram Dinstein, War Aggression and Self-Defense 249–52 (6th ed. 2017).

[99] *See Obama Framework Report, supra* note 77, at 9 (citing Daniel Bethlehem, *Self-Defense Against an Imminent or Actual Armed Attack by Nonstate Actors*, 106 Am. J. Int'l L. 769 (2012)).

[100] *Id.*

[101] *Id.*

traditional understanding.[102] The Report's concept of imminence is better understood as a reformulation of the principle of *necessity* related to self-defense. Adopted "in light of the modern-day capabilities, techniques, and technological innovations of terrorist organizations," the Report argues that these factors are "increasingly recognized by the international community."[103] In other words, the Report admits that its description of imminence, or of the "necessity" to resort to defensive force, is at best a developing norm rather than widely accepted customary law or treaty interpretation.[104]

The Report contains a related, controversial normative claim, positing that in "cases in which there is a reasonable and objective basis for concluding that the territorial State is unable or unwilling to confront effectively a non-State actor in its territory" it may be "necessary to act in self-defense against the non-State actor in that State's territory without [the territorial state's] consent."[105] The Report clarifies that this "unwilling or unable" doctrine applies only "if measures short of force have been exhausted or are inadequate to address the threat posed by the non-State actor emanating from the territory of another State."[106]

The Report then posits broad and malleable definitions of the terms "unable" and "unwilling." "Unable" includes situations in which "a State has lost or abandoned effective control over the portion of its territory where [a NSAG] is operating."[107] The Report utterly fails to clarify what constitutes "effective control" or the loss thereof.[108] "Unwilling" refers to circumstances in which "a State is colluding with or harboring a terrorist organization operating from within its territory and refuses to address the threat posed by the group."[109] Commentators who accept the possibility of an unwilling-or-unable doctrine emphasize the need to exhaust alternatives to a nonconsensual territorial incursion with the government of a territorial state.[110] The United States waives that requirement if doing so would be "inadequate to address the threat posed," but provides no

102 *See* Miller, *supra* note 97 and accompanying text.

103 *See Obama Framework Report*, *supra* note 77, at 9.

104 Regarding the unsettled state of international law regulating defensive responses to non-state actors, *see, e.g.*, Hakimi, *supra* note 76, at 3 ("Efforts to clarify the law on the use of defensive force against non-State actors are premature. The evident ambiguities and inconsistences in the practice reflect an ongoing struggle over the law's proper content."); W. Michael Reisman & Andrea Armstrong, *The Past and Future of the Claim of Pre-Emptive Self-Defense*, 100 AM. J. INT'L L. 525 (2003). *See generally* Franck, *supra* note 91.

105 *See Obama Framework Report*, *supra* note 77, at 10.

106 *Id.*

107 *Id.*

108 *Id.*

109 *Id.*

110 *See, e.g.*, NOAM LUBELL, EXTRATERRITORIAL USE OF FORCE AGAINST NON-STATE ACTORS 45–48 (2010); Ashley S. Deeks, *"Unwilling or Unable": Toward a Normative Framework for Extraterritorial Self-Defense*, 52 VA. J. INT'L L. 483, 519–33 (2012).

clarity regarding the precise circumstances under which such action might properly be considered futile.[111]

The Report then explains that the United States relies upon its reformulated right of self-defense, coupled with territorial state consent or the "unable or unwilling" doctrine, to pursue elements of non-state armed groups from one foreign state to another.[112] It first claims that "it is not necessary as a matter of international law to reassess whether an armed attack is occurring or imminent prior to every subsequent action taken against [a] group, provided that hostilities have not ended."[113] It next asserts that, "in armed conflicts with non-State actors that are prone to shifting operations from country to country, the United States does not view its ability to use military force against a non-State actor with which it is engaged in an ongoing armed conflict as limited to 'hot' battlefields."[114] In these circumstances, the Report argues that "the use of force in self-defense in an ongoing armed conflict is limited by respect for States' sovereignty and the considerations discussed above, including the customary international law requirements of necessity and proportionality when force could implicate the rights of other States."[115]

The most significant problem with this approach is that it conflates the norms of self-defense and armed conflict and then extends both to "associated forces" without providing clear legal or factual support for doing so.[116] For example, the Report suggests that its approach permits attacks on alleged "associated forces" that may have formed in another state without clarifying when distinct terrorist groups are properly considered "associated forces."[117] Such elements are then targeted, even if they do not present an imminent threat of harm at the time, so long as the intrusion upon the third state's territory is no more than is necessary to engage in an act of self-defense.[118] In other words, if a state considers one NSAG to be an associated force of another NSAG, it may target both groups. Doing so, however, conflates the threats posed by the groups and eschews analysis of the specific threat(s) that each distinctly poses.

The upshot is that the emerging norms do not limit transnational self-defense to circumstances involving immediate or even relatively certain and specific threats to US persons, property, or instrumentalities within US territory or abroad. It allows the United States to use lethal force to defend US citizens and

[111] *See Obama Framework Report*, *supra* note 77, at 10.
[112] *Id.*
[113] *Id.* 11.
[114] *Id.*
[115] *Id.*
[116] *Id.* 4–5.
[117] For example, Al Qaeda in the Arabian Peninsula formed well after September 11, 2001, but is nevertheless identified as an associated force of Al Qaeda and has been considered subject to lethal targeting on an equal basis. *Id.* 18, 22.
[118] *Id.* 19–21.

government organs or instrumentalities located anywhere in the world from "ongoing," indefinite, and indeterminate threats originating from anywhere in the world.[119] States have long asserted that defending nationals or government organs and instrumentalities in foreign countries from *local* and *immediate* non-state threats is an aspect of their inherent right of self-defense.[120] These allegedly emerging norms significantly enlarge that right by allowing for the defense of nationals or government instrumentalities abroad from nonlocal threats.[121] This "leapfrog" approach to preemptive self-defense substantially disregards state sovereignty. It also expands the number of individuals that may be subjected to lethal targeting based upon their alleged status as fighters in a NSAG involved in a NIAC rather than any immediate threat of harm that they pose.

The Report's discussion of the non-state group known as al-Shabaab in Somalia is illustrative of these inexact and potentially overbroad claims. The Report confirms that the United States is using force against al-Shabaab in Somalia "in the context of armed conflict" between al-Shabaab and Somali forces, as well as "in furtherance of U.S. national self-defense."[122] With regard to the self-defense claim, the Report states that al-Shabaab poses a direct threat to US persons and interests in the region.[123] Later, the Report describes al-Shabaab as an "associated force" of Al Qaeda,[124] because it allegedly "entered the fight alongside al-Qa'ida and is a co-belligerent with al-Qa'ida in hostilities against the United States."[125] The Report provides almost no factual basis for this claim, suggesting only ideological alignment rather than coordinated operations.[126] The Report thus provides three alternate justifications for using force against al-Shabaab: (1) US participation by invitation in an armed conflict between al-Shabaab and Somali forces; (2) an armed conflict between the United States and Al Qaeda, in which al-Shabaab is an associated force of Al Qaeda; and (3) an independent right of self-defense against threats al-Shabaab allegedly pose to US interests in the region.[127] While the first basis for the use of force is legally and factually plausible,

[119] *Id.* 11.

[120] *See, e.g.*, Franck, *supra* note 91, at 69–96; Schachter, *supra* note 96, at 1636–37.

[121] *See Obama Framework Report*, *supra* note 77, at 11.

[122] *Id.* 16–17.

[123] *Id.* 5.

[124] *Id.* 17.

[125] *Id.* 5.

[126] *Id.* ("[A]l-Shabaab has pledged loyalty to al-Qa'ida in its public statements; made clear that it considers the United States one of its enemies; and been responsible for numerous attacks, threats, and plots against U.S. persons and interests in East Africa."). For more information regarding the threats posed by the group, *see* Claire Felter et al., "Al-Shabab," Council on Foreign Relations, Jan. 9, 2018. <http://www.cfr.org/somalia/al-shabab/p18650>.

[127] *Obama Framework Report*, *supra* note 77, at 17. Asserting alternate bases for using armed force may also be designed to address domestic legal authority in addition to international law concerns. For example, the claim that the right of self-defense applies could provide domestic justification for participation in the NIAC involving al-Shabaab without express congressional authorization. The claim that al-Shabaab is an associated force of Al Qaeda supports an assertion that there is legislative

the "associated forces" claim is legally and factually unsupported and suspect. The self-defense claim against a poorly defined and indefinite regional threat is even more dubious.

Taken together, these claims strongly suggest that the United States asserts a broader right to resort to armed force in transnational self-defense than a healthy respect for settled international law and basic liberal values should allow. These claims are not only broad but also ambiguous in both their substance and application, potentially yielding an effectively unconstrained right to use force in self-defense against NSAGs.

B. Permissible Measures of Defensive Force

The overbroad assertions about the right to resort to defensive force aggravate errors regarding the permissible measures of defensive force. The Report and the PPG strongly but implicitly assert that international rules regulating war apply to every act of transnational self-defense. For example, the Report notes that, regardless of the legal justification for resorting to transnational force under the UN Charter, all military operations "are conducted consistent with the law of armed conflict, also known as the '*jus in bello*' or 'law of war.' "[128] In its later analysis of issues related to targeting, the Report also addresses only the law of war.[129] Most tellingly, the PPG specifies that "direct action will be taken only if there is near certainty that the action can be taken without injuring or killing non-combatants."[130] It then defines "non-combatants," a law-of-war term of art, as those "who may not be made the object of attack under the law of armed conflict," specifically excluding "an individual who is targetable as part of a belligerent party to an armed conflict, an individual who is taking a direct part in hostilities, or *an individual who is targetable in the exercise of national self-defense*."[131] This terminology clearly signals reliance on a law of war legal framework for all uses of force in transnational self-defense.[132]

authorization based in the September 18, 2001 Authorization for the Use of Military Force, Pub. L. No. 107-40, 115 Stat. 224 (2001) (authorizing use of "necessary and appropriate" military force in response to the attacks by Al Qaeda against the United States on September 11, 2001). Although the accuracy of these claims is beyond the scope of this project, the concern is that these claims may be inexact, overbroad or contrived in part to address concerns about domestic legal authority.

[128] *Id.* 8.

[129] *Id.* 21–24.

[130] *See 2013 PPG*, *supra* note 80, at 1.

[131] *Id.* (emphasis added).

[132] This conclusion is further supported by the fact that "[i]t is [Department of Defense] policy that [m]embers of the DoD Components comply with the law of war during all armed conflicts, however such conflicts are characterized, *and in all other military operations*." US Dept. of Def., *Dir. 2311.01E*, *DoD Law of War Program* (2006) para. 4.1 (emphasis added). *But see* Geoffrey S. Corn, *IV*

This broad view of the applicability of the law of war to violence with non-state actors is erroneous. States and commentators generally agree that international law defines a NIAC to which the law of war applies to include only violence of sufficient intensity and duration between a state and a sufficiently organized NSAG (or between two or more NSAGs).[133] Unless a NSAG meets the organization requirement, and until hostilities with that NSAG reach sufficient intensity, the law of war does not apply and cannot be invoked as authority for the use of measures such as lethal targeting (hereinafter law-of-war targeting) based solely upon membership in a NSAG.[134] Transnational violence by terrorist groups and responsive defensive measures may often involve situations that do not meet one or both of these threshold requirements. In such cases, applying the law of war to defensive military operations is clearly erroneous.[135] Coupling this error with a much broader right to resort to defensive force greatly expands the number of individuals who may be killed based merely upon their status as members of a terrorist group rather than any actual threat they pose at the time they are targeted.

Commentators have offered support for the view that the law of war might apply to some acts of transnational self-defense occurring outside of a NIAC. For example, Professor Adil Haque proposed that states may adopt a war paradigm for an initial use of force against a NSAG under certain conditions: "if an organized armed group has the capacity to sustain military operations then any military operation by or against that group should be constrained by the law of armed conflict."[136] Other commentators argue that international human rights law—and a law enforcement paradigm—apply if no NIAC exists at the

Self-Defense Targeting: Blurring the Line Between the Jus Ad Bellum and Jus In Bello, 88 Int'l L. Stud. 57, 58 (2012) (asserting the Obama administration approach intimates that "*jus ad bellum* self-defense principles regulate the execution of combat operations used to achieve [a] self-defense objective, obviating the need to assess whether and what *jus in bello* principles apply to these operations.").

133 *See, e.g.*, How Is the Term "Armed Conflict" Defined in International Law? 3–5 (Mar. 17, 2008) (noting congruence on this basic definition in treaties, the jurisprudence of international tribunals, and commentary). *See also* Commentary of 2016 to the First Geneva Convention of 1949 (Mar. 22, 2016), para. 387 ("A situation of violence that crosses the threshold of [non-international armed conflict] is a situation in which organized Parties confront one another with violence of a certain degree of intensity.").

134 *See* Expert Meeting: The Use of Force in Armed Conflicts: Interplay Between the Conduct of Hostilities and Law Enforcement Paradigms 4–8 (Gloria Gaggioli ed., 2013) [hereinafter IHL-HRL Report].

135 *See, e.g.*, Michael N. Schmitt, *Extraterritorial Lethal Targeting: Deconstructing the Logic of International Law*, 52 Colum. J. Transnat'l L. 77, 98 (2013) ("Although the threshold lacks exactitude, it is clear that extraterritorial operations directed against groups that engage in only a single (and last) act of violence, no matter how destructive, or that engage in violence on an infrequent basis, are not subject to international humanitarian law norms.").

136 *See* Adil Ahmad Haque, *Triggers and Thresholds of Non-International Armed Conflict*, Just Security, Sept. 29, 2016, <https://www.justsecurity.org/33222/triggers-thresholds-non-international-armed-conflict/>.

time defensive force is used.[137] One of Haque's motivating concerns, however, is that "according to some militarily active states"—by which he means the United States—"human rights law does not [apply or] constrain extraterritorial lethal targeting by state armed forces" in transnational self-defense.[138] Therefore, we should extend the application of the law of war because "such conduct should be constrained by international law."[139]

The concern that international law has no role and nothing to say if neither the law of war nor international human rights law regulates an act of transnational self-defense is misguided. The same fundamental legal principles that govern a resort to force in self-defense—necessity and proportionality—also govern the specifics of its use. Frequently ignored or overlooked aspects of the *Caroline* diplomatic correspondence confirm this understanding.

III. The *Caroline* Correspondence and the Role of Necessity and Proportionality

A. Principles in Transnational Self-Defense

Diplomatic correspondence related to the *Caroline* incident contains important insights into the substance and application of the legal principles that regulate the resort to and use of force in transnational self-defense. This correspondence receives significant, but typically narrow, attention in legal commentary on the topic. States and scholars often assert that Article 51 of the UN Charter preserved the inherent right of self-defense which existed in customary international law when the UN Charter was adopted.[140] Because the text of Article 51 limits self-defense to situations when an "armed attack occurs,"[141] the *Caroline* correspondence is invoked to support the view that states may resort to defensive force when it is imminent.[142] This correspondence, however, speaks to more than the circumstances justifying the resort to defensive force. As this section explains,

[137] *See, e.g.*, Jonathan Horowitz, *Laws of War: Humanitarian Stallion or Trojan Horse?*," JUST SECURITY, Nov. 3, 2016, <https://www.justsecurity.org/34128/laws-war-humanitarian-stallion-trojan-horse/>; Deborah Pearlstein, *The NIAC Threshold*, OPINIO JURIS, Oct. 4, 2016. <http://opiniojuris.org/2016/10/04/the-niac-threshold/>. *See also* Kevin Jon Heller, *First Strikes and NIAC: Thoughts on the Haque/Horowitz Debate*, OPINIO JURIS, Nov. 24, 2016, <http://opiniojuris.org/2016/11/24/first-strikes-and-niac-two-thoughts-on-haque/>.

[138] *See* Haque, *supra* note 136 (referencing Beth Van Schaack, *The United States' Position on the Extraterritorial Application of Human Rights Obligations: Now Is the Time for Change*, 90 INT'L L. STUD. 20 (2014)).

[139] *Id.*

[140] *See*, e.g., Schachter, *supra* note 96, at 1633–35.

[141] *See* UN Charter art. 51.

[142] *See*, e.g., Schachter, *supra* note 96, at 1633–35.

the correspondence also clarifies that necessity and proportionality also address the specific nature of permissible force in transnational self-defense.

A summary of the *Caroline* incident provides important context for the correspondence.[143] On December 29, 1837, the *Caroline*, a private, US-flagged vessel, allegedly carried men and arms across the Niagara River to support an insurrection in Canada.[144] It evidently had done so several times that day.[145] After returning to the port of Schlosser on the US side of the Niagara River that evening, twenty-three US citizens requested and received permission to stay aboard the *Caroline* for the night.[146] Around midnight, seventy to eighty British soldiers attacked the crew and passengers, killing and wounding many of them.[147] The attackers also lit the *Caroline* on fire and "set her adrift over Niagara Falls."[148] Several of the crew and guests were later missing and may have been wounded or dead aboard the *Caroline* as it plummeted over the falls.[149]

The United States protested these acts as unjustified.[150] After lower-level diplomatic exchanges, on July 27, 1842, US Secretary of State Daniel Webster penned a letter to the British Foreign Secretary, Lord Ashburton.[151] Webster enclosed an excerpt from an earlier letter he had sent the British minister in Washington, Mr. Fox, as well as an excerpt from a December 7, 1841, message to Congress from President John Tyler.[152] The oft-cited quote, that a resort to defensive force requires "a necessity of self-defence, instant, overwhelming, leaving no choice of means, and no moment for deliberation," was in Webster's letter to Fox.[153]

Much in that letter, and in the excerpt of President Tyler's related message to Congress, undermines the Report's reformulation of the necessity principle as well as the "unable or unwilling" doctrine. For example, Webster argued that when an alleged act of self-defense "has led to the commission of hostile acts within the territory of a Power at peace, nothing less than a clear and absolute necessity can afford ground of justification."[154] He also stated "it must be shewn [*sic*] that admonition or remonstrance to the persons on board the *Caroline* was impracticable, or would have been unavailing."[155] President Tyler's message

143 This summary is taken from the account in Miller, *supra* note 97, at 444. The relevant sections are reprinted at "British-American Diplomacy: The Caroline Case" (Yale L. Sch.: Avalon Project), <http://avalon.law.yale.edu/19th_century/br-1842d.asp>.
144 *See* Miller, *supra* note 97, at 444.
145 *Id.*
146 *Id.*
147 *Id.*
148 *Id.*
149 *Id.*
150 *Id.*
151 *Id.* 445.
152 *Id.* 446.
153 *Id.* 449.
154 *See* Miller, *supra* note 97, at 446.
155 *Id.* 449.

asserted that strict necessity was needed to justify infringing US territory even if—due to its extensive border—the United States was unable to arrest or suppress those adding the British rebels. He noted:

> To recognize it as an admissible practice that each Government in its turn, upon any sudden and unauthorized outbreak which, on a frontier the extent of which renders it impossible for either to have an efficient force on every mile of it, and which outbreak, therefore, neither may be able to suppress in a day, may take vengeance into its own hands, and without even a remonstrance, and in the absence of any pressing or overruling necessity may invade the territory of the other, would inevitably lead to results equally to be deplored by both.[156]

Additionally, Webster's letters also addressed how the necessity principle limits permissible measures of defensive force.[157] Webster asserted that Britain must show that it "did nothing unreasonable or excessive; since the act justified by the necessity of self-defence, must be limited by that necessity, and kept clearly within it."[158] He therefore argued, "it must be shewn [*sic*] that daylight could not be waited for," "that there could be no attempt at discrimination, between the innocent and the guilty," and "that it would not have been enough to seize and detain the vessel."[159] He posited that there must have been "a necessity, present and inevitable, for attacking her" as well as "then drawing her into the current, above the cataract, setting her on fire . . . careless to know whether there might not be in her the innocent with the guilty, or the living with the dead."[160] Webster concluded, "[a] necessity for all this the government of the United States cannot believe to have existed."[161]

Ashburton's response agreed with Webster's general view of the applicable legal principles but not with their application to the facts.[162] He asserted that the resort to armed force was proper because rebel forces and armaments were "hourly increasing" due to the *Caroline*'s activities.[163] He also argued that there

[156] *Id.* 450.

[157] This is often because the authors focus solely or primarily on *jus ad bellum*, or resort-to-force, issues. *See, e.g.*, Deeks, *supra* note 182, at 662 (reciting only imminence language of Mr. Webster's letter). *See also* Noam Lubell, *The Problem of Imminence in an Uncertain World in* THE OXFORD HANDBOOK ON THE USE OF FORCE IN INTERNATIONAL LAW 698 (Marc Weller ed., 2014); Schmitt, *supra* note 135, at 88–89; Reisman & Armstrong, *supra* note 104, at 535; Sean D. Murphy, *The Doctrine of Preemptive Self-Defense*, 50 VILL. L. REV. 699, 722–23 (2005).

[158] *See* Miller, *supra* note 97, at 449.

[159] *Id.*

[160] *Id.*

[161] *Id.* 450. Webster's arguments are a reminder that "proportionality" is implied from necessity. If one does more than strictly necessary to counter the reasonably perceived nature of a given threat, one's actions are disproportionate.

[162] *Id.* 451 ("It is so far satisfactory to perceive that we are perfectly agreed as to the general principles of international law applicable to this unfortunate case.").

[163] *Id.* 452.

was no prospect of timely intervention by American authorities to eliminate this ongoing activity and increasing threat.[164] Referring to the absence of US government intervention, Ashburton questioned how long a similarly situated government, "having the paramount duty of protecting its own people [can] be reasonably expected to wait for what they had then no reason to expect?"[165] He therefore claimed that the need to use defensive force existed to "as high a degree as . . . any case of a similar description in the history of nations."[166]

Ashburton also argued that the specific measures of force used were proper. He asserted that the territorial incursion occurred only because the *Caroline* was not where they expected her to be.[167] He also claimed that attacking the ship at night was an effort to minimize casualties, and that "the strength of the current not permitting the vessel to be carried off, and it being necessary to destroy her by fire, she was drawn into the stream for the express purpose of preventing injury to persons or property" of local residents ashore.[168]

These assertions, even if accurate, represent a rather flexible view of the necessity and proportionality principles. At the time of the attack, the *Caroline* was "moored to the shore" in US territory with crew and passengers largely asleep.[169] The threat of the *Caroline* resuming ferry operations at some point in the future provided no compelling need to attack it or those on board at that time.

In sum, Ashburton and Webster agreed that the principles of necessity and proportionality govern both the resort to force and the permissible measures of force in transnational self-defense. They disagreed only about the application of those principles to the *Caroline* incident. The American correspondence, however, clearly supported the view that the permissible measures of defensive force must be strictly necessary only to neutralize the nature of the threat existing at the time force is used. Because neither the *Caroline* nor those aboard her were, at the time of the attack, posing an imminent threat of harm to British territory or persons, Webster contended the ship, crew, and passengers should have at most been detained rather than destroyed, wounded, or killed.[170] In other words, for acts of transnational self-defense unrelated to an existing NIAC, the United States argued that fundamental self-defense principles of necessity and proportionality require using no more force than is clearly necessary to neutralize the nature of the threat reasonably believed to exist at the time force is used.

164 *Id.* ("I might safely put it to any candid man acquainted with the existing state of things, to say whether the military commander in Canada had the remotest reason on the 29th of December to expect to be relieved from this state of suffering by the protective intervention of any American authority.").

165 *Id.* 453.

166 *Id.*

167 *Id.*

168 *Id.*

169 *Id.* 449.

170 *Id.*

Both prior to and after the *Caroline* incident, US practice toward violent non-state entities was more consistent with the British approach to the *Caroline* incident and the Grotian tradition. As noted earlier in this chapter, it engaged in numerous and sometimes substantial defensive actions and punitive expeditions.[171] A 1934 report produced by the Solicitor of the US State Department, *Right to Protect Citizens in Foreign Countries by Landing Forces*, canvassed the views of international jurists on self-defense, including the defense of nationals abroad, and related topics and surveyed US practice.[172] Its analysis reveals that US practice toward non-state actors aligned with the British approach to the *Caroline*. This view rests quite firmly in the Grotian tradition on the use of force with respect to non-state entities.

Secretary Webster's arguments may have resonated through generations of geopolitical and international legal history precisely because they embrace and advance the basic liberal values to which the international system aspires. While current arguments in favor preemptive self-defense may seem inconsistent with them,[173] Vattel and other jurists postulated very limited conditions for its exercise.

IV. Necessity, Liberal Values, and Preemptive Self-Defense

Now that basic liberal values have been broadly incorporated into international law and the international system, Webster's views regarding their application to transnational self-defense should arguably prevail in the twenty-first century. This section further examines how basic liberal values should influence the behavior of states in the context of transnational self-defense.

A. Liberal Values and Self-Defense

There is substantial similarity between the liberal political values articulated in the US Declaration of Independence and Vattel's account of the rights and obligations of nations. Vattel posited that all nations are equal, possess perfect

[171] *See* US Dept. of State, Right to Protect Citizens in Foreign Countries by Landing Forces 51–78 (3d ed. 1933) [hereinafter Right to Protect]. For a survey of post-UN Charter US incidents, *see Contemporary Case Studies of United States Forcible Protection of Nationals Abroad*, 77 Int'l L. Stud. Ser. US Naval War Coll. 41 (2002). For a survey of non-US state practice, *see State Practice during the Pre-United Nations Period*, 77 Int'l L. Stud. Ser. US Naval War. Coll. 25 (2002).

[172] *See Right to Protect*, *supra* note 171, at 12–38.

[173] *See* James Thuo Gathii, *Assessing Claims of a New Doctrine of Preemptive War Under the Doctrine of Sources*, 43 Osgoode Hall L.J. 67 (2005)(explaining preeminence of contemporary norms prohibiting the use of force).

and imperfect rights and liberty, and are governed by laws only to which they consent. The Declaration stated: "that all men are created equal; that they are endowed by their Creator with certain unalienable rights; that among these are life, liberty, and the pursuit of happiness; that, to secure these rights, governments are instituted among men, deriving their just powers from the consent of the governed."[174] A properly circumscribed right of self-defense, or self-preservation, is a long-standing norm of international law and entirely consistent with the liberal values.[175]

Because the same principles support an inherent right of self-defense for both individuals and states, it is unsurprising that Webster's view of a state's right of self-defense resonates with individual self-defense in Anglo-American domestic common law.[176] States, like individuals, may repel intrusions upon their basic rights only when clearly necessary, using no more force than is reasonably necessary to do so.[177] As described by an American court: "The law of [individual] self-defense is a law of necessity; the right of self-defense arises only when the necessity begins, and equally ends with the necessity."[178] A right to act in self-defense therefore requires "a threat, actual or apparent," that the threat was "unlawful and immediate," that the defender honestly and reasonably "believed that he was in imminent peril," and "that his response was necessary to save himself" from that peril.[179] While all of these factors address the need to resort to defensive force, the fourth also speaks to permissible defensive measures. Lawful measures of defensive force include only those necessary to neutralize a specific and imminently impending threat of harm.

There is, however, a contextual adjustment in the application of these principles to states. The *Caroline* correspondence clarifies that when

[174] *See* The Declaration of Independence, para. 2 (US 1776).

[175] *See, e.g.*, George P. Fletcher & Jens David Ohlin, Defending Humanity 45–55 (2008) (retracing jurisprudential origins of an "inherent" or "natural" right of self-defense).

[176] This is not to suggest that Anglo-American common law perfectly incorporates and respects liberal political or natural law principles in all of its particulars. The common law's basic approach to rights and obligations between and among individuals, however, is informed by the same natural law principles that underlie Grotian and Lockean liberalism. *See* I William Blackstone, *Commentaries* *38–41. Distinctions about the role of natural law in the common law must be drawn carefully, however, because natural law principles inform not only the *substance* of individual rights and therefore some (but not all) conduct-regulating rules, but also what constitute legitimate *sources* of law, meaning, to what laws or law-making institutions individuals should be understood to have consented. *Id.* One commentator credits Blackstone's *Commentaries* with reconciling "not just in theory but in detail the principles of liberal political theory and the practices of English common law." James L. Stoner Jr., *Common Law and Liberal Theory* (1993) 163. For purposes of this analysis, it is sufficient to recognize that the Anglo-American common law of self-defense incorporates generally accepted natural law principles that reinforce basic liberal political values.

[177] *See* Fletcher & Ohlin, *supra* note 175, at 11–14 (justifying use of criminal law principles governing individual self-defense to reinterpret international law of self-defense between or among states).

[178] United States v. Peterson, 483 F.2d 1222, 1229 (D.C. Dist. 1973).

[179] *Id.* 1229–30.

properly observed, necessity and proportionality justify two distinct acts: (1) invading or intruding upon another state's territory to address a threat, and (2) abridging rights to life, liberty, and property interests of those who comprise that threat.[180] Consistent with liberal values, however, Webster argued that, at most, a use of defensive force is limited to what is strictly necessary to counter the specific nature of the threat reasonably perceived at the time force is used.[181]

B. Inattention to Law and Liberal Values

1. Resort to Force

Regarding the resort to force, the emerging norms allow lethal force against threats believed to be "ongoing" rather than imminent, at least if there is no prospect that the state in which the threat is then located will effectively intervene. This approach is indistinguishable from Ashburton's arguments related to the *Caroline* incident, which similarly argued in favor of what some commentators call preemptive self-defense.[182]

There are, however, earlier arguments related to self-defense between "civilized" states that are instructive. For example, when Vattel adapted the concept of self-defense to nations, he concluded that nations inherently possess a broader right to act defensively than do individuals. Even though he asserted that force could only be used when justified and absolutely necessary,[183] Vattel nevertheless posited that states might sometimes use preemptive defensive force under limited circumstances.

Vattel first argued that a state perceiving a threat from its neighbor must seek to peacefully resolve the situation:

> When a neighbor . . . makes preparations for war, — are we allowed to attack him, with a view to prevent the danger with which we think ourselves threatened? The answer greatly depends on the manner and character of that

[180] *See* Miller, *supra* note 97, at 446–57 (containing text of the *Caroline* Correspondence).

[181] *Id.* 449.

[182] *See, e.g.*, Ashley Deeks, *Taming the Preemption Doctrine*, *in* THE OXFORD HANDBOOK ON THE USE OF FORCE IN INTERNATIONAL LAW 661 (Marc Weller ed., 2014)(defining preemptive self-defense as a "use of force in self-defense to halt a particular, tangible course of action that the potential victim state perceives shortly will evolve into an armed attack against it"); *see generally* MICHAEL DOYLE, STRIKING FIRST: PREEMPTIVE AND PREVENTION IN INTERNATIONAL CONFLICT (2008).

[183] *See* Vattel, *supra* note 21, at bk. IV, 654, sec. 6. ("The love of peace should equally prevent [nations] from embarking in a war without necessity, and from persevering in it after the necessity has ceased to exist. When a sovereign has been compelled to take up arms for just and important reasons, he may carry on the operations of war till he has attained its lawful end, which is, to procure justice and safety.").

> neighbor. We must inquire into the reasons of those preparations, and bring him to an explanation . . . and if his sincerity be justly suspected, securities may be required of him.[184]

When no attack had yet occurred, however, Vattel explained that the right to act defensively depends upon the gravity and probability of the anticipated harm.

> As men are under a necessity of regulating their conduct in most cases by probabilities, those probabilities claim their attention in proportion to the importance of the subject: and (to make use of a geometrical expression) their right to obviate a danger is in a compound ratio of the degree of probability and the greatness of the evil threatened. If the evil in question be of a supportable nature—if it be only some slight loss—matters are not to be precipitated: there is no great danger in delaying our opposition to it till there be a certainty of our being threatened. But if the safety of the state lies at stake, our precaution and foresight cannot be extended too far. Must we delay to avert our ruin till it is become inevitable?[185]

Vattel limited preemptive defense force to situations in which it is necessary to neutralize a significant threat to the "safety of the state" that threatens its "ruin," perhaps meaning its very existence or, at the very least, significant harm to it. The German jurist Lassa Oppenheim would later assert similar preemptive self-defense norms between states.[186]

Emerging transnational self-defense norms do not fully resonate with Vattel.[187] First, Vattel's asserted right of preemptive self-defense existed only between states. Perhaps this is because only states then possessed the means to threaten substantial or existential harm to other states.[188] Although attacking non-state entities was far less constrained in the Grotian tradition adopted by Vattel, doing so today is inconsistent with the basic liberal values enshrined in contemporary international law. Of course, one might argue that NSAGs may now possess the destructive power of states, including the ability to project that power globally.[189] This may justify expanding the inherent right of self-defense

184 *Id.* bk. 3, ch. III, 499, § 50.

185 *Id.* 493, § 44.

186 *See* Gill & Tabori-Szabó, *supra* note 49, at 473 (citing 1 Lassa F.L. Oppenheim, International Law: A Treatise 178 (1905)).

187 *See* (n **Error! Bookmark not defined.**, 99–103, 106–110, 119–120) and accompanying text.

188 In this vein, recall Lord Ashburton's assertion of a sovereign's "paramount duty of protecting its own people." *See* Miller, *supra* note 97, at 453.

189 *See, e.g.*, The White House, The National Security Strategy of the United States of American 13 (Sept. 2002), <http://nssarchive.us/NSSR/2002.pdf> ("[N]ew deadly challenges have emerged from rogue states and terrorists. None of these contemporary threats rival the sheer destructive power that was arrayed against us by the Soviet Union. However, the nature and motivations of these new adversaries, their determination to obtain destructive powers hitherto available

to extraterritorial NSAGs in some limited circumstances. Conversely, states have vested the UN Security Council with the power to determine "any threat to the peace, breach of the peace, or act of aggression" along with the power "to decide what measures shall be taken" in response.[190] These powers might be used in a way that subsumes any theory of preemptive self-defense involving inchoate and indefinite extraterritorial threats of future harm. Any claimed right to act defensively against developing or ongoing but not yet imminent threats, whether posed by states or non-state actors, potentially subverts the Charter's collective security system. Doing so may not be in the best long-term interests of the international community, although there are contrary arguments.[191]

Additionally, Vattel required that states first attempt to resolve any security concerns peacefully.[192] Because terrorist NSAGs typically lurk in the global shadows and often attack without warning, states typically have no comparable opportunity to seek a peaceful resolution of a situation involving them. Nevertheless, commentators argue that states must make reasonable efforts to allow a territorial state to neutralize threats posed by a violent NSAG within its borders.[193] This may not always be feasible if a threat will likely manifest before the territorial government can effectively respond. To provide a simple example, it is surely the case that a border agent need not call a neighboring territorial state's government to address a threat posed by someone about to shoot the agent if its response is unlikely to be timely or otherwise adequate to prevent this harm.

This brings us to the concern regarding the lack of clarity regarding how the United States assesses the gravity and probability of the threat posed by a specific terrorist group before engaging in preemptive self-defense. Vattel's commentary suggests that a state may only use preemptive defensive force against emerging threats that are highly probable and significant. Although some terrorist NSAGs may actively seek weapons of mass destruction (WMD), it is uncertain how close any may be to actually obtaining them. It is also unclear whether all potential WMD attacks threaten harm of the type Vattel contemplated. If terrorist NSAGs might cause substantial but localized harm rather than a more significant loss of life or damage to state institutions or instrumentalities, the justification for using preemptive defensive force is reduced.

only to the world's strongest states, and the greater likelihood that they will use weapons of mass destruction against us, make today's security environment more complex and dangerous.").

[190] *See* UN Charter art. 39.

[191] *See, e.g.*, Doyle, *supra* note 182 at 33–34 (arguing that preventive force is sometimes justified because U.N. Security Council is not always willing or able to effectively deal with threats to the peace, necessitating self-help by states).

[192] *See* Vattel, *supra* note 21, at bk. 3, ch. III, 499, § 50.

[193] *See Obama Framework Report*, *supra* note 77, at 10.

Also unclear is how these developing norms attribute a significant threat posed by one non-state armed group to all alleged "associated forces" of that group. Returning to al-Shabaab, for example, the Report is vague regarding the precise nature of the regional threat it poses. It is therefore not clear whether that threat is sufficiently grave to justify preemptive defensive force by the United States. Regardless, it would be difficult to argue that any threat of harm to US citizens or instrumentalities on the African continent poses a significant threat to the United States itself, let alone threatens its "ruin" or very existence. If the gravity and probability of this regional threat does not justify preemptive defensive force, what does? Does the fact that al-Shabaab allegedly "entered the fight alongside al-Qa'ida" do so? Even assuming Al Qaeda or some of its "associated forces" actively seek WMD, it is not clear whether al-Shabaab participates in that effort. Unless al-Shabaab is somehow a part of a WMD threat against US bases or territories, preemptive defensive force may not be justified.[194]

Without knowing how the United States evaluates and attributes the gravity and probability of the threats that a NSAG poses, it is difficult to evaluate how closely its approach aligns the theory of preemptive self-defense posited by Vattel and others. The US government's opacity on these matters generates substantial ambiguity about the substance and application of relevant norms, which then creates the potential for abuse. Defending American "interests at home and around the world" is rhetorical, politically expedient shorthand that does not speak clearly to the circumstances that truly justify preemptive defensive force.[195]

In sum, emerging transnational self-defense norms allowing law-of-war targeting against all "ongoing" transnational threats regardless of their gravity or imminence is inconsistent with the basic liberal values that underlie earlier related jurisprudential thought and the contemporary international security system. Preemptive lethal force, if ever permitted, should not be used to address any threat that does not involve a relatively certain and grave harm. To the extent a less significant threat of harm might be thought to require immediate action to protect innocent lives, it must be remembered that Vattel, like Webster, would limit permissible measures only to those clearly necessary to neutralize the specific threat that exists at the time force is used.[196]

[194] A US administration would then likely rest on the Report's alternate claims, that attacks on al-Shabaab are part of one or more existing armed conflicts. *See supra* notes 50–53 and accompanying text.

[195] *See* Tuck, *supra* note 4 and accompanying text.

[196] Vattel does not directly address permissible measures of force but strongly suggests that states may only take necessary precautions unless it is clear the threatening neighbor will attack. He therefore appears to observe a fairly strict necessity principle with regard to not only the resort to force but also responsive measures. *See* Vattel, *supra* note 21, at bk. 3, ch. III § 50 at 499–500.

2. The Use of Force

Regarding the specifics of the force used in defensive operations, the adoption of a war paradigm for all transnational threats is clearly problematic. Doing so means that individuals may be targeted and killed even if they present no immediate threat of death or other significant harm. This, again, more closely aligns with Britain's approach to the *Caroline* than with Webster's objections grounded in basic liberal values. Adhering to international law's liberal values therefore requires observing a narrower concept of defensive necessity, at least when a NIAC does not (or does not yet) exist with respect to the targeted NSAG. According to Webster, defensive measures not occurring within the context of an armed conflict must be calibrated to the specific nature of the threat that exists at the time defensive force is used.

Outside of armed conflict, law-of-war targeting is inconsistent with this more limited approach. Unlike the necessity principle of self-defense, the military necessity principle of the law of war permits attacks that degrade or neutralize an enemy's *capacity* to inflict present *and future* harm rather than only immediately impending harm.[197] Under the law of war, the primary consideration is degrading or eliminating a collective entity's ability to successfully wage war, subject to humanitarian constraints on permissible means and methods of warfare and protections for the victims of the conflict.[198] As correctly stated in the Report, the necessity principle applicable in armed conflict therefore allows "all measures needed to defeat the enemy as quickly and efficiently as possible that are not prohibited by the law of [war]" and requires that such measures "be directed at accomplishing a legitimate military purpose."[199]

The breadth of permissible military purposes recognized by the law of war demonstrates how significantly its military necessity principle differs from defensive necessity. Under the law of war, enemy forces may be attacked at any time, even when sleeping, because they are a part of a nation's capacity to wage war.[200] Permissible objects of attack include things "that by their nature, location, purpose or use, make an effective contribution to military action and whose total

[197] *See* How Does Law Protect in War? 89 (Marco Sassoli et al. eds., 3d ed. 2011) ("The basic axiom underlying [the law of war is] that even in an armed conflict the only acceptable action is to weaken the military potential of the enemy.").

[198] *See, e.g.*, *IHL-HRL Report*, *supra* note 134, at iv ("The conduct of hostilities does not prohibit the killing of legitimate targets, provided that, among others, the IHL principles of proportionality and precautions are fulfilled.").

[199] *See Obama Framework Report*, *supra* note 77, at 21.

[200] *See, e.g.*, Jens David Ohlin, *The Duty to Capture*, 97 Minn. L. Rev. 1268, 1271 (2013) ("If IHL–and IHL alone–applies, then . . . there is no implied duty to capture [a member of an opposing armed force].").

or partial destruction, capture, or neutralization, in the circumstances ruling at the time, offers a definite military advantage."[201] The Report argues that this permits destruction of not only an enemy's "war-fighting" capabilities but also certain of its "war-sustaining" capabilities.[202] In other words, the concept of "military advantage" permits targeting a broad range of persons, things, and property that either currently or may prospectively contribute to an enemy's ability to fight.

Even more problematic from the standpoint of basic liberal values, the law of war allows for collateral harm to innocent persons and their property when not "excessive to the direct and concrete military advantage anticipated" from an attack.[203] Plainly stated, states can deprive individuals of their basic rights to life, liberty, and property regardless of their past or present actions. Mere proximity to a legitimate military target—whether intentional, knowing, or unknowing—allows for a knowing deprivation of those rights so long as an attacking force directs its attack to a valid military target and believes the anticipated military advantage justifies any anticipated collateral harm to innocent persons and their property. By relying upon a war paradigm and its military necessity principle rather than a defensive necessity principle, the emerging norms of transnational self-defense offend the basic liberal values that America and its allies purport to cherish and defend. Unless a NIAC exists with a targeted group, respect for individual rights and liberal values require observing a narrower, "Webster-ian" concept of necessity and proportionality for all uses of defensive force.

It is here worth noting that states may have originally adopted organization and intensity thresholds necessary to establish the existence of a NIAC in order to narrow its scope and avoid undertaking law of war obligations for all domestic disorders.[204] Perhaps they intended to preserve flexibility when responding to them. By limiting the scope of application of the law of war, however, these threshold requirements also limit the circumstances under which states may use law-of-war targeting to deprive individuals of their basic rights. In this narrow way, the threshold requirements of NIAC advance liberal values. Unless there is a NIAC, respect for basic liberal values

[201] *See* Protocol Additional to the Geneva Conventions of 12 August 1949, and Relating to the Protection of Victims of International Armed Conflicts (Protocol I) (8 June 1977) art. 1(2), 1125 U.N.T.S. 3, 7 [hereinafter Protocol I]. This rule is widely understood to reflect customary international law applicable to all armed conflicts. *See, e.g.*, *Customary IHL Study*, *supra* note 70, at 99–111.

[202] *See Obama Framework Report*, *supra* note 77, at 23–24.

[203] *See, e.g.*, Protocol I, *supra* note 201, at art. 51(5)(b), 26; *Customary IHL Study*, *supra* note 70, at 46–50.

[204] *See* Laura Perna, The Formation of the Treaty Law of Non-International Armed Conflicts 106–07 (2006).

requires lethal force should not be permitted unless a threat of grave harm is truly imminent.

V. Perpetuating the Grotian Tradition: Substituting Flawed Policy for Liberal Values

The Obama administration attempted to mitigate the effects of its overbroad embrace of a war paradigm by adopting policies that limited the use of lethal force outside areas of "active hostilities."[205] In these areas, according to the Report and the PPG, lethal targeting is permissible only when there is near certainty that a target is present, near certainty that no "non-combatants" are present, and a determination that capturing a targeted individual is not feasible.[206] Although it appears likely that Trump administration discarded these policy constraints in 2017,[207] they could still be thought to influence emerging norms of transnational self-defense and should therefore be carefully examined.

When an act of transnational self-defense does not occur within the context of an existing NIAC, these policy constraints are inconsistent with basic liberal values in at least four ways. First, they permit a use of lethal force based upon the status of an individual as a member in a NSAG even when not clearly necessary to counter a specific and imminent threat of harm from that individual or NSAG.[208] Second, they apply based only upon the location where force will be used rather than requiring the existence of a NIAC.[209] Third, although the policies purport to limit collateral deaths, they too broadly tolerate them.[210] This is in part because they are vague and in part because they are revocable policy rather than law.[211]

205 *See Obama Framework Report*, *supra* note 77, at 24.

206 *Id.* 25 (citing *2013 PPG*, *supra* note 80).

207 *See* Charlie Savage, *Trump Revokes Obama-Era Rule on Disclosing Civilian Casualties from U.S. Airstrikes Outside War Zones*, N.Y. Times, Mar. 6, 2019, <https://www.nytimes.com/2019/03/06/us/politics/trump-civilian-casualties- rule-revoked.html>.

208 *See* Adil Ahmad Haque, *Targeted Killing Under Trump: Law, Policy, and Legal Risk*, Just Security, Feb. 10, 2017, <https://www.justsecurity.org/37636/targeted-killing-trump-law-policy-legal-risk/> ("For its part, the Department of Defense has taken the extreme view that, '[u]nder customary international law, no legal presumption of civilian status exists for persons or objects.' That extreme view is probably incorrect [. . .].").

209 *See* Michael J. Adams & Ryan Goodman, *"Reasonable Certainty" vs "Near Certainty" in Military Targeting—What the Law Requires*, Just Security, Feb. 15, 2018, <https://www.justsecurity.org/52343/reasonable-certainty-vs-near-certainty-military-targeting-what-law-requires> ("If one determines, for example, that a group of enemy fighters (all of whom are lawful targets) are in a location and that the specific individual is, let's say, somewhat likely to be present (or even unlikely but possible), nothing in the law of armed conflict would forbid striking the group. The entire group is targetable, and it really is just a policy choice whether to restrict attacks only to when the specific individual is present (at whatever level of certainty or uncertainty).").

210 *See* Haque, *supra* note 206 ("However, outside areas of active hostilities, the military advantage of isolated or sporadic strikes may be insufficient to justify collateral harm to civilians.").

211 The Report asserts that its policies "are more restrictive than what would be required as a matter of law" and that "the United States maintains the right to change its policies and practices consistent with applicable law." *See Obama Framework Report*, *supra* note 77, at 19.

Finally, the imprecise "near certainty" standards allow lethal targeting, including weapons release,[212] decisions without carefully evaluating whether any potential collateral deaths are an unavoidable incident to a necessary use of force. This section briefly examines these issues.

A. Lethal Force

Even in places where they apply, policy constraints like those adopted in the PPG do not limit the use of lethal force to circumstances of defensive necessity. The PPG requires only "near certainty" that a targeted individual is even present at the location if a lethal attack.[213] Critically, it still allows targeting based upon an individual's membership in a NSAG posing an indefinite, ongoing threat of future harm rather than any actual or imminent threat that a targeted group or individual then poses. This is clearly inconsistent with Webster's articulation and application of the necessity principle.

Absent an existing armed conflict, and assuming that a resort to defensive force can be justified at all, the necessity principle of self-defense requires that individuals posing only indefinite, "ongoing" threats of future harm be captured rather than killed, just as Webster argued.[214] Capture sufficiently neutralizes an individual's prospective participation in, or support for, future acts of violence. Thus, essentially the same limitations that human rights law imposes upon preventive action restrict defensive measures in transnational self-defense. This is not because international human rights law is clearly applicable by its terms, although it could be in some circumstances.[215] It is because observing the self-defense principles of necessity and proportionality limit the permissible measures of defensive force in ways similar to human rights law.[216]

A necessity to use lethal force may arise during an attempt to capture members of a violent NSAG. For example, the use of lethal force would be permissible against those who, in the course of a capture operation, pose an immediate threat of death or serious injury to the would-be captors or others. Additionally, the use of lethal force may be permissible to stop violent criminals who are escaping

[212] "Weapons release" refers to firing, dropping, or launching weapons from their delivery platform, such as manned or unmanned aircraft. The person possessing decision-making authority to allow weapons release is a "weapons release authority." *See, e.g.*, Dept. of Def., *Joint Pub 3-09.3: Close Air Support* (Nov. 25, 2014) III 40.

[213] *See 2013 PPG, supra* note 80, at 1, 3.

[214] *See* Miller, *supra* note 97, at 449; *see supra* note 128 and accompanying text.

[215] *See* Ashley S. Deeks, *Consent to the Use of Force and International Law Supremacy*, 54 Harv. Int'l L.J., no. , 39–41 (2013) (arguing state acting with consent of territorial government should be bound by all laws applicable to that government, including international law).

[216] A thorough assessment of the extent to which the self-defense principles of necessity are identical to human rights law requirements when no non-international armed conflict exists is beyond the scope of this chapter.

capture or detention if there are no reasonable alternatives to prevent their escape. These are well-established bases for a necessary use of lethal force in a majority of legal systems and recognized by the General Assembly of the United Nations.[217]

Furthermore, although the PPG requires a determination that capture is not feasible, it does not explain how feasibility is determined. Short of actually attempting capture, determining the feasibility of capturing a specific individual in a remote foreign territory is an uncertain enterprise at best. The operation that resulted in the death of Osama bin Laden demonstrated the American military's impressive capability to infiltrate fortified compounds deep in foreign countries to confront dangerous individuals.[218] Assessing emerging transnational self-defense norms on this issue requires much more information about how the US government evaluates feasibility of capture and how that determination relates to a perceived necessity to use lethal force at a given time and place. Indeed, the fact that friendly forces are not placed at risk likely leads to the more frequent use of remote targeted killing against those presenting no immediate threat of death or grave bodily harm.

B. Location Rather than Nature of Violence

The parameters of the PPG policy constraints are further flawed because they are observed only "outside areas of active hostilities."[219] This might be understood to improperly substitute the nature of the location where an individual is targeted for a determination of whether an individual is subject to law-of-war targeting in an existing NIAC. This aspect of the PPG potentially misconstrues how the law of war regulates lethal force. Merely being on a battlefield does not render every human threat susceptible to law-of-war targeting.

[217] *See, e.g.*, UN Congress on Prevention of Crime and the Treatment of Offenders, Havana, Cuba, 27 August to 7 September 1990, *Basic Principles on the Use of Force and Firearms by Law Enforcement Officials*, para. 9, UN Doc. A/CONF.144/28/Rev.1 (1990). ("Law enforcement officials shall not use firearms against persons except in self-defense or defense of others against the imminent threat of death or serious injury, to prevent the perpetration of a particularly serious crime involving grave threat to life, to arrest a person presenting such a danger and resisting their authority, or to prevent his or her escape, and only when less extreme means are insufficient to achieve these objectives. In any event, intentional lethal use of firearms may only be made when strictly unavoidable in order to protect life."); European Convention for the Protection of Human Rights and Fundamental Freedoms, art. 2 (Nov. 4, 1950) Europ.T.S. No. 5, 213 U.N.T.S. 221 (entered into force Sept. 3, 1953) [hereinafter ECHR] ("Deprivation of life shall not be regarded as inflicted in contravention of this Article when it results from the use of force which is no more than absolutely necessary: (a) in defense of any person from unlawful violence; (b) in order to effect a lawful arrest or to prevent the escape of a person lawfully detained; (c) in action lawfully taken for the purpose of quelling a riot or insurrection.").

[218] *See*, e.g., Johnathan Mahler, *What Do We Really Know About Osama bin Laden's Death?*, N.Y. Times Magazine, Oct. 15, 2015.

[219] *See Obama Framework Report*, *supra* note 77, at 25.

Under well-settled international norms, only members of state armed forces or NSAGs that are parties to a specific IAC or NIAC may be targeted at any time.[220] Civilians not part of such armed forces or groups are generally protected from attack and only lose that protection if and "for such time as they take a direct part in" the hostilities of an armed conflict.[221] If no NIAC exists with a NSAG to which a targeted individual belongs, then the strict defensive necessity principle applies to any threat that the group or individual poses, even on an active battlefield.[222]

Regardless of its location, a state must assess each distinct threat of harm and the context of that threat to determine the applicable legal framework and the circumstances under which force, including lethal force, is lawful.[223] For example, a violent battlefield protest by a local population against foreign armed forces does not intrinsically permit the use of law-of-war targeting in response.[224] Unless NIAC thresholds are met, or unless violent individuals take a direct part in the hostilities of an existing NIAC, defensive force must be limited to that which is necessary and proportionate to the specific threats posed at the time force is used.[225] The PPG not only failed to adopt these constraints but also set the wrong criteria for the constraints it adopted.

C. Collateral Harm and Near Certainty

The PPG also allowed for collateral deaths without requiring a determination of whether those deaths would be unavoidably incident to a necessary use of defensive force. As the assertions of both Webster and Ashburton indicated, a necessity to use defensive force does not inherently justify collateral harm to innocent persons or property. Unforeseen or unintended harm may sometimes

[220] INTERPRETIVE GUIDANCE ON THE NOTION OF DIRECT PARTICIPATION IN HOSTILITIES UNDER INTERNATIONAL HUMANITARIAN LAW 31–35 (Nils Melzer ed., 2009).

[221] *Id.* 11–13.

[222] *See, e.g.*, *IHL-HRL Report*, *supra* note 134, at 13–17.

[223] *Id.* 18 ("[. . .] there had to be some type of test against which each situation would need to be assessed in order for the most adequate legal framework to be determined.") (citing HRC, Outcome of the Expert Consultation on the Issue of Protecting the Human Rights in Armed Conflicts: reports of the United Nations High Commissioner for Human Rights, Eleventh session (June 4, 2009) UN Doc. A/HRC/11/31, para. 14).

[224] *Id.* 26–27 ("[S]ituations of civilian unrest in the context of an armed conflict can be highly volatile and can turn into actual armed clashes amounting to hostilities. Thus, a situation . . . could become mainly governed by the conduct of hostilities paradigm if fighters or civilians directly participating in hostilities actually outnumber peaceful and rioting civilians (whose acts do not amount to direct participation in hostilities). In other words, a situation can change in nature and the predominant paradigm may not always be the same.").

[225] *Id.* 7.

be unavoidable and should be properly addressed.[226] Different legal and policy concerns arise when a state is practically certain that a use of defensive force will result in harm to innocent persons and property.

The precise extent to which knowingly causing harm to innocent persons or property is permissible outside of armed conflict is not entirely clear. Just as law enforcement officers should not shoot recklessly into a crowd through which a violent criminal is fleeing, a use of defensive force should not unnecessarily risk innocent lives.[227] The PPG, however, required only "near certainty" that targeted individuals would be present and "near certainty" that individuals not subject to attack were not present.[228] Logically, it would seem that these "near certainty" standards tolerate some erroneous target identification as well as some collateral harm that may be avoidable under the circumstances.[229] The use of these standards elides more difficult legal and moral questions about whether incidental death or destruction is justified or acceptable under the circumstance.

These ambiguities might also result in inconsistent application of the "near certainty" standards. The quantity and quality of the evidence deemed sufficiently "certain" may vary based upon the decision maker and his or her idiosyncratic perceptions of the situation, of the threat, or of acceptable collateral deaths or injuries. At a minimum, respect for liberal values requires a systematic and carefully calibrated approach to identifying and assessing the nature of a threat that a targeted individual or group poses and the necessity of any responsive measures that is practically certain to result in incidental harm to innocent persons and their property.

D. Replacing Flawed Law with Flawed Policies

The fact that these now-discarded policy constraints were policy rather than law amplifies the concern that they do not impose adequate constraints that a proper respect for basic liberal values require. Any state with such policies might: (1) change or eliminate the policies, (2) grant an exception to the policies for a

[226] It is beyond the scope of this chapter to discuss the extent to which international law and liberal principles require compensation or other remedies in these situations.

[227] *See, e.g.*, UN Congress, *supra* note 217, at para. 5 ("Whenever the lawful use of force and firearms is unavoidable, law enforcement officials shall: (a) Exercise restraint in such use and act in proportion to the seriousness of the offence and the legitimate objective to be achieved; (b) Minimize damage and injury, and respect and preserve human life.").

[228] *See 2013 PPG*, *supra* note 80, at 3.

[229] *See generally* Geoffrey S. Corn, *Targeting, Command Judgment, and a Proposed Quantum of Information Component: A Fourth Amendment Lesson in Contextual Reasonableness*, 77 BROOK. L. REV. 437 (2012).

specific operation, (3) determine that an area is now one of active hostilities, thus eliminating the precondition to the application of the policies, or (4) ignore or excuse violations of the policies. Reports indicate that the Trump administration leveraged most or all of these options.[230]

Relaxing the application of these policies may be consistent with the law of war but only when and where it applies. For example, in 2017, the Trump administration reportedly designated new areas in Somalia as areas of active hostilities.[231] Such designation is appropriate if the United States is engaged in an armed conflict in these areas of Somalia, such as against al-Shabaab.[232] Any targeted individuals must be members of a NSAG that is a party to that armed conflict or a civilian participating in the hostilities on its behalf at the time of the attack.[233] After the first publicly reported attack conducted pursuant to this designation, the US Department of Defense stated that it targeted an al-Shabaab command and logistics center, killing eight militants.[234] If these targets were properly identified and the United States is participating in an armed conflict against al-Shabaab, then the attack is likely consistent with the law of war and lawful. Such an attack would be inconsistent with settled law and basic liberal values if no armed conflict existed and if no harm to US forces or property was imminent at the time of the attack.

A state might also be tempted to suspend or rescind policies like these for reasons of expedience, as the Trump administration is reported to have done.[235] Or, a state might choose not to enforce such policies when violated, perhaps retaining them for the sake of appearances only. Thus, not only are the policies an inadequate alternative to strictly observing the self-defense principles of necessity and proportionality, their status as policy rather than

[230] *See* Charlie Savage & Eric Schmitt, *Trump Poised to Drop Some Limits on Drone Strikes and Commando Raids*, N.Y. TIMES, Sept. 21, 2017, <https://www.nytimes.com/2017/09/21/us/politics/trump-drone-strikes-commando-raids-rules.html>. *See also* Charlie Savage & Eric Schmitt, *Trump Administration Is Said to Be Working to Loosen Counterterrorism Rules*, N.Y. TIMES, Mar. 12, 2017, <https://www.nytimes.com/2017/03/12/us/politics/trump-loosen-counterterrorism-rules.html>.

[231] Charlie Savage & Eric Schmitt, *Trump Eases Combat Rules in Somalia Intended to Protect Civilians*, N.Y. TIMES, Mar. 30, 2017, <https://www.nytimes.com/2017/03/30/world/africa/trump-is-said-to-ease-combat-rules-in-somalia-designed-to-protect-civilians.html>.

[232] *See Obama Framework Report*, *supra* note 77, at 25 ("The determination as to whether a region constitutes an "area of active hostilities" does not turn exclusively on whether there is an armed conflict under international law taking place in the country at issue, but also takes into account, among other things, the size and scope of the terrorist threat, the scope and intensity of U.S. counterterrorism operations, and the necessity of protecting any U.S. forces in the relevant location.").

[233] *Id.* 19 ("It is well- and long-established that under the law of armed conflict, States may target specific, identified individual members of an enemy force as well as individuals directly participating in hostilities.").

[234] *See* Charlie Savage, Helene Cooper, & Eric Schmitt, *US Strikes Shabab, Likely a First since Trump Relaxed Rules for Somalia*, N.Y. TIMES June 11, 2017, <https://www.nytimes.com/2017/06/11/us/politics/us-airstrike-somalia-trump.html>.

[235] *See supra* notes 230–31.

law substantially diminishes their value as proxies for fully respecting basic liberal values.

VI. Conclusion

To the extent that the arguments of the United States and commentators supporting post–September 11, 2001, counterterrorism operations represent emerging transnational self-defense norms, this chapter has shown that they are inconsistent not only with relevant, settled international law but also with the basic liberal values that universally underlie the contemporary international system. This is at least true whenever they are relied upon outside the context of a NIAC in which a targeted individual or entity is subject to attack.

The legitimate concerns regarding the improper reliance on a war paradigm and the assertion of other questionable or ambiguous legal norms are amplified by the opacity surrounding their precise application. Whether it pertains to the imminence of an attack or its probability and gravity, to the ability or willingness of a territorial state to address a threat, or to the determination of whether an individual is part of a specific or associated NSAG, the assertion of these erroneous or dubious and ambiguous norms is troubling and problematic. Such concerns are significantly aggravated by the fact that the information supporting claims that these norms are satisfied with respect to a specific use of force is often almost entirely secret.

At bottom, the preceding analysis demonstrates that the legal and factual errors and ambiguities surrounding emerging transnational self-defense norms essentially permit states to engage in lethal punitive or defensive uses of force against NSAGs whenever and wherever they desire. These norms and their exceedingly loose application thus effectively perpetuate the Grotian tradition of sovereignty and human rights "haves" and "have-nots." Although an international system based upon universal respect for basic liberal values has been formally adopted by states, those values have not yet been fully realized in state practice. This is particularly so in the emerging state practice related to transnational self-defense.

13
Finding Peace in the Law of War

Bailey Brown[1]

I. Introduction

As a countdown reaches zero hour and tanks start crossing borders, amidst dust and smoke and the roar of engines, an intricately detailed legal order guides the beginning of war. National combatants know exactly what rules to follow because lawyers and military planners worked out the details ahead of time. The transition from peacetime civil law and the public international law of human rights to the *lex specialis* of the law of war is an orderly and planned event. The legal basis for the war and the rules for its conduct are developed in accordance with international law at both policy and operational levels.

The United States, for example, has in recent decades invoked arguments grounded in *jus ad bellum* for the liberation of Kuwait from Iraqi forces, the destruction of the Taliban and the Al Qaeda network in Afghanistan, and preemptive self-defense in Iraq. Though the original theories of *jus ad bellum* underpinning these conflicts remain controversial to some degree, the wars in Iraq and Afghanistan, rightly or wrongly entered, unquestionably manifested as high-intensity shooting wars with detailed legal justifications and rules of engagement. These were grounded in international law, and especially in the law of war.

Uncomfortably, recent wars have not shown the same administrative regularity and rigorous compliance with international law in their conclusions. Instead, conflicts often persist as difficult, occasionally bloody hybrids. Peacekeeping, nation building, and training efforts coexist alongside airstrikes, security cordons, raids, and assistance to partner nations' combat operations against various iterations of resistance, including terrorist actors such as ISIS and the Taliban. Despite declarations of victory, coalition partners and US forces

[1] Lieutenant Colonel (Ret.), US Army. Many thanks to the Center for Ethics and the Rule of Law (CERL) at the University of Pennsylvania Law School, and in particular to Claire Finkelstein, the Director and founder of CERL, for their support to this project. This article is not associated with the US government, the Department of Defense, or the US Army. The opinions reflected in the chapter are those of the author alone, in a personal capacity, and do not represent the opinions or policy of any element of the US government.

Bailey Brown, *Finding Peace in the Law of War* In: *Between Crime and War*. Edited by: Claire Finkelstein, Christopher Fuller, Jens David Ohlin, Mitt Regan, Oxford University Press. © Claire Finkelstein, Christopher Fuller, Jens David Ohlin, Mitt Regan 2023. DOI: 10.1093/oso/9780197638798.003.0014

remain involved in operations against persistent non-state belligerents in both Iraq and Afghanistan. These forces operate in a context of *jus in bello*, the law of war version of human rights law, looking to the Geneva Conventions and other sources of the law of war for guidance as to whom they can kill, capture, and detain even as they seek to stabilize regions and to restore (or to establish) peacetime civil regimes underpinned by accepted principles of human rights law.

This chapter will address the inability of positive international law to account effectively for how some modern armed conflicts end. It will examine the general framework of the law of armed conflict (LOAC), the problem of how wars end, and the historical experiences that have helped shape the current legal structures of conflict termination. It will then compare the conflict in Afghanistan and the conflict in Colombia as representative examples of a new paradigm for the transition to peace. Although shaped by very different historical experiences, very divergent religious and cultural norms, and completely dissimilar landscapes, Afghanistan and Colombia share some surprising commonalities. Comparison will reveal profound impacts of historical narrative, the importance of physical distance, and how cultural and religious factors can enable, or retard, recession of war's *lex specialis*. Ultimately, comparison will reveal a symbiotic relationship between civil law and LOAC in both countries. The chapter concludes that the experiences of Afghanistan and Colombia, despite their many differences, present a model for terminating armed conflict through the coexistence of civil law and LOAC for a protracted period of time. This hybrid condition should not be regarded as an accident of circumstance or an unforeseeable surprise to chagrined political and military leaders. It should be treated as an expected component of armed conflict, as deliberate and detailed as the original rules of engagement.

II. Legal Framework

The *lex generalis*, the public international law prevailing in the absence of international or non-international armed conflict, here called the law of peace or international human rights law (IHRL), extends fundamental protections to individuals and provides for basic human rights. These rights are perhaps best articulated in the United Nations' Universal Declaration of Human Rights, which asserts, in thirty articles, a set of commonly agreed upon rights that all nations are exhorted to pursue. These include the rights to "life, liberty and security of person" and the prohibition of torture and "cruel, inhuman or degrading treatment or punishment."[2] Although not specifically binding, the Universal Declaration establishes customary international law that serves as a basis for the

[2] United Nations General Assembly, "Universal Declaration of Human Rights" (adopted Dec. 10, 1948, GA . 217 A, Doc. A/810), <http://www.un.org/en/universal-declaration-human-rights/.

legitimacy of domestic criminal procedures. These are expected to punish past acts through a system of due process which recognizes basic human rights.

Another aspect of public international law deals with the *lex specialis* of war, or LOAC. The LOAC addresses both the just entry into war, *jus ad bellum*, and the lawful conduct of warfare once undertaken, known as *jus in bello*.[3] The LOAC is the subset of public international law that deals with the peculiar circumstances of war.[4] *Jus in bello* is based upon humanitarian law, similar in title but distinct from international human rights law. Humanitarian law, like LOAC, is specific to the conduct of hostilities. It derives from the experiences of nations in the depredations and horrors of war, and the efforts of states and nongovernmental organizations to redress them.[5]

Key multilateral treaties giving expression to the law of war are the Hague Conventions, the Geneva Conventions and their 1977 Additional Protocols, and the UN Charter.[6] Chapter VII of the UN Charter recites two bases for state use of force: enforcement actions under the auspices of the UN Security Council pursuant to Articles 39 through 42, and self-defense pursuant to Article 51. Where a breach of the peace by a state cannot be resolved through peaceful means, the UN Security Council

> may take such action by air, sea, or land forces as may be necessary to maintain or restore international peace and security. Such action may include demonstrations, blockade, and other operations by air, sea, or land forces of Members of the United Nations.[7]

[3] *See* "Charter of the United Nations and the Statute of the International Court of Justice" (San Francisco, 26 June 1945) art. 2(4), which states: "[a]ll members shall refrain in their international relations from the threat or use of force against the territorial integrity or political independence of any state, or in any other manner inconsistent with the Purposes of the United Nations." The exceptions begin from there.

[4] Department of the Army and United States Marine Corp, "The Commander's Handbook on the Law of the Land and Warfare" (FM 6-27/MCTP 11-10C, August 2019).

[5] Rules of Engagement (ROE) are not international law. Upon engaging in an armed conflict, or a peace operation, or any action involving US military forces, the United States develops ROE. ROE are policy based upon the exigencies of a particular conflict. They are consistent with, and grounded in, the law of war and US criminal law—violations of ROE may be punishable, for example, under the Uniform Code of Military Justice. ROE provide specific guidance for United States forces based upon the interests and objectives of the United States in a particular conflict. ROE are different in every campaign and can even be specific to particular missions. While ROE used for planning at operational or strategic headquarters elements generally are classified and often fill multiple binders, Soldiers are issued ROE that are distilled from fundamental principals of international law, are unclassified, and that fit on a single, laminated card the size of a standard playing card.

[6] The Hague Conventions are available in their entirety at International Committee of the Red Cross, "Treaties, States Parties and Commentaries," <https://ihl-databases.icrc.org/ihl/INTRO/195; the Geneva Conventions and their additional protocols are available in their entirely at International Committee of the Red Cross, "The Geneva Conventions and their Commentaries," <https://www.icrc.org/en/war-and-law/treaties-customary-law/geneva-conventions; *see also* United Nations, *supra* note 3.

[7] United Nations, *supra* note 3, at art. 42.

Alternatively, Article 51 states: "Nothing in the present Charter shall impair the inherent right of individual or collective self-defence if an armed attack occurs against a Member of the United Nations." Self-defense can be individual, meaning action by a state to protect its territory, independence, or its nationals. Self-defense can also be collective, allowing "victim States to receive assistance from other States in responding to and repelling an armed attack." This requires that the victim state have a legitimate right of self-defense, and that the victim state request the assistance. Sometimes states enter into collective self-defense agreements, such as the North Atlantic Treaty Organization (NATO) treaty, to help provide a framework for this type of self-defense.[8]

A narrow interpretation of Article 51 would stop with these two forms of self-defense. However, there is an increasingly relevant concept of anticipatory self-defense. This is the idea that "a State is not required to absorb the first hit" before acting in self-defense.[9] Anticipatory self-defense is particularly relevant where a state is unable or unwilling to stop an actor from launching an attack from the state's territory.[10] This broad interpretation of self-defense is controversial in international law because the language of the UN Charter recites individual and collective self-defense specifically, but says nothing of anticipatory self-defense. Somewhere between anticipatory self-defense and unprovoked attack lies preventive self-defense, or the use of force to prevent a future attack that is not imminent. This conduct is widely considered illegal under international law.[11]

Of special concern is the problem of non-state actors, particularly those who have not agreed to be bound by international law. International law developed on the basis of a system of treaties that arose at the conclusion in 1648 of Europe's Thirty Years' War. Known collectively as the Peace of Westphalia, these treaties more or less deliberately introduced the modern concept of the state and inaugurated the idea of checks and balances between states as normative. Over time, states became the focus of the international legal system. International law establishes four criteria that must be met for an entity to be regarded as a state: (1) a defined territory (even if disputed); (2) a permanent population; (3) a government; and (4) the capacity to conduct international relations.[12]

[8] International and Operational Law Department, Operational Law Handbook 5–6 (16th ed. 2016), < https://www.loc.gov/rr/frd/Military_Law/pdf/operational-law-handbook_2016.pdf.

[9] *Id.* 6.

[10] *See generally* Brian Egan, *International Law, Legal Diplomacy, and the Counter-ISIL Campaign*, *in* Benjamin Wittes, *State Department Legal Adviser Brian Egan's Speech at ASIL*, Lawfare, Apr. 8, 2016, <https://www.lawfareblog.com/state-department-legal-adviser-brian-egans-speech-asil.

[11] International and Operational Law Department, *supra* note 8, at note xx.

[12] *See* sec. 201, note 3 of Restatement of the Law Third, Foreign Relations Law of the United States, vol. 1, at 72, 74 (American Law Institute, 1987)

Contemporary conflicts involve adversaries capable of delivering violence sufficient to threaten states, by means and on scales not amendable to criminal prosecution under civil law, but without the qualifications of statehood and attendant status under international law. This creates significant problems of definition and legal status. To the extent that statehood is required for combatant immunity, for example, belligerents engaged in violence against states but who themselves act on behalf of a non-state actor may not enjoy such immunity. At the same time, it is impracticable to address the threat posed by some actors and organizations using the tools and institutions of domestic criminal law enforcement, not least because such actors are often located in areas where little or no state authority exists. This creates pressing legal challenges.

As Claire Finkelstein of the Center for Ethics and the Rule of Law has observed, the laws of war are "organized around the assumption that parties to an armed conflict are 'combatants,' meaning that they are members of a state military acting in the name of that state." Accordingly, norms of conduct with regard to non-state actors remain unclear and ill-defined with, as Finkelstein notes, "few consistent legal principles to provide guidance." Efforts to define non-state actors and their fighters as "unlawful combatants" creates a misleading framework of analysis that treats state-based definitions as qualification criteria for rights during armed conflict This dangerous cognitive error undermines coherent legal analysis of the issues involved in combating non-state actors in a manner properly constrained by the principles of *jus in bello*.

Despite these inconvenient and challenging ambiguities, continuing threats by non-state actors have compelled the United States to invoke principles of self-defense in response to non-state threats. The United States has interpreted Article 51's inherent right of self-defense to apply "to any 'armed attack,' not just attacks from state actors."[13] By this reasoning, an armed attack by a non-state actor within a state could trigger the right of another state to self-defense under Article 51, even if the state from which the attack originated did not intend or support the attack. Whether a cross border response to a non-state threat is legitimate under international law depends, according to many scholars and to the official policy of the United States, "on whether the host State is unwilling or unable to deal with the nonstate actors who are launching armed attacks from within its territory."[14]

[13] International and Operational Law Department, *supra* note 8, at 7, citing Department of Defense Law of War Manual, *supra* note 1, at § 1.11.5.4. *See also* The White House, "Report on the Legal and Policy Frameworks Guiding the United States' Use of Military Force and Related National Security Operations" 9 (Dec. 2016), < https://obamawhitehouse.archives.gov/sites/whitehouse.gov/files/documents/Legal_Policy_Report.pdf.

[14] *Id.* 10

III. Triggering and Terminating the Law of Armed Conflict: International and Non-International Frameworks

One approach to terminating LOAC is to reverse the conditions that triggered it. The Geneva Conventions contemplate two types, or levels, of armed conflict: international and non-international.[15] Common Article 2 of the Geneva Conventions is triggered by a "declared war or of any other armed conflict which may arise between two or more of the High Contracting Parties even if the state of war is not recognized by one of them."[16] The phrase "or any other armed conflict" can be read broadly. Would a brief spurt of violence on a remote border between two states not otherwise at war qualify as "other armed conflict?" The International Red Cross would argue that LOAC applies to "any dispute between two States involving the use of their armed forces. Neither the duration of the conflict nor its intensity plays a role."[17] The use of the phrase "other armed conflict," suggests that the framers of Common Article 2 intended a broad application of LOAC such that "the applicability of international humanitarian law was henceforth to be unrelated to the will of governments."[18]

The Geneva Conventions codify long-standing state practice for the termination of LOAC in Common Article 2 international armed conflict situations. Termination of hostilities occurs when:

a. All protected persons "who have fallen into the hands of the enemy" are repatriated;
b. Military operations have generally closed;
c. In cases of occupation of a belligerent state's territory by one or more other states, one year after the close of military operations, except that with occupational control come certain obligations to protect civilians continue.[19]

These conditions amount to a reversal of the conditions that gave rise to the application of the LOAC. In other words, because armed conflict triggers LOAC,

[15] Gertrude C. Chelimo, *Defining Armed Conflict in International Humanitarian Law*, 3 Inquiries J. 1 (2011).

[16] Common Article 2 of the Geneva Conventions I–IV; High Contracting Parties are state actors.

[17] International Committee of the Red Cross, Commentary on the Additional Protocols of 8 June 1977 to the Geneva Conventions of 12 August 1949 (Martinus Nijhoff 1987), *see* Article 1 of "Additional Protocol I," para. 62.

[18] Sylvain Vite, *Typology of Armed Conflicts in International Humanitarian Law: Legal Concepts and Actual Situations*, 91 Int'l Rev. Red Cross, no. 873, 72 (2009)

[19] *See* Article 5 of "Convention (I) for the Amelioration of the Condition of the Wounded and Sick in Armed Forces in the Field" (International Committee of the Red Cross, Aug. 12 1949) and "Convention (II) for the Amelioration of the Condition of Wound, Sick and Shipwrecked Members of Armed Forces at Sea" (International Committee of the Red Cross, Aug. 12, 1949). *See also* Article 6 of "Convention (IV) Relative to the Protection of Civilian Persons in Time of War" (International Committee of the Red Cross, Aug. 12, 1949).

the cessation of armed conflict terminates it. This framework contemplates only state actors as participants in war. Insurgencies and terrorist organizations fall outside Common Article 2 definitions.

Common Article 3 of the Geneva Conventions defines non-international armed conflict as "[a]rmed conflict not of an international character occurring in the territory of one of the High Contracting Parties." It contains specific minimum protections to be afforded all persons even when an armed conflict occurs within the territory or purview of one state. Common Article 3 is supplemented by Additional Protocol II and related jurisprudence from the International Criminal Court, and by judicial decisions from ad hoc tribunals.[20] These provide more detailed requirements for the protection of persons in situations of non-international armed conflict.[21]

Common Article 3 specifically applies to conflict between the armed forces of a state "and dissident armed forces or other organized armed groups which, under responsible command, exercise such control over a part of its territory as to enable them to carry out sustained and concerted military operations and to implement this Protocol."[22] Guerrilla warfare, rebellion, and transnational terrorist operations all can qualify as non-international armed conflict under this definition.[23]

Judicial decisions have further expanded range of circumstances which can trigger the LOAC. The International Criminal Tribunal for the former Yugoslavia (ICTY), in *Prosecutor v. Tadic* (*Tadic*), wrestled with a jurisdictional challenge asserting that the specific acts charged did not occur in a qualifying non-international conflict.[24] The Court reasoned that the "rules contained in [Common] Article 3 also apply outside the narrow geographical context of the actual theatre of combat operations" and can last "beyond the actual hostilities," until "a peaceful settlement is achieved."[25] On the basis of this reasoning, the Court found that armed conflict exists whenever there is "protracted armed

[20] Louise Arimatsu & Mohbuba Choudhury, "The Legal Classification of the Armed Conflicts in Syria, Yemen and Libya" 3–4 (International Law PP 2014/001, Chatham House, Mar. 2014).

[21] *Id.*

[22] United Nations, "Protocol Additional to the Geneva Conventions of 12 August 1949, and Relating to the Protection of Victims of Non-International Armed Conflicts (Protocol II), adopted 8 June 1977" (1979) 1125 United States Treaty Series 609, art. I, para. 1.

[23] International and Operational Law Department, *supra* note 8, at 15.

[24] That "Dusan" TADIC a/k/a "Dule" a/k/a "Dusko," participated in the collection and mistreatment, including killings, of Bosnian Muslims and Croats in Opstina Prijedor within Omarska camp and outside Omarska camp, as set forth below. The accused Goran Borovinica OROVNICA participated with Dusan TADIC in killings outside of Omarska camp." *See* Prosecutor v. Tadić, Initial Indictment (Case No. IT-94-1-T, International Criminal Tribunal for the Former Yugoslavia, Feb. 13, 1995), <https://www.icty.org/x/cases/tadic/ind/en/tad-ii950213e.pdf.

[25] Prosecutor v. Tadić, Decision on Defence Motion for Interlocutory Appeal on Jurisdiction (Case No. IT-94-1-T, International Criminal Tribunal for the Former Yugoslavia, Oct. 2, 1995) para. 69, <http://www.icty.org/x/cases/tadic/acdec/en/51002.htm.

violence between governmental authorities and organized armed groups or between such groups within a State."[26] This case is "widely accepted as establishing the two key criteria for qualification as a [non-international armed conflict]: i) intensity of the hostilities; and ii) the involvement of an organized armed group (OAG)."[27] When any of these conditions apply, the protections of Common Article 3 bind the conduct of all parties.

Usefully, Additional Protocol II provides examples of situations that do not rise to the level of armed conflict within a state. These are "internal disturbances and tensions, such as riots, isolated and sporadic acts of violence and other acts of a similar nature."[28] These situations are subject to the internal domestic law of the state in which they occur. They are treated as policing functions, and state responses are limited only by the peacetime public international law of human rights. The LOAC does not apply.

The distinction between situations that amount to policing functions and those that rise to the level of armed conflict within a state is important because the protections afforded by the Geneva Conventions pierce the veil of sovereignty enshrined in Article 2 of the UN Charter.[29] They constrain the actions of regimes contending with armed conflict inside their own borders. This leads to a significant political dimension in the decisions of states to recognize internal armed conflict in their own or in other states. To recognize an armed conflict is to supplement a sovereign's domestic law with the Geneva Conventions. Similarly, to recognize that no armed conflict exists is to deny the applicability of the public international law of armed conflict and to rest upon the *lex generalis*, with its fundamental respect for sovereignty.

The variety of standards used to determine whether armed conflict exists, and thus whether the LOAC is implicated, do not lend themselves to simple inversion for determining when the LOAC no longer applies. The conditions that give rise to an internal armed conflict will be fact specific and informed by the politics of the states involved. The law cannot specify exactly what degree of organization and intensity rises to the level of armed conflict, or how far the geographical and temporal borders of the conflict area may extend. By extension, the law cannot tell us exactly where the LOAC ends. As described in *Tadic*, once armed conflict exists, LOAC applies "until a general conclusion of peace is reached; or, in the case of internal conflicts, a peaceful settlement is achieved."[30] Mere reversal of the criteria for armed conflict does not define the absence of armed conflict.

[26] *Id.* para. 70.
[27] Arimatsu & Choudhury, *supra* note 20, at 4
[28] United Nations, *supra* note 22, at art. I, para. 2.
[29] Stating at paragraph 1, "[t]he Organization is based on the principle of the sovereign equality of all its Members."
[30] Prosecutor v. Tadić, *supra* note 25 at para. 70.

This ambiguity becomes more acute when non-state actors and terrorist organizations operate within or between the territories of states.

IV. The Old Way

The European tradition for ending wars involves the defeated sovereign or sovereigns agreeing to terms set by a prevailing sovereign or sovereigns. In limited wars, such as border clashes or conflicts over royal succession or religious alignment in Europe in the seventeenth through the nineteenth centuries, one or more belligerent sovereigns ultimately determines that the objectives of the war are not worth the costs of further conflict. A peace treaty results, and international order restored. This is war as "a true political instrument, a continuation of political intercourse," undertaken in a context of mutually assured national survival.[31]

In unlimited wars, such as the world wars, one or more belligerents are rendered incapable of imposing their will. The defeated sovereigns may find their governments, or their whole societies, upended and reorganized by the victors. Even here, the means of surrender are formal instruments executed by the sovereigns or their representatives, as in the surrender of the Japanese aboard the battleship *Missouri*. If a belligerent sovereign has been substantially eliminated as a governing authority—as Germany in the Second World War—peace is negotiated by the prevailing parties.

In either scenario, there is little ambiguity concerning the end of hostilities. On June 28, 1919, following six months of negotiations during which an armistice but not a cessation of hostilities provided breathing room for negotiations, the Treaty of Versailles and other instruments formally terminated World War I. With the implementation of each treaty, all parties and belligerents were on notice of the precise time when combatant immunity would cease to apply. Before the agreed time, the shooting on sight of a German soldier by an allied soldier was a legally sanctioned action on behalf of a state at war. After, it would be murder. World War II came to a similarly formal end. Although occupations, repatriations, and military restrictions would continue in the wakes of both conflicts, the governing international legal framework was no longer that of LOAC, but instead became the *lex generalis*, the international law of peace, as a result of formal legal actions by the sovereigns concerned.

Recent conflicts offer little of this legal clarity in the transition from LOAC to civil law. Governments in places such as Afghanistan and Colombia lack means to control their territories and are unable to assert civil authority following

[31] CARL VON CLAUSEWITZ, ON WAR 87 (Michael Howard & Peter Paret eds. & tr. 1989).

conflict. Non-state actors like Al Qaeda and ISIS in the Middle East, and the FARC in Colombia, operate in these ungoverned spaces. The factors that gave rise to armed conflict refuse fully to abate. Conditions in these conflict zones resemble the internal armed conflict contemplated by Common Article 3 of the Geneva Conventions, but without the framework of statehood and effective sovereignty contemplated by those instruments. These examples represent a category of armed conflict in which existing legal constructs for conflict termination fail to provide a workable framework to end the LOAC regime and transition to civil law. Some scholars consider victory in such conflicts to be a hopeless endeavor, arguing that in "the future, there will be no clear enemy surrenders. Instead of parades and flowers, there will be only exhaustion, suffering, and exasperatingly empty rhetoric."[32] As the General Counsel to the Department of Defense observed about the conflict in Afghanistan, and which could be said about any number of conflicts in which non-state actors operate in substantially ungoverned spaces, "it is highly unlikely that there will ever be an agreement to end the conflict. Unlike at the close of the World Wars, there will not be any instruments of surrender or peace treaties."[33]

V. A New Way

The enduring conflicts in Afghanistan and Colombia illustrate an alternative to traditional models of conflict termination. They are examples of gradual conflict mitigation. Examination of these two countries will show that war and peace, LOAC and civil law, are not always binary. They can exist in a dualistic continuum, with separate legal regimes simultaneously supporting efforts gradually to reduce armed conflict and to encourage civil order.

A. Afghanistan

In contrast to the assumptions underpinning the state sovereignty based, Westphalian framework of international relations that gave rise to international law as we know it, the failure of states has emerged as a significant trend in the last two decades.[34] Nowhere is this more visible than in Afghanistan. For

[32] Louis René Beres, *Wars Without Victory*, US NEWS & WORLD REPORTS, Mar. 8, 2013, <https://www.usnews.com/opinion/articles/2013/03/08/iraq-afghanistan-and-the-end-of-winning-wars.

[33] Stephen W. Preston, "The Legal Framework for the United States' Use of Military Force Since 9/11," US Dept. of Defense, Annual Meeting of the American Society of International Law, Washington, DC, Apr. 10, 2015, <https://www.defense.gov/News/Speeches/Speech-View/Article/606662.

[34] Dr. Ashraf Ghani, *How to Rebuild a Broken State*, TEDGLOBAL, July 2005, <https://www.ted.com/talks/ashraf_ghani_on_rebuilding_broken_states#t-108183.

hundreds of years, efforts at central government have "sought to impose a unified legal system on the vast, mountainous provinces," but have never been able "to displace local tribal mechanisms of adjudication and political control."[35] Most recently, the United States and its coalition partners have attempted to establish a recognizable state from amidst the physical and political rubble of a fifteen-year war against Al Qaeda and the Taliban, and more recently even groups claiming loyalty to ISIS. Recognizing that the destruction of the Taliban as a ruling organization and the continued pursuit of Al Qaeda and other terrorists in the region have foreclosed the possibility of a formal, conventional end to hostilities, the United States has taken the position that, "[h]ostilities against an enemy like al-Qa'ida are unconventional and presumably will not come to a conventional end," while acknowledging that "this war, like all wars, must end."[36]

Examination of the history and legal culture of Afghanistan will show that peaceful settlement among the factions involved deeply rooted challenges and is unlikely in the near term. Instead, a blended regime of LOAC and civil law, with some level of international military and civil support, is likely to persist long into the future.

Afghanistan last enjoyed peace in the mid-twentieth century, following its independence from British colonialism in 1919, when it was ruled by a monarchy. From the late 1920s until 1973, Afghanistan's rulers made efforts to modernize the country, including the construction of modern buildings and improving the rights of women.[37] In 1964, Afghanistan passed its third and most successful constitution, which "provided for a popularly elected parliament, elected city councils, provincial advisory councils, and an independent legislature."[38] During this time Afghanistan declined to align itself with the global agendas of either United States or the Soviet Union, but accepted aid from both.

It was during this period of relative stability and increasing secularity that both Islamist and communist movements began to grow in influence. This came to a head in 1973, when Afghanistan's last king, Muhhamed Zahir Shah, was in Rome for medical treatment.[39] His cousin, Mohammed Daoud Khan, led a bloodless coup and declared Afghanistan a republic.[40] The People's Democratic

[35] Faiz Ahmed, *Shari'a, Custom, and Statutory Law: Comparing State Approaches to Islamic Jurisprudence, Tribal Autonomy, and Legal Development in Afghanistan and Pakistan*, 7 GLOBAL JURIST, arts. 5, 3 (2007).

[36] The White House, *supra* note 13, at 11.

[37] Alan Taylor, *Afghanistan in the 1950s and 60s*, THE ATLANTIC, July 2, 2013, <https://www.theatlantic.com/photo/2013/07/afghanistan-in-the-1950s-and-60s/100544/.

[38] J. Alexander Thier, *The Making of a Constitution in Afghanistan*, 51 N.Y.L. SCH. L. REV. 557, 560 (2006–07).

[39] Mohammed Zahir Shah, called the Father of the Nation, returned to Afghanistan in 2002, after the fall of the Taliban. He was considered for election as the leader of Afghanistan, but was displaced by the US-backed Hamid Kharzi. *See* GILLES DORRONSORO, REVOLUTION UNENDING: AFGHANISTAN 1979 TO THE PRESENT 330 (John King tr., 2005).

[40] MICHAEL BARRY, KABUL'S LONG SHADOWS: HISTORICAL PERSPECTIVES 68 (Spring 2011).

Party of Afghanistan (PDPA), a Soviet-supported communist organization, was active in attempting to influence Afghanistan at this time, and Daoud took aggressive steps to repress it. This repression had the opposite effect, resulting in popular support for the PDPA and a communist coup in April 1978.[41] When the communists struggled to hold power, the Soviet Union sent troops to support them.[42] Islamist factions, alienated and incensed by the communists' secular reforms, were galvanized by the foreign occupation and took up arms.[43]

From December of 1979 until February 1989, Soviet forces sought to suppress the Islamic insurgency. They found themselves in conflict with the self-styled Mujahedin, loosely organized but devout Muslim fighters who saw themselves as engaged in a defensive struggle to protect Islam from infidel invaders.[44] They enjoyed financial backing from the United States and Saudi Arabia, and their guerrilla tactics proved highly effective against the cumbersome, heavy Soviet formations. The conflict became a quagmire. The Soviets could neither win nor easily escape.

The Mujahedin were split into no fewer than seven distinct movements and were incapable of large-scale planning or coordination. Their strength came from popular support, the ability to blend with the local populace, and material support from the United States and other Western countries that willingly overlooked the excesses of Islamic extremism in favor of blocking the expansion of communism.[45] The Soviet Forces finally withdrew in 1989.[46] Communists held on to power in Kabul, supported by the Soviet Union, until that regime's collapse at the end of 1991.[47]

From 1992 until 1996, civil war between various Mujahedin warlords, political parties, and ethnic groups dominated the country. It was during this period of chaos that the Taliban coalesced into an organized political force. Starting in 1994, it began to play a major role in the ongoing Afghan civil war. The Taliban was predominantly comprised of ethnic Pashtuns, generally from poor, rural backgrounds and with education only from madrasas.[48] However, they benefited from substantial support from Pakistan's intelligence service.[49] Taking control of

[41] Dorronsoro, *supra* note 39 at 80–92.

[42] Daryl Wortthington, *Communist Revolution in Afghanistan*, NEW HISTORIAN, Apr. 26, 2015, <http://www.newhistorian.com/communist-revolution-in-afghanistan/3610/.

[43] Dorronsoro, *supra* note 39 at 105–07.

[44] *Id.*

[45] Kenneth Katzman "Afghanistan: Post-Taliban Governance, Security, and U.S. Policy" (Congressional Research Service, RL30588, Jan. 12, 2017), 2–3.

[46] Dorronsoro, *supra* note 39, at 187–92.

[47] Katzman, *supra* note 45, at 1–5.

[48] Dorronsoro, *supra* note 39, at 257–73.

[49] See STEVE COLL, GHOST WARS: THE SECRET HISTORY OF THE CIA, AFGHANISTAN, AND BIN LADEN, FROM THE SOVIET INVASION TO SEPTEMBER 10, 2001, at 289–94 (2004) and WILLIAM MALEY, THE AFGHANISTAN WARS 182–86 (2d ed. 2009). Even as Pakistan's political leadership sought to access new markets, the ISI and other factions pursued an anti-India agenda, leveraging Taliban connections to foment insurgency in Kashmir.

the south and eastern sectors of the country, they practiced a strict form of sharia law and employed brutal tactics in competing for power. By 1996, the Taliban had extended substantial control over much of Afghanistan, especially in the urban districts. This continued until 2001.[50]

Taliban successes galvanized other factions, mainly ethnic Tajiks and Uzbeks in the rural north and west of the country, to form a united resistance. This became known as the Northern Alliance. The Northern Alliance doggedly clung to a shrinking area in the far northeastern sector of the country. Meanwhile, Osama bin Laden's Al Qaeda found welcome respite in the Taliban-controlled southern province of Kandahar and supported the regime with training and fighters. It was from here that Al Qaeda directed the attacks of September 11, 2001.[51]

Following the attacks on the World Trade towers and the Pentagon, the US Congress authorized the president "to use all necessary and appropriate force against those nations, organizations, or persons he determines planned, authorized, committed or aided the terrorist attacks."[52] This was more than a traditional declaration of war against a state, as illustrated by the open-ended inclusion of organizations and persons, as well as nations, as approved objects of the use of force.[53]

Within a matter of weeks, bombing began against Taliban forces. The United States worked with the Northern Alliance to lay the groundwork for invasion. Afghanistan's non-international armed conflict became international for the second time since 1979. By the end of 2001, the US-led invasion of Afghanistan had toppled the Taliban government. The next step was to install a friendly government in its place. To this end, the United Nations invited representatives of various Afghan factions, including its former king, to Germany. There they settled upon the Bonn Agreement, establishing an interim administration for the country.[54] This agreement preserved the international legal status of statehood for Afghanistan by declaring that "the Interim Authority shall be the repository of Afghan sovereignty."[55] It recited the Afghan constitution of 1964 as the applicable legal framework until a new constitution could be adopted.[56]

In December 2001, the UN Security Council passed Resolution 1386 to establish the International Security Assistance Force (ISAF). ISAF was authorized "to assist the Afghan Interim Authority in the maintenance of security in Kabul

50 Katzman, *supra* note 45, at 4.

51 *Id.* 5–18.

52 Authorization for Use of Military Force, Pub. L. No. 107 40, 115 Stat. 224.

53 Preston, *supra* note 33.

54 Mark Oliver, *The New Afghan Administration*, THE GUARDIAN, Dec. 5, 2001, https://www.theguardian.com/world/2001/dec/05/qanda.markoliver.

55 United Nations Security Council, "Agreement on Provisional Arrangements on Afghanistan Pending the Re-establishment of Permanent Government Institutions" (S/2001/1154, Dec. 5, 2001) para. I(3).

56 *Id.* para. II(1).

and its surrounding areas."[57] The resolution authorized member states of ISAF to "to take all necessary measures to fulfill its mandate,"[58] which is UN language for authorizing the use of force. Even as the Interim Authority sought to administer Afghanistan's civil law in accordance with IHRL, the LOAC was still in full effect.

Rapid tactical successes against the state apparatus of the Taliban led to exuberance among the United States and its coalition partners, and the mission expanded into an effort to build a stable and democratic Afghanistan[59] in which terrorist organizations no longer could thrive.[60] The United States committed to rebuilding Afghanistan over the long term, in an effort compared by some to the Marshall Plan of World War II.[61] This represented a state-building approach to counterterrorism in which "humanitarian, political, economic, and security assistance" would supplement military force.[62]

In mid-2002, an emergency meeting of prominent leaders from around Afghanistan, called a *loya jirga*, established a new Afghan Transitional Authority and installed Hamid Karzai as provisional president.[63] By mid-2003, senior US officials had declared an end to major combat operations and sought to refocus efforts on reconstruction.[64] With only about eight thousand US soldiers remaining on the ground, in August 2003, NATO took over responsibility for ISAF. It appeared that civil law was gaining traction, and the role of LOAC was coming rapidly to a close.

Yet the conflict refused to comply with the rules of international law for the termination of war. The recently established government in Kabul controlled, for the most part, Kabul.[65] Elsewhere, local warlords, faction leaders, and commanders held sway, "each valley a law unto itself."[66] Throughout Afghanistan in 2003, insurgents continued to battle the US-led coalition. Major counterinsurgency combat operations failed to halt the deterioration of the security environment in Afghanistan, and "by autumn security had already deteriorated to the point that 13 of the country's 32 provinces had become too dangerous for the

[57] United Nations Security Counsel, Res. 1386 (S/RES/1386, Dec. 20, 2001) para. 1.

[58] *Id.* para. 3.

[59] George W. Bush, "Remarks to the George C Marshall ROTC Award Seminar on National Security," Virginia Military Institute, Apr. 17, 2002, < https://georgewbush-whitehouse.archives.gov/news/releases/2002/04/20020417-1.html.

[60] Katzman, *supra* note 45, at 9, table 1.

[61] Bush, *supra* note 59.

[62] The White House, "National Security Strategy of the United States of America" (Sept. 2002), 7, < https://georgewbush-whitehouse.archives.gov/nsc/nss/2002/.

[63] "Afghan Government," Institute for the Study of War, <http://www.understandingwar.org/afghan-government.

[64] *Bush Makes Historic Speech Aboard Warship*, CNN.com, May 1, 2003, <http://www.cnn.com/2003/US/05/01/bush.transcript/.

[65] Daniel Bolger, Why We Lost: A General's Inside Account of the Iraq and Afghanistan Wars 289–90 (2014).

[66] *Id.* 290.

U.N. and non-governmental organizations (NGOs) to work."[67] A situation that, in 2002, seemed like a decisive victory to be quickly followed by a new, agreeable civil government had, just one year later, emerged as the beginning of a long conflict against non-state actors in uncharted strategic and legal territory.

At the time of this writing, US and coalition actors have simultaneously conducted military operations and supported the development of Afghan civil governance institutions, including a constitution and an independent judiciary, for over fifteen years. The application of LOAC to insulate a nascent civil law regime has occurred by default, rather than by design.[68] These efforts have failed to purge LOAC from Afghanistan or to extend international human rights law across the country. This failure stems in part from a clash of legal cultures both within Afghanistan and between the local traditions and Western expectations.[69]

Afghanistan is a multi-ethnic country with a history described by Faiz Ahmed, a leading expert in Islamic history and law at Brown University, as "turbulent center-vs.-provinces conflict." Control of the country is handicapped by "extremely complex politics and ethnically diverse societies, and multiple adjudicatory mechanisms that govern, de facto, in rural areas." Over centuries, Ahmed explains, "Islamic jurisprudence meshed with diverse indigenous cultures [that] make up the predominant language of legal discourse." The eleventh century's widespread blossoming of Islam "did not wipe out Afghanistan's diverse indigenous cultures, even in the realm of law," assesses the scholar, who instead notes that the injection of Islamic thought promoted "a dynamic fusion of the various details of customary law with general principles of Islamic jurisprudence."[70]

In addition to the complex blend of law, culture, religion, and politics, people in Afghanistan experience distance in a manner perhaps foreign to most Western observers.[71] Seemingly small distances on a map result in profound regionalization and isolation of areas outside the urban centers.[72] Even the stern Taliban government was unable fully to exercise control over the country and instead "was forced to negotiate with local elites and accept a degree of local autonomy."[73] The effects of this temporal and geographic isolation on legal development in Afghanistan are profound. Throughout the countryside, in isolated villages and towns where travel to, or even communication from, central urban authorities is

[67] Larry Goodson, *Afghanistan in 2003: The Taliban Resurface and a New Constitution Is Born*, 44 Asian Survey 14, 15 (2004).

[68] *See generally* Bolger, *supra* note 65, at note xx.

[69] *See generally* Special Inspector General for Afghanistan Reconstruction, "Rule of Law in Afghanistan" (15-68 Audit Report, July 2015), 1.

[70] Ahmed, *supra* note 35, at 1–13.

[71] Gregory Feifer, The Great Gamble: The Soviet War in Afghanistan 262 (2009).

[72] Ghani, *supra* note 34.

[73] Ahmed, *supra* note 35, at 1, quoting J. Alexander Thier.

both time consuming and rare, local and regional actors control the instruments of governance.[74] This has been true throughout the country's history.[75]

One result is that individual tribes, villages, and communities have evolved detailed, and primarily oral, local legal traditions. These traditions have combined over several centuries with the divine revelation–based aspects of Islamic law—sharia[76]—to produce community-level jurisprudence for the resolution of common community matters.[77] These localized, hybrid traditions result from, and therefore resonate with, the life experience of the people in the communities. Because local culture and belief are blended with the Quran and other religious texts as interpreted by local holy men, local law is perceived and expected to flow directly from God.[78]

It is within the context of this deeply embedded, highly traditional legal culture that the US-led, predominantly Western coalition sought, and in many ways still seeks, to introduce a written criminal code grounded in international human rights law. The basis for the official, codified criminal law in Afghanistan is its 1976 Criminal Code. This code was consolidated under the country's previous president, Mohammed Daoud Khan. It purported to cover "all of the behaviors that were considered crimes in Afghanistan," unifying sectarian principles and Islamic law.[79] It was suspended by the Taliban and restored by the December 2001 Bonn Agreement.[80] It is the official law of the land, but given the dispersed nature of authority and importance of local traditions and interpretations, does not represent the de facto norms that govern the lives of the majority of the Afghan populace.[81]

Unsurprisingly, local leaders resist replacing their adjudicative roles with a foreign criminal code.[82]

More subtly, but perhaps more importantly, efforts to introduce a national criminal code are perceived as undermining Islam. The Western legal tradition values codification of the law because it creates predictability, ensures accountability to a known standard rather than the whims of individuals, and offers

[74] *Id.* 12.

[75] Feifer, *supra* note 71, at 120.

[76] Islamic Law derives from both divine revelation of the "path to righteousness," called Shari'a, and from human reasoning on the "practicalities of conduct," called Fiqh. *See* Mohammad Hashim Kamali, *The Interplay of Revelation and Reason in the Shariah," The Oxford History of Islam* 107–10 (1999).

[77] Ahmed, *supra* note 35, at 1.

[78] *Id.* 11, quoting Wael B. Hallaq.

[79] Eli Sugarman et al., An Introduction to the Criminal Law of Afghanistan 18 (2d ed. 2012).

[80] *Id.* 19.

[81] Martin Lau, "Islamic Law and the Afghan Legal System" (Presentation, State Reconstruction and International Engagement in Afghanistan, Bonn, May 30–June 1, 2003), <http://eprints.lse.ac.uk/28366.

[82] Ahmed, *supra* note 35, at 11.

equality before the law of various groups within society. Another effect of written legal codes, central to combating terror through law, is the extension of "the centralized state structure through law to the outlaying provinces."[83]

Contrast these principles with Islamic traditions in Afghanistan, where "codifying Shari'a amounts to imposing human limits on law of the Divine."[84] Local legal regimes draw their legitimacy precisely from the professed origin of their legal customs in divine law, which cannot be contained or limited in a fixed code. In other words, the indigenous legal culture is one of faith and rule by holy men, not a legal culture of transparent process or uniform law. Efforts to codify national laws in accordance with international human rights law fail to satisfy local legal cultures. From the perspective of many in Afghanistan, imposing the rule of law would shut out the rule of God.

Efforts by foreign actors to build national institutions that will govern according to written law tend to evoke a long history of colonial brutality suffered by Muslim countries in general and by Afghanistan more acutely than most. The imposition of international human rights law in the form of a codified law can be perceived as an effort by Western powers to further an existential conflict between colonial powers and Islam. This perception is not limited to Afghanistan but extends throughout the Islamic world, where efforts to impose Western-style legal codes have too often occurred in the context of colonialism. This has helped split societies between local elites who benefited and general populations which clung to traditional Islamic norms. Such divides continue to this day.[85] This deep-seated conflict between Islamic norms and Western legal traditions is at the heart of Afghanistan's collective refusal to embrace national legal reforms.[86]

Both the physical terrain and the sociolegal norms present in Afghanistan impede the evolution of a stable, centralized civil regime.[87] Where the coalition-supported government cannot assert a legal regime consistent with international human rights law, it is unable to impose norms and penalties sufficient to suppress terrorist violence. Here, the regime must rely on the LOAC to suppress terrorist and insurgent threats until it can attain and extend legitimacy throughout its territory.

Since the fall of the Taliban, the creation of structures of governance, the holding of elections, and activism by local and international groups and institutions, all have aided the development of an Afghan civil society and domestic government.[88] In December 2014, NATO called an official end to the

[83] *Id.* 7–8, quoting "Stabilizing Afghanistan."
[84] *Id.* 11.
[85] Ahmed, *supra* note 35, at 29.
[86] Wael B. Hallaq, *"Muslim Rage" and Islamic Law*, 54 Hastings L.J. 1712–13 (2003).
[87] Special Inspector, *supra* note 69, at 1.
[88] Katzman, *supra* note 45, 1.

combat mission in that country, drawing down international forces from a peak of 150,000 to less than 20,000, not including 5,500 US troops.[89] Yet, just over a year later, again to the surprise of Western leaders, combat operations resumed after US officials recognized that, in the words of General John Nicholson, "what is on the ground right now just isn't working."[90] To this day, Kabul rules Kabul, while locally defined cultural and legal norms, alongside the LOAC, rule the countryside.

The United States has spent over a billion dollars on rule of law programs alone in Afghanistan, with few discernable results. More than 80 percent of disputes continue to be resolved through local councils rather than formal courts.[91] As a result, civil law is weak, and extremism continues to simmer in remote areas. In many cases local leaders prefer to work with the insurgents instead of the central government.[92] This may be in part due to their presence and ability to exercise control over the area, but is also informed in part by distrust of rampant corruption in the central government.[93]

After ISAF stood down at the end of 2014, it was replaced by a new NATO mission called Resolute Support. The intent of Resolute Support was to turn international forces from combat to "training, advice and assistance for the Afghan security forces and institutions."[94] The idea is that ISAF will support both security forces and government institutions. The goal is to enable the Afghan government to extend the rule of law while increasingly providing for its own security.[95] This effort has not been entirely successful, with only about two-thirds of the country under the control of the central government by late 2016, down from almost three-fourths in late 2015.[96] The Afghan government lacks the means to extend governance to the rural provinces, with the result that threats from organized groups remain active. These threats continue to trigger a right to self-defense by international actors and to require continued counterinsurgency operations by Afghan forces.

Although official combat operations have ended, approximately thirteen thousand troops, mostly made up of American service personnel, remain in

[89] Sune Engel Rasmussen, *Nato Ends Combat Operations in Afghanistan*, THE GUARDIAN, Dec. 28, 2014, <https://www.theguardian.com/world/2014/dec/28/nato-ends-afghanistan-combat-operations-after-13-years.

[90] Carlo Muñoz, *Obama Effectively Restarts Afghanistan Combat Operations a Year After Officially Ending Them*, WASH. TIMES, June 14, 2016, quoting General John Nicholson, <http://www.washingtontimes.com/news/2016/jun/14/obama-effectively-restarts-afghanistan-combat-oper/.

[91] Special Inspector, *supra* note 69, at 1.

[92] Katzman, *supra* note 45, at 1.

[93] Maley, *supra* note 49, at 254–58.

[94] North Atlantic Treaty Organization, "Resolute Support Mission in Afghanistan," Apr. 15, 2021, http://www.nato.int/cps/en/natohq/topics_113694.htm.

[95] North Atlantic Treaty Organization http://www.rs.nato.int/mission.html.

[96] Daniel Wasserbly, *Widespread Corruption, Lagging Capabilities Continue to Thwart Afghan Progress*, JANES DEFENCE WEEKLY, Jan. 11, 2017.

the country in support of Afghan forces. The Afghans continue to incur heavy casualties in ongoing efforts to suppress Taliban insurgents and secure regional capitals in the provinces.[97] The government of Afghanistan continues to invite international forces, and international forces continue to support, the LOAC campaign to suppress international terrorist groups and violent threats to the developing Afghan state. Far from marking the end of hostilities, two years on from the official drawdown of ISAF forces, the United States has loosened the rules of engagement for its forces in Afghanistan.[98] This amounts to a de facto continuation of combat operations, even as civil law norms gradually take hold in the capital.

Conditions in Afghanistan resemble an internationalized form of the Common Article 3 non-international armed conflict. Terrorist groups continue to find safe haven in unsecured provinces and continue to resist the capital's influence with armed force. They are less than "dissident armed forces or other organized armed groups which, under responsible command, exercise such control over a part of its territory as to enable them to carry out sustained and concerted military operations," such as would amount to war inside the state.[99] Yet conditions are also greater than "internal disturbances and tensions, such as riots, isolated and sporadic acts of violence and other acts of a similar nature," that could be dealt with as internal police actions without triggering the LOAC.[100]

The *Tadic* standard would capture conditions in Afghanistan under the rubric of non-international conflict under international law. Afghanistan continues to suffer "protracted armed violence between governmental authorities and organized armed groups or between such groups within a State."[101] The widely accepted criteria of "intensity of the hostilities" and "involvement of an organized armed group" are in place.[102] As discussed earlier and as demonstrated in Afghanistan, LOAC applies "until a general conclusion of peace is reached; or, in the case of internal conflicts, a peaceful settlement is achieved."[103]

The engaged states agree that the path forward for the Afghanistan state is stability, improved security forces, and rule of law. The combination of the entrenched legal cultures in the Afghan provinces and the Afghan government's inability to cope with enduring threats has created conditions where these goals

[97] Micheal R. Gordon, *U.S. General Seeks "a Few Thousand" More Troops in Afghanistan*, N.Y. Times, Feb. 9, 2017, <https://www.nytimes.com/2017/02/09/us/politics/us-afghanistan-troops.html.

[98] Lucas Tomlinson, *Pentagon Loosens Rules of Engagement Against ISIS in Afghanistan*, Military.com, Jan. 22, 2016, < https://www.military.com/daily-news/2016/01/22/pentagon-loosens-rules-of-engagement-against-isis-in-afghanistan.html.

[99] United Nations, *supra* note 22, at art. I, para 1.

[100] *Id.* para. 2.

[101] Prosecutor v. Tadić, *supra* note 25, at para. 70.

[102] Arimatsu & Choudhury, *supra* note 20, at 4.

[103] Prosecutor v. Tadić, *supra* note 25, at para. 70.

seem far away. No *Tadic*-style peaceful settlement seems imminent. The two international legal regimes, the *lex generalis* and the *lex specialis*, the civil law and the LOAC, may coexist indefinitely in Afghanistan. Despite these challenges, the situation is Afghanistan has improved, albeit slowly. The progress of another, very different country on the other side of the world demonstrates that simultaneous LOAC and civil law regimes can, over time, overcome seemingly intractable challenges.

B. Colombia

This heavily forested, predominantly Catholic, South American country faces challenges strikingly similar to those confronting Afghanistan. Unlike Afghanistan, however, Colombia has managed to become one of the wealthiest and most democratic states in its region. This was possible in significant part due to the application of a dual LOAC and civil law regime, in conjunction with international support, for a long period of time and as a matter of deliberate strategy. Colombia has developed innovative methods to leverage the two systems of law. Its experience illustrates that the relationship between the civil law and the LOAC can be one of symbiosis rather than tension.

Colombia's approximately forty-seven million inhabitants enjoy civil liberties, democratic institutions, and peaceful elections.[104] Yet, like the people of Afghanistan, they have also endured decades of violence. "In nearly two centuries since independence," reflects Colonel Philip Abbott, a US Army counterterrorism expert with experience serving in Latin America, "Colombia has experienced only 47 years of peace."[105] Also like Afghanistan, Colombia bears a legacy of colonialism. The nation was formed as an independent state after almost ten years of revolutionary war against Spain, from 1810 to 1819, led by Simon Bolivar. Even after the decisive battle in Boyaca in 1819, internal violence continued for four more years.[106]

Following independence, Colombia's national legal and political experience has been a fundamentally European one. The first constitution of Colombia, enacted in 1821, established a republican government, separation of powers between branches of government, and guaranteed certain individual rights. This

[104] Central Intelligence Agency, *Columbia*, The World Fact Book (Apr. 15, 2021, <https://www.cia.gov/the-world-factbook/countries/colombia/.

[105] Phillip Abbott, *Colombian Peace Negotiations: A Critical Juncture for Positive Change?*, Small Wars Journal, Feb. 17, 2015, <https://smallwarsjournal.com/jrnl/art/colombian-peace-negotiations-a-critical-juncture-for-positive-change.

[106] John Dugas, *Colombia*, *in* Politics of Latin America: The Power Game 504 (Harry Vanden & Gary Prevost eds., 2d ed. 2006).

constitution aspired to elevate individual liberty and to limit the church and state.[107]

From the beginning of its existence as a state, the seeds of conflict were sown into Colombian political life. The new republic quickly split between conservative followers of Simon Bolivar and liberal adherents of his vice president, and later president, Francisco de Paula Santander. By the end of the 1840s, followers of these two revolutionary leaders had coalesced into the Liberal and Conservative Parties of Colombia, "which today are among the oldest continuously functioning parties in all of Latin America."[108]

The Liberal and Conservative Parties vied for control of the state in a winner-takes-all pattern of governance, with the victorious party often completely excluding the other faction for the duration of its administration. This binary ideological split polarized the political landscape, giving rise to seven civil wars between 1851 and 1902.[109] Resentments fomented by this cycle of violence and reciprocal oppression created conditions for near a collapse of the state in 1946, when a split between two candidates in the Liberal Party resulted in the election of the conservative candidate.[110] The ensuing chaos has become known as La Violencia.[111] It began as merely a repetition of the recriminations common to power shifts between the two parties.[112] But, with the assassination on April 9, 1948, of a prominent Liberal leader, what Latin America scholar Grace Livingstone describes as "a wave of angry protest and mass rioting" shook Bogota.[113] From the streets of the capital, La Violencia spiraled into a broad, chaotic national conflict that drew from a complex mix of social factors.[114] For example, La Violencia could be attributed in part to a vast inequality of wealth between the poor majority and the wealthy elites.[115]

Human rights law was among the early casualties of La Violencia. Between 1946 and 1957, approximately two hundred thousand Colombians were killed in a civil war that devolved routinely into lawlessness, banditry, and plunder.[116] Torture, mutilation, rape, and the razing of villages were common practices, with each outrage fueling further reprisals.[117] A military junta finally deposed the

[107] David Bushnell, The Making of Modern Colombia: A Nation in Spite of Itself 52 (1993)

[108] Dugas, *supra* note 106, at 505.

[109] *Id.* 505–06. The last of these, known as the War of a Thousand Days, helped create the conditions for the U.S. backed secession of modern Panama from Colombian control.

[110] Bushnell, *supra* note 107, at 196–200.

[111] Dugas, *supra* note 106, at 506.

[112] Bushnell, *supra* note 107, at 201.

[113] Grace Livingstone, Inside Colombia: Drugs, Democracy, and War 42 (2004).

[114] *Id.* 42.

[115] *Id.* 43.

[116] Dugas, *supra* note 106, at 506–08.

[117] Livingstone, *supra* note 113, at 42.

last partisan president in 1957, ending La Violencia and setting the stage for the National Front.[118]

According to the American historian and famed "Father of the Colombianists" David Bushnell, the military junta "never aspired to anything more than a caretaker role."[119] It managed the election of a civilian government under power-sharing rules designed to compel the two traditional parties to manage peacefully their disagreements and to facilitate execution of government. This rigid coalition remained in control of Colombia until the 1970s.[120] The apparent stability of the National Front regime, especially in the cities, enabled wealthy landowners and business owners to consolidate power.[121] Violence continued among peasant farmers in the countryside.[122]

La Violencia also created a class of experienced military leaders, some of whom were able to organize rural peasant self-defense forces around left-wing ideologies. Several groups formed to resist the clientelist, capitalist government in Bogota.[123] The most successful and notorious was the Fuerzas Armadas Revolucionarias de Colombia (Colombian Armed Revolutionary Forces), or FARC. Espousing a communist ideology mixing anti-imperialism and agrarianism, Livingstone has described the FARC as a "grassroots peasant army."[124] The organization espoused improved conditions for the rural population and protection from the capitalists in Bogota. To finance its efforts to control territory, provide services, and train fighters, the FARC kidnapped and ransomed members of the wealthy and ruling political classes.[125] Partly in response to this threat from the left, the National Front regime gradually succumbed in the late 1970s to an increasingly right-wing national government, in which power sharing was abandoned. In this context the guerilla movements became the de facto voice of the opposition in Colombian politics.[126]

These events developed simultaneously with a surge in the cultivation of illegal drug plants in rural, outlying areas. As Livingstone has sought to explain, peasant farmers discovered in the drug trade an opportunity to accumulate the capital necessary to compete with large farms owned by Colombia's elites.[127]

[118] Dugas, *supra* note 106, at 506–08.
[119] Bushnell, *supra* note 107, at 223.
[120] *Id.* 224.
[121] Livingstone, *supra* note 113, at 43.
[122] *Id.* 45.
[123] Dugas, *supra* note 106, at 509, stating that "[b]y the 1970s, four principal guerilla movements were active in Colombia: the Colombian Armed Revolutionary Froces, or FARC . . . ; the Army of National Liberation, or ELN . . . ; the Popular Liberation Army, or EPL . . . ; and the April 19th Movement, or M-19."
[124] Livingstone, *supra* note 113 at 48.
[125] "Revolutionary Armed Forces of Colombia (FARC)," Center for International Security and Cooperation, 2019, http://web.stanford.edu/group/mappingmilitants/cgi-bin/groups/view/89.
[126] Livingstone, *supra* note 113, at 52.
[127] *Id.* 53.

The FARC was initially concerned that participating in the criminal drug trade would create its own wealthy class and undermine its moral credibility, but succumbed to the trade because it brought many benefits to the peasant farmers that the FARC sought to champion. The organization even taxed the trade's earnings in areas under its control.[128] From the late 1970s through the 1980s, cocaine profits financed FARC's activities and growth.[129] The drug money flooding the countryside allowed insurgents to become increasingly well organized and well equipped, and to effectively resist and threaten the central government. This is similar to the role of opium in Afghanistan.

At the same time, the central government was engaged in law enforcement efforts against powerful drug cartels whose influence and organizations resembled those of the insurgents. Narco-terrorism by major drug cartels, specifically the Medellin Cartel and the Cali Cartel, arguably rose to the level of internal armed conflict in its own right. Attacks included the destruction of the headquarters of the liberal, anti-cartel newspaper *El Espactador*, assassinations of civic and government leaders, the destruction of an Avianca airliner, and the destruction by car bomb of the state intelligence headquarters building.[130]

As in Afghanistan, in Colombia, the central government "has never been in control of all of its territory."[131] It is in the isolated spaces that guerillas, drug cartels, and criminal gangs displace the authority of the state. There they enforce their own forms of stability and maintain self-sustaining economic ecosystems. According to one researcher's conversations with military and civilian leaders in Colombia, this dynamic can create a perception among rural populations that state forces cause, rather ameliorate, systemic violence in the country. Just as in Afghanistan, "the disconnection and isolation of rural Colombia from the central government remains one of the leading contributors to violence and sustained insurgency."[132]

By the 1990s, a toxic combination of high-level drug trafficking combined with incidents of terrorism, kidnapping, and murder had put the Colombian state at risk. Colombian institutionalized corruption, a dramatic economic downturn, brain drain, and endemic violence contributed to a perilous breakdown of civil law.[133] By 1997, the FARC had grown sufficiently in strength to pose a conventional military threat to Colombia's armed forces, defeating them in battalion-sized battles.[134] In 1999 alone, Colombia suffered roughly five thousand acts of

[128] *Id.*
[129] "Revolutionary Armed Forces of Colombia," *supra* note 125.
[130] *See generally* Dugas, *supra* note 106, at 510–15.
[131] Livingstone, *supra* note 113, at 35.
[132] Abbott, *supra* note 105.
[133] GABRIEL MARCELLA, DEMOCRATIC GOVERNANCE AND THE RULE OF LAW: LESSONS FROM COLOMBIA 15 (2009).
[134] *Id.* 16.

terrorism and kidnapping. Sixty out of every one hundred thousand people died by murder. The government controlled only about one half of Colombia's territory.[135] The survival of the state was in doubt.[136] A US Army War College report later described the situation at that time as "a paradigm of the failing state."[137]

Colombia's disintegration into government, military, revolutionary, and narco-terrorist factions reflected, and arguably resulted from, a failure of rule of law. Colombia's legal culture descends from that of Spain and the Romans, and Colombia has been prolifically legislative since independence.[138] A new constitution in 1991 "opened the door to broad changes in the administration of justice in Colombia and to a strengthening of judicial review," including an independent judiciary with the power of constitutional review.[139] It was hoped the new constitution would improve the rule of law in Colombia, but the government proved incapable of effective administration or enforcement of the law.[140] A backlog of over one million cases rolled over from year to year.[141]

Failure of justice in Colombia meant impunity for criminal actors, as well as for terrorists and insurgents. Even in areas the government controlled, legal process was slow, corrupt, and generally failed to deliver justice. Only in 7 percent of homicide cases did a conviction result, and only in 38 percent did an investigation even take place. Ponderous procedures, corruption, and violence made justice largely inaccessible to citizens.[142] It is not surprising that populations denied justice turned to extralegal means of redress, or relied on drug cartels or guerilla organizations to provide order.

In response to this crisis of stability, and to help stem the flow of narcotics entering the United States, the Clinton administration turned from the previous US strategy of low-level covert intervention and announced Plan Colombia. Plan Colombia delivered funds, training, equipment, and troops in support of government efforts to defeat the drug cartels. Of $860 million provided to Colombia under the plan in 2000, $622 million was devoted to "improving the capabilities of the armed forces and police to conduct counter-narcotics activities."[143] Another $120 million was aimed at human rights assistance and the administration of justice. Although the focus was on the counter-narcotics mission,

[135] Michael Shifter, *Plan Colombia: A Retrospective*, AMERICAS Q., July 18, 2012, <http://www.americasquarterly.org/node/3787.

[136] PETER DESHAZO, TANYA PRIMIANI, & PHILLIP MCLEAN, BACK FROM THE BRINK: EVALUATING PROGRESS IN COLOMBIA, 1999–2007, at v (2007).

[137] Marcella, *supra* note 133, at 1.

[138] *Id.* 24.

[139] DeShazo, Tanya, & McLean, *supra* note 137 at 33.

[140] Marcella, *supra* note 133, at 70, quoting Ana Maria Bejarano.

[141] DeShazo, *supra* note 137, at 33.

[142] Marcella, *supra* note 133, at 25.

[143] DeShazo, *supra* note 137, at 10–11.

Congress imposed strict conditions on the Colombian military to comply with the rule of law and to punish violators within its ranks.[144]

With the onset of Plan Colombia and the support and commitment of the Colombian government, the Colombian military has become increasingly professionalized and several times larger. This has translated into tactical successes against guerillas in the early 2000s, which resulted in large-scale desertions from the FARC and other groups, the demobilization of paramilitary groups, and a steep decline in terrorist attacks.[145] Guerilla forces have been forced into decline, with the FARC agreeing to a ceasefire in June of 2016, after the "15-year, US-backed military offensive thinned the rebels' ranks and forced its ageing leaders to the negotiating table in 2012."[146] Despite rejection of the initial peace accord in a popular referendum, in February 2017, the FARC began surrendering its arms and reintegrating into society.[147]

Since about 2005, the Colombian military leadership has undertaken a purposeful program to instill professionalism in state forces, with a particular focus on adhering to international humanitarian law.[148] This program has included embracing the dual systems of civil law and LOAC down to the tactical level, where distinct military and law enforcement functions merge. It is common for soldiers to carry rules of engagement (ROE) cards. These are about the size of an ordinary playing card and supply simple rules for the use of force against the enemy in a particular situation. Colombia has gone one step further, equipping its soldiers with a card for each of the two operative legal regimes. A blue card explains the use of force for law enforcement in compliance with domestic civil law. This card explains that force must be proportional to the threat and that deadly force is a last resort. A red card contains rules to engage enemy combatants that are based on the LOAC. On the red card, lethal force is not a last resort. The two legal regimes operate symbiotically to empower government forces both to enforce the law and to maintain territorial control.[149]

Colombian military forces now bear significant accountability for adherence to the appropriate legal regime—LOAC or civil law—sometimes to the point where soldiers face prosecution for mistaking the law while under fire.[150] These

[144] *Id.*

[145] *Id.* 11–27.

[146] *Colombian Government and Farc Rebels Announce Ceasefire Deal to End War*, THE GUARDIAN, June 22, 2016, <https://www.theguardian.com/world/2016/jun/22/colombian-government-farc-rebels-ceasefire-deal.

[147] *Colombia's FARC Rebels to Begin Surrendering Weapons*, VOA, Feb. 28, 2017, <http://www.voanews.com/a/colombia-farc-rebels-begin-surrendering-weapons/3744114.html.

[148] Thomas E. Ayers, *Truth, Reconciliation and the Laws of War in Colombia*, SMALL WARS JOURNAL, Feb. 8, 2017, <https://smallwarsjournal.com/jrnl/art/truth-reconciliation-and-the-laws-of-war-in-colombia.

[149] *Id.*

[150] *Id.*

legal norms enhance the legitimacy of the regime. They are consistent with the legal culture of Colombia, which is substantially European in character and constitutional in its formal form. They also reflect confidence in the Colombian government's ability to respond effectively to guerilla and narcotics related threats.

Plan Colombia coincided with concerted efforts by the government of Colombia to "reassert state control over more national territory."[151] President Alvaro Uribe, elected in 2002, developed a Democratic Defense and Security Policy, which leveraged the support of Plan Colombia. Among its lines of effort was a concerted focus on the rule of law, supported by an interagency effort by the United States. A key innovation of the Democratic Defense and Security Policy was the introduction of an accusatory criminal justice "system modeled on Anglo-American practice and procedures."[152] This replaced a traditional inquisitorial system.[153]

Simultaneously, with assistance from the US Agency for International Development and the US Department of Justice, large investments were made in making justice accessible. This has involved two major efforts. First, the government has trained hundreds of justices of the peace and conciliators of justice specializing in alternative dispute resolution. Second, legal service facilities, called Casas de Justica, have been built in both urban and rural areas to improve access to justice services. In the context of improved security and expanded control of territory by the central government, these efforts had, by 2007, enabled the provision of services in response to more than five million requests.[154] These innovations "have helped transparently alleviate grievances and enhance citizen confidence in the justice sector, making people less inclined to take the law into their own hands."[155]

After fifteen years and roughly $8 billion, Plan Colombia largely failed in its stated purpose of ending the smuggling of cocaine into the United States. It resulted mainly in the displacement of cocaine production from one area to another, or into other countries where enforcement efforts are weaker.[156] In this respect, it fails to offer a convincing model for countering the opium trade in

[151] *Id.* 12.

[152] Marcella, *supra* note 133, at 27–28.

[153] *Id.* 34.

[154] *Id.*

[155] Jorge Luis Silva Mendez & Camilo Andres Avila Ceballos, *How Colombia is Improving Access to Justice Services*, World Bank Blogs, Oct. 14, 2015, <http://blogs.worldbank.org/governance/how-colombia-improving-access-justice-services, stating "[a]s one user explained, it had taken her two hours and several costly bus rides to access the justice system. Now she can access services in less time, with the opportunity to appear before a judge, and to process routine cases without traveling far from home."

[156] Shifter , *supra* note 135. *See also* Natalio Cosoy, *Has Plan Colombia Really Worked?*, BBC News, Feb. 4, 2016, <http://www.bbc.com/news/world-latin-america-35491504.

Afghanistan.[157] However, even though the policy was sold to the domestic US audience as a counter-narcotics program for political expediency, its primary objective was always counterinsurgency.[158]

Plan Colombia may not have crushed the cocaine trade, but, as Professor of Latin American politics Michael Shifter observed, it demonstrated a successful model for sustained involvement in a foreign country to mitigate internal conflict. Colombia still faces significant social and political problems, but the existential crisis has passed.[159] Plan Colombia's sustained support to security, law enforcement, human rights, and judicial institutions, over a period roughly the same as the US and coalition engagement in Afghanistan, has helped "transform a nation on the verge of collapse into a strong institutional democracy with historically low levels of violence."[160] These conditions have enabled the civil government to increase its reach within its borders—one of the basic criteria of statehood. Although Colombia now faces a new challenge in reconciling citizens on both sides of the civilian-FARC divide, its experience has proved that LOAC and civil law can, and have, successfully mitigated intractable conflict involving non-state actors.[161]

VI. Conclusion

Despite many differences, the examples of Afghanistan and Colombia illustrate that the simultaneous coexistence of LOAC and civil law regimes can increase the reach of the rule of law and gradually undermine terrorist, insurgent, and criminal non-state actors. They also demonstrate that the legal structures of conflict termination contemplated in the UN Charter and the Geneva Conventions may not translate to effective strategies against such actors. Both countries faced conflicts that have not ended with formal peace agreements between High Contracting Parties, but instead with transition to persistent semi-international conflict gradually mitigated by international support and a dual legal regime.

The experiences of Colombia and Afghanistan demonstrate that the existence of civil law, and its ability meaningfully to order societies in accordance with international human rights law, is emergent, rather than binary. In other words,

[157] *See* Cosoy, *supra* note 157, quoting an official from the Washington Office on Latin America. For a contrary view, *see* George Phillips, *Afghanistan Needs Its Own Plan Colombia*, WASH. EXAMINER, Apr. 9, 2015, <http://www.washingtonexaminer.com/afghanistan-needs-its-own-plan-colombia/article/2562702.

[158] *A New Plan For Colombia*, 418 THE ECONOMIST 30 (2016).

[159] Shifter, *supra* note 135.

[160] John Kerry, *Getting the Endgame Right in Colombia*, MIAMI HERALD, Jan. 30, 2016, <http://www.miamiherald.com/opinion/op-ed/article57352418.html.

[161] *A New Plan for Colombia*, *supra* note 158.

civil law is not a light switch that, by its activation, dispels the darkness of war. Instead, civil law sometimes progresses from a nascent and weak impulse to a progressively more normative and enforceable regime. Its emergence does not necessarily displace the LOAC from simultaneous application in the same society or state. Instead, the LOAC can be seen as a shield to protect the civil regime as it matures, protecting civilians from military violence while providing the security and public confidence needed to enable the rule of civil law. As the civil law matures, the LOAC continues to apply as needed to suppress those threats that have the capacity to overwhelm it.

There are differences between Afghanistan and Colombia that may help explain why the latter's progress seems to have, thus far, outstripped that of the former. The indigenous legal culture in Colombia is favorable to rule of law. The people of Colombia perceive governance according to a written constitution and codified law as politically and socially legitimate. Their preferred legal values are consistent with international human rights law. It is not necessary to overcome culture to establish rule of law in Colombia, though it remains necessary to overcome a colonial history of social division and nearly continuous internal armed conflict for almost two hundred years.

Although governed by a legal code and a constitution on paper, the indigenous legal culture presents a barrier to widespread political and social acceptance of a civil law that is codified and consistent with international human rights law. In the absence of politically viable civil law, it is unsurprising that the institutional architecture of law is correspondingly weak. Afghanistan lacks the means to enforce its formal legal code. Compounding this problem, large areas of the country remain beyond the reach of central authority. Isolated provinces allow terrorist and criminal actors to operate beyond the reach of the rule of law.

Afghanistan may enjoy one distinct, important, and somewhat ironic, advantage over Colombia. Precisely because the state is comprised of multiple, fractious ethnic groups and religious sects, and precisely because these groups have little history of national unity and lack a strong civil culture, the atrocities of some groups or individuals, whether conducted in the name of religion, for economic gain, or for ethnic dominance, are more likely to be forgiven. The fractured nature of Afghan society renders unlikely the need for a long-term truth-and-reconciliation process to render an accounting for the various acts of violence committed by fighters. Questions of who supported the Taliban, Pakistan, the Soviets, the Northern Alliance, or the United States in Afghanistan are of secondary importance to the challenge of extending inclusion in civil society to the entire population, especially in the lawless regions outside the cities. By contrast, Colombia's comparatively robust civil society may require generations fully to recover from the violence committed by those who have supported the FARC and other violent groups.

Because the LOAC is grounded in public international law and, in its application, effectuates humanitarian law principles, the very act of complying with the LOAC is normatively favorable to the development of civil law. This normative aspect symbiotically enhances legitimacy by demonstrating the benefits of rule of law, while strengthening the civil law by demonstrating accountability to it. The professionalization and accountability of Colombia's armed forces has contributed both to security and to civil law.

Combining LOAC and civil law regimes is not necessarily a question of massive military intervention, but can require sustained commitment to rule of law efforts aimed at both the culture and the architecture of justice and stability. Political, sectarian, and ethnic strife can transition from kinetic in nature to political in nature through frameworks of governance and infrastructure that provide access to justice. This may not always require helicopters and battalions. It will always require multidisciplinary institution building efforts. Such efforts may be frustrating and expensive. They may iterate in fits and starts. They are likely to leave many observers unsatisfied much of the time. However, the goal of LOAC-enabled civil law is not an immediate end to conflict, but the creation of civil institutions that can increasingly be seen as more legitimate than violence and isolation.

At a time when failed states and violent non-state actors have tragically become more common, the models for conflict termination envisioned by international law, and its definitions of international and non-international armed conflict, have lost much of their meaning. Formal peace treaties between High Contracting Parties to the UN Charter are rarely seen in the wild. In the early twenty-first century, LOAC-based security regimes increasingly must incubate rule of law efforts grounded in human rights law—potentially for many decades. This is finding peace in the law of war.

14
From Armed Conflict to Countering Threat Networks
Counterterrorism and Social Network Analysis

Todd Huntley & Mitt Regan

I. Introduction

Transnational non-state armed groups have emerged as prominent national security threats in the last few decades or so. The most notable attack was on the United States on September 11, 2001, but other attacks have occurred in London, Madrid, Bali, Paris, Brussels, Mogadishu, Baghdad, Kabul, Nigeria, and other locations.

The US response to this threat has been distinctive compared to most other states. It has declared itself a party in an armed conflict against Al Qaeda and associated forces, in which it is authorized to operate under the laws of war. This permits using lethal force as a first resort against persons designated as members of these groups and against civilians directly participating in hostilities. In addition, it means authority to use force that causes unintended civilian casualties, as long as they are not excessive in comparison to anticipated military advantage. The law of war also permits destruction of civilian infrastructure if it is being used for military purposes by enemy forces. The level of force that the United States has used has waxed and waned with different rules of engagement at different times in different locations during this conflict. Nonetheless, the United States has regarded itself at war with non-state armed groups for twenty years.

Is this likely to be the template for combating transnational armed groups in the future? President George W. Bush stated in an address to Congress on September 20, 2001, "Our 'war on terror' begins with al Qaeda, but it does not end there. It will not end until every terrorist group of global reach has been found, stopped and defeated."[1] Given the far-flung operations of many of these

[1] George W. Bush, "Address to a Joint Session of Congress and the American People," The White House: President George W. Bush, Archived, Sept. 20, 2001, <http://georgewbush-whitehouse.archives.gov/news/releases/2001/09/20010920-8.html.

Todd Huntley & Mitt Regan, *From Armed Conflict to Countering Threat Networks* In: *Between Crime and War.* Edited by: Claire Finkelstein, Christopher Fuller, Jens David Ohlin, Mitt Regan, Oxford University Press. © Claire Finkelstein, Christopher Fuller, Jens David Ohlin, Mitt Regan 2023. DOI: 10.1093/oso/9780197638798.003.0015

groups, this is a sobering prospect. It raises the possibility that numerous locations around the globe may effectively be battlefields in non-international armed conflicts. Since a surrender of enemy forces or any other clear end to these conflicts is unlikely, the result could be ongoing levels of significant violence for an indefinite period.

The United States has retreated to some extent from the idea of the war on terror, however, and in the last several years has emphasized reliance on a range of measures to address transnational terrorism.[2] In particular, there are indications that the United States is moving away from the idea that non-state armed groups are comparable to state military forces who can be engaged and defeated in a war of definite duration. This evolution is reflected in US adoption of an approach to terrorism known as "Countering Threat Networks." The doctrine implementing this approach is set forth most prominently in Joint Publication 3-25 (JP 3-25) of the Department of Defense.[3] This doctrine emphasizes monitoring potential threats and using a variety of non-kinetic and kinetic means to deprive them of the resources they need to pose a serious threat. JP 3-25 candidly acknowledges that completely defeating a threat network is unlikely; the focus is on continuously applying pressure with all the tools of the US government to keep it as weak as possible. As we will describe, social network analysis (SNA) provides a powerful analytical tool in support of this approach. Furthermore, as artificial intelligence progresses, it is likely to enable more rapid analytical capabilities to inform identification of threat networks and anticipation of their activities.

This shift in emphasis toward focusing on threat networks offers a potentially promising alternative to engaging in the intense levels of violence that are authorized under the armed conflict paradigm. At the same time, it poses the danger that the United States may use force to prevent, rather than preempt, armed attacks by attempting to reduce risks to the United States as much as possible at the expense of persons elsewhere.

JP 3-25 reflects what has been called an "information-age" approach to conflict, in contrast to an "industrial-age" strategy.[4] The latter approach is based on the paradigm of conflict between states, in which the parties are located in a particular territory, constituted by a center of gravity consisting of various military and industrial assets subject to hierarchical command and control. This

[2] *See, e.g.*, White House, "National Strategy for Counterterrorism in the United States" (October 2018); White House, "National Strategy for Counterterrorism" (June 2011).

[3] Joint Chiefs of Staff, "Countering Threat Networks," Department of Defense Joint Publication 3–25, Dec. 21, 2016.

[4] Christopher Fussell & D.W. Lee, *Networks at War: Organizational Innovation and Adaptation in the Twenty-First Century*, *in* BEYOND CONVERGENCE: WORLD WITHOUT ORDER 369, 371, 373 (Hilary Matfess & Michael Miklavic eds., Oct. 2016).

paradigm informed the US invasion of Afghanistan. That country was seen as the territorial headquarters of Al Qaeda by virtue of the Taliban's protection, much as a state would invade an enemy state during wartime with the goal of bringing hostilities to an end by defeating it.

While the United States succeeded in removing the Taliban from government in Afghanistan and removing a sanctuary for Al Qaeda, the operation did not result in the defeat of Al Qaeda. This is not simply because high-level Al Qaeda leaders were able to evade efforts to capture or kill them. More fundamentally, it is because Al Qaeda is not an entity that conforms to conventional notions of an enemy. It is comprised of a network of individuals and resources located in multiple countries that are loosely connected rather than integrated into a hierarchical command structure. Cells in various countries consisting of a small number of individuals acquire resources by drawing on this network and have considerable autonomy in determining when and where they will launch attacks.

This point was brought home even more emphatically after the US invasion of Iraq. That operation succeeded in defeating Iraq and removing Saddam Hussein from power. While this was the principal goal of that operation, the United States also hoped that it would weaken Al Qaeda by depriving it of a potential source of support.

Within roughly a year, however, the United States was contending with substantial violence by radical jihadists who ultimtely pledged fealty to Al Qaeda. The United States eventually appreciated that it was dealing not with a conventional enemy but with a network, which required a departure from the industrial-age conception of warfare. This required an understanding of how seemingly disparate individuals and assets were linked, and how each of them contributed to furthering Al Qaeda's mission.

In order to combat this network, the United States engaged in an information-age campaign. It drew on and refined SNA as an integral instrument in this campaign, and it sought to fuse intelligence and operations in order to place persistent pressure on the most important nodes in Al Qaeda's networks. This reflected realization that Al Qaeda did not have a center of gravity comparable to that of a conventional nation-state military force.

The next section provides an overview of SNA, while the section that follows describes in more detail the evolution in the US approach to combatting Al Qaeda that began under General Stanley McChrystal in Iraq. The chapter then discusses US military doctrine growing out of that experience that conceptualizes counterterrorism as operations to counter threat networks, and how it reflects a hybrid approach that draws on both law enforcement and armed conflict paradigms. The conclusion assesses the implications of this approach to counterterrorism.

II. Social Network Analysis

SNA is a methodology that analyzes data about what may appear to be random interactions between and among individuals that can be used to identify a network that is engaged in various activities.[5] It is based on the recognition that that individuals don't act in a vacuum. The world may seem to be made up of separate, physically bounded, individuals who act on their own. If we pay closer attention, however, we can see that how people behave, what they say, and what they believe are powerfully influenced by their interactions with other people. SNA thus provides a distinctive lens through which to view the social world.

One prominent definition of a network is "any collection of actors . . . that pursue repeated, enduring exchange relations with one another and, at the same time, lack a legitimate organizational authority to arbitrate and resolve disputes that may arise during the exchange."[6] The relationships between persons are based on their ability to provide and receive benefits, so that there is some degree of interdependence between and among actors. As one scholar describes it,

[5] The discussion in this section draws on several sources relating to social networks in general and terrorist networks in particular. These include JOHN ARQUILLA & DAVID RONFELDT, NETWORKS AND NETWARS: THE FUTURE OF TERROR, CRIME, AND MILITANCY (2001); SEAN F. EVERTON, DISRUPTING DARK NETWORKS (2012); MARC SAGEMAN, UNDERSTANDING TERROR NETWORKS (2004); John Arquilla, *The End of War as We Knew It? Insurgency, Counterinsurgency and Lessons From The Forgotten History of Early Terror Networks*, 28 THIRD WORLD Q. 369 (2007); Stephen P. Borgatti et al., *Network Analysis in the Social Sciences*, 323 SCIENCE 892 (2009); Stephen P. Borgatti, *Centrality and Network Flow*, 27 SOC. NETWORKS 55 (2005); Kathleen M. Carley, Ju-Sung Lee, & David Krackhardt, *Destabilizing Networks*, 24 CONNECTIONS 79 (2002); Paul K. Davis & Brian Michael Jenkins, *A System Approach to Deterring and Influencing Terrorists*, 21 CONFLICT MGMT. & PEACE SCI. 3 (2004); John Hardy & Paul Lushenko, *The High Value of Targeting: A Conceptual Model for Using HVT against a Networked Enemy*, 12 DEFENCE STUD. 413 (2012); Scott Helfstein & Dominick Wright, *Covert or Convenient? Evolution of Terror Attack Networks*, 55 J. CONFLICT RES. 785 (2011); Roy Lindelauf, Peter Borm, & Herbert Hamers, *Understanding Terrorist Network Topologies and Their Resilience Against Disruption*, *in* COUNTERTERRORISM AND OPEN SOURCE INTELLIGENCE (Uffe Kock Wiil ed., 2011); Tim Minor, *Attacking the Nodes of Terrorist Networks*, 3 GLOBAL SEC. STUD., no. 2, 1 (2012); Assaf Moghadam, *How Al Qaeda Innovates*, 22 SEC. STUD. 466 (2013); Peter Neumann, Ryan Evans, & Raffaello Pantucci, *Locating Al Qaeda's Center of Gravity: The Role of Middle Managers*, 34 STUD. IN CONFLICT & TERRORISM 825 (2011); Steve Ressler, *Social Network Analysis as an Approach to Combat Terrorism: Past, Present, and Future Research*, 2 HOMELAND SECURITY AFFAIRS ARTICLE 8 (2006); Nancy Roberts & Sean F. Everton, *Strategies for Combating Dark Networks*, 12 J. SOC. STRUCTURE, no. 2, 1 (2011); Burgert A. Seneka, *Mapping a Dark Network With Social Network Analysis (SNA): The Right Wing Vaal Dam Bomb Plot*, 39 J. CONTEMP. HIST. 95 (2014); Maksim Tsvetovat & Kathleen M. Carley, *Structural Knowledge and Success of Anti-Terrorist Activity: The Downside of Structural Equivalence*, 6 J. SOC. STRUCTURE, no. 2, 1 (2005); Philip vos Felman, *The Complexity of Terror Networks*, *in* UNIFYING THEMES IN COMPLEX SYSTEMS (Ali A. Minai, Dan Braha, & Yaneer Bar-Yam eds., 2011); Olivier J Walther & Dimitris Christopoulos, *Islamic Terrorism and the Malian Rebellion*, 27 TERRORISM & POL. VIOLENCE 497 (2015); Uffe Kock Wiil, Jolanta Gniadek, & Nasrullah Memon, *Measuring Link Importance in Terrorist Networks*, *in* 2010 INTERNATIONAL CONFERENCE ON ADVANCES IN SOCIAL NETWORKS ANALYSIS AND MINING (Nasrullah Memon & Reda Alhajj eds., 2010).

[6] Joel Polodny & Karen Page, *Network Forms of Organization*, 24 ANN. REV. SOC. 57, 59 (1998).

the "glue congealing networked ties may include authority bonds, exchange relations and coalitions based on common interest."[7]

Interactions among individuals can constitute a network of persons who have something in common; interact with one another based on that common interest, commitment, or belief; and whose behavior in some cases is explained by their membership in that network. People in ordinary life thus typically are members of several networks based on family, friendship, work, neighborhood, ethnic, avocational, and other ties. Such ties are the basic units of analysis in SNA, and individuals connected by these ties are conceptualized as "nodes."[8] Sometime the networks comprised by such ties may overlap; other times not. A dark network may draw on ties in various of these networks in order to conduct its operations, thereby creating a network that itself is comprised of various networks. "Ties between actors can function as conduits for goods such as information, feelings, financial resources, norms, opinions, and trust."[9]

Strong ties "are those where actors have repeated and relatively intense interactions with one another, while weak ties are those where actors see one another occasionally or rarely."[10] Analysts may attempt to assess the intensity of a tie by focusing on the content of communications, behavior during an interaction, intelligence about the relationship between or among actors, or events preceding or following the interaction. One challenge in characterizing ties among members of groups engaged in illegal activity is that "clandestine networks may be forged on strong ties that remain mostly dormant for the purposes of operational security. The opposing needs for security and communication can cause inactive social ties to appear weak even when they are strong."[11]

SNA can be especially helpful in identifying the existence and activity of these "dark networks" that seek to avoid detection. The challenge in attempting to identify such networks is that a network is not a directly observable entity. What may be visible features of a terrorist group, for instance, are a few leaders who make public declarations, the terrorist attacks that are the results of the network's operations, and individuals in areas where the group operates who may or may not be connected to it. One may suspect that there is some kind of organizational structure that enables the group to function, but there is little publicly available information about what it is. There are lots of dots, but it's not clear how to connect them.

[7] Laurence J. O'Toole, *Treating Networks Seriously: Practical and Research-Based Agendas in Public Administration*, 57 PUB. ADMIN. REV. 45, 45 (1997).

[8] Sageman, *supra* note 5.

[9] Everton, *Disrupting Dark Networks*, *supra* note 5.

[10] *Id.*

[11] Hardy & Lushenko, *supra* note 5, at 419.

This opacity reflects the fact that groups engaged in illegal conduct must solve a fundamental dilemma: how to stay secret while ensuring the necessary coordination and control of their members. This is known as the security/efficiency trade-off.[12] Because they need to avoid detection by authorities, these groups can't engage in processes available to legal groups to conduct their activities. First, almost all exchanges—of money, goods, and services—especially over borders become dangerous and difficult. While legal businesses can use the services of global financial institutions and international transportation companies, illegal organizations must devote much of their attention and resources to activities such as arranging secret transportation and money laundering.

Second, legal organizations are able to coordinate their operations efficiently by means of formal authority structures in which directives by leadership are carried out by people at lower levels, subject to some exercise of discretion by lower levels. Multiple levels of increasingly specialized operations are linked through a formal command structure. It is risky, however, for illegal groups to operate this way. The larger the number of links among people in a group, the greater is the risk that the group will be detected. If authorities arrest one person in the structure, they have the chance to bring down the entire organization by getting each person to lead them to the next highest leader in the organization, all the way up to the top leadership. It's not necessary for each person to know the entire structure of the organization. It's enough that they simply know who is above them in the hierarchy, that each of these people has the same information, and that each is in a line of authority that ultimately reaches top leadership. Illegal organizations must be structured in a way that minimizes this risk.

In the first part of the twentieth century, for instance, drug cartels tried to maintain control of their products through the entire chain of manufacturing, distribution, and sale to consumers, in order to maximize coordination and control of operations. They found, however, that as law enforcement became more sophisticated, this made them vulnerable. Identifying a single link had the potential to bring down the entire organization.[13]

Finally, illegal organizations face challenges in resolving disputes because they cannot rely on either a conventional hierarchical system of authority or legal proceedings to do so. This puts a premium on ties between members that are based on familiarity and trust, which can both reduce the likelihood of disputes and help ensure that when they occur they will be resolved relatively smoothly.

These challenges stemming from the security/efficiency trade-off tend to lead groups to use the network as their form of organization. A dark network that

[12] Hardy & Lushenko, *supra* note 5; Jorge Raab & H. Brinton Milward, *Dark Networks as Problems*, 13 J. Pub. Admin. Res. & Theory, no. 4, 413–439 (2003).

[13] Raab & Milward, *supra* note 12, at 430.

comprises an illegal organization generally is separated into cells comprised of individuals who have close ties with one another but few ties with other cells in the network.[14] Cell members often do not know of the existence of other cells or of other levels in the organization. Each member of a cell may have only intermittent contact with other members until an operation is imminent, and may not even know who all members of the cell are. The person who provides a link to the larger organization will be in contact only occasionally, and only one person in the cell knows him or her.

This structure is designed to enhance security, in that cell members who are apprehended typically will not be able to provide much information about the larger network. It also furnishes redundancy, in that the neutralization of one cell will usually not deprive the network of a crucial resource because other cells will be able to provide it. Each of the cells has considerable autonomy to engage in operations that are consistent with the mission of the organization. It receives instruction and material resources from the organization through persons who have access to varying levels of leadership.

The trust that is crucial between members of illegal groups is maximized by careful selection of members, especially at the level of the cell. Ties based on family or tribal relationships, or on shared experiences such as training in group military camps or religious centers, often are a significant basis for selection.[15] Members in individual cells thus often have strong ties based on common experiences. Even if they may be motivated to engage in acts of terrorism on behalf of a cause, however, they may not have sufficient training, sophistication, or resources to do so effectively. Their close ties with one another can serve to isolate them from persons outside their cell who can provide these resources.

They therefore need to make connections to the larger organization. This is where weak ties are important. A member of the cell may have an acquaintance with whom he or she has a weak tie. That acquaintance then has ties with one or more members of the larger terrorist organization. These one or more members have ties with more senior members of the organization. In this way, the weak tie between the nodes that are the cell member and the acquaintance can serve as a conduit for the provision of training, guidance, and resources from other networks whose nodes are more senior members who can enable the cell to act on its aims. These broader networks of leaders provide some direction, but generally will leave it to the cell to determine when, where, and how to attack based on its assessment of local conditions. Taken together, each of these ties and the nodes that they connect are part of a network, which is connected by one or more

[14] Moghadam, *supra* note 5; Neumann, Evans, & Pantucci, *supra* note 5; Raab & Milward, *supra* note 12; Sageman, *supra* note 5.

[15] Hardy & Lushenko, *supra* note 5, at 417–20.

nodes to other nodes who constitute another network, so that the terrorist group effectively consists of a network of networks.[16]

People who play a crucial role in linking these networks together are called "hubs." This is a particular type of node in the network. A hub is someone who has a larger set of ties than most people in the network, or who provides crucial connections between people in the network who otherwise would not be connected. We can think of him or her as the intersection of ties with several different people, who is in a position to connect individuals who otherwise would not be in contact with one another. Hubs are nodes who can connect small networks with larger ones within an overall terrorist network. They span gaps in the network by providing "bridges" to separate and relatively self-contained parts of it.

In what is called a scale-free network, a handful of actors known as hubs have many connections, but most actors have very few because they work in secret and are connected to relatively few other people who know of their work.[17] Because most actors in a scale-free network have very few ties, scale-free networks are relatively immune to random targeting. They are vulnerable, however, to attacks targeted against nodes. Reflecting the crucial role of hubs, research suggests that the removal of 10 to 15 percent of the hubs in a scale-free network will generally disconnect the network.[18]

A study of what the authors call "Al Qaeda middle managers" illustrates these dynamics.[19] Middle managers are not part of what experts and security practitioners have variously referred to as "core Al Qaeda," "Al Qaeda Central," or the "top leadership." Nor are middle managers grassroots foot soldiers who consist of individuals who are inspired by Al Qaeda and often "participate" through internet forums; low-level members of jihadist cells and their activist leaders; and those who have been to a training camp and returned to their home countries without having developed lasting ties to the leadership. With rare exceptions, these grassroots members are relatively unskilled and have not participated in fighting. They may proclaim the desire to join a foreign battlefront and subscribe to the idea of a global jihad, but their focus is mostly local or national. They ordinarily are unknown to the leadership, and their networks do not extend much beyond their places of origin.

[16] The classic source on the important function of weak ties is Mark Granovetter, *The Strength of Weak Ties*, 78 AM. J. SOC. 1360 (1973). On the role of weak ties in dark networks, *see* Sageman, *supra* note 5, at Kindle location 2183–89. *See also* Jose Rodriguez, "The March 11th Terrorist Network: In Its Weakness Lies Its Strength," Working Papers EPP-LEA 03, Universitat de Barcelona, 2005.

[17] Albert-Laszlo Barabasi & Eric Bonabeau, *Scale-Free Networks*, 288 SCI. AM., no. 5, 60 (2003). On the application of this concept to terrorism, *see* Sageman, *supra* note 5.

[18] Barabasi & Bonabeau, *supra* note 17.

[19] Neumann, Evans, & Pantucci, *supra* note 5.

Middle managers can provide both grassroots forces and top leadership with valuable resources. From the grassroots perspective, middle managers are the most senior Al Qaeda persons they will have come in contact with and are likely respected because of their experience and connections. They can provide skills and expertise from higher levels of Al Qaeda, and may arrange for access to finance and training camps. They can also offer strategic direction to grassroots members and give them a sense of being part of Al Qaeda.

For the top leadership, the middle managers provide grassroots connections that they can broker. This enables leadership to use foot soldiers to turn strategy into practice. Middle managers provide an efficient and trusted channel through which to facilitate connections, screen potential applicants, and reduce the risks involved in reaching out to the grassroots members.

Middle managers therefore are hubs who are critical to forging linkages and facilitating the flow of information, resources, skills, and strategic direction between the top and bottom of the organization. If middle management is removed, the top leadership lacks the reach and opportunities for implementing its global designs. The grassroots members may have large ambitions, but will fail to acquire the needed resources to carry out effective campaigns. It is only through their mutual connection to middle managers that both the grassroots members and top leadership become one coherent strategic entity. Middle managers thus help turn prospective terrorists into reasonably competent operators, integrating their activities into Al Qaeda's wider strategy in making their plans more likely to succeed.

SNA can provide a portrait of the "topography" of a dark network such as Al Qaeda that identifies hubs and their ties, the existence and intensity of other nodes and their ties, and the different types of resources that these ties and the networks they comprise make available to the overall network.[20] This is based on the use of various metrics that indicate the relative importance of individuals in a network.[21] One basic metric, "degree centrality," simply determines the number of links a node has two other nodes in the network. Another, "betweenness centrality," measures the number of times a node lies on the shortest path between other nodes, indicating nodes that act as bridges between others. "Closeness centrality" calculates the shortest paths between all nodes and then assigns each node a score based on it some of shortest paths. Finally, "Eigen Centrality" measures a node's influence based on the number of links it has to other nodes within the network and then weights those according to how many links those nodes have two other nodes within the network.

[20] Helfstein & Wright, *supra* note 5; Lindelauf, Borm, & Hamers, *supra* note 5; vos Felman, *supra* note 5.

[21] Borgatti, "Centrality and Network Flow," *supra* note 5; Everton, *Disrupting Dark Networks*, *supra* note 5; Wiil, Gniadek, & Memon, *supra* note 5.

These and other metrics can help establish priorities for counterterrorism operations that, for instance, focus on neutralizing the contributions that the most important hubs provide.[22] This may include persuading a hub to defect; neutralizing crucial parts of the hub's network that provide key resources that they need to play their role; or direct action involving capture or use of lethal force. The goal is to weaken the ability of the larger network to operate by removing a hub on which it relies for vital resources such as communication, recruits, control of a smuggling route, weapons, or funds.

Reliance on sophisticated SNA underlies the shift in US counterterrorism toward an information-age approach to conflict as expressed in the Countering Threat Networks doctrine in JP 3-25. As the volume of information from human, signals, geospatial, open-source, and other sources of intelligence proliferates, the potential for identifying threat networks exponentially increases. The task of analyzing this information and making connections among it, however, can be overwhelming. As the next section describes, US Joint Task Force 714 in Iraq confronted this issue in attempting to use intelligence to identify terrorist networks. The next section describes how its response served as an especially significant impetus for using SNA for counterterrorism operations.

III. Information-Age Conflict and Joint Task Force 714

US Counterterrorist Joint Task Force (JTF) 714 operated in Afghanistan and Iraq after the terrorist attacks of 9/11. It was the latest version of the JTF that had been established in December 1980 after the failed attempt to rescue the hostages held at the US embassy in Tehran. The role of this entity was to provide mission planning and support, exercise command and control, and provide intelligence support for specialized counterterrorism missions.[23]

The JTF that deployed into Afghanistan to hunt down Osama bin Laden and other Al Qaeda senior leaders had years of experience conducting similar missions in Panama, Somalia, Colombia, and the Balkans. In the course of these operations, they used rudimentary versions of what we now call SNA.[24]

[22] *See, e.g.*, Carley, Lee, & Krackhardt, *supra* note 5; Hardy & Lushenko, *supra* note 5; Minor, *supra* note 5; Ressler, *supra* note 5; Roberts & Everton, *supra* note 5.

[23] For a discussion of *Operation Eagle Claw* and how JSOC was formed as a result, *see* Sean Naylor, Relentless Strike: The Secret History of Joint Special Operations Command 2–14 (2015); Steven Emerson, Secret Warriors 22, 26, 44–45 (1988); Joint Chiefs of Staff, "Special Operations Review Group, Iran Hostage Rescue Mission Report" (Aug. 23, 1980), 60–61, < https://nsarchive2.gwu.edu//NSAEBB/NSAEBB63/doc8.pdf.

[24] Sean Naylor, Not a Good Day to Die 33 (2005), describing JSOC members' experience in man hunting in Colombia, Somalia, and the Balkans. *See also* Marc Bowden, Killing Pablo: The Hunt for the World's Greatest Outlaw 95–96 (2001); Naylor, *Relentless Strike*, *supra* note 23, at 51–64.

In 1992 to 1993, elements of the JTF used SNA to assist the Colombian military in finding, and killing, drug cartel leader Pablo Escobar. Other elements of the JTF were using SNA in 1993 to hunt down and capture Farrah Aidid and other Somali militia leaders. From the mid-1990s to 2001, the JTF was also using SNA to find and capture indicted war criminals in Bosnia.[25] Similar to a prosecutor working her way up the chain of a Mafia family, the JTF would identify the operational leaders and track them until they were able to identify the location of the senior leader. In the terminology of the JTF, this effort to "find and fix" the target, would ultimately result in a "finish"—that is, a mission to kill or capture.[26]

With the invasion of Iraq in March 2003, the JTF's main focus shifted from Al Qaeda in Afghanistan to Iraq. Initially, the mission was to find and capture Saddam Hussein and other senior Iraqi leaders.[27] Late 2003, however, brought about two significant developments—the emergence of a deadly insurgent group, Al Qaeda in Iraq (AQI), led by Abu Musab al-Zarqawi, and the arrival of a new JTF commander, General Stanley McChrystal.[28]

AQI's attacks became even more frequent and deadly in 2004. McChrystal and his staff realized that they were fighting a foe that had fully embraced the information age while the JTF had remained very much an industrial-age CT organization.[29] Previous targeted organizations may have operated in small cells, but they were still hierarchical organizations.[30] Whether the mission was to find, and then capture or kill, indicted war criminals, Farrah Aidid, or Pablo Escobar, the JTF, would identify members of the organization through intelligence assets, track them as they met with other members of the organization, and establish a pattern of life based on such activity that would illuminate the leadership structure of the organization.[31] AQI was different in that it operated as a decentralized network of networks rather than as a collection of cells arranged in a hierarchical leadership structure.[32]

[25] For a fuller description of these early missions, *see* Naylor, *Relentless Strike*, *supra* note 23, at 41–68.

[26] Department of the Army, "Army Doctrine Reference Publication 3-05: Special Operations," 3-12 (Jan. 2018). *See also* AKI PERITZ & ERIC ROSENBACH, FIND, FIX, FINISH: INSIDE THE COUNTERTERRORISM CAMPAIGNS THAT KILLED BIN LADEN AND DEVASTATED AL QAEDA 4–5 (2013); RICHARD SCHULTZ, MILITARY INNOVATION IN WAR: IT TAKES A LEARNING ORGANIZATION, A CASE STUDY OF TASK FORCE 714 IN IRAQ 38 (JSOU Report 16-6, 2016).

[27] Schultz, *supra* note 26.

[28] GENERAL STANLEY MCCHRYSTAL, MY SHARE OF THE TASK: A MEMOIR 93–94 (2013). Then Major General (MG), McChrystal was no stranger to the TF, having served as the commander of the 75th Ranger Regiment and been assigned for missions conducted by the JTF in the past.

[29] *Id.* 92 "This is a story about how an organization of units and people that began in the wake of Desert One in 1980 radically transformed to fight a new threat." *See also* Schultz, *supra* note 26.

[30] Schultz, *supra* note 26, at 16.

[31] *See* Naylor, *Relentless Strike*, *supra* note 23, at 46–65.

[32] Schultz, *supra* note 26, at 16–17.

As earlier described, Al Qaeda middle managers, including those in AQI, provided the resources and expertise for the organization.[33] They coordinated execution of the organization's operations, while al-Zarqawi provided strategic guidance and attracted new recruits through his online messaging.[34] As the organization grew in size, these middle managers were able to integrate new fighters into their respective networks, increasing both the number and lethality of attacks.[35] This organizational structure gave AQI an operational advantage in that it could plan and carry out attacks faster than the JTF could react.[36]

The JTF had more experienced personnel and more resources than ever before. Yet no matter how many fighters the JTF captured and killed, the enemy stayed one step ahead.[37] The JTF, however, had access to new intelligence capabilities that produced an increasing amount of intelligence. Scores of both manned and unmanned aircraft with full-motion video capability patrolled the skies over Iraq. These assets could loiter overhead for hours, tracking individuals of interest for days and weeks. They identified meeting places and safe houses and could record the individuals, their vehicles, and their travel patterns. This created the possibility of establishing the pattern of life of multiple AQI members.[38]

Perhaps the most significant intelligence development was the use of signals intelligence (SIGINT) technology that allowed for electronic surveillance and interception of communications, particularly cell phones. These SIGINT tools could not only intercept and record the content of calls but also identify the location of specific cell phones and identify linkages between the target phone and phones that had called and been called by it.[39]

Intelligence was also being collected by the various JTF teams operating across Iraq.[40] As the teams conducted raids on AQI facilities, they captured AQI members and seized material that was likely to be of intelligence value. This often included computer hard drives, cell phones, thumb drives, and documents, as well as improvised explosive device components and weapons. This material was often dumped into bags onsite, with few or no descriptive notes.[41] Once the team returned to base, they would put it into a storage room, where local intelligence analysts would later review it.[42] Much of the material, especially the computer

[33] *See* Neumann, Evans, & Pantucci, *supra* note 5.
[34] McChyrstal, *My Share of the Task*, *supra* note 28, at 114–15.
[35] *Id.*
[36] Mark Bowden, The Finish: The Killing of Osama Bin Laden 105 (2012).
[37] Schultz, *supra* note 26, at 19–20.
[38] Schultz, *supra* note 26, at 43. *See also* Bowden, *The Finish*, *supra* note 36, at 111.
[39] McChrystal, *My Share of the Task*, *supra* note 28, at 157. *See also* Naylor, *Relentless Strike*, *supra* note 23, at 260–64.
[40] Schultz, *supra* note 26, at 38.
[41] *Id.*
[42] Stanley McChrystal et al., Team of Teams: New Rules of Engagement for a Complex World 120 (2015).

media, was sent to the JTF headquarters or back to the United States for processing and analysis, which could take weeks or months.[43] Detainees would be processed and interrogated, before any analysis could be completed on the material.[44] Even after the analysts completed their reviews of the materials and interrogations, it was often not shared with other teams in the JTF.[45]

The JTF was overwhelmed with the volume of information being collected from these diverse sources. Intelligence seized on raids was often not analyzed in a timely manner, rendering it useless for local team operations.[46] Further, it was not being shared with other elements of the JTF or with other organizations.[47] Often, the element that could have used the collected intelligence not only did not have access to it but were not even aware it had been collected.

Intelligence fuels operations, but raw intelligence must be analyzed, shared, and presented in a form that enables operators to achieve their missions as effectively as possible. This was not the case in 2003 and most of 2004. Instead, the various JTF elements were conducting their operations in "silos," that is, they focused on intelligence relevant to their assigned areas of responsibility, with little sharing of information across the teams.[48]

The JTF may have been the most capable CT organization in existence, but it was not organized to face an information-age threat.[49] Each element within it could operate independently and accomplish extremely difficult missions, but there was little coordination between those elements.[50] They communicated with and were controlled by the JTF headquarters, but there was little information shared among teams within the JTF. In addition, the focus on operational security prevented most intelligence sharing with organizations outside of the Task Force, even those supporting it. McChrystal explained how the JTF came to understand this limitation: "The unexpected revelation [was] that our biggest challenges lay not in the enemy, but in the dizzyingly new environment in which we were operating, and within the carefully crafted attributes of our own organization."[51] To be successful, the JTF would have to become an information-age

43 Bowden, *The Finish*, *supra* note 36, at xi. The story of the raid that killed an AQ terrorist, Muthanna, as told by author Marc Bowden, illustrates the changing nature of the CT fight from the industrial to information age. More important than the killing of Muthanna was the capture of what Bowden referred to as the "mother lode." He states: "[i]n another war in a different time, the "mother lode" might have been a huge cache of valuable weapons or a collection of battlefield maps showing enemy troop movements and positions. In the twenty-first century, the raiders of JSOC had discovered something of equivalent value: a Rolodex."

44 Schultz, *supra* note 26, at 41–42.

45 *Id.* 27.

46 *Id.* 38.

47 McChrystal, *Team of Teams*, *supra* note 42, at 120–22.

48 *Id.* 83.

49 Schultz, *supra* note 26, at 24.

50 McChrystal *Team of Teams*, *supra* note 42, at 116–18.

51 *Id.* 6.

organization. In McChrystal's words, it would "take a network to defeat a network."[52]

McChrystal and his staff soon realized that the Task Force would have to rethink how it analyzed, shared, and integrated intelligence into operations. This would involve both restructuring the relationship of the elements within the JTF, as well as establishing new, closer relationships with outside organizations, particularly in the intelligence community.[53] McChrystal saw these changes as critical for the JTF to be able to bring to bear intelligence and operational capabilities faster than AQI could operate. A key element of this approach was the use of SNA to not only identify key AQI nodes but also to determine where and what type of force would be most effective in disrupting the AQI network's operations.[54]

The JTF first needed to increase its analytical capability.[55] This could be accomplished by merely increasing the number of internal intelligence analysts, but that would not, by itself, improve the sharing of information across the Task Force. McChrystal took the additional step of reaching out to the leaders of other intelligence organizations and offering to share information. Furthermore, rather than simply exchanging information, he suggested that analysts from these organizations be placed directly inside the JTF.[56] He invited a senior member of the intelligence community to join the JTF staff as a senior intelligence advisor. McChrystal also provided outside agencies expanded access to the information collected by the JTF.[57] This included sharing access to the material gathered during sensitive site exploitation on missions, as well as detainee interrogations, information that before may not have been readily available outside the Task Force.[58]

Analysts from across the intelligence community joined their JTF counterparts throughout Iraq and Afghanistan.[59] These analysts were now able to track JTF operations and intelligence requirements. They could help spot issues, including gaps in intelligence, and reach back to their home agencies to request additional intelligence relevant to these operations, which previously would have been unknown to the JTF.[60]

The JTF augmented its own internal analytical capabilities as well. Operators began photographing or videotaping targets, noting the location of materials seized on missions. Instead of sending computers, thumb drives, and cell phones

52 *Id.* 84.
53 Fussell & Lee, *supra* note 4, at 377; *see also* Schultz, *supra* note 26, at 25–26.
54 Schultz, *supra* note 26, at 52.
55 *Id.* 37–38.
56 McChrystal, *My Share of the Task*, *supra* note 28, at 117–19.
57 Schultz, *supra* note 26, at 52.
58 *See* McChrystal, *Team of Teams*, *supra* note 42, at 167.
59 *Id.* 117, 168–69.
60 *Id.* 167.

back to the United States, analysis was done at the forward operating locations or JTF forward headquarters.[61] Operators were able to meet with the analysts to provide additional information and to rapidly find out what the analyst had learned.[62] This information was also shared with interrogators, who would then be able to ask the detainees about its significance.[63]

Increasing both access to intelligence from across the intelligence community and internal analytical capability was an important step in developing a network within the JTF. For those developments to have a significant operational impact, however, the intelligence and its analysis needed to be shared as widely as possible across the JTF. This was especially important when conducting SNA of AQI operations coordinated by middle managers. A JTF raid on an AQI safehouse in Fallujah, for instance, might uncover information useful for JTF operations in Mosul. The importance of this information by itself might not be readily apparent to those operators seizing it. Unless the analysts in Fallujah were aware of the relevance or JTF personnel in Mosul found out about it, that information would not be shared and put to use. In order to ensure that information was shared and brought to the attention of those who needed it, McChrystal instituted Operations and Intelligence Updates (O&I) that were held six days a week.[64]

These O&I, often lasting two hours or more, provided an opportunity for everyone in the JTF to receive the latest operations and intelligence updates from all the JTF elements, including liaisons from outside organizations.[65] Rather than simply a briefing of McChrystal with senior officers, these events gave everyone attending an opportunity to share information and ask questions.[66] Both junior analysts and subject matter experts therefore would provide updates in addition to senior Task Force members. These focused not solely on Iraq, but included updates on the broader fight against Al Qaeda. Elements of the JTF across the world would participate via secure video conferencing so that relevant information could be shared across the entire network.[67]

The O&I went into great detail about what intelligence had been uncovered during interrogations, who had been captured, and what operations had been carried out since the last meeting.[68] The main focus was to construct the social networks of AQI and other Al Qaeda associated groups—who had met with whom, how the networks were resourced, and the patterns of life

61 *See* Schultz, *supra* note 26, at 42–43.
62 McChrystal, *Team of Teams*, *supra* note 42, at 166.
63 Schultz, *supra* note 26, at 42.
64 McChrystal, *My Share of the Task*, *supra* note 28, at 163–64.
65 Schultz, *supra* note 26, at 48.
66 *Id.* 49.
67 *Id.*
68 Fussel & Lee, *supra* note 4, at 378–79.

for middle managers. The change in information sharing did not stop with the O&I updates. On the view that one could not be certain who needed what information, hundreds of different people were copied on emails between McChrystal and other senior leaders.[69] It was not unusual for several mid-level team members or analysts to be copied on an email from McChrystal to the Commander of US Central Command or the Chairman of the Joint Chiefs of Staff.

Through such measures, the JTF, with the support of other intelligence agencies, had the potential to develop what McChrystal referred to as an "unblinking eye."[70] Manned and unmanned aircraft with full-motion video could provide weeks of uninterrupted video monitoring.[71] Signals intelligence tools could intercept communications, locate specific cell phones, and identify the cell numbers of those calling and being called. Data collected by these capabilities could be stored and analyzed to find connections that might otherwise go unnoticed. This technical intelligence was augmented by detainee interrogations and materials seized during raids. Most important, all this information was now being shared across the JTF so that it could be put into the hands of those who could use it—the operational team leaders who had the authority to execute operations.[72] The process that had begun as "find, fix, finish" had developed into "find, fix, finish, exploit, analyze, disseminate."[73] "[T]he Task Force's continual adaptation had transformed it into a fundamentally new organization—one that functioned using distinctly different processes and relationships."[74]

These changes allowed the JTF to substantially increase the number of operations it conducted against AQI. In mid-2004, it was conducting about eighteen missions a month.[75] By mid-2006, the JTF was conducting thirty missions a night, with some teams conducting multiple raids in a single period of darkness.[76] In essence, McChrystal had created his own hyper-enabled network that could process information and carry out operations faster than the enemy could react.

[69] McChrystal, *My Share of the Task*, *supra* note 28, at 151–52.

[70] *See* McChrystal, *Team of Teams*, *supra* note 42, at 238–39.

[71] *See* Bowden, *The Finish*, *supra* note 36, at 111. "[T]he movements of that vehicle could be followed over a small city for months, or even years, permitting a detailed map of the suspect's travels. Combine that map with cell phone tracking, with human intelligence, and you can begin to assemble a detailed and accurate chart of your target's connections, or his network."

[72] McChrystal, *Team of Teams*, *supra* note 42, at 83.

[73] Schultz, *supra* note 26, at 39. *See also* Bowden, *The Finish*, *supra* note 36, at 149, describing F3EAD as being "essential for feeding the targeting engine."

[74] McChrystal, *Team of Teams*, *supra* note 42, at 3.

[75] Schultz, *supra* note 26, at 7.

[76] *Id.* 8.

These measures also enabled the JTF to conduct more effective operations. Applying available intelligence to SNA, the JTF could specifically target individuals for capture based on their connections and the potential information they could provide about those connections. The preference was to capture targets, since the intelligence provided during interrogation, along with the analysis of the sensitive site exploitation material, would allow the Task Force to gain a fuller picture of the AQI network. This in turn enabled targeting individuals or networks that would have the greatest disruptive effect on the organization.

As SNA continued to develop, the JTF began turning to host-nation law enforcement to execute missions. Operations became "warrant based," in that evidence was presented to a local judge, who would review it to determine whether a legal basis existed for an operation against an individual. Much of this evidence came from intelligence collected by the JTF and connected to the target. SNA also often enabled identification of Al Qaeda members who were supporting AQI from other countries.[77] In such cases, intelligence would be turned over to host-nation law enforcement authorities to remove the threat via law enforcement and judicial means. The interaction between law enforcement and the JTF continued to grow with the emergence of ISIS. SNA was used to identify ISIS members from numerous countries who had traveled to Syria and Iraq to join the organization, which was turned over to the governments of those countries.[78]

The shift to intelligence-intensive SNA-based operations is perhaps best characterized by McChrystal's description of the JTF headquarters in Balad, Iraq. He noted that when he arrived, the walls of the headquarters were covered in maps. This reflected the conventional industrial-age focus of the military, that is, the physical location of the enemy. He goes on to describe the shift that then took place, where the maps that had been used to depict battle locations were replaced with whiteboards mapping out the enemy organization, showing not geographic features but relationships and connections—"connections between things rather than the things themselves."[79] In this respect, the shift within the Task Force was the harbinger of an eventual shift in counterterrorism strategy to information-age conflict. The next section describes the doctrine that currently expresses this approach.

[77] McChrystal, *My Share of the Task*, *supra* note 28, at 169.

[78] *See* Jim Garamone, "Australia, U.S. Discussions Ranged the Globe, Dunford Says," U.S. Dept of Defense, June 7, 2017, < https://www.defense.gov/Explore/News/Article/Article/1205625/australia-us-discussions-ranged-the-globe-dunford-says/.

[79] McChrystal, *Team of Teams*, *supra* note 42, at 24.

IV. Countering Threat Networks

A. US Military Doctrine

The US military formalized its approach to dealing with threat networks in December 2016 in JP 3-25.[80] The publication describes the new challenges posed by these networks in this way:

> In a world increasingly characterized by volatility, uncertainty, complexity, and ambiguity, a wide range of local, national, and transnational irregular challenges to the stability of the international system have emerged. Traditional threats like insurgencies and criminal gangs have been exploiting weak or corrupt governments for years, but the rise of transnational extremists and their active cooperation with traditional threats has changed the global dynamic. Successful deterrence and elimination of these illicit networks is more complicated and less predictable than in the past.[81]

JP 3-25 notes that these networks create significant uncertainty and ambiguity with respect to their capabilities and their intent, and that "analysis of their strengths, weaknesses, and centers of gravity (COGs) differs greatly from traditional nation-state adversaries."[82] Advances in technology that permit the rapid flow of information provide opportunities for these networks to plan and coordinate attacks through the "high-speed, high-volume exchange of ideas, people, goods, money, and weapons."[83] As a result, "determining the strategic, operational, and tactical COGs and decisive points of multiple threat networks will be more challenging than analyzing a traditional military force."[84] Because of the transnational nature of these networks, "CTN [countering threat networks] is not a localized fight within identifiable geographical boundaries."[85]

Threat networks may use a combination of both legal and illegal financial, transportation, and distribution networks in their operations. This underscores that they are linked with other networks that may be friendly or neutral and that may wittingly or unwittingly enable threat networks to sustain themselves. In addition, threat networks may be linked to criminal, insurgent, or terrorist networks on which they can draw for resources and to expand the geographical scope of their operations. As JP 3-25 observes, "threat networks may be formally

[80] Joint Chiefs of Staff, "Countering Threat Networks," *supra* note 3.
[81] *Id.* III-1.
[82] *Id.* I-1.
[83] *Id.* I-4.
[84] *Id.* I-7.
[85] *Id.* V-1.

intertwined or come together when mutually beneficial. This convergence (or nexus) between threat networks has greatly strengthened regional instability and allowed threats and alliances to increase their operational reach and power to global proportions."[86]

"Because of the large number of networks," JP 3-25 says, "the problem is to find the given threats buried within an operating environment across multiple networks."[87] This requires close monitoring of the operational environment by the intelligence community and evaluation of that intelligence by various agencies. SNA can use this information to provide a picture of the operational environment by identifying friendly, neutral, and threat networks and the links among them. Since both friendly and threat groups both may use many neutral networks, such as transportation and communication systems, "the difficult part is determining what networks are a threat and what networks are not."[88] Analysis of intelligence can enable such identification, and furnish an understanding of the intentions, capabilities, and influences of different networks, their key nodes and links, and how they draw on other networks to acquire the resources they need to sustain themselves.

Continuous monitoring of these networks enables recognition of when a network may change its orientation, such as from neutral to threat, or from friendly to neutral. As the doctrine notes, "A threat network can be operating for years in the background and suddenly explode on the scene."[89] Commanders therefore must "determine not only which networks are within an operational area, but also which pose the greatest threat."[90] As networks that are regarded as threats gain in influence, planning begins for possible operations to counter the network. This involves intensive effort to identify what JP 3-25 describes as the political, military, economic, social, information, and infrastructure (PMESII) resources that could enable it to conduct operations.[91]

Traditional adversaries such as nation-states and their military forces acquire and exercise command over a large portion of the resources they need to engage in hostilities. This made plausible the notion that an adversary possesses a single or primary center of gravity that conformed to Clausewitz's definition: "the hub of all power and movement, on which everything depends . . . the point at which all our energies should be directed."[92] While military doctrine has evolved to refine this concept, the most current Department of Defense Dictionary of Military Terms also uses the definite article in defining a center of gravity as "[t]he source

86 *Id.* III-8.
87 *Id.* III-2.
88 *Id.* III-9.
89 *Id.* V-1.
90 *Id.* III-9.
91 *Id.* III-9-10.
92 Carl von Clausewitz, On War 595–96 (Michael Howard & Peter Paret eds. & tr., 1976).

of power that provides moral or physical strength, freedom of action, or will to act. Also called COG. See also decisive point."[93]

JP 3-25 emphasizes, however, that a network's fluid and opportunistic reliance on multiple sources of support means that "when analyzing networks, there will never be a single COG."[94] There will be different COGs at different levels of a network and for different functions, and the network may be linked with criminal, insurgent, or terrorist networks that have their own different COGs. This means that "[a] COG for networks will often be difficult to target directly due to complexity and accessibility."[95] Since a network's COGs may be embedded in neutral and even friendly networks, analysis of possible interventions to counter the network must take account of the effects on these networks.

Understanding the threat network therefore requires analysis of the "critical factors" that affect the ability of it to sustain itself and conduct activities.[96] Examples include leaders and planners; fighters, operatives, and followers; bomb-makers; intelligence; finance; communication; logistics; freedom of movement; safe haven; training; and ideological narrative, which could include spiritual leaders in some cases. This analysis must be informed by identification of the network's goals, the courses of action that can achieve them, the functions that the network possesses to carry out these courses of action, the resources available and necessary for the network to perform these functions, and the capabilities the network has to use these resources.

This must be followed by identification of "critical variables," based on an assessment of how important and accessible different resources are to the network and how easily they may be repaired or replaced if degraded or removed.[97] Furthermore, a full understanding requires situating the network within the other friendly, neutral, and threat networks within the operational environment and mapping its relationships with them. The purpose of this exercise is to identify priorities for which resources of the network should be targeted through "network engagement" to most effectively impair its ability to function.[98]

The fundamental aim of targeting is to deprive the network of the most important resources that it needs to function. As JP 3-25 puts it, "identification and systematic strangulation of threat resources is the fundamental principle for CTN [countering threat networks]."[99] Each of these sources may be vulnerable to different types of engagement, which typically will require coordination

[93] Department of Defense, "DOD Dictionary of Military and Associated Terms" (2020), 30, < https://www.jcs.mil/Portals/36/Documents/Doctrine/pubs/dictionary.pdf>.
[94] Joint Chiefs of Staff, "Countering Threat Networks," *supra* note 3, at I-8.
[95] *Id.* IV-4.
[96] *Id.* IV-1.
[97] *Id.* IV-7.
[98] *Id.* V-4.
[99] *Id.* III-3-4.

with nonmilitary elements of the US government. The doctrine emphasizes the difference between this form of engagement and conventional military operations: "One major difference that must be noted is that conventional targeting is usually done during military operations/conflict, [while] much of the threat network targeting is done by USG [US government] departments and agencies and PN [partner nations]."[100]

This process also involves partnering with and strengthening friendly networks or engaging with neutral ones, depending upon the links that the threat network has in the environment. Thus, "[w]hile the commander engages one portion of a network to achieve an objective related to a friendly group or to create an effect on that friendly group to achieve an objective, the commander may be simultaneously engaging another portion of the network to affect a threat group."[101]

The goal is to apply simultaneous and continuous pressure on various nodes and links of the network that are correlated with its sources of vital resources. "The most effective operations pressure and influence elements of these networks at multiple fronts and target multiple nodes and links."[102] A campaign may, for instance, involve working with host-nation law enforcement to interdict supplies and close smuggling routes for weapons and for goods used to generate funds, engaging in information campaigns to discredit the threat network and increase opposition to it, using cyber operations to disrupt communications, raiding network training camps, strengthening host nation security forces, and using local law enforcement to disrupt the production of illegal drugs that produce revenues, with training and support that enhances partner law enforcement effectiveness.

While engaging targets may take the form of lethal force, JP 3-25 emphasizes, "it is important to remember that nonlethal actions can also have a desired effect when use against threat networks,"[103] and also emphasizes throughout the publication the contribution that such measures can make. "For example," it says, "a traditional JTF [Joint Task Force] does not normally have civilian financial experts on its staff to identify and assist in attacking threat financial network activities. Likewise, a JTF fires cell may require mainly MISO [military information support operations] and/or IO [information operations] specialists rather than field artillery and joint terminal attack controllers."[104] In addition, "the JTF requires active support and participation by USG, HN [host nation], nongovernmental agencies, and partners, particularly when it comes to addressing

[100] *Id.* V-2.
[101] *Id.* I-2.
[102] *Id.*
[103] *Id.* III-5.
[104] *Id.* III-1.

cross-border sanctuary, arms flows, and the root causes of instability."[105] Furthermore, "[w]hen commanders decide to generate an effect on a network through engaging specific nodes, the intent may not be to cause damage, but to shape conditions of a mental or moral nature."[106]

JP 3-25 emphasizes this point in discussion of how CTN takes a form that is different from conventional military operations during what is known as Phase Two of military operations, "seizing the initiative." In a passage worth quoting at length, it states:

> In traditional combat operations, this involves executing offensive operations at the earliest opportunity, forcing the adversary to offensive culmination, and setting the conditions for decisive operations. In CTN, direct offensive confrontation is often less effective or desirable than indirect approaches. Threat networks rarely present open targets. Destruction of a single node or cell might do little to impact network operations when assessed against the cost of operations and/or the potential for collateral damage. This does not mean that lethal power is never used, but it does mean that the application of force without the intent for death or gross physical destruction integrated across PMESII systems and against multiple threat network links and nodes often will constitute a majority of operations.[107]

The doctrine emphasizes that deterring threat networks "is a complex and difficult challenge that is significantly different from classical notions of deterrence."[108] JP 3-25 notes, "Deterrence is most classically thought of as the threat to impose such high costs on an adversary that restraint is the only rational conclusion. When dealing with violent extremist organizations and other threat networks, deterrence is likely to be ineffective due to radical ideology, diffuse organization, and lack of ownership of territory."[109]

This note of caution reflects a striking difference between operations to counter threat networks and conventional military operations: the assumption that the former typically will not be able to defeat a network in the way that traditional military campaigns seek to defeat an enemy. As JP 3-25 states, "[n]either all threats nor all elements of their supporting networks can be defeated, particularly if they have a regional or global presence. Certain elements of the network can be deterred, other parts neutralized, and some portions defeated."[110]

105 *Id.* III-1.
106 *Id.* xii.
107 *Id.* IV-20.
108 *Id.* I-4.
109 *Id.* I-4.
110 *Id.* I-2.

This point is reiterated throughout the publication. For instance: "Neutralization of an entire network may not be feasible, but through analysis, the staff has the ability to identify key parts of the threat network's structure to target that will result in the neutralization of specific functions that may interfere with a particular operation."[111] Similarly: "Identifying the defeat of a threat network is difficult due to the nature of how a threat network is organized and its ability to be located across a broad geographic area,"[112] and "Operations will rarely be possible against an entire threat or its supporting networks."[113]

JP 3-25 identifies a range of effects that targeting may have on networks. The first of these is to *neutralize* the ability of a network to perform certain functions. This renders a network incapable of interfering with a particular operation. The second is to *degrade* the effectiveness or efficiency of a network to function by eliminating critical resources that it needs to do so. The third is to *disrupt* a network's timetable or cause it to commit prematurely or attack in a piecemeal fashion. This should consider the potential impact and amount of time that disruption will provide in terms of opportunities for friendly forces to exploit a potential opportunity.

A fourth effect is to *destroy* the ability of a network to conduct certain tasks until it is reconstituted. JP 3-25 observes, "destroying the threat network that is adaptive and transnationally established is an extreme challenge," and "[i]solated destruction of cells may be more plausible."[114] Next, a *defeat* is an outcome that occurs when a network has temporarily "has temporarily or permanently lost the physical means or the will to fight."[115] An operation also may *deny* a network the use of territory, personnel or facilities through destruction, removal or creation of obstacles. Finally, one may *divert* a network from a course of action by drawing attention away from the point of the principal operation, which requires it to use resources unproductively.[116]

The fact that threat networks commonly are intertwined with friendly and neutral networks in the operational environment generally further constrains CTN operations more than conventional military ones. "To successfully accomplish mission goals," JP 3-25 says, "the JFC [joint forces commander] should equally consider the impact of actions on multinational and friendly forces, local population, criminal enterprises, as well as the adversary. Intelligence may provide the commander with the location of the adversary, but if planning does not consider the impact of a strike on the local population, the adversary could

[111] *Id.* V-5.
[112] *Id.* V-7.
[113] *Id.* II-1.
[114] *Id.* V-6.
[115] *Id.* V-7.
[116] *Id.* V-5-8.

gain twice the number of combatants lost during the attack."[117] The best course of action may not be to destroy a network or cells, since "friendly or neutral populations may use the same network or cells, and to destroy it would have a negative effect."[118] In considering targeting network affiliations associated with a particular critical resource, "[e]valuating a potential target from the perspective of each affiliated network will provide the joint staff with potential second- and third-order effects on both the targeted threat networks and other interrelated networks within the OE."[119]

This description of doctrine on countering threat networks illuminates several ways in which information age conflict differs from industrial age conflict. The differences are not absolute and categorical, but are differences of degree. Nonetheless, together they result in distinctive approaches to addressing hostile actors. First, the operational environment in the information age contains several different networks among which one or more threat networks may not be fully distinguishable. This is different from a situation in which there is a clearly identifiable enemy who is the target of military operations.

Second, the environment described in JP 3-25 is subject to multiple influences that are continuously shaping the structure, activities, and orientations of these networks. The characterization of networks as friendly, neutral, or threat, therefore, must always be tentative and subject to revision based on new information. This is in contrast to the ascription of consistent hostility on the part of enemy forces in traditional operations.

Third, countering threat networks requires coordination among multiple instruments of US government power and friendly networks within the operational environment to monitor and respond to the emergence of threats and to attempt to deprive them of critical resources. While military operations in conventional conflicts are supplemented by various nonmilitary efforts, the military takes the lead in these situations.

Fourth, the targeting process is more complex in countering threat networks than it is in industrial-age hostilities. It must consider the effects of targeting not only on the threat network but on other networks in the operational environment to which that network is linked. In addition, it needs to determine which instrument of US power is most appropriate to engage the target and whether friendly networks such as the host nation or partner nations should be utilized as well. Such targeting may often involve nonlethal or nonkinetic forms of engagement, depending upon this analysis. In contrast, targeting in industrial-age conflicts generally focuses on kinetic engagement by the military. Force may be

[117] *Id.* III-6-7.
[118] *Id.* IV–1.
[119] *Id.* IV-13.

deployed only against combatants or military objects, but the assumption is that such deployment serves the purpose of defeating the enemy as quickly as possible. The only significant constraint on this is that civilian casualties must not be excessive compared to the anticipated military advantage.

Fifth, countering threat networks is rarely likely to completely extinguish them, in contrast to industrial-age warfare, which aims to defeat the enemy and destroy its will to continue. The goal realistically is to reduce as much as possible the ability of the network to carry out its operations by depriving it of the resources it needs to do so. The decentralized nature of a network, and its complex relationships with other networks that may provide resources, means that there generally is no single center of gravity against which force can be concentrated to vanquish the network. As a result, operations focus on continuously applying pressure simultaneously on various nodes and links of the network, and revising targeting priorities on an ongoing basis as the network adapts to changes in its environment.

Finally, understanding what is called the "human domain" in the form of formal and informal relationships plays an especially prominent role in determining how to counter threat networks. US Special Operations Command defines this domain as "the people (individuals, groups, and populations) in the environment, including their perceptions, decision-making, and behavior."[120] This domain, it says, "has a disproportionate role during population-centric conflicts, which are confrontations in which the perceptions and behavior of the relevant populations affect the conduct and outcome of hostilities."[121] As a result, "[t]o prevent or succeed in these types of conflicts, SOF and its partners must build influence and legitimacy with an increasing number of entities, each with their own perspective and interests."[122] As JP 3-25 notes, compared to conventional military conflict operations, "[a]dding a social dynamic complicates use of mathematical and deterministic formulas when human nature and social interactions play a major part in the OE."[123]

V. A Hybrid Approach

Doctrine on countering threat networks represents a hybrid approach that draws on restrictive elements of law enforcement while going beyond them in some respects. It resembles law enforcement first in that, as with potential

[120] United States Special Operations Command, "Operating in the Human Domain Version1.0," 2 (NSI, Aug. 3, 2015), 3–4, https://nsiteam.com/operating-in-the-human-domain-1-0/.

[121] *Id.* 6.

[122] *Id.* 6.

[123] *Id.* VI–5.

criminals, it conceptualizes dark networks as situated within a complex environment that contains many innocent individuals and legitimate social organizations. Just as criminals may draw on resources in this environment to accomplish their aims, so may threat networks. The doctrine emphasizes that operations to counter threats therefore must be mindful of the potential effects of such operations on individuals and organizations who may be unwittingly linked to threat networks or who rely on the same resources as they do.

This requirement to carefully analyze harmful effects on innocent parties places constraints on efforts to combat threats that are more akin to those applicable to law enforcement operations than to operations in armed conflict. The latter are limited by the requirement that civilian harms not be excessive in comparison to anticipated military advantage, but are subject to criticism by some that they do not consider second and third order effects. By contrast, CTN directs attention to such effects.

Second, doctrine on countering threat networks calls for individualized determinations for each group, which considers the level of threat that a group poses at any given time. This is intended to give the United States an opportunity to calibrate and refine the measures that it believes will be most effective in reducing that threat. These measures include several operations drawn from law enforcement efforts to reduce crime, such as surveillance, arrest, interdiction of contraband, seizure of property, cultivation of informers, and cutting off flows of financial resources. JP 3-25 emphasizes the important role of these and other nonlethal efforts to degrade the capabilities of threat networks. Ideally, the United States will work with partner governments and help enhance their capability to carry out such law enforcement operations.

Third, the use of lethal force depends upon the gravity of the threat that a group poses and the role of an individual in enabling the group to engage in hostilities. There is always the possibility that a group may present such a coordinated dangerous threat that the United States will designate it as a hostile force under the laws of armed conflict, as it has done with Al Qaeda and associated forces. In this case, of course, the United States would regard any member of the group as a combatant who is subject to lethal force at any time. Operations to counter threat networks, however, are intended to avoid allowing a group to reach that stage. This means that the use of lethal force generally will be based on individualized threat determinations rather than on a categorical presumption that every member of a group poses a serious threat to the United States.

It is true that the United States regards the law of armed conflict as governing all of its military operations abroad and does not accept that its forces outside the United States may be subject as a matter of law to human rights law as reflected in law enforcement standards. US policy based on the Presidential Policy Guidance issued by President Barack Obama,[124] however, and continued in some form under President Donald Trump in what is known as Principles, Standards, and Procedures,[125] is that outside areas of active hostilities, the United States will use lethal force based on individualized threat assessments, and only when capture is infeasible. This reflects appreciation that perceptions of the legitimacy of using lethal force in the international community rest upon confining status-based targeting to zones of armed conflict. While JP 3-25 does not refer to US policy, its measured approach to the use of lethal force is consistent with it.

At the same time, CTN departs from a strict law enforcement approach.

First, individuals may be targeted with lethal force in some cases because of the effect of doing so on the network rather than because they themselves pose an imminent threat to life. Someone who has specialized skills, for instance, may be several steps removed from the conduct of an attack, but may provide resources to the network that are crucial to enabling it to conduct attacks. This could be someone who is a trusted link between otherwise separate parts of the network—that is, someone who bridges what is known as a "structural hole" in the network.[126] Or it could be a person in a position of authority who allows territory to be used for entry of foreign fighters into a country. Using lethal force against these persons would not be authorized under law enforcement standards, but doing so may be the most effective feasible way to deprive the network of critical resources.

This touches on another respect in which CTN is more similar to operations in armed conflict than law enforcement activities. Persons or objects that may be attacked in order to counter the threat network are effectively treated as military objectives under Additional Protocol I of the Geneva Conventions. Such objectives are defined as those who "by their nature, location, purpose or use make an effective contribution to military action and whose total or partial destruction, capture or neutralization, in the circumstances ruling at the time, offers a definite military advantage."[127]

A military advantage is one that reflects targeting based on military necessity. The International Committee of the Red Cross (ICRC) states that "[t]he principle of military necessity permits measures which are actually necessary to accomplish a legitimate military purpose and are not otherwise prohibited

[124] The White House, "Report on the Legal and Policy Frameworks Guiding the United States' Use of Military Force and Related National Security Operations" (Dec. 2016), 24–26.

[125] Charlie Savage & Eric Schmitt, *Trump Poised to Drop Some Limits on Drone Strikes and Commando Raids*, N.Y. TIMES, Sept. 21, 2017, < https://www.nytimes.com/2017/09/21/us/politics/trump-drone-strikes-commando-raids-rules.html>.

[126] ROBERT BURT, STRUCTURAL HOLES: THE SOCIAL STRUCTURE OF COMPETITION (1992).

[127] "Protocol Additional to the Geneva Conventions of 12 August 1949, and Relating to the Protection of Victims of Internationally Armed Conflicts (Protocol I)" (International Committee of the Red Cross, June 8, 1977) art. 52(2), < https://ihl-databases.icrc.org/ihl/INTRO/470

by international humanitarian law."[128] The ICRC continues, "In the case of an armed conflict the only legitimate military purpose is to weaken the military capacity of the other parties to the conflict."[129] In the case of CTN, the purpose is to weaken the capacity of a threat network to execute attacks. Targeting any person or object that contributes to this capacity thus serves this purpose. In this respect, CTN may involve the kind of status-based targeting that occurs in armed conflict.

This illuminates another way in which CTN is not fully aligned with law enforcement standards but reflects a hybrid approach. The traditional primary focus of law enforcement is not to prevent threats of criminal activity from arising but to detect and apprehend those who engage in it. Police officers, for instance, may obtain a search warrant only upon probable cause to believe that a crime has been, is being, or will be committed. They may arrest someone only upon probable cause that the person has committed a crime or will soon do so.

It is true that, with respect to counterterrorism, law enforcement has been more aggressive in the last several years in charging people with lesser crimes or violations of, for instance, immigration law to target suspected terrorists. Nonetheless, if we think of a criminal act as involving several different stages on a spectrum in preparation for the crime, from the moment it is committed backward in time, the probable cause requirement means that criminal law intervenes only at a relatively late stage. The fact that someone may desire to commit a crime, and that they have some of the resources that might enable them to do so, means that they may be a threat to some extent. Except in rare cases, however, this is not sufficient for apprehension or criminal liability unless they take significant steps toward committing a crime. While a person could be under surveillance in some cases, police could not, for instance, damage their computer or prevent them from purchasing legal items in order to reduce the threat that they could pose. The aim of law enforcement is not to do whatever is necessary to reduce as much as possible the threat of criminal activity in society.

By contrast, CTN involves monitoring networks in an operational environment on an ongoing basis and assessing the level of threat that they may pose. The aim is to prevent threats from materializing in the first place and to prevent them from becoming more serious if they emerge. As JP 3-25 says, "The intelligence community maintains watch on [the operational environment], while the Department of State (DOS), Department of Defense (DOD), and interagency partners consider their relative equities to determine if action is warranted."[130] It continues, "When they detect a change that can have potential adverse

[128] International Committee of the Red Cross, "How Does Law Protect in War? Military Necessity," <https://casebook.icrc.org/glossary/military-necessity>.

[129] *Id.*

[130] Joint Chiefs of Staff, "Countering Threat Networks," *supra* note 3, at I-1.

consequences to the US's interests, they begin planning tailored responses as part of the broader instruments of national power to prevent a threat network from fully developing."[131]

Even before this, in what the military has traditionally called shaping operations in Phase Zero, "[t]he goal is to deny the threat network the resources needed to expand their operations and reduce it to a point where they no longer pose a direct threat to regional/local stability, while influencing the network to reduce or redirect its threatening objectives."[132] Unlike law enforcement operations, the core goal of CTN therefore is prevention, with action taken at an early point to prevent potential threats from materializing.

To this point, we have been discussing how CTN compares to law enforcement standards and the law of armed conflict with respect to discrete operations. With respect to the use of force, we can broadly characterize each of these legal regimes as establishing the *jus in bello* for these two kinds of activities. As a threshold matter, however, each individual use of force outside the United States to counter a threat network with which the United States does not regard itself as in an armed conflict must satisfy the requirements of *jus ad bellum*, in order to avoid violating UN Charter Article 2(4) and customary international law prohibition on the use of force. Assuming that the United States will not wait until the threat network actually attacks, this requires justifying the use of force in each case as an act of anticipatory self-defense to avert an imminent attack.

The United States set forth its understanding of imminence in the White House Frameworks published in December 2016. This states:

> When considering whether an armed attack is imminent under the jus ad bellum for purposes of the initial use of force against another State or on its territory, the United States analyzes a variety of factors. These factors include "the nature and immediacy of the threat; the probability of an attack; whether the anticipated attack is part of a concerted pattern of continuing armed activity; the likely scale of the attack and the injury, loss, or damage likely to result therefrom in the absence of mitigating action; and the likelihood that there will be other opportunities to undertake effective action in self-defense that may be expected to cause less serious collateral injury, loss, or damage."[133]

The Frameworks continue, "Moreover, 'the absence of specific evidence of where an attack will take place or of the precise nature of an attack does not preclude a conclusion that an armed attack is imminent for purposes of the exercise of the

[131] *Id.* I-1.
[132] *Id.* IV-17.
[133] The White House, "Frameworks," *supra* note 123.

right of self-defense, provided that there is a reasonable and objective basis for concluding that an armed attack is imminent.' "[134] Finally, "the traditional conception of what constitutes an 'imminent' attack must be understood in light of the modern-day capabilities, techniques, and technological innovations of terrorist organizations."[135]

To the extent that emphasis on prevention in CTN reflects policy, it could mean even greater US reliance on anticipatory self-defense to justify the use of force and potential expansion of it to situations even more temporally distant from an actual attack than the current US formulation. CTN aims to limit the ability of threat networks to increase capabilities that may eventually enable them to launch attacks. As JP 3-25 declares, this involves ongoing persistent efforts to disrupt a network and deprive it of resources by whatever means are most effective and feasible. The approach is to intervene early and often to prevent potential threats from maturing into more immediate ones.

Targeting, broadly defined as efforts to "engage" or disrupt the network, therefore ideally occurs well before there is imminent danger of an attack by a network in any meaningful temporal sense. The doctrine emphasizes that nonkinetic and nonlethal means often may be the best way of doing this. These will involve a number of "grey zone" tactics, or efforts to disadvantage states and non-state actors that often have ambiguous status under international law.[136]

At the same time, JP 3-25 consistently notes that both lethal and nonlethal measures must always be available. "In all CTN activities," the doctrine says, "lethal actions directed against the network should also be combined with nonlethal actions to support the legitimate government and persuade neutrals to reject the adversary."[137] Imagine, for instance, that a charismatic leader emerges who is effective at mobilizing resentment and resources that may eventually coalesce into a significant threat network. Eliminating that leader at an early stage could be the most effective way to reduce the risk that this network will materialize.

The earlier that force is used to deprive a network of resources that it could use to launch an attack, the more it resembles preventive, rather than preemptive, self-defense. The goal in these cases is not to avert an attack in the near future but to reduce the risk that one will ever occur. States that do this are using force in an effort "to transfer all risk from themselves to the people of other nations."[138] Yet, as Gabriella Blum and David Luban note, "life is inherently risky business, and

[134] *Id.* Quoting Daniel Bethlehem, *Self-Defense Against an Imminent or Actual Armed Attack by Nonstate Actors* 106 AM. J. INT'L L, 769 (2012).

[135] *Id.*

[136] On grey zone conflict, *see* MICHAEL J. MAZARR, MASTERING THE GRAY ZONE: UNDERSTANDING A CHANGING ERA OF CONFLICT (Dec. 2015).

[137] "Countering Threat Networks," V-16.

[138] Gabriella Blum & David Luban, *Degrees of Risk and the Jus ex Bello*, 125 ETHICS 751, 766 (2015).

nations must accept that some background risk is inevitable."[139] What level of such background risk is acceptable is a complex question, but using force abroad to minimize risk as much as possible at home is morally questionable and is not consistent with the authorization to use force in self-defense under Article 51 of the UN Charter.

Further, it is at least conceivable that someone may serve as a node in a network without fully appreciating that he is one. Terrorist networks share information only on a need-to-know basis because of the need for concealment. A courier, or someone else who links otherwise separate parts of the network, may not be aware that this is the function that he is performing. Indeed, he may not even be aware of the structure and topography of the network, or even think about the interaction that he has as communication within a larger network that enables it to function. This can raise concerns about the possibility of targeting an individual based upon minimal, if any, moral responsibility for posing a threat.

In addition, networks do not exist in the world in the same way as physical armed forces do. They are constructions based on analytical techniques, which are created by persons who are not disinterested in the activities they are analyzing. Furthermore, depending on how it is employed, increasing use of artificial intelligence to characterize individuals as members of networks and to anticipate the threat they pose could diminish reliance on human judgment. Networks are emergent phenomena that can be identified as products of various interactions among individuals. To identify someone as a node in a network and subject him to lethal targeting by virtue of that status does is not the same as identifying a member of a state armed force who has a readily identifiable function in an armed conflict that integrates his activity with that of others in the organization. Basing targeting decisions on network topography may challenge our moral notions of the bases for liability to lethal force.

JP 3-25 does not clarify the conditions under which lethal measures are appropriate in CTN operations. It indicates that such measures may be infeasible in some cases for practical reasons. These may include "diplomatic or political constraints,"[140] or the fact that "[d]estruction of a single node or cell might do little to impact network operations when assessed against the cost of operations and/or the potential for collateral damage."[141] SNA "will usually reveal a web of interconnected relationships and associations of which only a small percentage can be affected by lethal targeting and actions."[142] The doctrine does not, however, discuss other considerations that should inform the decision whether to

139 *Id.*
140 Joint Chiefs of Staff, "Countering Threat Networks," *supra* note 3, at IV-15.
141 *Id.* IV-20
142 *Id.* IV-12

use lethal force. Ideally, a decision maker will consider the gravity of this step and will regard it as a last resort, but this is not articulated at least in JP 3-25.

Presumably, the use of force in CTN operations outside areas of active hostilities would be governed as a policy matter by some version of the Principles, Standards, and Procedures (PSP) regarding direct action that the Trump administration adopted in 2017. These in turn reflected revisions of the Presidential Policy Guidance (PPG) issued by the Obama administration.[143] The Trump administration did not publicly disclose the PSP, but they became public in 2021. These provisions eliminated the PPG requirement that a target pose a "continuing imminent threat" to US persons, providing instead that direct action could be taken against targets "whose removal, either independently or as part of a broader campaign, is assessed to be reasonably necessary to US efforts to address the threat posed by the terrorist group."[144]

This effectively permitted targeting of "foot-soldier jihadists with no special skills or leadership roles."[145] Luke Hartig, who served in the Obama administration, observes:

> [C]ounterterrorism professionals have become adept at analyzing the structure of terrorist networks and targeting them based on the understanding that there are particular nodes that, if removed, could have a devastating impact on the entire network. In many cases, those nodes may be couriers, bodyguards, or propagandists who, while lawful military targets under the laws of war, may not pose a continuing, imminent threat to U.S. persons. The new policy appears to give operators greater leeway to target according to what will be considerably more effective in disrupting and defeating terrorist networks.[146]

As Hartig's comment reflects, both the PPG and the PSP were formulated mainly to provide policy guidance on targeting members of Al Qaeda and associated forces under the Authorization for the Use of Military Force outside of hot battlefields. In such cases, the United States reserves the right to engage in targeting under the law of armed conflict. CTN operations against other threat networks with whom the United States in not engaged in such a conflict should be more constrained.

143 *See* Savage & Schmitt, *supra* note 124.

144 White House. (no date). Principles, standards, and procedures for direct action against terrorist targets. American Civil Liberties Union, 1. https://www.aclu.org/foia-document/psp-foia-document-april-30-2021, p. 4.

145 *Id.*

146 Luke Hartig, *Trump's New Drone Strike Policy: What's Any Different? Why It Matters*, Just Security, Sept. 22, 2017, < https://www.justsecurity.org/45227/trumps-drone-strike-policy-different-matters/.

At the same time, however, the United States takes the position that all military operations, regardless of their intensity, are governed by the law of armed conflict. It is thus not entirely clear what standard the United States might follow in determining whether to use lethal force in CTN operations against threat networks with whom the United States is not engaged in an armed conflict. Clarifying this would be an important step in helping establish a coherent framework for CTN doctrine, and more generally for states in combating transnational non-state armed groups outside of armed conflict.

VI. Conclusion

US doctrine on countering threat networks draws on SNA to provide an approach to counterterrorism that is a salutary alternative to US reliance in the last two decades on the paradigm of armed conflict. This has the potential to limit the use of violence that has been such a controversial element of US strategy. Mapping a broad set of relationships that furnish various types of resources to terrorist groups enables policymakers to identify nonkinetic means to deprive these groups of such resources. More generally, SNA ideally should direct attention to addressing the social, economic, and political conditions that can give rise to terrorism. In these respects, CTN doctrine represents an opportunity to move beyond the predominant kinetic focus of US counterterrorism.

At the same time, this shift raises potential concerns. At its most ambitious, it purports to use SNA to monitor potential risks to the United States across the entire world and to intervene in various ways when reducing that risk seems advisable. Such an early warning system can be valuable, but also could lead to a tendency to regard other countries simply as the location of sets of risks that the United States must attempt to minimize. This may be especially likely with a pivot shift toward great power competition and its assumption of an ongoing struggle for global influence.

In addition, it may be tempting to seek as much as possible to drive risk down to zero if SNA appears to identify measures that may do so. This could lead to the implicit adoption of an unrealistic benchmark for US security in a world that necessarily poses at least some risk. Such a benchmark would be problematic in light of CTN doctrine's emphasis on prevention and its focus on persons as nodes within networks. Capturing or killing an individual may be effective in reducing the amount of risk that a group may present, even though there are no grounds for taking such action under law enforcement standards and moral principles of liability to harm.

These potential benefits and risks of CTN reflect the challenges of fashioning counterterrorism strategy in an age in which terrorist groups have the potential to conduct transnational operations. Tools such as SNA can enable more discriminating initiatives than are available under an armed conflict approach. At this chapter suggests, however, these tools cannot free decision makers from the task of identifying and addressing the legal and ethical issues raised by their deployment.

PART IV

CRIME AND WAR: PROSECUTING TERRORISM AND WAR CRIMES

15

Counting the Ripples

The Challenge of Extraterritorial Jurisdiction to Prosecute Non-State Actors

Evan R. Seamone[*]

> *It is [] entirely foreseeable that an indiscriminate attack on civilians in a crowded metropolitan center such as [Jerusalem] will cause injury to persons who reside in distant locales—including tourists and other visitors to the city, as well as relatives of individuals who live in the area. The ripples of harm that flow from such barbarous acts rarely stop at the banks of the Mediterranean Sea or the Jordan River, and those who engage in this kind of terrorism should hardly be surprised to find that they are called to account for it in the courts of the United States—or, for that matter, in any tribunal recognized by civilized peoples.*[1]

I. Introduction

We live in an increasingly global sphere, characterized by botnet attacks that could foreseeably involve the hijacking of thousands of computers in several different states to perpetrate denial of services or other consequences on a victim.[2] Countries are scrambling to develop the legal framework to prosecute non-state actors. Of five recognized principles for prescriptive jurisdiction—the jurisdiction to punish actors and acts—only one, the Protective Principle (hereinafter, the Principle), permits a state to extend the reach of criminal laws to failed

* The author extends tremendous thanks to Professor Richard Meyer of Mississippi College School of Law and Professor Iain Pedden of the Judge Advocate General's Legal Center & School for their insights and suggestions.

1 Sissov v. Islamic Republic of Iran, 448 F. Supp. 2d 76, 90 (D. D.C. 2006).

2 *See, e.g.*, Paul N. Stockton & Michelle Golabek-Goldman, *Prosecuting Cyberterrorists: Applying Traditional Jurisdictional Frameworks to a Modern Threat*, 25 Stan. L. & Poly Rev. 212, 233–34 (2014) (describing the widespread implications of the 2009 Stuxnet virus and other botnet attacks).

Evan R. Seamone, *Counting the Ripples* In: *Between Crime and War*. Edited by: Claire Finkelstein, Christopher Fuller, Jens David Ohlin, Mitt Regan, Oxford University Press. © Claire Finkelstein, Christopher Fuller, Jens David Ohlin, Mitt Regan 2023. DOI: 10.1093/oso/9780197638798.003.0016

terrorism attempts or planning activities entirely involving aliens.[3] In short, the Principle allows prosecution of aliens who commit offenses in foreign lands when the aliens have engaged in conduct that threatens "security or other vital interests" of the prosecuting state.[4] Arguably, the full parameters of this Principle are yet to be known[5] because its codifications in the 1935 Draft Convention on Jurisdiction With Respect to Crime and the Restatement of the Foreign Relations Law of the United States occurred at times when the reporters could not comprehend the magnitude and reach of current technological advancements.[6] While scholars have recognized that the Protective Principle offers the best chance to respond to non-state actors in the current global sphere and to deter them from future acts against states,[7] they also recognize that this Principle offers the greatest potential for abuse by states.[8]

Considering the unanswered questions that surround the Protective Principle as a means to prosecute non-state actors for acts of terrorism, this chapter explores two important aspects of the discussion: (1) the Principle's prerequisite for an offense that reaches the level of interference with important government interests, and (2) the nexus between the alien and those state interests. Of many questions, the former inquiry is important because of the relationships between private and governmental organizations in the contemporary global economy.[9] A representation of the latter inquiry would be whether a stateless or foreign-flagged vessel containing a large amount of narcotics was close enough to the United States to implicate its interests in preventing drug smuggling.[10] Clarity on these two fundamental concerns in Protective Principle jurisprudence will contribute greatly to the effective use of the Principle to help leverage an affected

[3] *Id.* 251 ("The protective doctrine is the only jurisdictional basis under international law that authorizes extraterritorial jurisdiction over crimes that pose a potential danger to the security of a state.").

[4] Dapo Akande, *Protective Principle (Jurisdiction)*, *in* The Oxford Companion to International Criminal Justice 474 (Antonio Cassese ed., 2009), 474. *See, e.g.*, United States v. Clark, 315 F. Supp. 2d 1127, 1130 (W.D. Wa. 2004) (noting the applicability of the Protective Principle when acts committed by aliens abroad "impinge on the territorial sovereignty, security, or political independence of the United States").

[5] Akande, *supra* note , at 474 ("Although the protective principle is unquestionably accepted in international law, there is no certainty as to the activities which may be regarded as against the vital interests of the state[.]"). *See also* United States v. Reumayr, 530 F. Supp. 2d 1210, 1222 (D. N.M. 2008) ("Cases discussing the extent of the protective principle are few.").

[6] Stockton & Colabek-Goldman, *supra* note 2, at 230.

[7] *Id.* 249.

[8] *See, e.g.*, Iain Cameron, The Protective Principle of International Criminal Jurisdiction 2 (1994) (suggesting that Protective Principle jurisdiction claims "should . . . be restricted as far as possible").

[9] *See, e.g.*, Austen Parrish, *The Effects Test: Extraterritoriality's Fifth Business*, 61 Vand. L. Rev. 1455, 1457 (2008) ("In an age of globalization, . . . law should fin national and political borders of little significance.").

[10] Part III, *infra*.

state's judicial system to hold non-state actors accountable for terrorism, thereby deterring terrorist acts.

This chapter does recognize that other important considerations may ultimately preclude the application of the Principle, even if a state can demonstrate a threat to its vital interest. Accordingly, this chapter makes the following three assumptions. First, it assumes that the United States is engaged in these sorts of prosecutions at a higher rate than other states and focuses on use of the Principle by the United States, even though other states have taken divergent approaches to this Principle regarding specific offenses.[11] The United States may be specially situated for the purpose of enforcing this Principle because it is the object of a high volume of attacks. Second, in discussing US prosecution of an alien, this chapter assumes no conflict with another state wishing to exert jurisdiction over the alien for the same conduct.[12] While some commentators have voiced concern over states' competing claims for jurisdiction over a crime affecting multiple states,[13] in many instances, countries have been willing to relinquish such claims in favor of US prosecution based on its optimal resources and capacity for such prosecutions. The final assumption is that the assertion of Protective jurisdiction will comply with due process requirements or their equivalents. This concern is important because, increasingly, US courts have recognized a requirement for the offender to have sufficient "notice" that his or her conduct as perpetrated in foreign lands could still lead to potential prosecution in the United States.[14] The Ninth Circuit Court of Appeals, for example, uses the most "robust" notice formulation.[15] The assumption of sufficiency of notice should be less alarming given an apparent relationship in which notice increases with the magnitude of a threat to US security. As the Southern District of New York aptly recognized, "defendants surely cannot suggest that they suddenly learned that mass murder was illegal in the United States or anywhere else."[16]

This chapter adopts a three-part approach to explore the question of US vital interests and the nexus between an alien and those interests. First, it briefly explores the changing trajectory of the Principle over time, from an initial position of rejection to increasing acceptance and expansion, ultimately embracing diplomatic issues, narcotics, bombings of airlines, and interference with financial and oil markets. During this evaluation, it is important to consider the manner in

[11] This is true especially in the area of export controls. Cameron, *supra* note 8, at 276–79.

[12] Stockton & Golabek-Goldman, *supra* note 2, at 259–67.

[13] *Id.* (exploring the dynamics of such conflicts and recommending sequential prosecutions).

[14] Sara A. Solow, *Prosecuting Terrorists as Criminals and the Limits of Extraterritorial Jurisdiction*, 85 St. John's L. Rev. 1483, 1549 (2011).

[15] *Id.*

[16] United States v. Al Kassar, 582 F. Supp. 2d 488, 495 (S.D.N.Y. 2008) (citing United States v. Bin Laden, 92 F. Supp. 2d 189, 218 (S.D.N.Y. 2000)). *See also* United States v. Carvajal, 924 F. Supp. 2d 219, 263 (D. D.C. 2013) ("[L]arge-scale Columbian drug traffickers cannot have been surprised by United States prosecution.").

which terrorist acts influenced the expansion of not only the Protective Principle but also other jurisdictional principles, signaling the flexibility of international law to respond to the threat of transnational terrorism perpetrated by non-state actors. The second section of this chapter explores the concept of a "vital interest" by examining various judicial opinions. This section concerns applications of the Principle to interests that can loosely be defined as economic, political, policy, and national security related, with the hope of identifying the Principle's limits. The final section of this chapter uses a hypothetical scenario involving a transnational terrorist organization, similar to the hacker group "Anonymous," to explore the contours of the Protective Principle as applied to contemporary threat. The scenario assists in demonstrating the utility of the Precautionary Principle to prosecute non-state actors who threaten the United States within the global financial and telecommunications sectors.

II. Evolution of the Protective Principle as a Means to Prosecute Non-State Actors

The first codification of the Protective Principle dates to the 1808 French Code of Criminal Procedure.[17] Yet, scholars have traced its inception back to at least the time of thirteenth-century Italian city-states.[18] Stripped to its basic components, the Principle permits a state to take measures to defend itself against hostile forces abroad, especially when the prosecuting state would not be able to rely on other states to protect its interests.[19] Often confused with the Effects Principle,[20] the Protective Principle is distinct as a means of exercising prescriptive jurisdiction in the way that it attaches to aliens abroad even when their hostile acts are inchoate.[21]

> If a state chooses to rely upon the protective principle it can assert jurisdiction over a crime notwithstanding the fact that it was completed or frustrated wholly abroad. All that is necessary is for the state asserting jurisdiction to

[17] Arthur Lenhoff, *International Law and Rules on International Jurisdiction*, 50 CORNELL L. REV. 5, 12 (1964) (citing *Code d'Instruction Criminelle* (1808), arts. 5–6).

[18] *See, e.g.*, Monika B Krizek, Note, *The Protective Principle of Extraterritorial Jurisdiction: A Brief History and an Application of the Principle to Espionage as an Illustration of Current United States Practice*, 6 B.U. INT'L L.J. 337, 339 (1988).

[19] Cameron, *supra* note 8, at 31 ("The *raison d'être* of the protective principle is quite simply the fact that state A cannot really rely upon state B to protect A's vital interests, or to protect them to the extent which A considers to be necessary or desirable.").

[20] *Id.* 64, 222; *id.* 212 ("The effects principle has . . . been invoked when the protective principle would have been more appropriate.").

[21] *Id.* 218 (describing the appropriateness of the Principle for "potential effects" on a state or "frustrated rather than completed crimes.").

> show a nexus between itself and the offense, i.e. that the offense was aimed, or directed, or intended to impact or actually impacted upon . . . its central protected interests.[22]

Accordingly, some have proclaimed this to be "the most important exception to the territoriality principle."[23] Early on, the United States and Great Britain eschewed the Protective Principle, instead operating from the Territorial Principle, which attaches jurisdiction to offenses committed within a nation's geographic territory. In the aftermath of World War II, nations shifted positions with the United States supporting the Principle "to cover the acts of alien war criminals and collaborators committed outwith the territory of a state against the interests of the state, or even the interests of allied states."[24] Increasing acts of terrorism began to influence jurisdictional principles across the globe. As one example, the Third Restatement of U.S. Foreign Relations explicitly recognized how the Passive Nationality Principle of extraterritorial jurisdiction was "increasingly applied to terrorist and other organized attacks."[25] By 2009, in a comprehensive study of extraterritorial jurisdiction across the globe, the International Law Association observed that twenty-two of twenty-seven surveyed states had "enacted legislation based on some form of the protective principle."[26] Notably, some of these states have applied the principle to crimes of , while others have required a greater mens rea of knowledge or specific intent.[27]

Despite favorable laws on their books, many states avoid application of the Protective Principle or use the measure only as a last resort. Problems arise when states use the Principle to effectuate "vague penal legislation on economic and ideological matters."[28] The chief reason for this reluctance is the Principle's serious potential for abuse. As early as 1988, courts described a very real risk that the Principle would be applied so broadly that it would "allow the United States to police *any* international conduct" under the moniker of important state interests.[29] Scholars have pointed to various international court opinions in which the Principle had been used in an abusive manner. One example existed

[22] *Id.* 65.

[23] Lenhoff, *supra* note 18, at 12.

[24] Cameron, *supra* note 8, at 44.

[25] Restatement (Third) of Foreign Relations Law § 402 cmt g.

[26] International Law Association, Report of the Task Force on Extraterritorial Jurisdiction 150 (2009). Some of the areas of coverage include: "national security," "acts of war," "arms offenses," "counterfeiting the state's currency or seal," "treason," "interference with a state's democratic rule, constitution, or independence," "arms control laws," and "perjury before consuls." *Id.* 150. *See also* Peter Malanczuk, Akenhurst's Modern Introduction to International Law 112 (7th rev. ed. 1997) ("Most countries use this principle to some extent[.]").

[27] *Supra* note 8, at 49.

[28] *Id.* 44.

[29] *Peralza*, 439 F.3d at 1162 (citing United States v. Robinson, 843 F.2d 1, 3 (1st Cir. 1988)).

in the enforcement of racial purity rules prior to the end of World War II.[30] More recently, critics have mentioned concerns about the Principle's use in the prosecution of aliens for the offense of providing material support to terrorism.[31] For example, they identify an individual who contributes medical supplies to the health services arm of a designated foreign terrorist organization with concern that the foreign donor may find himself subject to US prosecution merely because he has aided certain humanitarian operations.[32] Under such circumstances, the chief criticism is the "indiscriminate" and "unfair" application of the Principle.[33]

III. Tracing the Contours of the Protective Principle in US Jurisprudence

Harvard Law School conducted an extensive study of extraterritorial jurisdiction in 1935, recognizing certain principles in US jurisprudence that aligned with the Protective Principle.[34]

The study published Article 7 of a Draft Convention on Jurisdiction with Respect to Crime, which provided:

> *Protection Security of the State*
> A State has jurisdiction with respect to any crime committed outside its territory by an alien against the security, territorial integrity, or political independence of that State, provided that the act or omission which constitutes the crime was not committed in exercise of a liberty guaranteed the alien by the law of the place where it was committed.[35]

Nearly a generation later, the 1960 case of *United States v. Rodriguez* marked the very first time that a US court "explicitly recognized" the Protective Principle.[36]

[30] Michael Akehurst, *Jurisdiction in International Law*, 46 BRIT. Y.B. INT'L L. 145, 158 (1972–1973) (describing other examples).

[31] *See, e.g.*, Solow, *supra* note 14, at 1502 (citing cases prosecuted under the "material support" statute, 18 U.S.C. § 2339B, including United States v. Shah, 47 F. Supp. 2d 492, 498–99 (S.D.N.Y. 2007), and Singh-Kaur v. Ashcroft, 385 F.3d 294, 294 (3d Cir. 2004)).

[32] *Id.* 1555:

> For instance, when a person (located abroad) donates food to a group classified as an FTO (also located abroad), and it is reasonably foreseeable that the group will use its shared resources to subsequently harm the United States, has the donor displayed sufficient mens rea to make him a criminal under United States law?

[33] Krizek, *supra* note 17, at 356.

[34] *See generally* Harvard Research in International Law, *Jurisdiction with Respect to Crime*, 29 AM. J. INT'L L. 435 (1935 Supp.), reprinted in 2 HARVARD RESEARCH ON INTERNATIONAL LAW: ORIGINAL MATERIALS 439 (John P. Grant & J. Craig Barker eds., 2008).

[35] *Id.* 440.

[36] Krizek, *supra* note 17, at 346 (citing United States v. Rodriguez, 182 F. Supp. 479 (S.D. Cal. 1960)).

Another court viewed a false statement on a visa application as "an affront to the very sovereignty of the United States."[37] A series of related cases recognized a US interest in "the control of immigration" sufficient to prosecute a full range of misrepresentations, including sham marriages.[38]

Beginning in the 1970s and through the 1980s, during a surge in drug smuggling, US courts applied these same principles to the vital function of regulating narcotics. At the most general level, courts noted that "vessels in close proximity to the United States, full of illegal drugs, represent a real potential for harm to the effective administration of United States' customs and narcotics laws, which reflect a strong governmental interest."[39] However, courts did recognize some limitations. As Oppenheim observed: "[I]t seems probable that in the absence of any direct and substantial connection between the state exercising jurisdiction and the matter in relation to which jurisdiction is exercised, the exercise of jurisdiction would be a violation of international law."[40] Accordingly, whether in the context of the Protective Principle, under notions of Fifth Amendment Due Process, or somewhere in between, courts observed the requirement for some evidence of knowledge or intent to transport narcotics into the United States.[41]

Building on the standards established by US courts applying the Protective Principle to narcotics smuggling, the District of Massachusetts applied the rule to a charge of espionage in 1985.[42] In *Zehee*, the court reasoned that the Protective Principle attaches where the prohibited activity "directly obstructs a government function,"[43] emphasizing in substance how the rules could easily encompass other types of state interests. Courts also recognized Protective Jurisdiction in cases involving murder or physical harm to US representatives on the basis that an attack on an elected representative constituted an attack on US "constitutional structure," thus the "integrity of our nation."[44]

Also in the 1980s, the Fifth Circuit Court of Appeals refused to extend the Protective Principle to an alien who agreed to fence a car in Mexico, which he knew had been stolen by the original thief in El Paso, Texas.[45] The *Columba-Colella* court's reason for rejecting the Protective Principle in that case included

[37] United States v. Pizzarusso, 388 F.2d 8, 9 (2d Cir. 1967).

[38] United States v. Khalje, 658 F.2d 90 (2d Cir. 1981).

[39] In re Extradition of Demjanjuk, 612 F. Supp. 544, 558 n.13 (N.D. Ohio 1985).

[40] 1 Oppenheim's International Law 468 (9th ed. Robert Jennings & Arthur Watts eds., 2008) (1905).

[41] *See, e.g.*, Solow, *supra* note 14, at 1552 ("[W]hen a boat is hundreds of miles from the United States and there is no circumstantial or direct evidence that the narcotics aboard were likely to wind up within United States borders, . . . jurisdiction does not lie.").

[42] United States v. Zehe, 601 F. Supp. 196 (D. Mass. 1985).

[43] *Id.* 196.

[44] United States v. Layton, 509 F. Supp. 212, 218 (N.D. Cal. 1981).

[45] United States v. Columba-Colella, 604 F.2d 356, 360 (5th Cir. 1979).

the fact that the individual, an accomplice, had not originally participated in the theft.[46] While recognizing that the Mexican authorities surely retained jurisdiction to prosecute the alien for his offense within that state's territory, the court reasoned:

> It is difficult to distinguish the present case from one in which the defendant had attempted not to fence a stolen car but instead pick pockets of American tourists in Acapulco. No one would argue either that Congress would be competent to prohibit such conduct or that the courts of the United States would have jurisdiction to enforce such a prohibition were the offender in their control.[47]

As noted by Iain Cameron, "[A] crime can seriously damage state interests without being specifically directed against the state. And an interest in prosecuting a criminal is not the same as a 'protected interest of the state.' "[48] The crime of fencing a stolen US car, therefore, did not rise to the level of an important state interest of the United States, emphasizing a clear limitation on the United States' extraterritorial reach: "[A]n act that affects the citizen of a state is not sufficient basis for that state to assert jurisdiction over the act."[49]

Even in the prosecution of drug smugglers, courts increasingly rejected the notion that *all* vessels containing large amounts of drugs could be prosecuted by the United States. Although some courts reasoned that a sufficient *potential* for implicating US interests existed if a portion of the drugs would have eventually found their way into the United States,[50] other courts demanded evidence of intent or knowledge. In an oft-cited passage, the Ninth Circuit, in *United States v. Peterson*, commented: "[T]he notion that [the] 'protective principle' could be applied to 'prohibiting foreigners on foreign ships 500 miles offshore from possessing drugs that . . . might be bound for Canada, South America, or Zanzibar' . . . has been repeatedly called into question by our Court and others."[51] In this vein, courts have recognized: "Never in a published opinion of an American court has a potential generalized effect, which might or might not also be an effect on the United States, been found sufficient to invoke the protective principle of international law."[52] Yet, courts found sufficient indicia of knowledge or intent of distribution to the United States in a host of contextual and

[46] *Id.*
[47] *Id.*
[48] Cameron, *supra* note 8, at 240.
[49] *Columba-Colella*, 604 F.2d at 360.
[50] *See, e.g.*, United States v. Medjuck, 156 F.3d 916, 919 (9th Cir. 1997).
[51] United States v. Peralza, 439 F.3d 1149 (9th Cir. 2006) (internal citations omitted).
[52] United States v. James-Robinson, 515 F. Supp. 1340, 1344 (S.D. Fla. 1981). *See also id.* 1346 (addressing "[p]roximity to U.S. territory").

circumstantial factors, including: (1) proximity of a mothership to a "stopping point for marijuana on its way to the United States";[53] (2) whether markings on the drugs matched markings on drugs that had been seized in the United States;[54] (3) "[t]he location of the ship and [whether] the kind of navigational maps on board were consistent with the cocaine being bound for the United States";[55] and (4) whether "the foreign defendants kn[e]w or intend[ed] that their illegal cargo w[ould] be distributed in this country."[56]

Many of these same factors would also be valuable in demonstrating other threats to US security and governmental interests as the Protective Principle continued to evolve.

In the late 1990s and early 2000s, International Conventions on the Suppression of Terrorist Bombings and Financing of Terrorism embraced this Principle.[57] Not surprisingly, in 2003, the Second Circuit turned to the Ninth Circuit's maritime drug-smuggling precedent to inform its application of the Protective Principle to an alien's training runs in preparation for eventual bombings of US airlines. In *United States v. Yousef*, a member of Al Qaeda practiced bombing techniques on Philippine airlines, causing the death of Japanese passengers.[58] Although the defense protested that the crime did not have a sufficient nexus to the United States given the lack of US victims or perpetrators, the court approved of jurisdiction under the Protective Principle. By this time, the court recognized that "[t]he protective principle generally is invoked to obtain jurisdiction over politically motivated acts . . . ," seemingly in recognition of its expanding use to fight terrorism.[59]

The *Yousef* court evaluated the activities of the bombers in conducting their "test-runs" and relied upon various written statements demonstrating the ultimate aim of the defendant to harm the United States.[60] Ultimately, "the flight schedules and paths of the United States-flag aircraft and detailed plans for planting bombs on these flights, conformed that the co-conspirators intended to bomb United States-flag aircraft using a *modus operandi* identical to that

[53] United States v. Angola, 514 F. Supp. 933, 936 (S.D. Fla. 1981) (further commenting how this fact would demonstrate "an inherent and necessary effect threatening the United States with the eventual flow of illicit drugs into this country").

[54] United States v. Klimavicius-Viloria, 144 F.3d 1249, 1258 (9th Cir. 1998).

[55] *Id.*

[56] *Id.*

[57] Akande, *supra* note 4 at 474 (citing art. 6(2)(b) and (d) of the 1998 International Convention for the Suppression of Terrorist Bombings, and art. 7(2)(b) and (c) of the 2000 International Convention for the Suppression of Financing Terrorism).

[58] United States v. Yousef, 327 F.3d 56 (2d Cir.), cert. denied, 540 U.S. 933 (2003).

[59] *Id.* 110.

[60] *Id.* 110. For example, one letter contained the following proclamation: "[W]e will consider all American nationals as part of our legitimate targets because they are responsible for the behavior of their government and its foreign policies." *Id.* 110, citing Letter from the Fifth Division of the Liberation Army (Nov. 19, 1994).

which permitted them to place the bomb on Philippine Airlines Flight 434."[61] Because the crime involved a plot to destroy US commercial aircraft with the aim of "influenc[ing] United States foreign policy," this implicated a vital "government function" sufficient to invoke the Protective Principle.[62] Commentators have remarked that *Yousef* was the seminal case in which "a U.S. court upheld prescriptive jurisdiction based on the Protective Principle" relating to terrorism.[63] An important consideration in *Yousef* is the increase in the potential consequences from a written false statement to the loss of human life. In this regard, a subsequent opinion found that arms suppliers threatened US interests just as the actual attackers in *Yousef*.[64] Along these lines, other courts have reasoned that the Protective Principle must surely apply to violent acts of terrorism if it applies to conduct as minor as lying to a consular official.

For example, in 2008, US jurisprudence witnessed a further expansion of the Protective Principle to terrorist activity. In the *Reumayr* case, a Canadian citizen planned an attack on the Trans-Alaska Oil Pipeline that would be perpetrated entirely from Canada.[65] Because the United States was part of that oil production and transport scheme, with the private Prudhoe Bay oil field connected to the pipeline, the US government argued that the plan to blow up the pipeline and stop the flow of oil implicated an oil and financial security interest of the United States.[66] Reumayr countered that the United States could not invoke its own governmental interest in the disruption of private businesses.[67] The District of New Mexico rejected this objection and held that "an attempt to destroy an important conduit of petroleum located within the United States [is] a crime which clearly implicates the fuel security and financial security of the United States." The court specifically reasoned that the intent to "disrupt" the US oil supply was "a corollary" of disrupting US financial markets, which was cognizable under the Protective Principle.[68]

Even though *Reumayr* did involve a potential threat of violent explosions as a means to disrupt the flow of oil across borders, commentators have noted the significance of the opinion more for its position that US state interests may be implicated by the acts of non-state actors against private companies in the United States so long as there are tangible threats to economic or oil security.[69] In

[61] *Id.* 111.
[62] *Id.* 110.
[63] Stockton & Golabeck-Goldman, *supra* note 2, at 254–55.
[64] *See Al Kassar*, 582 F. Supp. 2d at 494.
[65] United States v. Reumayr, 530 F. Supp. 2d 1210, 1212 (D. N.M. 2008).
[66] *Id.* 1212.
[67] *Id.* 1214.
[68] *Id.* 1222 & n.17.
[69] Stockton & Golabek-Goldman, *supra* note 2, at 255 (linking this private/public distinction to cyberterrorism).

this instance, the Prudhoe Bay oil field produced approximately 8 percent of the nation's oil.[70]

On balance, different courts have applied the Protective Principle inconsistently, with some describing judicial confusion over the Principle's interaction or interchangeability with other Principles. While some US courts have situated the discussion of the Protective Principle under the moniker of jurisdiction to try a case,[71] others have limited the principle to a nonjurisdictional issue.[72] Some of the courts that have applied the Principle prior to addressing the question of due process applied the Third Restatement's reasonableness standards laid out in Section 403(2) as a precursor to the exercise of subject matter jurisdiction to try the case.[73] These factors include:

(a) the link of the activity to the territory of the regulating state, i.e., the extent to which the activity takes place within the territory, or has substantial, direct, and foreseeable effect upon or in the territory;
(b) the connections, such as nationality, residence, or economic activity, between the regulating state and the person principally responsible for the activity to be regulated, or between that state and those whom the regulation is designed to protect;
(c) the character of the activity to be regulated, the importance of regulation to the regulating state, the extent to which other states regulate such activities, and the degree to which the desirability of such regulation is generally accepted.
(d) the existence of justified expectations that might be protected or hurt by the regulation;
(e) the importance of the regulation to the international political, legal, or economic system;
(f) the extent to which the regulation is consistent with the traditions of the international system;
(g) the extent to which another state may have an interest in regulating the activity; and
(h) the likelihood of conflict with regulation by another state.[74]

[70] *Reumayr*, 530 F. Supp. 2d at 1212.

[71] *See, e.g.*, *James-Robinson*, 515 F. Supp. at 1347 n.10 ("To act without jurisdiction would be a denial of due process.").

[72] *See, e.g.*, United States v. Yousef, 750 F.3d 254, 262 (2d Cir. 2014) ("[I]n the criminal context, 18 U.S.C. § 3231 is all that is necessary to establish a court's power to hear cases involving a federal offense, whether or not the conduct charged proves beyond the scope of Congress's concern or authority in enacting the statute at issue.").

[73] *See, e.g.*, *Clark*, 315 F. Supp. 2d at 1127.

[74] *Restatement (Third) of Foreign Relations Law* § 403(2).

However, in all cases leading up to 1994, among "those U.S. cases . . . in which courts found the protective principle to be applicable, no court found that an exercise of jurisdiction under the principle was unreasonable."[75] Beyond this, as of December 2020, only six US criminal courts have remotely mentioned the reasonableness factors of Section 403(2) in the same opinion as a Protective Principle issue.[76] Within the Fifth Circuit, as of 2009, the court noted, "there is no Fifth Circuit precedent making these factors a mandatory part of the threshold inquiry to determine whether a statute may be applied extraterritorially. The Court declines to do so here."[77] While such balancing is supposed to happen immediately following the determination that the Protective Principle applies to conduct, critics note that the potential for bias minimizes the value of the reasonableness test in international criminal cases.[78]

The greatest concern regarding US courts' application of the protective principle is on-demand definitions of state interests that encompass a given offender's conduct even if that individual's act "does not cast a sufficient shadow on the United States."[79] Clearly, such exercises of extraterritorial jurisdiction violate the sovereign rights of the state in which those acts have been committed. Thus, when the issue turns to the prosecution of non-state actors for cyberterrorism, some still question the application of the Protective Principle as a means of extraterritorial jurisdiction on the basis that governments lack an objective list of the specific types of conduct that "would warrant jurisdiction under the protective principle."[80] Ultimately, it appears that "so long as states are the ultimate arbiters of their security and other vital interests and so long as the protective principle may be used to criminalize extraterritorial conduct against such interests, the threat of abuse is ever present."[81]

IV. An Applied Example Involving Telecommunications

Although the United States and the international community await further guidelines and standards to improve the implementation of a state's exercise

[75] Cameron, *supra* note 8, at 336.

[76] Lexis-Nexis search conducted on Dec. 2, 2020, using search terms "403(2) and 'Protective Principle.' " The search identified: United States v. Yousef, 327 F.3d 56, 109 n.44 (2d Cir. 2003); United States v. McVicker, 979 F. Supp. 2d 1154, 1175 n.7 (D. Or. 2013); United States v. Vasquez-Velasco, 15 F.3d 833, 840 n.6 (9th Cir. 1994); *Bin Laden*, 92 F. Supp. at 222–24; *Clark*, 315 F. Supp. 2d at 1127; and United States v. Martinez, 591 F. Supp. 2d 784, 801 n9 (W. D. Tex. 2009).

[77] *Martinez*, 591 F. Supp. 2d at 801.

[78] *See, e.g.*, Cameron, *supra* note 8, at 336 (observing that "the process of balancing can never be impartial").

[79] *Columba-Colella*, 604 F.2d at 360.

[80] Stockton & Golabek-Goldman, *supra* note 2, at 259.

[81] Cameron, *supra* note 8, at 348.

of extraterritorial jurisdiction, it is helpful to consider a hypothetical threat as a means to identify the areas of greatest concern and potential uses of the Protective Principle to combat the terrorist acts of non-state actors. The hypothetical follows.

A. Background

Digital Liberation Front (DLF) consists of a group of computer hacktivists[82] *with anonymous members throughout the Globe. Much like "hacking collectives" Anynomous and LulzSec,*[83] *the DLF aims to effect social and political change, in part, by interfering with global computing and telecommunications. In the past, the DLF gained notoriety by launching a number of targeted Denial of Service (DOS) attacks*[84] *on various transnational businesses in order to discourage mergers and acquisitions between companies that have allegedly violated human rights in their labor practices. The DLF has, in the past, claimed credit for installing malware and ransomware in a number of US Wall Street brokerage firms' accounts to siphon service fees into the accounts of public pension funds. However, the DLF has evaded an official US designation as a foreign terrorist organization.*[85]

Recently, the United States proposed a multinational agreement that would promote expansion of international agribusiness throughout Europe. For the purposes of this hypothetical, Switzerland happens to be the top international producer of organic foods, with certain farming arrangements that have limited exposure of crops to some of the most ubiquitous pesticides and preservatives. The DLF publicly objects to Swiss participation in this international agribusiness agreement on grounds that it will lead to the introduction of genetically modified organisms into Swiss organic food sources. After posting DLF propaganda that briefly remained on the websites in the US Department of Agriculture and the Swiss Ministry of

[82] *See, e.g.*, Andrew T. Illig, Comment, *Computer Age Protesting: Why Hactivism Is a Viable Option for Modern Social Activists*, 119 PENN. ST. L. REV. 1033, 1036 (2015) ("Hacktivism is, predictably, created by combining the words "hack" and "activism." Generally, hacktivism is defined as using computers to promote social or political ends or to effect social or political change. The politics of civil disobedience are combined with the technological innovations and techniques of an increasingly computer-savvy public to create hacktivism.").

[83] *See* Swathi Padmanabhan, Note, *Hacking for Lulz: Employing Expert Hackers to Combat Cyberterrorism*, 15 VAND. J. ENT. & TECH. L. 191, 194–95 (2012) (describing the common activities and aims of hacking collectives).

[84] *See* Michael S. Urcuyo, Note & Comment, *From Internet Trolls to Seasoned Hackers: Protecting Our Financial Interests from Distributed-Denial-of-Service-Attacks*, 42 RUTGERS COMP. & TECH. L.J. 299, 300 (2016) (defining a Denial of Service attack as a situation "where a hacker or group of hackers employ malicious programs to infect a series of networks or individual computers, which are known as bots, and use the bots to overload a server. Essentially, the hacker is creating artificial traffic to flood the targeted server to crash and deny access to other users.").

[85] *See* 8 U.S.C. § 1189 (discussing the designation of Foreign Terrorist Organizations).

Agriculture, the DLF decided to exert pressure on the Swiss government in another way.

With the World Cup competition set to commence days after to the planned signing of the international agribusiness agreement, 6,871,171 Swiss viewers, approximately 82 percent of the Swiss population, are expected to watch their national team play soccer against international competitors in the United States. US firm Giant Telecommunications will be broadcasting the World Cup games to Switzerland and several other European states. The DLF recently communicated a threat to the Swiss government that it will block all transmissions of Swiss participation in the World Cup games if Switzerland signs on to the International Agribusiness Agreement. As an example of its technological abilities, the DLF blocked transmission of other US stations for five minutes at a designated time resulting in a static screen on nearly all Swiss cable and satellite television sets.

Acting on a tip from a confidential informant within the DLF, a team of US Special Forces apprehended a DLF network administrator as he left a casino in Zurich and transported him to the United States for prosecution under general terrorism provisions[86] *and the Computer Fraud and Abuse Act.*[87] *US personnel obtained a DLF manifesto in the administrator's attaché case, which stated, in part, "The DLF can no longer stand by idly as American agricultural industries poison the last pure food sources in the world. The Swiss government must protect its organic reserves at all costs, or risk losing its most popular pastime—soccer!" The US Attorney General has cited the Protective Principle in support of the prosecution.*

B. Considerations for Extraterritorial Jurisdiction

This hypothetical poses a number of important questions. With the thwarting of the attack on Swiss telecommunications networks, the common principles of extraterritorial jurisdiction would not apply in this case. Similarly, a five-minute disruption to television programs would not likely constitute the type of effect in the United States, let alone Switzerland, that rises to the level of an "important government interest."

A genuine question arises regarding the nature of the potential threat to the United States if the DLF had followed through with its threat to block the World Cup. Would the blockage of transmission of a signal for coverage of a recreational sports competition constitute a potential threat to US economic, financial, or security interests? Would the DLF's intent to prevent transmission of signals into Switzerland prevent the United States from arguing that its interests were

[86] Acts of Terrorism Transcending National Boundaries, 18 U.S.C. § 2332b (2012).
[87] Computer Fraud and Abuse Act, 18 U.S.C. § 1030(a)(3)(5)(1).

implicated since US business satellites were still capable of transmitting television signals? Would the DLF's intent to frustrate the efforts of US private businesses limit the claim that US government interests would even be implicated? Can a US court presume that, if enacted, the DLF's plan would have resulted in Swiss withdrawal from the agreement? Each of these questions would likely relate to the determination of applicability of the Protective Principle or the "nexus" between the DLF defendant and the United States.

1. The Public/Private Distinction

In addressing the blockage of a signal emanating from a US private company, *Reumayr* confirms that it is still possible for US interests to be implicated when aliens influence private rather than public services. As the court noted, even private entities can implicate important government interests when they are inextricably tied to the fuel and economic security of the nation.[88] Thus, Protective jurisdiction could still attach as long as the threat posed by the activity involving the private business interfered with a US interest.

2. The Nature of a Blocked Signal

A more serious concern arises with the nature of the blocked signal. If a court views the blockage of an outgoing signal as something similar to an export control, there would be little support for invoking protective jurisdiction.[89] Arguably, there must be some sort of tangible relationship between the activity that is limited and US vital interests. National security, though a popular basis for jurisdiction, is not likely implicated. While in *Reumayr*, the ultimate act would have resulted in oil production and transport within the United States, arguably having some effect on the plant that generated 8 percent of the nation's oil, even a successful blockage of the satellite signal would not prevent the United States from transmitting the signal to other countries besides Switzerland or receiving communications from other countries' satellites. Along these lines, commentators have suggested that collateral damage to computer systems caused by the Stuxnet virus attack against Iran's nuclear facility would not implicate those eleven countries' important interests for protective jurisdiction because the result was limited to "reversible minor collateral damage."[90]

The limited set of vital US interests implicated by the potential effect of the DLF would have to be rooted in US effects. In this situation, US foreign policy interests exist in multinational agreements relating to food. Thus, if the evidence

[88] *Reumayr*, 530 F. Supp. 2d at 1216 ("To the extent Defendant argues that the Government can have no security interest in private property, the Court roundly rejects such a contention.").

[89] Cameron, *supra* note 8, at 276–77.

[90] Stockton & Golabek-Goldman, *supra* note 2, at 250–51 ("[S]uch relatively minor economic costs and inconvenience did not rise to the level of threatening these nations' vital security interests.").

supported a potential effect on US food security or US food commerce, in the potential withdrawal of Switzerland from an agreement with the United States, this effect could logically fall in line with other types of interests that have been recognized by US courts. Notably, *Reumayr* recognized the US interest in "fuel security and financial security" that would result from a disruption to the US oil supply.[91]

A related question would be whether a court could reasonably and reliably consider a chain of successive hypothetical effects that might ultimately result in a US impact. What if Switzerland rebuffed the threat and entered the agreement despite the blocked signal? What if the United States could recover from Switzerland's withdrawal by importing and exporting food goods through a surrogate? In an interesting discussion, Michael Akehurst raised concerns over where to draw such lines:

> If, for instance, a man commits arson against a factory and the company owning the factory becomes insolvent as a result, the effects may be felt all over the world—losses may be suffered by the company's suppliers, customers, and creditors, not to mention the dependents of the employers of the creditors. Clearly the line must be drawn somewhere. But where?[92]

In some drug smuggling cases, even though the vessel containing large sums of narcotics was not anywhere near the United States, the courts still accepted the possibility that some of the drugs might eventually be introduced into the United States. For example, although the Ninth Circuit Court of Appeals acknowledged a lack of intent to deliver drugs directly to the United States, it upheld exercise of Protective jurisdiction over the defendant because "both economics and geography dictate that at least some portion of the hashish would at some point be found in the United States."[93] Others have sustained perceived connections by reasoning that the harm involved was more severe than that threatened by a false statement to a consular official or a forged customs document.[94] On either of these grounds it seems plausible that a US court could and would find a sufficient nexus between the acts of the DLF and important state interests.

[91] *Reumyr*, 530 F. Supp. 2d at 1222 & n.17.
[92] Akehurst, *supra* note 30, at 154.
[93] *Medjuck*, 156 F.3d at 919.
[94] For an example of this position, *see* Stockton & Golabek-Goldman, *supra* note 2, at 256: "If mere perjury in an immigration proceeding is sufficiently dangerous to warrant protective jurisdiction, then an attack that incapacitates the nation's power grids leaving millions of Americans in the dark for weeks, should also warrant jurisdiction under this doctrine."

3. Defendant's Mens Rea

A final concern posed by the above hypothetical scenario is the mental state of the DLF network administrator. While his intent to cause potential harm in Switzerland is manifest, he could likely argue that he lacked the requisite intent to take any action in the United States. Although his confiscated letter references "American agricultural industries," the letter does not speak of any harm to the United States, and rather focuses upon Switzerland as the object of its threats. This claim would fall on deaf ears. Jurisdiction under the Protective Principle can be applied if the ultimate purpose of the defendant's act is to cause the necessary effect in US territory, or the defendant knew or should have known that the act would have the necessary effect on US interests. As applied to this hypothetical scenario, the pivotal fact, however, is not the secondary aim of the blockage, but rather the primary motive. The DLF is an organization opposed to US trade agreements with other nations. By pressuring Switzerland to withdraw from a US agreement, DLF members' purpose is to impact the United States and limit its interaction with emerging food markets.

Even if DLF's purpose had not been to cause effects in the United States, but the perpetrators had knowledge that their blockage of the signal could likely affect the vital government interest of food security, jurisdiction would still apply. Further, as in narcotics smuggling cases, the defendant need not be certain regarding every consequence of his or her act. Rather, the defendant must intend or know that some of the consequences are likely to take seat in US territory. Lack of access to food is little different from lack of access to oil in this regard, raising similar justifications for application of Protective jurisdiction based on the defendant's mens rea.

This hypothetical is just one example of how wide the barn door has been opened in the application of the Protective Principle.

V. Conclusion

The Protective Principle is now more necessary than ever due to the prevalence of non-state actors committing criminal acts abroad for political purposes. However, it remains the most controversial of all bases for extraterritorial jurisdiction and prone to abuse. For example, this chapter posed a semi-realistic hypothetical involving the threatened blockage of US satellite signals to Switzerland during the World Cup competition. Thus, a private hacktivist who never left his home in Bern, Switzerland, could face prosecution at a courtroom in Peoria.

This hypothetical should hopefully assist in contemplating the incredibly nuanced Protective jurisdiction tool against non-state actors who are still in the planning stages of their transborder terrorist activities.

16

Diversifying the Sources of Evidence in Terrorism Cases before Criminal Courts in (Post-)Conflict and High-Risk Situations

The Role of the Military

Bibi van Ginkel, Christophe Paulussen, & Tanya Mehra[1]

I. Introduction

A. General Context

A key component of global counterterrorism efforts since 2001 has been the promotion of effective criminal justice responses to terrorism that fully comply with the rule of law and international law. The ultimate aim of this approach is to end impunity for terrorist suspects by bringing them to justice. Yet bringing terrorism suspects to justice for the full scope of the crimes committed can be difficult. This

[1] This chapter is heavily based on earlier publications by the authors on this topic, including B. van Ginkel & C. Paulussen, *The Role of the Military in Securing Suspects and Evidence in the Prosecution of Terrorism Cases before Civilian Courts: Legal and Practical Challenges*, 6 The International Centre for Counter-Terrorism—The Hague, no. 4 (2015), available at https://www.icct.nl/download/file/ICCT-Van-Ginkel-Paulussen-The-Role-Of-The-Military-In-Securing-Suspects-And-Evidence-In-The-Prosecution-Of-Terrorism-Cases-Before-Civilian-Courts.pdf; B. van Ginkel, *Prosecuting Foreign Terrorist Fighters: What Role for the Military?*, 7 The International Centre for Counter-Terrorism—The Hague, no. 1 (2016), available at http://icct.nl/app/uploads/2016/05/ICCT-VanGinkel-Prosecuting-Foreign-Terrorist-Fighters-May2016-2.pdf, as well as their involvement in the development of instruments such as UN CTED, *Guidelines to facilitate the use and admissibility as evidence in national criminal courts of information collected, handled, preserved and shared by the military to prosecute terrorist offences*, Dec. 2019, available at https://www.un.org/sc/ctc/wp-content/uploads/2020/01/Battlefield_Evidence_Final.pdf; and GCTF, *Abuja Recommendations on the Collection, Use and Sharing of Evidence for Purposes of Criminal Prosecution of Terrorist Suspects*, 2018, available at https://www.thegctf.org/Portals/1/Documents/Framework%20Documents/2018/GCTF-Abuja-Recommendations_ENG.pdf?ver=2018-09-21-122246-523&timestamp=1580219129062.

Bibi van Ginkel, Christophe Paulussen, & Tanya Mehra, *Diversifying the Sources of Evidence in Terrorism Cases before Criminal Courts in (Post-)Conflict and High-Risk Situations* In: *Between Crime and War*. Edited by: Claire Finkelstein, Christopher Fuller, Jens David Ohlin, Mitt Regan, Oxford University Press. DOI: 10.1093/oso/9780197638798.003.0017

can be the case in purely domestic situations or in situations where the prosecuting state is not the same as the state where the crimes were committed.

Indeed, investigators and prosecutors may face a number of challenges when securing evidence in such situations: it may be impossible to physically travel to war-torn regions to collect evidence, the prosecuting state may not have entered into a judicial cooperation agreement with the state where the crime has been committed, there may not be a legitimate government with which such agreements can be concluded, or the government in place does not have effective control over the area in which the evidence is located. This challenge has received considerable attention in relation to the alleged crimes committed by foreign terrorist fighters (FTFs), especially in Syria and Iraq. It is important to state, however, that the challenge already existed prior to this phenomenon.

B. Facing the Challenge

To face this challenge, new policies and new practices have emerged to improve the evidence collection in areas that are not easily accessible for law enforcement officers. On the international policy level, the United Nations (UN) has first referenced to this challenge and the potential role the military can play in this respect in the 2015 Madrid Guiding Principles.[2] This reference was followed by a paragraph in the preamble of UN Security Council Resolution 2396 (2017) in which the Council recognized that member states "face challenges in obtaining admissible evidence (. . .) from conflict zones that can be used to help prosecute and secure the conviction of foreign terrorist fighters and those supporting foreign terrorist fighters."[3] This has ultimately led to the development, by the United Nations Counter-Terrorism Committee Executive Directorate (UN CTED), of the "Guidelines to facilitate the use and admissibility as evidence in national criminal courts of information collected, handled, preserved and shared by the military to prosecute terrorist offences" (hereinafter UN CTED's Military Evidence Guidelines).[4] These guidelines, as is explicitly stated in the preface, are a first attempt at the international level to address this issue, and they should be understood to be a living document, which requires review based on evolving experiences and views of relevant stakeholders. Beyond the context

[2] UN CTC, *Madrid Guiding Principles- A practical tool for Member States to stem the flow of foreign terrorist fighters*, Dec. 23, 2015, U.N. Doc. S/2015/939, at 16 available at https://www.un.org/sc/ctc/wp-content/uploads/2016/10/Madrid-Guiding-Principles_EN.pdf.

[3] UN Security Council Resolution 2396 of Dec. 21, 2017 (S/RES/2396 (2017)), Preamble.

[4] UN CTED, *Guidelines to facilitate the use and admissibility as evidence in national criminal courts of information collected, handled, preserved and shared by the military to prosecute terrorist offences*, Dec. 2019, available at https://www.un.org/sc/ctc/wp-content/uploads/2020/01/Battlefield_Evidence_Final.pdf.

of the UN, the Global Counterterrorism Forum (GCTF) also referenced to the role of the military in the collection, use, and sharing of evidence in the "Abuja Recommendations on the Collection, Use and Sharing of Evidence for Purposes of Criminal Prosecution of Terrorist Suspects."[5] At the regional level, one could refer to the recent "Eurojust Memorandum on Battlefield Evidence,"[6] or the NATO Battlefield Evidence Policy and NATO Practical Framework for Technical Exploitation.[7] At the national level, the United States (US) has developed "Non-Binding Guiding Principles on Use of Battlefield Evidence in Civilian Criminal Proceedings."[8] Inspired by all these developments, also other organizations, such as the Organization for Security and Co-operation in Europe (OSCE), are currently developing their own guidelines.[9] Moreover, the Council of Europe has established a Working Group on the Gathering of Evidence from Conflict Zones for the Purpose of Criminal Prosecutions.[10]

The scope of all these initiatives differs. Some focus on so-called "military evidence," whereas others refer to the term "battlefield evidence." Military evidence refers to information that has been collected by the military in (post-)conflict or high-risk situations. This could be the national military, foreign military, or international forces, such as the Global Coalition against Da'esh. Battlefield evidence, on the other hand, refers to information from the conflict zone collected by a variety of actors other than regular law enforcement actors. This could include the military, but also other actors such as International Commissions of Inquiry, Independent Fact-Finding Missions, international mechanisms mandated to collect evidence, and finally, specialized nongovernmental organizations (NGOs) that document international humanitarian law and international human rights law violations and abuses.

An example is the International, Impartial and Independent Mechanism (IIIM), which has been established based on UN General Assembly Resolution 71/248 (2016)[11] to assist in the investigation and prosecution of persons

[5] GCTF, *Abuja Recommendation on the Collection, Use and Sharing of Evidence for Purposes of Criminal Prosecution of Terrorist Suspects*, Sept. 2018, available at https://www.thegctf.org/Portals/1/Documents/Framework%20Documents/2018/GCTF-Abuja-Recommendations_ENG.pdf?ver=2018-09-21-122246-523&timestamp=1580219129062.

[6] Eurojust, *Eurojust Memorandum on Battlefield Evidence*, Sept. 2020, available at https://www.eurojust.europa.eu/sites/default/files/2020-09/2020-09-14-Eurojust-Memorandum-on-Battlefield-Evidence.pdf.

[7] NATO, *NATO Allies agree Policy on Battlefield Evidence from operational theatres to boost efforts against terrorism*," Oct. 22 and 23, 2020, available at https://www.nato.int/cps/en/natohq/news_179194.htm?selectedLocale=en.

[8] Available at https://theiij.org/wp-content/uploads/Non-Binding-Guiding-Principles-on-Use-of-Battlefield-Evidence-EN.pdf.

[9] Representatives of this organization have confirmed this to the authors.

[10] See the Terms of Reference of the Council of Europe Working Group on the Gathering of Evidence from Conflict Zones for the Purpose of Criminal Prosecutions, available at https://rm.coe.int/cdct-ge-2019-01rev-eng-terms-of-reference-/168096f748.

[11] U.N. Doc. A/RES/71/248, Jan. 11, 2017.

responsible for the most serious crimes under international law committed in the Syrian Arab Republic since March 2011.[12] The scope of the IIIM is broader in the sense that it focuses on the most serious crimes under international law, and not only on terrorism crimes. It also diversifies the sources of evidence that it can investigate and works with different partners and actors that collect the information, including the Independent International Commission of Inquiry on the Syrian Arab Republic, other international and regional organizations, UN entities, state actors, NGOs, foundations, and individuals. This information will be shared only with countries that will provide a fair trial and are able to prosecute the alleged crimes as international crimes. According to its latest report, the IIIM has received a total of sixty-six requests for assistance from eleven countries.[13] A similar but certainly not identical mechanism is the UN Investigative Team to Promote Accountability for Crimes Committed by Da'esh/Islamic State in Iraq and the Levant (UNITAD), which is mandated to only investigate and collect information and evidence committed by Da'esh/ISIL. After the call for assistance by the Iraqi government, UNITAD was established by the UN Secretary-General at the request of the UN Security Council (UN Security Council Resolution 2379 (2017)).[14] Although the primary recipient of the information and evidence collected by UNITAD are the Iraqi authorities, UNITAD has provided assistance to other domestic authorities as well, such as those in Finland.[15]

C. Scope and Structure

The preceding examples show there is a proliferation of international, regional, and national initiatives trying to address the challenges regular law enforcement actors face, considering the (post-)conflict and high-risk circumstances in which collecting information that can serve as evidence in terrorism cases sometimes needs to take place. The scope of this chapter is limited to the role of the military in collecting such information for the purpose of terrorism cases before national civilian criminal courts.

[12] *See* the terms of reference of the IIIM, available at https://iiim.un.org/terms-of-reference-of-iiim/.

[13] Report of the International, Impartial and Independent Mechanism to Assist in the Investigation and Prosecution of Persons Responsible for the Most Serious Crimes under International Law Committed in the Syrian Arab Republic since March 2011, A/75/311, Aug. 13, 2020, para. 3.

[14] U.N. Doc. S/RES/2379 (2017), Sept. 21, 2017.

[15] Fourth report of the Special Adviser and Head of the United Nations Investigative Team to Promote Accountability for Crimes Committed by Da'esh/Islamic State in Iraq and the Levant, S/2020/386, May 11, 2020, para. 83.

In our view, the reality that the military—whether national forces, foreign forces, or international troops—are often the first to arrive at a scene where they may find information that could be of relevance in later terrorism trials justifies a closer look at the potential role the military could play in this context. However, because the military is not an actor particularly trained or equipped to fulfill this task, allowing the military to collect information that could be used as evidence in terrorism cases raises both legal and practical challenges that will be addressed in this chapter.

Although, as mentioned before, the international community started to pay attention to this topic especially when confronted with the challenges of prosecuting FTFs, our scope focuses on the use of information collected by the military for terrorism crimes more generally, not limited to crimes committed by FTFs. Furthermore, and while admitting that the information collected by the military could be used by various end users (including tribunals), we will focus on national criminal courts, either in the country in which the crimes were committed, or in a foreign state, such as the state of the nationality of the perpetrator. The scope of his chapter is thus limited with regard to the actor performing the information collection, the alleged crimes for which this information is used, and the court ruling on the admissibility of the information as evidence.

In this chapter, we will discuss a select number of legal and practical challenges that this topic engenders and provide recommendations to overcome these challenges. We understand the topic is controversial, and we realize that criticism is possible from various sides: the military itself may not be too happy with yet additional tasks, whereas especially human rights lawyers will be wary about providing the military with tasks that should be within the domain of law enforcement specialists. Before we delve into the specifics, it is therefore important to stress, from the start, that the rule of thumb should always be: as civilian as possible and only as military as needed. Moreover, our normative framework in thinking about counterterrorism was, is, and will always remain compliance with international law and the rule of law. In the words of the UN Security Council:

> *Reaffirming* that Member States must ensure that any measures taken to counter terrorism comply with all their obligations under international law, in particular international human rights law, international refugee law, and international humanitarian law, *underscoring* that respect for human rights, fundamental freedoms and the rule of law are complementary and mutually reinforcing with effective counter-terrorism measures, and are an essential part of a successful counter-terrorism effort and notes the importance of respect for the rule of law so as to effectively prevent and combat terrorism, and *noting* that failure to comply with these and other international obligations, including

> under the Charter of the United Nations, is one of the factors contributing to increased radicalization and fosters a sense of impunity[.][16]

This chapter is structured as follows. In section II, we will explain the current context of terrorism prosecutions and the challenge of securing evidence, in particular in relation to the conflict in Syria and Iraq. In section III, we will discuss a number of scenarios in which the military can be involved. This includes information related to previous and comparable situations in which the military has played a role, and from which lessons can be learned. In section IV, the focus will be on a number of legal and practical military challenges, whereas in section V, we will offer some concluding observations.

II. Contextualizing the Problem

From the moment the conflict started in Syria in 2011, some forty thousand men and women from practically all corners of the world traveled to the conflict zone to join the different parties in the conflict, including terrorist organizations such as Al Nusra and the organization that calls itself the Islamic State (IS), also referred to as ISIL, ISIS, or Da'esh (hereinafter: IS). [17] Allegedly one-third of these FTFs or foreign fighters (FFs)[18] have returned, and taking into account the military collapse of IS, the question is of course what will happen with the rest of these individuals. These FTFs may join other conflicts, relocate, or return home. In view of the terrorist attacks inspired or carried out by IS outside Syria and Iraq, such as the attacks in Brussels,[19]

[16] U.N. Security Council Resolution 2178 of Sept. 24, 2014 (S/RES/2178 (2014)), Preamble.

[17] This section is heavily based on B. van Ginkel, *Prosecuting Foreign Terrorist Fighters: What Role for the Military?*, 7 The International Centre for Counter-Terrorism—The Hague, no. 1 (2016), available at http://icct.nl/app/uploads/2016/05/ICCT-VanGinkel-Prosecuting-Foreign-Terrorist-Fighters-May2016-2.pdf.

[18] The UN and the GCTF, for instance, refer to FTFs, whereas the European Union rather uses the term foreign fighter (FFs). The GCTF refers to "individuals who travel abroad to a State other than their States of residence or nationality to engage in, undertake, plan, prepare, carry out or otherwise support terrorist activity or to provide or receive training to do so." The UN , inspired by the GCTF, defines FTFs as "individuals who travel to a State other than their States of residence or nationality for the purpose of the perpetration, planning, or preparation of, or participation in, terrorist acts or the providing or receiving of terrorist training, including in connection with armed conflict." (UN Security Council 2178 of Sept. 24, 2014 (S/RES/2178 (2014)), Preamble).

[19] On May 24, 2014, Mehdi Nemmouche shot dead two men and a woman at the Brussels Jewish Museum. A few days later he was arrested in Marseille by the French authorities. The French counterterrorism police claimed that Nemmouche had returned from Syria in 2013 and that they since then had him under surveillance. *See Brussels Fatal Gun Attack at Jewish Museum*, BBC News, May 24, 2014, available at http://www.bbc.com/news/world-europe-27558918; and A. Penketh, *Brussels Jewish Museum Shooting: Suspect with Islamist Links Arrested*, The Guardian, June 1, 2014, available at http://www.theguardian.com/world/2014/jun/01/suspect-arrest-brussels-jewish-museum-shooting.

Beirut,[20] Paris,[21] Istanbul,[22] and Manchester,[23] the urgency to take effective action was highly felt at the international, regional, and national level. The involvement of (returning) FTFs might range from inspiring, planning, plotting, coordinating, recruiting, or directly being involved in carrying out terrorist attacks. In some cases, FTFs may be involved in helping other FTFs to relocate to a third country and help establish a terrorist cell or organization.[24]

Many European states are reluctant to repatriate their own citizens, due to the security risk FTFs may pose but also because of the perceived legal challenges. In 2015, prosecutors indicated several challenges in successfully bringing FTFs to justice. Many relied on preexisting ordinary crimes as some countries had, by then, not yet implemented UN Security Council Resolution 2178 (2014), which allowed prosecutors more than before to charge FTFs for preparatory offences. Moreover, prosecutors were experiencing many difficulties in generating admissible evidence.[25]

Some states have stressed the importance of prosecution of suspects of terrorist crimes in the region itself. In Iraq, indeed, a significant number of terrorist cases have been brought before Iraqi criminal courts. These trials are, however, heavily criticized by human rights organizations for the lack of respect for fair trial principles.[26] There have also been proposals tabled to set up

[20] On November 12, 2015, a suicide-bomber committed a terrorist attack on behalf of IS in Beirut, killing 43 people, and leaving 239 wounded. *See* G. Botelho, P. Cruickshank, & C.E. Shoichet, *Beirut Suicide Bombings Kill 43; Suspect Claims ISIS Sent Attackers*, CNN, Nov. 16, 2015, available at http://edition.cnn.com/2015/11/12/middleeast/beirut-explosions/.

[21] On November 13, 2015, seven coordinated terrorist attacks were executed in Paris targeting a football stadium where an international match took place between France and Germany, people in restaurants and on terraces, and a concert hall. The ten attackers killed 130 people and wounded 368. IS claimed responsibility for the attacks. Many of the perpetrators had previously been in Syria. See more elaborate on the Paris attack: G. Chauzal et al., *Paris 11/13/15: Analysis and Policy Options*, Clingendael Policy Brief, Nov. 2015, available at http://www.clingendael.nl/sites/default/files/Policy_Brief_Clingendael_ICCT-Paris111315Analysis_and_Policy_Options_November%202015_final.pdf.

[22] A suicide bomber killed 22 persons during an Ariane Grande concert in Manchester. IS claimed responsibility for the attack. *See* L. Dearden, *Manchester Arena Attack: Isis Claims Responsibility for Suicide Bombing That Killed at Least 22 People*, The Independent, May 23, 2017, available at https://www.independent.co.uk/news/uk/home-news/manchester-arena-attack-isis-responsible-claim-suicide-bombing-islamic-state-ariana-grande-concert-a7751221.html.

[23] Just shortly after midnight on January 2017 a gunman shot 39 persons in a nightclub in Istanbul. IS claimed responsibility for the attack. *See* J. Grierson, *Isis Claims Istanbul Nightclub Attack as Perpetrator Remains at Large*, The Guardian, Jan. 3, 2017, available at https://www.theguardian.com/world/2017/jan/02/isis-group-claims-responsibility-for-istanbul-nightclub-attack.

[24] UN CTED, *The Challenge of Returning and Relocating Foreign Terrorist Fighters: Research Perspectives*, CTED Trends Report, Mar. 2018, available at https://www.un.org/sc/ctc/wp-content/uploads/2018/04/CTED-Trends-Report March-2018.pdf

[25] Report of the Counter-Terrorism Committee to the UN Security Council on the Sixth Prosecutors Seminar on Bringing Terrorists to Justice, U.N. Doc. S/2015/123, Feb. 23, 2015, available at https://www.un.org/sc/ctc/wp-content/uploads/2015/09/S_2015_123_EN.pdf.

[26] *See, e.g.*, Human Rights Watch, *Flawed Justice; Accountability for ISIS Crimes in Iraq*," Dec. 5, 2017, available at https://www.hrw.org/report/2017/12/05/flawed-justice/accountability-isis-crimes-iraq. *See also* United Nations Assistance Mission for Iraq and Office of the United Nations High

a special international(ized) criminal tribunal in the region,[27] but so far there is not enough international support to make that a reality.[28]

In this situation, one also considered the role that other domestic courts could play in adjudicating the crimes committed by terrorists. But as indicated, several challenges can be identified in this process. One of these is obviously the still continuing chaotic and insecure situation in the region and the implications this has for collecting evidence. Local prosecutors might get overwhelmed with the sheer number of cases, meaning they lack the capacity to organize themselves properly. Besides this practical issue, there are also political challenges for foreign prosecutors and courts that could make cooperation with the local law enforcement authorities problematic. In the case of crimes committed in Syria and Iraq, these political challenges relate to the problem that, for instance, many governments do not recognize Assad's government in Syria to be the legitimate authority. The same goes for cooperation with the Kurdish authorities (and possible implications for states vis-à-vis their relationship with Turkey).[29] The region controlled by the Kurdish authorities is not internationally recognized as a distinct country, making it difficult to conclude cooperation agreements. Moreover, it is also not clear which laws they would apply in relation to local prosecutions and whether their courts would be able to render justice in accordance with international fair trial standards.[30]

Foreign prosecutors could base their case on testimonies of fellow FTFs or on data obtained from a confiscated mobile phone, and—when very lucky—on

Commissioner for Human Rights, *Human Rights in the Administration of Justice in Iraq: Trials under the anti-terrorism laws and implications for justice, accountability and social cohesion in the aftermath of ISIL*, Jan. 2020, available at https://reliefweb.int/sites/reliefweb.int/files/resources/Iraq_-_ISIL_trials_under_the_anti-terrorism_laws_and_the_implications_for_justice_28012020.pdf.

[27] The Dutch Minister of Foreign Affairs Blok announced an initiative to explore the options to set up "an international trial in the region" for crimes committed by IS during the UN GA Summit of September 2019 in New York, see The Government of the Netherlands, *The Netherlands: ISIS cannot go unpunished*, Sept. 26, 2019, available at https://www.government.nl/latest/news/2019/09/26/the-netherlands-isis-cannot-go-unpunished.

[28] See for an overview of the legal and political challenges regarding the establishment of a special court for terrorist crimes, B. van Ginkel, *Special Court for Terrorism Crimes*, Max Planck Encyclopedia of International Law, Mar. 2020, available at https://opil.ouplaw.com/view/10.1093/law-mpeipro/e3229.013.3229/law-mpeipro-e3229?rskey=YFDZWM&result=1&prd=OPIL.

[29] *See also* Eurojust, "Foreign Fighters: Eurojust's Views on the Phenomenon and the Criminal Justice Response," Updated Report, Summary of Main Findings, Jan. 2015, at 3 available at https://www.statewatch.org/media/documents/news/2015/feb/eu-eurojust-foreign-fighters.pdf, and the Note from the EU Counter-Terrorism Coordinator to the Council, "Foreign Fighters And Returnees: Discussion Paper," Dec. 2, 2014, 15715/2/14 REV 2, at 4.

[30] *See* N. Harley, *Swedish Female ISIS Supporters May Be Tried in Syria for Terrorism Offences*, The National News, Oct. 12, 2020, available at https://www.thenationalnews.com/world/swedish-female-isis-supporters-may-be-tried-in-syria-for-terrorism-offences-1.1092495?utm_campaign=1607733_&utm_medium=email&utm_source=iterable.

data stemming from registration forms of new IS recruits.[31] Due to the presence of a large number of refugees and asylum seekers, some foreign prosecutors are seeking help from refugees to investigate terrorist crimes committed in Syria and Iraq.[32] But in most cases, the prosecutor is faced with many difficulties in collecting the necessary evidence, and might need to rely on internet-based information or social media postings—which has its own set of challenges.[33] Alternatively, prosecutors might need to base their case on intelligence information[34] that subsequently needs to be transposed into information that can be used in a civilian court case, respecting the rights of the defendant who should have the possibility to challenge the evidence.[35]

Due to all these evidentiary obstacles, a prosecutor might decide on a prosecutorial strategy that avoids or limits having to deal with most of these issues, yet allows for sufficient possibilities to at least secure a conviction.

Prosecutors may settle for a prosecutorial strategy merely based on proving conspiracy to commit a terrorist attack or preparatory acts to commit murder or manslaughter.[36] An example is the conviction of Maher H. by a Dutch Appeals Court to four years' imprisonment.[37] Neither the District Court nor the Appeals

[31] In March 2016, a former IS operative handed over a memory stick with the files of 22,000 IS recruits to Sky news. The memory stick was stolen from the head of IS's internal security police. *See* S. Ramsay, *IS Documents Identify Thousands of Jihadis*, Sky News, Mar. 9, 2016, available at https://news.sky.com/story/is-documents-identify-thousands-of-jihadis-10198557.

[32] T. Mehra, *Bringing (Foreign) Terrorist Fighters to Justice in a Post-ISIS Landscape, Part II: Prosecution by Foreign National Courts*, ICCT Perspective, Jan. 12, 2018, available at https://icct.nl/publication/bringing-foreign-terrorist-fighters-to-justice-in-a-post-isis-landscape-part-ii-prosecution-by-foreign-national-courts/.

[33] Electronic evidence may often be encrypted or stored in multiple locations, posing significant challenges for the prosecutors to identify the location of the service providers in order to submit a data preservation request. In addition, electronic evidence is easily volatile and easily altered and can raise issues regarding the reliability of electronic evidence in court. *See, e.g.*, the list of challenges put together by Eurojust: Eurojust, "Foreign Fighters: Eurojust's Views on the Phenomenon and the Criminal Justice Response," Updated Report, Summary of Main Findings, Jan. 2015, at 6–7, available at https://www.statewatch.org/media/documents/news/2015/feb/eu-eurojust-foreign-fighters.pdf.

[34] See on the use of intelligence in court more elaborately Q. Eijkman & B. van Ginkel, *Compatible or Incompatible? Intelligence and Human Rights in Terrorist Trials*, 2 The International Centre for Counter-Terrorism—The Hague, no. 3 (2011), available at http://dx.doi.org/10.19165/2011.1.03.

[35] The principle of equality of arms, as an element of the right to a fair trial, is included in various international human rights documents, such as Article 14 of the International Covenant on Civil and Political Rights, and Article 6 of the European Convention on Human Rights.

[36] As part of the *Sharia4Belgium* case against 36 suspects, the Court of First Instance of Antwerp based part of the convictions on the testimonies of Jejoen Bontinck, who returned from Syria. *See* Rechtbank van eerste aanleg Antwerpen, Press Release on the "Syria Fighters Trial," Jan. 14, 2015, available at http://www.rechtbankeersteaanlegantwerpen.be/index.php/83-persinformatie/110-terro. And more elaborate on the *Sharia4Belgium* case, C. Paulussen & E. Entenmann, *National Responses in Select Western European Countries to the Foreign Fighter Phenomenon*, *in* Foreign Fighters under International Law and Beyond 391–422 (A. de Guttry, F. Capone, & C. Paulussen eds., 2016).

[37] Judgment of the Appeals Court of The Hague of July 7, 2016, Case 22-005306-14 (in Dutch); see for an English summary of the case in first instance: Judgment of the District Court of The Hague

Court could prove whether he had actually committed terrorist attacks in Syria, but the Court argued that merely traveling to Syria and joining jihadi groups in Syria was enough to convict him for preparing to commit terrorist crimes, including murder and manslaughter.[38]

In an Austrian case, a person was found guilty of membership of a terrorist organization[39] and a Dutch court in the so-called *Context* case against nine suspects convicted four of them for, inter alia, participating in a terrorist training camp and conspiracy to commit murder or manslaughter with a terrorist motive in Syria.[40] Conspiracy crimes are easier to prove than actual murder with terrorist intent, since one does not need, for instance, to prove the identity of the person who is murdered, which in many instances is not possible. The verdict was based on evidence retrieved from social media, tapped phone calls, and testimonies of fellow FTFs who returned to the Netherlands and were subsequently questioned by the prosecutor.[41]

In December 2015, a Swedish court convicted two FTFs to life for their participation in the fighting in Syria in 2013. Interestingly, the Court was able to establish that the two suspects were in Syria in 2013 and participated in the fighting, but was not able to prove to what group the two had pledged their allegiance. Video evidence was used featuring two killings, one of which was a beheading. The two men were seen in the two videos, but did not participate in the actual killings but rather in the celebrations in the background. The court argued that even though there was no proof that the two had pledged allegiance to a specific terrorist group, "the purpose of the crime was to incite fear in people in Syria and other countries," which was apparently enough to convict them for terrorist crimes.[42]

of Dec. 1, 2014, Case 09/767116-14, available at http://www.internationalcrimesdatabase.org/Case/3278.

[38] C. Paulussen & E. Entenmann, *National Responses in Select Western European Countries to the Foreign Fighter Phenomenon*, *in* FOREIGN FIGHTERS UNDER INTERNATIONAL LAW AND BEYOND 413–14 (A. de Guttry, F. Capone, & C. Paulussen (eds.), 2016).

[39] The suspect traveled to Syria in 2013 in order to join a training camp of Jabhat al-Nusra. The prosecutor only managed to prove his presence in the training camp, not the concrete activities that took place in this camp, nor his intention to commit terrorist attacks, see Europol, European Union Terrorism Situation and Trend Report (TE-SAT) 2015, at 15, available at https://www.europol.europa.eu/activities-services/main-reports/european-union-terrorism-situation-and-trend-report-2015.

[40] *Context* case, Judgement of the District Court of The Hague of Dec. 10, 2015, available at http://www.internationalcrimesdatabase.org/Case/3270.

[41] *See* for more information on the case, Dec. 17, 2015, http://www.internationalcrimesdatabase.org/home/newsarchive. The Judgment (in Dutch) can be found at http://deeplink.rechtspraak.nl/uitspraak?id=ECLI:NL:RBDHA:2015:14365.

[42] Europol, *European Union Terrorism Situation and Trend Report (TE-SAT)*, 2016, at 18–19 available at https://www.europol.europa.eu/sites/default/files/documents/europol_tesat_2016.pdf.

In Belgium, several trials have taken place. The *Sharia4Belgium* case is so far considered Europe's biggest trial against forty-six suspects of Islamist violent extremism in Syria.[43] Of these suspects, thirty-six were tried in absentia. Some of these suspects were also convicted for terrorist activities in Syria, based on evidence collected on social media, tapped phone calls, and testimonies of returnees.

These examples[44] show that prosecutors are able to conclude successful prosecutions but mostly have to rely on evidence found elsewhere than on the battlefield, and that the prosecuted crimes focus on membership of a terrorist organization, inchoate offences, or ordinary crimes, leaving the actual terrorist crimes untouched.

From the perspective of the victims of these terrorist acts, who understandably want to know what happened exactly to their loved ones, this lack of focusing on the actual crimes, while maybe understandable from a prosecutorial perspective, is unsatisfying. Nonetheless, the (physical) defeat the caliphate, and thus the improved access to the various crime scenes, may lead to more court cases in which the suspect is charged with specific and actual crimes. Also the work of the already-discussed IIIM and UNITAD has already assisted in that respect. And this brings us back again to the role that the military can play in this context.

III. A Role for the Military

A. Introduction

As indicated earlier, the start of an investigation into terrorist crimes should ideally be fully dealt with by civil authorities alone and not by the military. However, realities on the ground might on occasion render this very difficult or simply impossible. At the same time, military personnel might be confronted with significant and even crucial evidence of terrorist crimes in (post-)conflict and

[43] Rechtbank van eerste aanleg Antwerpen (Court of First Instance in Antwerp), Press Release on the "Syrian Fighters Trial," Jan. 14, 2015, available at http://www.rechtbankeersteaanlegantwerpen.be/index.php/83-persinformatie. *See* for a detailed analysis of this judgment, C. Paulussen & E. Entenmann, *National Responses in Select Western European Countries to the Foreign Fighter Phenomenon*, *in* Foreign Fighters under International Law and Beyond 396–99 (A. de Guttry, F. Capone, & C. Paulussen eds., 2016).

[44] *See* for more examples the International Crimes Database's special section on foreign fighters, http://www.internationalcrimesdatabase.org/ForeignFighters; *see also* C. Paulussen & K. Pitcher, *Prosecuting (Potential) Foreign Fighters: Legislative and Practical Challenges*, 8 The International Centre for Counter-Terrorism—The Hague, no. 13 (2018), available at https://icct.nl/wp-content/uploads/2018/01/ICCT-Paulussen-Pitcher-Prosecuting-Potential-Foreign-Fighters-Legislative-Practical-Challenges-Jan2018.pdf.

high-risk situations. This could be documents containing relevant information about membership of terrorist organizations, cell phones and forensic information, such as fingerprints on improvised explosive devices (IEDs), or weapons retrieved from the battlefield.

An illustrative case is the UK *Sardar* case. London's Woolwich Crown Court convicted Sardar of murder and conspiracy to commit murder in 2015 in relation to the IEDs that he and another terrorist had built in Syria. An American soldier, Randy Johnson, was killed by one of these devices during the 2007 "Surge" Operation in Iraq. An American Army Explosive Ordinance Disposal (EOD) Team had examined the bomb components in Iraq and took fingerprints. When Sardar arrived at Heathrow Airport two months after the attack, his fingerprints were taken. In 2012, during a separate investigation, police officers found bomb-making instructions on a computer during a search of his house. Yet it took seven years before officials at the FBI's terrorist explosive device analytical center found Sardar's fingerprints on two of the bombs, but not on the bomb that killed Johnson. All four bombs had the prints of his co-conspirator, and Sardar admitted to being part of the bomb-making cell.[45]

The military may be confronted with such information and objects in different situations: they may run into it accidentally, while on a regular military mission, they may be the first responders after a terrorist attack, and they may be on a specific anti-terrorism mission with the objective to collect information, based on prior (intelligence) information that triggered the specific assignment.

This is not just theory. US troops, during one of their operations, confiscated a large set of IS membership cards at the battlefield, filled out by FTFs upon entry into the terrorist organization. The membership card information was shared with intelligence services of various other states.[46] A first conviction based on this information in Europe was issued in Denmark by the District Court of Glostrup. According to Europol this membership card information:

> (. . .) offered the possibility to indicate one's role for IS and was made available by foreign authorities. It contained information on a Danish citizen charged with terrorist offences. In the form, he had been registered as a fighter. Reference to the form was made when questioning the accused about his role

[45] *See* H. Siddique, *London Cab Driver Guilty of Making Bombs to Kill US Soldiers in Iraq*, The Guardian, May 21, 2015, available at https://www.theguardian.com/uk-news/2015/may/21/london-cab-driver-guilty-ied-bombs-us-soldiers-iraq.

[46] Europol, *European Union Terrorism Situation and Trend Report (TE-SAT) 2018*, https://www.europol.europa.eu/activities-services/main-reports/european-union-terrorism-situation-and-trend-report-2018-tesat-2018, p. 18; Eurojust, *Foreign Terrorist Fighters: Eurojust's Views on the Phenomenon and the Criminal Justice Response*, Fourth Eurojust Report, Nov. 2016, at 14, available at http://statewatch.org/news/2017/mar/eu-eurojust-foreign-fighters-legal-response-report-restricted-11-16.pdf.

> within the terrorist organisation. The court held that his statement about his tasks, mainly cooking and serving food, was not reliable. Based on this and other evidence, the accused was found guilty, amongst other charges, of joining a terrorist organisation and sentenced to 6 years' imprisonment.[47]

The information retrieved from these membership cards has contributed to inter alia the in absentia conviction of a Dutch FTF to a prison sentence of six years, even though the individual is still believed to be in Syria.[48]

Hence, the question is therefore not so much *whether* the military will and can play a role in these situations—they will and can—but rather to ensure that the conditions are fulfilled so that they can effectively contribute to successful law enforcement efforts to end impunity for terrorist crimes in full conformity with international law and the rule of law

B. Lessons Learned from Previous Experiences

Given their role, mandates, and current tasks, it is understandable that not only human rights lawyers but also the military *themselves*—even if they realize assistance in this context may have operational value[49]—may not be very enthusiastic about taking on new responsibilities. Nonetheless, history shows that the military has in fact *already* been engaged in the sort of tasks discussed in this chapter—and that certain lessons can be learned from these situations.

For example, the military has already been involved in collecting information that could be used later as evidence in trials, not related to alleged crimes committed by terrorists that will lead to civilian trials before regular criminal courts—the focus of this chapter—but related to alleged crimes committed by military personnel themselves that will lead to trials before military courts. Best practices stemming from these latter investigations, conducted by the military police or provosts—such as the *Koninklijke Marechaussee* in the Netherlands or the *Gendarmerie Nationale* in France—could be used for this new context as well. For instance, to make prosecution possible, countries often sign a Status

[47] Europol, *European Union Terrorism Situation and Trend Report (TE-SAT) 2017*, at 19, available at https://www.europol.europa.eu/sites/default/files/documents/tesat2017_0.pdf.

[48] Europol, *European Union Terrorism Situation and Trend Report (TE-SAT) 2019*, at 22–23, available at https://www.europol.europa.eu/publications events/main-reports/terrorism-situation-and-trend-report-2019-te-sat.

[49] Indeed, being able to provide proper assistance in this context will also have operational value. After all, a correct evidence collection will enable a status determination of the detainee (operational interest), a failure to adhere to proper evidence collection will lead to an inability to prosecute (which is also an operational interest) and to correctly assist in local criminal proceedings is a critical element in counter-insurgency operations (which is again an operational interest). *See* Van Ginkel & Paulussen, *supra* note 1, at 16.

of Forces Agreement (SOFA), which is "[a]n agreement concluded between a troop-sending State or an international organization and the troop-receiving State, regulating the status of the troop-sending State's forces while present in the troop-receiving State."[50] Although these SOFAs usually "prescribe the exclusive right for the troop sending States to bring their soldiers to justice in their home country for offences committed on the territory of the receiving State,"[51] they could also regulate other powers, including the authority to collect information in relation to terrorist crimes. If so, it would be important to be as specific as possible in describing the relevant powers, as the context of regular SOFAs has demonstrated that even if such agreements "authorize visiting military law enforcement officers to use investigative powers,"[52] these powers may be limited to, for example, the personnel of the sending state, which of course "heavily affects investigations regarding incidents which require access to local victims, witnesses or the collection of evidence which is not under the ownership of the sending State."[53]

Whereas this example is focused on bringing the suspect to justice in the troop-sending state, foreign military troops could also be of assistance in bringing the suspect to justice in the troop-receiving (or host) state. Such operations are called evidence-based operations (EvBOs), a term that was first defined in the context of ISAF in Afghanistan, to mean "operations, where Afghan law enforcement authorities, supported by ISAF, effectively investigate, apprehend, search and seize criminal suspects and affiliated property in accordance with Afghan law."[54] This means that the military forces should have a reasonable knowledge of the local criminal law practice and should be able to rely on a legal advisor with knowledge of the domestic law and local procedures.[55] These challenges can be somewhat overcome by joint operations between the foreign forces and the local partners.[56] This process, involving local and international actors, in turn, can also assist in strengthening the role of evidence in local procedures that may otherwise be based primarily on confessions.[57]

Another interesting example stems from counterpiracy operations, where military forces were often the first responders to incidents that later saw a follow-up in a regular civilian criminal court. During piracy operations, "evidence grids

[50] UN CTED's Military Evidence Guidelines, at 19, n.38.

[51] B. Van Hoek, J. Nijhof, & J. Voetelink, *The Scope of Jurisdiction Provisions in Status of Forces Agreements Related to Crisis Management Operations*, 51/2 MILITARY L. & THE L. OF WAR REV. 337 (2012).

[52] *Id.* 338.

[53] *Id.* 356.

[54] J. Voetelink, *Evidence-Based Operations; How to Remove the Bad Guys from the Battlefield*, 182 MILITAIRE SPECTATOR, no. 10, 440–41 (2013).

[55] *Id.* 443.

[56] *Id.*

[57] *Id.*

have been developed which help the military on board of navy vessels who make arrests of alleged pirates to know what type of evidence needs to be collected to pass the different penal law thresholds of a variety of coastal states."[58] Such evidence grids, which should of course comply with international law, could also be of interest to (joint) military forces patrolling the various border areas of regions popular to transboundary terrorism, such as the Lake Chad region,[59] where depending on where the suspect is apprehended or the information collected different standards will become relevant. Moreover, "experiences with detention on the high seas, where conditions to bring suspects before a judge are challenging, have shown that solutions can be found through videoconferencing or by having a law enforcement official on board."[60] Such best practices could also be considered for comparable terrorist operations, whether on sea or land.

The final example concerns the context of the international criminal tribunals (ICTs), such as the International Criminal Tribunal for the former Yugoslavia (ICTY) and the permanent International Criminal Court (ICC). In the context of these ICTs, military forces have assisted the Office of the Prosecutor (OTP) to be able to conduct investigations in (post-)conflict situations. During a 2014 expert meeting on this topic, it was indicated that despite an initial reluctance among the military to have investigators accompany them, the degree and quality of collaboration improved quickly, with approximately "65 percent" of the evidence being secured by the ICTY OTP stemming from operations conducted with military support.[61] Nonetheless, challenges remain, which became quite visible in the context of the ICC's very first case against Thomas Lubanga. In this case, there was a "strong reliance on confidential information from the UN Peacekeeping Mission in the DRC,"[62] but because the OTP refused to disclose this information, the case was nearly dismissed.

The role of military forces in the context of these ICTs went, and still goes, beyond assisting in the securing of information and could include the arrest and detention of fugitives. An example is the arrest of Slavko Dokmanović, who was arrested by the ICTY OTP and UN Transitional Authority in Eastern Slavonia, Baranja and Western Sirmium (UNTAES) soldiers on June 27, 1997.[63] And also in the context of the ICC, it is clear that UN peacekeeping forces can be involved

[58] Van Ginkel & Paulussen, *supra* note 1, at 5. *See also* UN CTED's Military Evidence Guidelines, at 21.

[59] *See* C. Casola, *Multinational Joint Task Force: Security Cooperation in the Lake Chad Basin*, ISPI Commentary, Mar. 19, 2020, available at https://www.ispionline.it/en/pubblicazione/multinational-joint-task-force-security-cooperation-lake-chad-basin-25448.

[60] Van Ginkel & Paulussen, *supra* note 1, at 5.

[61] *Id.*

[62] H. Fujiwara & S. Parmentier, *Investigations*, *in* International Prosecutors 597 (L. Reydams, J. Wouters, & C. Ryngaert eds., 2012).

[63] *See* for a detailed account C. Paulussen, Male captus bene detentus? Surrendering Suspects to the International Criminal Court 383 (2010).

in the arrest of suspects—examples are the UN Multidimensional Integrated Stabilization Mission in the CAR[64] and the UN Organization Stabilization Mission in the DRC[65]—as long as the mandates allow for this possibility.

C.. Concerns: The Situation in Africa

While IS has territorially been defeated in Iraq and to a large extent in Syria, at the same time Islamic insurgencies are on the rise in Africa. The number of terrorist attacks has increased significantly since 2019, in, for instance, Mozambique and the Sahel.[66] The security situation in these regions can be described as high-risk situations and, in some countries, the conflict can even be qualified as a non-international armed conflict. In Mozambique, Mali, Burkina Faso, and Niger, the military has often been the target of terrorist attacks, while at the same time playing a role in combating terrorism to secure the situation or when the high-risk situations do not allow civil criminal justice actors to fulfill their roles. Some cases from Africa—but examples can also be found from other continents—show that, while the military can find themselves in a position to play a role in assisting the criminal justice sector in its response to terrorism, their involvement often goes hand in hand with international humanitarian law and international human rights law violations.

For instance, Mozambique has been dealing with an increasing terrorist threat since 2017, posed by an Islamic terrorist group, known locally known as al-Shabaab, and the terrorist group Ahlu Sunnah Wa-Jamaa (with ties to IS).[67] The military of Mozambique has played a role in the government response, but is struggling to effectively contain and address the growing influence of Islamic terrorism in the country.[68] Amnesty International reported that the security forces in Cabo Delgado province have been involved in torture and dismemberment of alleged jihadi fighters .[69]

[64] *See* UN Security Council Resolution 2301 of July 26, 2016 (S/RES/2301 (2016)), para. 35 (a).

[65] *See* UN Security Council Resolution 2348 of Mar. 31, 2017 (S/RES/2348 (2017)), para 34 (f).

[66] D. Paquette, S. Mekhennet, & J. Warrick, *ISIS Attacks Surge in Africa Even as Trump Boasts of a "100-percent" Defeated Caliphate*, Wash. Post, Oct. 19, 2020, available at https://www.washingtonpost.com/national-security/islamic-state-attacks-surging-africa/2020/10/18/2e16140e-1079-11eb-8a35-237ef1eb2ef7_story.html. *See also Mozambique: Is Cabo Delgado the Latest Islamic State Outpost?*, BBC News, May 4, 2020, available at https://www.bbc.com/news/world-africa-52532741.

[67] J. Burke, *Mozambique Army Surrounds Port Held by Isis-linked Insurgents*, The Guardian, Aug. 16, 2020, available at https://www.theguardian.com/world/2020/aug/16/mozambique-army-surrounds-port-captured-by-isis-linked-insurgents.

[68] T. Mukeredzi, *Mozambique Can't Contain Its Insurgency Alone*, Foreign Policy, Sept. 11, 2020, available at https://foreignpolicy.com/2020/09/11/mozambique-contain-insurgency-counterterrorism-strategy-assistance/.

[69] *Mozambique: Torture by Security Forces in Gruesome Videos Must Be Investigated*, Amnesty International, Sept. 9, 2020, available at https://www.amnesty.org/en/latest/news/2020/09/mozambique-torture-by-security-forces-in-gruesome-videos-must-be-investigated/.

Across the continent, Mali—but increasingly Niger and Burkina Faso—is suffering from jihadist terrorist attacks and intercommunal violence, which have contributed to a deteriorating regional stability in the Sahel and larger West Africa.

In Niger, a state of emergency has existed since early 2018, and several security measures have been imposed in the Tilaberi region, where over 150 military have been killed in a wave of terrorist attacks.[70] In February 2020, the national army of Niger, together with the French army, killed 120 alleged terrorists and seized materials that are being used to make bombs.[71] In the military response, serious human rights violations have been committed, including allegedly the involvement by the military in enforced disappearances.[72]

Finally, the situation in Mali deteriorated after the attempted coup by the army of President Keita. Despite the increased presence of the United Nations Multidimensional Integrated Stabilization Mission in Mali (MINUSMA) and renewed pledges to Operation Barkhane led by France, the situation in Mali remains very unstable. Most of the terrorist attacks were carried out by Jama'a Nusrat ul-Islam wa al-Muslimin or Islamic State in the Greater Sahara against the international forces and national security forces.

According to Amnesty International, two hundred human rights violations incidents have been recorded showing involvement of the armed forces of Mali, Burkina Faso, and Niger between February and May 2020, some of which may amount to war crimes in Mali and Burkina Faso.[73] The alleged human rights violations include torture and ill-treatment of prisoners, extrajudicial killings and enforced disappearances. Overall there is a culture of impunity and lack of willingness to initiate investigations. One exception is that in July 2020, "prosecution orders were signed for military personnel suspected of involvement in serious crimes in central Mali."[74]

The role played by the military in these African examples in combating terrorism paints a grim picture. The military are underresourced, may have limited

[70] *Death Toll in Niger Army Base Attack "Rises to 89,"* Al Jazeera, Jan. 12, 2020, available at https://www.aljazeera.com/news/2020/1/12/death-toll-in-niger-army-base-attack-rises-to-89; *Niger Military Operation "Kills 120 Terrorists" after Jihadist Attacks*, The Guardian, Feb. 22, 2020, available at https://www.theguardian.com/world/2020/feb/22/niger-military-operation-kills-120-terrorists-after-jihadist-attacks.

[71] F. Kelly, *Joint Niger-Barkhane Operation "Neutralizes" 120 Terrorists, Defense Ministry Says*, The Defense Post, Feb. 22, 2020, available at https://www.thedefensepost.com/2020/02/22/niger-france-operation-terrorists-tillaberi-120-neutralized/.

[72] S. Fröhlich, *Niger: Fear of Terror—And the Military*, Deutsche Welle, Sept. 16, 2020, available at https://www.dw.com/en/niger-fear-of-terror-and-the-military/a-54947989.

[73] *"They Executed Some and Brought the Rest with Them"—Human Rights Violations by Security Forces in the Sahel*, Amnesty International, June 2020, available at https://www.amnesty.org/download/Documents/AFR3723182020ENGLISH.pdf.

[74] "Situation in Mali," Report of the Secretary-General, S/2020/952, Sept. 29, 2020, para. 42, available at https://minusma.unmissions.org/sites/default/files/s_2020_952_e.pdf.

experience and understanding of how the terrorist organizations operate and recruit members, and they are often targeted themselves by the different terrorist groups. The primary response to terrorism is thus a military response, and the continued state of emergency in several of the Sahel countries is creating a situation in which the exception is becoming the norm. The military are not held accountable for the alleged international humanitarian law and international human rights law violations and the mandate of the military does not clearly define the tasks and responsibilities. The fact that the army has been implicated in several abuses clearly raises doubts regarding the ability and credibility of some military to be involved in the collection of evidence and making of arrests in accordance with the rule of law.[75] It would therefore be paramount to provide training, clear mandates, and proper instructions on how to operate in a rule of law compliant manner.

IV. Legal Challenges

A. Introduction

The previous section has demonstrated that the military can have a role in assisting bringing terrorism suspects to justice and that valuable lessons can be drawn from earlier experiences that have some overlap with this new task. At the same time, the experiences from some African states—but comparable examples can also be found in other continents—show that there are serious concerns with regard to the adherence to international law obligations. Therefore, even if the military is willing to take on new tasks, various legal challenges will need to be considered, some of which we have already touched upon briefly in the previous pages. In the current section, a selection of legal challenges will be discussed in more detail,[76] related to mandates (B), applicable legal frameworks (C), cooperation (D), and fair trial issues (E).

B. (Inter)national Legal Mandate

Whereas all military forces need to have a national mandate to assist in law enforcement tasks (whether these tasks take place abroad or in one's own state), foreign troops need to have a clear international legal mandate as well to be able

[75] Human Rights Watch, *World Report 2019, Mozambique: Events of 2018*, available at https://www.hrw.org/world-report/2019/country-chapters/mozambique.

[76] For more information, *see* Van Ginkel & Paulussen, *supra* note 1, and UN CTED's Military Evidence Guidelines.

to operate on another state's territory.[77] This is only possible in three situations, namely, when there is consent of the territorial state, a case of lawful self-defense or authorization by the UN Security Council. When the UN Security Council provides authorization, it is recommended that the resolution in question does not use general formulations that may leave room for different interpretations,[78] but stipulates as explicitly as possible that the mandate can be used to prevent impunity for terrorist crimes committed in the designated area and that the military are authorized to assist civilian law enforcement authorities to contribute to that aim.

Furthermore, the powers and authorities of the military are further specified in the rules of engagement (ROE) for specific operations. Although the ROE are commonly used to specify under what circumstances the use of force is legitimized, mission-specific ROE could authorize the collection and preservation of information and evidence for use in national court proceedings. In addition, standard operating procedures (SOPs) and instructions on tactics, techniques, and procedures (TTPs) can provide further detailed instructions on how military troops during an operation, and in various situations of conflict intensity, can assist in this process.[79]

But rules on paper will not be enough. As explained earlier, in the context of questioning witnesses,

> [t]he prevailing cultural norms might also dictate that not the actual witness but the village elder will step forward to give testimony (even if he was not present at the scene). Details might also get lost in translation, or be altered by the translators because of their own analysis of the situation. Testimonies might furthermore be coloured by perceptions towards the military. And there

[77] This section is heavily based on Van Ginkel & Paulussen, *supra* note 1, at 6–8. *See also* UN CTED's Military Evidence Guidelines, at 13–14.

[78] Examples are UN Security Council Resolution 1973 of Mar. 17, 2011 (related to Libya), and UN Security Council Resolution 2085 of July 13, 2012 (related to Mali). For more information, *see* Van Ginkel & Paulussen, *supra* note 1, at 8.

[79] These instructions could relate to "(i) indicating the appropriate level of military command at which information-collection decisions are to be made; (ii) identifying the military personnel best situated and trained to carry out or supervise these tasks; (iii) setting out how and when the military can conduct information-collection activities; (iv) setting out operational scenarios where the collection of information for potential use as evidence in civilian criminal-justice proceedings is required (e.g., sensitive site exploitation (SSE), IED strikes, suicide bombings); (v) setting out effective independent oversight mechanisms; (vi) providing an outline of investigation liaison between civilian criminal-justice actors and the military; (vii) encouraging the integration into the military of civilian law-enforcement officers and prosecutors where possible; and (viii) procedures for the military regarding the collection of information in a manner that meets rule-of-law and due-process requirements for civilian criminal-justice proceedings (e.g., establishing a secure environment, cordoning off the area and restricting access by locals, and the recording and maintenance of a chain of custody of information)." (UN CTED's Military Evidence Guidelines, at 14). Not better to have the full stop before the parenthesis?

> could also be genuine fears for retaliation once a testimony is given. When determining the reliability of evidence, it is important to consider unintentional intimidation of witnesses and detainees. Therefore, the military may not be the best to interrogate a detainee.[80]

Indeed, it might be easier to bridge the knowledge gap by particularly authorizing special branches of the military, such as the gendarmerie, military police, or designated law enforcement officers, with executing or overseeing these tasks. Such units are much better equipped in ensuring that evidence is collected in accordance with the rule of law and can also monitor any international humanitarian law and international human rights law violations committed by the military.[81] Another option could be to appoint embedded police investigators to the military mission, or have remote prosecutorial assistance or mobile forensic teams on standby. An example is the decision of the G5 Sahel to create a police component, which would assist in the prosecution of terrorists apprehended by the G5 Sahel Force.[82] Other options that could be useful is appointing an evidence custodian or police advisor or embedding a prosecutor within the military. Alternatively, a hotline can provide the military expert assistance in how to collect, identify, handle, and preserve information in these situations, without jeopardizing the admissibility as evidence later on.[83]

It might also be an option, if appropriate, to set up a dual track for information processing, right after the first step of information collection. This would imply that the same piece of information would on the one hand be processed as intelligence that is of operational interest in full respect of the rules of confidentiality that apply to the processing of intelligence, and on the other hand be processed as information that is potentially of interest for the law enforcement trajectory and thus in full respect of the rules dictated by the criminal justice chain.[84]

Finally, and given the uncertainties involved, it is good to "play safe" and always abide by the highest standards. As explained before, and again taking the example of questioning witnesses:

> [I]t is important to ensure that if someone is interrogated, it is clear to the suspect or witness whether this is done by an intelligence officer or by a law

[80] Van Ginkel & Paulussen, *supra* note 1, at 15.

[81] *See* A. Ngari, *The Threat of Violent Extremism Has Seen Disproportionate Resources Given to Military and Security Actions*, ISS, Aug. 5, 2020, available at https://issafrica.org/iss-today/niger-and-mali-should-reconcile-justice-and-military-responses-to-terrorism.

[82] UNODC, *The G5 Sahel Police Component: A Unique Mechanism for the Restoration of Justice*, undated, available at https://www.unodc.org/westandcentralafrica/en/2019-12-06-unodc-composante-police-g5-sahel.html.

[83] *See* UN CTED's Military Evidence Guidelines, at 30.

[84] *See* Van Ginkel & Paulussen, *supra* note 1, at 19.

enforcement officer who will read out the rights to the suspect or witness. Sometimes, a "cooling down" period between the intelligence interview and the criminal justice interview can clarify to the interviewee that the second interview is done by different actors with different backgrounds and roles. However, it remains to be seen whether such a construction, which has probably been applied in the ship-based detention of Abu Khatallah,[85] is in conformity with a person's right not to incriminate him/herself.[86] Given the fact that there is often uncertainty surrounding the purpose of interrogations, it would be recommendable from the outset to respect the requirement to conduct all interrogations and gathering of evidence, to the maximum extent possible, as though the statements/evidence will eventually be presented in a civilian criminal prosecution.[87]

C. Applicable Legal Frameworks

As explained, the military may find themselves required to collect information that can be used as evidence not only while engaged in combat, during armed conflicts, but also in non-conflict settings. [88] During armed conflict, international human rights law and international humanitarian law apply, with international humanitarian law usually being the *lex specialis*, whereas in peacetime, only international human rights law applies. It should be stressed that international human rights law is not limited to a state's own territory: it applies extraterritorially when a state exercises effective power or control over persons or territory.[89] Several human rights law provisions

[85] Abu Khatallah is considered to be the brains behind the attack on the US Mission in Benghazi, Libya, on September 11, 2012. *See* D. Wise, *The Capture of Khatallah: How Things Went Down in Libya*, Reuters, June 20, 2014, available at http://blogs.reuters.com/great-debate/2014/06/20/the-capture-of-khatallah-how-things-went-down-in-libya/.

[86] Additionally, problematic in the Khatallah case is that he was captured in Libya and detained on a Navy ship in the Mediterranean. Hafetz notes that such "detentions, due to their inherent isolation and inaccessibility, (. . .) create a risk of diluting presentment and *Miranda* rights, particularly given the government's increased latitude to gather intelligence in terrorism cases." *See* J. Hafetz, *Abu Khattalah and the Evolution of Ship-Based Detention*, Just Security, June 28, 2014, available at https://www.justsecurity.org/12395/abu-khattalah-evolution-ship-based-detention/. The Miranda warning is an "[e]xplanation of rights that must be given before any custodial interrogation, stemming largely from the Fifth Amendment privilege against self-incrimination. The person detained and interrogated must be made aware of the right to remain silent, the right to consult with an attorney and have the attorney present during questioning, and the right to have an attorney appointed if indigent." Explanation available at the Legal Information Institute of Cornell University Law School's website: https://www.law.cornell.edu/wex/miranda_warning.

[87] Van Ginkel & Paulussen, *supra* note 1, at 14.

[88] This section is heavily based on Van Ginkel & Paulussen, *supra* note 1, at 9.

[89] *See, e.g.*, International Court of Justice, *Legal Consequences of the Construction of a Wall in the Occupied Palestinian Territory (Advisory Opinion)*, July 9, 2004, para. 109, available at https://

affect the collection and use of evidence (such as Article 7 (prohibition of torture) and Article 9 (right to liberty and security) of the International Covenant on Civil and Political Rights), but international human rights law regulates less closely the mechanisms by which evidence is gathered and preserved. This falls within the purview of domestic law. Eventually, the procedural thresholds that follow from domestic law are guiding with respect to the admissibility, reliability, and credibility of the evidence in a court case, although these domestic standards should of course be in line with international law.

If international humanitarian law applies, to what extent might this legal regime affect the collection of evidence during a particular operation? Restrictions and provisions include Common Article 3 to the Geneva Conventions (prohibiting torture and other ill-treatment, but also elaborating on personal dignity), and Article 75 of Additional Protocol I of the Geneva Conventions (prohibiting ill-treatment and requiring humane treatment of detainees). In addition, it could be argued that in cases where the main legal framework (for instance, international humanitarian law) does not regulate how evidence can be secured for the purpose of criminal prosecution, domestic law and the *lex generalis* international human rights law can complement the *lex specialis* international humanitarian law.

Regardless of how information was obtained on the battlefield, by whom, under what mandate, or during what type of operation, prosecutors will use only information that they find reliable and that is likely to be found admissible in court. In the end a judge will decide on the admissibility, reliability, and credibility of the evidence based mainly on domestic procedural law or practice, informed by relevant international law standards. The military forces that are collecting information may not know in what court case the information might eventually be submitted as evidence, and henceforth what admissibility standards will apply. As explained earlier, they are therefore well advised to ensure they minimize the risk that the evidence will be dismissed, or rather to maximize the chance that the evidence will be considered, by making sure they fully comply with everything that has been presented earlier, from international legal mandates, to national legal mandates, ROE, SOPs, TTPs, and all applicable (international) legal frameworks.

www.icj-cij.org/public/files/case-related/131/131-20040709-ADV-01-00-EN.pdf; and International Court of Justice, *Case Concerning Armed Activities on the Territory of the Congo (Democratic Republic of the Congo v. Uganda)*, Dec. 19, 2005, para. 216, available at https://www.icj-cij.org/public/files/case-related/116/116-20051219-JUD-01-00-EN.pdf.

D. Cooperation

Terrorism-related crimes often have an international dimension. For instance, FTFs cross (multiple) borders to join a terrorist organization in another country or move on to another conflict zone, whereas other may return home or plan an attack in a third country. Investigation of terrorist acts and efforts to track FTFs thus require international cooperation and the sharing of information among law enforcement officials and prosecutors from different states. This kind of cooperation, typically taking form through the use of mutual legal assistance (MLA) requests, allows for exchange of evidence, requests to hear suspects or witnesses, and, eventually, the extradition of suspects. However, and especially during (post-)conflict and high-risk situations, such cooperation may not always be effective or possible. [90] The *Sardar* case discussed earlier, for example, already shows that considerable time may elapse between the act under investigation and the ultimate trial in court. Moreover, the information may pass through several actors, as has been explained by Ester Natus, who works as a federal magistrate at the counterterrorism department of the Belgian Federal Prosecutor's Office:

> Belgium heavily relies on the collaboration with partner nations better equipped to collect evidence on the battlefield. The USA, for example, deploy their troops together with the Federal Bureau of Investigation (FBI) and prosecutors in order to ensure that the military personnel are well advised with regard to evidence gathering. The material seized by the US military will then digitally transit through many different services before it reaches the Office of the Belgian Federal Prosecutor: it will first be transferred to the FBI; then, to the Belgian military intelligence services which will, in turn, transfer the information to the civil intelligence services; and, finally, it will reach the Federal Prosecutor's Office. It is important to note that Belgium will never possess the original items that were seized on the battlefield. Battlefield evidence is however essential to the prosecutors since it is the only link they have with the conflict zone.[91]

Hence, a question that immediately comes to mind is how the information can be stored in such a way that the judge may still qualify it as admissible evidence in court years later and after it has passed so many actors and services? In this context, the UN Security Council has encouraged member states to share biometric data "responsibly" among relevant member states, as

[90] *See also* UN CTED's Military Evidence Guidelines, at 14–19.

[91] Report of the Third "Silent Leges Inter Arma?" International Conference held in Bruges from 18 to 20 September 2019, at 5, available at https://www.ismllw.org/wp-content/uploads/2020/04/ISMLLW-1041-N-E-3.pdf.

appropriate, and with Interpol and other relevant international bodies.[92] It can be argued that states need to adopt strong legal safeguards with respect to the type of data that can be collected, the period the data can be retained, and procedures for deleting data. For instance, in the event of data exchange, there should be an agreement of how such data is to be preserved, for what purpose, for what period, and who is responsible for the destruction of the information once deemed redundant. Using the databases of international organizations that ensure that the chain of custody is not broken and that data protection is respected can be of use in this context.[93] For example, "INTERPOL pioneered military-to-law enforcement information exchange, starting in 2005 with Project Vennlig in Iraq, and later in Afghanistan through Project Hamah."[94] Another question is how to ensure that information is not obtained by another state through serious human rights violations or torture. In some countries specific guidelines have been adopted to overcome these challenges. For example, in November 2017, the government of Canada adopted a Ministerial Direction that prohibits

> a. the disclosure of information that would result in a substantial risk of mistreatment of an individual by a foreign entity; b. the making of requests for information that would result in a substantial risk of mistreatment of an individual by a foreign entity; and c. certain uses of information that was likely obtained through the mistreatment of an individual by a foreign entity.[95]

At the national level, cooperation between the different actors is of course of vital importance as well. As explained earlier, given the specialist skills required to best ensure that the chain of custody is respected, and thus that the "bagging and tagging" of material evidence is done properly, it might be easier to cooperate with and bring in special branches of the military, such as the gendarmerie or military police. Other options are embedding law enforcement specialists to the military mission or having remote prosecutorial assistance or mobile forensic teams on standby, if need be via a hotline.

[92] UN Security Council Resolution 2396 of Dec. 21, 2017 (S/RES/2396 (2017)), para. 15.

[93] UN CTED's Military Evidence Guidelines, at 16.

[94] Interpol, *G7 Ministers Call for Sharing of Battlefield Data on Terrorists via INTERPOL*, Oct. 20, 2017, available at https://www.interpol.int/News-and-Events/News/2017/G7-Ministers-call-for-sharing-of-battlefield-data-on-terrorists-via-INTERPOL.

[95] Government of Canada, *Ministerial Direction to the Department of National Defence and the Canadian Armed Forces: Avoiding Complicity in Mistreatment by Foreign Entities*, Nov. 24, 2017, available at https://www.canada.ca/en/department-national-defence/corporate/ministerial-directions/avoiding-complicity.html.

E. Fair Trial Issues

Some military involved in gathering the information—such as special forces—may not be willing or authorized to testify in court, which could potentially undermine the right of the defense to cross-examine the evidence brought against the suspect, thus violating the principle of equality of arms, while in some countries rules on hearsay might affect the admissibility of their written statements.[96] Creative solutions could help to balance the interests of both the defense and the need to conceal the identity of the military for security reasons. This may include video-conferencing, partly concealing the identity of the witness and other techniques, while still allowing the defense to effectively challenge the evidence.[97] In some countries, a third party, with both a foot in the intelligence community and in the law enforcement community, such as an independent commission or a special intelligence prosecutor, may review the intelligence and decide whether or not certain information can be declassified and turned over.[98] In yet other countries, including many common law countries, law enforcement officials will work with the intelligence officers to identify which information is relevant for the case, after which the prosecutor will decide in what form the information will be disclosed to the court.[99]

An example of such a creative solution took place during a trial in the Netherlands against members of the Liberation Tigers of Tamil Eelam (LTTE). In this case, the Dutch prosecutor received several pages of a document, which contained membership cards of LTTE. This document was uncovered by the Sri Lankan Army. To assert whether these documents were genuine, the Dutch prosecutor wanted to hear, in a Dutch court, one of the military officers who found them. The mutual legal assistance request, however, was denied, but the Sri Lankan authorities agreed that the military officer could be heard as a witness through a video link. The Dutch prosecutor needed to be sure that the documents were genuine and not obtained illegally, but also needed to ascertain whether the witness was credible. The Dutch court concluded that documents deriving from Sri Lanka could be used as evidence but cautioned to do so carefully for the following reasons. First, Sri Lanka is part of the conflict and may have an interest in seeing the LTTE suspects convicted. Second, there is no bilateral agreement on

[96] *See* UN CTED's Military Evidence Guidelines, at 22–24.

[97] *See* S. Crowther, *The UN Security Council Is About to Dangerously Undermine Fair Trial Guarantees*, Just Security, Aug. 20, 2020, available at https://www.justsecurity.org/72118/the-un-security-council-is-about-to-dangerously-undermine-fair-trial-guarantees/.

[98] Global Counterterrorism Forum (GCTF), Criminal Justice Sector and Rule of Law Working Group, *Recommendations for Using and Protecting Intelligence Information In Rule of Law-Based, Criminal Justice Sector-Led Investigations and Prosecutions*, Sept. 19, 2014, at 5, available at https://www.thegctf.org/documents/10162/159887/14sept19_gctf+rabat+gp+6+recommendations.pdf.

[99] *Id.* 4.

MLA with Sri Lanka, so that less attention can be placed on the principle of trust. And last, there were credible sources that Sri Lankan authorities committed human rights violations that could potentially be of influence to the assessment of the acquired documents.[100]

Due to the insecure and chaotic circumstances under which militaries have to operate, it is imaginable that certain irregularities occur during the collection of information. These kinds of irregularities might have consequences for the admissibility, reliability, and credibility of the information as evidence. Clearly, each national legal system is different in how they assess these irregularities and what the consequences might be. In the end it will be the judge who makes the final judgment. However, judges, when deciding upon the seriousness of the irregularity and its consequences, might consider (1) the situation on the ground and what can be demanded from the military in that particular time and place; (2) who was involved in the irregularity (the closer the irregularity is perpetrated by an organ of the prosecuting state, the more serious the consequences will probably be); and (3) what kind of norm was violated. Clearly information obtained through torture should lead to another remedy (the dismissal of the case) than, for example, a violation of a SOP. As a form of remedy to correct the irregularity, a judge can consider various options, including a reduction of the sentence, the exclusion of a certain piece of evidence, or in the most serious situations, the dismissal of the case.

V. Conclusions

There is not just a moral obligation but also a legal obligation to bring terrorists to justice. An integral part of the international community's efforts to counter terrorism is to hold the perpetrators of terrorist acts accountable for their actions, in accordance with international law and the rule of law. The difficulties in securing admissible, reliable, and credible evidence from the battlefield entails that some of the terrorist suspects, including FTFs, are not being prosecuted for the actual crimes they have committed, but only for "lesser" crimes such as membership of a terrorist organization or preparatory acts. One of the consequences of this somewhat practical approach is that the terrorists serve relatively shorter prison

[100] The Hague Court of Appeal, Case No. 22-005123-11, Apr. 30, 2015, at para. 9.2, available at http://deeplink.rechtspraak.nl/uitspraak?id=ECLI:NL:GHDHA:2015:1082. *See also* T. Mehra, *Bringing (Foreign) Terrorist Fighters to Justice in a Post-ISIS Landscape Part III: Collecting Evidence from Conflict Situations*, ICCT Perspective, June 12, 2018, available at https://icct.nl/publication/bringing-foreign-terrorist-fighters-to-justice-in-a-post-isis-landscape-part-iii-collecting-evidence-from-conflict-situations.

sentences.[101] According to the 2017 European Union Terrorism Situation and Trend Report, the average prison sentence for jihadist and separatist terrorist offences across the European Union was five years,[102] and according to Globsec, a significant number of European jihadists convicted for "lesser" crimes will be released in 2023.[103]

By utilizing the information that can be obtained from (post-)conflict and high-risk situations within a rule of law framework, the chances of prosecuting terrorist suspects for their actual deeds will increase. This not only helps to bring terrorists to justice but also does justice to the victims.

However, collecting information as part of a military mission or by other actors from the battlefield in order to use it as evidence in terrorism cases is new for many countries. The international, regional, and national policy developments presented at the beginning of this chapter, however, show that organizations and states become more aware of the need and possibilities to do so. As indicated, Eurojust, in September 2020, published the *Eurojust Memorandum on Battlefield Evidence*, in which it provides an overview of the few cases in which battlefield evidence was used in judicial proceedings.[104] The inventory of cases nevertheless shows that battlefield information has led to convictions in some cases. Battlefield evidence has also been used to determine the existence of an armed conflict, or to clarify the nature and level of participation of a national of a state in the operation of terrorist organizations, and has been corroborated by other evidence. At the same time, the examples from the African continent show that there is a serious risk for abuse and that operating in a rule of law compliant manner is not a given, underlining the need for better preparations, cooperation, guidance, instructions, and accountability.

Indeed, military units engaged in counterterrorism operations, either as part of a foreign deployment in another country in either a conflict or non-conflict situation or as (inter)national forces in the role of emergency powers as a result of highly insecure situations and/or a lack of civilian capacities, need to prepare themselves properly. Preparation should include gaining a good understanding of the legal frameworks that govern the collection of information and training of skills. These are important steps to take, in order to ensure that during operations, key principles of evidence collection can be respected, just

101 UN CTED, *The Challenge of Returning and Relocating Foreign Terrorist Fighters: Research Perspectives*, CTED TRENDS REPORT, Mar. 2018, at 13, available at https://www.un.org/sc/ctc/wp-content/uploads/2018/04/CTED-Trends-Report-March 2018.pdf.

102 Europol, *European Union Terrorism Situation and Trend Report 2017*, at 52, available at https://www.europol.europa.eu/sites/default/files/documents/tesat2017.pdf.

103 Globsec, *Who Are the European Jihadis?*, PROJECT MIDTERM REPORT, Sept. 2018, at 8, 10, & 16, available at https://www.globsec.org/wp-content/uploads/2018/09/GLOBSEC_WhoAreTheEuropeanJihadis.pdf.

104 Eurojust, *Eurojust Memorandum on Battlefield Evidence*, Sept. 2020, available at https://www.eurojust.europa.eu/publication/eurojust-memorandum-battlefield-evidence.

like the authorities traditionally involved in collecting evidence and arresting and detaining suspects for prosecution before a civilian criminal court would. Furthermore, the military authorities must work as closely as possible with (national) civilian investigators and prosecutors, and learn from experiences with embedded prosecutors or gendarmerie officers. Thus, it is important that the military authorities engage (also prior to the start of an operation) with the (national) prosecutors and vice versa in order to know how they can best cooperate in a specific situation and what kind of information prosecutors are looking for. A good practice identified in section III.B in the context of EvBOs shows that joint operations between foreign forces and their local partners can also lead to a better understanding of the importance of proper evidence collection, thus reducing the risk of international law violations.

We come to a conclusion. It is of the utmost importance to stress again that the arguments presented in this chapter are not meant and should not be used as a justification to simply increase the power of the military without seriously reflecting about its possible ramifications. To the contrary: we highly believe in the rule of thumb "as civilian as possible and only as military as needed." However, at the same time, we must be cognizant of the reality that sometimes, this need may present itself: if military personnel stumble across information and are not in the position to call in their colleagues with a law enforcement background, then reality dictates that it is useful if they know how to at least secure this information so that their colleagues are not put in a difficult position afterward by discovering a demolished crime scene. In addition, our normative framework has always been, and should always be, international law. Yes, we should aim to increase the chance that the judge finds the information admissible, reliable, and credible during the criminal trial, but obviously not at all costs: serious violations of international humanitarian law and international human rights law should lead to the dismissal of the evidence and perhaps even to the collapse of the entire case. In the end, and that would be our final message, this is not merely about bringing to justice suspects of terrorism as such, but about bringing to justice suspects of terrorism *in full compliance with international law and the rule of law.*[105]

[105] *See, e.g.*, C. Paulussen, *Impunity for International Terrorists? Key Legal Questions and Practical Considerations*, 3 The International Centre for Counter-Terrorism—The Hague, no. 3 (2012), available at https://www.icct.nl/download/file/ICCT-Paulussen-Impunity-April-2012.pdf; and C. Paulussen, *Repressing the Foreign Fighters Phenomenon and Terrorism in Western Europe: Towards an Effective Response Based on Human Rights*, 7 The International Centre for CounterTerrorism—The Hague, no. 10 (2016), available at https://icct.nl/app/uploads/2016/11/ICCT-Paulussen-Rule-of-Law-Nov2016-4.pdf.

17

US Military Prosecutions during Non-International Armed Conflict

Chris Jenks[1]

I. Introduction

Since the September 11 attacks, the United States has been at war, however characterized, for longer than at any point in its 244-year history. Between first invading Afghanistan in 2001 and then Iraq in 2003, the US military has been engaged in one, and often more than one, armed conflict for over nineteen straight years. Between 2001 and 2015, the Rand Corporation estimates that some 2.77 million US service members served on more than 5.4 million deployments.[2]

With so many service members deployed for so long, there were instances where US service members committed crimes. For example, US service members wrongfully killed civilians, individuals who either never participated in hostilities or had participated but had been captured or detained. Some of the more high-profile incidents include US Marines killing twenty-four unarmed Iraqi civilians in 2005 in what became known as the Haditha massacre;[3] a group of US Army soldiers raping a fourteen-year-old Iraqi girl and then murdering her as well as her parents and sister in 2006;[4] a group of US Army soldiers conspiring to and actually murdering Afghan civilians in 2011 in what became known as the Kill Team;[5] and a US Army sergeant murdering sixteen Afghan civilians in

[1] Associate Professor of Law & Criminal Clinic Director, SMU Dedman School of Law. The author would like to thank the SMU Statistics Center for assistance in understanding military-specific law enforcement data.

[2] Jennie W. Wenger, Caolionn O'Connell, & Linda Cottrell, "Examination of Recent Deployment Experience Across the Services and Components," Rand Corporation, 2018, <https://130.154.3.25/content/dam/rand/pubs/research_reports/RR1900/RR1928/RAND_RR1928.pdf>.

[3] Charlie Savage & Elisabeth Bumiller, *An Iraqi Massacre, a Light Sentence and a Question of Military Justice*, N.Y. Times, Jan. 27, 2012, A 17.

[4] James Dao, *Ex-Soldier Gets Life Sentence for Iraq Murders*, N.Y. Times, May 21, 2009, < https://www.nytimes.com/2009/05/22/us/22soldier.html>

[5] Mark Boal, *The Kill Team: How US Soldiers in Afghanistan Murdered Innocent Civilians*, Rolling Stone, Mar. 26, 2011, < https://www.rollingstone.com/politics/politics-news/the-kill-team-how-u-s-soldiers-in-afghanistan-murdered-innocent-civilians-169793/>

Chris Jenks, *US Military Prosecutions during Non-International Armed Conflict* In: *Between Crime and War*. Edited by: Claire Finkelstein, Christopher Fuller, Jens David Ohlin, Mitt Regan, Oxford University Press. DOI: 10.1093/oso/9780197638798.003.0018

2012.[6] The US military investigated and prosecuted these and thousands of other US service members, charging them with various violations of the Uniform Code of Military Justice (UCMJ) and prosecuting them via a military court-martial.

Over this same period, the US military captured and prosecuted enemy belligerents. Shortly after invading Afghanistan, the US military captured, or had transferred into their control, thousands of suspected insurgents. The United States transported several hundred of these detainees to Naval Station Guantánamo in Cuba.[7] The detainees included suspected members of the Al Qaeda terrorist group and of the Taliban.[8]

The US military has prosecuted (or attempted to prosecute) twenty-nine detainees, charging them with violations of the initial 2002 Military Commissions Order (MCO)[9] and/or the Military Commissions Act (MCA) of 2006[10] and/or the MCA of 2009[11] and prosecuting them via a military commission.

On its face, there is nothing remarkable about the proposition that the United States, while a party to one or more armed conflicts, prosecuted both its own service members (internal prosecutions) as well as captured enemy belligerents (external prosecutions). This has occurred at several points in US history as far back as the beginnings of the country and the Revolutionary War.[12] Yet while the United States has continuously conducted internal prosecutions, the last external prosecutions were during World War II.[13]

[6] Jack Healy, *Soldier Sentenced to Life Without Parole for Killing 16 Afghans*, N.Y. Times, Aug. 23, 2013, A 10.

[7] Katharine Q. Seelye, *A Nation Challenged: The Prisoners; First 'Unlawful Combatants' Seized in Afghanistan Arrive at US Base in Cuba*, N.Y. Times, Jan. 12, 2002, A7.

[8] *The Guantánamo Docket: A History of the Detainee Population*, N.Y. Times, Jan. 21, 2020, < https://www.nytimes.com/interactive/projects/guantanamo>.

[9] US Dep't of Defense, Military Commissions Order No. 1 (Mar. 21, 2002) reprinted at 41 ILM 725 (2002).

[10] Military Commissions Act of 2006, Pub. L. No. 109-366, 120 Stat. 2600 (2006) (codified at 10 USC §§ 948a-950p).

[11] Military Commissions Act of 2009, Pub. L. No. 111-84, 123 Stat. 2190 (2009) (codified as amended at 10 USC §§ 948a-950t).

[12] *See* William Winthrop, Military Law and Precedents 831 (2d ed. 1920)

[13] Most of the post–World War II armed conflicts in which the United State was a party did not last long enough for criminal justice mechanisms to be implemented. There were armed conflicts seemingly long enough, Korea and Vietnam, but the United States did not employ external prosecutions (prosecutions of the enemy) in either. Detlev Vagts, *Military Commissions: A Concise History*, 101 AJIL 35, 47 (2007). In Korea, "the United Nations Command in Korea had set up military commissions on paper. They were never activated." Jordan Paust, *Antiterrorism Military Commissions: Courting Illegality*, 23 Mich. J. Int'l L. 1, 4 (2001). Of note Korean War military commissions "would have guaranteed the same procedural rights to due process that existed in general courts-martial in the US military and that are required under the 1949 Geneva Convention Relative to the Treatment of Prisoners of War." *Id.* As will be discussed, the Korean War was an international armed conflict, while the armed conflicts in which the United States has engaged in for the last nineteen years, with brief exceptions, have been non-international, with different and less applicable international law. In the Vietnam War, while members of the North Vietnamese Army and Viet Cong were prosecuted, South Vietnam, not the United States, conducted the proceedings. *See generally* Cheryl Benard et al., The Battle Behind the Wire: US Prisoner and Detainee Operations from World War II to Iraq, ch. 4 (2011).

When the United States last conducted internal *and* external prosecutions, while often styled with different labels,[14] as a matter of policy the proceedings followed the same rules.[15] Up to and during World War II, those rules were the Articles of War.[16] Following the war, the United States enacted the UCMJ, which, through Article 36, required that whatever the military justice proceeding was called, "to the extent practicable" the proceedings shall "apply the principles of law and the rules of evidence generally recognized in the trial of criminal cases in the United States District Courts, but which shall not be contrary to or inconsistent with [the UCMJ]."[17] Yet, on November 13, 2001, President George W. Bush issued an executive order that determined, among other findings, that it was not practicable to apply those principles of law and the rules of evidence in military commissions (external prosecutions).[18] Those principles and rules would however continue to apply to internal prosecutions.

All of this to say that for the last nineteen years the US military, for the first time since World War II, has conducted internal and external prosecutions and done so without a process equivalency requirement. This chapter considers the results of those prosecutions, comparing external and internal proceedings both qualitatively and quantitatively.

Section II establishes the international law predicate for external prosecutions, states prosecuting captured enemy belligerents for pre-capture offenses during armed conflict, and how the predicate varies depending on the armed conflict characterization. In essence, there is an international law–based equivalency requirement for external prosecutions during an international armed conflict (IAC) but not during a non-international armed conflict (NIAC). Section III then establishes the US legal foundation for external prosecutions. Section IV then transitions to considering the external prosecutions since 2001, the relatively small number of military commissions that have yielded a finding of guilt and imposed a punishment. The point of this consideration is to compare the maximum possible punishment for analogous offenses under the UCMJ and the MCA of 2009. For several offenses, the maximum punishment authorized by the

[14] At various times up to and including World War II, the United States has labeled internal and external prosecutions as courts-martial, boards of inquiry, tribunals, and commissions.

[15] The policy application of an equivalency requirement for external prosecutions refers to pre-capture misconduct. For post-capture misconduct, crimes committed while a prisoner of war, the 1929 Geneva Conventions requires equivalency in external and internal prosecutions. *See* Geneva Convention Relative to the Treatment of Prisoners of War (adopted July 27, 1929, entered into force June 19, 1931), 118 LNTS 343 art. 63 (stating that "sentence shall only be pronounced on a prisoner of war by the same tribunals and in accordance with the same procedure as in the case of persons belonging to the armed forces of the detaining Power").

[16] Articles of War (1912–1920) (Library of Congress), https://www.loc.gov/rr/frd/Military_Law/AW-1912-1920.html.

[17] Uniform Code of Military Justice, 10 USC §§ 801–940 (1958) (UCMJ).

[18] Detention, Treatment, and Trial of Certain Non-Citizens in the War Against Terrorism, 66 Fed. Reg. 57,833 § 1(a) (Nov. 16, 2001).

UCMJ is relatively light, months or one to two years of confinement; however, for similar if not identical offenses under the MCA 2009, the maximum authorized punishment is generally confinement for life or the death penalty punishment. From there, section IV considers the actual punishment imposed in military commissions and offers a theory as to why, in several cases, that punishment was only a fraction of what it could have been. Section V then segues to internal prosecutions. Relying on US Army law enforcement data, this section compares the final outcomes when a criminal investigation initiated in Afghanistan or Iraq determines probable cause exists that a deployed US Army soldier committed a homicide offense with when the homicide investigation originates outside the combat zone. This exercise roughly compares how the US Army holds soldiers accountable for when they commit a homicide offense against an Afghan or Iraqi civilian (aka the enemy) with when they commit that same offense against a non-Afghan or Iraqi civilian (aka a neutral or a friend).

The chapter then concludes by highlighting that while removing the equivalency requirement has not yet yielded maximum disparities between external and internal prosecutions, relying solely on individual discretion for punishment is ill-advised.

II. External Prosecutions under International Humanitarian Law

The quantity and specificity of the international humanitarian law (IHL) governing external prosecutions for pre-capture misconduct during armed conflict depends on the characterization of the armed conflict as international or non-international.

A. International Armed Conflict

A state on either side of the armed conflict results in an IAC.[19] In turn, the existence of an IAC triggers the largest amount of IHL applicable as a matter of law.[20]

[19] *See* International Committee of the Red Cross, "How Is the Term 'Armed Conflict' Defined in International Humanitarian Law?," Opinion Paper, 2008, https://www.icrc.org/en/doc/assets/files/other/opinion-paper-armed-conflict.pdf.

[20] *See* Geneva Convention Relative to the Treatment of Prisoners of War (adopted Aug. 12, 1949, entered into force Oct. 21, 1950) 75 U.N.T.S. 135 art. 2 (GPW) (stating that "the present convention shall apply to all cases of declared war or of any other armed conflict which may arise between two or more of the High Contracting Parties, even if the state of war is not recognized by one of them"). The United States, Afghanistan, and Iraq, like every state in the world, have either signed and ratified or acceded to the 1949 Geneva Conventions.

This includes all four of the 1949 Geneva Conventions (totaling over two hundred pages) and a series of eighteen Hague Conventions from 1899 and 1907.[21] In short, IACs trigger the application of the largest amount of IHL.

The 1949 Geneva Conventions were a response to a number of legal issues arising during World War II, including when and how captured enemy belligerents could be prosecuted for their pre-capture misconduct during an armed conflict. The Commentary to the 1949 Conventions explains part of the impetus for what would become process equivalency requirements:

> It was mainly during the Second World War and the years which followed it that the problem of punishing war criminals arose. The very numerous violations of the laws of war committed during the war had made the question an urgent one, which engaged the attention of public opinion and the authorities in the various countries. The absence of any international regulation of this matter and the small number of national laws concerned with it led most States to pass special legislation to punish the war crimes committed by the enemy against their people and troops. Although in most cases public opinion considered it normal and fair to punish those who were condemned on the basis of these laws, there remained a certain feeling of uncertainty as to whether the verdicts given were lawful or not. Furthermore, the various penal systems are not based on the same principles. In the Anglo-Saxon countries in general, it seems that the existence of a rule of international law, whether in writing or merely customary, even if it does not include mention of penalties, enables the courts of the country to condemn those who have violated that rule, whereas in other countries, particularly on the Continent, penal law, if it is to be applicable, must include not only formal regulations but also provisions determining the nature and seriousness of the punishment. In these countries, the saying "nulla poena sine lege" remains fully valid.[22]

The 1949 Geneva Conventions introduced the concept of "grave breaches"—the most serious treaty violations of the treaties. [23] A grave breach is so serious an offense against international law that it offends all states, thereby vesting all states with an interest in prosecution.[24]

[21] Laws and Customs of War on Land (signed July 29, 1899, entered into force Sept. 4, 1900) USTS 403.

[22] Oscar M. Uhler et al., Commentary Geneva Convention Relative to the Protection of Civilian Persons in Time of War 584 (Jean S. Pictet ed., 1958) [hereinafter Commentary GCC].

[23] *See* Jean de Preux et al., Commentary Geneva Convention Relative to the Treatment of Prisoners of War 626 (Jean S. Pictet ed., 1960) [hereinafter Commentary GPW].

[24] *But see* Marko Divac Öberg, *The Absorption of Grave Breaches into War Crimes Law*, 91 Int'l Rev. Red Cross 163 (2009) (comparing war crimes and grave breaches and suggesting that the grave breach regime is "likely to become confined to history"). *Id.* 163.

The 1949 Geneva Conventions also impose affirmative obligations on states parties with regard to grave breaches. States must implement a regime to prosecute grave breaches through domestic penal law. More specifically, states must enact legislation to provide "effective penal sanctions for persons committing, or ordering to be committed, any of the grave breaches."[25]

The Commentary to the grave breach provisions in each of the four 1949 Geneva Conventions is clear on the equivalency requirement, stating:

> The court proceedings should be carried out in a uniform manner, whatever the nationality of the accused. Nationals, friends, enemies, all should be subject to the same rules of procedure and judged by the same courts. There is therefore no question of setting up special tribunals to try war criminals of enemy nationality.[26]

The Commentary is the work of Jean Pictet of the International Committee of the Red Cross (ICRC). Pictet led the ICRC's efforts to revise the 1929 Conventions, authored many of the preparatory documents for the conferences and meetings in which the 1949 Convention was drafted, attended those meetings, and is the editor of the Commentaries to the 1949 Convention.[27] But it is not just Pictet who claims that the states parties intended equivalency. The grave breach paragraph of the 1949 Conventions was proposed during a joint Committee meeting by the French delegation to the Conference because of "the importance of applying the same system to all accused, whatever their personal status."[28] The Committee adopted the French proposal by twenty-four votes to ten with one abstention, and it was later endorsed by the Conference.[29] Research of the negotiation documents related to what became the grave breach articles has not revealed any state party positions contrary to either Pictet's Commentary language or the stated French rationale for proposing the grave breach provisions.

Thus, when an enemy belligerent commits a grave breach of the 1949 Geneva Conventions and is subsequently captured, the capturing state has an obligation

[25] Geneva Convention for the Amelioration of the Condition of the Wounded and Sick in Armed Forces in the Field (adopted Aug. 12, 1949, entered into force Oct. 21, 1950) 75 U.N.T.S. 31 art. 49 (GCW); Geneva Convention for the Amelioration of the Condition of Wounded, Sick and Shipwrecked Members of Armed Forces at Sea (adopted Aug. 12, 1949, entered into force Oct. 21, 1950) 75 U.N.T.S. 85 art. 50 (GWS Sea); GPW (n. 20) art. 129; Geneva Convention Relative to the Protection of Civilian Persons in Time of War (adopted Aug. 12, 1949, entered into force Oct. 21, 1950) 75 U.N.TS. 287 art. 146 (GCC).

[26] Commentary GPW (n. 23) 623. *See also* Jean S. Pictet et al., Commentary Geneva Convention for the Amelioration of the Condition of the Wounded and Sick in Armed Forces in the Field 264–65, 366 (Jean S. Pictet ed., 1952); Commentary GCC (n. 22) 593.

[27] *See* Alexandre Hay et al., *A Tribute to Jean Pictet*, 19 Int'l Rev. Red Cross 115 (1979)

[28] Commentary GPW (n. 23) 625.

[29] Conferénce Diplomatique 1949: Stenogrammes de la Commission Mixte: Full text 11éme séance du 19 Juliet 1949 à 10h; *see* pp. 4–8.

to either prosecute or transfer the individual, and if the state elects to prosecute, it must do so using the same rules of procedure and courts that the state employs against its own service members. Thus, at least during an IAC, a state should conduct external prosecutions in the same manner as internal ones. Therein lies the rub—an IHL equivalency requirement for external prosecutions exists but only during an IAC.

B. Non-international Armed Conflict

The United States has been engaged in armed conflict for over nineteen years, fighting in Afghanistan since 2001 and on again, off again for over a decade in Iraq. The international nature of these conflicts was short-lived, as the United States and its coalition partners toppled Taliban-ruled Afghanistan in roughly twelve weeks and Saddam Hussein's Iraq in less than six weeks. Armed conflict most certainly continued, but in a non-international form—the United States and other countries partnered with the new interim governments of Afghanistan and Iraq to fight insurgencies comprised of non-state actors.[30] These conflicts were (and remain) NIACs. With the change in conflict classification came vastly less IHL, including the equivalency requirement, applicable as a matter of law.

The change in conflict classification in Afghanistan and Iraq from IAC to NIAC meant that with the exception of Common Article Three, none of the 1949 Geneva Conventions, including the equivalency requirement, have been legally operable.[31]

The paucity of law applicable to NIACs yields a profound regulatory gap. This problem is exacerbated because NIACs occur far more frequently than IACs. Estimates are that, over the past fifty years, over 90 percent of the armed conflicts have been NIACs.[32]

The only portion of the 1949 Geneva Conventions applicable to NIACs as a matter of law is Common Article Three (CA 3), so named because the article is common to each of the four conventions.[33] Common Article Three mandates humane treatment of persons taking no active part in hostilities, including those in detention. Specifically, CA 3 prohibits "the passing of sentences and

[30] *See* Jens David Ohlin, *The Nature and Scope of the War in Afghanistan*, OpinioJuris, May 28, 2015, < opiniojuris.org/2015/05/28/the-nature-and-scope-of-the-war-in-afghanistan/>.

[31] In terms of IHL applicable to NIAC, Additional Protocol II to the Geneva Conventions is another source of law, but the United States is not a party to AP II. Even if it were, it is not clear that the NIACs in Afghanistan and Iraq would qualify as AP II conflicts for reasons outside the scope of this chapter.

[32] Uppsala Conflict Data Program, Armed Conflicts by Type and Year Armed Conflict By Type, 1946–2016 Uppsala Conflict Data Program 2017.

[33] *See* GCW (n. 25) art. 3; GWS Sea (n. 25) art. 3; GPW (n. 20) art. 3; GCC (n. 25) art. 3.

the carrying out of executions without previous judgment pronounced by a regularly constituted court, affording all the judicial guarantees which are recognized as indispensable by civilized peoples."[34] Neither the text of CA 3 nor the original commentary elaborates on or explains the qualifications of a "regularly constituted court" or what judicial guarantees civilized people recognize as indispensable.[35]

III. Domestic Law Basis for External Prosecutions

The starting point for the president's authority to conduct external prosecutions is UCMJ Article 21, which states:

> The provisions of this code conferring jurisdiction upon courts-martial shall not be construed as depriving military commissions, provost courts, or other military tribunals of concurrent jurisdiction in respect of offenders or offenses that by statute or by the law of war may be tried by such military commissions, provost courts, or other military tribunals.[36]

Following the September 11, 2001, terrorist attacks, Congress responded by adopting the Authorization for Use of Military Force (AUMF).[37] The US Supreme Court would later state its assumption that the AUMF "activated" the president's wartime powers, which included the authority to convene military commissions.[38]

As referenced in the introduction, in November 2001, President Bush issued an executive order directing the establishment of military commissions for external prosecutions. Among other findings, the president determined the UCMJ Article 36 requirement for equivalent external and internal prosecutions was impracticable.

Which differences between external and internal prosecution pass constitutional muster has been the subject of much litigation and multiple Supreme Court opinions. The process for external prosecution has undergone considerable change from the MCO to the MCA of 2006 to the currently operable MCA

[34] *Id.*

[35] In 2016, the ICRC updated the commentary to CA 3. While the updates did address "regularly constituted court" and what was meant by indispensable judicial guarantees, there is no mention of an equivalency requirement. *See* Jean-Marie Henckaerts et al., Commentary Geneva Convention for the Amelioration of the Condition of the Wounded and Sick in Armed Forces in the Field (2016), art. 3, § G.

[36] UCMJ, § 821.

[37] Authorization for Use of Military Force, Pub. L. No. 107-40, 115 Stat. 224 (2001).

[38] Hamdi v. Rumsfeld, 542 US 507, 518 (2004).

of 2009. But differences between courts-martial under the UCMJ and military commissions under the MCA of 2009 remain. Indeed, President Bush's determination that equivalent external and internal prosecutions are impracticable has been added to Article 36 of the UCMJ.[39] While the specific procedural differences are outside the scope of this chapter, the MCA of 2009 provides a framework from which to assess the import of removing the equivalency requirement.

IV. Qualitative Analysis of US External Prosecutions

This section conducts a qualitative assessment of external prosecutions. Using the MCA of 2009, this section first compares the maximum authorized punishment for analogous offenses in military commissions and courts-martial.

A. Comparing Maximum Authorized Punishment for Analogous Offenses

The first point of comparison is substantive offenses as reflected in Table 17.1.

As Table 17.1 reflects, there is minimal variation among the military commissions' punishments. Committing an offense yields either a capital case for which the death penalty is a potential outcome or, in the alternative, a potential sentence of confinement for life without the possibility of parole. In contrast, offenses at court-martial often have gradations and/or include a lower sentence range.

Obviously, the difference between the death penalty and confinement for life is significant. Further, for several offenses, for example mutilating or maiming, an enemy prosecuted by a military commission could receive the death penalty, while a US service member tried by court-martial could not. Yet the disparity is not necessarily as significant is it may appear. Where an individual has committed the actus reus of mutilation or maiming and the result is death, in nearly all circumstances the crime committed would be considered murder. The only circumstances in which murder could not be charged would be where, while death was a result, the mutilation or maiming was not both the actual and legal cause of that death. The same point would apply to offenses like intentionally causing serious bodily injury.

Yet even separating out the death penalty, Table 17.1 reflects disparity between maximum possible punishments. An enemy belligerent is subject to possible

[39] *See* UCMJ, § 836 (stating that "[a]ll rules and regulations made under this article shall be uniform insofar as practicable, except insofar as applicable to military commissions.").

Table 17.1 Analogous Substantive MCA vs. UCMJ Offenses (in the order listed in the MCA)

MCA Offense	Commissions Maximum Punishment	Court-Martial Maximum Punishment	UCMJ Offense
Murder of protected persons[1]	Death	Death	Murder[2]
Cruel or inhuman treatment[3]	If death results to one or more victims, death; otherwise life sentence without possibility of parole	Two years' confinement, dishonorable discharge (DD)	Cruelty and maltreatment [of subordinates][4]
Intentionally causing serious bodily injury[5]	If death results to one or more victims, death; otherwise life sentence without possibility of parole	With a loaded firearm: ten years' confinement, DD; other cases: three years confinement, DD	Assault in which grievous bodily harm is intentionally inflicted[6]
Mutilating or maiming[7]	If death results to one or more victims, death; otherwise life sentence without possibility of parole	Twenty years' confinement, DD	Maiming[8]
Destruction of property in violation of the law of war[9]	Life sentence without possibility of parole	Property of a value of \$500 or less: one year confinement, bad conduct discharge (BCD); property of a value more than US\$500: two years confinement, DD	Property other than military property of the US: waste, spoilage, or destruction[10]
Rape[11]	Life sentence without possibility of parole	Life sentence without possibility of parole; DD	Rape[12]
Sexual assault or abuse[13]	If death results to one or more victims, death; otherwise life sentence without possibility of parole	Thirty years' confinement; DD	Sexual assault[14]
Hijacking or hazarding a vessel or aircraft[15]	If death results to one or more victims, death; otherwise life sentence without possibility of parole	Life sentence without possibility of parole; DD	Improper hazarding of vessel or aircraft[16]

Table 17.1 Continued

MCA Offense	Commissions Maximum Punishment	Court-Martial Maximum Punishment	UCMJ Offense
Wrongfully aiding the enemy[17]	Life sentence without possibility of parole	Death	Aiding the enemy[18]
Spying[19]	Death	Death	Espionage[20]
Cruel or inhuman treatment[22]	If death results to one or more victims, death; otherwise life sentence without possibility of parole	Two years confinement, DD	Cruelty and maltreatment [of subordinates][23]
Intentionally causing serious bodily injury[24]	If death results to one or more victims, death; otherwise life sentence without possibility of parole	With a loaded firearm: ten years confinement, DD; other cases: three years confinement, DD	Assault in which grievous bodily harm is intentionally inflicted[25]
Mutilating or maiming[26]	If death results to one or more victims, death; otherwise life sentence without possibility of parole	Twenty years confinement, DD	Maiming[27]
Destruction of property in violation of the law of war[28]	Life sentence without possibility of parole	Property of a value of $500 or less: one year confinement, BCD; Property of a value more than $500: two years confinement, DD	Property other than military property of the US: waste, spoilage, or destruction[29]
Rape[30]	Life sentence without possibility of parole	Life sentence without possibility of parole; DD	Rape[31]
Sexual assault or abuse[32]	If death results to one or more victims, death; otherwise life sentence without possibility of parole	Thirty years confinement; DD	Sexual assault[33]
Hijacking or hazarding a vessel or aircraft[34]	If death results to one or more victims, death; otherwise life sentence w/out possibility of parole	Life sentence without possibility of parole; DD	Improper hazarding of vessel or aircraft[35]

(*continued*)

Table 17.1 Continued

MCA Offense	Commissions Maximum Punishment	Court-Martial Maximum Punishment	UCMJ Offense
Wrongfully aiding the enemy[36]	Life sentence without possibility of parole	Death	Aiding the enemy[37]
Spying[38]	Death	Death	Espionage[39]

[1]10 USC § 950t(1).
[2]UCMJ, § 918.
[3]10 USC § 950t(12).
[4]UCMJ, § 893.
[5]10 USC § 950t(13).
[6]UCMJ, § 928(b).
[7]10 USC § 950t(14).
[8]UCMJ, § 928a.
[9]10 USC § 950t(16).
[10]UCMJ, § 909.
[11]10 USC § 950t(21).
[12]UCMJ, § 120(a).
[13]10 USC § 950t(22).
[14]UCMJ, § 920(b).
[15]10 USC § 950t(23).
[16]UCMJ, § 910.
[17]10 USC § 950t(26).
[18]UCMJ, § 903b.
[19]10 USC § 950t(27).
[20]UCMJ, § 903a.
[21]UCMJ, § 918.
[22]10 USC § 950t(12)
[23]UCMJ, § 893
[24]10 USC § 950t(13).
[25]UCMJ, § 928(b).
[26]10 USC § 950t(14).
[27]UCMJ, § 928a.
[28]10 USC § 950t(16).
[29]UCMJ, § 909.
[30]10 USC § 950t(21).
[31]UCMJ, § 120(a).
[32]10 USC § 950t(22).
[33]UCMJ, § 920(b).
[34]10 USC § 90t(23).
[35]UCMJ, § 910.
[36]10 USC § 950t(26).
[37]UCMJ, § 903b.
[38]10 USC § 950t(27).
[39]UCMJ, § 903a.

lifetime confinement for intentionally causing serious bodily injury, regardless of the instrumentality used to inflict that injury. In contrast, where a US service member uses a loaded firearm to intentionally inflict grievous bodily harm, the maximum punishment is ten years' confinement. And with any other instrumentality, for example, a knife or a hammer, the maximum punishment is three years' confinement. If one engages in the macabre exercise of imagining a knife-wielding enemy and a knife-wielding US service member, each intentionally inflicting substantial bodily harm on a victim, that the enemy faces a possible sentence of lifetime confinement without the possibility of parole while the US service member faces a possible sentence of three years confinement seems a significant disparity.

Table 17.1 also reflects another difference: UCMJ offenses have gradated punishments, unlike the MCA. The potential punishment for a US service member who destroys non-US government property is predicated on the value of that property. Not surprisingly, the greater the value of the property destroyed, the greater the potential criminal sanction. The use of $500 as a delineating benchmark for property value is relatively arbitrary. It could just as easily have been $250 or $1000, but $500 is not an unreasonable amount through which to delineate low versus higher value property in terms of whether the US service member faces a maximum potential punishment of one-year confinement for lower-valued property compared to two years' confinement for higher-valued property. None of that exists, however, within the MCA punishment for a similar offense, destruction of property in violation of the law of war.[40] For the enemy who intentionally destroys property, regardless of the value of that property, the maximum punishment is confinement for life without the possibility of parole.

Table 17.1 also reflects several offenses—rape, hijacking or hazarding a vessel, and spying—for which the maximum punishments are exactly the same. For sexual abuse, the MCA authorizes confinement for life without the possibility of parole, while the UCMJ authorizes confinement for thirty years. As a reference point, thirty years' confinement is generally thought of as a sentence of lifetime confinement. Thus, the difference between the two punishment regimes is that under the MCA an offender may potentially never be eligible to receive parole from their life sentence, while under the UCMJ, a US service member would. Finally, in an interesting twist, the UCMJ authorizes greater punishment (death) for a US service member who aids the enemy than the MCA does for the offense of wrongfully aiding the enemy (confinement for life without the possibility of parole).[41]

Turning to inchoate offenses, Table 17.2 compares the maximum punishment for analogous offenses under the MCA and the UCMJ.

[40] The offense "destruction of property in violation of the law of war" is committed by the intentional destruction of property belonging to another person. 10 USC § 950t(16).

[41] The offense of wrongfully aiding the enemy is predicated on the offender having allegiance or a duty to the United States and knowingly and intentionally aiding an enemy of the United States.

Table 17.2 Analogous Inchoate MCA vs. UCMJ Offenses

MCA Offense	Commissions Maximum Punishment	Court-Martial Maximum Punishment	UCMJ Offense
Attempts[1]	Life sentence without possibility of parole	Punishment is the same as for commission, except punishment may not include death, or a mandatory minimum and other than for attempted murder may not exceed twenty years' confinement	Attempt[2]
Conspiracy[3]	If death results to one or more victims, death; otherwise life sentence without possibility of parole	If death results to one or more victims, death; otherwise life sentence without possibility of parole	Conspiracy[4]
Solicitation[5]	If offense solicited is attempted or committed, punishment is that provided for commission of the offense; otherwise life sentence without possibility of parole	If offense solicited is attempted or committed, punishment is that provided for commission of the offense; otherwise life sentence without possibility of parole dishonorable discharge	Solicitation[6]

[1]10 USC § 950t(28).

[2]UCMJ, § 880.

[3]10 USC § 950t(29).

[4]UCMJ, § 881.

[5]10 USC § 950t(30).

[6]UCMJ, § 882.

When closely examined, attempt offenses reflect significant punishment disparity, while the punishment for the other inchoate offenses is identical. For attempt offenses, the MCA's maximum punishment is confinement for life without the possibility of parole. Under the UCMJ, only the punishment for attempted murder

See UCMJ, § 903b. The overwhelming majority of those who have allegiance or a duty to the United States are US citizens who work for the US government. Under the MCA, US citizens are not subject to trial by military commission. It is difficult, though not impossible, to envision someone having an allegiance or duty to the United States while not being a US citizen. Suffice to say this is an exceedingly small subgroup of potential offenders.

may exceed twenty years' confinement. There is a disparity between the maximum punishment of twenty years' confinement for all other offenses under the UCMJ as compared to the MCA. For example, under the MCA, attempting to destroy (but not actually destroying) someone's private property in violation of the law of war, regardless of the value of that property, subjects the offender to confinement for life without the possibility of parole.[42]

There are a number of MCA offenses for which there is not an analogous punitive article of the UCM; however, the UCMJ allows for the assimilation of federal offenses—violations of the United States Code (USC). The subject matter of a number of MCA offenses is criminalized in this manner. Thus, a military prosecutor could assimilate or incorporate the USC provision in charging a US service member at court-martial. As a result, this allows for additional potential punishment comparison, as reflected in Table 17.3.

There is minimal potential punishment disparity between MCA and USC offenses. Many of the USC offenses derive from the war crimes statute, which criminalizes grave breaches of the 1949 Geneva Conventions (including CA 3), a number of articles from the Hague Convention IV, as well as the Protocol on Prohibitions or Restrictions on the Use of Mines, Booby-Traps and Other Devices.[43] The other USC offenses are from separate statutes criminalizing hostage-taking,[44] torture,[45] terrorism,[46] and material support to terrorism.[47]

The difference in potential punishment between the MCA and USC for terrorism where death has not resulted is one of degree. Under the MCA, the maximum punishment is confinement for life without the possibility of parole, while under the USC the maximum punishment could be as "low" as twenty-five years' confinement for terrorism resulting in property damage. That disparity is sufficiently less than with material support to terrorism not resulting in death. Once again, the maximum MCA punishment is confinement for life without the possibility of parole,[48] while under the USC the maximum punishment is limited to fifteen years' confinement.[49] Other than those offenses, for the remainder of the MCA offenses there are analogous USC offenses with the exact same maximum punishment.

In toto, all the MCA offenses except one have either a direct UCMJ analog or a USC analog, which may be assimilated into a court-martial charge. The one

42 See 10 USC § 950t(16)
43 18 USC § 2441(c).
44 18 USC § 1203.
45 18 USC §§ 2340-2340A.
46 18 USC §§ 2331, 2332b.
47 18 USC § 2339A.
48 10 USC § 950t(25).
49 18 USC § 2339A.

Table 17.3 Substantively Analogous MCA vs. USC Offenses

MCA Offense	Commissions Maximum Punishment	Court-Martial Maximum Punishment	USC Offense
Attacking civilians[1]	If death results to one or more victims, death; otherwise life sentence without possibility of parole	If death results to one or more victims, death; otherwise life sentence without possibility of parole	War crimes[2]
Attacking civilian objects [3]	Life sentence without possibility of parole	Life sentence without possibility of parole	War crimes[4]
Attacking protected property[5]	Life sentence without possibility of parole	Life sentence without possibility of parole	War crimes[6]
Pillaging[7]	Life sentence without possibility of parole	Life sentence without possibility of parole	War crimes[8]
Denying quarter[9]	Life sentence without possibility of parole	Life sentence without possibility of parole	War crimes[10]
Taking hostages[11]	If death results to one or more victims, death; otherwise life sentence without possibility of parole	If death results to one or more victims, death; otherwise life sentence without possibility of parole	Hostage-taking[12]
Employing poison or similar weapons[13]	If death results to one or more victims, death; otherwise life sentence without possibility of parole	If death results to one or more victims, death; otherwise life sentence w/out possibility of parole	War crimes[14]
Using protected persons as a shield[15]	If death results to one or more victims, death; otherwise life sentence without possibility of parole	If death results to one or more victims, death; otherwise life sentence without possibility of parole	War crimes[16]
Torture[17]	If death results to one or more victims, death; otherwise life sentence without possibility of parole	If death results to one or more victims, death; otherwise life sentence without possibility of parole	Torture[18]

Table 17.3 Continued

MCA Offense	Commissions Maximum Punishment	Court-Martial Maximum Punishment	USC Offense
Terrorism[19]	If death results to one or more victims, death; otherwise life sentence without possibility of parole	If death results to one or more persons, death; if kidnapping, life sentence without possibility of parole; maiming, limited to thirty-five years' confinement; for assault with a dangerous weapon or assault resulting in serious bodily injury, limited to thirty years' confinement; for destroying or damaging any structure, conveyance, or other real or personal property, limited to twenty-five years' confinement	Terrorism[20]
Providing material support for terrorism[21]	If death results to one or more victims, death; otherwise life sentence without possibility of parole	If death results to one or more victims, life sentence without possibility of parole; otherwise limited to fifteen years' confinement	Providing material support to terrorists[22]
Cruel or inhuman treatment[23]	If death results to one or more victims, death; otherwise life sentence without possibility of parole	If death results to one or more victims, death; otherwise life sentence without possibility of parole	War crimes[24]
Using treachery or perfidy[25]	If death results to one or more victims, death; otherwise life sentence without possibility of parole	If death results to one or more victims, death; otherwise life sentence without possibility of parole	War crimes[26]

(*continued*)

Table 17.3 Continued

MCA Offense	Commissions Maximum Punishment	Court-Martial Maximum Punishment	USC Offense
Improperly using a flag of truce[27]	Life sentence without possibility of parole	Life sentence without possibility of parole	War crimes[28]
Improperly using a distinctive emblem[29]	Life sentence without possibility of parole	Life sentence without possibility of parole	War crimes

[1]10 USC § 950t(2)

[2]18 USC § 2441

[3]10 USC § 950t(3).

[4]18 USC § 2441.

[5]10 USC § 950t(4).

[6]18 USC § 2441.

[7]10 USC § 950t(5).

[8]18 USC § 2441.

[9]10 USC § 950t(6).

[10]18 USC § 2441.

[11]10 USC § 950t(7).

[12]18 USC § 1203.

[13]10 USC § 950t(8).

[14]18 USC § 2441.

[15]10 USC § 950t(9).

[16]18 USC § 2441.

[17]10 USC § 950t(11).

[18]18 USC §§ 2340–2340A.

[19]10 USC § 950t(24).

[20]18 USC §§ 2331, 2332b.

[21]10 USC § 950t(25).

[22]18 USC § 2339A.

[23]10 USC § 950t(12).

[24]18 USC § 2441.

[25]10 USC § 950t(17).

[26]18 USC § 2441.

[27]10 USC § 950t(18).

[28]18 USC § 2441.

[29]10 USC § 950t(19).

exception is the MCA offense of intentionally mistreating a dead body. This offense is committed by the intentional mistreatment of a dead person without justification by legitimate military necessity and is subject to a maximum punishment of confinement for life without the possibility of parole.[50] There is no UCMJ or USC analog to this offense, despite the fact that, while there is not a detainee facing charges of intentionally mistreating a dead body, there is at least one instance of US service members doing so. In 2011, US Marines videotaped themselves urinating on Taliban corpses.[51] The Marine Corps charged the Marines with dereliction of duty, the maximum authorized punishment for which is two years' confinement.[52]

The discussion thus far has been one of potentiality, of the possible disparity between the quantum of punishment in external versus internal prosecutions. While disparity of potential punishment is a factor to be considered, its utility is primarily in framing the disparity between actual punishment imposed.

B. Actual Punishment Imposed in External Prosecutions

Actual punishment imposed may be viewed both from the perspective of the enemy belligerent under the MCA and that of the US service member under the UCMJ. The relatively small number of completed military commissions allows for consideration of all imposed punishments, while the larger number of UCMJ actions militates toward representative case study examples as explained later.

Military commission prosecutors have charged twenty-nine individuals with violations of the initial Military Commissions Order, the 2006 MCA, and/or the 2009 MCA.[53] Of those twenty-nine, twenty-two, for different reasons, did not result in punishment.[54] This analysis factors in punishment imposed by a military commission and does not consider possible modifications to that sentence or to a finding of guilt on appeal. The individuals who determined what, if any, punishment to impose were the military commission members—the military equivalent of a jury.

The military cases for which punishment was imposed are depicted in Table 17.4:

[50] 10 USC § 950t(20).

[51] *See, e.g.*, United States v. Chamblin, No. 201500388, 2017 CCA Lexis 694, at *1 (N-M Ct. Crim. App. Nov. 8, 2017). While urinating on the corpses, the Marines made comments including "have a great day buddy." Graham Bowley & Matthew Rosenberg, *Video Inflames a Delicate Moment for US in Afghanistan*, N.Y. TIMES, Jan. 12, 2012, A 4; *Corpse Abuse a "War Crime,"* SYDNEY MORNING HERALD, Jan. 15, 2002, < https://www.smh.com.au/world/corpse-abuse-a-war-crime-20120114-1q0j1.html>; Lee Ferran, *Marine Who Urinated on Taliban Dead Says He'll Do It Again*, ABC NEWS, July 17, 2013, < https://www.abcnews.go.com/Blotter/marine-urinated-taliban-dead-hed/story?id=19687916>.

[52] UCMJ, § 892.

[53] *See* "The Guantanamo Trials," Human Rights Watch, < https://www.hrw.org/guantanamo-trials>.

[54] These reasons include defendants still involved in pretrial litigation, defendants for whom the convening authority dismissed (dropped) charges, one defendant (Ghailani) whose case was transferred to a US Federal District Court, and one defendant (Majid Khan) for whom punishment has yet to be imposed. *Id.*

Table 17.4 Military Commissions Potential vs Actual Punishment Comparison

Name	MCA Offenses	Guilty Plea/ Contested Trial	Potential Punishment	Actual Punishment
al Bahlul[1]	Conspiracy, providing material support to terrorism & solicitation	Contested trial	Confinement for life x 3	Confinement for life
al Darbi[2]	Attacking civilian objects, hazarding a vessel, terrorism, attempts	Guilty plea	Confinement for life x 4	Confinement for thirteen years
Hicks[3]	Providing material support to terrorism	Guilty plea	Confinement for life	Confinement for seven years
Khadr[4]	Murder, attempted murder, conspiracy, providing material support to terrorism, spying	Guilty plea	Death	Confinement for forty years
al Qosi[5]	Providing material support to terrorism, conspiracy	Guilty plea	Confinement for life x 2	Confinement for fourteen years
Hamdan[6]	Providing material support to terrorism, conspiracy	Contested trial	Confinement for life x 2	Confinement for sixty-six months
Muhammed[7]	Providing material support to terrorism, conspiracy	Guilty plea	Confinement for life x 2	Confinement for fourteen years

[1] United States v. Al Bahlul, 820 F. Supp. 2d 1141, 1156–57 (USCMCR 2011), vacated, No. 11-1324, 2013 WL 297726 (D.C. Cir. Jan. 25, 2013), reh'g en banc granted, order vacated (Apr. 23, 2013), on reh'g en banc, 767 F.3d 1 (D.C. Cir. 2014), and aff'd in part, vacated in part, remanded, 767 F.3d 1 (D.C. Cir. 2014), and vacated in part, 792 F.3d 1 (DC Cir 2015), reh'g en banc granted, judgment vacated (Sept. 25, 2015), and aff'd sub nom Bahlul v. United States, 840 F.3d 757 (D.C. Cir. 2016).

[2] "Ahmed Mohammed Ahmed Haza al Darbi," (US Department of Defense Office of Military Commissions) https://www.mc.mil/Cases.aspx?caseType=omc&status=1&id=46.

[3] "Military Commission Order No 1" (United States v. Hicks, US Department of Defense Office of Military Commissions, May 1, 2007), < https://www.mc.mil/Portals/0/pdfs/Hicks/Hicks%20(Convening%20Authority%20Post-trial%20Action,%20Service%20on%20the%20accused).pdf>.

[4] United States v. Khadr, 717 F. Supp. 2d 1215, 1219 (USCMCR 2007); *see also* "United States of America v Omar Ahmed Khadr," International Crimes Database, < https://www.internationalcrimesdatabase.org/Case/810>.

[5] United States v. al Qosi, 28 F. Supp. 3d 1198, 1200 (USCMCR 2017).

[6] "United States v Hamdan" (Report of Result of Trial, *US Department of Defense Office of Military Commissions* Aug. 7, 2008), <https://www.mc.mil/Portals/0/pdfs/Hamdan/Hamdan%20(AE326).pdf>.

[7] "Military Commission Order Number 1-15" (United States v Muhammed, *US Department of Defense Office of Military Commissions* Jan. 9, 2015), < https://www.mc.mil/Portals/0/pdfs/NoorUthman/Noor%20(CA%20Action%20MEMO%20and%20Promulgating%20Order).pdf>.

With the exception of al Bahlul (life sentence) and Khadr (forty-year sentence), the remaining military commissions defendants received actual punishment that was a fraction of the potential punishment they could have received. The most glaring example of this is Hamdan, who served as Osama bin Laden's driver and bodyguard.[55] Hamdan faced a potential punishment of two life sentences. While Hamdan should not be (and was not) punished for not pleading guilty and forcing the US government to prove the case against him, had he pled guilty, he could have entered into a pretrial agreement with the convening authority. In doing so, Hamdan could have agreed to spare the government some portion of the time, effort, and expense of a contested trial, and the convening authority could have agreed to take some favorable action—usually in the form of limiting the sentence. The point being that, for several reasons, one might have expected an individual like Hamdan to be severely punished, yet despite the potential of two life sentences, he received a sentence of sixty-six months.[56]

Without an equivalency requirement, the captured enemy faces the potential of much more punishment through a military commission than a US service member who committed an analogous offense could receive through a court-martial. Yet the removal of the governor of an equivalency requirement has not resulted in that potential being realized, at least not uniformly.

Is there an explanation for why five of seven defendants received a fraction of the maximum potential sentences, while the other two defendants received substantial sentences? One key difference is that the five defendants (al Qosi; al Darbi; Hicks; Hamdan; Muhammed) either committed a crime without a physical victim (al Qosi; Hicks; Hamdan; Muhammed) or, where there was a victim (al Darbi), that victim was not a US service member or US national.

Contrast that with the two defendants who received very long sentences, al Bahlul (confinement for life) and Khadr (confinement for forty years). In the case of Khadr, he was involved in an attack which killed a US special operator, Sergeant First Class Christopher Spears.[57]

While al Bahlul was not directly involved in the killing of a US service member or US national, he was indirectly involved. Al Bahlul admitted to being a member of Al Qaeda and to producing an Al Qaeda propaganda video celebrating the attack on the USS *Cole*, which killed seventeen US sailors.[58] He knew of and wanted to participate in the 9/11 attacks but was denied the opportunity by Osama bin Laden, instead administering loyalty oaths to two of the hijackers.

[55] *See* United States v. Hamdan, 801 F. Supp. 2d 1247, 1256 (USCMCR 2011).

[56] *See* "United States v Hamdan" (Report of Result of Trial) (n. 115).

[57] *Stipulation of Fact (United States v. Omar Ahmed Khadr)*, Miami Herald, Oct. 13, 2010, <http://media.miamiherald.com/smedia/2010/10/26/10/stip.source.prod_affiliate.56.pdf>; *see also Khadr*, *supra* note 57, at 1219.

[58] Samantha Arrington Sliney, *US v al Bahlul, Where It's Been and Where It's Going*, Harv. Nat'l Sec. J. (2016), https://www.harvardnsj.org/2016/03/us-v-al-bahlul/#_ftnref1.

While detained, al Bahlul "wrote several letters to al Qaeda leaders 'renewing his pledge of bayat, restating his resolve to fight to the end, and reaffirming his belief that war is the only way to secure al Qaeda's objectives.' "[59] Finally, at sentencing, al Bahlul delivered an unsworn statement in which he stated that "we are the only ones on earth who will stand against you."[60] He also

> blamed the US for the deaths of innocent civilians over the past 50 years and for the 9/11 attacks, and "declared that al Qaeda does not submit to any Arab government or to international law, only to God." He also "expressed his willingness to die in prison and belief that al Qaeda will prevail in its war against the [US]."[61]

Thus, al Bahlul appears to have repeatedly provided a number of compelling reasons for the military commission to sentence him to be confined for life.

The limited number of external prosecutions resulting in punishment does not allow for any statistical analysis, which is why the preceding discussion was more qualitative in nature. There is, on the other hand, considerable data regarding internal prosecutions (US courts-martial of US service members) that allows for quantitative analysis.

V. Internal Prosecutions

Another way to gauge the importance of the equivalency requirement removed from external prosecutions is to compare outcomes from internal prosecutions. This means comparing internal prosecution outcomes where the underlying crime is committed by a US service member either against "the enemy" (for these purposes an Afghan or Iraqi civilian) or an individual who is not the enemy.

The very limited number of external prosecutions suggests that while the presence of an equivalency requirement may have led to a more standardized sentencing range, the absence of that requirement did not necessarily yield long sentences of confinement. That suggests that the military members serving on the military commissions did not impose punishment out of emotion stemming from the defendant being the enemy. A study of internal prosecutions may inform the inverse of the external prosecution question: Does the US military handle or treat US service members the same or similarly when they commit an offense against the enemy versus when they commit that same offense against an individual who is not the enemy?

59 *Id.*
60 *Id.*
61 *Id.*

This comparison requires US military law enforcement data. This section first explains how the law enforcement data was requested, the categories within the data, how the data was queried, and, finally, the results. The end focus of this inquiry is on what, if any, action did a unit commander take against a service member under his or her command who was alleged to have committed a crime. If there are disparities, are they based on the location of the crime and status of the victim?

A. US Army

For reasons outside the scope of this chapter there is no such thing as joint military law enforcement data, meaning combined law enforcement data reflecting the Army, Navy, Air Force, Marine Corps, and Coast Guard. Each of the services utilizes different systems, forms, and reporting processes. In terms of selecting which service to focus on, as noted in the introduction, the US Army contributed by far the greatest number of service members to the armed conflicts in Afghanistan and Iraq.[62] Thus, a threshold assumption is that more service members deployed to combat would yield more internal investigations and prosecutions. Accordingly, records requests were submitted to the US Army's Criminal Investigation Command (CID).

B. US Army CID

To obtain data on US Army criminal justice efforts in order to facilitate the comparison, records requests were submitted to CID, which is the sole law enforcement entity in the US Army responsible for the criminal investigation of felony crimes—offenses for which the maximum punishment includes confinement for more than one year.[63] Submitting the request to CID meant any results would concern only felony investigations, as opposed to misdemeanor investigations, which in the US Army are the purview of the Provost Marshall (military police), or disciplinary infractions, which are the purview of the unit commander. The rationale for requesting Army CID data was that, as further explained in the following, the most useful offense for attempting to differentiate among internal prosecutions is homicide, a felony.

[62] *See* Dan Lamothe, *How 775,000 US Troops Fought in One War: Afghanistan Military Deployments by the Numbers*, WASH. POST, Sept. 11, 2019, < https://www.washingtonpost.com/national-security/2019/09/11/how-us-troops-fought-one-war-afghanistan-military-deployments-by-numbers/>.

[63] *See, e.g.*, US DEP'T OF ARMY, REG. 190-45, LAW ENFORCEMENT REPORTING (Oct. 27, 2016); US DEP'T OF ARMY, REG. 195-2, CRIMINAL INVESTIGATION ACTIVITIES (July 21, 2020).

C. Records Request Time Frame

The records request utilized a ten-year time frame, 2003–2013, in order to capture data for the time period when the largest number of US service members were deployed to Afghanistan and Iraq.[64]

D. US Army Law Enforcement Data Results

The records request yielded data for every felony investigation US Army CID initiated/opened, anywhere in the world, between 2003–2013. This section provides a brief overview and explanation of the most relevant data categories.

1. Name and Location of the CID Office Opening the Investigation and the Date when the Investigation Was Initiated

Army CID has offices around the world, collocated where US Army soldiers are stationed. Thus, there are CID offices in the United States, overseas in countries where there is not an armed conflict (Germany, Italy, etc.), and overseas in countries where there is an armed conflict (Afghanistan and Iraq). The date CID initiates an investigation is the day that the relevant CID office learned of or had reported to it an allegation that a felony had been committed. The investigation initiation date has nothing to do with the date the alleged crime was committed.

One of the first steps taken to analyze the data is to reorganize it depending on the location of the CID office opening the investigation. Specifically, two categories are created: "combat zone" and "not combat zone." The CID offices included in the combat zone category are reflected in Appendix 1.

2. Description of the Offense

Criminal Investigation Command uses a series of codes to describe the various manners by which a soldier may violate a punitive UCMJ article. This analysis focused on homicide offenses, the offense codes for which are reflected in Appendix 2.

3. Report of the Investigation

Where a CID investigation determines that there is probable cause that a felony was committed, CID categorizes the investigation as "founded." Where a CID

[64] *See* Amy Belasco, "Troop Levels in the Afghan and Iraq Wars, FY2001-FY2012: Cost and Other Potential Issues," R40682, Congressional Research Service 2009 (reported troop levels for FY02–FY08, estimated troop levels FY09–FY12); Heidi M. Peters & Sofia Plagakis, "Department of Defense Contractor and Troop Levels in Afghanistan and Iraq: 2007-2018," R44116, Congressional Research Service 2019.

report of investigation (ROI) determines that there was not probable cause that a felony was committed, CID categorizes the investigation as "unfounded." Where CID has credible information as to who may have committed the offense, the individual is "titled" or named as a subject in the report. Where the subject is a US Army service member, CID relays facts of the case to that service member's commander using an Army Form, Department of the Army (DA) Form 4833. This form

> represents the Army's *only* record of Soldier disciplinary and administrative action. The DA Form 4833 is essentially a commander's "court record", which provides the outcome of disciplinary and administrative proceedings including information on crime, sentencing, [and] punishment imposed.[65]

When commanders comply with the requirement to return the form,[66] the CID is then able to include the action taken in the data set. One significant qualification to the data is that the return rate for unit commanders submitting the DA Form 4833 has varied over time. In 2010, the Army reflected a "noncompliance rate of 36%."[67] That noncompliance rate is not constant nor is it clear if the unsubmitted forms were from combat zone or not combat zone investigations.

4. Action Taken

The unit commander is required to complete the DA Form 4833 and indicate what, if any, action was taken against the soldier who was the subject of the CID. The range of options in terms of action taken are: no action, administrative, nonjudicial punishment, and judicial. No action is self-explanatory. Administrative action refers to actions like a letter of reprimand. Nonjudicial punishment refers to punishment imposed through a process within the chain of command which, as the name suggests, does not involve a judge. Judicial means that the soldier was formally charged with one or more criminal charges subject to trial by court-martial. So, unlike external prosecutions where, for an admittedly small group of defendants, the specific punishment is known, here what is known, for a much larger group, is the route the final action took. Given the parameters of the categories other than judicial, that route itself could be very telling.

[65] US Department of the Army, "Army 2020: Generating Health & Discipline in the Force Ahead of the Strategic Reset," Report, 2012, at 162, <https://apps.dtic.mil/dtic/tr/fulltext/u2/a554745.pdf> (emphasis added).

[66] *See* US Department of the Army, "Health Promotion Risk Reduction Suicide Prevention," Report, 2010, at 59, < https://www.armyg1.army.mil/hr/suicide/docs/Commanders%20Tool%20 Kit/HPRRSP_Report_2010_v00.pdf.

[67] *Id.*

The data does not include either the name of the soldier suspected of committing the offense or the names, or even nationalities, of any victims. To mitigate (but not eliminate) those limitations, the data was organized into two categories: final action from homicide investigations initiated in a combat zone and final action from homicide investigations initiated not in a combat zone. There is an important assumption imbedded in this approach. The assumption is that homicide investigations initiated in a combat zone most likely involved an Afghan or an Iraqi as a victim. Conversely, homicide investigations initiated not in a combat zone are assumed to involve a US citizen as a victim. This assumption is thought to be valid a large percentage of the time, but it is certainly not valid all the time. In terms of when the assumption is invalid, an example would be CID opening a combat zone investigation of US Army soldier A for allegedly killing US Army soldier B in Mosul, Iraq.[68] That would be a combat zone homicide investigation where the victim is not an Afghan or an Iraqi. Similarly, if a stateside unit deployed to Afghanistan or Iraq then returned to the United States and CID learned of an alleged murder of a detainee during the deployment and opened an investigation in Fort Hood, Texas, the result would be a non-combat zone initiated homicide investigation where the victims were Afghan or Iraqi.

Both of these "counter assumption" examples did in fact occur in the time period reflected in the data set.[69] They occurred more than once, though how many times is unknown. One way the analysis sought to mitigate the challenge of these counter-assumption cases was in parsing out the homicide offense codes. For example, one of the offense codes is for murder by narcotics or dangerous drugs. It seems unlikely that a deployed soldier would kill an Afghan or Iraqi by narcotics or dangerous drugs. It seems far more likely that soldier A might kill soldier B by narcotics or dangerous drugs. So the analysis excluded that (and other) categories of homicide which were not likely to be committed by deployed soldiers against Afghan or Iraqi civilians.

E. Data Query Results

The Criminal Investigation Command initiated a total of 2,229 homicide investigations between 2003 and 2013, among which 265 cases (11.90%) were

[68] The most common method by which a US Army soldier kills another US Army soldier during combat operations is through a negligent discharge of a weapon. *See* Terry Boyd, *Tank Commander Guilty in Iraq "Friendly-Fire" Death*, STARS & STRIPES, Nov. 30, 2005, https://www.stripes.com/news/tank-commander-guilty-in-iraq-friendly-fire-death-1.41736.

[69] *See, e.g., id.*; Gail Gibson, *Deaths of Detainees held by US Tend to Occur Under the Radar*, BALTIMORE SUN, Dec. 19, 2004, https://<www.baltimoresun.com/news/bs-xpm-2004-12-19-0412190114-story.html>.

initiated in a combat zone. The remaining 1,964 (88.10%) were initiated in non-combat zones.

The percentage of founded homicide ROIs was 3.22 percent higher in non-combat zones (91.9%) compared to founded homicide ROIs initiated in combat zones (88.68%). This difference, however, was not statistically significant.

> Founded homicide ROIs initiated in non-combat zones were 1.84 times as likely to result in no action compared to cases initiated in combat zones.

Compared to founded homicide ROIs initiated in combat zones, founded homicide ROIs initiated in non-combat zones were:

- 4.36 times as likely to result in an administrative action;
- 1.03 times as likely to result in a judicial action; and
- 0.80 times as likely to result in a non-judicial action.

Lastly, when CID completed an ROI but did not find probable cause that a homicide offense had been committed, if the ROI originated in a combat zone, the command still took action against a soldier in 1 out of the 23 unfounded cases (4.35%). If the ROI originated in a non-combat zone, the command took some form of action in 8 out of 136 unfounded cases (5.15%).

F. Interpreting Data Results

To be clear, there are enough issues or qualifications with the internal prosecution data that this chapter is only making the relative comparisons previously listed. The data does not support, and this chapter does not assert, causation. In interpreting the data, this chapter maintains the assumption that the victim of a homicide ROI initiated in a combat zone was an Afghan or Iraqi civilian while the victim of a homicide ROI initiated outside of a combat zone was not.

The internal prosecution data suggests that commanders were not more lenient toward a soldier under their command who allegedly committed a homicide offense against "the enemy." If anything, commanders were more likely to take action against the solider when the homicide offense was against the enemy. As reflected earlier, commanders were almost twice as likely to take some kind of action when the victim was Afghan or Iraqi than when they were not.

In terms of action taken, judicial action was the outcome in 90.3 percent of the combat cases and 79.77 percent of the non-combat cases. By contrast, commanders took (lower) administrative action almost four times more often in non-combat cases than combat. In terms of nonjudicial punishment, there was not much disparity with 5.22 percent of the combat cases yielding that action and 3.59 percent of the non-combat cases.

Another challenge in comparing external to internal prosecutions is that, for the former, the decision maker is a group—the military commissions panel. For the latter, the decision maker is one individual—the unit commander. Nonetheless, the analysis of both offer at least suggested insights.

The external prosecutions suggest that the absence of a legal equivalency requirement do not yield severe punishments. What the internal prosecutions may offer is the "why"; why did the removal of the governor (the equivalency requirement) not lead to spiraling sentences? The internal prosecutions suggest that commanders are not significantly influenced by the victim's status. Whatever influence there may be, it appears that commanders believed action is more appropriately taken when the victim was an Afghan or Iraqi civilian than when they were not; however, this is not to suggest that there is no need for equivalency requirements.

VI. Conclusion

That nineteen years of combat operations do not appear to have inappropriately biased US military officers, whether serving on a military commissions panel or as commander of a soldier suspected of committing a crime (either against Afghan or Iraqi civilians or US service members), is commendable—if it is correct. It is also surprising.

Relying exclusively on a military officer's temperament and judgment to achieve relative equivalence in internal and external military prosecutions in NIACs is ill-advised. Not only is a legal equivalency requirement for external prosecutions lacking, the maximum authorized punishments at the military commissions facilitate the as of now mostly unrealized potential of massively disproportionate punishment for the captured enemy compared to a US service member committing the same or similar offense.

The check against the risk of arbitrary dispensation of punishment should be something more than panel member or officer temperament or judgment, which, while nice if it is present, provides little stability or predictability—fundamental aspects of the rule of law.[70] In a sense, the United States has been

[70] Stefanie A. Lindquist & Frank C. Cross, "Stability, Predictability and the Rule of Law: *Stare Decisis* as Reciprocity Norm," Measuring the Rule of Law Conference, Austin, Mar. 2010, < https://law.utexas.edu/conferences/measuring/The%20Papers/Rule%20of%20Law%20Conference.crosslindquist.pdf>.

whistling past the proverbial graveyard in conducting so many internal and external prosecutions for so many years without a legal equivalency requirement. Yet that assumes the United States cares about even the perception of equivalence, perhaps the most flawed assumption of all.

Appendix 1

The combat zones were defined according to Investigation_Installation_Name (column F); specifically, "Combat" was defined to be any of the following: LSA Anaconda, Al Assad, Bagram Airfield, Bagram CID Office, Balad CID Office, Basrah Office, Buehring CID office, Camp Bucca, Camp Cropper, Camp Deh Dadi, Camp Eggers, Camp Kunduz, Camp Liberty, Camp Marmal, Camp Phoenix, Camp Slayer, Camp Spann, Camp Taji, COB Adder, COB Speicher, FOB Salerno, FOB Sharana, FOB Warrior, International Zone Branch, International Zone Baghdad, Iraq Fraud Det, Jalalabad Airfield, Kabul CID Office, Kandahar Airfield, Kandahar CID Office, Kirkuk CID Office, Mosul CID Office, Sharana CID Office, Taji, Talil, Tikrit.

Appendix 2

Offense Code Counts and Descriptions

Obs	Offense_Code	COUNT	PERCENT	Offense_Description
1	5H1A	593	26.6039	Murder - Act Dangerous to Others - Shooting
594	5H1B	155	6.9538	Murder - Intent to Kill or Harm - Cutting, Stabbing or Mutilation
749	5H1C	36	1.6151	Murder - Intent to Kill or Harm - Strangulation
785	5H1D	43	1.9291	Murder - Intent to Kill or Harm - Bludgeoning
828	5H1F	3	.1346	Murder - Intent to Kill or Harm - Poisoning
831	5H1G	4	.1795	Murder - Intent to Kill or Harm - Grenades
835	5H1H	4	.1795	Murder - Intent to Kill or Harm - Explosives
839	5H1J	6	.2692	MURDER - INVOLVING NARCOTICS OR DANGEROUS DRUGS
845	5H1K	11	.4935	Murder - Premeditation
856	5H1L	4	.1795	Murder - Act Dangerous to Others - Drowning
860	5H1M	18	.8075	Murder - With Specific Offenses - Suffocation or Asphyxiation
878	5H1N	26	1.1664	MURDER - BY TRAFFIC
904	5H1P	135	6.0565	Murder - Intent to Kill or Harm - Other Means
1039	5H2A	12	.5384	Voluntary Manslaughter With Intent to Kill or Harm - Shooting
1051	5H2B	2	.0897	Voluntary Manslaughter With Intent to Kill or Harm - Cutting, Stabbing or Mutilation
1053	5H2D	3	.1346	Voluntary Manslaughter With Intent to Kill or Harm - Bludgeoning
1056	5H2J	2	.0897	Voluntary Manslaughter While Attempting Offense - Narcotics and Dangerous Drugs
1058	5H2L	1	.0449	VOLUNTARY MANSLAUGHTER - BY DROWNING
1059	5H2M	1	.0449	Voluntary Manslaughter With Intent to Kill or Harm - Suffocation or Asphyxiation
1060	5H2N	5	.2243	VOLUNTARY MANSLAUGHTER - BY TRAFFIC
1065	5H2P	12	.5384	Voluntary Manslaughter With Intent to Kill or Harm - Other Means
1077	5H3A	55	2.4675	INVOLUNTARY MANSLAUGHTER - BY SHOOTING
1132	5H3B	1	.0449	Involuntary Manslaughter - Cutting, Stabbing or Mutilation
1133	5H3C	1	.0449	INVOLUNTARY MANSLAUGHTER - BY STRANGULATION
1134	5H3D	3	.1346	Involuntary Manslaughter - Bludgeoning
1137	5H3J	12	.5384	Involuntary Manslaughter - Narcotics and Dangerous Drugs
1149	5H3L	3	.1346	Involuntary Manslaughter - Drowning
1152	5H3M	20	.8973	Involuntary Manslaughter - Suffocation or Asphyxiation
1172	5H3N	125	5.6079	Involuntary Manslaughter - Traffic
1297	5H3P	37	1.6599	Involuntary Manslaughter - Other Means
1334	5H3Q	23	1.0319	ASSAULT - WITH INTENT TO MANSLAUGHTER
1357	5H4A	60	2.6918	NEGLIGENT HOMICIDE - BY SHOOTING
1417	5H4B	7	.3140	Negligent Homicide - Cutting, Stabbing or Mutilation
1424	5H4C	4	.1795	Negligent Homicide - Poisoning
1428	5H4E	2	.0897	Negligent Homicide - Explosives
1430	5H4F	22	.9870	Narcotics and Dangerous Drugs
1452	5H4G	1	.0449	Negligent Homicide - Arson
1453	5H4H	5	.2243	Negligent Homicide - Drowning
1458	5H4J	23	1.0319	Negligent Homicide - Suffocation or Asphyxiation
1481	5H5	228	10.2288	Negligent Homicide - Traffic
1709	5H7	521	23.3737	Assault With Intent to Murder

18
Conclusion

Jens David Ohlin & Mitt Regan

The chapters in this volume provide a rich and wide-ranging discussion of the ways in which states may combat non-state violence by eschewing rigid reliance on the paradigms of crime and war. This approach challenges the assumption that adopting the war paradigm is the only alternative available to states that must respond to non-state violence whose scope and intensity exceeds ordinary criminal behavior. It suggests that drawing on each paradigm may provide a more sensitive response to particular contexts of violence that enables finer calibration of state use of force.

At the same time, this approach raises important issues about the predictability and accountability of state conduct, and the extent to which proceeding in this contextual way can be consistent with commitment to the rule of law. Greater flexibility may create more opportunity for abuse and the risk of ad hoc justifications that ultimately rest simply on state interests. This conclusion situates the chapters based on their engagement with these issues, with the aim of both clarifying the concerns they raise and suggesting directions for further research to address them.

First, it is essential to appreciate what motivates rejection of a categorical approach and a turn to contextual analysis. As Seth Cantey, Christopher J. Fuller, and John C. Dehn argue, conceptualizing counterterrorism as warfare has significant material and psychological effects. The law of war provides permissions to use force and take life that are dramatically more expansive than the law that governs law enforcement activities. In addition, conceptualizing non-state groups as enemy forces elevates perceptions of the threat that they present, which can be used to justify restrictions on rights that are in tension with the professed commitments of liberal democracies. Furthermore, the war paradigm can create an unrealistic expectation of absolute protection against terrorism, rather than a focus on ensuring resilience in the face of unavoidable risk. In these respects, treating counterterrorism as warfare expands the authority of the state both within and outside its borders, and provides a cognitive framework in which such expansion is likely to be regarded as acceptable.

Claire Finkelstein also expresses concern about relying on the war framework to characterize non-state actors as combatants. She focuses in particular on

Jens David Ohlin & Mitt Regan, *Conclusion* In: *Between Crime and War.* Edited by: Claire Finkelstein, Christopher Fuller, Jens David Ohlin, Mitt Regan, Oxford University Press. © Claire Finkelstein, Christopher Fuller, Jens David Ohlin, Mitt Regan 2023. DOI: 10.1093/oso/9780197638798.003.0019

how this characterization has been used to justify targeting such actors outside theaters of armed conflict. Finkelstein argues that this has potentially problematic implications for treatment of state actors and treatment of non-state actors in the domestic context. She suggests that the targeted strike against Iranian Quds Force leader Qasem Soleimani implicitly characterized him as a dangerous individual rather than a state official, comparable to the treatment of leaders of terrorist groups such as Al Qaeda. This ostensibly elided a claim that the strike was an unlawful act of aggression against another state.

Finkelstein maintains that adopting this approach with respect to other state officials who may work with irregular or non-state actors would undermine international law limitations on the use of force by one state against another. In addition, she suggests, status-based targeting of non-state actors outside areas of armed conflict risks extension of the war paradigm to violent non-state actors in the domestic setting. She suggests that individuals in theaters of conflict not affiliated with the state should be regarded as subject to attack based on direct participation in hostilities, but that outside this setting such persons should be regarded as members of transnational criminal conspiracies under the crime paradigm. Their treatment would thus depend upon the setting in which they operate, rather than on a categorical judgment independent of context.

One response to criticism of reliance on binary paradigms is to attempt to salvage the traditional approach by arguing that the crime paradigm is not as restrictive as critics assert. That paradigm authorizes escalation of force based on the threat at hand, and thus enables the state to use intensive force in some cases that significantly depart from ordinary law enforcement settings. As Kenneth Watkin has noted, the human rights law that establishes standards for the use of force and law enforcement operations provides flexibility to state officers in responding to violence. The requirements of both necessity and proportionality have been interpreted to permit a state to use the level of force that is commensurate with the nature of a threat posed by non-state groups. Perhaps the most striking example of this is the jurisprudence of the European Court of Human Rights in reviewing military operations by Russia during hostilities with Chechen rebels. One might claim that these cases demonstrate that the crime paradigm is sufficiently capacious to support a continued reliance on a categorical approach. This would ensure that the presumption against taking life is preserved even in situations of intense violence, but provide flexibility in determining under what conditions a state can rebut this presumption.

This approach is promising in forestalling recourse to the war paradigm as soon as non-state violence exceeds what is common in ordinary law enforcement operations. As Watkin suggests, however, at some point it also may pose a risk of militarizing law enforcement. The further we move from the standard conceptions of necessity and proportionality under human rights law, the more contorted the application of those requirements may seem. When hostilities are substantively but not formally an armed conflict, as was the case with Russia and Chechen rebels, a court must necessarily grant considerable deference to military judgment. There is also a risk that influence may work in the other direction, serving to increase the level of force that is deemed acceptable in ordinary police operations. In other words, there may be costs to encompassing responses to street crime and to intense organized non-state violence within the same paradigm.

If rigid reliance on the two paradigms is inadvisable, what would a contextual approach involve? Joshua Andresen offers seven factors to consider in placing hostilities on a continuum that ranges from active combat with readily distinguishable combatants and civilians to areas away from active battlefields where the two are intermingled. He suggests that the gravity of the threat, whether a state exercises affective control or right area, and whether decisions must be made in the heat of battle are among the factors that are relevant. This approach thus identifies several features of a situation that should guide a highly refined analysis of what level of force should be deployed in a given instance.

At the same time, how plausible is it to expect that such multifactor assessments can be subject to meaningful evaluation? How much consistency is there likely to be among different decision makers who weigh the relative importance of these factors? In addition, how can we prevent contextual analysis from serving simply as a fig leaf for state decisions governed by expediency rather than law? Some of the authors in this volume suggest various ways in which decision-making might be guided by a principled contextualism that is responsive to these concerns.

One approach, as Watkin proposes, is to adopt a presumption of proceeding under the crime paradigm until the restrictions of that paradigm prevent an effective response to violence. This would reflect default reliance on human rights law and the flexibility it provides, placing the burden on the state to justify moving beyond that to the law of armed conflict. A state might adopt the war paradigm for a limited period of time if intensification of hostilities make this necessary, but would be expected to revert to law enforcement standards once violence abates. The state thus would have flexibility to move back and forth between paradigms as circumstances dictate, but would be required to justify departing from the default crime paradigm.

Geoffrey S. Corn argues that states should adopt this approach even during a non-international armed conflict itself. There may be situations in such conflicts, he suggests, in which it is not necessary to use force as expansively as the law of war permits. When that is the case, a state should rely on law enforcement standards to govern its operations. Corn thus would adopt the crime paradigm as a default even within an armed conflict, with state authority to deploy force more expansively when the need arises. As does Watkin, he also contemplates the possibility of temporary armed conflicts of limited duration that would justify reliance on the law of war.

Both Watkin and Corn envisage decisions being made on the operational level, where appreciation of contextual nuances is most keen. This seems sensible. It raises the question, however, of how best to ensure accountability when fine-grained judgments are based on military expertise and on information that it may not be possible to fully share with the public. An analogy may be rules of engagement, which militaries use to constrain the use of force based on a range of situational considerations. Such rules generally are classified, which means that the public may not know what governs the use of force in a particular instance. How might we minimize the risk of such opacity? To what extent might institutionalizing rigorous procedures provide some reassurance of good faith decision-making even if not all the substantive considerations taken into account can be disclosed? Rigorous research, including empirical studies of decision-making, are worth undertaking in order to answer these questions.

Laurie R. Blank suggests that the need for the kind of contextual flexibility that Watkin and Corn describe is likely to be of increasing importance because of the ways that hostilities with non-state groups, unlike those between state actors, tend to ebb and flow without a definitive end. This raises the challenge of determining whether a surge of violence is part of an ongoing armed conflict or is an episode that must be analyzed under the standards for initiation of a new armed conflict. Blank suggests that a state should first rely on law enforcement authority to address violence when hostilities are internal, resorting to military force only when it becomes so intense and organized that it is necessary to rely on the law of war. When hostilities are with external non-state groups, however, it may be less feasible to adopt this presumption. This effectively reflects an effort to rely on principled contextualism by establishing a presumption based on the location from which non-state violence is emanating.

Bailey Brown observes that the fact that non-international armed conflicts may not involve a clear end to hostilities means that there may be a gradual rather than sharp transition from war to peace. During this transition, a nascent central government may be attempting to establish its authority by providing protection and stability to the local population. The hope is that this process will culminate in a situation in which law enforcement operations are sufficient to address violence.

For this to occur, however, there may be a need to continue military operations under the war paradigm to reduce hostilities in some parts of the country that can threaten the legitimacy of the embryonic government. In this respect, armed conflict and a regime of fragile civil law may need to coexist for some period of time. In such circumstances, it would be unwise to adopt a categorical approach that assumes that a diminution in hostilities below the level of armed conflict warrants reversion to the crime paradigm. Instead, it will be necessary to determine when reliance on each paradigm is appropriate, and to calibrate the use of force accordingly. Brown points to experiences in Afghanistan and Columbia as examples of this phenomenon.

The kinds of situations that Brown describes can present substantial challenges to forces that may need to shift back and forth between the crime and war paradigms. European Court of Human Rights cases reviewing claims of human rights violations by the International Security Assistance Force (ISAF) in Iraq highlight these challenges. ISAF personnel often were performing policing functions in areas over which neither they nor the host country exercised the type of control that exists in a typical law enforcement setting. While these constabulary forces were operating in the midst of an armed conflict, they also had the obligation to respect the right to life of innocent members of the local population. Such situations may recur if non-state violence continues to be the most prominent form, and it will be important to learn from ground-level efforts to regulate the use of force in places such as Afghanistan and Columbia.

As Laura A. Dickinson notes, another way to combine elements of the crime and war paradigms is to rely on policy to guide operations. The Obama administration, for instance, did this by adopting Presidential Policy Guidance (PPG) that constrained the use of force outside areas of active hostilities, and by adopting a Periodic Review Board process for continued detention of enemy combatants that resembles the process afforded to detained civilians during wartime. In each case, the administration reserved the right to proceed under the law of armed conflict. Policy in such cases is established on the national rather than the operational level. It therefore can be formulated in terms that are more rule-like and transparent than may be feasible on the operational level, which can enhance external evaluation of compliance.

At the same time, of course, policy can be overridden in some cases, or reversed by a successor. It also does not contribute to the creation of customary international law because it does not reflect action taken based on a sense of legal obligation. Dickinson suggests, however, that policy may become institutionalized and regularly incorporated into decision-making in ways that may be difficult to change. It would be valuable for research to examine the extent to which policy can bring about sustained and enduring change. In addition, to what extent may even policy generate public expectations that can effectively constrain behavior because assessments of legitimacy come to rest on perceived compliance with that policy? The PPG requirement of near certainty of no civilian casualties in drone strikes outside areas of active hostilities, for instance, may reflect this process. It would be useful for research to explore the extent to which policy may affect perceptions of legitimacy, notwithstanding its failure to contribute to the creation of customary international law.

Another set of issues involves the treatment of terrorism as a distinctive category within criminal law. On the one hand, this may seem to represent an effort to introduce flexibility into the crime paradigm by devising rules that take account of the ways in scale and psychological effects of terrorist violence are distinct from ordinary criminal conduct. Thus, for instance, states have sought to intervene earlier in the process ostensibly leading to the commission of a crime by criminalizing certain preparatory behavior. On the other hand, as Fionnuala Ní Aoláin describes, the surge in such regulation spearheaded by resolutions of the UN Security Council, along with the absence of a common definition of terrorism, have created opportunities for states to use counterterrorism measures to stifle political dissent and opponents. The United Nations also has neglected to emphasize the importance of protecting human rights while combating terrorism.

The result in some cases is to license substantial restrictions on expression, association, assembly, and mobility, as well as substantial violence by the state. Such steps in the name of counterterrorism may offer a cautionary tale about drawing on both paradigms. The role played by the UN Security Council in treating terrorism as a threat to international peace and security arguably urges states to incorporate at least some elements of the war paradigm into criminal law and law enforcement operations. Ní Aoláin's chapter underscores the need for any efforts to address terrorism within the crime paradigm to ensure continued meaningful protection of human rights. Her careful analysis of state practices can serve as a model for the detailed examination of counterterrorism measures that is important in assessing the extent to which states have achieved an appropriate balance.

Evan R. Seamone also notes how states may use the crime paradigm for counterterrorism purposes by asserting extraterritorial jurisdiction to prosecute non-state actors accused of terrorism. The protective principle permits exercise of such jurisdiction when an actor has threatened the security or other vital interests of the state. This can enhance the likelihood that a state will rely on criminal prosecution rather than the use of military force to respond to terrorist threats abroad. Seamone cautions, however, that the protective principle may be subject to abuse by powerful states that take an expansive view of what threatens their interests. This highlights that considerations of sovereignty need to inform reliance on more aggressive measures within the crime paradigm to address terrorism. Empirical research can be useful in providing insight into whether there has been a greater tendency to rely on the protective principle based on terrorism, and whether this has occurred with due regard for the sovereignty of less powerful states.

Advances in technology also can shape responses to non-state violence. Jens David Ohlin describes how the use of drones to target terrorists represent a form of violence directed at particular individuals that bears some similarity to law enforcement operations. This perception has been reinforced by US policy on drone strikes outside of areas of active hostilities, which imposes restrictions similar to those that apply under human rights law. To the extent that this results in a tendency to view such operations through the lens of the crime paradigm, however, such strikes are likely to be regarded as extrajudicial executions—eventhough the United States regards them as operations during wartime.

Ohlin suggests that this may create an incentive for a state to use more intensive force in an operation order to underscore its character as warfare rather than law enforcement. The conundrum that the chapter highlights illustrates the interaction between the state's choice of counterterrorism measures and public expectations about their deployment. As weapons become more precise, expectations may emerge that they be used based on individualized threat assessments and that they cause no civilian casualties. To the extent this occurs, military claims of legal compliance may not be sufficient to avoid public criticism. This possibility suggests that further research would be fruitful on the relationship between law and perceptions of legitimacy when a state attempts to draw on both the crime and war paradigms, as with the PPG, and when it uses precise weapons even during a full-blown armed conflict.

Another form of technology that has become increasingly prominent in counterterrorism operations is the use of social network analysis. Todd Huntley and Mitt Regan describe the elements of this technology, its use during conflicts in Iraq and Afghanistan, and its potential to provide insight into the emergence of threats at an early stage around the world. They argue that this analytical tool is furthering a shift in US policy from counterterrorism conceptualized as armed conflict to counterterrorism framed as countering threat networks. The latter model cautions that completely defeating a network is unlikely, and emphasizes the importance of nonkinetic measures to disrupt the flow of resources on which networks rely. In these respects, social network analysis is enabling a salutary shift away from the war paradigm.

At the same time, Huntley and Regan suggest that a focus on threat networks could have the potential for periodic use of lethal force to prevent a network from gaining strength when the threat it poses is not yet imminent. In other words, the emphasis on continuous monitoring and disruption may ultimately lead to use of kinetic means to prevent, rather than preempt, threats based on the desire to minimize risk as much as possible. This reduction in risk may come at the expense of populations in other countries, and would be in serious tension, if not conflict, with international law. It is worth monitoring the shift to countering threat networks to see whether this occurs, and whether it leads the United States to attempt to define an imminent threat even more expansively than it already does.

Chapters by Bibi van Ginkel, Christophe Paulussen, and Tanya Mehra, and by Chris Jenks illuminate that one element of the crime paradigm explicitly operates during war, which is prosecution for war crimes. Van Ginkel and co-authors note that military forces are often first to the site of a possible war crime and may be best situated to investigate it. Such forces, however, are not trained to do so. The chapter describes ways to remedy this situation in order to enhance the likelihood of effective war crimes prosecutions. This would reflect the acquisition of competencies utilized under the crime paradigm by forces who otherwise operate according to the war model.

Jenks notes the substantial differences between prosecution of state and non-state combatants for war crimes. This rests on the distinction between international and non-international armed conflicts. Such a distinction, he argues, is insufficient to warrant disparate treatment. He maintains that non-state defendants should have the same protections as state defendants, thus ensuring that basic elements of the crime paradigm apply regardless of the formal status of an enemy defendant. Such a step would enable the use of war crimes prosecution to further counterterrorism by enhancing the perceived legitimacy of prosecutions under international law.

Finally, Orde Kittrie reminds us that nonkinetic measures may be available in some cases to combat terrorism, and may even avoid reliance on military force. He describes how the US treasury has taken the lead in using what he calls "financial warfare" to deprive adversaries of resources. This has involved tools such as using regulatory authority to block access to the US financial system, prohibiting private parties from engaging in transactions with designated parties, and imposing economic sanctions. Kittrie describes in detail the ways in which the United States has taken this approach with respect to Iran. He also suggests that, given the continued importance of the United States in the global economy, there needs to be careful consideration of the full impact of such financial warfare. One important question that may warrant further exploration is the consequences that may flow from conceptualizing this instrument as warfare.

Issues surrounding the choice of legal frameworks to guide responses to non-state violence are likely to remain urgent in light of the fact that hostilities between states and non-state groups comprise the majority of modern conflicts. As this volume has underscored, the categories that international law uses to govern the use of force have not been devised with such conflicts in mind. This means that mechanical reliance on these categories may not be sensitive to contextual features that should be considered in balancing state interests and the potential loss of human life. States necessarily must experiment with flexible approaches that are more sensitive to this balance, while providing assurance that such experimentation is guided by fundamental principles.

The need for such creativity arises as part of a larger trend toward displacement of states as the sole actors of concern under international law. Non-state armed groups are of course a prominent example of this. Furthermore, even during wartime, individuals now may be held liable for war crimes. Beyond this setting, human rights organizations, civil society entities, business corporations, and international organizations all are non-state actors that are exercising increasing influence and gaining recognition in international relations. In this sense, the challenge that this volume discusses is but one instance of the need to rethink a range of issues under international law. Meeting it, however, is especially crucial for the protection of life and preservation of the rule of law.

Index

For the benefit of digital users, indexed terms that span two pages (e.g., 52–53) may, on occasion, appear on only one of those pages.

Note: Tables and figures are indicated by *t* and *f* following the page number

Abbott, Philip, 426
active combat
  gravity of the threat, 551
  IHRL obligations, 107–8, 115, 116–18
  introduction to, 6–7
  non-combat *vs.*, 109–11
  use of force in, 91–92, 93–94, 124, 253–54
active hostilities
  areas of, 352–54, 362, 400, 402–3, 404–5
  cessation of, 4, 13, 117, 136, 159, 415
  by civilians engaged in a NIAC, 166, 173–74
  CTN operations, 462–63, 468
  drone strikes, 553, 554–55
  under ECtHR, 104–5
  end to in Afghanistan, 239–40
  IHRL, 104–7, 110–11, 116–17
  introduction to, 12
  Obama policy guidance, 91–92
  use of force and, 122–24, 553
Aerospace Industries Organization (Iran), 287
Afghan Interim Authority, 419–20
Afghanistan
  airstrikes for counterinsurgency, 95–96
  Al Qaeda's capabilities in, 239–40
  codified criminal law in, 422
  destruction of Taliban and Al Qaeda, 407
  displaced persons, 37–38
  drone strikes in, 96–97
  external prosecutions and, 525
  introduction to, 13, 21
  Kill Team, 519–20
  NIACs in, 121–22
  peace in the law of war, 416–26
  Project Hamah, 513–14
  as sanctuary for Al Qaeda, 438–39
  target killings, 64–65
  US invasion of, 438–39
  violent non-state actors in, 154–55
Afghan National Army, 201
Afghan National Police (ANP), 209–10, 213–14
Afghan Special Police Unit, 209
Afghan Transitional Authority, 420
African evidence sources in terrorism cases, 506–8
Ahlu Sunnah Wa-Jamaa group, 506
Ahmadinejad, Mahmoud, 265–66, 283
Ahmed, Faiz, 421
Aidid, Farrah, 447
Akehurst, Michael, 488
al-Assad, Bashar, 38n.69
al-Awlaki, Abdulrahman, 87–88
al-Awlaki, Anwar, 70, 73–89, 155, 156, 165
Al-Muqrin, Adb Al-'Aziz, 191
Al Qaeda
  Anwar al-Awlaki case, 76–77
  armed conflict with, 71–72
  associated force of, 385–86
  bombing of US embassies, 320–21
  characterization of operations against, 257
  civilian casualties, 95
  civilian law enforcement model and, 179–80
  combatancy status, 158–59
  declaration of war by, 31–32
  destruction in Afghanistan, 407
  drone strikes against, 68, 70
  financial lawfare against, 273–74
  humane treatment of, 173
  identification of members, 453
  illegal membership status, 178
  indefinite detainment of, 245–46
  jihadist strategy of, 317–19
  lethal force obligations against, 342–43
  middle managers, defined, 444–45
  military commission against, 259–60
  operational strategy of, 122–24
  organization factor in, 147–48
  Philippine airlines bombings, 481–82
  policy guidance on targeting, 468
  reconstitution or re-emergence of, 144–45
  sanctuary in Afghanistan, 438–39

Al Qaeda (*cont.*)
 September 11, 2001 attacks, 321–22
 social network analysis, 438–39
 strategic response flexibility against, 253
 as terrorists, 32–34
 as unlawful combatants, 8, 159–61, 171–72
 US armed conflict against, 12–13, 227–29, 237, 239–40, 245–46
Al Qaeda in Iraq (AQI), 447–48, 451
Al Qaeda in the Arabian Peninsula (AQAP), 76–77, 81, 88, 95, 165
Al-Qaida/Taliban Sanctions Committee, 50
Al-Saadoon v. Secretary of State for Defence, 104–6, 112, 117–18, 338–39
al-Shabaab in Somalia, 385–86, 405
al-Suri, Abu Mus'Ab, 195–96
alternative models of conflict termination, 416–33
al-Zarqawi, Abu Musab, 196, 447
al-Zawahiri, Ayman, 318–19
American Airlines Flight 63 attempted bombing, 320–21
American exceptionalism, 69
American Muslims, 74
American Society of International Law, 97–98
Amnesty International, 507
analogies in policymaking, 28–29
Andreou v. Turkey, 103–4, 117–18
Anglo-American domestic common law, 393
anti-coalition violence, 193
anti-money-laundering (AML), 276–77
anti-money laundering/combating the financing of terrorism (AML/CFT), 296–97
anti-Muslim demonstrations, 323–24
apology of terrorism, 54n.46
armed conflict classified after resurgence of hostilities
 in brief, 131–37
 characteristics of, 134–36
 framing problem and legal landscape, 128–30
 identifying international armed conflict, 138–41
 identifying non-international armed conflict, 131–37, 141–48
 impact of renewed violence, 128–30, 138–48
 indicators of intensity, 142–46
 introduction to, 125–28
 organization factor in, 146–48
 summary of, 148–49
Armed Forces Logistics (Iran), 287
Ashcroft, John, 36, 37
Ashford, Mary, 63–64
assassination of a state actor, 166–67
associated forces, 159n.11, 166, 384–86
Associated Press, 95
Atomic Energy Organization of Iran, 287, 295
Austro-Hungarian Empire, 166–67
Authorization for Use of Military Force (AUMF), 241–42, 526
autonomous entities, 177

Bail Reform Act (1984), 258
Bank Melli, 287–88, 295
Bank Saderat, 286–87
Bank Sepah, 295
Bar, Bill, 21
Barron, David, 86–87
battlefield misconduct, 261
Baxter, Richard, 203
bazaaris, 282
Belgian Federal Prosecutor, 513
Belgium, 501
Bethlehem, Daniel, 92–93
bin Laden, Osama, 64–65, 81–82, 175–76, 446–47
Black Lives Matter, 8–9
Blair, Dennis C., 95
Blair, Tony, 327–28
blocking assets tool, 286
Blum, Gabriella, 466–67
BNP Paribas, 301
Bobbitt, Philip, 26, 32, 33–34
Bockstette, Carsten, 25
Bolivar, Simon, 427
bomb-diffusing robots, 182
Bonn Agreement (2001), 419, 422
Border Protection Group 9 (GSG-9), Germany, 215–16
Brennan, John, 86–87, 97–98, 284, 307
British Special Air Service, 333–34
Burkina Faso, 507
Bush, George W.
 combating transnational armed groups, 437–38
 establishment of military commissions, 526
 introduction to, 21, 30–31
 Islamic radicalization concerns, 74
 military commission against Al Qaeda and Taliban, 259–61
 on 9/11 attacks, 21, 30–31, 155–56
 Obama repudiation of, 40
 Rendition, Detention, and Interrogation (RDI) program, 159–60
 UCMJ and, 521
 unlawful combatancy designation by, 161
 War on Terror, 317, 437–38

Bush Doctrine, 159–62
Bushnell, David, 428

Cali Cartel, 429
Calvar, Patrick, 326–27
Cameron, Iain, 480
Canadian Armed Forces, 3
Canadian Special Operations Task Force, 209
Capone, Al, 278
Caroline incident, 167–68, 381, 388–92
Case Concerning Armed Activities on the Territory of the Congo (advisory opinion), 102–3
Center for Ethics and the Rule of Law, 411
Center for Strategic and International Studies, 53–55
centers of gravity (COGs), 454
Central Bank of Iran (CBI), 291–92
Central Intelligence Agency (CIA), 65, 78–79, 80–81, 82
cessation of hostilities, 4, 13, 117, 136, 159, 415
Charter of the United Nations, 48–49, 167–68, 181, 369, 376–79, 380–86, 388–92, 465
Chechen warriors, 186–87
Cheney, Dick, 161
Christmas Day "underwear-bomber," 76–77
civilian casualties/deaths
  absent *vs.* distinguishable, 111–12
  in counterterrorism, 92–93, 96–97
  as justifiable, 114–15
  kinetic approach and, 194–95
  reliability of information on, 114–15
  violence against civilians, 144
  warnings with active combat, 111
civilian internment, 258
civilians directly participating, 164, 172–77
civil law
  Afghanistan, 411, 415–16, 417, 419–20, 421, 425–26, 433–35
  Colombia, 431–32, 433–35
civil wars, 26, 75, 121–22, 418–19, 427–28
Clinton, Bill, 30
coercing the target, 273
Cohen, David, 270–72, 283, 291–93, 299
Cohen, Eliot, 32, 33
Cold War, 32, 33
collateral damage
  by airstrikes, 194
  to computer systems, 487
  concerns over, 309–10, 336–37, 467–68
  as lawful, 77
  prevention/reduction of, 6, 66–67, 337–38, 339–40
  as proportionate/disproportionate, 72
  use of force and, 458
  Yemen campaign and, 81, 87
collective self-defense, 168
Colombia, 13, 408, 426–33
combatancy, 156, 157–62
combating the financing of terrorism (CFT), 276–77
combat zones, defined, 547
Committee of the Security Council (Counter-Terrorism Committee), 49
common law of war, 215–16, 260
Comprehensive Iran Sanctions, Accountability, and Divestment Act of 2010 (CISADA), 289–91
Computer Fraud and Abuse Act, 486
conflict characterization
  Common Article III and NIACs, 232–47
  introduction to, 7, 223–32
  policy presumption impact, 257–62
  primacy approach to, 247–57
  summary of, 262–64
Congressional Research Service, 374
Conservative Parties of Colombia, 427
conspiracy crimes, 500
constraining the target, 273
CONTEST strategy (UK), 327–29
continuous combat function, 164
Convention on Torture, 159–60
Correlates of War (COW) project, 26
Council of Europe, 492–93
Council of European Union, 59
countering threat networks (CTN), 454–70
"Countering Threat Networks" (US Department of Defense), 14
counterterrorism. *See also* military force in counterterrorism under IHL/IHRL; post-9/11 counterterrorism; social network analysis (SNA) in counterterrorism
  colonialism in, 3–4
  determinations, 6–7
  global counterterrorism, 45–47, 53–57, 61–62
  under IHL/IHRL, 97–118
  legalistic policy path in counterterrorism, 351, 352–60
  perceived legality of, 15
  violations, 5
  as war, 38–39, 41
Counter-Terrorism Committee (CTC), 46–47, 49, 50–53
Counter-Terrorism Executive Directorate (CTED), 46–47, 50–53, 57

Counter-Terrorism Implementation Task Force (CTITF), 50–51
counterterrorism work by UN Security Council
human rights effects of, 53–57
impact of ignoring human rights, 58–61
introduction, 5, 45–47
Resolution 1368, 47–48
Resolution 1373, 47–53
Resolution 1456, 49
Resolution 1535, 50
Resolution 1566, 50
summary of, 61–62
covert sabotage, 265–66
Crenshaw, Martha, 322–23
criminal enforcement with war, 7–11
criminal gangs, 13, 189–91, 216, 232n.55
Criminal Investigation Command (CID) (US Army), 541–46
criminalization of non-state actors, 210–12
criminal justice system, 1, 70, 211
Cronin, Audrey, 322
Cuban Missile Crisis, 28, 29

Daily Mail, 331–32
Dean, Howard, 37
Declaration of War Against the Americans Occupying the Land of the Two Holy Places (Al Qaeda), 31–32
Defense Security Cooperation agreement, 315–16
defensive force measures, 386–88
de jure sovereignty, 102–3
Denial of Service (DOS) attacks, 485
Denmark's Criminal Code, 53–55
Digital Liberation Front (DLF), 485–89
Dinstein, Yoram, 25, 382
"direct participation" standard, 163–64
disinformation campaigns, 38–39
displaced persons, 37–38, 38n.69, 187–88
Doctors without Borders, 251–52
doctrine of counterinsurgency (COIN), 39
doctrine of unlawful combatancy, 156
domestic criminal law, 14–15, 72–73, 155–56, 157, 181, 411
domestic terrorism, 58n.68, 156, 182
Draft Convention on Jurisdiction With Respect to Crime and the Restatement of the Foreign Relations Law of the United States (1935), 473–74, 478
drone strikes
as active hostilities, 553, 554–55
active hostilities and, 553, 554–55
in Afghanistan, 96–97
against Al Qaeda, 68, 70
as human rights violations, 72–73
international humanitarian law and, 72–73, 154–55
introduction to, 6, 40
against ISIS, 315–16
Obama administration policy, 66–67, 68–69
in Pakistan, 95
Predator drone, 70
RAF Reaper drones, 331–32
by UK, 315–16, 342–43
by US, 64–65, 66–71
in Yemen, 96–97, 165, 337–38, 352
drug cartels, 13, 178
drug smuggling, 194–95
dual-hatted argument, 169, 181
Due Process Clause of the US Constitution, 83
Dunlap, Charles W., Jr., 270

economic sanctions, 265–66
Effects Principle, 476
Einhorn, Robert, 278
Eisenhower, Dwight D., 324–25
El Salvador, 168
Emergency Response Division (ERD), 209
Emmerson, Ben, 40–43
Escobar, Pablo, 446–47
Esper, Mark, 21
Eurojust Memorandum on Battlefield Evidence, 517
European Commission, 296
European Convention on Human Rights (ECHR)
counterinsurgency and, 204–6
lethal force obligations, 316, 335–39
military operations and, 103–7
Operation Falvius (UK), 333–35
right of self-defense, 11
European Court of Human Rights (ECtHR), 98–99, 103–7, 117–18, 334–35, 550
European models of policing, 218
European tradition for ending war, 415–16
European Union Terrorism Situation and Trend Report, 516–17
EU Strategy for Combatting Radicalization and Recruitment to Terrorism, 59
evidence-based operations (EvBOs), 504, 517–18
evidence sources in terrorism cases
in Africa, 506–8
contextualizing problem of, 496–501
cooperation and, 513–14
facing challenges in, 492–94

fair trial concerns, 515–16
general context, 491–92
introduction to, 491–96
legal challenges, 508–16
lessons learned, 503–6
mandates and, 508–11
military role in, 501–8
scope and structure of, 494–96
summary of, 516–18
Ex parte Milligan, 121–22
Ex parte Quirin, 160–61
Explosive Ordinance Disposal (EOD), 502
external prosecutions
actual punishment imposed, 537–40
domestic law basis for, 526–27
internal armed conflict and, 522–25
under international humanitarian law, 522–40
maximum authorized punishment for analogous offenses, 527–37, 528*t*, 532*t*, 534*t*
non-international armed conflicts and, 525–26
qualitative analysis of, 527–40
extrajudicial killings
combatancy notion and, 157–59
law of armed conflict and, 157
by Obama administration, 87, 166
in post-9/11 counterterrorism, 157
Trump administration, 166–70
by Trump administration, 166–70
extra-systemic wars, 26
extraterritorial jurisdiction, 79, 477, 478–84, 486–89

fair trial concerns, 515–16
Fakhrizadeh, Mohsen, 153–54
Fall, Bernard, 189
Fallon, Michael, 10–11
fast-tracked executions, 197–98
fast-tracking practice, 56n.56
feasibility of capture, 175
Feaver, Peter, 32–33
Federal Bureau of Investigation (FBI), 513
Ferdinand, Franz, 166–67
Fidler, David, 213
Fifth Amendment of US Constitution, 79, 86–87, 479
Fighting at the Legal Boundaries: Controlling the Use of Force in Contemporary Conflict (Watkin), 3, 223–24
Fillmore, Charles, 28
Financial Action Task Force (FATF), 276–77, 293, 296–98
financial warfare against Iran
challenge of unwinding, 310–12
collateral damage concerns, 309–10
in conceptual context, 269–75
executive orders and designations, 285–89
future role in US strategy, 312–13
impact of, 281–85
implementation of, 285–305
incomplete success of, 306–9
innovative design of, 277–81
international financial system use by Iran, 275–77
by international organization and foreign countries, 293–99
introduction to, 10, 265–69
lessons learned from, 306–13
outreach to foreign governments, 298–99
pre-JCPOA US economic lawfare, 269–75, 307, 312
prosecuting foreign banks, 305
statutory measures, 289–93
targeting nuclear and terrorism sponsorship activities, 285–93
UN Security Council Resolutions, 274–75, 293–99
warning meetings with foreign banks, 299–305
First Amendment of US Constitution, 75–76
First East Export Bank, 295
focoists, defined, 186
force authority, 256–57, 263
foreign terrorist fighters, 211–12
Foreign Terrorist Fighters (FTFs), 495, 496–97, 498–99, 500, 502–3
Forfeiture Theory, 161
formal surrender, 4
Fourth Amendment of US Constitution, 79
frames, defined, 28
freedom of expression, 53–55
Free Speech Clause of the US Constitution, 75–76
French Code of Criminal Procedure (1808), 476
French counterterrorism against ISIS, 325–27
French law on apology of terrorism, 54n.46
Fuerzas Armadas Revolucionarias de Colombia (Colombian Armed Revolutionary Forces), 428–30

Gates, Robert, 79
Gearty, Conor, 24

Geneva Conventions
  Additional Protocol I, 51–52, 77–78, 173, 174, 178–79, 180, 203, 512
  Additional Protocol II, 51–52, 203, 413–14
  adoption of, 377–78
  combatancy status, 157
  Common Article II, 412–13
  Common Article III, 159, 178–79, 232–47, 260, 413–14, 512, 525–26
  domestic law with, 414
  external prosecutions and, 522–25
  interrogation techniques illegal under, 159–60
  introduction to, 14–15, 16–17
  law of armed conflict and, 126, 131–37
  law of war and, 409
  LOAC *vs.*, 161–62n.16
  POW status under, 172–73
  problems with, 42n.81
Gentili, Alberico, 371–72
German U-boat operators, 160–61
G5 Sahel Force, 510
Glaser, Daniel, 266, 270–71, 275, 302–4
global counterterrorism, 45–47, 53–57, 61–62
Global Counter-Terrorism Coordination Compact, 51n.25
Global Counterterrorism Forum (GCTF), 492–93
globalization, 313
Global North, 3–4
Goldberg, Jeffrey, 37n.67
Goldsmith, Jack, 161
grave breaches, 523
Grotian tradition, 369, 370–74, 395–96, 400–6
Grotius, Hugo, 370–72
Guantánamo Bay, 12, 15, 40
Guantánamo Bay detainees, 79–80, 162–64, 352–60, 520
guerillas/guerrilla warfare, 13, 187, 195, 197–98, 431

Haditha massacre, 519–20
Hague Conventions, 374, 375, 377–78, 409
Hakimi, Monika, 250–51
Hamas organization, 286–87
Hamdi, Yaser, 82
Hamdi v. Rumsfeld, 245–46, 262
Hammer, Craig, 36–37
Haque, Adil, 387–88
Hartig, Luke, 468
Hasan, Nidal, 76–77
Hellfire missile, 70
Hezbollah, 139–40, 273–74
High Contracting Parties, 126, 131–32
high-explosive ordnances, 207–8
Hitler, Adolf, 176
Hizballah organization, 286–87
Hoffman, Bruce, 22
Holder, Eric, 84–85, 86
Hollande, François, 326–27
Hostage Rescue Team (FBI), 211–12
hostage taking, 193
Howard, Michael, 35
human domain, 461
humanitarian assistance funds, 192
humanitarian law. *See* international humanitarian law
Human Rights Committee, 100–1, 106–7
human rights law
  as alternative to *jus in bello*, 315–16
  in Colombia, 427–28
  effects of global counterterrorism work structure, 53–57
  establishing correct paradigm against terrorism, 317–20
  governing use of force, 8
  impact of ignoring, 58–61
  introduction to, 1, 2–3
  lethal force obligations, 335–39
  militarization of, 9
  policing and use of force, 201–10
  in UK drone strikes, 342–43
  urban warfare law enforcement, 184
  using force under, 7
human rights violations, 41–42, 46–47, 59–61, 72–73, 199–200
human trafficking, 192–93
HUMINT (human intelligence), 65–66
Hussein, Saddam, 447, 525
"hybrid" legal response, 245

Ignatius, David, 265–66
illegal immigration, 194–95
illegal interrogation techniques, 159–60
immediate non-state threats, 384–85
imminent threat evaluation, 85–86
improvised explosive devices (IEDs), 501–2
industrial age model of armed conflict, 14
information-age approach to conflict, 438–39, 446–53
information operations (IO) specialists, 457–58
institutionalism, 51–52
insurgency. *See* urban insurgency and warfare law enforcement
intensity indicators in armed conflict classification, 142–46
internal displacement of persons, 38n.69

internal prosecutions, 540–46
International, Impartial and Independent Mechanism (IIIM), 493–94, 501
international armed conflict (IAC)
  assassination of a state actor, 166–67
  conflict characterization, 224–25
  external prosecutions and, 522–25
  ICTY and, 132–34, 135
  identification of, 138–41
  internal prosecutions, 521–22
  LOAC and, 138–41
  overview, 138–41
International Atomic Energy Agency, 267, 274
International Committee of the Red Cross (ICRC), 121–22, 172, 174, 206–7, 463–64, 524
International Conventions on the Suppression of Terrorist Bombings and Financing of Terrorism, 481
International Court of Justice (ICJ), 98–103, 168
International Covenant on Civil and Political Rights (ICCPR)
  fighting terrorism, 97–98, 99, 100–1
  human rights under, 378
  lethal force obligations, 335–43
  right of self-defense, 11
  targeting killing and, 316
International Criminal Court (ICC), 142–43, 505
international criminal law, 3
International Criminal Tribunal for Rwanda (ICTR), 134
International Criminal Tribunal for the former Yugoslavia (ICTY)
  conduct of organized armed groups, 169
  context of, 505
  fighting terrorism and, 119–22
  indicators of intensity, 142–43
  international armed conflict and, 132–34, 135
  LOAC and, 413–14
  Office of the Prosecutor, 505–6
  organization factor in, 146
International Emergency Economic Powers Act (IEEPA), 285–86, 287
international financial system use by Iran, 275–77
international humanitarian law (IHL). *See also* military force in counterterrorism under IHL/IHRL; policymaking in international law
  assessing boundaries of armed conflict, 347–48
  conflict characterization, 247–51
  counterterrorism under, 97–118
  defined, 234–35n.70
  determinant use of force, 7
  drone strikes and, 72–73, 154–55
  evidence sources in terrorism cases, 511–12
  external prosecutions under, 522–40
  extraterritorial counterterror operations, 362
  full application of, 6–7
  introduction to, 2–3
  legalistic policy path in counterterrorism, 351, 352–60
  lethal force reductions, 6
  low-intensity conflict and, 60–61
  PPG framework, 352–55
  PRB framework, 352–60
  tailored authority, 9–10
  triggered by armed conflict, 126
  urban warfare and, 184, 201–10
international human rights law (IHRL). *See also* military force in counterterrorism under IHL/IHRL
  active combat and, 107–8, 115, 116–18
  active hostilities and, 104–7, 110–11, 116–17
  conflict characterization, 223–32, 247–62
  counterterrorism under, 97–118
  evidence sources in terrorism cases, 511–12
  law of peace and, 408–9
  norms and values embedded in, 347–52
  policy presumption impact, 257–62
  primacy approach, 247–57
  right to life, 100
  US non-applicability of, 97–99
International Law Commission, 119–21
International Red Cross, 412
International Security Assistance Force (ISAF), 96–97, 419–20, 424–25, 504, 553
International Standards on Combating Money Laundering and the Financing of Terrorism & Proliferation, 296
international terrorism, defined, 23–24
inter-state wars, 26, 194–95
Iran. *See also* financial warfare against Iran
  nuclear weapons program, 269, 272
  Quds Forces, 8–9, 156, 168–70
  use of international financial system, 275–77
  US war with, 154, 166–67
Iran Threat Reduction and Syria Human Rights Act, 292–93
Iraq
  conflict with ISIS in, 125–26
  crowd-control capabilities of army, 209–10
  external prosecutions and, 525

Iraq (*cont.*)
  foreign terrorist fighters, 211–12
  insurgent forces in, 186–87
  liberation of Kuwait, 407
  police, as insurgency targets, 199
  Project Vennlig in, 513–14
  Sunni-Shia tensions, 197–98
  "Surge" Operation in, 502
  target killings, 64–65
  US invasion of, 21, 34, 447
  violent non-state actors in, 154–55
Irish Republican Army (IRA), 198–99, 332–33
"iron fist" approach to counterinsurgency, 199–200
Isayeva v. Russia I case, 250–51
Islamic insurgency, 418
Islamic radicalization, 74–81
Islamic Republic of Iran Shipping Lines, 295
Islamic Revolutionary Guard Corps (IRGC), 153, 287, 295, 303
Islamic State (ISIS)
  armed conflict with, 125–26
  civilian casualties, 95
  civilian law enforcement model and, 179
  drone technology against, 315–16
  evidence sources in terrorism cases, 496–501
  fighting terrorism and, 32–33, 34–35, 37, 91–92
  financial capacity of, 193–94
  foreign terrorist fighters, 211–12
  French counterterrorism against, 325–27
  identification of members, 453
  impact of renewed violence, 128
  jihadist strategy of, 317–19
  lethal force obligations against, 342–43
  organization factor in, 147–48
  Paris 2015 attack, 321–22
  RAF Reaper drones against, 331–32
  reconstitution or re-emergence of, 144–45
  social media platforms of, 322–23
  US armed conflict against, 227–28
Islamophobia, 329–30
Israel Defense Forces (IDF), 240–41
Israeli Supreme Court, 173–74

Jenkins, Brian, 37, 39, 317–18
jihadist movement, 195–98, 317–18
Joint Comprehensive Plan of Action (JCPOA), 266–69, 284–85, 293–95, 307, 308–9, 311–12
Joint Human Rights Committee (UK), 11
Joint Plan of Action (JPA), 292
Joint Special Operations Command (JSOC), 65
Joint Task Force (JTF), 446–53
Joint Terminal Air Controller (JTAC), 252–53
Jones, Rupert, 331–32
Journey to Extremism in Africa, 59–60
JP 3-25 publication (US), 454–61, 466, 467–68
judicial preapproval, 82–83
jus ad bellum
  armed attack meaning, 238–39
  countering threat networks, 465
  doctrine of LOAC, 169–70
  IHRL right to life, 100
  introduction to, 2–3
  liberation of Kuwait from Iraq, 407
  military force and, 106–8
  public international law, 409
  retribution for past wrongs, 168
  targeted killing and, 167
jus in bello
  absent *vs.* distinguishable civilians, 111–12
  countering threat networks, 465
  defensive force and, 386
  IHRL right to life, 100
  introduction to, 2–3, 10, 15, 17
  law of war and, 407–8
  military force and, 106–8
  public international law, 409
  unlawful combatants definition and, 411
Justice Select Committee (UK), 10–11

Karzai, Hamid, 420
Keegan, John, 201–2
Kellogg-Briand Pact, 374–75
Kennedy, Bobby, 324–25
Kennedy, John F., 28, 29, 324–25
Kerry, John, 37–38, 268
Khamenei, Ayatollah, 284, 307
Khan, Mohammed Daoud, 417–18, 422
Khan, Rayeed, 10–11, 331
Khorasan Group, 144–45
Kilcullen, David, 187
Kill Team, 519–20
kinetic intelligence activity, 38–39
King, Martin Luther, Jr., 324–25
Koh, Harold, 97–98
Kolenda, Christopher, 96–97
Kunduz Treatment Facility (KTF), 251–53, 254
Kurdish authorities, 498
Kuwait, 407

Lakoff, George, 28–29
large-scale military campaigns, 6
La Violencia conflict, 427–28
lawfare, defined, 8

Law of Armed Conflict (LOAC)
in Afghanistan, 425–26, 433–35
in Colombia, 13, 408, 426–35
Common Article III and NIACs, 232–47
conduct of war and, 77
conflict characterization, 223–32, 251–57
defined, 126–27, 347–48
extrajudicial killing and, 157
extraterritorial counterterror operations, 362
fighting terrorism and, 91–92
Geneva Conventions *vs.*, 161–62n.16
ICTY and, 413–14
indicators of intensity, 142–43
international armed conflict and, 138–41
introduction to, 3
jus ad bellum and, 169–70
necessity-based justifications for, 230–31
non-international armed conflict and, 129–30, 131–37
organization factor in, 145–46
policy presumption impact, 257–62
positive international law, 408, 409
PPG framework, 352–55
PRB framework, 352–60
purpose of, 131–37
triggering and terminating, 412–15
UK operations under, 349–50
US operations under, 349–51, 462–63
League of Nations, 374–75
Lee, Judith, 266
legal armed insurgency, 204–5
The Legal Consequences of the Construction of a Wall in the Occupied Palestinian Territory (advisory opinion), 100–1, 204
legalistic policy path in counterterrorism, 351, 352–60
The Legality of the Threat or Use of Nuclear Weapons (advisory opinion), 99–100, 101–2, 107–9, 119–21
Leiter, Michael, 322
"Lessons" from the Past (May), 29
Levey, Stuart, 273, 280
Lew, Jacob J., 265
lex generalis, 408–9, 415, 425–26
lex lata, 250
lex specialis, 99, 228, 407, 409, 425–26, 511–12
Liberal Parties of Colombia, 427
liberal values and transnational self-defense, 370–79, 392–400
Liberation Tigers of Tamil Eelam (LTTE), 515–16
Libya, 21, 37–38, 40, 64–65, 128–29, 143–44
Lieberman, Joseph, 308
The Limits of International Law (Goldsmith, Posner), 161
Livingstone, Grace, 427
local non-state threats, 384–85
low-key weapons, 265–66
Luban, David, 466–67
Lyall, Jason, 95–96

Madison, James, 315, 320–21
Madrid Guiding Principles (2015), 492–93
Maharashtra State Anti-Terrorism Squad, 206–7
Malcom X, 324–25
Mali, 507
The Management of Savagery: The Most Critical Stage Through Which the Umma Will Pass (Salafi jihadist doctrine), 186–87, 195–96
Marighella, Carlos, 186
Marine Commando counterterrorism (MARCO), India, 206–7
materially supported hostilities, 210–11
Mattis, James, 337–38, 357
maximum authorized punishment for analogous offenses, 527–37, 528*t*, 532*t*, 534*t*
Maxwell, Mark, 322
May, Earnest, 29
McCarthy, Joseph, 37
McChrystal, Stanley, 439, 446–53
McMaster, H.R., 153–54
Medellin Cartel, 429
metaphors in thinking about problems, 27–29
middle managers, defined, 444–45
Military Commission Act (MCA) (2006), 241–42, 260–61, 526–27, 537–40
Military Commission Act (MCA) (2009), 520, 521–22
Military Commissions Order (MCO), 520, 526–27, 537–40
military force in counterterrorism under IHL/IHRL
absent *vs.* distinguishable civilians, 111–12
active combat *vs.* non-combat, 109–11
counterterrorism operations, 97–118
criteria for, 115–18
debate over, 119–22
ECHR application, 103–7
effective control by a state, 112–14
gravity of threat, 109
ICJ application, 98–103
impact of military force, 91–97
impact on terrorism, 91–97

military force in counterterrorism under IHL/IHRL (*cont.*)
  introduction to, 6–7, 91–94
  reliability of information on use of force, 114–15
  summary of, 122–24, 123*f*
military information support operations (MISO), 457–58
military organization membership, 1–2
The Military Theory of the Global Islamic Resistance Call (al-Suri), 195–96
Miller, Stephen, 42
Milley, Mark, 153
Ministry of Defense (Iran), 287
MINUSMA, 507
Montevideo Convention on the Rights and Duties of States (1933), 34
Mothana, Ibrahim, 95
Mozambique, 506
Mueller, John, 318–19
Mujahedin, 418–19
Multinational Specialist Units, Balkans, 217
mutual legal assistance (MLA) requests, 513

Nagan, Winston, 36–37
Nagel, John, 35
narco-terrorism, 429
National Counterterrorism Center, 322
National Defense Appropriation Act (2012), 357
National Defense Authorization Act (NDAA), 291–92
National Defense University, 97–98
National Front regime, 428
National Gendarmerie Intervention Group (GIGN), France, 215–16
National Security Guard, Mumbai, 206–7
nation building, 198–200, 315, 407–8
Natus, Ester, 513
necessity-based justifications for LOAC, 230–31
Neilson, George, 63
Netherlands, 515–16
Newsweek, 266, 280
The New York Times, 40, 266, 282
Nicaragua v. United States, 168
Nicholson, Jack, 423–24
Niger, 507
nonderogable rights, 59
nongovernmental organizations (NGOs), 409, 420–21, 493
non-international armed conflicts (NIACs)
  civilians directly participating, 164, 172–77
  civilians engaged in, 166
  Common Article III and, 232–47
  conflict characterization, 223–32, 247–51
  conflict classification, 126–27, 129–30, 131–37
  defined, 387
  external prosecutions, 521–22, 525–26
  fighting terrorism and, 119–21
  identification of, 126–27, 129–30, 131–37
  non-state actors as part of, 165
  transnational self-defense, 400–6
non-state armed group (NSAG), 384–86, 387–88, 395–97, 400–2, 406
Normandy Invasion, 82–83
North Atlantic Treaty Organization (NATO), 423–24, 492–93
North Korea, 273–74

Obama, Barack. *See also* financial warfare against Iran
  countering threat networks, 467–68
  counterterrorism policies under, 347–48
  diplomatic outreach to Iran, 301
  drone policy, 66–67, 68–69
  executive order against Iran, 288
  extrajudicial killings, 87, 166
  fighting terrorism, 37
  Guantánamo Bay detainees, 356–57, 358–59
  hope for ending armed conflict, 239–40, 315
  legalistic policy path in counterterrorism, 351, 352–60
  military force by, 107–18, 124
  national security policy after 9/11, 40–43
  obligation to reduce casualties, 66–67
  strategy against ISIS, 322–23
  targeted killings by, 40, 78–79, 80–82, 97–98, 157, 162–66
  terrorists among civilian populations, 91–92
Obama Doctrine, 162–66
Office of Counter-Terrorism (OCT), 50–51
Office of Foreign Assets Control (OFAC), 280–81
Office of Legal Counsel (OLC), 78, 84–85, 86–88, 155, 165
Office of the Prosecutor (OTP), 505–6
Office of the UN High Commissioner for Human Rights on Libya, 143–44
Oklahoma City bombing (1995), 30, 320–21
open-ended war, 10
Open Society Foundations, 96–97

operational domain of authority, 225–26, 236, 243, 244, 246–47
operational-level presumption, 231
Operation Falvius (UK), 333–35
Operations and Intelligence Updates (O&I), 451–52
Oppenheim, Lassa, 25, 395
organization factor in armed conflict classification, 146–48
organized armed group (OAG), 413–14
organized crime, 189, 193
Osman v. UK, 335–36

Pakistan, 21, 40, 95
Palestinian Islamic Jihad, 286–87
Palestinians-Israeli conflict, 240–41
Panetta, Leon, 79, 175
para-military organizations, 213–14
Paris 2015 attack, 321–22, 497n.21
Passive Nationality Principle of extraterritorial jurisdiction, 477
Paul, Rand, 68–69, 71–72, 86–87
Paulson, Henry, 278, 279–80, 299–305, 309–10
peace in the law of war
  in Afghanistan, 416–26
  alternative models of conflict termination, 416–33
  in Colombia, 13, 408, 426–33
  European tradition for ending war, 415–16
  introduction to, 13, 407–8
  legal framework, 408–11
  summary of, 433–35
  triggering and terminating LOAC, 412–15
Peel, Robert, 215
People's Democratic Party of Afghanistan (PDPA), 417–18
Periodic Review Board (PRB) framework, 12, 352–68
Perles, Steven, 267
Permanent Court of Arbitration, 374
PFLP-GC organization, 286–87
Philippine airlines bombings, 481–82
Pictet, Jean, 524
piracy, 194–95, 504–5
Plan Colombia, 430–31, 432–33
police operations, 1
police primacy approach to counterinsurgency, 184, 198–201
policing and use of force, 201–10
policymaking in international law
  advantages and disadvantages of, 360–67
  analogies in policymaking, 28–29
  introduction to, 12
  legalistic policy path in counterterrorism, 351, 352–60
  PPG framework, 352–68
  PRB framework, 352–68
political, military, economic, social, information, and infrastructure (PMESII), 455
political assassinations, 181–82
political effects of crime, 2
political violence, 58–59, 60–61
positive international law, 408
Posner, Eric, 161
post-9/11 counterterrorism
  Authorization for the Use of Military Force, 241–42
  extrajudicial killing and, 157
  introduction to, 10–11, 91–92
  jihadist movement response to, 195–96
  self-defense against non-state actors, 119–21
  status of violent non-state actors, 170–71, 170*t*
  US response, 238n.76, 419
post-9/11 terrorism
  global counterterrorism architecture, 45–47
  impact on US, 37n.67, 38
  introduction to, 5, 21–22
  making a case for war, 30–35
  metaphors in thinking about problems, 27–29
  war and terrorism, defined, 22–27
A Practical Course for Guerrilla War (al-Suri), 196
Predator drone, 70
preemptive defensive force, 397
Presidential Policy Guidance on Procedures for Approving Direct Action Against Terrorist Targets Located Outside the United States and Areas of Active Hostilities (PPG)
  fighting terrorism, 106–7, 164–65, 179
  introduction to, 12
  overview on, 352–68
  summary of, 553
  transnational self-defense and, 379–86, 401–4
principled contextualism, 1–4, 551, 552
prisoner of war (POW) status, 172–73, 180, 210–11
Project Hamah, 513–14
Project Vennlig in Iraq, 513–14
proliferation networks, 276

prosecution proceedings by US
combat zones, defined, 547
external prosecutions, 522–40
internal prosecutions, 540–46
introduction to, 16–17, 519–22
offense code counts and descriptions, 548
summary of, 546–47
Prosecutor v. Tadić case, 119–21, 121n.113, 127–28, 134, 135–36, 141, 169, 206, 413–14
Protective Principle jurisprudence by US
background on, 485–86
Digital Liberation Front, 485–89
evolution of, 476–78
extraterritorial jurisdiction, 477, 478–84, 486–89
introduction to, 16, 473–76
studies on, 478–84
summary of, 489
telecommunications example, 484–89
Provincial Response Company-Kandahar (PRC-K), 209
psychological effects of crime, 2

Quds Forces, 8–9, 156, 168–70

RAF Reaper drones, 331–32
refugee flows, 38n.69
regions of savagery, 186–87, 188
Reid, Richard, 320–21
Rendition, Detention, and Interrogation (RDI) program, 159–60
renewed violence classification, 128–30, 138–48
Report of Investigation (ROI), 251–52, 545
Research Handbook on Remote Warfare (Ohlin), 236–37
Resolute Support (NATO mission), 424
right of self-defense, 11
"risk of release" assessments, 258
Rouhani, Hassan, 284
Royal Air Force (RAF), 315–16
Royal Canadian Mounted Police, 201
rule of law, 59, 155
rules of engagement (ROE), 116–17, 225, 249–50, 251–57, 409n.5, 431, 509
Rumsfeld, Donald, 159, 160–61
Russia, 273–74

Salafi jihadists, 186–87, 195–98
Saudi Arabia, 53–55, 418
scale-free network, 444
Schmitt, Michael, 121–22
Schumer, Charles, 284–85
second Cold War, 32
secret military organizations, 195–96
segregated battlefields, 4
self-defense authority, 251–52, 263
self-defense norms. *See* transnational self-defense
September 11, 2001 attacks, 321–22
Serbia, 273–74
Shah, Muhhamed Zahir, 417–18
Sharia4Belgium case, 501
Shifter, Michael, 433
"shoot to kill" policy, 201–2
SIGINT (signal intelligence), 65–66
signals intelligence (SIGINT) technology, 448
Singer, J. David, 26
Small, Melvin, 26
Snake Eaters, 192
social network analysis (SNA) in counterterrorism
countering threat networks, 454–70
defined, 440–46
hybrid approach to, 461–69
introduction to, 14, 437–39
summary of, 469–70
US Joint Task Force and, 446–53
US military doctrine, 454–69
social order, 1–2
social solidarity network, 51–52
socio-economic marginalization, 58
Soleimani, Qasem, 8–9, 21, 139–40, 156, 168–69, 181, 549–50
Somalia
active hostilities, 405
al-Shabaab in, 385–86, 405
insurgent forces in, 186–87
invasions of, 21
piracy in, 194–95
surge in US military operations, 40
targeted killing in, 337–38
target killings, 64–65
Soviet Union, 32, 418
Special Air Service, Britain, 215–16, 219–20
"special law" principle, 204
Special Police Units (SPUs), Kosovo, 217
Special Weapons and Tactics (SWAT) units, 209, 217
standing army, 33–34
Standing Rules of Engagement (SROE), 247–48, 250–57
Status of Forces Agreement (SOFA), 503–4
street-to-street fighting, 209
suicide bombers/bombings, 24, 497n.22
"Surge" Operation in Iraq, 502

Syria
  conflict with ISIS in, 34, 125–26
  displaced persons from, 37–38
  evidence sources in terrorism cases, 496–501
  financial lawfare against, 273–74
  foreign terrorist fighters, 211–12
  insurgent forces in, 186–87
  surge in US military operations, 40
  target killings, 64–65
Szasz, Paul, 47–48
Szubin, Adam, 270–71, 306–8

tailored authority, 9–10, 223–32
Taliban
  combatancy status, 158–59
  destruction of, 407, 416–17
  drug activities by, 194–95
  fighting terrorism and, 96–97
  humane treatment of, 173
  illegal membership status, 178
  indefinite detainment of, 245–46
  military commission against, 259–60
  as organized political force, 418–19
  as unlawful combatants, 159–61
  US response to attacks, 419–20
targeted killings
  Anwar al-Awlaki case, 70, 73–89
  counterproductive nature of, 337–38
  introduction, 6, 63–66
  judicial preapproval, 82–83
  jus ad bellum and, 167
  by Obama, Barack, 40, 78–79, 80–82, 97–98, 157, 162–66
  obligation to reduce casualties, 66–71
  paradox for US, 71–74
  in Somalia, 337–38
  summary of, 88–89
territorial integrity, 1–2, 376, 409n.3, 478
Terror and Consent: The Wars for the Twenty-First Century (Bobbitt), 33
terrorism. *See also* post-9/11 terrorism
  apology of, 54n.46
  defined, 22–23
  domestic terrorism, 58n.68, 156, 182
  establishing correct paradigm against, 317–20
  funding of, 192–95
  global regulation of, 45–46
  identifying causes of, 58–60
  impact on freedom, 320–27
  impact on US, 37n.67, 38
  interface with urban insurgency, 212–16
  interface with urban insurgency policing, 212–16
  introduction to, 5, 21–22
  law enforcement responsibility, 184–85
  narco-terrorism, 429
  overview of, 22–27
  prosecution of, 14–17
  terrorism, defined, 22–23
  transnational terrorism, 1–4, 227–28, 437–39
  USA PATRIOT Act and, 23–24
  US State Department and, 23
  as world war, 33
Thatcher, Margaret, 332–33
Thornton, Abraham, 63–64, 70
Thornton, Sean, 280–81
threats by collective actors, 1–2
transnational self-defense
  Caroline incident, 167–68, 381, 388–92
  Charter of the United Nations, 369, 376–79, 380–86
  collateral harm, 403–4
  defensive force measures, 386–88
  emerging norms, 379–88
  flaws with, 404–6
  Grotian tradition and, 369, 370–74, 395–96, 400–6
  inattention to law, 394–400
  introduction to, 12–13, 369–70
  lethal force and, 401–2
  liberal values and, 370–79, 392–400
  location of violence, 402–3
  PPG report and, 379–86, 401–4
  principles of, 388–92
  resorting to force, 394–97
  summary of, 406
  use of force, 394–400
transnational terrorism, 1–4, 227–28, 437–39
travaux préparatoires of the ICCPR, 100–1
Treasury's War: The Unleashing of a New Era of Financial Warfare (Zarate), 270–71, 280
Treaty of Versailles, 415
trial by combat, 63–66
Truman, Harry S., 324–25
Trump, Donald
  civilian casualties under, 95
  extrajudicial killings, 166–70
  fighting terrorism, 21, 37–38
  Guantánamo Bay detainees, 357
  JCPOA withdrawal, 268–69
  Muslim bans and, 42
  promises to bring troops home, 317–18, 319–20
Tuck, Richard, 371–72
typology of war, 26

"unable or unwilling" doctrine, 176
UN buffer zone, 104
UN Committee on Human Rights, 97–98
UN Comprehensive Anti-Terrorism Treaty, 25
unconventional insurgency-type threats, 245
UN Global Counter-Terrorism Strategy, 58
UN Human Rights Committee, 53–55
Uniform Code of Military Justice (UCMJ), 259–60, 519–20, 521, 526–40
UN Investigative Team to Promote Accountability for Crimes Committed by Da'esh/Islamic State in Iraq and the Levant (UNITAD), 493–94, 501
United Against Nuclear Iran, 308
United Kingdom (UK)
  CONTEST strategy, 327–29
  counterterrorism by, 315–16, 327–30
  drone strikes by, 315–16, 342–43
  human rights law obligations, 335–38
  human rights law protections, 333–42
  lethal force obligations, 335–43
  LOAC under, 349–50
  national terrorism threat level, 331–33
  Operation Falvius, 333–35
  RAF Reaper drones, 331–32
United States (US). *See also* prosecution proceedings by US; Protective Principle jurisprudence by US
  Al Qaeda bombing of US embassies, 320–21
  armed conflict against Al Qaeda, 12–13, 227–29, 237, 239–40, 245–46
  armed conflict against ISIS, 227–28
  drone strikes by, 64–65, 66–71
  invasion of Afghanistan, 438–39
  invasion of Iraq, 21, 34, 447
  LOAC under, 349–51, 462–63
  military operations in Yemen, 40
  non-applicability of IHRL, 97–99
  post-9/11 counterterrorism response, 238n.76, 419
  post-9/11 terrorism impact on, 37n.67, 38
  Presidential Policy Guidance, 106–7
  response to Taliban attacks, 419–20
  social network analysis doctrine, 454–61
  target killings by, 64–65, 66–88
  terrorism impact on, 37n.67, 38
  war with Iran, 154, 166–67
United States v. Peterson, 480–81
United States v. Reumayr, 482–84, 487–88
United States v. Rodriguez, 478–79
United States v. Salerno, 258–59
United States v. Yousef, 481–82
unlawful combatants characterization
  combatancy, traditional notion, 157–59
  distinction between war and crime, 4–11, 170–77
  fighting terrorists and, 159–62
  introduction to, 8–9
  Obama Doctrine, 162–66
  overview, 1–4
  summary of, 180–82
  Trump administration extrajudicial killings, 166–70
  unlawful combatancy, 159–62
UN Multidimensional Integrated Stabilization Mission in the CAR, 505–6
UN Office of Counter-Terrorism, 46–47
UN Organization Stabilization Mission in the DRC, 505–6
UN Security Council. *See also* counterterrorism work by UN Security Council
  Article 51 and, 409–10, 411
  evidence sources in terrorism cases, 495–96, 508–11, 513–14
  financial lawfare against Iran, 274
  financial warfare against Iran, 277
UN Security Council Resolutions, 210, 274–75, 293–99, 419–20, 492–94, 497
UN Special Rapporteur on Counter-Terrorism, 50, 55–57
UN Transitional Authority in Eastern Slavonia, Baranja and Western Sirmium (UNTAES), 505–6
UN Universal Declaration of Human Rights, 408–9
urban insurgency and warfare law enforcement
  criminalization of non-state actors, 210–12
  funding of, 192–95
  guerillas/guerrilla warfare, 13, 187, 195, 197–98
  introduction to, 9, 183–84
  jihadist movement, 195–98
  legal frameworks, 201–12, 216–20
  overview, 184–88
  police primacy approach to counterinsurgency, 184, 198–201
  policing and use of force, 201–10
  summary of, 220–21
  terrorism interface, 212–16
  threat of, 189–92
  in unstable security environments, 212–20
  urbanization challenges, 184–88
US Agency for International Development, 432
USA PATRIOT Act, 23–24, 289

US Army internal prosecutions, 541–46
US Code, 23–24
US Constitution, 82
US Counterinsurgency Manual, 208–9
US Declaration of Independence, 372n.26, 392–93
US Department of Defense, 96–97, 405
US Department of Justice (DOJ), 162–63, 432
US embassy bombing, 30
use of force
  in active combat, 91–92, 93–94, 124, 253–54
  active hostilities and, 122–24, 553
  collateral damage and, 458
  human rights law and policing, 201–10
  human rights law governing, 8
  international humanitarian law and, 7
  transnational self-defense, 370–79, 394–400
  urban insurgency and, 201–10
US Special Operations Command, 461
US State Department, 23
US Supreme Court, 79, 245–46, 258
US Treasury Department, 10, 271, 279–81

Vattel, Emmerich de, 372–74, 394–96
Vietcong, 159
Vietnam War, 159, 170

war. *See also* financial warfare against Iran; peace in the law of war; urban insurgency and warfare law enforcement
  civil wars, 26, 75, 121–22, 418–19, 427–28
  Cold War, 32, 33
  common law of, 215–16, 260
  counterterrorism as, 38–39, 41
  criminal enforcement with, 7–11
  defined, 21–22, 25–27
  expanding accepted definitions of, 38–40
  extra-systemic wars, 26
  guerillas/guerrilla warfare, 13, 187, 195, 197–98, 431
  inter-state wars, 26, 194–95
  making a case against, 35–40
  making a case for, 30–35
  open-ended war, 10
  terrorism and, 22–27
  terrorism as world war, 33
  typology of, 26
  World War I, 28
"war-fighting" capabilities, 398–99
war obligations, 93–94
War on Terror, 11, 22, 36, 317–20, 322, 437–38
war paradigm
  conferring legitimacy against enemy, 35–36
  as criminal enforcement, 7–11
  distinguishing from crime paradigm, 4–7
  expands accepted definitions of war, 38–40
  fostering division among people of good will, 36–37
  magnifying threat beyond proportion, 37–38
  overview, 1–4
  unresolved questions over, 40–43
war permissions, 93–94
War Powers Resolution (1973), 26
war restrictions, 93–94
war sustaining activities, 193–94, 398–99
Washington Post, 265–66
weapons-of-mass-destruction (WMD), 271, 287, 396–97
Webster, Daniel, 382, 389–91, 393
Wilkinson, James, 278
Williams, Paul, 192
Williamson, Gavin, 331–32
Wittes, Benjamin, 26
Wolfowitz, Paul, 317–18
World War I, 28

Yemen
  displaced persons, 37–38
  drone strikes in, 96–97, 165, 337–38, 352
  NIACs in, 121–22
  target killings, 64–65, 70, 73–81
  US military operations against, 21, 40
Yoo, John, 10
Yuen Foong Khong, 28, 29

Zarate, Juan, 270–71, 280, 304
zone of combat, 85–86